Northern Tanzania

Serengeti • Kilimanjaro • Zanzibar

the Bradt Travel Guide

Philip Briggs
Chris McIntyre

edition
3

www.bradtguides.com

Bradt Travel Guides Ltd, UK
The Globe Pequot Press Inc, USA

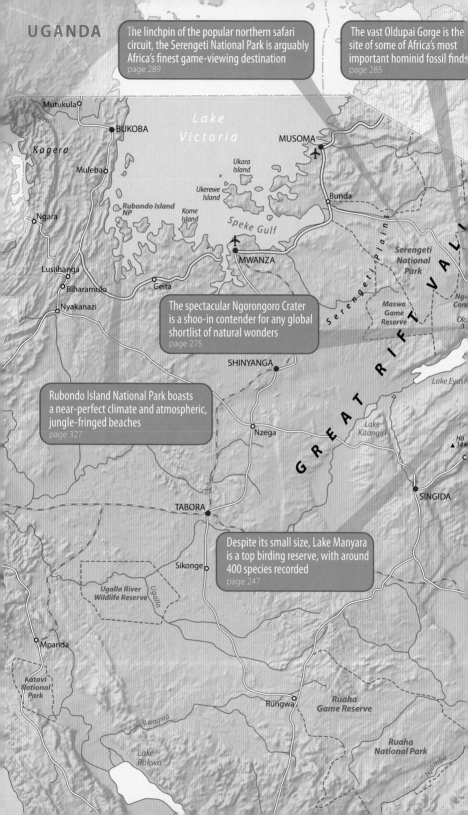

UGANDA

The linchpin of the popular northern safari circuit, the Serengeti National Park is arguably Africa's finest game-viewing destination
page 289

The vast Oldupai Gorge is the site of some of Africa's most important hominid fossil find
page 285

Mutukula

Kagera

BUKOBA

Lake Victoria

MUSOMA

Muleba

Ukara Island

Ukerewe Island

Bunda

Rubondo Island NP

Kome Island

Ngara

Speke Gulf

Serengeti Plains

Serengeti National Park

Lusahanga

MWANZA

Ng Con

Biharamulo

Geita

The spectacular Ngorongoro Crater is a shoo-in contender for any global shortlist of natural wonders
page 275

Nyakanazi

Maswa Game Reserve

Olo 3

GREAT RIFT VALL

SHINYANGA

Lake Eyasi

Rubondo Island National Park boasts a near-perfect climate and atmospheric, jungle-fringed beaches
page 327

Nzega

Lake Kitangiri

Ha 34

SINGIDA

TABORA

Despite its small size, Lake Manyara is a top birding reserve, with around 400 species recorded
page 247

Sikonge

Ugalla River Wildlife Reserve

Ugalla

Mpanda

Katavi National Park

Rungwa

Ruaha Game Reserve

Rungwa

Ruaha National Park

Lake Rukwa

Njombe

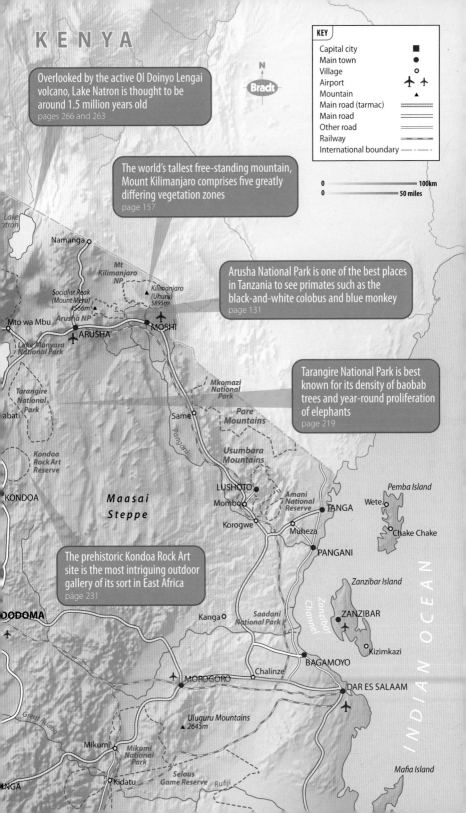

KENYA

KEY

Capital city	■
Main town	●
Village	○
Airport	✈ ✈
Mountain	▲
Main road (tarmac)	
Main road	
Other road	
Railway	
International boundary	

Overlooked by the active Ol Doinyo Lengai volcano, Lake Natron is thought to be around 1.5 million years old
pages 266 and 263

The world's tallest free-standing mountain, Mount Kilimanjaro comprises five greatly differing vegetation zones
page 157

Arusha National Park is one of the best places in Tanzania to see primates such as the black-and-white colobus and blue monkey
page 131

Tarangire National Park is best known for its density of baobab trees and year-round proliferation of elephants
page 219

The prehistoric Kondoa Rock Art site is the most intriguing outdoor gallery of its sort in East Africa
page 231

0 _____ 100km
0 _____ 50 miles

Lake Natron

Namanga

Mt Kilimanjaro NP

Socialist Peak (Mount Meru) 4566m

Kilimanjaro (Uhuru) 5895m

Arusha NP

Mto wa Mbu

ARUSHA

MOSHI

Lake Manyara National Park

Tarangire National Park

abati

Mkomazi National Park

Same

Pare Mountains

Pangani

Kondoa Rock Art Reserve

KONDOA

Maasai Steppe

Usumbara Mountains

LUSHOTO

Mombo

Amani National Reserve

Korogwe

Muheza

TANGA

Wete

Pemba Island

Chake Chake

PANGANI

DODOMA

Kanga

Saadani National Park

Zanzibar Channel

Zanzibar Island

ZANZIBAR

Kizimkazi

INDIAN OCEAN

MOROGORO

Chalinze

BAGAMOYO

DAR ES SALAAM

Uluguru Mountains 2645m

Great Ruaha

Mikumi

Mikumi National Park

NGA

Kidatu

Selous Game Reserve

Rufiji

Mafia Island

N

Bradt

Northern Tanzania

Don't miss...

Traditional culture
The primal scenery of the Hanang plains is enhanced by the colourful presence of traditional pastoralists such as the Barabaig

pages 227 & 232

Hiking and climbing
Whether you summit the mighty Mount Kilimanjaro, go rambling in the Usambara or scale the active Ol Doinyo Lengai volcano, northern Tanzania is rife with hiking opportunities

pages 160, 173 & 266

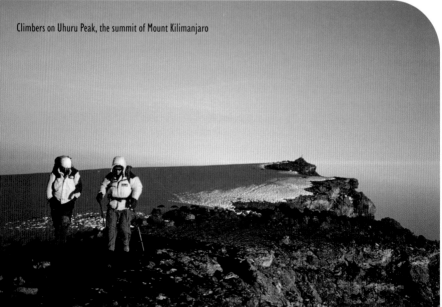

Climbers on Uhuru Peak, the summit of Mount Kilimanjaro

The 'Big Five'
Tanzania's northern safari circuit offers an excellent opportunity for viewing the famous 'Big Five'
page 21

Coastal delights
Northern Tanzania offers some of Africa's finest beaches, from the jungle-fringed shores of Lake Victoria to Zanzibar's endless tropical beaches
pages 311 & 341

Mbweni Beach, Zanzibar

Kondoa Rock Art
The fascinating and myriad painted shelters around Kondoa allow you to explore this enigmatic facet of Tanzania's prehistory
pages 231

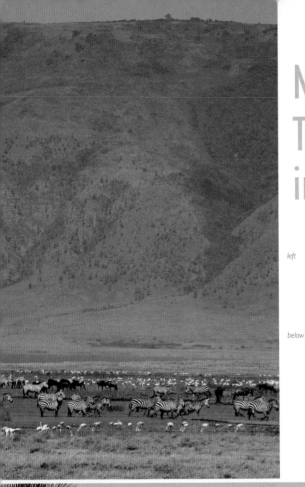

Northern Tanzania in colour

left   The Ngorongoro Crater is a mesmerising safari experience – made all the more spectacular by the striking backdrop of the 600m-high crater wall page 280

below   Lake Manyara National Park is a compact but ecologically varied area known for its tree-climbing lions, plentiful giraffes and prodigious birdlife page 247

above left Stone Town's Anglican Cathedral stands on the site of a 19th-century slave market. Pictured, a sculpture of slaves chained in a pit page 365

above right Nungwi is the centre of Zanzibar's dhow-building industry; generations of skilled craftsmen have worked on the beach outside the village page 373

below Zanzibari locals descend on a beach for a game of sunset football

AUTHORS

Philip Briggs is a travel writer specialising in Africa. Raised in South Africa, where he still lives, Philip first visited East Africa in 1986 and has since spent an average of six months annually exploring the highways and back roads of the continent. His first Bradt Travel Guide, to South Africa, was published in 1991, and he has subsequently written Bradt guides to Tanzania, Uganda, Ethiopia, Malawi, Mozambique, Ghana, Rwanda and East African wildlife. Philip has contributed to more than a dozen other books about Africa, and his work regularly appears in magazines  such as *Africa Geographic*, *Travel Africa* and *Wanderlust*. He also acts as an advisor to specialist tour operator Expert Africa, helping to develop their programmes.

Chris McIntyre went to Africa in 1987, after reading Physics at Queen's College, Oxford. He taught with VSO in Zimbabwe for almost three years and travelled extensively, before writing his first guidebook in 1990. He has since written Bradt guides to Namibia, Botswana and Zambia, and co-authored (with his wife, Susan) the last three editions of Bradt's *Zanzibar* guide – the latest of which was thoroughly revised at the same time as this book. Chris now runs specialist tour operator Expert Africa, where he leads a team of dedicated  Africa addicts who provide impartial advice and organise great safaris to Africa, including Tanzania. He can be contacted on **e** chris.mcintyre@expertafrica.com.

PUBLISHER'S FOREWORD   *Hilary Bradt*

Over 30 years ago George and I spent two fruitless days trying to hitchhike through the Serengeti. We were also bitten to distraction by mosquitoes in Mto wa Mbu ('River of Mosquitoes') and arrested in Tabora because, the official said, it was illegal to take photographs in Tanzania without a permit. George sourly wrote in *Backpacker's Africa* (1977): 'We hope someday it will all come together and be the most enlightened and productive country in Africa, but that's not going to happen for a while.' It's happened. The northern safari circuit in Tanzania is widely considered to be the best in East Africa, with an excellent infrastructure and some of the friendliest and most welcoming people in Africa. Philip once wrote: 'I've visited most corners of Tanzania … and I have to confess that were my time in the country limited to a couple of weeks, then my first priorities would undoubtedly be the Serengeti, Ngorongoro and Zanzibar. They are very special places.' In this book, Philip has been able to indulge himself – and his fans – with the detailed descriptions that these special places deserve.

Third edition June 2013   First published February 2006

Bradt Travel Guides Ltd
IDC House, The Vale, Chalfont St Peter, Bucks SL9 9RZ, England
www.bradtguides.com
Print edition published in the USA by The Globe Pequot Press Inc,
PO Box 480, Guilford, Connecticut 06437-0480

Text copyright © 2013 Philip Briggs
Zanzibar and Pemba sections copyright © 2013 Chris McIntyre and Susan McIntyre
Maps copyright © 2013 Bradt Travel Guides Ltd
Town maps content copyright © 2013 Philip Briggs
Illustrations copyright © 2013 Individual photographers and artists (see below)
Project Managers: Greg Dickinson and Kelly Randell
Cover image research: Pepi Bluck

British Library Cataloguing in Publication Data
A catalogue record for this book is available from the British Library
ISBN-13: 978 1 84162 457 0 (print)
e-ISBN-13: 978 1 84162 750 2 (e-pub)
e-ISBN-13: 978 1 84162 651 2 (mobi)

Photographs All photos in guidebook and on covers by Ariadne Van Zandbergen
Front cover Elephant, Serengeti National Park
Back cover Hot air balloons over the Serengeti, Lilac-breasted roller
Title page Barabaig man, Traditional dhow, Zanzibar, Cheetah in the Serengeti

Illustrations Annabel Milne
Maps David McCutcheon FBCart.S; colour relief base by Nick Rowland FRGS

Typeset from the authors' disk by Wakewing
Production managed by Jellyfish Print Solutions; printed in India
Digital conversion by the Firsty Group

CONTRIBUTORS

Ariadne Van Zandbergen, who took most of the photographs in this book and did much of the research for the sections on Kilimanjaro and Ol Doinyo Lengai, is a Belgian-born freelance photographer who first travelled through Africa from Morocco to South Africa in 1994–95 and is now resident in Johannesburg. Her photographs have appeared in numerous travel and wildlife guides, coffee-table books, magazines and newspapers. She runs an online photo library: www.africaimagelibrary.com.

Susan McIntyre is co-author of Bradt's *Zanzibar*. She has worked in public relations for the travel industry since 1999, and created media campaigns for tourist boards worldwide before focusing on some of southern Africa's finest independent safari camps and boutique hotels. Susan continues to travel and to advise on Expert Africa's programme of trips to the Zanzibar archipelago and the Seychelles, with an increasing interest in adventurous family travel, thanks to the young McIntyres.

Emma Thomson (*www.ethomson.co.uk*), former Commissioning Editor at Bradt Travel Guides, is a freelance writer and Fellow of the Royal Geographical Society. She has spent time living with Rangi, Chagga and Maasai communities in Tanzania and is a trustee of Serian UK, a registered charity that supports Monduli Juu's Noonkodin Secondary School, which provides shelter and education to FGM runaways. Emma is also the author of Bradt's award-winning *Flanders* guide.

We go back a bit, Tanzania and I. Our first stilted encounter was back in 1986, when as a nervous novice traveller heading from Kenya to Zambia, I'd heard so much about the nightmarish black market, appalling public transport and obtuse officials that I decided to nip through Tanzania in less than a week, stopping only to catch my breath in the spectacularly rundown port of Dar es Salaam.

Two years later, I returned to Tanzania on a less intimidated footing, and followed a more adventurous route that incorporated side trips to somnambulant Tanga and the fabulous ferry ride down Lake Tanganyika. But I guess the real romance began in 1992, when I spent four unforgettable months bussing the length and breadth of Tanzania to research what would become the first dedicated guidebook to this extraordinarily diverse – and at the time vastly underrated – country.

Updating duties have recalled me to Tanzania regularly since then, and every time I'm struck afresh at how much it has blossomed over the course of our acquaintance. The Tanzania I first encountered in 1986 was seemingly stuck in inextricable economic decline, with every aspect of its infrastructure – from roads and public transport to electricity and water supplies – tottering on the verge of collapse. Meanwhile, manufacture had ground to a standstill – simply tracking down a warm beer in Dar was an exercise that could take on epic proportions.

Back then, tourist facilities, such as they existed, were barely functional. And an insane fixed exchange rate ensured that travel was dominated by a risky black market. Had anybody suggested that Tanzania might one day rank as the most diverse, friendliest and arguably the best safari destination anywhere in Africa, I'd have thought they were insane.

And how wrong I'd have been … for today, almost 25 years on, that's exactly what Tanzania is!

Acknowledgements

PHILIP BRIGGS

I received an enormous amount of assistance from within the safari industry during the course of researching all editions of this book, as well as earlier editions of the Bradt guide to *Tanzania*, and I would like to express my gratitude to the many safari companies and airlines that have helped ferry us around the country, and to the myriad lodges, hotels and camps that have accommodated us over the years – this would be a poor guidebook indeed were it not for the support and hospitality that has made it possible for me to explore the region so thoroughly.

I am also indebted to my wife, travel companion and photographic collaborator Ariadne Van Zandbergen; to my co-author Chris McIntyre, his wife Susan McIntyre and the staff of Expert Africa; to Kim Wildman for her collaboration on the previous edition of Bradt's *Tanzania* guide; to my parents Roger and Kay Briggs for shuttling us to and from O R Tambo Airport so many times I've lost count; and to various Bradt staffers past and present, notably Tricia Hayne, Adrian Phillips and Emma Thomson.

CHRIS MCINTYRE

Primarily my thanks go to Philip Briggs, my co-author, for kindly allowing me to have a modest input into what was his creation and has always been his book. Then to numerous people in Tanzania, mostly on the islands, who I know will forgive me for only crediting them properly in the *Zanzibar* book. In the UK, thanks to Angela Griffin and Eleanor Dunkels of Expert Africa, who both helped extensively with parts of this text. Finally to my love, Susie, who worked so hard and delivered so well.

Contents

LIST OF MAPS

KEY TO SYMBOLS

——·—·	International boundary
▬▬▬	Tarred roads (town plans)
═══	Tarred roads (regional maps)
═══	Other roads (regional maps)
------	Tracks/4x4 (regional maps)
▬▬	Railway
··········	Footpath
--⛴--	Pedestrian ferry & route
✈ ✚	Airport/airstrip
☐	Railway station
🚌	Bus station
⛽	Filling station/garage
✕—✕	Gate/barrier
🛈	Tourist information
🏺	Museum
⊞	Important/historic building
$	Bank/ATM
✉	Post office
✚	Hospital/clinic
✚	Pharmacy
⌂	Hotel/inn/guesthouse etc
▲	Campsite
♦	Resthouse/hut

⚲	Bar
✕	Restaurant, etc
☕	Café
☆	Nightclub/casino
@	Internet access
✝	Church/cathedral
☾	Mosque
☬	Sikh temple
⊞	Cemetery
⁖	Archaeological site
⌓	Cave
❋	Viewpoint
﹀	Waterfall
♆	Woodland feature
▲	Summit (height in metres)
○	Spring/waterhole
●	Other place of interest
	Crater/escarpment
⚐	Sports facility
	Glacier
	Marsh
	National park
	Forest park/reserve
	Urban market
	Urban park

Introduction

Tanzania is a statistician's dream. Within its borders lie Africa's highest and fifth-highest mountains, the world's largest intact volcanic caldera, what is widely agreed to be Africa's greatest national park, as well as the lion's share of the continent's most expansive lake. Yet this vast East African country also boasts a litany of evocative place names to touch the heart of any poet: Kilimanjaro, Serengeti, Ngorongoro Crater, Olduvai Gorge, Lake Victoria, Zanzibar, the Indian Ocean, the Great Rift Valley, the Maasai Steppes …

More remarkable still is that this enviable list of landmarks – with the exception of offshore Zanzibar – is concentrated within a mere 10% of the country's surface area abutting the border with Kenya. And here too, bookended by Lake Victoria in the west and Kilimanjaro in the east, a bloc of contiguous national parks, game reserves and other conservation areas forms what is almost certainly the most expansive safari circuit in Africa, and arguably the finest.

At the heart of this near-pristine ecosystem lies the Serengeti National Park and adjacent Ngorongoro Conservation Area, possibly the most publicised pair of game reserves in the world. And justifiably so: the Serengeti Plains host Africa's greatest wildlife spectacle, the annual migration of perhaps two million wildebeest and zebra, while also supporting remarkably dense populations of predators such as lion, cheetah, leopard and spotted hyena. The floor of the spectacular Ngorongoro Crater is if anything even more densely packed with large mammals, and is the best place in East Africa to see the endangered black rhino.

Less celebrated components of this safari circuit include Lake Manyara and Tarangire national parks, the former protecting a shallow but expansive lake on the Rift Valley floor, the latter a tract of dry acacia woodland notable for its innumerable ancient baobabs and dense elephant population. Then there is the caustic expanse of alkaline water known as Lake Natron, breeding site to millions of flamingos. There is East Africa's most active volcano, the fiery Ol Doinyo Lengai. There is remote Lake Eyasi, its hinterland home to the region's last remaining hunter-gatherers. Dotted amid the savanna, there is jungle-covered Rubondo Island on Lake Victoria, lush montane forest in Arusha National Park, and sodden groundwater forest rising from the shores of lakes Duluti and Manyara. And, when the clouds lift, towering above the twin safari capitals of Arusha and Moshi stand the jagged peaks of Mount Meru and the even taller Kilimanjaro itself.

In short, northern Tanzania is the Africa you have always dreamed about: vast plains teeming with wild animals; rainforests alive with cackling birds and monkeys; Kilimanjaro's snow-capped peak rising dramatically above the flat scrubland; colourful Maasai guiding their cattle alongside fields of grazing wildebeest; perfect palm-lined beaches lapped by the clear warm waters of the Indian Ocean stretching as far as the eye can see – all supported by a tourist infrastructure that has recovered from an immediate post-independence economic free-fall to rank as one of the finest anywhere in Africa.

Northern Tanzania has always boasted an incomparable natural abundance and these days it is serviced by a selection of genuinely world-class game lodges, bush camps and beach resorts. But travel isn't simply about ticking off the sights in comfort. When you spend time in a country, your feelings towards it are determined more than anything by the mood of its inhabitants. I have no hesitation in saying that, on this level, my affection for Tanzania is greater than for any other African country I have visited. Tanzania is an oasis of peace and egalitarianism in a continent stoked up with political and tribal tensions, its social mood embodying all that I respect in African culture. Its people, as a rule, are polite and courteous, yet also warm and sincere, both among themselves and in their dealings with foreigners.

The one thing I can say with near certainty is that you will enjoy Tanzania. Whether you decide to stick to the conventional Serengeti–Ngorongoro–Zanzibar tourist circuit or strike out to the more offbeat likes of lakes Natron and Eyasi; whether you visit the mysterious rock art of Kondoa or track chimps through the remote forests of the Usambara Mountains, you will find Tanzania to be a truly wonderful country.

NOTE ABOUT MAPS

Several maps use grid lines to allow easy location of sites. Map grid references are listed in square brackets after listings in the text, with page number followed by grid number, eg: [105 F6].

Part One

GENERAL INFORMATION

TANZANIA AT A GLANCE

Location East Africa, between 1° and 11°45′S, and 29°20′ and 40°35′E

Size 945,166km²

Climate Tropical along coast; temperate in the highlands

Status Republic

Ruling party Chama Cha Mapinduzi (CCM)

President Jakaya Kikwete

Population 46 million (2012 estimate)

Life expectancy 51.45

Capital Dodoma

Largest city Dar es Salaam

Major exports Coffee, cotton, cashew nuts, sisal, tobacco, tea, diamonds, gold

Languages KiSwahili and English; over 100 regional variations

Religion 30–45% Muslim, 30–40% Christian, 15–30% traditional or other beliefs

Currency Tanzanian shilling (Tsh)

Exchange rate £1 = Tsh2,446, US$1 = Tsh1,620, €1 = Tsh2,094 (March 2013)

International telephone code +255

Time GMT + 3 hours

Electrical voltage 230v (60Hz). Round or square three-pin British-style plugs

Weights and measures Metric

Flag Blue and green, with diagonal black-and-yellow stripe

Public holidays 1 January, 12 January, 7 April, 26 April, 1 May, 7 July, 8 August, 14 October, 9 December, 25–26 December. See also *Public Holidays*, page 77.

1

Background Information

GEOGRAPHY

The bulk of East Africa is made up of a vast, flat plateau rising from a narrow coastal belt to an average height of about 1,500m. This plateau is broken dramatically by the 20-million-year-old Great Rift Valley, which cuts a trough up to 2,000m deep through the African continent from the Dead Sea to Mozambique. The main branch of the Rift Valley bisects Tanzania. A western branch of the Rift Valley forms the Tanzania–Congo border. Lakes Natron, Manyara, Eyasi and Nyasa/Malawi are all in the main rift, Lake Tanganyika lies in the western branch, and Lake Victoria lies on an elevated plateau between them.

East Africa's highest mountains (with the exception of the Ruwenzori Mountains in Uganda) are volcanic in origin, created by the same forces that caused the emergence of the Rift Valley. Kilimanjaro is the most recent of these: it started to form about one million years ago, and was still growing as recently as 100,000 years ago. Mount Meru is older. Ngorongoro Crater is the collapsed caldera of a volcano that would once have been as high as Kilimanjaro is today. The only active volcano in Tanzania, Ol Doinyo Lengai, rises from the rift floor to the north of Ngorongoro.

SIZE AND LOCATION The United Republic of Tanzania came into being in 1964 when Tanganyika on the African mainland united with the offshore state of Zanzibar, the latter comprising the Indian Ocean islands of Unguja (Zanzibar) and Pemba. It lies on the East African coast between 1° and 11°45'S and 29°20' and 40°35'E, and is bordered by Kenya and Uganda to the north, Rwanda, Burundi and the Democratic Republic of the Congo to the west, and Zambia, Malawi and Mozambique to the south. The country extends over 945,166km² (364,929 square miles), making it one of the largest countries in sub-Saharan Africa, covering a greater area than Kenya and Uganda combined. To place this in a European context, Tanzania is more than four times the size of Britain, while in an American context it's about 1.5 times the size of Texas.

This book concentrates mostly on the northeast of Tanzania, running southward from the Kenyan border to a latitude of around 4°, and between 31.5° and 37.5°E, a total area of around 120,000km², about half the size of Britain.

CAPITAL Dodoma was earmarked as the future capital of Tanzania in 1973. It has subsequently displaced Dar es Salaam as the official national capital, and is also where all parliamentary sessions are held. Some government departments, however, are still based in Dar es Salaam, which remains the most important and largest city in the country, and is the site of the main international airport, many

ARUSHA	Jan	Feb	Mar	Apr	May	Jun	Jul	Aug	Sep	Oct	Nov	Dec
Max (°C)	29	29	28	25	22	21	20	22	25	27	28	28
Min (°C)	10	12	12	14	11	10	10	9	9	10	10	10
Rain (mm)	50	85	180	350	205	20	10	15	15	20	105	100

MOSHI	Jan	Feb	Mar	Apr	May	Jun	Jul	Aug	Sept	Oct	Nov	Dec
Max (°C)	36	35	34	30	29	29	28	30	31	32	34	34
Min (°C)	15	15	15	16	14	13	12	12	13	14	14	15
Rain (mm)	50	60	120	300	180	50	20	20	20	40	60	50

MWANZA	Jan	Feb	Mar	Apr	May	Jun	Jul	Aug	Sep	Oct	Nov	Dec
Max (°C)	33	34	33	31	31	30	29	29	30	32	32	31
Min (°C)	15	16	16	16	14	13	12	13	15	16	15	15
Rain (mm)	105	110	165	160	100	20	15	25	30	45	105	120

ZANZIBAR TOWN	Jan	Feb	Mar	Apr	May	Jun	Jul	Aug	Sep	Oct	Nov	Dec
Max (°C)	32	32	33	30	29	28	27	28	29	30	31	31
Min (°C)	25	25	26	26	25	24	23	23	23	25	25	26
Rain (mm)	50	65	140	310	290	45	25	25	35	60	180	135

diplomatic missions to Tanzania, and most large businesses. The main commercial centre and unofficial safari capital of northern Tanzania is the town of Arusha at the southern base of Mount Meru.

CLIMATE

The coast and Lake Victoria hinterland are hot and humid, with temperatures least comfortable from November to March. Otherwise, northern Tanzania is far cooler than many visitors expect. The Ngorongoro Crater rim and Usambara Mountains tend to be chilly at night and misty in the morning, and the former receives a sufficiently high annual rainfall to support a belt of montane rainforest. The crater floor and Serengeti Plains are warmer but, since they lie above the Rift Valley escarpment at elevations of well over 1,000m, they are far from being oppressively hot and can be quite chilly in the early morning and after dark. Tarangire and Lake Manyara national parks lie at lower elevations and are considerably warmer, with Tarangire in particular sometimes becoming seriously hot in the afternoon. Both areas cool down after dusk, however, and most visitors to Manyara will sleep at one of the lodges on the cool, breezy escarpment. Alpine conditions and sub-zero temperatures are characteristic of the higher slopes of Mount Meru and especially Kilimanjaro after dark.

Tanzania is too near the Equator to experience the sort of dramatic contrast between summer and winter experienced in much of Europe or North America, but the months between October and April are marginally hotter than May to September. The rainy season is generally split into the short rains or *mvuli*, over November and December, and the long rains or *masika* from late February to early May, although the exact timing of these seasons varies considerably from one year to the next.

Tanzania has a rich and fascinating history, but much of the detail is highly elusive. Specialist works often contradict each other to such an extent that it is difficult to tell where fact ends and speculation begins, while broader or more popular accounts are commonly riddled with obvious inaccuracies. This is partly because there are huge gaps in the known facts; partly because much of the available information is scattered in out-of-print or difficult-to-find books; and partly because once an inaccuracy gets into print it tends to spread like a virus through other written works. For whatever reason there is not, as far as I am aware, one concise, comprehensive and reliable book about Tanzanian history in print.

The following account attempts to provide a reasonably comprehensive and readable overview of the country's history. It is, to the best of my knowledge, as accurate as the known facts will allow, but at times I have had to decide for myself the most probable truth among a mass of contradictions, and I have speculated freely where speculation seems to be the order of the day. My goals are to stimulate the visitor's interest in Tanzanian history, and to give easy access to information that would have greatly enhanced my formative travels in Tanzania. Many of the subjects touched on in this general history are given more elaborate treatment elsewhere in the book, under regional history sections or in tinted boxes.

PREHISTORY OF THE INTERIOR The part of the Rift Valley passing through Ethiopia, Kenya and northern Tanzania is almost certainly where modern human beings and their hominine ancestors evolved. The two most common hominine genera on the fossil record are *Australopithecus* and *Homo*, the former extinct for at least a million years, and the latter now represented by only one species – *Homo sapiens* (modern man). The paucity of hominine fossils collected before the 1960s meant that for many years it was assumed that *A. africanus* (the most common Australopithecine in the fossil record) evolved directly into the genus *Homo* and was thus man's oldest identifiable ancestor.

This linear theory of human evolution became blurred when Richard and Mary Leakey, who were excavating Olduvai Gorge in northern Tanzania, discovered that at least two *Australopithecus* species had existed. Carbon dating and the skeletal structure of the two species indicated that the older *A. robustus* had less in common with modern man than its more lightly built ancestor *A. africanus*, implying that the *Australopithecus* line was not ancestral to the *Homo* line at all. This hypothesis was confirmed in 1972 with the discovery of a two-million-year-old skull of a previously undescribed species *Homo habilis* at Lake Turkana in Kenya, providing conclusive evidence that *Australopithecus* and *Homo* species had lived alongside each other for at least one million years. As more fossils have come to light, including older examples of *Homo erectus* (the direct ancestor of modern humans), it has become clear that several different hominine species existed alongside each other in the Rift Valley until perhaps half a million years ago.

In 1974, Donald Johansen discovered an almost complete hominine skeleton in the Danakil region of northern Ethiopia. Named Lucy (the song 'Lucy in the Sky with Diamonds' was playing in camp shortly after the discovery), this turned out to be the fossil of a 3.5-million-year-old Australopithecine of an entirely new species dubbed *A. afarensis*. Lucy's anatomy demonstrated that bipedal hominines (or rather semi-bipedal, since the length of Lucy's arms suggest she would have been as comfortable swinging through the trees as she would have been on a morning jog) had evolved much earlier than previously assumed.

In the 1960s it was widely thought that humans and apes diverged around 20 million years ago. More recent molecular studies indicate that modern man and chimpanzees are far more closely related than previously assumed, and that the two evolutionary lines diverged from a common ancestor between eight and six million years ago. The Afar region of Ethiopia has yielded the world's oldest undisputed hominine *Ardipithecus kadabba* (thought to be around 5.5 million years old). More controversial candidates for the title of the world's oldest known hominine fossil include the seven-million-year-old *Sahelanthropus tchadensis*, discovered in Chad in 2001, and the arboreal *Orrorin tugenensis*, which lived in Kenya about six million years ago and might represent a common ancestor of chimpanzees and hominines.

The immediate ancestor of modern man is *Homo erectus*, which appeared about 1.5 million years ago. *Homo erectus* was the first hominine to surmount the barrier of the Sahara and spread into Europe and Asia, and is credited with the discovery of fire and the first use of stone tools and recognisable speech. Although modern man, *Homo sapiens*, has been around for at least half a million years, only in the last 10,000 years have the African races recognised today more or less taken their modern form. Up until about 1000BC, East Africa was populated exclusively by hunter-gatherers with a physiology, culture and language similar to the modern-day Khoisan (or Bushmen) of southern Africa. Rock art accredited to these hunter-gatherers is found throughout East Africa, most notably in the Kondoa-Irangi region of central Tanzania.

The pastoralist and agricultural lifestyles that were pioneered in the Nile Delta in about 5000BC spread to parts of sub-Saharan Africa by 2000BC, most notably to the Cushitic-speaking people of the Ethiopian Highlands and the Bantu-speakers of West Africa. Cushitic-speakers first drifted into Tanzania in about 1000BC, closely followed by Bantu-speakers. Familiar with Iron Age technology, these migrants would have soon dominated the local hunter-gatherers. By AD1000, most of Tanzania was populated by Bantu-speakers, with Cushitic-speaking pockets in areas such as the Ngorongoro Highlands.

There is no detailed information about the Tanzanian interior prior to 1500, and even after that details are sketchy. Except for the Lake Victoria region, which supported large authoritarian kingdoms similar to those in Uganda, much of the Tanzanian interior is too dry to support large concentrations of people. In most of Tanzania, an informal system of **ntemi** chiefs emerged. The ntemi system, although structured, seems to have been flexible and benevolent. The chiefs were served by a council and performed a role that was as much advisory as it was authoritarian. By the 19th century there are estimated to have been more than 200 ntemi chiefs in western and central Tanzania, each with about 1,000 subjects.

The ntemi system was shattered when southern Tanzania was invaded by **Ngoni** exiles from what is now South Africa, refugees from the rampantly militaristic Zulu Kingdom moulded by Shaka in the early 19th century. The Ngoni entered southern Tanzania in about 1840, bringing with them the revolutionary Zulu military tactics based on horseshoe formations and a short stabbing spear. The new arrivals attacked the resident tribes, destroying communities and leaving survivors no option but to turn to banditry. Their tactics were observed and adopted by the more astute ntemi chiefs, who needed to protect themselves, but had to forge larger kingdoms to do so. The situation was exacerbated by the growing presence of Arab slave traders. Tribes controlling the areas that caravan routes went through were able to extract taxes from the slavers and to find work with them as porters or organising slave raids. This situation was exploited by several chiefs, most notably Mirambo of Unyamwezi and Mkwawa of the Uhehe, charismatic leaders who dominated the interior in the late 19th century.

THE COAST TO 1800 There have been links between the East African coast and the rest of the world for millennia, but only the barest sketch of events before AD1000 is possible. The ancient Egyptians believed their ancestors came from a southerly land called **Punt** and in about 2500BC an explorer called Sahare sailed off in search of this mysterious place. Sahare returned laden with ivory, ebony and myrrh, a booty that suggests he had landed somewhere on the East African coast, most likely in the north of present-day Somalia (but possibly further south). There is no suggestion that Egyptian boats traded regularly with Punt, but they did visit it again on several occasions. Interestingly, an engraving of the Queen of Punt, made after an expedition in 1493BC, shows her to have distinctly Khoisan features. The Phoenicians first explored the coast in about 600BC. According to the 1st-century *Periplus of the Ancient Sea* they traded with a town called Rhapta, which is thought to have lain upriver of a major estuary, possibly the Pangani or the Rufiji Delta.

Bantu-speakers arrived at the coast about 2,000 years ago. It seems likely they had trade links with the **Roman Empire**: Rhapta gets a name check in Ptolemy's 4th-century *Geography*, and a few 4th-century Roman coins have been found at the coast. The fact that the Romans knew of Kilimanjaro, and of the great lakes of the interior, raises some interesting questions. One hypothesis is that the coastal Bantu-speakers were running trade routes into the interior and that these collapsed at the same time as the Roman Empire, presumably as a result of the sudden dearth of trade partners. This notion is attractive and not implausible, but the evidence seems rather flimsy. The Romans could simply have gleaned the information from Bantu-speakers who had arrived at the coast recently enough to have some knowledge of the interior.

Historians have a clearer picture of events on the coast from about AD1000, by which time trade between the coast and the Persian Gulf was well established. The earliest known Islamic buildings on the coast, which stand on Manda Island off Kenya, have been dated to the 9th century AD. Items sold to Arab ships at this time included ivory, ebony and spices, while a variety of oriental and Arabic goods were imported for the use of wealthy traders. The dominant item of export, however, was **gold**, mined in the Great Zimbabwe region, transported to the coast at Sofala (in modern-day Mozambique) via the Zambezi Valley, then shipped by local traders to Mogadishu, where it was sold to the Arab boats. The common assumption that Swahili language and culture was a direct result of Arab traders mixing with local Bantu-speakers is probably inaccurate. KiSwahili is a Bantu language, and although it did spread along the coast in the 11th century, most of the Arabic words that have entered the language did so at a later date. The driving force behind a common coastal language and culture was almost certainly not the direct trade with Arabs, but rather the internal trade between Sofala and Mogadishu.

More than 30 Swahili city-states sprung up along the East African coast between the 13th and 15th century, a large number of which were in modern-day Tanzania. This period is known as the **Shirazi era** after the sultans who ruled these city-states, most of whom claimed descent from the Shiraz region of Persia. Each city-state had its own sultan; they rarely interfered in each other's business. The Islamic faith was widespread during this period, and many Arabic influences crept into coastal architecture. Cities were centred on a great mosque, normally constructed in rock and coral. It has long been assumed that the many Arabs who settled on the coast before and during the Shirazi era controlled the trade locally, but this notion has been questioned in recent years. Contemporary descriptions of the city-states suggest that Africans formed the bulk of the population. It is possible that some African traders claimed Shirazi descent in order to boost their standing both locally and with Shirazi ships.

In the mid 13th century, probably due to improvements in Arab navigation and ship construction, the centre of the gold trade moved southward from Mogadishu to the small island of Kilwa. Kilwa represented the peak of the Shirazi period. It had a population of 10,000 and operated its own mint, the first in sub-equatorial Saharan Africa. The multi-domed mosque on Kilwa was the largest and most splendid anywhere on the coast, while another building, now known as Husuni Kubwa, was a gargantuan palace, complete with audience courts, several ornate balconies and even a swimming pool.

Although Mombasa had possibly superseded Kilwa in importance by the end of the 15th century, coastal trade was still booming. It came to an abrupt halt in 1505, however, when the **Portuguese** captured Mombasa, and several other coastal towns, Kilwa included, were razed. Under Portuguese control the gold trade collapsed and the coastal economy stagnated. It was dealt a further blow in the late 16th century when a mysterious tribe of cannibals called the Zimba swept up the coast to ransack several cities and eat their inhabitants before being defeated by a mixed Portuguese and local army near Malindi in modern-day Kenya.

In 1698, an Arabic naval force under the Sultan of Oman captured Fort Jesus, the Portuguese stronghold in Mombasa, paving the way for the eventual Omani takeover of the coast north of modern-day Mtwara. Rivalries between the new Omani and the old Shirazi dynasties soon surfaced, and in 1728 a group of Shirazi sultans went so far as to conspire with their old oppressors, the Portuguese, to overthrow Fort Jesus. The Omani recaptured the fort a year later. For the next 100 years an uneasy peace gripped the coast, which was nominally under Omani rule, but dominated in economic terms by the Shirazi Sultan of Mombasa.

SLAVERY AND EXPLORATION IN THE 19TH CENTURY The 19th century was a period of rapid change in Tanzania, with stronger links established between the coast and the interior as well as between East Africa and Europe. Over the first half of the 19th century, the most important figure locally was **Sultan Seyyid Said of Oman**, who ruled from 1804 to 1854. Prior to 1804, Britain had signed a treaty with Oman, and relations between the two powers intensified in the wake of the Napoleonic Wars, since the British did not want to see the coast fall into French hands. In 1827, Said's small but efficient navy captured Mombasa and overthrew its Shirazi sultan, to assert unambiguous control over the whole coast, with strong British support.

Having captured Mombasa, Sultan Said chose Zanzibar as his East African base, partly because of its proximity to Bagamoyo (the terminus of a caravan route to Lake Tanganyika since 1823) and partly because it was more secure against attacks from the sea or the interior than any mainland port. Said's commercial involvement with Zanzibar began in 1827 when he set up a number of clove plantations there, with scant regard for the land claims of local inhabitants. Said and his fellow Arabs had come totally to dominate all aspects of commerce on the island by 1840, the year in which the sultan permanently relocated his personal capital from Oman to Zanzibar.

The extent of the East African **slave trade** prior to 1827 is unclear. It certainly existed, but was never as important as the gold or ivory trade. In part, this was because the traditional centre of slave trading had always been West Africa, which was far closer than the Indian Ocean to the main markets of the Americas. In the early 19th century, however, the British curbed the slave trade out of West Africa, leaving the way open for Said and his cronies. By 1839, over 40,000 slaves were being sold from Zanzibar annually. These came from two sources: the central caravan route between Bagamoyo and the Lake Tanganyika region, and a southern route between Kilwa Kivinje and Lake Nyasa.

The effects of the slave trade on the interior were numerous. The **Nyamwezi** of the Tabora region and the **Yua** of Nyasa became very powerful by serving as porters along the caravan routes and organising slave raids and ivory hunts. Weaker tribes were devastated. Villages were ransacked; the able-bodied men and women were taken away while the young and old were left to die. Hundreds of thousands of slaves were sold in the mid 19th century. Nobody knows how many more died of disease or exhaustion between being captured and reaching the coast. Another long-term effect of the slave trade was that it formed the driving force behind the second great expansion of KiSwahili, which became the *lingua franca* along caravan routes.

Europeans knew little about the African interior in 1850. The first Europeans to see Kilimanjaro (Rebmann in 1848) and Mount Kenya (Krapf in 1849) were ridiculed for their reports of snow on the Equator. The Arab traders must have had an intimate knowledge of many parts of the interior that intrigued Europeans, but, oddly, at least in hindsight, nobody seems to have thought to ask them. In 1855, a German missionary, **James Erhardt**, produced a map of Africa, based on third-hand Arab accounts, which showed a large slug-shaped lake in the heart of the continent. Known as the Slug Map, it was wildly inaccurate, yet it did serve to fan interest in a mystery that had tickled geographers since Roman times: the source of the Nile.

The men most responsible for opening up the East African interior to Europeans were **David Livingstone**, **Richard Burton**, **John Speke** and, later, **Henry Stanley**. Livingstone, who came from a poor Scots background, left school at the age of ten, and educated himself to become a doctor and a missionary. He arrived in the Cape in 1841 to work in the Kuruman Mission, but, overcome by the enormity of the task of converting Africa to Christianity, he decided he would be of greater service opening up the continent so that other missionaries could follow. Livingstone was the first European to cross the Kalahari Desert, the first to cross Africa from west to east and the first to see Victoria Falls. In 1858, Livingstone stumbled across Africa's third-largest lake, Nyasa. Later in the same year, on a quest for the source of the Nile funded by the Royal Geographical Society, Burton and Speke were the first Europeans to see Lake Tanganyika, and Speke continued north to Lake Victoria. Speke returned to the northern shore of Lake Victoria in 1863 and concluded – correctly, although it would be many years before the theory gained wide acceptance – that Ripon Falls in modern-day Uganda formed the source of the Nile.

Livingstone had ample opportunity during his wanderings to witness the slave caravans at first hand. Sickened by what he saw – the human bondage, the destruction of entire villages, and the corpses abandoned by the traders – he became an outspoken critic of the trade. He believed the only way to curb it was to open up Africa to the three Cs: Christianity, commerce and civilisation. Though not an imperialist by nature, Livingstone had seen enough of the famine and misery caused by the slavers and the Ngoni in the Nyasa area to believe the only solution was for Britain to colonise eastern Africa.

In 1867, Livingstone set off from Mikindani to spend the last six years of his life wandering between the great lakes, making notes on the slave trade and trying to settle the Nile debate. He believed the source of the Nile to be Lake Bangweulu (in northern Zambia), from which the mighty Lualaba River flowed. In 1872, while recovering from illness at Ujiji, Livingstone was met by Henry Stanley and became the recipient of perhaps the most famous words ever spoken in Africa: 'Dr Livingstone, I presume.' Livingstone died near Lake Bangweulu in 1873. His heart was removed and buried by his porters, who then carried his cured body over 1,500km via Tabora to Bagamoyo, a voyage as remarkable as any undertaken by the European explorers.

Livingstone's quest to end the slave trade met with little success during his lifetime, but his death and highly emotional funeral at Westminster Abbey seem to have acted as a catalyst. Missions were built in his name all over the Nyasa region, while industrialists such as William Mackinnon and the Muir brothers invested in schemes to open Africa to commerce (which Livingstone had always believed was the key to putting the slavers out of business).

In the year Livingstone died, **John Kirk** was made the British Consul in Zanzibar. Kirk had travelled with Livingstone on his 1856–62 trip to Nyasa. Deeply affected by what he saw, he had since spent years on Zanzibar hoping to find a way to end the slave trade. In 1873, the British navy blockaded the island and Kirk offered Sultan Barghash full protection against foreign powers if he banned the slave trade. Barghash agreed. The slave market was closed and an Anglican church built over it. Within ten years of Livingstone's death, the volume of slaves was a fraction of what it had been in the 1860s. Caravans reverted to ivory as their principal trade, while many of the coastal traders started up rubber and sugar plantations, which turned out to be just as lucrative as their former trade. Nevertheless, a clandestine slave trade continued on the mainland for some years – 12,000 slaves were sold at Kilwa in 1875 – and even into the 20th century, only to be fully eradicated in 1918, when Britain took control of Tanganyika.

THE PARTITIONING OF EAST AFRICA The so-called **scramble for Africa** was entered into with mixed motives, erratic enthusiasm and an almost total lack of premeditation by the powers involved. Britain, the major beneficiary of the scramble, already enjoyed a degree of influence on Zanzibar, one that arguably approached informal colonisation, and it was quite happy to maintain this mutually agreeable relationship unaltered. Furthermore, the British government at the time, led by Lord Salisbury, was broadly opposed to the taking of African colonies. The scramble was initiated by two events. The first, the decision of King Leopold of Belgium to colonise the Congo Basin, had little direct bearing on events in Tanzania. The partitioning of East Africa was a direct result of an about-face by the German premier, Bismarck, who had previously shown no enthusiasm for acquiring colonies and probably developed an interest in Africa in the hope of acquiring pawns to use in negotiations with Britain and France.

In 1884, a young German metaphysician called **Carl Peters** arrived inauspiciously on Zanzibar and then made his way to the mainland to sign a series of treaties with local chiefs. The authenticity of these treaties is questionable, but when Bismarck announced claims to a large area between the Pangani and Rufiji rivers, it was enough to set the British government into a mild panic. Britain had plans to expand the Sultanate of Zanzibar, its informal colony, to include the fertile lands around Kilimanjaro. Worse, large parts of the area claimed by Germany were already part of the sultanate. Not only was Britain morally bound to protect these, it also did not want to surrender control of Zanzibar's annual import–export turnover of two million pounds.

Despite pressure put on the British government by John Kirk, angry that his promises to Barghash would not be honoured, there was little option but to negotiate with Germany. A partition was agreed in 1886, identical to the modern border between Kenya and Tanzania. (You may read that Kilimanjaro was part of the British territory before Queen Victoria gave it to her cousin, the Kaiser, as a birthday present. This amusing story, possibly dreamed up by a Victorian satirist to reflect the arbitrariness of the scramble, is complete fabrication.) In April 1888, the Sultan of Zanzibar unwillingly agreed to lease Germany the coastal strip south of the Umba River. Germany mandated this area to Carl Peters's **German East Africa Company (GEAC)**, which placed agencies at most of the coastal settlements north of Dar es Salaam. These agents demanded heavy taxes from traders and were encouraged to behave high-handedly in their dealings with locals.

The GEAC's honeymoon was short. Emil Zalewski, the Pangani agent, ordered the sultan's representative, the Wali, to report to him. When the Wali refused, Zalewski had him arrested and sent away on a German war boat. In September 1888, a sugar plantation owner called **Abushiri Ibn Salim** led an uprising against the GEAC. Except for Dar es Salaam and Bagamoyo, both protected by German war boats, the GEAC agents were either killed or driven away. A horde of 20,000 men gathered on the coast, including 6,000 Shambaa who refused to relinquish their right to claim tax from caravans passing the Usambara. In November, the mission at Dar es Salaam was attacked. Three priests were killed and the rest captured. The coast was in chaos until April 1889 when the Kaiser's troops invaded Abushiri's camp and forced him to surrender. The German government hanged Abushiri in Pangani; they withdrew the GEAC's mandate and banned Peters from ever setting foot in the area.

The 1886 agreement only created the single line of partition north of Kilimanjaro. By 1890, Germany had claimed an area north of Witu, including Lamu, and there was concern in Britain that they might try to claim the rich agricultural land around Lake Victoria, thereby surrounding Britain's territory. Undeterred by the debacle at Pangani (and with a nod and a wink from Bismarck), Carl Peters decided to force the issue. He slipped through Lamu and in May 1890, after a murderous jaunt across British territory, he signed a treaty with the King of Buganda entitling Germany to most of what is now southern Uganda. This time, however, Peters's plans were frustrated. Bismarck had resigned in March of the same year and his replacement, Von Kaprivi, wanted to maintain good relations with Salisbury's government. In any case, Henry Stanley had signed a similar treaty with the Baganda when he passed through the area in 1888 on his way from rescuing the Emin Pasha in Equatoria.

Germany had its eye on Heligoland, a small but strategic North Sea island that had been seized by Britain from Denmark in 1807. To some extent, German interest in Africa had always been related to the bargaining power it would give them in Europe. In 1890, Salisbury and Von Kaprivi knocked out the agreement that created the modern borders of mainland Tanzania (with the exception of modern-day Burundi and Rwanda, German territory until after World War I). In exchange for an island of less than 1km² in extent, Salisbury was guaranteed protectorateship over Zanzibar and handed the German block north of Witu, and Germany relinquished any claims it might have had to what are today Uganda and Malawi.

GERMAN EAST AFRICA The period of German rule was not a happy one. In 1891, Carl Peters was appointed governor. Peters had already proved himself an unsavoury and unsympathetic character: he boasted freely of enjoying killing Africans and, under the guise of the GEAC, his lack of diplomacy had already instigated one uprising. Furthermore, the 1890s were plagued by a series of natural disasters: a rinderpest epidemic at the start of the decade, followed by an outbreak of smallpox, and a destructive plague of locusts. A series of droughts brought famine and disease in their wake. Many previously settled areas reverted to bush, causing the spread of tsetse fly and sleeping sickness. The population of Tanganyika is thought to have decreased significantly between 1890 and 1914.

It took Peters a decade to gain full control of the colony. The main area of conflict was in the vast central plateau where, led by **Mkwawa**, the Hehe had become the dominant tribe. In 1891, the Hehe ambushed a German battalion led by Emil Zalewski. They killed or wounded more than half of Zalewski's men, and made off with his armoury. Mkwawa fortified his capital near Iringa, but the Germans razed it in 1894. Mkwawa was forced to resort to guerrilla tactics, which he used with some success until 1898, when he shot himself rather than face capture by the Germans.

Germany was determined to make the colony self-sufficient. Sugar and rubber were well established on parts of the coast, coffee was planted in the Kilimanjaro region, a major base for settlers, and cotton grew well around Lake Victoria. The colony's leading crop export, sisal, was grown throughout the rest of the country. In 1902, Peters decided that the southeast should be given over to cotton plantations. This was an ill-considered move: the soils were not suitable for the crop and the scheme was bound to cause great hardship. It also led to the infamous and ultimately rather tragic **Maji-Maji rebellion**, which proved to be perhaps the most decisive event in the colony during German rule.

Carl Peters was fired from the colonial service in 1906. He believed his African mistress had slept with his manservant, so he flogged her close to death then hanged them both. After that, the German administration introduced a series of laws protecting Africans from mistreatment. To the disgust of the settler community, it also created an incentive-based scheme for African farmers. This made it worth

TRIBES

The word 'tribe' has fallen out of vogue in recent years, and I must confess that for several years I rigorously avoided the use of it in my writing. It has, I feel, rather colonial connotations, something to which I'm perhaps overly sensitive having lived most of my life in South Africa. Some African intellectuals have argued that it is derogatory, too, in so far as it is typically applied in a belittling sense to non-European cultures, where words such as 'nation' might be applied to their European equivalent.

All well and good to dispense with the word tribe, at least until you set about looking for a meaningful substitute. Nation, for instance, seems appropriate when applied in a historical sense to a large and cohesive centralised entity such as the Zulu or Hehe, but rather less so when you're talking about smaller and more loosely affiliated tribes. Furthermore, in any modern sense, Tanzania itself is a nation (and proud of it), just as are Britain and Germany, so that describing, for instance, the modern Chagga as a nation would feel as inaccurate and contrived as referring to, say, the Liverpudlian or Berliner nation.

It would be inaccurate, too, to refer to most African tribes in purely ethnic, cultural or linguistic terms. Any or all of these factors might come into play in shaping a tribal identity, without in any sense defining it. All modern tribes contain individuals with a diverse ethnic stock, simply through intermarriage. Most modern Ngoni, for instance, belong to that tribe through their ancestors having been assimilated into it, not because all or even any of their ancestors were necessarily members of the Ngoni band who migrated up from South Africa in the 19th century. And when the original Bantu-speaking people moved into present-day Tanzania thousands of years ago, local people with an entirely different ethnic background would have been assimilated into the newly established communities. Likewise, the linguistic and cultural differences between two neighbouring tribes are often very slight, and may be no more significant than dialectal or other regional differences within either tribe. The Maasai and Samburu, for instance, their while to grow cash crops and allowed the colony's exports to triple in the period leading up to World War I.

When war broke out in Europe, East Africa also became involved. In the early stages of the war, German troops entered southern Kenya to cut off the Uganda Railway. Britain responded with an abortive attempt to capture Tanga. The balance of power was roughly even until **Jan Smuts** led the Allied forces into German territory in 1916. By January 1918, the Allies had captured most of German East Africa and the German commander, Von Lettow, retreated into Mozambique. The war disrupted food production, and a serious famine ensued. This was particularly devastating in the Dodoma region. The country was taken over by the League of Nations. The Ruanda-Urundi District, now the states of Rwanda and Burundi, was mandated to Belgium. The rest of the country was renamed Tanganyika and mandated to Britain.

TANGANYIKA The period of British rule between the wars was largely uneventful. Tanganyika was never heavily settled by Europeans so the indigenous populace had more opportunity for self-reliance than it did in many colonies. Nevertheless, settlers were favoured in the agricultural field, as were Asians in commerce. The Land Ordinance Act of 1923 secured some land rights for Africans, otherwise

share a long common history, are of essentially the same ethnic stock, speak the same language, and are culturally almost indistinguishable. Yet they perceive themselves to be distinct tribes, and are perceived as such by outsiders.

A few years ago, in mild desperation, I settled on the suitably nebulous term ethno-linguistic group as a substitute for tribe. Clumsy, ugly and verging on the meaningless it might be, but it does sound impressively authoritative, without pinning itself exclusively on ethnicity, language or culture as a defining element, and it positively oozes political correctness. It's also, well, a little bit silly! Just as Tanzanians are unselfconscious about referring to themselves as black and to *wazungu* as white, so too do they talk about their tribe without batting an eyelid. For goodness sake, at every other local hotel in Tanzania, visitors are required to fill in the 'Tribe' column in the standard-issue guesthouse visitors' book. And if it's good enough for Tanzanians, who am I to get precious about it?

More than that, it strikes me that even in an African nation as united as Tanzania certainly is, the role of tribe in shaping the identity of an individual has no real equivalent in most Western societies. We may love – or indeed loathe – our home town, we might fight to the death for our loved ones, we might shed tears when our football team loses or our favourite pop group disbands, but we have no equivalent to the African notion of tribe. True enough, tribalism is often cited as the scourge of modern Africa, and when taken to fanatical extremes that's a fair assessment, yet to damn it entirely would be rather like damning English football, or its supporters, because of the actions of a fanatical extreme. Tribalism is an integral part of African society, and pussyfooting around it through an overdeveloped sense of political correctness strikes me as more belittling than being open about it.

So, in case you hadn't gathered, Tanzania's 120 ethno-lingual-cultural groupings are tribes for this edition of the guide, a decision that will hold at least for as long as I'm expected to fill in my tribe – whatever that might be – every time I check into a Tanzanian guesthouse.

they were repeatedly forced into grand but misconceived agricultural schemes. The most notorious of these, the **Groundnut Scheme** of 1947, was an attempt to convert the southeast of the country into a large-scale mechanised groundnut producer. The scheme failed through a complete lack of understanding of local conditions; it caused a great deal of hardship locally and cost British taxpayers millions of pounds. On a political level, a system of indirect rule based around local government encouraged African leaders to focus on local rivalries rather than national issues between the wars. A low-key national movement called the **Tanganyika Africa Association (TAA)** was formed in 1929, but it was as much a cultural as a political organisation.

Although it was not directly involved in World War II, Tanganyika was profoundly affected by it. The country benefited economically. It saw no combat so food production continued as normal, while international food prices rocketed. Tanganyika's trade revenue increased six-fold between 1939 and 1949. World War II was a major force in the rise of **African nationalism**. Almost 100,000 Tanganyikans fought for the Allies. The exposure to other countries and cultures made it difficult for them to return home as second-class citizens. They had fought for non-racism and democracy in Europe, yet were victims of racist and non-democratic policies in their own country.

The dominant figure in the post-war politics of Tanganyika/Tanzania was **Julius Nyerere** (1922–99). Schooled at a mission near Lake Victoria, he went on to university in Uganda and gained a Master's degree in Edinburgh. After returning to Tanzania in 1952, Nyerere became involved in the TAA. This evolved into the more political and nationalist **Tanganyika African National Union (TANU)** in 1954. Nyerere became the president of TANU at the age of 32. By supporting rural Africans on grass-roots issues and advocating self-government as the answer to their grievances, TANU gained a strong national following. By the mid 1950s, Britain and the UN were looking at a way of moving Tanganyika towards greater self-government, although over a far longer time-scale than TANU envisaged. The British governor, Sir Edward Twining, favoured a multi-racial system that would give equal representation to whites, blacks and Asians. TANU agreed to an election along these lines, albeit with major reservations. Twining created his own 'African party', the UTC.

In the 1958 election, there were three seats per constituency, one for each racial group. Electors could vote for all three seats, so in addition to putting forward candidates for the black seats, TANU indicated their preferred candidates in the white and Asian seats. Candidates backed by TANU won 67% of the vote; the UTC did not win a single seat. Twining's successor, Sir Richard Turnball, rewarded TANU by scrapping the multi-racial system in favour of open elections. In the democratic election of 1960, TANU won all but one seat. In May 1961, Tanganyika attained self-government and Nyerere was made prime minister. Tanganyika attained full **independence** on 9 December 1961. Not one life had been taken in the process. Britain granted Zanzibar full independence in December 1963. A month later the Arab government was toppled and in April 1964 the two countries combined to form Tanzania.

TANZANIA At the very core of Tanzania's post-independence achievements and failures lies the figure of Julius Nyerere, who ruled Tanzania until his retirement in 1985. In his own country, where he remains highly respected, Nyerere is called *Mwalimu* – the teacher. In the West, he is a controversial figure, often portrayed as a dangerous socialist who irreparably damaged his country. This image of Nyerere doesn't bear scrutiny. He made mistakes and was intolerant of criticism – at one point Tanzania had more political prisoners than South Africa – but he is also one of the few genuine statesmen to have emerged from Africa, a force for positive change both in his own country and in a wider African context.

In 1962, TANU came into power with little policy other than their attained goal of independence. Tanganyika was the poorest and least economically developed country in East Africa, and one of the poorest in the world. Nyerere's first concerns were to better the lot of rural Africans and to prevent the creation of a money-grabbing elite. The country was made a one-party state, but had an election system that, by African standards, was relatively democratic. Tanzania pursued a policy of non-alignment, but the government's socialist policies and Nyerere's outspoken views alienated most Western leaders. Close bonds were formed with socialist powers, most significantly China, who built the Tanzam Railway (completed in 1975).

Relations with Britain soured in 1965. Nyerere condemned the British government's tacit acceptance of the Unilateral Declaration of Independence (UDI) in Rhodesia. In return, Britain cut off all aid to Tanzania. Nyerere also gave considerable vocal support to disenfranchised Africans in South Africa, Mozambique and Angola. The ANC and Frelimo both operated from Tanzania in the 1960s.

Nyerere's international concerns were not confined to white supremacism. In 1975, Tanzania pulled out of an Organisation of African Unity (OAU) conference in Idi Amin's Uganda saying: 'The refusal to protest against African crimes against Africans is bad enough … but … by meeting in Kampala … the OAU are giving respectability to one of the most murderous regimes in Africa.' Tanzania gave refuge to several Ugandans, including the former president Milton Obote and the current president Yoweri Museveni. Amin occupied part of northwest Tanzania in October 1978, and bombed Bukoba and Musoma. In 1979, Tanzania retaliated by invading Uganda and toppling Amin. Other African leaders condemned Tanzania for this action, despite Amin having been the initial aggressor. Ousting Amin drained Tanzania's financial resources, but it never received any financial compensation, either from the West, or from any other African country.

At the time of independence, most rural Tanzanians lived in scattered communities. This made it difficult for the government to provide such amenities as clinics and schools and to organise a productive agricultural scheme. In 1967, Nyerere embarked on a policy he called **villagisation**. Rural people were encouraged to form *Ujamaa* (familyhood) villages and collective farms. The scheme met with some small-scale success in the mid 1970s, so in 1975 Nyerere decided to forcibly re-settle people who had not yet formed villages. By the end of the year 65% of rural Tanzanians lived in Ujamaa villages. In many areas, however, water supplies were inadequate to support a village. The resultant mess, exacerbated by one of Tanzania's regular droughts, ended further villagisation. Ujamaa is often considered to have been an unmitigated disaster. It did not achieve what it was meant to, but it did help the government improve education and healthcare. Most reliable sources claim it did little long-term damage to agricultural productivity.

By the late 1970s Tanzania's economy was a mess. There were several contributory factors: drought, Ujamaa, rising fuel prices, the border closure with Kenya (to prevent Kenyan operators from dominating the Tanzanian safari industry), lack of foreign aid, bureaucracy and corruption in state-run institutions, and the cost of the Uganda episode. After his re-election in 1980 Nyerere announced he would retire at the end of that five-year term. In 1985, **Ali Hassan Mwinyi** succeeded Nyerere as prime minister. Nyerere remained chairman of the **Chama Cha Mapinduzi (CCM)**, the party formed when TANU merged with the Zanzibari ASP in 1975, until 1990.

Under President Mwinyi, Tanzania moved away from socialism. In June 1986, in alliance with the IMF, a three-year Economic Recovery Plan was implemented. This included freeing up the exchange rate and encouraging private enterprise. Since then Tanzania has achieved an annual growth rate of around 4% (in real terms). Many locals complain that the only result they have seen is greater inflation. In 1990 attempts were made to rout corruption from the civil service, with surprisingly positive results.

The first multi-party election took place in October 1995. The CCM was returned to power with a majority of around 75% under the leadership of Benjamin Mkapa, who stood down in December 2005 following the country's third multi-party election. This, once again, was won by the CCM, which polled more than 80% of the 11.3 million votes under its new leader, Jakaya Kikwete. The CCM retained power under the 60-year-old Kikwete in the 2010 election, but with a vastly reduced majority, polling only 63% of the vote amongst the 42% of registered voters who turned out for the election. The main beneficiary of this significant electoral shift was the conservative **Chama cha Demokrasia na Maendeleo (CDM, popularly known as Chadema)**, meaning Party for Democracy and Progress, whose leader Dr Willibrord Slaa took 27% of the vote. Widespread corruption is among the main reasons cited for this swing away from the CCM, and it remains to be seen whether this was just a one-off protest against the status quo, or if – as many experts predict – the upstart CDM will emerge as a serious contender for the next elections due in 2015.

As Africa enters the sixth decade of post-colonialism, much of the continent suffers from the same tribal divisions it had at the time of independence. Tanzania is a striking exception to this generalisation, and hindsight demonstrates that Nyerere's greatest achievement was the tremendous sense of **national unity** he created by making KiSwahili the national language, by banning tribal leaders, by forcing government officials to work away from the area in which they grew up, and by his own example. True, Tanzania remains one of the world's least-developed countries, but most sources agree that the economic situation of the average Tanzanian has improved greatly since independence, with unusually high economic growth shown over the past 15 years, as have adult literacy rates and healthcare. Furthermore, Tanzania has thus far navigated the tricky path from British colony to independent state to socialist dictatorship to free-market democracy with remarkably little internal conflict and bloodshed. This long history of adaptability, tolerance and stability stands the country in good stead as the CCM faces the first genuine challenge to its long period of total political dominance.

GOVERNMENT AND POLITICS

The ruling party of Tanzania since independence has been **Chama Cha Mapinduzi (CCM)**. Up until 1995, Tanzania was a one-party state, under the presidency of Julius Nyerere and, after his retirement in 1985, Ali Hassan Mwinyi. Tanzania has held four multi-party elections since 1995, with the CCM winning them all – the first two under President Benjamin Mkapa, the more recent two under President Jakaya Kikwete. The president and unicameral National Assembly of Tanzania are elected concurrently by popular vote, with 236 of the 324 seats in the National Assembly being elected directly, while 75 are allocated to women chosen by their parties (proportionate to each party's share of the electoral vote), another ten are nominated by the president, and five are selected by the Zanzibar House of Representatives. The National Assembly is led by a prime minister, who is appointed by the president along with the cabinet. Eighteen parties contested

ADMINISTRATIVE REGIONS

Region	Capital	Population (millions)	Area (km²)	People (per km²)
Dar es Salaam	Dar es Salaam	2.6	1,393	1,870
Zanzibar & Pemba	Zanzibar	1.0	2,460	406
Mwanza	Mwanza	3.0	19,592	153
Kilimanjaro	Moshi	1.8	13,309	135
Mtwara	Mtwara	1.4	16,707	83
Mara	Musoma	1.5	19,566	76
Tanga	Tanga	2.0	26,808	75
Kagera	Bukoba	2.1	28,388	74
Shinyanga	Shinyanga	2.8	50,781	55
Dodoma	Dodoma	2.0	41,311	48
Mbeya	Mbeya	2.4	60,350	40
Kigoma	Kigoma	1.4	37,037	38
Iringa	Iringa	1.9	56,864	33
Pwani	Bagamoyo	1.0	32,407	31
Morogoro	Morogoro	1.9	70,799	29
Arusha	Arusha	2.1	82,306	25
Singida	Singida	1.2	49,341	24
Tabora	Tabora	1.7	76,151	22
Ruvuma	Songea	1.2	63,498	18
Rukwa	Sumbawanga	1.1	68,635	16
Lindi	Lindi	1.0	66,046	15

the 2010 election, and since then the CCM has held 259 seats on the National Assembly, the **Chama cha Demokrasia na Maendeleo (CDM)** has 48 seats and the Civic United Front has 36. The other six seats are split between three parties.

ADMINISTRATIVE REGIONS Tanzania is divided into 21 administrative regions, each with a local administrative capital. These are listed in the box above in descending order of population density based on the most recent national census, undertaken in 2002.

ECONOMY

Immediately after independence, Tanzania became one of the most dedicated socialist states in Africa, and its economy suffered badly as a result of a sequence of well-intentioned but misconceived or poorly managed economic policies. By the mid 1980s, Tanzania ranked among the five poorest countries in the world. The subsequent swing towards a free-market economy, making the country more attractive to investors, has resulted in dramatic improvement, and Tanzania today – while hardly wealthy – has managed to ascend out of the list of the world's 20 poorest countries. The mainstay of the economy is agriculture, and most rural Tanzanians are subsistence farmers who might also grow a few crops for sale. The country's major exports are traditionally coffee, cotton, cashew nuts, sisal, tobacco, tea and diamonds. Tanzania is also now the third-largest gold producer in Africa (after South Africa and Ghana), and a unique gem called tanzanite is of increasing importance to the export economy. Zanzibar and Pemba are important clove producers. The tourist industry that practically collapsed in the mid 1980s has since grown steadily. Over the past few years, up to one million visitors per year have generated around US$1.7 billion annually in foreign revenue, a tenfold increase since 1990, accounting for about a quarter of the country's hard currency income.

PEOPLE

The total population of Tanzania is estimated at around 46 million in 2012. The most densely populated rural areas tend to be the highlands, especially those around Lake Nyasa and Mount Kilimanjaro, and the coast. The country's largest city is Dar es Salaam, whose population, estimated at almost three million, exceeds that of the country's next ten largest towns combined. The only northern Tanzanian towns with a population in excess of 100,000 are Arusha, Moshi and Mwanza.

There are roughly 120 tribes in Tanzania, each speaking their own language, and none of which exceeds 10% of the country's total population. The most numerically significant tribes are the Sukuma of Lake Victoria, Haya of northwest Tanzania, Chagga of Kilimanjaro, Nyamwezi of Tabora, Makonde of the Mozambique border area, Hehe of Iringa and Gogo of Dodoma.

LANGUAGE

More than 100 different languages are spoken across Tanzania, but the official languages are KiSwahili and English. Until recently, very little English was spoken

TRADITIONAL MUSICAL INSTRUMENTS

Tanzania's tribal diversity has meant that a vast array of very different – and, for that matter, very similar – traditional musical instruments are employed around the country under a bemusing number of local names. Broadly speaking, however, all but a handful of these variants can be placed in one of five distinct categories that conform to the classes of musical instrument used in Europe and the rest of the world.

The traditional music of many Tanzanian cultures is given its melodic drive by a *marimba* (also called a *mbira*), a type of instrument that is unique to Africa but could be regarded as a more percussive variant of the familiar keyboard instruments. The basic design of all marimbas consists of a number of metal or wooden keys whose sound is amplified by a hollow resonating box. Marimbas vary greatly in size from one region to the next. Popular with several pastoralist tribes of the Rift Valley and environs are small hand-held boxes with six to ten metal keys that are plucked by the musician. In other areas, organ-sized instruments with 50 or more keys are placed on the ground and beaten with sticks, like drums. The Gogo of the Dodoma region are famed for their marimba orchestras consisting of several instruments that beat out a complex interweave of melodies and rhythms.

The most purely melodic of Tanzanian instruments is the *zeze*, the local equivalent to the guitar or fiddle, used throughout the country under a variety of names. The basic zeze design consists of between one and five strings running along a wooden neck that terminates in an open resonating gourd. The musician rubs a bow fiddle-like across the strings, while manipulating their tone with the fingers of his other hand, generally without any other instrumental accompaniment, but

SWAHILI NAMES

In KiSwahili, a member of a tribal group is given an 'M' prefix, the tribe itself gets a 'Wa' prefix, the language gets a 'Ki' prefix, and the traditional homeland gets a 'U' prefix. For example, an Mgogo person is a member of the Wagogo tribe who will speak Kigogo and live in Ugogo. The 'Wa' prefix is commonly but erratically used in English books; the 'M' and 'Ki' prefixes are rarely used, except in the case of KiSwahili, while the 'U' prefix is almost always used. There are no apparent standards; in many books the Swahili are referred to as just the Swahili while non-Swahili tribes get the 'Wa' prefix. I have decided to drop most of these prefixes: it seems as illogical to refer to non-Swahili people by their KiSwahili name when you are writing in English as it would be to refer to the French by their English name in a German book. I have, however, referred to the Swahili language as KiSwahili on occasion. I also refer to tribal areas – as Tanzanians do – with the 'U' prefix, and readers can assume that any place name starting with 'U' has this implication; in other words that Usukuma is the home of the Sukuma, and Unyamwezi is the home of the Nyamwezi.

outside of the larger towns, but this is changing rapidly and visitors can be confident that almost anybody involved in the tourist industry will speak passable English. KiSwahili, indigenous to the coast, spread through the region along the 19th-century caravan routes, and is today spoken as a second language by most Tanzanians.

sometimes as part of an orchestra. Less widespread stringed instruments include the zither-like *enanga* of the Lake Tanganyika region and similar *bango* and *kinubi* of the coast, all of which are plucked like harps rather than stroked with a bow, to produce more defined melodic lines than the zeze.

The most important percussive instrument in African music is the drum, of which numerous local variations are found. Almost identical in structure and role to their European equivalent, most African drums are made by tightly stretching a membrane of animal hide across a section of hollowed tree trunk. A common and widespread type of drum, which is known in most areas as a *msondo* and is often reserved for important rituals, can be up to 1m tall and is held between the drummer's legs.

Percussive backing is also often provided by a variety of instruments known technically as idiophones. Traditionally, these might include the maraca-like *manyanga*, a shaker made by filling a gourd with dry seeds, as well as metal bells and bamboo scrapers. A modern variant on the above is the *chupa*: a glass soda bottle scraped with a piece of tin or a stick.

Finally, in certain areas, horned instruments are also used, often to supply a fanfare at ceremonial occasions. These generally consist of a modified animal horn with a blowing hole cut into its side, through which the musician manipulates the pitch using different mouth movements.

Readers with an interest in traditional music are pointed towards an excellent but difficult-to-locate booklet, *The Traditional Musical Instruments of Tanzania*, written by Lewis and Makala (Music Conservatoire of Tanzania, 1990), and the primary source of this boxed text.

Islam has had a long history on the coast and islands of Tanzania as evidenced by the presence of numerous ruined medieval mosques, some of which date back to the 12th century or earlier. It remains the main religion along the coast, and it also has a stronghold in inland towns such as Ujiji and Tabora, which were founded by Arabic traders along the 19th-century caravan routes. It has been estimated that up to 40% of Tanzanians follow Islam today, though no exact figures are available. Around 85% of the Islamic population is Sunni.

Christianity is the dominant religion of the interior, also accounting for about 35–40% of the total population of Tanzania. Among the more common denominations are Roman Catholic, Lutheran, Anglican and Methodist. Tanzanians of Islamic and Christian persuasion generally live side by side without noticeable rancour, though both are often uncomfortable with the concept of atheism.

Traditional animist beliefs are also still followed by many Tanzanians, in particular the Nilotic-speaking pastoralists of the Rift Valley. The Maasai traditionally worship a dualistic deity, Engai, who resides in the volcanic crater of Ol Doinyo Lengai, while Aseeta, the God of the Datoga, is said to live on Mount Hanang. Many practising Muslims or Christians in Tanzania concurrently adhere to traditional beliefs and will consult local healers and spiritualists in times of ill health or misfortune.

2

Natural History

For more on wildlife in northern Tanzania check out Bradt's East African Wildlife. *See page x for a special discount offer.*

There are plenty of good reasons to visit northern Tanzania – the beautiful coastline, fascinating history and magnificent scenery – but for most people one attraction overwhelms all others, and that is the wildlife. Tanzania is Africa's prime game-viewing country, best known for the deservedly well-publicised Serengeti and the Ngorongoro Crater, highlights in a mosaic of national parks and other conservation areas that cover almost 25% of the country and protect an estimated 20% of Africa's large mammals.

HABITATS AND VEGETATION

The bulk of Tanzania is covered in open grassland, savanna (lightly wooded grassland) and woodland. The Serengeti Plains are an archetypal African savanna: grassland interspersed with trees of the acacia family – which are typically quite short, lightly foliated and thorny. Many have a flat-topped appearance. An atypical acacia, the yellow fever, is one of Africa's most striking trees. It is relatively large, has yellow bark and is often associated with water. Combretum is another family of trees typical of many savanna habitats. The dry savanna of central Tanzania can be so barren during the dry season that it resembles semi-desert.

Woodland differs from forest in lacking an interlocking canopy. The most extensive woodland in Tanzania is in the *miombo* belt, which stretches from southern and western Tanzania to Zimbabwe. Miombo woodland typically grows on infertile soil, and is dominated by broad-leafed brachystegia trees. You may come across the term mixed woodland: this refers to woodland with a mix of brachystegia, acacia and other species. Many woodland habitats are characterised by an abundance of baobab trees.

True closed-canopy forest covers less than 1% of Tanzania's surface area, but it is the country's most ecologically diverse habitat, represented along the northern circuit by the montane forests of Kilimanjaro, Meru, Ngorongoro Crater rim and various lesser mountains, as well as the groundwater forests around Lake Duluti and in Lake Manyara. Other interesting but localised vegetation types are mangrove swamps (common along the coast, particularly around Kilwa) and the heath and moorland found on the higher slopes of Kilimanjaro and Meru.

WILDLIFE

MAMMALS More than 80 large mammal species are resident in Tanzania. On an organised safari your guide will normally be able to identify all the mammals you see. For serious identification purposes – or a better understanding of an animal's lifestyle and habits – it is worth investing in a decent field guide or a book on animal behaviour.

Such books are too generalised to give much detail on distribution in any one country, so the section that follows is best seen as a Tanzania-specific supplement to a field guide. In the listings overleaf, an animal's scientific name is given in parentheses after its English name, followed by the Swahili (Sw) name. The Swahili for animal is *nyama* (plural *wanyama*); to find out what animal you are seeing, ask '*Nyama gani?*'

For most first-time safari-goers, a major goal is to tick off the so-called 'Big Five' – and even if doing so isn't a priority when you first arrive in Tanzania, conversations with lion-obsessed driver-guides and with other travellers are likely to make it one.

ANIMAL TAXONOMY

In this book, I've made widespread use of taxonomic terms such as genus, species and race. Some readers may not be familiar with these terms, so a brief explanation follows.

Taxonomy is the branch of biology concerned with classifying living organisms. It uses a hierarchical system to represent the relationships between different animals. At the top of the hierarchy are kingdoms, phyla, sub-phyla and classes. All vertebrates belong to the animal kingdom, phylum Chordata, sub-phylum Vertebrata. There are five vertebrate classes: Mammalia (mammals), Aves (birds), Reptilia (reptiles), Amphibia (amphibians) and Pisces (fish). Within any class, several orders might be divided in turn into families and, depending on the complexity of the order and family, various sub-orders and sub-families. All baboons, for instance, belong to the Primate order, sub-order Catarrhini (monkeys and apes), family Cercopithecoidea (Old World monkeys) and sub-family Cercopithecidae (cheek-pouch monkeys, ie: guenons, baboons and mangabeys).

Taxonomists accord every living organism a Latin binomial (two-part name) indicating its genus (plural genera) and species. Thus the savanna baboon *Papio cyenephalus* and hamadrayas baboon *Papio hamadrayas* are different species of the genus *Papio*. Some species are further divided into races or sub-species. For instance, taxonomists recognise four races of savanna baboon: yellow baboon, olive baboon, chacma baboon and Guinea baboon. A race is indicated by a trinomial (three-part name), for instance *Papio cyenephalus cyenephalus* for the yellow baboon and *Papio cyenephalus anubis* for the olive baboon. The identical specific and racial designation of *cyenephalus* for the yellow baboon make it the nominate race – a label that has no significance other than that it would most probably have been the first race of that species to be described by taxonomists.

Taxonomic constructs are designed to approximate the real genetic and evolutionary relationships between various living creatures, and on the whole they succeed. But equally the science exists to help humans understand a reality that is likely to be more complex and less absolute than any conceptual structure used to contain it. This is particularly the case with speciation – the evolution of two or more distinct species from a common ancestor – a gradual process that might occur over many thousands of generations and lack for any absolute landmarks.

Simplistically, the process of speciation begins when a single population splits into two mutually exclusive breeding units. This can happen as a result of geographic isolation (for instance mountain and lowland gorillas), habitat differences (forest and savanna elephants) or varied migratory patterns (the six races of yellow wagtail intermingle as non-breeding migrants to Africa during the northern winter, but they all have discrete Palaearctic breeding grounds). Whatever the reason, the two breeding communities will share an identical gene

Ironically, given its ubiquity in modern game-viewing circles, the term 'Big Five' originated with the hunting fraternity and it refers to those animals considered to be the most dangerous (and thus the best sport) back in the colonial era, namely lion, elephant, buffalo, leopard and black rhino. Of these, the first three are likely to be seen with ease on a safari of any significant duration, but leopard are more elusive (the most reliable site in northern Tanzania is the Serengeti's Seronera Valley) and the only part of northern Tanzania where black rhino remain reasonably visible is the Ngorongoro Crater.

pool when first they split, but as generations pass they will accumulate a number of small genetic differences and eventually marked racial characteristics. Given long enough, the two populations might even deviate to the point where they wouldn't or couldn't interbreed, even if the barrier that originally divided them was removed.

The taxonomic distinction between a full species and a sub-species or race of that species rests not on how similar the two taxa are in appearance or habit, but on the final point above. Should it be known that two distinct taxa freely interbreed and produce fertile hybrids where their ranges overlap, or it is believed that they would in the event that their ranges did overlap, then they are classified as races of the same species. If not, they are regarded as full species. The six races of yellow wagtail referred to above are all very different in appearance, far more so, for instance, than the several dozen warbler species of the genus *Cisticola*, but clearly they are able to interbreed, and they must thus be regarded as belonging to the same species. And while this may seem a strange distinction on the face of things, it does make sense when you recall that humans rely mostly on visual recognition, whereas many other creatures are more dependent on other senses. Those pesky cisticolas all look much the same to human observers, but each species has a highly distinctive call and in some cases a display flight that would preclude crossbreeding whether or not it is genetically possible.

The gradual nature of speciation creates grey areas that no arbitrary distinction can cover – at any given moment in time there might exist separate breeding populations of a certain species that have not yet evolved distinct racial characters, or distinct races that are on their way to becoming full species. Furthermore, where no conclusive evidence exists, some taxonomists tend to be habitual 'lumpers' and others eager 'splitters' – respectively inclined to designate any controversial taxon racial or full specific status. For this reason, various field guides often differ in their designation of controversial taxa.

Among African mammals, this is particularly the case with primates, where in some cases up to 20 described taxa are sometimes lumped together as one species and sometimes split into several specific clusters of similar races. The savanna baboon is a case in point. The four races are known to interbreed where their ranges overlap but they are also all very distinctive in appearance, and several field guides now classify them as different species. The olive baboon, for instance, is designated *Papio anubis* as opposed to *Papio cyenephalus anubis*. Such ambiguities can be a source of genuine frustration, particularly for birdwatchers obsessed with ticking 'new' species, but they also serve as a valid reminder that the natural world is, and will always be, a more complex, mysterious and dynamic entity than any taxonomic construct designed to label it.

Cats, dogs and hyenas

Lion (*Panthera leo*) Sw: *simba*. Shoulder height: 100–120cm; weight: 150–220kg. Africa's largest predator, the lion is the one animal that everybody hopes to see on safari. It is a sociable creature, living in prides of five to ten animals and defending a territory of between 20 and 200km². Lions hunt at night, and their favoured prey is large or medium antelope such as wildebeest and impala. Most of the hunting is done by females, but dominant males normally feed first after a kill. Rivalry between males is intense, and battles to take over a pride are frequently fought to the death, for which reason two or more males often form a coalition. Young males are forced out of their home pride at three years of age, and male cubs are usually killed after a successful takeover. When not feeding or fighting, lions are remarkably indolent – they spend up to 23 hours of any given day at rest – so the anticipation of a lion sighting is often more exciting than the real thing. Lions naturally occur in any habitat but desert and rainforest, and once ranged across much of the Old World, but these days they are all but restricted to the larger conservation areas in sub-Saharan Africa (one remnant population exists in India). Essentially terrestrial, they seldom take to trees in most of their range, but this unusual behaviour is observed quite regularly in Lake Manyara and parts of the Serengeti National Park. Recent surveys indicate that Tanzania might host around 50% of the world's surviving free-ranging lions, and the Serengeti and the Ngorongoro Crater are arguably the best places in Africa to see these charismatic beasts.

Leopard (*Panthera pardus*) Sw: *chui*. Shoulder height: 70cm; weight: 60–80kg. The powerful leopard is the most solitary and secretive of Africa's large cat species. It hunts using stealth and power, often getting to within 5m of its intended prey before pouncing, and it habitually stores its kill in a tree to keep it from hyenas and lions. The leopard can be distinguished from the superficially similar cheetah by its rosette-like spots, lack of black 'tear marks' and more compact, powerful build. Leopards occur in all habitats, favouring areas with plenty of cover such as

Leopard

riverine woodland and rocky slopes. There are many records of individuals living in close proximity to humans for years without being detected. The leopard is the most common of Africa's large felines, found throughout Tanzania, yet a good sighting must be considered a stroke of fortune. One relatively reliable spot for leopard sightings is the Seronera Valley in the Serengeti. An endemic race of leopard did occur on Zanzibar, although recent research suggests that it is probably extinct on the island, and that the handful of local reports of leopard sightings were probably the result of confusion with the African civet and introduced Java civet.

Cheetah (*Acinonyx jubatus*) Sw: *duma*. Shoulder height: 70–80cm; weight: 50–60kg. This remarkable spotted cat has a greyhound-like build, and is capable of running at 70km/h in bursts, making it the world's fastest land animal. It is often seen pacing the plains restlessly, either on its own or in a small family group comprising a mother

Cheetah

and her offspring. A diurnal hunter, favouring the cooler hours of the day, the cheetah's habits have been adversely affected in areas where there are high tourist concentrations and off-road driving is permitted. Males are territorial, and generally solitary, though in the Serengeti they commonly defend their territory in pairs or trios. Despite superficial similarities, you can easily tell a cheetah from a leopard by its simple spots, disproportionately small head, streamlined build, diagnostic black 'tear marks', and preference for relatively open habitats. Widespread, but thinly distributed and increasingly rare outside of conservation areas, the cheetah is most likely to be seen in savanna and arid habitats such as the Serengeti Plains (where sightings are regular on the road to Seronera) and the floor of the Ngorongoro Crater.

Similar species The **serval** (*Felis serval*) is smaller than a cheetah (shoulder height: 55cm) but has a similar build and black-on-gold spots giving way to streaking near the head. It is widespread and quite common in moist grassland, reed beds and riverine habitats, but tends to be very secretive. The Serengeti is probably the best place in Africa for serval sightings.

Caracal (*Felis caracal*) Sw: *simbamangu*. Shoulder height: 40cm; weight: 15–20kg. The caracal resembles the European lynx with its uniform tan coat and tufted ears. It is a solitary hunter, feeding on birds, small antelope and livestock, and ranges throughout the country favouring relatively arid savanna habitats. It is nocturnal and seldom seen.

Caracal

Similar species The smaller **African wild cat** (*Felis sylvestris*) ranges from the Mediterranean to the Cape of Good Hope, and is similar in appearance to the domestic tabby cat. Like the caracal, it is common, but nocturnal, and infrequently seen.

African wild dog (*Lycaon pictus*) Sw: *mbwa mwitu*. Shoulder height: 70cm; weight: 25kg. Also known as the African hunting dog or painted dog, the wild dog is distinguished from other African canids by its large size and cryptic black, brown and cream coat.

African wild dog

Highly sociable, living in packs of up to 20 animals, the wild dog is a ferocious hunter that literally tears apart its prey on the run. Threatened with extinction as a result of its susceptibility to diseases spread by domestic dogs, it is indeed extinct in several areas where it was formerly abundant, for instance in the Serengeti and most other reserves in northern Tanzania. The global population of around 4,000 wild dogs is spread across much of eastern and southern Africa, but the Selous Game Reserve is the most important stronghold (estimated population 1,300) and Ruaha National Park also hosts a viable population. The one place in northern Tanzania where wild dogs are regularly observed is Mkomazi National Park, where a recently reintroduced population is thriving. Wild dogs have been reported denning in Loliondo annually since 2008, and scattered sightings in Tarangire, Lake Manyara and the northern Serengeti suggest that this endangered creature might yet re-colonise the northern safari circuit.

Black-backed jackal (*Canis mesomelas*) Sw: *mbweha*. Shoulder height: 35–45cm; weight: 8–12kg. The black-backed (or silver-backed) jackal is an opportunistic feeder capable of adapting to most habitats. Most often seen singly or in pairs at dusk or dawn, it is ochre in colour with a prominent black saddle flecked by a varying amount of white or gold. It is probably the most frequently observed small predator in Africa south of the Zambezi, and its eerie call is a characteristic sound of the bush at night. It is the commonest jackal in most Tanzanian reserves.

DANGEROUS ANIMALS

The dangers associated with Africa's wild animals have frequently been overstated since the days of the so-called Great White Hunters – who, after all, rather intensified the risk by shooting at animals that are most likely to turn nasty when wounded – and others trying to glamorise their chosen way of life. Contrary to the fanciful notions conjured up by images of rampaging elephants, man-eating lions and psychotic snakes, most wild animals fear us more than we fear them, and their normal response to human proximity is to flee. That said, many travel guides have responded to the exaggerated ideas of the dangers associated with wild animals by being overly reassuring. The likelihood of a tourist being attacked by an animal is indeed very low, but it can happen and there have been a number of fatalities caused by such incidents in recent years, particularly in southern Africa.

The need for caution is greatest near water, particularly around dusk and dawn, when hippos are out grazing. Hippos are responsible for more human fatalities than any other large mammal, not because they are aggressive but because they tend to panic when something comes between them and the safety of the water. If you happen to be that something, then you're unlikely to live to tell the tale. Never consciously walk between a hippo and water, and never walk along riverbanks or through reed beds, especially in overcast weather or at dusk or dawn, unless you are certain that no hippos are present.

Watch out, too, for crocodiles. Only a very large crocodile is likely to attack a person, and then only in the water or right on the shore. Near towns and other settlements, you can be fairly sure that any such crocodile will have been consigned to its maker by its potential human prey, so the risk is greatest away from human habitation.

There are areas where hikers might still stumble across an elephant or a buffalo, the most dangerous of Africa's terrestrial herbivores. Elephants almost invariably mock charge and indulge in some hair-raising trumpeting before they attack in earnest. Provided that you back off at the first sign of unease, they are unlikely to take any further notice of you. If you see them before they see you, give them a wide berth, bearing in mind they are most likely to attack if surprised at close proximity. If an animal charges you, the safest course of action is to head for the nearest tree and climb it. Black rhinos are prone to charging without apparent provocation, but they're too rare in Tanzania to be a cause for concern. Elephants are the only animals to pose a potential danger to a vehicle, and much the same advice applies – if an elephant evidently doesn't want you to pass, then back off and wait until it has crossed the road or moved further away before you try again. In general, it's a good idea to leave your engine running when you are close to an elephant, and you should avoid letting yourself be boxed in between an elephant and another vehicle.

There are campsites in Tanzania where vervet monkeys and baboons have become pests. Feeding these animals is highly irresponsible, since it encourages

Similar species The **side-striped jackal** (*Canis adustus*) is more cryptic in colour, and has an indistinct pale vertical stripe on each flank and a white-tipped tail. Nowhere very common, it is distributed throughout Tanzania, and most likely to be seen in the southern reserves. The cryptically coloured **common jackal** (*Canis aureus*), also known as the Eurasian or golden jackal, is relatively pale with a black tail tip. Primarily a Eurasian and North African species, its range extends as far south as the Serengeti and the Ngorongoro Crater, and it is probably more

them to scavenge and may eventually lead to them being shot. Vervet monkeys are too small to progress much beyond being a nuisance, but baboons are very dangerous and have often killed children and maimed adults with their teeth. Do not tease or underestimate them. If primates are hanging around a campsite and you wander off leaving fruit in your tent, don't expect the tent to be standing when you return. Chimpanzees are also potentially dangerous but are unlikely to be encountered except on a guided forest walk when there is little risk as long as you obey your guide's instructions at all times.

The dangers associated with large predators are often exaggerated. Most predators stay clear of humans and are only likely to kill accidentally or in self-defence. Lions are arguably the exception, but it is unusual for a lion to attack a human without cause. Should you encounter one on foot, the important thing is not to run since this is likely to trigger the instinct to give chase. Of the other cats, cheetahs represent no threat and leopards generally attack only when they are cornered. Hyenas are often associated with human settlements, and are potentially very dangerous but in practice aren't aggressive towards people and will most likely to slink off into the shadows when disturbed. A slight but real danger when sleeping in the bush without a tent is that a passing hyena or lion might investigate a hairy object sticking out of a sleeping bag, and you might be decapitated through predatory curiosity. In areas where large predators are still reasonably common, sleeping in a sealed tent practically guarantees your safety – but don't sleep with your head sticking out and don't at any point put meat in the tent.

All manner of venomous snakes occur in Tanzania, but they are unlikely to be encountered since they generally slither away when they sense the seismic vibrations made by a walking person. You should be most alert to snakes on rocky slopes and cliffs, particularly where you risk putting your hand on a ledge that you can't see. Rocky areas are the favoured habitat of the puff adder, which is not an especially venomous snake but is potentially lethal and unusual in that it won't always move off in response to human footsteps. Wearing good boots when walking in the bush will protect against the 50% of snake bites that occur below the ankle, and long trousers will help deflect bites higher up on the leg, reducing the quantity of venom injected. Lethal snake bites are a rarity – in South Africa, which boasts almost as many venomous snakes as Tanzania, more people are killed by lightning than by snake bites – but some discussion of treatment is included in the *Health* section, page 85.

When all is said and done, the most dangerous animal in Africa, exponentially a greater threat than everything mentioned above, is the Anopheles mosquito, which carries the malaria parasite. Humans – particularly when behind a steering wheel – run them a close second!

readily seen than the black-backed jackal on the crater floor, since it is more diurnal in its habits.

Bat-eared fox (*Otocyon megalotis*) Sw: *bweha masikio.* Shoulder height: 30–35cm; weight: 35kg. This small, silver-grey insectivore, unmistakable with its huge ears and black eye-mask, is most often seen in pairs or small family groups during the cooler hours of the day. Associated with dry open country, the bat-eared fox is quite common in the Serengeti and likely to be encountered at least once in the course of a few days' safari, particularly during the denning season (November and December).

Bat-eared fox

Spotted hyena (*Crocuta crocuta*) Sw: *fisi.* Shoulder height: 85cm; weight: 70kg. Hyenas are characterised by their bulky build, sloping back, brownish coat, powerful jaws and dog-like expression. Despite looking superficially canine, they are more closely related to mongooses and bears than to cats or dogs. Contrary to popular myth, hyenas are not exclusively scavengers: the spotted hyena in particular is an adept hunter capable of killing an animal as large as a wildebeest. Nor are they hermaphroditic, an ancient belief that stems from the false scrotum and penis covering the female hyena's vagina. Sociable animals, and fascinating to observe, hyenas live in loosely structured clans of about ten animals, led by females who are stronger and larger than males. The spotted hyena is the largest hyena, distinguished by its blotchily spotted coat, and it is probably the most common large predator in eastern and southern Africa. It is most frequently seen at dusk and dawn in the vicinity of game reserve lodges, campsites and refuse dumps, and is likely to be encountered on a daily basis in the Serengeti and the Ngorongoro Crater.

Similar species The North African **striped hyena** (*Hyaena hyaena*) is pale brown with several dark vertical streaks and an off-black mane. It occurs alongside the spotted hyena in dry parts of Tanzania, but is scarce and secretive. The equally secretive **aardwolf** (*Proteles cristatus*) is an insectivorous striped hyena, not much bigger than a jackal, occurring in low numbers in northern Tanzania.

Civets, mongoose and mustelids

African civet (*Civettictis civetta*) Sw: *fungo.* Shoulder height: 40cm; weight: 10–15kg. This bulky, long-haired, rather feline creature of the African night is primarily carnivorous, feeding on small animals and carrion, but will also eat fruit. It has a similarly coloured coat to a leopard or cheetah, and this is densely blotched with large black spots becoming stripes towards the head. Civets are widespread and common in many habitats, but very rarely seen.

Similar species The smaller, more slender **tree civet** (*Nandinia binotata*) is an arboreal forest animal with a dark-brown coat marked with black spots. The **small-spotted genet** (*Genetta genetta*) and **large-spotted genet** (*Genetta tigrina*) are the most widespread members of a group of similar small predators, all of which are very slender and rather feline in appearance, with a grey to golden-brown coat marked with black spots and an exceptionally long ringed tail. Most likely to be seen on nocturnal game drives or scavenging around game reserve lodges, the large-spotted genet is golden brown with very large spots and a black-tipped tail, whereas the small-spotted genet is greyer with rather small spots and a pale tip to the tail.

Banded mongoose (*Mungos mungo*) Shoulder height: 20cm; weight: around 1kg. The banded mongoose is probably the most commonly observed member of a group of small, slender, terrestrial carnivores. Uniform dark brown except for a dozen black stripes across its back, it is a diurnal mongoose occurring in family groups in most wooded habitats and savanna.

Banded mongoose

Similar species Several other mongoose species occur in Tanzania, though some are too scarce and nocturnal to be seen by casual visitors. The **marsh mongoose** (*Atilax paludinosus*) is large, normally solitary and has a very scruffy brown coat. It's widespread in the eastern side of Africa where it is often seen in the vicinity of water. The **white-tailed ichneumon** (*Ichneumia albicauda*) is another widespread, solitary, large brown mongoose, easily identified by its bushy white tail. The **slender mongoose** (*Galerella sanguinea*) is as widespread and also solitary, but it is very much smaller (shoulder height: 10cm) and has a uniform brown coat and black tail tip. The **dwarf mongoose** (*Helogale parvula*) is a diminutive (shoulder height: 7cm) and highly sociable light-brown mongoose often seen in the vicinity of termite mounds, particularly in Tarangire National Park.

Ratel (*Mellivora capensis*) Sw: *nyegere*. Shoulder height: 30cm; weight: 12kg. Also known as the honey badger, the ratel is black with a puppyish face and grey-to-white back. It is an opportunistic feeder best known for its symbiotic relationship with a bird called the honeyguide which leads it to a beehive, waits for it to tear the nest open, then feeds on the scraps. The ratel is among the most widespread of African carnivores, but it is thinly distributed and rarely seen.

Similar species Several other mustelids (mammals of the weasel family) occur in the region, including the **striped polecat** (*Ictonyx striatus*), a common but rarely seen nocturnal creature with black underparts and bushy white back, and the similar but much scarcer **striped weasel** (*Poecilogale albinucha*). The **Cape clawless otter** (*Aonyx capensis*) is a brown freshwater mustelid with a white collar, while the smaller **spotted-necked otter** (*Lutra maculicollis*) is darker with white spots on its throat.

Primates
Chimpanzee (*Pan troglodytes*) Sw: *sokwe-mtu*. Standing height: 100cm; weight: up to 55kg. This distinctive black-coated ape, along with the bonobo (*Pan paniscus*) of the southern Congo, is more closely related to man than to any other living creature. The chimpanzee lives in large troops based around a core of related males dominated by an alpha male. Females aren't firmly bonded to their core group, so emigration between communities

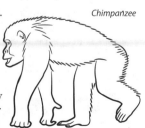

Chimpanzee

is normal. Primarily frugivores (fruit-eaters), chimpanzees eat meat on occasion, and though most kills are opportunistic, stalking of prey is not unusual. The first recorded instance of a chimp using a tool was at Gombe Stream in Tanzania, where modified sticks were used to 'fish' in termite mounds. In West Africa, chimps have been observed cracking open nuts with a stone and anvil. In the USA, captive chimps have successfully been taught sign language and have created compound words such as 'rock-berry' to describe a nut. A widespread and common rainforest resident, the chimpanzee is thought to number 200,000 in the wild. In East Africa, chimps occur in western Uganda and on the Tanzanian shore of Lake Tanganyika, where they can be seen at the research centre founded by primatologist Jane Goodall in Tanzania's Gombe Stream, as well as at Mahale Mountains. The only chimpanzee population to fall within the scope of this book is the introduced (but to all intents and purposes wild) community that can be visited on Rubondo Island.

Baboon (*Papio* spp) Sw: *nyani*. Shoulder height: 50–75cm; weight: 25–45kg. This powerful terrestrial primate, distinguished from any other monkey by its much larger size, inverted U-shaped tail and distinctive dog-like head, is fascinating to watch from a behavioural perspective. It lives in large troops that boast a complex, rigid social structure characterised by matriarchal lineages and plenty of inter-troop movement by males seeking social dominance. Omnivorous and at home in almost any habitat, the baboon is the most widespread

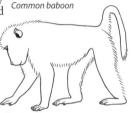
Common baboon

GALAGO DIVERSITY IN TANZANIA

The Prosimian galago family is the modern representative of the most ancient of Africa's extant primate lineages, more closely related to the lemurs of Madagascar than to any other mainland monkeys or apes. With their wide round eyes and agile bodies, they are also – as their alternative name of bushbaby suggests – uniquely endearing creatures, bound to warm the heart of even the least anthropomorphic of observers. And no natural history lover could fail to feel some excitement at the revolution in the taxonomy of the galago family that has taken place over recent years, largely due to research undertaken in the forests of Tanzania by the Nocturnal Primate Research Group (*www.nprg.org*) of Oxford Brookes University.

In 1975, only six species of galago were recognised by specialists. Today, it is thought there may be as many as 40 species, a quarter of which are confirmed or likely to occur in Tanzania, including three national endemics. The reasons behind this explosion of knowledge probably lie in the animals' nocturnal habits, which makes casual identification tricky, particularly in relatively inaccessible forested habitats. Previously biologists based their definition of galago species largely on superficial visual similarities. It has recently been recognised, however, that the distinctive vocal repertoires of different populations, as well as differences in the penile structure, provide a more accurate indicator of whether two populations would or indeed could interbreed given the opportunity – in other words, whether they should be regarded as discrete species.

By comparing the calls, penile structures and DNA of dwarf galago populations around Tanzania, the Nocturnal Primate Research Group has discovered several previously undescribed species since the early 1990s. These are Grant's galago primate in Africa, frequently seen in most Tanzanian game reserves. There are several species of baboon in Africa, regarded by some authorities to be full races of the same species. Two species are present in northern Tanzania: you're most likely to see the olive or anubis baboon (*P. anubis*), which is the darker and hairier green-brown baboon found in the west, but in areas such as West Kilimanjaro you might encounter the yellow baboon (*P. cynocephalus*), a more lightly built and paler yellow-brown race whose range lies to the east of the Rift Valley.

Vervet monkey (*Cercopithecus aethiops*) Sw: *tumbili*. Length (excluding tail): 40–55cm; weight: 4–6kg. Also known as the green or grivet monkey, the vervet is probably the world's most numerous monkey and certainly the most common and widespread representative of the *Cercopithecus* guenons, a taxonomically controversial genus associated with African forests. An atypical guenon in that it inhabits savanna and woodland rather than true forest, the vervet spends a high proportion of its time on the ground and in most of its range could be confused only with the much larger and heavier baboon. However, the vervet's light-grey coat, black face and white forehead band should be diagnostic – as should the male's garish blue genitals. The vervet is abundant in Tanzania, and might be seen just about anywhere, not only in reserves.

Vervet monkey

Similar species The terrestrial **patas monkey** (*Erythrocebus patas*), larger and more spindly than the vervet, has an orange-tinged coat and black forehead stripe.

(*Galago granti*; coastal woodland south of the Rufiji River), Matundu galago (*G. udzungwensis*; Udzungwa Mountains), Zanzibar galago (*G. zanzibaricus*; Zanzibar), Uluguru galago (*G. orinus*; Uluguru and Usambara mountains) and Rondo galago (*G. rondoensis*). The last of these species was initially thought to be confined to the Rondo Plateau inland of Lindi but has recently been discovered living in the Pugu Hills, right outside the country's largest city. Nevertheless, it is regarded as critically endangered and has been listed as one of the 'World's 25 Most Endangered Primates'. It is not so much possible as certain that further galago species await discovery: in East Africa alone populations that require further study are found in southeast Tanzania, in the isolated forests of Mount Marsabit in northern Kenya, and in the mountains along the northern shores of Lake Nyasa-Malawi.

Simon Bearder of the Nocturnal Primate Research Group argues convincingly that the implications of these fresh discoveries in galago taxonomy might extend to other 'difficult' groups of closely related animals. He points out that our most important sense is vision, which makes it easiest for us to separate species that rely primarily on vision to recognise or attract partners. It becomes more difficult for us to separate animals that attract their mates primarily by sound and scent, more so if they use senses we do not possess such as ultrasound or electric impulses. 'Such "cryptic" species', Bearder writes, 'are no less valid than any other, but we are easily misled into thinking of them as being much more similar than would be the case if we had their kind of sensitivity. The easiest way for us to distinguish between free-living species is to concentrate on those aspects of the communication system that the animals themselves use to attract partners.'

Essentially a monkey of the dry northwestern savanna, the patas occurs in low numbers in the Mbalageti River region of the western Serengeti.

Blue monkey (*Cercopithecus mitis*) Sw: *kima*. Length (excluding tail): 50–60cm; weight: 5–8kg. This most variable of African monkeys is also known as the samango, golden, silver and Sykes' monkey, or the diademed or white-throated guenon. Several dozen races are recognised, divided by some authorities into more than one species. Taxonomic confusion notwithstanding, *C. mitis* is the most common forest guenon in eastern Africa, with one or another race occurring in just about any suitable habitat. Unlikely to be confused with another species in Tanzania, the blue monkey has a uniformly dark blue-grey coat broken by a white throat, which in some races extends all down the chest and in others around the collar. It lives in troops of up to ten animals and associates with other primates where their ranges overlap. It is common in Arusha and Lake Manyara national parks and in many forest reserves.

Blue monkey

Black-and-white colobus (*Colobus guereza*)
Sw: *mbega mweupe*. Length (excluding tail): 65cm; weight: 12kg. This beautiful jet-black monkey has bold white facial markings, a long white tail and in some races white sides and shoulders. Almost exclusively arboreal, it is capable of jumping up to 30m, a spectacular sight with white tail streaming behind. Several races have been described, and most authorities recognise more than one species. The black-and-white colobus is a common resident of forests in Tanzania, often seen in the forest zone of Kilimanjaro and in Arusha National Park.

Black-and-white colobus

Galagos (Bushbabies) (*Galago and Otolemur* spp) Sw: *komba*. Length (excluding tail): up to 45cm; weight: up to 500g. This taxonomically controversial family (see box *Galago diversity in Tanzania*, page 30), distantly related to the lemurs of Madagascar, is widespread in Tanzania, where around a dozen species in two genera are recognised. Most commonly seen, and easily identified due to their size, are the three species of greater galago (*Otolemur* spp). They occur all along the eastern side of Africa and produce a terrifying scream so loud you'd think it was emitted by a chimpanzee or gorilla. The lesser bushbabies of the genus *Galago* are more widespread and common but less readily seen, though they can sometimes be picked out by tracing the cry to a tree and shining a torch or spotlight in its general direction to look for its large eyes.

Large antelope
Roan antelope (*Hippotragus equinus*) Sw: *korongo*.
Shoulder height: 120–150cm; weight: 250–300kg. This handsome equine antelope is uniform fawn-grey with a pale belly, short de-curved horns and a light mane. It could be mistaken for the female sable antelope, but this has a well-defined white belly, and lacks the roan's distinctive black-and-white facial markings. The roan is widespread but thinly distributed in southern Tanzania, though rare in the north, with one small population known to occur (yet seldom seen) in the Serengeti.

Roan antelope

Sable antelope (*Hippotragus niger*) Sw: *pala hala*. Shoulder height: 135cm; weight: 230kg. The striking male sable is jet black with a distinct white face, underbelly and rump, and long de-curved horns. The female is chestnut brown and has shorter horns. The main stronghold for Africa's sable population is the *miombo* woodland of southern Tanzania; it is virtually absent from northern Tanzania.

Oryx (*Oryx gazella*) Sw: *choroa*. Shoulder height: 120cm; weight: 230kg. This regal, dry-country antelope is unmistakable with its ash-grey coat, bold black facial marks and flank strip, and unique long, straight horns. The fringe-eared oryx is the only race found in Tanzania, where it is most common (though still scarce) in Mkomazi and Tarangire national parks, and the Lake Natron region.

Oryx

Waterbuck (*Kobus ellipsiprymnus*) Sw: *kuro*. Shoulder height: 130cm; weight: 250–270kg. The waterbuck is easily recognised by its shaggy brown coat and the male's large lyre-shaped horns. The Defassa race of the Rift Valley and areas further west has a full white rump, while the eastern race has a white U on its rump. The waterbuck is frequently seen in small family groups grazing near water in all but the most arid of game reserves in Tanzania.

Waterbuck

Blue wildebeest (*Connochaetes taurinus*) Sw: *nyumbu*. Shoulder height: 130–150cm; weight: 180–250kg. This rather ungainly antelope, also called the brindled gnu, is easily recognised by its dark coat and bovine appearance. The superficially similar buffalo is far more heavily built. Immense herds of blue wildebeest occur on the Serengeti Plains, where the annual migration of more than a million heading into Kenya's Maasai Mara forms one of Africa's great natural spectacles. There are also significant wildebeest populations in the Ngorongoro Crater and Tarangire.

Blue wildebeest

Hartebeest (*Alcelaphus buselaphus*) Shoulder height: 125cm; weight: 120–150kg. Hartebeests are ungainly antelopes, readily identified by the combination of large shoulders, a sloping back, red-brown or yellow-brown coat and smallish horns in both sexes. Numerous races are recognised, all of which are generally seen in small family groups in reasonably open country. The race found in northern Tanzania, Coke's hartebeest or kongoni, is common in open parts of the Serengeti and Ngorongoro.

Hartebeest

Similar species The **topi** or **tsessebe** (*Damaliscus lunatus*) is basically a darker version of the hartebeest with striking yellow lower legs. Widespread but thinly and patchily distributed, the topi occurs alongside the much paler kongoni in the Serengeti National Park, where it is common.

Common eland (*Taurotragus oryx*) Sw: *pofu*.
Shoulder height: 150–175cm; weight: 450–900kg.
Africa's largest antelope, the common eland is
light brown in colour, sometimes with a few
faint white vertical stripes. It has a somewhat
bovine appearance, accentuated by the relatively
short horns and large dewlap. It is widely distributed
in east and southern Africa, and small herds may be
seen almost anywhere in grassland or light woodland.
The eland is fairly common in Serengeti and Mkomazi
national parks, but difficult to approach closely.

Eland

Greater kudu (*Tragelaphus strepsericos*) Sw: *tandala*. Shoulder height: 140–
155cm; weight: 180–250kg. In many parts of Africa, the greater kudu is the most
readily observed member of the genus *tragelaphus*, a group of
medium to large antelopes characterised by the male's large
spiralling horns and a dark coat generally marked with several
vertical white stripes. The greater kudu is very large, with a
grey-brown coat and up to ten stripes on each side,
and the male has magnificent double-spiralled horns.
A widespread animal occurring in most wooded
habitats except for true forest, the greater kudu
is rare in northern Tanzania, but small numbers
persist in Tarangire.

Greater kudu

Similar species The thinly distributed and skittish **lesser kudu** (*Tragelaphus
imberbis*) is an East African species largely restricted to arid woodland. In Tanzania,
it often occurs alongside the greater kudu, from which it can be distinguished by its
smaller size (shoulder height: 100cm), two white throat patches and greater number
of stripes (at least 11). Nowhere common, it is most likely to be encountered in
Tarangire and Mkomazi national parks. The semi-aquatic **sitatunga** (*Tragelaphus
spekei*) is a widespread but infrequently observed inhabitant of west and central
African swamps from the Okavango in Botswana to the Sudd in Sudan. Tanzania's
Rubondo Island is one of the few places where it is readily observed. The male,
with a shoulder height of up to 125cm and a shaggy fawn coat, is unmistakable in
its habitat. The smaller female might be mistaken for a bushbuck (see below) but is
much drabber.

Medium and small antelope

Bushbuck (*Tragelaphus scriptus*) Sw: *pongo*. Shoulder
height: 70–80cm; weight: 30–45kg. This attractive
antelope, a member of the same genus as the kudu and
sitatunga, shows great regional variation in colouring.
The male is dark brown, chestnut or in parts of Ethiopia
black, while the much smaller female is generally pale
red-brown. The male has relatively small, straight horns
for a *Tragelaphus* antelope. Both sexes have similar throat
patches to the lesser kudu, and are marked with white
spots and sometimes stripes. One of the most widespread
antelope species in Africa, the bushbuck occurs in forest
and riverine woodland throughout Tanzania, where it is

Bushbuck

normally seen singly or in pairs. It tends to be secretive and skittish except where it is used to people, so it is not as easily seen as you might expect of a common antelope.

Thomson's gazelle (*Gazella thomsoni*) Shoulder height: 60cm; weight: 20–25kg. Gazelles are graceful, relatively small antelopes that generally occur in large herds in open country, and have fawn-brown upper parts and a white belly. Thomson's gazelle is characteristic of the East African plains, where it is the only gazelle to have a black horizontal stripe. It is common to abundant in the Serengeti and surrounds.

Similar species Occurring alongside Thomson's gazelle in many parts of East Africa, the larger **Grant's gazelle** (*Gazella granti*) lacks a black side stripe and has comparatively large horns. An uncharacteristic gazelle, the **gerenuk** (*Litocranius walleri*) is a solitary, arid country species of Ethiopia, Kenya and northern Tanzania, similar in general colour to an impala but readily identified by its very long neck and singular habit of feeding from trees standing on its hind legs. Nowhere common in Tanzania, the gerenuk is present in small numbers in Mkomazi, Tarangire, West Kilimanjaro and the Loliondo area.

Impala (*Aepeceros melampus*) Sw: *swala pala*. Shoulder height: 90cm; weight: 45kg. This slender, handsome antelope is superficially similar to some gazelles, but in fact belongs to a separate family. Chestnut in colour, the impala has diagnostic black and white stripes running down its rump and tail, and the male has large lyre-shaped horns. One of the most widespread antelope species in sub-equatorial Africa, the impala is normally seen in large herds in wooded savanna habitats, and it is one of the most common antelope in many Tanzanian reserves.

Impala

Reedbuck (*Redunca* spp) Sw: *tohe*. Shoulder height: 65–90cm; weight: 30–65kg. The three species of reedbuck are all rather nondescript fawn-grey antelopes generally seen in open grassland near water. The mountain reedbuck (*Redunca fulvorufula*) is the smallest and most distinctive, with a clear white belly, tiny horns and an overall grey appearance. It has a broken distribution, occurring in mountainous parts of eastern South Africa, northern Tanzania, Kenya and southern Ethiopia. The Bohor reedbuck is found in northern Tanzania, whereas the southern reedbuck occurs in southern Tanzania.

Reedbuck

Klipspringer (*Oreotragus oreotragus*) Sw: *mbuze mawe*. Shoulder height: 60cm; weight: 13kg. The klipspringer is a goat-like antelope that's normally seen in pairs and is easily identified by its dark, bristly grey-yellow coat, slightly speckled appearance and unique habitat preference. Klipspringer means 'rock jumper' in Afrikaans, an apt name for an antelope that occurs exclusively in mountainous areas and rocky outcrops. It is found throughout Tanzania, and is often seen around the Lobo Hills in the Serengeti and the Maji Moto area in Lake Manyara.

Klipspringer

Steenbok (*Raphicerus cempestris*) Sw: *tondoro*. Shoulder height: 50cm; weight: 11kg. This rather nondescript small antelope has red-brown upper parts and clear white underparts, and the male has short straight horns. It is probably the most commonly observed small antelope in Africa, though it has a broken range, and is absent from southern Tanzania despite being common in the north of the country and in areas further south. Like most other antelopes of its size, the steenbok is normally encountered singly or in pairs and tends to 'freeze' when disturbed.

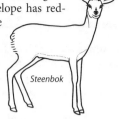
Steenbok

Similar species The **oribi** (*Ourebia ourebi*) is a widespread but uncommon grassland antelope that looks much like a steenbok but stands about 10cm higher at the shoulder and has an altogether more upright bearing. **Kirk's dik-dik** (*Madoqua kirki*), smaller than the steenbok and easily identified by its large white eye-circle, is restricted primarily to Tanzania and Kenya, and it is particularly common in Arusha National Park.

Red duiker (*Cephalophus natalensis*) Sw: *nsya*. Shoulder height: 45cm; weight: 14kg. This is the most likely of Africa's 12–20 'forest duikers' to be seen by tourists. It is deep chestnut in colour with a white tail and, in the case of the east African race *C. n. harveyi* (sometimes considered to be a separate species), a black face. The red duiker occurs in most substantial forest patches along the eastern side of Africa, though it is less often seen than it is heard crashing through the undergrowth.

Similar species The **blue duiker** (*Cephalophus monticola*) is widespread in Africa and the only other forest duiker to occur in countries south of Tanzania. It can easily be told apart from the red duiker by its greyer colouring and much smaller size (it is the smallest forest duiker, about the same size as a suni – dwarf antelope). **Abbott's duiker** (*Cephalophus spadix*) is a large duiker, as tall as a klipspringer, and is restricted to a handful of montane forests in Tanzania, including those on Kilimanjaro and the Usambara, Udzungwa and Poroto mountains. The endangered **Ader's duiker** (*Cephalophus adersi*) is presumably restricted to forested habitats on Zanzibar Island, where as few as 1,000 animals may survive, most of them in the Jozani Forest. Recent reports suggest that this duiker is extinct in the only other locality where it has been recorded, the Sokoke Forest in Kenya.

Common duiker (*Sylvicapra grimmia*) Sw: *nysa*. Shoulder height: 50cm; weight: 20kg. This anomalous duiker holds itself more like a steenbok and is the only member of its family to occur outside of forests. Generally grey in colour, the common duiker can most easily be separated from other small antelopes by the black tuft of hair that sticks up between its horns. It occurs throughout Tanzania, and tolerates most habitats except for true forest and very open country.

Common duiker

Other large herbivores
African elephant (*Loxodonta africana*) Sw: *tembo*. Shoulder height: 2.3–3.4m; weight: up to 6,000kg. The world's largest land animal, the African elephant is intelligent, social and often very entertaining to watch. Female elephants live in close-knit clans in which the eldest female plays matriarch over her sisters,

daughters and granddaughters. Mother–daughter bonds are strong and may last for up to 50 years. Males generally leave the family group at around 12 years to roam singly or form bachelor herds. Under normal circumstances, elephants will range widely in search of food and water, but when concentrated populations are forced to live in conservation areas, their habit of uprooting trees can cause serious environmental damage. Elephants are widespread and common in habitats ranging from desert to rainforest and, despite heavy poaching, they are likely to be seen on a daily basis in most of Tanzania's larger national parks.

Black rhinoceros (*Diceros bicornis*) Sw: *kifaru*. Shoulder height: 160cm; weight: 1,000kg. This is the more widespread of Africa's two rhino species, an imposing, sometimes rather aggressive creature that has been poached to extinction in most of its former range. It occurs in many southern African reserves, but is now very localised in Tanzania, where it is most likely to be seen in the Ngorongoro Crater.

Black rhinoceros

Hippopotamus (*Hippopotamus amphibius*) Sw: *kiboko*. Shoulder height: 150cm; weight: 2,000kg. Characteristic of Africa's sizeable rivers and lakes, this large, lumbering animal spends most of the day submerged, but emerges at night to graze. Strongly territorial, herds of ten or more animals are presided over by a dominant male who will readily defend his patriarchy to the death. Hippos are abundant in most protected rivers and water bodies, and they are still quite common outside of reserves, where they kill more people than any other African mammal.

African buffalo (*Syncerus caffer*) Sw: *nyati*. Shoulder height: 140cm; weight: 700kg. Frequently and erroneously referred to as a water buffalo (an Asian species), the African buffalo is a distinctive ox-like animal that lives in large herds on the savanna and occurs in smaller herds in forested areas. Common and widespread in sub-Saharan Africa, herds of buffalo are likely to be encountered in most Tanzanian reserves and national parks. The best place to see large buffalo herds is on the Ngorongoro Crater floor.

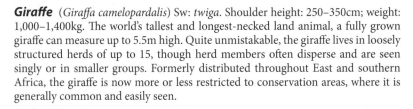

African buffalo

Giraffe (*Giraffa camelopardalis*) Sw: *twiga*. Shoulder height: 250–350cm; weight: 1,000–1,400kg. The world's tallest and longest-necked land animal, a fully grown giraffe can measure up to 5.5m high. Quite unmistakable, the giraffe lives in loosely structured herds of up to 15, though herd members often disperse and are seen singly or in smaller groups. Formerly distributed throughout East and southern Africa, the giraffe is now more or less restricted to conservation areas, where it is generally common and easily seen.

Common zebra (*Equus burchelli*) Sw: *punda milia*. Shoulder height: 130cm; weight: 300–340kg. This attractive striped horse is common and widespread throughout most of East and southern Africa, where it is often seen in large herds alongside wildebeest. The common zebra is the only wild equine to occur in Tanzania, and is common in most conservation areas, especially the Serengeti where the population may be as high as half a million.

Warthog (*Phacochoreus africanus*) Sw: *ngiri*. Shoulder height: 60–70cm; weight: up to 100kg. This widespread and often conspicuously abundant resident of the African savanna is grey in colour with a thin covering of hairs, wart-like bumps on its face, and rather large upward-curving tusks. Africa's only diurnal swine, the warthog is often seen in family groups, trotting off briskly with its tail raised stiffly (a diagnostic trait) and a determinedly nonchalant air.

Warthog

Similar species Bulkier, hairier and browner, the **bushpig** (*Potomochoerus larvatus*) is as widespread as the warthog, but infrequently seen due to its nocturnal habits and preference for dense vegetation. Larger still, weighing up to 250kg, the **giant forest hog** (*Hylochoerus meinertzhageni*) is primarily a species of the West African rainforest. It does occur in certain highland forests in northern Tanzania, but the chance of a sighting is practically non-existent.

Small mammals

Aardvark (*Orycteropus afer*) Shoulder height: 60cm; weight: up to 70kg. This singularly bizarre nocturnal insectivore is unmistakable with its long snout and huge ears. It occurs practically throughout the region, but sightings are extremely rare, even on night drives.

Aardvark

Similar species Not so much similar to an aardvark as equally dissimilar to anything else, **pangolins** are rare nocturnal insectivores with distinctive armour plating and a tendency to roll up in a ball when disturbed. Most likely to be seen in Tanzania is **Temminck's pangolin** (*Manis temminckii*). Also nocturnal, but spiky rather than armoured, several **hedgehog** and **porcupine** species occur in the region, the former generally no larger than a guinea pig, the latter generally 60–100cm long.

Rock hyrax (*Procavia capensis*) Sw: *pimbi*. Shoulder height: 35–30cm; weight: 4kg. Rodent-like in appearance, hyraxes are more closely related to elephants. The rock hyrax and similar bush hyrax (*Heterohyrax brucei*) are often seen sunning in rocky habitats and become tame when used to people, for instance at Seronera and Lobo lodges in the Serengeti. The less common **tree hyrax** (*Dendrohyrax arboreus*) is a nocturnal forest creature, often announcing its presence with an unforgettable shrieking call.

Rock hyrax

Similar species The **elephant shrews** (Sw: *sange*) are rodents that look like miniature kangaroos with elongated noses. A number of species are recognised, but they are mostly secretive and nocturnal, so rarely seen. The smaller species are generally associated with savanna habitats, but the much larger chequered elephant shrew is a resident of Eastern Arc forests – I've only ever seen it in Amani and Udzungwa.

Scrub hare (*Lepus saxatilis*) Weight: 2.7–4.5kg. This is the largest and most common African hare or rabbit. In some areas a short walk at dusk or after nightfall might reveal three or four scrub hares. They tend to freeze when disturbed.

Ground squirrel

Unstriped ground squirrel (*Xerus rutilus*) Weight: 1.4kg. An endearing terrestrial animal of arid savanna, the unstriped ground squirrel is grey to grey-brown with a prominent white eye-ring and silvery black tail. It spends much time on its hind legs, and has the characteristic squirrel mannerism of holding food in its forepaws. In Tanzania, it is most likely to be seen in the Serengeti.

Bush squirrel (*Paraxerus cepapi*) Weight: 1kg. This is the typical squirrel of the eastern and southern savanna, rusty brown in colour with a silvery black back and white eye-rings. A great many other arboreal or semi-arboreal squirrels occur in the region, but most are difficult to tell apart in the field.

BIRDS Tanzania is a birdwatcher's dream, and it is impossible to do justice to its rich avifauna in the confines of a short introduction. Casual visitors will be stunned at the abundance of birdlife: the brilliantly coloured lilac-breasted rollers and superb starlings, the numerous birds of prey, the giant ostrich, the faintly comic hornbills, the magnificent crowned crane – the list could go on forever. For more dedicated birdwatchers, Tanzania, following an explosion in ornithological knowledge of the country over the past two decades, must now surely rank with the top handful of birding destinations in Africa.

The national checklist, which stood at below 1,000 species in 1980, now stands at more than 1,100 species, according to a working checklist compiled by Neil and Liz Baker of the Tanzania Bird Atlas Project. This astonishing gain is exaggerated by the Bakers' admitted bias towards splitting controversial species, but it also reflects an unparalleled accumulation of genuine new records. In 1987, the Minziro Forest on the Uganda border yielded 17 additions to the national checklist, and at least 60 new species have been recorded since then. As a result, Tanzania now vies with Kenya as the African country with the second most varied avifauna (after the Democratic Republic of the Congo).

Virtually anywhere in Tanzania offers good birding, and species of special interest are noted under the relevant site throughout the main body of this guide. In many areas a reasonably competent novice to East African birds could hope to see between 50 and 100 species in a day. Any of the northern reserves are recommended: Arusha and Lake Manyara national parks are both good for forest and water birds; the Serengeti and Tarangire are good for raptors and acacia and grassland species.

Recent new discoveries now place Tanzania second to South Africa for its wealth of national endemics – species that are unique to the country. At present, up to 34 endemic species are recognised, including a couple of controversial splits, three species discovered and described in the 1990s, and four that still await formal description. Six of the national endemics are readily observed on the northern safari circuit, but a greater number are restricted to the Eastern Arc Mountains, together with about 20 eastern forest and woodland species whose core range lies within Tanzania. The forests of the Eastern Arc Mountains must therefore rank as the country's most important bird habitat, with the Amani Nature Reserve the most accessible site for seeing some of the Eastern Arc specials.

For a downloadable checklist of Tanzania's birds, visit www.tanzaniabirding. com. A comprehensive and regularly updated checklist of Tanzania's birds, together with atlas maps for a growing number of species, is posted on the Tanzania Bird Atlas Project website (*www.tanzaniabirdatlas.com*). Experienced birders who wish to fill in species cards for the Atlas Project based on their observations are also welcome to contact them through the website. Field guides are discussed in *Appendix 2*, page 421.

Endemics Brief details of those confirmed and probable endemics present along the northern Tanzania safari circuit follow:

WEAVERS

Placed by some authorities in the same family as the closely related sparrows, the weavers of the family Ploceidae are a quintessential part of Africa's natural landscape, common and highly visible in virtually every habitat from rainforest to desert. The name of the family derives from the intricate and elaborate nests – typically but not always a roughly oval ball of dried grass, reeds and twigs – that are built by the dextrous males of most species.

It can be fascinating to watch a male weaver at work. First, a nest site is chosen, usually at the end of a thin hanging branch or frond, which is immediately stripped of leaves, probably to prevent snakes from reaching the nest undetected. The weaver then flies back and forth to the site, carrying the building material blade by blade in his heavy beak, first using a few thick strands to hang a skeletal nest from the end of a branch, then gradually completing the structure by interweaving numerous thinner blades of grass into the main frame. Once completed, the nest is subjected to the attention of his chosen partner, who will tear it apart if the result is less than satisfactory, and so the process starts all over again.

All but 12 of the 113 described weaver species are resident on the African mainland or associated islands, with at least 45 represented within Tanzania, all but six of which have a range extending into the north of the country. A full 20 of these Tanzanian species are placed in the genus *Ploceus* (true weavers), which is surely the most characteristic of all African bird genera. Most of the *Ploceus* weavers are slightly larger than a sparrow, and display a strong sexual dimorphism. Females are with few exceptions drab buff- or olive-brown birds, with some streaking on the back, and perhaps a hint of yellow on the belly.

Most male *Ploceus* weavers conform to the basic colour pattern of the 'masked weaver' – predominantly yellow, with streaky back and wings, and a distinct black facial mask, often bordered with orange. Seven Tanzanian weaver species fit this masked weaver prototype more or less absolutely, and a similar number approximate it rather less exactly, for instance by having a chestnut-brown mask, or a full black head, or a black back, or being more chestnut than yellow on the belly. Identification of the masked weavers can be tricky without experience – useful clues are the exact shape of the mask, the presence and extent of the fringing orange, and the colour of the eye and the back.

The golden weavers, of which only four species are present in Tanzania, are also brilliant yellow and/or light orange with some light streaking on the back, but they lack a mask or any other strong distinguishing features. Forest-associated *Ploceus* weavers, by contrast, tend to have quite different and very striking colour patterns, and although sexually dimorphic, the female is often as boldly marked as the male. The most aberrant among these is Vieillot's black weaver, the males of which are totally black except for their eyes, while the extralimital black-billed weaver reverses the prototype by being all black with a yellow face-mask.

Grey-breasted spurfowl (*Francolinus rufopictus*) Game bird with distinctive combination of a red mask under which is a white stripe. Confined to the Serengeti and immediate vicinity, where it is common in the woodland in the Seronera area.

Tanzanian red-billed hornbill (*Tockus ruahae*) Recently 'split' from other red-billed hornbills, from which it can be distinguished by the unique combination

Among the more conspicuous *Ploceus* species in northern Tanzania are the Baglafecht, spectacled, vitelline masked, lesser masked and black-headed weavers – for the most part gregarious breeders forming single- or mixed-species colonies of hundreds, sometimes thousands, of pairs, often in reed beds and waterside vegetation. Most weavers don't have a distinctive song, but they compensate with a rowdy jumble of harsh swizzles, rattles and nasal notes that can reach deafening proportions near large colonies. One more cohesive song you will often hear seasonally around weaver colonies is a cyclic 'dee-dee-dee-Diederik', often accelerating to a hysterical crescendo when several birds call at once. This is the call of the Diederik cuckoo, a handsome green-and-white cuckoo that lays its eggs in weaver nests.

Oddly, while most East African *Ploceus* weavers are common, even abundant, in suitable habitats, seven highly localised species are listed as range-restricted, and three are regarded to be of global conservation concern. These include the Taveta palm weaver, which is restricted to the plains immediately below Kilimanjaro and is most common in the West Kilimanjaro–Amboseli area and around Lake Jipe, and the Usambara and Kilombero weavers, both endemic to a limited number of sites in eastern Tanzania.

Most of the colonial weavers, perhaps relying on safety in numbers, build relatively plain nests with a roughly oval shape and an unadorned entrance hole. The nests of certain more solitary weavers, by contrast, are far more elaborate. Several weavers, for instance, protect their nests from egg-eating invaders by attaching tubular entrance tunnels to the base – in the case of the spectacled weaver, sometimes twice as long as the nest itself. The grosbeak weaver (a peculiar larger-than-average, brown-and-white weaver of reed beds, distinguished by its outsized bill and placed in the monospecific genus *Amblyospiza*), constructs a large and distinctive domed nest, which is supported by a pair of reeds, and woven as precisely as the finest basketwork, with a neat raised entrance hole at the front.

By contrast, the scruffiest nests are built by the various species of sparrow- and buffalo-weaver, relatively drab but highly gregarious dry-country birds that occur throughout northern Tanzania. The most striking bird in the group is the white-headed buffalo-weaver, which despite its name is most easily identified by its unique bright red rump. The endemic rufous-tailed weaver, a close relative of the buffalo-weavers, is a common resident of Tarangire, Serengeti and the Ngorongoro Conservation Area.

of a black (not red) face-mask and pale (not black) eyes, this central Tanzanian endemic is a resident of acacia woodland in the Babati-Kondoa and it may also range into Tarangire National Park.

Fischer's lovebird (*Agapornis fischeri*) Stunning and colourful parrot-like bird with bright red head and white eyes, most often first noticed when a flock passes overhead squawking and screeching. Its natural range is centred on the Serengeti, where it is common. A popular caged bird in Europe, a feral population of this lovebird occurs in Naivasha (Kenya) where it regularly interbreeds with the next species.

Yellow-collared lovebird (*Agapornis personatus*) Another endemic lovebird – with a black rather than red head – that has gone feral in Naivasha (Kenya). Naturally confined to the Maasai Steppes and other semi-arid parts of central Tanzania, the yellow-collared lovebird is common in Tarangire National Park.

Beesley's lark (*Chersomanes beesleyi*) Recently split from the widespread spike-heeled lark, this endangered species is confined to a single population of fewer than 1,000 individuals in short grasslands west of Kilimanjaro.

Ashy starling (*Cosmopsarus unicolor*) A drab but nevertheless distinctive member of this normally colourful group of birds, the ashy starling is associated with semi-arid parts of central Tanzania. It's common in Tarangire National Park, and can be seen at the southern end of its range in Ruaha National Park.

Rufous-tailed weaver (*Histurgops ruficauda*) Large, sturdily built weaver of the central savanna, whose scaly feathering, pale eyes and habit of bouncing around boisterously in small flocks could lead to it being mistaken for a type of babbler, albeit one with an unusually large bill. It is a common and visible resident of the Serengeti, Ngorongoro and Tarangire national parks.

Endemics in the Usambara and/or Pare Mountains In addition to those above, the following endemics occur in the Usambara and/or Pare Mountains:

- **Nduk eagle-owl** (*Bubo vosseleri*)
- **Usambara nightjar** (*Caprimulgus guttifer*)   Recent debatable split from mountain nightjar
- **Yellow-throated mountain greenbul** (*Andropadus chlorigula*) Recent split from mountain greenbul
- **Usambara thrush** (*Turdus roehli*) Recent split from olive thrush
- **Usambara Akalat** (*Sheppardia montana*)
- **Mrs Moreau's Winifred's warbler** (*Bathmocercus winifredae*)
- **Usambara hyliota** (*Hyliota usambarae*)
- **Banded green sunbird** (*Anthreptes rubritorques*)
- **Moreau's sunbird** (*Cinnyris moreaui*)
- **Usambara double-collared sunbird** (*Cinnyris usambararicus*)
- **South Pare white-eye** (*Zosterops winifredae*) Controversial split from mountain white-eye
- **Usambara weaver** (*Ploceus nicolli*)

And the following are restricted to the island of Pemba:

- **Pemba Green Pigeon** (*Treron pembaensis*)
- **Pemba scops-owl** (*Otus pembae*)
- **Pemba sunbird** (*Cinnyris pembae*)
- **Pemba white-eye** (*Zosterops vaughani*)

REPTILES

Nile crocodile The order *Crocodilia* dates back at least 150 million years, and fossil forms that lived contemporaneously with dinosaurs are remarkably unchanged from their modern counterparts, of which the Nile crocodile is the largest living reptile, regularly growing to lengths of up to 6m. Widespread throughout Africa, the Nile crocodile was once common in most large rivers and lakes, but it has been exterminated in many areas in the past century – hunted professionally for its skin as well as by vengeful local villagers. Contrary to popular legend, Nile crocodiles generally feed mostly on fish, at least where densities are sufficient. They will also prey on drinking or swimming mammals where the opportunity presents itself, dragging their victim under water until it drowns, then storing it under a submerged log or tree until it has decomposed sufficiently for them to eat. A large crocodile is capable of killing a lion or wildebeest, or an adult human for that matter, and in certain areas such as the Mara or Grumeti rivers in the Serengeti, large mammals do form their main prey. Today, large crocodiles are mostly confined to protected areas within Tanzania.

Snakes A wide variety of snakes are found in Tanzania, though – fortunately, most would agree – they are typically very shy and unlikely to be seen unless actively sought. One of the snakes most likely to be seen on safari is Africa's largest, the **rock python**, which has gold-on-black mottled skin and regularly grows to lengths exceeding 5m. Non-venomous, pythons kill their prey by strangulation, wrapping their muscular bodies around it until it cannot breathe, then swallowing it whole and dozing off for a couple of months while it is digested. Pythons feed mainly on small antelopes, large rodents and similar animals. They are harmless to adult humans, but could conceivably kill a small child. A slumbering python might be encountered almost anywhere in northern Tanzania.

Of the venomous snakes, one of the most commonly encountered is the **puff adder**, a large, thick resident of savanna and rocky habitats. Although it feeds mainly on rodents, the puff adder will strike when threatened, and it is rightly considered the most dangerous of African snakes, not because it is especially venomous or aggressive but because its notoriously sluggish disposition means it is more often disturbed than other snakes. The related **Gabon viper** is possibly the largest African viper, growing up to 2m long, very heavily built, and with a beautiful cryptic, geometric gold, black and brown skin pattern that blends perfectly into the rainforest litter it inhabits. Although highly venomous, it is more placid and less likely to be encountered than the puff adder.

Several cobra species, including the **spitting cobra**, are present in Tanzania, most with characteristic hoods that they raise when they're about to strike, though they are all very seldom seen. Another widespread family is the mambas, of which the **black mamba** – which will only attack when cornered, despite an unfounded reputation for unprovoked aggression – is the largest venomous snake in Africa, measuring up to 3.5m long. Theoretically, the most toxic of Africa's snakes is said to be the **boomslang**, a variably coloured and, as its name – literally tree snake – suggests, largely arboreal snake that is reputed not to have accounted for one known human fatality, as it is back-fanged and very non-aggressive.

Natural History WILDLIFE

2

Most snakes are in fact non-venomous and not even potentially harmful to any other living creature much bigger than a rat. One of the non-venomous snakes in the region is the **green tree snake** (sometimes mistaken for a boomslang, although the latter is never as green and more often brown), which feeds mostly on amphibians. The **mole snake** is a common and widespread grey-brown savanna resident that grows up to 2m long, and feeds on moles and other rodents. The remarkable **egg-eating snake** lives exclusively on bird eggs, dislocating its jaws to swallow the egg whole, before eventually regurgitating the crushed shell in a neat little package. Many snakes will take eggs opportunistically, for which reason large-scale agitation among birds in a tree is often a good indication that a snake (or small bird of prey) is around.

Lizards All African lizards are harmless to humans, with the arguable exception of the **giant monitor lizards**, which could in theory inflict a nasty bite if cornered. Two species of monitor occur in East Africa, the water and the savanna, the latter growing up to 2.2m long and occasionally seen in the vicinity of termite mounds, the former slightly smaller but far more regularly observed by tourists, particularly in the vicinity of Lake Victoria. Their size alone might make it possible to fleetingly mistake a monitor for a small crocodile, but their more colourful yellow-dappled skin precludes sustained confusion. Both species are predatory, feeding on anything from bird eggs to smaller reptiles and mammals, but will also eat carrion opportunistically.

Visitors to Tanzania will soon become familiar with the **common house gecko**, an endearing, bug-eyed, translucent white lizard, which as its name suggests reliably inhabits most houses as well as lodge rooms, scampering up walls and upside down on the ceiling in pursuit of pesky insects attracted to the lights. Also very common in some lodge grounds are various **agama** species, distinguished from other common lizards by their relatively large size of around 20–25cm, basking habits, and almost plastic-looking scaling – depending on the species, a combination of blue, purple, orange or red, with the flattened head generally a different colour from the torso. Another common family are the **skinks**: small, long-tailed lizards, most of which are quite dark and have a few thin black stripes running from head to tail.

Chameleons Common and widespread in Tanzania, but not easily seen unless they are actively searched for, chameleons are arguably the most intriguing of African reptiles. True chameleons of the family Chamaeleontidae are confined to the Old World, with the most important centre of speciation being the island of Madagascar, to which about half of the world's 120 recognised species are endemic. Aside from two species of chameleon apiece in Asia and Europe, the remainder are distributed across mainland Africa.

Chameleons are best known for their capacity to change colour, a trait that has often been exaggerated in popular literature, and which is generally influenced by mood more than the colour of the background. Some chameleons are more adept at changing colour than others, with the most variable being the common chameleon *Chamaeleo chamaeleon* of the Mediterranean region, with more than 100 colour and pattern variations recorded. Many African chameleons are typically green in colour but will gradually take on a browner hue when they descend from the foliage to more exposed terrain, for instance while crossing a road. Several change colour and pattern far more dramatically when they feel threatened or are confronted by a rival of the same species. Different chameleon species also vary greatly in size, the largest being Oustalet's chameleon of Madagascar, which is known to reach a length of almost 80cm.

A remarkable physiological feature common to all true chameleons is their protuberant round eyes, which offer a potential 180° vision on both sides and are able to swivel around independently of each other. Only when one of them isolates a suitably juicy-looking insect will the two eyes focus in the same direction as the chameleon stalks slowly forward until it is close enough to use the other unique weapon in its armoury. This is its sticky-tipped tongue, which is typically about the same length as its body and remains coiled up within its mouth most of the time, to be unleashed in a sudden, blink-and-you'll-miss-it lunge to zap a selected item of prey. In addition to their unique eyes and tongues, many chameleons are adorned with an array of facial casques, flaps, horns and crests that enhance their already somewhat fearsome prehistoric appearance.

In Tanzania, you're most likely to come across a chameleon by chance when it is crossing a road, in which case it should be easy to take a closer look at it, since most chameleons move painfully slowly and deliberately. Chameleons are also often seen on night game drives, when their ghostly nocturnal colouring shows up clearly under a spotlight – as well as making it pretty clear why these strange creatures are regarded with both fear and awe in many local African cultures. More actively, you could ask your guide if they know where to find a chameleon – a few individuals will be resident in most lodge grounds.

The **flap-necked chameleon** (*Chamaeleo delepis*) is probably the most regularly observed species in savanna and woodland habitats in East Africa. Often observed crossing roads, the flap-necked chameleon is generally around 15cm long and bright green in colour with few distinctive markings, but individuals might be up to 30cm in length and will turn tan or brown under the right conditions. Another closely related and widespread savanna and woodland species is the similarly sized **graceful chameleon** (*Chamaeleo gracilis*), which is generally yellow-green in colour and often has a white horizontal stripe along its flanks.

Characteristic of East African montane forests, **three-horned chameleons** form a closely allied species cluster of some taxonomic uncertainty. Typically darker than the savanna chameleons and around 20cm in length, the males of all taxa within this cluster are distinguished by a trio of long nasal horns that project forward from their face. The most widespread three-horned chameleon in Tanzania is Johnston's chameleon (*Chamaeleo johnstoni*), while the most localised is the Ngosi three-horned chameleon (*Chamaeleo fuelleborni*), confined to the forested slopes of Ngosi Volcano in the Poroto Mountains. Perhaps the most alluring of East Africa's chameleons is the **giant chameleon** *Chamaeleo melleri*, a bulky dark-green creature with yellow stripes and a small solitary horn, mainly associated with the Eastern Arc forests, where it feeds on small reptiles (including snakes) as well as insects.

Tortoises and terrapins
These peculiar reptiles are unique in being protected by a prototypal suit of armour formed by their heavy exoskeleton. The most common of the terrestrial tortoises in the region is the **leopard tortoise**, which is named after its gold-and-black mottled shell, can weigh up to 30kg, and has been known to live for more than 50 years in captivity. It is often seen motoring along in the slow lane of game reserve roads in northern Tanzania. Four species of terrapin – essentially the freshwater equivalent of turtles – are resident in East Africa, all somewhat flatter in shape than the tortoises, and generally with a plainer brown shell. They might be seen sunning on rocks close to water or peering out from roadside puddles. The largest is the **Nile soft-shelled terrapin**, which has a wide, flat shell and in rare instances might reach a length of almost 1m.

BUTTERFLIES Tanzania's wealth of invertebrate life, though largely overlooked by visitors, is perhaps most easily appreciated in the form of butterflies and moths of the order Lepidoptera. Almost 1,000 butterfly species have been recorded in Tanzania, as compared to roughly 650 in the whole of North America, and a mere 56 on the British Isles. Several forests in Tanzania harbour 300 or more butterfly species, and one might easily see a greater selection in the course of a day than one could in a lifetime of exploring the English countryside. Indeed, I've often sat at one roadside pool in an East African forest and watched ten to 20 clearly different species converge there over the space of 20 minutes.

The Lepidoptera are placed in the class Insecta, which includes ants, beetles and locusts among others. All insects are distinguished from other invertebrates, such as arachnids (spiders) and crustaceans, by their combination of six legs, a pair of frontal antennae, and a body divided into a distinct head, thorax and abdomen. Insects are the only winged invertebrates, though some primitive orders have never evolved wings, and other more recently evolved orders have discarded them. Most flying insects have two pairs of wings, one of which, as in the case of flies, might have been modified beyond immediate recognition. The butterflies and moths of the order Lepidoptera have two sets of wings and are distinguished from all other insect orders by the tiny ridged wing scales that create their characteristic bright colours.

The most spectacular of all butterflies are the **swallowtails** of the family Papilionidae, of which roughly 100 species have been identified in Africa. Named for the streamers that trail from the base of their wings, swallowtails are typically large and colourful, and relatively easy to observe when they feed on mammal dung deposited on forest trails and roads. Sadly, this last generalisation doesn't apply to the African giant swallowtail (*Papilio antimachus*), a powerful flier that tends to stick at canopy level and seldom alights on the ground. With a wingspan known to exceed 20cm, this black, orange and green gem is the largest butterfly on the continent, and possibly the world.

The Pieridae is a family of medium-sized butterflies, generally smaller than the swallowtails and with wider wings, of which almost 100 species are present in Tanzania, several as seasonal intra-African migrants. Most species are predominantly white in colour, with some yellow, orange, black or even red and blue markings on the wings. One widespread member of this family is the oddly named **angled grass yellow** (*Eurema desjardinsii*), which has yellow wings marked by a broad black band, and is likely to be seen in any savanna or forest fringe habitat. The orange and lemon *Eronia leda* also has yellow wings, but with an orange upper tip, and it occurs in open grassland and savanna countrywide.

The most diverse of African butterfly families is the Lycaenidae, which accounts for almost one-third of the continental tally of around 1,500 recorded species. Known also as **gossamer wings**, this varied family consists mostly of small- to medium-sized butterflies, with a wingspan of 1–5cm, dull underwings, and brilliant violet blue, copper or rufous-orange upper wings. The larvae of many Lycaenidae species have a symbiotic relationship with ants – they secrete a fluid that is milked by the ants and are thus permitted to shelter in their nests. A striking member of this family is *Hypolycaena hatita*, a small bluish butterfly with long tail streamers, often seen on forest paths throughout Tanzania.

Another well-represented family in Tanzania is the Nymphalidae, a diversely coloured group of small to large butterflies, generally associated with forest edges or interiors. The Nymphalidae are also known as brush-footed butterflies, because their forelegs have evolved into non-functional brush-like structures. One of the more distinctive species is the **African blue tiger** (*Tirumala petiverana*), a large black butterfly with about two dozen blue-white wing spots, often observed on forest paths, near puddles or feeding from animal droppings. Another large member of this family is the **African queen** (*Danaus chrysippus*), which has a slow, deliberate flight pattern, orange or brown wings, and is as common in forest edge habitats as it is in cultivated fields or suburbia.

The family Charaxidae, regarded by some authorities to be a subfamily of the Nymphalidae, is represented by roughly 200 African species. Typically large, robust, strong fliers with one or two short tails on each wing, the butterflies in this family vary greatly in coloration, and several species appear to be scarce and localised since they inhabit forest canopies and are seldom seen. Rather less spectacular are the 200–300 **grass-skipper** species of the family Hersperiidae, most of which are small and rather drably coloured, though some are more attractively marked in black, white and/or yellow. The grass-skippers are thought to form the evolutionary link between butterflies and the generally more nocturnal moths, represented in Tanzania by several families of which the most impressive are the boldly patterned **giant silk moths** of the family Saturniidae.

3

Practical Information

WHEN TO VISIT

Tourist arrivals to Tanzania are highest during the northern hemisphere winter, but the country can be visited throughout the year, since every season has different advantages, depending strongly on which parts of the country you plan to include in your travel itinerary. A regional overview follows, but for those with the option, it is worth emphasising that there is much to be said for trying to avoid peak tourist seasons, as the parks and other main attractions will be less crowded.

NORTHERN SAFARI CIRCUIT The focal point of most northern circuit safaris is Serengeti National Park, and wildlife movement here is highly seasonal. The most accessible part of the Serengeti from Arusha, particularly for those on budget and midrange safaris, is the southern plains, which peak in wildlife activity over the rainy seasons, between early November and the end of May. The wildebeest migration disperses into the southern plains at this time of year, usually calving in February, and there is plenty of predator activity. It is also when the countryside is greenest, and it offers the best birdwatching, with resident species supplemented by a number of Palaearctic and intra-African migrants.

A few years back, the entire period between the Easter weekend and the end of September was regarded as low season in the Serengeti and elsewhere in northern Tanzania. However, a steady increase in tourist volumes, as well as the opening of several new camps in the far north and the western corridor, has resulted in more loosely defined tourist seasons. Indeed, many of the smaller camps and lodges in the western, central and northern Serengeti are actually busiest season between June and October, since the migration is usually in the west/central Serengeti over June and July, and in the far north over August to October.

April and May are usually the wettest months in northern Tanzania, and thus the quietest time of the year in touristic terms. This has its advantages. For one, most lodges and camps offer significantly cheaper low-season rates, which can greatly reduce the cost of a safari. And there is nothing wrong with the game viewing: plenty of wildlife can be seen in the south-central Serengeti over April and May, while the Ngorongoro Crater and Lake Manyara, which are incorporated into most northern safaris, are not so strongly seasonal in terms of wildlife movements, but they are far les crowded with 4x4s and more enjoyable to visit outside of peak tourist seasons.

Aside from the Serengeti, the most seasonal of the northern circuit parks is Tarangire, where animal concentrations generally peak between July and the start of the rains in November or early December.

49

MOUNT KILIMANJARO AND MERU Trekking conditions are best in the dry seasons, which run from January to early March and from August to October. There are several advantages to the period January to early March. The first is that it tends to be quieter in terms of tourists, an important consideration if you are following one of the more popular routes. The second is that it is probably the most beautiful time of year to climb, with the best chance of clear skies at higher altitudes. On the downside, it is also the coldest time of year on the mountain, though this does mean the snow cap tends be more extensive than in warmer months. The worst months for climbing in terms of weather are November and December.

ZANZIBAR AND THE COAST The coast can be visited throughout the year. However, the most pleasant time to be there is the long dry season, which runs from June to October. This is when temperatures are most comfortable (though still hot by European standards) and the humidity is lowest. There is also less chance of your holiday being disrupted by rain, and it is considerably safer than the wet season in terms of malaria and other mosquito-borne diseases. The wettest months of April and May are best avoided, while January to March, though drier, tend to be hot.

SOUTHERN AND WESTERN SAFARI CIRCUITS The parks of the south and west have a more clearly defined seasonal character than their northern counterparts. The best time to visit Selous, Ruaha, Mikumi and Katavi is during the long dry season, which runs from June to October or early November. This is when wildlife is most easily spotted as it congregates around perennial water sources, and also when road condition are best, and the risk of contracting malaria is lowest. Late November to early March sees showers, especially in the first two months. This makes wildlife more difficult to locate, but the scenery tends to be greener and avian activity peaks as migrant birds arrive from the northern hemisphere and resident birds go into breeding plumage. Late February to the end of May is best avoided, and roads are often washed out – indeed many camps and lodges in the south close for some or all of this period. Chimp tracking in Mahale and Gombe is also best during the dry season, though Gombe in particular could be visited at any time of year. For more on the southern and western safari circuits check out Bradt's *Tanzania Safari Guide*.

HIGHLIGHTS

Tanzania is truly a country of highlights, most of which are centred in the north, and it also contains a wealth of off-the-beaten track opportunities. The list below, broken down by category, only skims the surface:

BEST PUBLIC WILDLIFE DESTINATIONS
Serengeti National Park The linchpin of the popular northern safari circuit, this world-renowned park harbours large numbers of predators, as well as being the site of a legendary migration comprising million-strong herds of wildebeest and zebra. Overcrowding in this popular park is restricted to the southeast, so those with sufficient time and a suitable budget are advised to explore the more remote west and north.

Ngorongoro Crater Centrepiece of the Ngorongoro Conservation Area, the world's largest intact caldera is superb Big Five territory. Lion, buffalo and large tuskers are all common, and it's the best place in Tanzania to look for the endangered black rhinoceros.

Tarangire National Park Less celebrated than the Serengeti – and, as a consequence, less heavily touristed – Tarangire preserves a classic chunk of dry savanna studded with plentiful baobabs and home to prodigious elephant herds, along with plenty of other wildlife.

BEST EXCLUSIVE WILDLIFE CONCESSIONS

Klein's Camp Offering exclusive access to 1,000km² of hilly country bordering the northeast Serengeti, this superlative private reserve combines outright luxury and superb guiding with some of the finest game viewing in Tanzania – it's particularly good for leopard and lion.

Grumeti Reserve North of the Serengeti National Park's Western Corridor lies an area of largely flat plains with the occasional hill. There are three very chic, high-quality lodges here: the grand, hilltop Sasakwa; the minimalist Faru Faru; and the old-Africa style tented camp, Sabora Plains. Marketed by South Africa's smart Singita team, these lodges command Tanzania's highest costs.

West Kilimanjaro Effectively the Tanzanian counterpart to Kenya's Amboseli National Park, but with little tourist traffic and no restrictions on walking, this game controlled area is home to plenty of elephant alongside dry country antelope such as gerenuk and oryx. It also lies right at the base of Kilimanjaro, offering fantastic views of the snow-capped icon along with several other distinctive northern Tanzania mountains.

BEST HIKING AND WALKING

Mount Kilimanjaro National Park Encompassing the peaks and forested slopes of the continent's highest mountain, Kilimanjaro is climbed by thousands of tourists every year, not only to stand on the snow-capped pinnacle of Africa, but also to experience the other-worldly Afro-montane moorland habitat of the upper reaches.

West Usambara Mountains An affordable low-key alternative to Kilimanjaro, as well as being a good place to adapt to higher altitudes prior to a Kili climb, this beautiful mountain range southeast of Moshi offers unlimited opportunities for casual rambling.

Ol Doinyo Lengai Assuming it's not actually erupting when you visit, the affordable overnight ascent of Africa's most active volcano passes through some of the most dramatic rockscapes in the country.

BEST FOR BIRDS

Lake Manyara National Park All of the northern safari circuit offers good birding, but for first-time visitors to Africa this is the jewel in the region's avian crown, offering a good opportunity to tick off 100 species – from flamingos and storks to eagles and barbets – in a day.

Amani Nature Reserve This reserve in the Eastern Usambara Mountains, inland of Tanga, protects some of the most important montane forest in Tanzania along with a wealth of rare and endemic birds. There's inexpensive accommodation and a good range of walking trails – and it's easily accessible by public transport, too.

Lake Victoria Basin Rich in species not found elsewhere in Tanzania, Africa's largest lake is a great destination for birders, whether you chill out at Speke Bay or fly to remote Rubondo Island, where African grey parrots vie for attention with fish eagles and herons.

BEST FOR CULTURE AND HISTORY

Zanzibar Stone Town Like a living embodiment of 1001 nights, this traditional quarter of Zanzibar is as notable for its lovely Arab-influenced architecture as it is the pervasive laid-back vibe associated with traditional Swahili culture. It's emphatically worth spending a night or two here before heading out to one of the idyllic beaches that surround the island.

Kondoa Rock Art Site Probably the least publicised of Tanzania's several UNESCO World Heritage Sites, the fascinating and myriad painted shelters around Kondoa make for a great add-on to a northern Tanzania safari, offering a good opportunity to stretch the legs whilst exploring this enigmatic facet of the country's rich prehistory.

Cultural Programmes Numerous official cultural programmes operate around northern Tanzania, allowing visitors to interact with traditional pastoralists, farmers and hunter-gatherers. These range from hunting with the Hadza at Lake Eyasi to taking a camelback trip with the Maasai of Mkuru.

ITINERARY PLANNING

Tanzania has a well-defined tourist circuit. It would be no exaggeration to say that as many as 90% of visitors divide their time in the country between the northern safari circuit and the island of Zanzibar. If this is what you plan on doing, then any tour operator or safari company in Arusha will be able to put together a package to meet your requirements. A ten- to 14-day trip is ideal for the Zanzibar/safari combination. You might want to read the section *Organising a safari*, below, before making contact with a tour operator. With Zanzibar, the main decision you need to make in advance is whether you want to be based at a hotel in the old Stone Town, or out on one of the beaches, or a combination of the two. For a short trip to Tanzania, it is advisable to fly between Arusha (the springboard for safaris in northern Tanzania) and Zanzibar. If you are really tight for time, you'll get more out of your safari by flying between lodges. A fly-in safari will also be less tiring than the more normal drive-in safari.

After the northern safari circuit and Zanzibar, Tanzania's main tourist attraction is Kilimanjaro, which is normally climbed over five to seven days. A Kilimanjaro climb is one of those things that you either do or don't want to undertake: for a significant minority of travellers, climbing Kilimanjaro is the main reason for visiting Tanzania, but for the majority it is of little interest. If you want to do a Kili climb, it can be organised in advance through any number of tour operators and safari companies, and there is a lot to be said for arranging the climb through the same operator that organises your safari. As with budget safaris, it is generally possible to get cheaper prices on the spot. To combine a Kili climb with a few days on safari and a visit to Zanzibar you would need an absolute minimum of two weeks in the country, and even that would be very tight, allowing for no more than two nights on Zanzibar.

ORGANISING A SAFARI Several types of safari are on offer, with the major variables being accommodation type (budget camping, larger lodges such as those operated

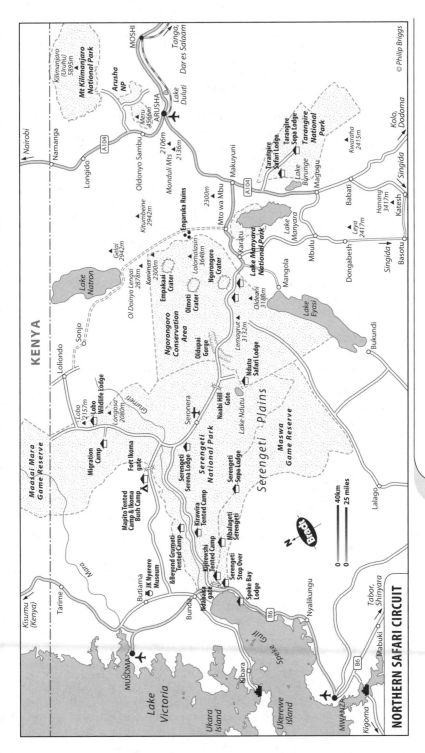

NORTHERN SAFARI CIRCUIT

© Philip Briggs

by the Sopa and Serena chains, or more exclusive lodges and tented camps), transportation (ie: whether you drive between the reserves using one vehicle throughout, or fly between reserves and go on game drives provided by the lodge or camp). There is some room for overlap between these types of accommodation and transport, and there are also a few more offbeat options. For instance, you might want to travel with a company that specialises in walking safaris, spend part or all of your time in exclusive private concessions bordering the parks (which typically offer extras such as guided game walks and night drives), or visit more far-flung areas such as Lake Eyasi (home to the Hadza hunter-gatherers) or Lake Natron.

Accommodation

Budget camping safaris These are generally designed to keep costs to a minimum, so they tend to make use of the cheapest camping options, often outside the national parks, and clients are normally expected to set up their own tents. Most backpackers and volunteers working in Tanzania go on budget camping safaris, although even with these there is a gap between the real shoestring operators (who'll skimp on everything) and those operators who offer a sensible compromise between affordability and adequate service. Given that high park fees and a recent escalation in fuel costs have pushed the lowest realistic rate for a budget safari to US$160–200 per person per day, it really isn't worth going with a dodgy company to save a few dollars.

Group safaris staying at larger lodges These are usually fixed-itinerary trips that accommodate the largest volume of visitors, and generally costs around double the price of a budget camping safari. For the extra outlay you get a roof over your head at night, restaurant food and a far higher level of comfort. If you decide to go on a lodge safari, the probability is that the operator will decide which lodges you stay at. Should you have the choice, however, it's worth noting that the former government 'Wildlife Lodge' chain generally has the best natural settings but the poorest standards of accommodation and service, while Sopa Lodges are more luxurious and well-run and slightly more expensive (but only the Ngorongoro Sopa Lodge has a setting to compare to its Wildlife Lodge equivalent). The lodges in the Serena chain are more upmarket still, with modern facilities, good locations and attractive décor.

Safaris to small lodges or tented camps If you think sleeping under canvas and eating under the stars might not cost much more, think again. Camping allows for a far more holistic and integrated safari experience than one will ever have sleeping in institutionalised and monolithic 'hotels in the bush' designed to keep the wilderness at bay, especially after dark. So this third and most costly type of safari accommodation in Tanzania comprises a multiplying selection of smaller and more exclusive lodges and seasonal, mobile or semi-permanent tented camps. These are generally as luxurious as any large lodge and provide food, service and (where game drives are included) guiding to a higher standard. They are, however, usually unfenced, have few permanent structures and are designed to maximise the bush experience. The most nervous of first-time safari-goers may therefore find them a little daunting.

The cost of a safari like this depends on your exact requirements, but it will usually be a lot more than a comparable lodge safari. Indeed, the best mobile and tented camps (as operated by the likes of &Beyond, Asilia and Nomad), although absolutely superlative, are generally more than double the price of larger chain lodges, so not within most safari-goers' means. Fortunately, there are also a small

The combination of steep national park entrance and camping fees, and the expense of running 4x4 vehicles in northern Tanzania, places the northern safari circuit pretty much out of bounds for travellers on a very tight budget. It is possible, however, to see parts of the circuit relatively cheaply by using public transport and/or hiring vehicles locally.

The most affordable way of traversing the Serengeti National Park is on one of the buses and Land Rovers that run daily along the B144 between Mwanza and Arusha. This route passes through conservation areas for a total of about 250km, firstly the Serengeti's Western Corridor and Seronera Plains, then the plains of the western Ngorongoro Conservation Area and over the Ngorongoro Crater rim. You should get a good feel for the scenery and landscapes from the bus window, and between November and July you can see plenty of game, including large predators but of course the vehicle cannot be expected to stop for special sightings. The trip will entail paying US$100 in park entrance fees on top of the bus fare. In theory, it is possible to make advance arrangements for one of these buses to drop you off at Seronera, and pick you up at a later date but it's difficult to see any reason why anybody would want to do this.

A more satisfying option for travellers who specifically want to see the Serengeti, have time on their hands, and cannot afford a safari of several days' duration, is to approach the park from the western side. This cuts out the long drive and overnight stops coming from Arusha, and allows you to get within 1km of the entrance gate on public transport and to visit the park as a day or overnight trip rather than as part of a longer safari. The best place to set up something like this is the Serengeti Stopover, a private campsite situated right next to the entrance gate to the Serengeti's Western Corridor and alongside the main road between the Lake Victoria ports of Mwanza and Musoma. The Western Corridor itself generally offers good game viewing, particularly when the migration passes through between May and July, and the game-rich Seronera Plains and campsite are only about two hours' drive from the western entrance gate. Serengeti Stop Over charges around US$150 per day for a vehicle that can carry up to five people into the park, which means that a day trip would work out at around US$125 per person for two people including park fees, and about US$90 per person for four people. For further details, see page 305.

On the eastern side of the northern safari circuit, affordable local buses run daily from Arusha to Karatu, stopping at Mto wa Mbu near the entrance of Lake Manyara National Park. Several lodges in Karatu and Mto wa Mbu rent out 4x4 vehicles for half- or full-day visits to Lake Manyara or Ngorongoro Crater. Worth noting, too, is that safari vehicles are found in abundance in Mto wa Mbu and Karatu, so there's every chance you could make cheaper private arrangements to hire a vehicle for a day. Were you to do something like this, you should be very clear about what the deal covers and how long you will spend in the game reserve – ambiguities at the negotiating stage often result in frayed tempers later in the day.

Hitching into any reserves in Tanzania is problematic; aside from being illegal there are numerous practical obstacles. And even if you were to catch a lift, you may well get stuck in the Serengeti or Ngorongoro and although you will see little game from a campsite or lodge, you will still have to pay park fees.

Practical Information   ITINERARY PLANNING

3

handful of tented or other more low-key camps that offer a bush atmosphere at rates comparable to the chain lodges – Tarangire Safari Lodge, Kirurumu Tented Camp and Ndutu Lodge stand out, as do the mobile camps operated by Wayo Africa, Wild Frontiers and Tanganyika Wilderness Safaris – and these are highly recommended to those seeking a bush experience at a relatively affordable price.

Getting around Regular scheduled flights connect all the main reserves in northern Tanzania, and an increasingly high proportion of safari-goers choose to fly around rather than bump along the long, dusty roads that separate the parks. Flying around will be particularly attractive to those who have bad backs or who tire easily, but it is more expensive and does dilute the sense of magic attached to driving through the vast spaces that characterise this region. Fly-in safaris allow you to see far more wildlife in a shorter space of time, because you don't lose hours on the road. Now that the road from Arusha is surfaced as far as Ngorongoro Conservation Area, a popular compromise is to cover the closer parks (Manyara, Tarangire and the NCA) by road, fly on to one or two locations in the Serengeti Ecosystem, then fly directly back to Arusha, or possibly to drive one-way, into the Serengeti, and then fly out at the end.

Group size One factor that all visitors should consider is the size of the group doing the safari. It is almost invariably cheaper to go on safari as part of a group, but it can also ruin things if the people in that group are not compatible. A group safari will be highly frustrating to those who have a special interest such as birding or serious photography. And, frankly, I think it is unfair to impose this sort of interest on other passengers, who will have little interest in identifying every raptor you drive past, or in waiting for two hours at a lion kill to get the perfect shot. Another consideration is that non-stretch Land Rovers can feel rather cramped with four people in the back, especially when the luggage is in the vehicle, and jostling for head room out of the roof can be a nightmare when four cameras are vying for the best position.

A small proportion of companies – generally the large package tour operators – use minibuses as opposed to conventional 4x4s. In my opinion, minibuses have several disadvantages, notably that the larger group size (typically around eight people) creates more of a package tour atmosphere, and that it is difficult for a large group to take proper advantage of the pop-up roofs that are usually found on safari vehicles. In any event, bouncing around rutted roads in a Land Rover is an integral part of the safari experience – it just wouldn't be the same in a minibus.

Finally, there is the question of aesthetics. Without wishing to wax too lyrical, the thrill of being on safari doesn't derive merely from the animals you see. There is an altogether more elusive (some might say spiritual) quality attached to simply being in a place as wild and vast and wonderful as the Serengeti, one that is most easily absorbed in silence, whether you travel on your own or with somebody with whom you feel totally relaxed. It isn't the same when you have to make small talk to new acquaintances, crack the rote jokes about who should be put out of the vehicle to make the lion move, decide democratically when to move on, listen to the driver's educational monotones, and observe social niceties that seem at odds with the surrounding wilderness.

Activities Visitors are generally restricted to two daily game drives in the national parks or the Ngorongoro Conservation Area (NCA), one in the morning and one in the afternoon. This is due to park rulings that forbid walking except in special circumstances and that also preclude driving after dark. Whilst a diet of two daily game drives is undoubtedly the best way to see the most wildlife, it can become quite restrictive if you are used to incorporating a little more exercise into your daily routine. For this reason, there is a lot to be said for mixing up the national park visits with stays in bordering concessions where guided walks and/or night drives are permitted (for instance Chem Chem or Manyara Ranch near Tarangire, or Klein's Camp in Loliondo), or other areas suited to walking (the Lake Eyasi and Natron hinterland, the lovely Empakaai Crater in the northern NCA, or the West Kilimanjaro region). For more dedicated walking safaris, Wayo Africa and Wild Frontiers are among the only operators licensed to take guided walking safaris through the national parks.

Tipping   In all categories of safari, the price you are quoted should include the vehicle and driver/guide, fuel, accommodation or camping equipment and fees, meals and park entrance fees. You are expected to tip the driver and cook. Around US$10 per day per party seems to be par, but you should check this with the company. Drivers and cooks are poorly paid; if they have done a good job, be generous.

Planning your itinerary

Planning your itinerary   Your itinerary will depend on how much time and money you have, and also the time of year. There are endless options, and most safari companies will put together the package you ask for. They know the ground well and can advise you on what is possible, but may tend to assume you will want to cover as many reserves as possible. This is not always the best approach.

Most budget safaris will take only five or six days to cover Ngorongoro, Serengeti, Manyara and Tarangire. A typical three-day trip takes in all these reserves except for the Serengeti. In the dry season (July to October) there is little game in the Serengeti and most safari companies will suggest you spend more time in Tarangire. The distances between these reserves are considerable and the roads are poor, so you will have a more relaxed trip if you visit fewer reserves. On a five-day safari, I would drop either the Serengeti or Tarangire. To visit all four reserves, six days is very rushed, seven or more would be better.

Three days isn't long enough to get a good feel for Tarangire, Manyara and Ngorongoro; four or even five days would be better. The combination of Ngorongoro and Tarangire would make an unhurried four-day safari. If you are limited to two days, you could either visit Tarangire on its own or do a combined trip to Manyara and Ngorongoro. If your budget is really limited, Tarangire can be visited as a day trip from Arusha; it is less than two hours' drive each way.

With all of the above, bear in mind that a fast driving itinerary will give you few chances to get away from the busier areas – as the busy areas are the ones which are most easily reached. For example, on a short one- or two-day trip to Tarangire, you're only ever likely to see the relatively busy north of the park; give yourself three nights and you can explore the park in much more detail, leave the crowds and reach the almost deserted southern half of the park. Similarly, if you pop into Manyara for a quick visit, then expect to be confined to the north side of the park, with plenty of other vehicles. Take a full day to see it, or stay inside the park and you can get much deeper in, and leave many of the crowds behind.

If your time is more limited than your budget, then a fly-in safari may be the answer. Then you can easily hop to the small lodges and safari camps deep within the parks, spending minimal time getting between them. Working like this, a trip of two nights in southern Tarangire, two nights at the Crater, and two in the northern Serengeti suddenly becomes viable.

Doing this area justice really requires both more time and more money. There's enough to see and do to warrant a safari of two weeks in duration, or even longer.

You could easily spend three nights in Tarangire, three between Manyara and the Crater, and a further five or six in the Serengeti. On a two-week guided safari, you could also visit Lake Natron and Ol Doinyo Lengai, the Kondoa Rock Art Sites and/ or the Lake Eyasi area.

MISCELLANEOUS TIPS AND WARNINGS **Malaria** is present in most parts of the region, with the notable exception of the Ngorongoro Crater rim, and the normal precautions should be taken. Aside from malaria, there are no serious health risks attached to visiting this area.

Tsetse flies are seasonally abundant in well-wooded areas such as Tarangire and the Western Corridor of the Serengeti. Sleeping sickness is not a cause for serious concern, but the flies are sufficiently aggravating that it is worth applying insect repellent to your arms and legs before game drives (though this doesn't always deter tsetse flies) and avoiding the dark (in particular blue) clothing that tends to attract them.

Tarangire can be reached via a good tar road, and so too can Lake Manyara and the eastern entrance gate to Ngorongoro Conservation Area. By contrast, roads between the Ngorongoro Crater and Serengeti are very rough, for which reason safari-goers with serious back problems or a low tolerance for bumping around in the back of a vehicle might want to consider flying between the reserves. If one member of a safari party has a particular need to avoid being bumped around, they will be best off in the front passenger seat or the central row of seats – the seats above the rear axle tend to soak up the most punishment.

The combination of **dust and glare** may create problems for those with sensitive eyes. Sunglasses afford some protection against dust and glare, and if you anticipate problems of this sort, then don't forget to pack eye drops. Many people who wear contact lenses suffer in these dusty conditions, so it is a good idea to wear glasses on long drives, assuming that you have a pair. For more health-related subjects, see *Chapter 4, Health*, on page 85.

Dust and heat can damage sensitive **camera equipment and film**, so read over the precautions mentioned in the *Photographic tips* box, pages 82–3.

Safari drivers earn a **commission** when their clients buy something from one of the many curio stalls in Mto wa Mbu and elsewhere in the region. There's nothing inherently wrong with this arrangement, but you might find that your safari driver is very keen to stop at a few stalls along the way. If this isn't what you want, then the onus is on you to make this clear the first time it happens – there's no need to be rude or confrontational, just explain gently that this isn't why you're on safari. Even if you do want to buy curios, don't fall into the obvious trap of assuming that you'll get a better deal buying locally. Many of the curios you see in places like Mto wa Mbu probably found their way there from outside, and they will generally be cheaper in Arusha than they will be at roadside stalls dealing exclusively with tourists.

Travellers on a budget camping safari who want to keep down their extra costs should be aware that drinks, although available at all game lodges, are very expensive. A beer at a lodge will typically cost around US$4, as opposed to about US$1 in a shop or local bar, and prices of sodas are similarly inflated. Those travellers who don't want to spend the extra money should ask their driver where to buy drinks to bring back to the campsite – there are bars aimed at drivers near to all the budget safaris' campsites, and the prices are only slightly higher than in Arusha. It is definitely worth stocking up on **mineral water** in Arusha (at least one 1.5-litre bottle per person per day), since this will be a lot more expensive on the road.

Finally, and at risk of stating the obvious, it is both illegal and foolhardy to get out of your safari vehicle in the presence of any wild animal, and especially buffalo, elephant, hippo and lion.

TOURIST INFORMATION

The Tanzania Tourist Board (TTB) (*www.tanzaniatouristboard.com*) has improved greatly over recent years, and its offices in London, New York, Stockholm, Milan and Frankfurt may be able to supply you with an information pack and leaflets about the country.

There are TTB offices in Dar es Salaam and in Arusha. Both are reasonably helpful and well informed when it comes to tourist-class hotels and major tourist attractions, but neither can offer much help when it comes to more remote destinations. The TTB in Arusha is a good source of information about the various cultural tourism programmes that have been established in northern Tanzania over the past few years. Its list of registered and blacklisted safari companies is a useful resource for travellers working through cheap safari companies.

Update information can also be accessed at http://bradttanzania.wordpress.com.

TOUR OPERATORS

Northern Tanzania is featured by a vast spectrum of tour operators. At the lower-end of the price scale are companies that sell a handful of their own trips, and these are usually group trips with fixed itineraries and departure dates. If you're on a budget and are considering one of these trips, spend time comparing the companies who run them, as well as the actual itineraries, and see how past travellers have rated them.

At the higher-cost end of the market, many tour operators offer enticing trips to Tanzania, and some will be specialists with good knowledge of the country, backed by personal experience. Of those, a few will genuinely listen to what you want and do a good job of helping you choose the right places for your trip – offering a wide choice and unbiased advice. These companies are worth seeking out if you want the best trip possible.

Here we must, as authors, admit some personal interests in the tour-operating business. Chris runs Expert Africa (see page 60), which is one of the leading tailor-made operators for Tanzania that organises trips for travellers to Africa from all over the world. Philip acts as an adviser to Expert Africa, complementing the company's team and helping to develop its programmes with the benefit of his high country knowledge. Booking your tailor-made trip with Expert Africa (or, indeed, many other tour operators) will usually cost you the same as, or less than, if you contacted Tanzania's upmarket camps directly – plus you have the benefit of independent advice, full financial protection and experts to make the arrangements for you.

For a fair comparison, the following international tour operators specialise in Tanzania. Safari companies based in Tanzania are found under their different regions in *Part Two, The Guide*.

UK
Abercrombie & Kent ☏0845 618 2200; e info@ abercrombiekent.co.uk; www.abercrombiekent. co.uk. Worldwide individual & group holidays; upmarket selection & prices to match.

Africa Odyssey ☏020 8704 1216 or (USA) +1 866 356 4691; e info@africaodyssey.com; www. africaodyssey.com; see also advert on page 48. Tailor-made tours throughout Africa, including Tanzania. (Also known as Tanzania Odyssey, Botswana Odyssey, Zambia Odyssey, etc ...)

3

Africa Travel 0845 450 1520; e info@ africatravel.co.uk; www.africatravel.co.uk. Substantial operator to all of Africa, with specialist sports travel & flight-only sections.

Africa Travel Resource 01306 880770; e info@ africatravelresource.com; www.africatravelresource. com. Web-based operator for southern & East Africa giving brief quips on a vast array of properties; their trips concentrate on just a few.

Alpha Travel 020 8423 0220; e alpha@alphauk. co.uk; www.arpsafaris.com. Part of the same group as Ranger Safaris in Tanzania, which is all they sell.

Baobab – Alternative Roots to Travel 0121 314 6011; e enquiries@ baobabtravel.com; www. baobabtravel.com. Africa specialist with strong ethical credentials; focuses on ecotourism with some offbeat destinations.

Cazenove & Loyd Safaris 020 7384 2332; e info@cazloyd.com; www.cazloyd.com. Top-end, tailor-made operator with worldwide options, including Africa.

Expert Africa 020 8232 9777 or (USA) +1 800 242 2434; e info@expertafrica.com; www. expertafrica.com; see also adverts on pages I & 218. Specialists to southern & East Africa & Seychelles, with a comprehensive website & an ethical ethos. Run by one of this book's authors (Chris) & advised on Tanzania by the other (Philip), it has probably the most complete & detailed choice of the best Tanzanian lodges, camps & destinations available anywhere. Safaris are flexible & start from about US$3,000/£2,000 per person for a week, including accommodation, meals & game activities, but excluding flights.

Explore Worldwide 0845 013 1537; e hello@ explore.co.uk; www.explore.co.uk. Market leader in small-group, escorted trips worldwide.

Footloose 01943 604030; e info@ footlooseadventure.co.uk; www.footlooseadventure. co.uk. Tailor-made tours, safaris & treks throughout Tanzania, including Zanzibar.

Gane & Marshall 01822 600 600; e info@ ganeandmarshall.com; www.ganeandmarshall. com. Long-established specialist to Africa with particularly strong ethics on Kilimanjaro climbs.

Hartley's Safaris 01673 861600; e info@ hartleys-safaris.co.uk; www.hartleys-safaris.co.uk. Reliable safaris to East & southern Africa, as well as diving & island holidays in the region.

Imagine Africa 020 7622 5114; USA 1 888 882 7121; e info@imagineafrica.co.uk; www.

imagineafrica.co.uk. Award-winning tour operator specialising in luxury travel & beach holidays in Africa.

Journeys by Design 01273 623 790; e info@ journeysbydesign.com; www.journeysbydesign. com. Stylish approach to safaris across southern & East Africa.

Okavango Tours & Safaris 020 8347 4030; e info@okavango.com; www.okavango.com. Small, long-established tailor-made specialists to East & southern Africa.

Rainbow Tours 020 7666 1250; e info@ rainbowtours.co.uk; www.rainbowtours.co.uk; see also advert on page 20. Africa & Latin America specialists, recently bought by a worldwide travel group.

Safari Consultants 01787 888590; e info@ safariconsultantuk.com; www.safari-consultants. co.uk; see also advert in colour section, page xvii. Long-established, knowledgeable tailor-made specialists to East & southern Africa, & the Indian Ocean islands.

Safari Drive 01488 71140; e info@ safaridrive.com; www.safaridrive.com. Self-drive Land Rover safaris & expedition with their own fleet, & tailor-made safaris; they know the ground very well.

Steppes Africa 01285 880 980; e safaris@ steppestravel.co.uk; www.steppestravel.co.uk. Worldwide tailor-made specialists with a long Africa history.

Tribes Travel 01473 890499; e info@tribes. co.uk; www.tribes.co.uk; see also advert on page 47. Consciously ethical range covering the globe, including some unique Tanzania offerings.

Wildlife Worldwide 0845 130 6982; e sales@ wildlifeworldwide.com; www.wildlifeworldwide. com. Tailor-made & small group trips worldwide.

World Odyssey 01905 731373; e info@ world-odyssey.com; www.world-odyssey.com. Tailor-made trips across the globe (a different company from Africa Odyssey).

US

Aardvark Safaris 1 888 776 0888; e info@ aardvarksafaris.com; www.aardvarksafaris.com. Tailored trips to southern & northern Tanzania, including walking safaris.

Abercrombie & Kent 1 800 554 7016; www.abercrombiekent.com. A leader in luxury adventure travel.

Adventure Center ✆1 800 228 8747; www.
adventurecenter.com. Provides safaris, treks,
expeditions & active vacations worldwide.
Represents Explore Worldwide (opposite).
Africa Adventure Consultants ✆1 866 778
1089; e info@adventuresinafrica.com; www.
adventuresinafrica.com. Small Africa specialist
with good ethics.
Big Five Tours & Expeditions ✆1 800 244
3483; e info@bigfive.com; www.bigfive.com.
Luxury operator to Asia, Africa & South America.
Eco-resorts ✆1 866 326 7376; e info@ eco-
resorts.com; www.eco-resorts.com. Small team
focusing on ecotourism destinations in East Africa.
Ker & Downey USA ✆1 800 423 4236; e info@
kerdowney.com; www.kerdowney.com. Long-
established operator with Africa focus, now goes
worldwide.
Micato Safaris ✆1 800 642 2861; e inquiries@
micato.com; www.micato.com. Smart, family-
owned company, based in New York & Nairobi.
Naipenda Safaris ✆1 888 404 4499; e jo@
naipendasafaris; www.naipendasafaris.com; see
also advert on page 48. Small English- & French-
speaking specialist operator to Tanzania, with
bases in USA & Arusha.
Next Adventure ✆1 800 562 7298; e safari@
nextadventure.com; www.nextadventure.com.

Small California-based operator with strong ties to
Tanzania; also India & South America.
Thomson Safaris ✆1 800 235 0289; e info@
thomsonsafaris.com; www.thomsonsafaris.com.
Long-established Tanzania specialist operating
mostly set-departure small groups on fixed
itineraries.

SOUTH AFRICA
Wild Frontiers ✆(South Africa) +27 (0)11
7012 2035; m 0786 642466/0754 842466;
e reservations@wildfrontiers.com; www.
wildfrontiers.com. Experienced Johannesburg-
based tour operator notable for its range of air
tickets & set-departure group trips, including
specialist ornithological safaris to East Africa.

AUSTRALASIA
Classic Safari Company ✆(Australia) +612
9327 0666; e info@classicsafaricompany.com.au;
www.classicsafaricompany.com.au. Reliable old-
school tour operator now organising tailor-made
trips across Africa, India & Latin America.
Expert Africa ✆(New Zealand) 04 894 6885 or
(Australia) + 1 800 995 397; e info@expertafrica.
com; www.expertafrica.com. Antipodean office of
African specialists whose Tanzania programme is
run & updated by this book's authors.

RED TAPE

Check well in advance that you have a valid **passport** and that it won't expire
within six months of the date on which you intend to leave Tanzania. Should your
passport be lost or stolen, it will generally be easier to get a replacement if you have
a photocopy of the important pages.

If you want to drive or hire a vehicle while you're in the country, either bring
your normal driving licence or organise an **international driving licence** through
the AA. You may sometimes be asked at the border or international airport for an
international health certificate showing you've had a yellow fever shot.

For security reasons, it's advisable to keep a record of all your important
information. You can do this by detailing it on one sheet of paper, photocopying it,
and distributing a few copies in your luggage, your money-belt, and among relatives
or friends at home. Or alternatively, you can email yourself and a few close friends or
family the relevant information. The sort of things you want to include are your travel
insurance policy details and 24-hour emergency contact number, passport number,
details of relatives or friends to be contacted in an emergency, bank and credit card
details, camera and lens serial numbers, etc. See also *Documentation*, page 68.

For up-to-the-minute advice, also check www.fco.gov.uk/knowbeforeyougo.

VISAS Visas are required by most visitors to Tanzania, including UK and USA
passport holders, and cost US$30–60, depending on your nationality. Visas can

3

be obtained on arrival at any international airport, or at any border post. This is a straightforward procedure: no photographs or other documents are required, but the visa must be paid for in hard currency. The visa is normally valid for three months after arriving in the country, and it allows for multiple crossings into Uganda and Kenya during that period. For current information about visa requirements, visit www.tanzaniatouristboard.com.

EMBASSIES AND DIPLOMATIC MISSIONS

A selection of embassies and high commissions in Dar es Salaam is listed below. Most are open mornings only and closed at weekends. Typical hours are 09.00 to 12.30, but this varies considerably.

🅔 **Belgium** 5 Ocean Rd, Upanga; ☏022 211 2688; www.diplomatie.be/dar-es-salaam

🅔 **Burundi** Lugalo Rd, Upanga; m 0742 767006; e burundemb@raha.com

🅔 **Canada** 38 Mirambo St; ☏022 216 3300; www.canadainternational.gc.ca

🅔 **China** 2 Kajifcheni St; ☏022 266 8063; http://tz.china-embassy.org/eng

🅔 **Denmark** Ghana Av; ☏022 216 5200; m 0784 558885; http://tanzania.um.dk/

🅔 **France** Ali Hassan Mwinyi Rd; ☏022 219 8800; www.ambafrance-tz.org

🅔 **Germany** Cnr Mirambo St & Garden Av; ☏022 211 7409; www.daressalam.diplo.de

🅔 **Ireland** 353 Toure Drive; ☏022 260 2355; www.embassyofireland.or.tz

🅔 **Italy** 316 Lugalo Rd; ☏022 211 5935/6; www.ambdaressalaam.esteri.it

🅔 **Japan** 1081 Ali Hassan Mwinyi Rd; ☏022 211 5827; www.tz.emb-japan.go.jp

🅔 **Kenya** Ali Hassan Mwinyi Rd; ☏022 266 8285/6; www.kenyahighcomtz.org

🅔 **Malawi** Zambia Hse, Ohio/Sokoine Rd; ☏022 212 4623

🅔 **Mozambique** 25 Garden Av; ☏022 212 4673

🅔 **Netherlands** Umoja Hse, Garden Av; ☏022 211 0000; http://tanzania.nlembassy.org

🅔 **Norway** Cnr Mirambo St & Garden Av; ☏022 216 3100; www.norway.go.tz

🅔 **Russia** 73 Ali Hassan Mwinyi Rd; ☏022 266 6005/6; www.russianembassy.net

🅔 **Rwanda** 32 Ali Hassan Mwinyi Rd; ☏022 212 0703; www.tanzania.embassy.gov.rw

🅔 **South Africa** Mwaya Rd, Msasani; ☏022 260 1800; www.dirco.gov.za

🅔 **Spain** 99B Kinondoni Rd; ☏022 266 6936/6018; e embesptz@mail.mae.es

🅔 **Sweden** Cnr Mirambo St & Garden Av; ☏022 219 6500; www.swedenabroad.com

🅔 **Uganda** Extelcom Bldg, Samora Machel Av; ☏022 266 7391; f 022 266 7224

🅔 **UK** Umoja Hse, Garden Av; ☏022 229 0000; http://ukintanzania.fco.gov.uk

🅔 **USA** 686 Old Bagamoyo Rd; ☏022 229 4000; http://tanzania.usembassy.gov

🅔 **Zambia** Cnr Ohio Rd & Sokoine Drive; ☏022 211 2977

GETTING THERE AND AWAY

BY AIR There are two international airports on the Tanzanian mainland. **Julius Nyerere International Airport** in Dar es Salaam (airport code DAR) is the normal point of entry for international airlines, and it is generally convenient for business travellers but less so for tourists; many visitors who arrive in Dar transfer directly onto a flight to elsewhere in the country. **Kilimanjaro International Airport** (often abbreviated to KIA although its official airport code is JRO), which lies midway between Moshi and Arusha, is the more useful point of entry for tourists, and it may catch on with more international airlines.

Major international airlines that fly to Dar es Salaam and/or Kilimanjaro include the following: British Airways (*www.britishairways.com*), EgyptAir (*www.egyptair. com*), Emirates (*www.emirates.com*), Ethiopian Airlines (*www.flyethiopian.com*),

Kenya Airways (*www.kenya-airways.com*), KLM (*www.klm.com*), South African Airways (*www.flysaa.com*), Swiss (*www.swiss.com*) and Turkish Airlines (*www.turkishairlines.com*).

Budget travellers looking for flights to East Africa may well find it cheapest to use an airline that takes an indirect route. London is the best place to pick up a cheap ticket; many continental travellers buy their tickets there. It is generally cheaper to fly to Nairobi than to Dar es Salaam, and getting from Nairobi to Arusha by shuttle bus is cheap, simple and quick. Several airlines also operate daily flights between Nairobi and Kilimanjaro International Airport.

Flight specialists

From the UK

Flight Centre 13 The Broadway, Wimbledon SW19 1PS; \020 8296 8181; www.flightcentre.co.uk. An independent flight provider with over 450 outlets worldwide. They also have offices in Australia, New Zealand, South Africa & Canada.

Quest Travel Stoneham Hse, 17 Scarbrook Rd, Croydon, Surrey CR0 1SQ; \0845 263 6963; www.questtravel.com. An independent agent that has been in operation for over a decade offering competitive prices, specialising in long-haul flights.

STA Travel 2 Grosvenor Gdns, Victoria, London SW1W 0AG; \0871 468 0649; e enquiries@statravel.co.uk; www.statravel.co.uk. STA has 10 branches in London & 30 or so around the country & at different university sites. STA also has several branches & associate organisations around the world.

Trailfinders 194 Kensington High St, London W8 7RG; \020 7938 3939; www.trailfinders.com. Also has several other offices in the UK. With origins in the discount flight market, Trailfinders now provides a one-stop travel service including visa & passport service, travel clinic & foreign exchange.

Travel Bag 2–3 High St, Alton, Hants GU34 1TL; \0207 810 6831 & at 373–5 The Strand, London WC2R 0JE; \0844 880 4436; www.travelbag.co.uk. Provides tailor-made flight schedules & holidays for destinations throughout the world.

Travel Mood 24 Islington Green, London N1 8DU; \0844 815 9560; e sales@travelmood.com; www.travelmood.com. Provides flights & tailor-made holidays.

WEXAS 45–49 Brompton Rd, Knightsbridge, London SW3 1DE; \020 7589 3315; e mship@wexas.com; www.wexas.com. More of a club than a travel agent. Membership is inexpensive, but for frequent fliers the benefits are many.

From the USA

Airtech \1 212 219 7000; e fly@airtech.com; www.airtech.com. Standby seat broker that also deals in consolidator fares, courier flights & a host of other travel-related services.

Council on International Educational Exchange \1 207 553 4000; e contact@ciee.org; www.ciee.org. Although the Council focuses on work-exchange trips, it also has a large travel department.

Net Fare \(freephone) 1 800 766 3601; e qdmin@netfare.net; www.netfare.net. Provides fares for destinations throughout the world.

STA Travel \(freephone) 1 800 781 4040; e go@statravel.com; www.statravel.com. Has several branches around the country.

Worldtek Travel \(freephone) 1 800 243 1723; e info@worldtek.com; www.worldtek.com. Operates a network of rapidly growing travel agencies.

From Canada

Flight Centre \(freephone) 1 877 967 5302; www.flightcentre.ca. Has a network of branches around the country.

Travel CUTS \(freephone) 1 866 246 9762; www.travelcuts.com. A Canadian student-based travel organisation with 60 offices throughout Canada.

From Australia

Flight Centre \(freephone) 133 133; www.flightcentre.com.au. An independent flight operator with offices around the country. They also have offices in the UK, New Zealand, South Africa & Canada.

STA Travel \134 782; www.statravel.com.au. A student travel specialist with a network of branches around Australia.

From New Zealand

Flight Centre \0800 2435 44; www.flightcentre.co.nz. A good starting point for cheap air fares.

From South Africa
Flight Centre 📞0860 400 727; www.
flightcentre.co.za. Part of the international chain
with a number of branches around the country.

Student Flights 📞0860 400 700; www.
studentflights.co.za. This outfit is linked to the
Flight Centre network.

Web-based flight sites

www.expedia.com Worldwide with a number
of local websites

www.lastminute.com Made its name selling
distressed last-minute trips

DAR ES SALAAM

Situated about 550km southeast of Moshi by road, Dar es Salaam – often referred to as plain 'Dar' – is Tanzania's capital in all but name. With a population estimated at 2.5 million in 2012, it is far and away the country's largest city and most important commercial centre. A lively bustling Indian Ocean port, it is rivalled in regional maritime significance only by Mombasa in Kenya. Unfortunately, however, Dar es Salaam cannot claim to be a tourist centre of any great note. On the contrary, the increasing ease with which visitors can fly into KIA directly, or fly straight on to Zanzibar or elsewhere after landing at Dar means that only a relatively small proportion of fly-in tourists ever set foot in the city itself.

Whether or not this is a good thing is a matter of opinion. Dar es Salaam is one of those cities that tends to draw extreme reactions from travellers, a real 'love it or hate it' kind of place, and its many detractors would probably regard any Dar-free itinerary through Tanzania as a highly desirable state of affairs. Personally, however, I enjoy Dar es Salaam, more perhaps than any other major East African city, since it boasts all the hustle and bustle of somewhere such as Nairobi yet has none of that city's underlying aggression or bland architectural modernity.

If nothing else, Dar is imbued with a distinctive sense of place, one derived from the cultural mix of its people and buildings, not to mention a torpid coastal humidity that permeates every aspect of day-to-day life. Architecturally, the city boasts German, British, Asian and Arab influences, but it is fundamentally a Swahili city, and beneath the superficial air of hustle, a laid-back and friendly place. People are willing to pass the time in idle chat and will readily help out strangers, and tourists will find they are rarely hassled except in the vicinity of the New Africa Hotel, where a resident brigade of hissing money-changers froths into action every time a *mzungu* (white person) walks past.

ARRIVING AND DEPARTING DAR ES SALAAM If you decide to fly into Dar es Salaam, the international airport is situated 13km from the city centre, a 20-minute taxi ride that costs up to US$25 depending on how hard you bargain. Almost all long-distance buses leave Dar es Salaam from the vast Ubungo Bus Station, situated out of town along the Morogoro road. This means you will be forced to make a special trip out of town a day ahead of your departure to book tickets. A taxi from the city centre to Ubungo will cost up to US$8, depending on how receptive the driver is to negotiation. The best coach service for Arusha and other destinations along the B1 is the Dar Express (m *0754 946155*), and buses depart every 30 minutes between 05.30 and 08.30, as well as at 10.00 and 14.30. Tickets costs US$18–20 depending on the type of coach and the trip takes about 12 hours.

OVERLAND The viability of the established overland routes between Europe and East Africa depends on the current political situation. In recent years, it has often been possible to reach East Africa via Egypt, Sudan and Ethiopia. However, it's not easy to predict the local political situation in advance, so do some online research and talk to several companies operating in the area before setting off.

WHERE TO STAY If you need to overnight in Dar there are plenty of hotels in and around the city to suit all budgets. A few recommendations, in descending order of price and quality, follow:

🏠 **Oyster Bay Hotel** (8 rooms) ☎ (UK) +44 1932 260618; e reservations@theoysterbayhotel.com; www.theoysterbayhotel.com. The super-exclusive Oyster Bay Hotel, boasting a peaceful location just off Toure Drive on the peninsula, is all billowing white drapes, stylish sculptures & African minimalism. The idea here is to feel part of a stylish house party, & food is tailored around guests' preferences but typically includes luxuries like lobster. There is a swimming pool. *US$525/800 sgl/dbl inc all meals & drinks.*

🏠 **Sea Cliff Hotel** (93 rooms) m 0764 700600; e information@hotelseacliff.com; www.hotelseacliff.com. This comfortable & stylish seafront hotel on Msasani Peninsula is only 20 mins by taxi from the city centre. Facilities include a franchise of the popular Alcove Restaurant, Karambezi coffee shop & cake counter, a swimming pool & gym, a business centre, & free Wi-Fi. A nearby mall has ATMs, several good restaurants & cafés, & a massage centre. *From US$320 dbl (main hotel), or US$180–200 at the nearby Village complex.*

🏠 **Southern Sun Dar es Salaam** (152 rooms) ☎ 022 213 7575; e reservations@southernsun.co.tz; www.southernsuntz.com. This smart, centrally located South African chain hotel stands in lush grounds on Garden Avenue. Facilities include a business centre, Wi-Fi, 2 good restaurants, 16-hr room service, non-smoking rooms, facilities for the disabled, an on-site travel centre, a good curio & book shop, a swimming pool & a fitness centre. *US$220/243 sgl/dbl, with discounts over w/ends.*

🏠 **Best Western Coral Beach Hotel** (62 rooms) ☎ 022 260 1928; e info@coralbeach-tz.com; www.coralbeach-tz.com. This new hotel on the Msasani Peninsula offers good value sea-facing en-suite accommodation with king-size beds, satellite TV, Wi-Fi & all the other amenities you'd expect of an international chain. *From US$160 dbl B&B.*

🏠 **Protea Courtyard Hotel** (52 rooms) ☎ 022 213 0130; m 0784 555130; e info@phcourtyard.com; www.proteahotels.com/courtyard. This comfortable international chain hotel on Ocean Drive is very reasonably priced by comparison to places of a similar standard. Facilities include a business centre, a restaurant, a coffee shop, DSTV in all the rooms, a swimming pool, conference centre & library. *US$155/195 sgl/dbl B&B.*

🏠 **Palm Beach Hotel** (32 rooms) ☎ 022 213 0985/212 2931; e info@pbhtz.com; www.pbhtz.com. About 20 mins' walk from the city centre on Ali Hassan Mwinyi Road, this rambling old 1950s hotel was undergoing its second major restoration in recent memory in late 2012. In the process it has sacrificed its Art Deco exterior & former time-warped charm, but modernised facilities A pleasant garden bar/restaurant serves good meals. En-suite rooms with mini-safe, hot water, TV & internet access are good value. *US$95/120 sgl/dbl.*

🏠 **Econo Lodge** (61 rooms) ☎ 022 211 6048/9; m 0741 270800; e econolodge@raha.com; www.econohotel.8m.com. This comfortable & well established hotel has a convenient central location off Libya Street, & is outstandingly good value in the budget range. *En-suite rooms with fans US$15/20/25 sgl/dbl/trpl; with AC US$25/30/35.*

A route via the Sahara and West Africa used to be favoured by several overland truck companies but unfortunately it has been impassable since the mid 1990s. At first this was due to banditry, then a major bridge collapsed in what was then Zaire, and then there was the civil war in the Democratic Republic of the Congo. This route has always been tough going for independent travellers, whether or not they have a vehicle, and in the present climate of instability it should not be considered.

The most popular overland route in Africa these days connects Kenya to South Africa via Tanzania and a combination of Mozambique, Malawi, Zambia, Zimbabwe, Botswana and Namibia. It is a good route for self-drivers, can be covered with ease using public transport, but is also serviced by a proliferation of overland truck companies – recommendations include **Acacia Expeditions** (*www.acacia-africa. com*), **Dragoman** (*www.dragoman.co.uk*) and **Exodus** (*www.exodus.co.uk*).

Border crossings Tanzania borders eight countries. A brief outline of frequently used border crossings into/from the three countries to its north follows:

To/from Kenya The most popular crossing is between Nairobi and Arusha via Namanga. A number of shuttle companies such as Riverside and Impala run twice-daily minibus transfers between Arusha, Moshi and Nairobi. You can also travel between Nairobi and Arusha more cheaply (and more masochistically) in stages, catching a minibus between Nairobi and Namanga (these leave Nairobi from Ronald Ngala Road), crossing the border on foot, and then catching a shared taxi to Arusha. Expect this to take around six hours.

Provided that your papers are in order, Namanga is a very straightforward border crossing. There is a bank where you can change money during normal banking hours but at other times you'll have to change money with private individuals – don't change more than you need, as there are several con artists about.

An increasingly popular route between Kenya and Tanzania is from Mombasa to Tanga (three to four hours) or Dar es Salaam. Again, this is straightforward enough, and a couple of buses do the run every day. Another route is between Kisumu and Mwanza on Lake Victoria. There are several buses daily along this route, leaving in the early morning and taking around 12 hours.

To/from Uganda The best way to cross from Uganda to Tanzania depends on which part of Tanzania you want to visit. If your main interest is the coast and the eastern parts of Tanzania, then the easiest option would be to catch an overnight bus from Kampala to Nairobi, from where it is relatively easy to travel on to Arusha (see above). The longer and more adventurous alternative is to travel by road from Masaka to Bukoba, by ferry from Bukoba to Mwanza, and then by road to Dar es Salaam or Arusha. For more details on this route see the *Lake Victoria* chapter, page 335.

To/from Rwanda The only route between Kigali and Mwanza is by road, crossing at the Rusumu border post. Plenty of minibuses zoom along the road between Kigali, the capital of Rwanda, and the border. From there, you'll need to catch a bus to Mwanza over a few days. For further details see http://bradttanzania. wordpress.com.

SAFETY

Crime exists in Tanzania as it does practically everywhere in the world. There has been a marked increase in crime in Tanzania over recent years, and tourists are inevitably at risk because they are far richer than most locals, and are conspicuous in their dress, behaviour and (with obvious exceptions) skin colour. For all that, Tanzania remains a lower crime risk than many countries, and the social taboo on theft is such that even a petty criminal is likely to be beaten badly should they be caught in the act. With a bit of care, you would have to be unlucky to suffer from more serious crime while you are in Tanzania. Indeed, a far more serious concern is reckless and drunk driving, particularly on public transport along major roads. Generally buses are regarded to be safer than light vehicles such as minibuses, though this cannot be quantified statistically. Safari drivers are generally a lot more sedate and safe behind the wheel than bus and minibus drivers. Self-drivers should take a far more defensive attitude to driving than they would at home, and be alert to the road hog mentality of many local drivers.

MUGGING There is nowhere in Tanzania where mugging is as commonplace as it is in, say, Nairobi or Johannesburg, but there are certainly several parts of the country where walking around alone at night would place you at some risk of being mugged. Mugging is generally an urban problem, with the main areas of risk being Dar es Salaam, Arusha and Zanzibar Town. Even in these places, the risk is often localised, so ask local advice at your hotel, since the staff there will generally know of any recent incidents in the immediate vicinity. The best way to ensure that any potential mugging remains an unpleasant incident rather than a complete disaster is to carry as little as possible on your person. If you are mugged in Tanzania, the personal threat is minimal provided that you promptly hand over what is asked for.

CASUAL THEFT The bulk of crime in Tanzania consists of casual theft such as bag-snatching or pickpocketing. This sort of thing is not particularly aimed at tourists (and as a consequence it is not limited to tourist areas), but tourists will be considered fair game. The key to not being pickpocketed is not having anything of value in your pockets; the key to avoiding having things snatched is to avoid having valuables in a place where they could easily be snatched. Most of the following points will be obvious to experienced travellers, but they are worth making:

- Many casual thieves operate in bus stations and markets. Keep a close watch on your belongings in these places, and avoid having loose valuables in your pocket or daypack.
- Keep all your valuables – passport, money, etc – in a money-belt. One you can hide under your clothes has obvious advantages over one of the currently fashionable codpieces that are worn externally.
- Never carry spending money in your money-belt. A normal wallet is fine provided it contains only a moderate sum of money. Better still is a wallet you can hang around your neck. If I plan to visit a risky area such as a busy market, I sometimes wear shorts under my trousers and keep my cash in the pockets of the shorts. In my opinion, it is difficult for somebody to stick a hand in the front pocket of a shirt unobserved, for which reason this is normally my favourite pocket for keeping ready cash.
- Distribute your money throughout your luggage. I always keep the bulk of my foreign currency in my money-belt, but I like to keep some cash hidden in various parts of my pack and daypack.
- Many people prefer to carry their money-belt on their person at all times. I think it is far safer to leave it locked away in a bag or safe in your hotel room.

It's not impossible for a locked hotel room to be broken into, but I've not heard of it happening in Tanzania, whereas I have met countless people who have been pickpocketed, mugged or had possessions snatched from them on the street. Circumstances do play a part here: in a large city, I would be far happier with my valuables locked away somewhere, whereas in a game lodge the risk of theft from a room has to be greater than that of theft from your person. One factor to consider is that some travellers' cheque companies won't issue refunds on cheques stolen from a hotel room.

- If you have jewellery that is of high personal or financial value, leave it at home.
- If you are robbed, think twice before you chase the thief, especially if the stolen items are of no great value. An identified thief is likely to be descended on by a mob and quite possibly beaten to death. I have met a few travellers who found themselves in the bizarre position of having to save someone who had just ripped them off.

DOCUMENTATION The best insurance against complete disaster is to keep things well documented. If you carry a photocopy of the main page of your passport, you will be issued a new one more promptly. In addition, email yourself and a few close friends or family a chart with full details of your passport, flights, bank, credit card travel insurance policy, travellers cheques (if you have them) and camera and other electronic equipment (including serial numbers). See also, *Red tape*, page 61.

You will have to promptly report to the police the theft of any item against which you wish to claim insurance.

SECURITY Tanzania is a very secure country, with a proud record of internal stability since independence. The bombing of the US embassies in Dar es Salaam and Nairobi resulted in large-scale cancellations of US tours to Tanzania in late 1998, despite a mass of evidence that would provide any rational human with greater cause to give a wide berth to US embassies than to cancel a holiday in East Africa. Aside from this, those parts of Tanzania regularly visited by tourists have a good safety record, although occasional armed robberies might occur anywhere.

Tanzania shares a western border (comprised entirely of Lake Tanganyika) with the troubled Democratic Republic of the Congo. So far as we are aware, the ongoing civil war here has had little direct effect on Tanzania.

WOMEN TRAVELLERS Women travellers in Tanzania have little to fear on a gender-specific level. Over the years, I've met several women travelling alone in Tanzania, and none had any serious problems in their interactions with locals, aside from the hostility that can be generated by dressing skimpily. Otherwise, an element of flirtation is about the sum of it, perhaps the odd direct proposition, but nothing that cannot be defused by a firm 'No'. And nothing for that matter that you wouldn't expect in any Western country, or – probably with a far greater degree of persistence – from many male travellers.

It would be prudent to pay some attention to how you dress in Tanzania, particularly in the more conservative parts of the Swahili coast. In areas where people are used to tourists, they are unlikely to be deeply offended by women travellers wearing shorts or other outfits that might be seen to be provocative. Nevertheless, it still pays to allow for local sensibilities, and under certain circumstances revealing clothes may be perceived to make a statement that's not intended from your side.

More mundanely, tampons are not readily available in smaller towns, although you can easily locate them in Dar es Salaam and Arusha, and in game lodge and

Tsh1,200, a drop of around 10% annually. It is reasonable to expect a similar trend will persist during the lifespan of this edition. For rates of exchange, see page 2.

Most upmarket hotels and safari companies in Tanzania quote rates in US dollars. Some will also demand payment in this or another prominent hard currency, although some hotels and lodges actually prefer payment in local currency. The situation with national parks and other conservation areas is variable, but if you expect to pay fees directly rather than through an operator, then you'll need enough hard currency to cover the full amount (see box, *Paying park fees*, below). These exceptions noted, most things in Tanzania are best paid for in local currency, including restaurant bills, goods bought at a market or shop, mid-range and budget accommodation, public transport and most other casual purchases. Indeed, most service providers geared towards the local economy will have no facility for accepting any currency other than the Tanzanian shilling.

Note that most prices in this book are quoted in US dollars rather than Tanzanian shillings, This is because of the local currency's propensity for devaluation against hard currencies, which means that even where prices are quoted locally in shillings, a US dollar price is more likely to hold steady over the book's lifespan. However, in the few instances where a hotel quotes its rates in euros or sterling, we have followed suit.

CASH, TRAVELLERS' CHEQUES AND CREDIT CARDS Traditionally, there are three ways of carrying money in Africa: hard currency cash, travellers' cheques or a credit card. Over recent years, **travellers' cheques** have been rendered all but obsolete as credit cards have become more widely accepted in East Africa. In any case, they are now difficult to exchange in Tanzania, so are best avoided altogether.

Far more convenient are **credit or debit cards**, which can be used to draw local currency at 24-hour ATMs in most towns of any size, as well as for paying bills at upmarket hotels, and for paying national park fees. Depending on the bank, a daily withdrawal limit of between Tsh400,000 (around US$250) and Tsh1.2 million (around US$750) will be imposed. It is important to note that the only widely accepted cards are Visa and to a lesser extent MasterCard. Other cards will be of little or no use. Note, too, that ATM facilities are not available in any national parks, or in smaller towns and beach resorts. Budget travellers can safely assume that hotels and other facilities within their reach cannot process credit card payments.

3

PAYING PARK FEES

Although it won't affect travellers on organised safaris, anybody doing a self-drive safari should be aware that the national parks on the northern circuit no longer accept cash payments for entrance or other fees. The only options accepted at the gate are Visa or MasterCard, or Tanapa smartcards, which can be bought at any Exim Bank. So if you only have cash, it's best to buy one of the Tanzania National Park (Tanapa) pre-paid cards in Arusha, and load it up with enough funds to cover all your park fees. There are two Exim bank branches in Arusha: the main branch on Sokoine Avenue near the Clock Tower (⊕ *09.00–15.00 Mon–Fri, 09.00–12.30 Sat*) and the subsidiary branch in the TFA (Shoprite) Centre at the other end of Sokoine Avenue (⊕ *09.00–16.30 Mon–Fri, 09.00–14.30 Sat*).

Paying fees for the Ngorongoro Conservation Area is a lot more complex, see box on page 274.

It's advisable to take along more than one card (i.e: a credit and a debit) as banks have an annoying habit of freezing your card at inopportune moments without telling you. And just in case that happens, include an overseas number for your bank's fraud department with your emergency contacts so that you can call and get any freeze lifted as soon as possible.

It is still a good idea to carry some of your funds in hard currency **cash**, ideally US dollars, although euros and pounds sterling are also widely accepted. Note that US$100 and US$50 bills usually attract a significantly better exchange rate than smaller denominations, and that US dollar bills printed before 2006 will be refused by almost all outlets that accept or exchange foreign currency.

Carry your hard currency and credit cards, as well as your passport and other important documentation, in a money-belt that can be hidden beneath your clothing. Your money-belt should be made of cotton or another natural fabric, and everything inside the belt should be wrapped in plastic to protect it against sweat.

FOREIGN EXCHANGE Foreign currencies can be changed into Tanzanian shillings at any bank or bureau de change (known locally as forex bureaux). Most banks are open from around 09.00 to 12.30 on weekdays and in many larger towns they stay open until 15.00 or later. They open from 09.00 to at least 11.30 on Saturdays. Most private forex bureaux stay open until 16.00 or later. You can normally change money at any time of day at Julius Nyerere International Airport (Dar es Salaam) or Kilimanjaro International Airport (between Arusha and Moshi). Most private forex bureaux deal in cash only, for which reason you'll probably be forced to change your travellers' cheques at a bank. The rate for this is often slightly lower than the cash rate and a small commission is also charged.

Generally, private forex bureaux offer a better rate of exchange than banks, although this is not as much the case as it was a few years ago, and some forex bureaux actually give notably lower rates than the banks. It's worth shopping around before a major transaction. The private bureaux are almost always far quicker for cash transactions than the banks, which might be a more important consideration than a minor discrepancy in the rate they offer. Before you change a large sum of money, check the bank or forex bureau has enough high denomination banknotes, or you'll need a briefcase to carry your local currency.

The legalisation of private forex bureaux has killed off the black market that previously thrived in Tanzania. Private individuals may give you a slightly better rate than the banks, but the official rate is so favourable it seems unfair to exploit this. In Dar es Salaam or Arusha you will be offered exceptionally good rates on the street, but if you are stupid or greedy enough to accept these, you can expect to be ripped off. There are plenty of forged US$100 bills floating around Tanzania, and you can assume that anyone who suggests a deal involving a US$100 bill is trying to unload a forgery.

GETTING AROUND

BY AIR Several private airlines run scheduled flights around Tanzania, most prominently Regional Air Services, Precision Air, Coastal Travel and Zanair. Between them, these carriers offer reliable services to most parts of the country that regularly attract tourists, including Dar es Salaam, Zanzibar, Pemba, Mafia, Kilimanjaro, Arusha, Serengeti, Ngorongoro, Lake Manyara, Mwanza, Rubondo Island, Kigoma and most of the southern parks. There are also regular flights between Kilimanjaro and the Kenyan cities of Mombasa and Nairobi. Several of the airlines now offer a straightforward online booking service. Contact details are as follows:

✈ **Coastal Travel** www.coastal.cc
✈ **Fastjet** www.fastjet.com/tz
✈ **Precision Air** www.precisionairtz.com

✈ **Regional Air Services** www.
regionaltanzania.com
✈ **Zanair** www.zanair.com

BY PUBLIC TRANSPORT Good express coach services, typically travelling at faster than 60km/h, connect Arusha and Moshi to Dar es Salaam and Nairobi (Kenya). **Dar Express** is particularly recommended, approaching (although far from attaining) Greyhound-type standards, and it operates several buses daily between Dar es Salaam and Arusha. Express coaches also connect Arusha to Moshi, Lushoto, Tanga, Mwanza and Dar es Salaam.

For long trips on major routes, ensure that you use an 'express bus', which should travel directly between towns, stopping only at a few prescribed places, rather than stopping wherever and whenever a potential passenger is sighted or an existing passenger wants to disembark. Be warned that as far as most touts are concerned, any bus that will give them commission is an express bus, so you are likely to be pressured into getting onto the bus they want you to get on. The best way to counter this is to go to the bus station on the day before you want to travel, and make your enquiries and bookings in advance, when you will be put under less pressure and won't have to worry about keeping an eye on your luggage.

The alternative to buses on most routes is a **dala-dala** – a generic name that seems to encompass practically any light public transport. On the whole, dala-dalas tend to be overcrowded by comparison with buses, and they are more likely to try to overcharge tourists, while the manic driving style results in regular fatal accidents.

When you check bus times, be conscious of the difference between Western time and Swahili time. Many Tanzanians will translate the Swahili time to English without making the six-hour conversion – in other words, you might be told that a bus leaves at 11.00 when it actually leaves at 05.00.' The best way to get around this area of potential misunderstanding is to confirm the time you are quoted in Swahili – for instance ask '*saa moja?*' if you are told a bus leaves at 13.00. See *Swahili time* in *Appendix 1, Language*, page 414, for more details.

BY PRIVATE SAFARI AND CAR RENTAL The most normal way of getting around northern Tanzania is on an **organised safari** by Land Cruiser, Land Rover or any other similarly hardy 4x4 with high clearance. It is standard procedure for safari companies to provide a driver/guide with a fair knowledge of local wildlife and road conditions, as well as some mechanical expertise. **Self-drive car hire** isn't a particularly attractive or popular option in northern Tanzania, but it is widely available in Zanzibar and Dar es Salaam.

 # ACCOMMODATION

The number of hotels in major urban tourist centres such as Zanzibar Town, Arusha, Moshi and Dar es Salaam is quite remarkable. So, too, is the variety in standard and price, which embraces hundreds of simple local guesthouses charging a couple of US dollars a night, as well as fantastic exclusive beach resorts and lodges charging upwards of US$1,000 for a room – and everything in between.

All accommodation listings in this guidebook are placed in one of six categories: exclusive, upmarket, moderate, budget, shoestring, and camping. The purpose of this categorisation is twofold: to break up long hotel listings that span a wide price range, and to help readers isolate the range of hotels that will best suit their budget and taste. The application of categories is not meant to be rigid. Aside from an inevitable element of subjectivity, I have categorised hotels on their feel as much as their rates (the prices are quoted anyway), and this might be influenced by the standard of other accommodation options in the same place.

Before going into more detail about the different accommodation categories, it's worth noting a few potentially misleading quirks in local hotel-speak. In Swahili, the word *hoteli* refers to a restaurant while what we call a hotel is generally called a lodging, guesthouse or *gesti* – so if you ask a Tanzanian to show you a hotel you might well be taken to an eatery. Another local quirk is that most Tanzanian hotels in all ranges refer to a room with an en-suite shower and toilet as being self-contained. Finally, at most hotels in the moderate category or below, a single room will as often as not be one with a three-quarter or double bed, while a double room will be what we call a twin, with two single or double beds. 'B&B' refers to bed and breakfast, 'HB' to half board, 'FB' to full board.

EXCLUSIVE This category does not generally embrace conventional international-style hotels, but rather small and atmospheric tented camps, game lodges and beach resorts catering to the most exclusive end of the market. Lodges in this category typically (but not invariably) contain significantly fewer than 20 accommodation units built and decorated in a style that complements the surrounding environment. The management will generally place a high priority on personalised service and quality food and wine, with the main idea being that guests are exposed to a holistic 24-hour bush or beach experience, rather than just a hotel room and restaurant in a bush/beach location. In several instances, lodges that fall into the exclusive category might be less conventionally luxurious, in terms of air conditioning and the like, than their competitors in the upmarket category. It is the bush experience and not the range of facilities that lends lodges in this category a quality of exclusivity. Rack rates are typically upwards of US$800 all-inclusive for a double room, but many cost twice as much as that (with substantial discounts for operators). This is the category to look at if you want authentic, atmospheric bush or beach accommodation and have few financial restrictions.

UPMARKET This category includes most hotels, lodges and resorts that cater almost entirely to the international tourist or business travel market. Hotels in this range would typically be accorded a two- to four-star ranking internationally, and they offer smart accommodation with en-suite facilities, mosquito netting, air conditioning or fans depending on the local climate, and satellite television in cities and some beach resorts. Hotels in this bracket might charge anything from under US$100 to upwards of US$500 for a double room, depending on quality and location, but they are generally at the higher end of that range in national parks and other safari destinations. As a rule, upmarket hotels in areas that see few foreign visitors are far cheaper than equivalent hotels in or around urban tourist centres such as Dar es Salaam or Arusha, which are in turn cheaper than beach hotels and lodges in national parks and game reserves. Room rates for city and beach hotels invariably include breakfast, while at game lodges they will also normally include lunch and dinner. Most package tours use accommodation in this range.

MODERATE In Tanzania, as in many African countries, there is often a wide gap in price and standard between the cheapest hotels geared primarily towards tourists and the best hotels geared primarily towards local travellers and budget travellers. For this reason, the moderate bracket is rather more nebulous than other accommodation categories, essentially consisting of hotels which, for one or another reason, couldn't really be classified as upmarket, but equally are too expensive or of too high quality to be considered budget lodgings. Many places listed in this range are superior local hotels that will suffice in lieu of any genuinely upmarket accommodation in a town that sees relatively few tourists. The category also embraces decent lodges or hotels in recognised tourist areas that charge considerably lower rates than their upmarket competitors, but are clearly a notch or two above the budget category. Hotels in this range normally offer comfortable accommodation in self-contained rooms with hot water, fan and possibly satellite television, and they will have decent restaurants and employ a high proportion of English-speaking staff. Prices for moderate city and beach hotels are generally in the US$50–120 range, more in some game reserves. This is the category to look at if you are travelling privately on a limited or low budget and expect a reasonably high but not luxurious standard of accommodation.

BUDGET Hotels in this category are aimed largely at the local market and definitely don't approach international standards, but are still reasonably clean and comfortable, and a definite cut above the basic guesthouses that proliferate in most towns. Hotels in this bracket will more often than not have a decent restaurant attached, English-speaking staff, and comfortable rooms with en-suite facilities, running cold or possibly hot water, fans (but not air conditioning) and good mosquito netting. The hotels in this category typically charge well under US$50 for a self-contained double room, and may charge as little as US$8–10 in relatively out-of-the-way places. This is the category to look at if you are on a limited budget, but want to avoid total squalor!

SHOESTRING This category is aimed at travellers who want the cheapest possible accommodation irrespective of quality. In most Tanzanian towns, this will amount to a choice of dozens of small private guesthouses, which are almost exclusively used by locals, are remarkably uniform in design, and generally charge below US$15 for an uncluttered room, often a lot less. The typical guesthouse consists of around ten cell-like rooms forming three walls around a central courtyard, with a reception area or restaurant at the front. Toilets are more often than not long-drops. Washing facilities often amount to nothing more than a lockable room and a bucket of water, although an increasing number of guesthouses do have proper showers, and a few have hot water. There are several cheap church-run guesthouses and hostels in Tanzania, and these are normally also included under the shoestring listings.

CAMPING There are surprisingly few campsites in Tanzania, and those that do exist tend to be in national parks, where camping costs US$20–30 per person. Along the coast north of Dar es Salaam and in Moshi and Arusha, several private sites cater to backpackers and overland trucks. If you ask at moderate hotels in out-of-the-way places, you may sometimes be allowed to camp in their grounds for a small fee.

✕ EATING AND DRINKING

FOOD Most tourists will eat 90% of their meals at game lodges or hotels that cater specifically to tourists and whose kitchens serve Western-style food, ranging in standard from adequate to excellent. Game lodges tend to offer a daily set menu with a limited selection, so it is advisable to have your tour operator specify in advance if you are a vegetarian or have other specific dietary requirements. First-time visitors to Africa might take note that most game lodges in and around the national parks have isolated locations, and driving within the parks is neither

TRADITIONAL MBEGE BANANA BEER
Emma Thomson

This party brew is prepared for many different Chagga ceremonies, but it is always drunk from a dried squash plant that has been hollowed out to form an enormous chalice, with the village landlord's clan name engraved upon it. Below is a rough recipe, as the measurements are only approximate.

INGREDIENTS
1kg mashed banana
1 litre water
1kg finger millet

METHOD Boil bananas in water until they turn red, and then cover for three days.

Meanwhile, wash the finger millet, cover and leave in a wet, warm and dark place for three to four days until the millet begins to sprout. Then grind the millet into flour.

From this, make porridge by mixing two parts flour to one part water. Next add ten parts of the boiled banana to one part porridge, mix and cover until the next day.

Let the celebrations begin. (The longer you leave it, the stronger the brew.)

permitted nor advisable after dark, so that there is no realistic alternative to eating at your lodge. You will rarely be disappointed.

Most game lodges offer the option of a packaged breakfast and/or lunch box, so that their guests can eat on the trot rather than having to base their game-viewing hours around set meal times. The standard of the packed lunches is rather variable (and in some cases pretty awful) but if your first priority is to see wildlife, then taking a breakfast box in particular allows you to be out during the prime game-viewing hours immediately after sunrise. Packed meals must be ordered the night before you need them. It is best to ask your driver-guide to make this sort of arrangement, rather than doing it yourself.

When you are staying in towns such as Arusha and Moshi, there is a fair selection of eating-out options. Indian eateries are particularly numerous in most towns, thanks to the high resident Indian population, and good continental restaurants and pizzerias are also well represented. Seafood is excellent on the coast. Options tend to be more limited in smaller towns such as Lushoto or Tanga, and very basic in villages off the main tourist trail. A selection of the better restaurants in each town is listed in the main part of the guide.

As for the local cuisine, it tends to consist of a bland stew eaten with one of four staples: rice, chapati, *ugali* or *batoke*. Ugali is a stiff maize porridge eaten throughout sub-Saharan Africa. Batoke or *matoke* is cooked plantain, served boiled or in a mushy heap. In the Lake Victoria region, batoke replaces ugali as the staple food. The most common stews are chicken, beef, goat and beans, and the meat is often rather tough. In coastal towns and around the great lakes, whole fried fish is a welcome change. The distinctive Swahili cuisine of the coast makes generous use of coconut milk and is far more spiced than other Tanzanian food.

Mandaazi, the local equivalent of doughnuts, are tasty when freshly cooked. They are served at *hotelis* and sold at markets. You can eat cheaply at stalls around markets and bus stations. Goat kebabs, fried chicken, grilled groundnuts and potato chips are often freshly cooked and sold in these places. A very popular and filling (though not exactly healthy) street dish throughout Tanzania is *chipsi mayai*, which essentially consists of potato chips cooked in an omelette-like mix of eggs (mayai).

KiSwahili names for various foods are given in *Appendix 1, Language*, page 415.

DRINKS The most widely drunk beverage is *chai*, a sweet tea where all ingredients are boiled together in a pot. Along the coast chai is often flavoured with spices such as ginger. In some places chai is served *ya rangi* or black; in others *maziwa* or milky. Sodas such as Coke, Pepsi, Sprite and Fanta are widely available, and normally cost less than US$0.50 in outlets geared towards locals, and up to five times that price in tourist-oriented lodges. In large towns you can often get fresh fruit juice. On the coast and in some parts of the interior, the most refreshing, healthy and inexpensive drink is coconut water, sold by street vendors who will decapitate the young coconut of your choice to create a natural cup, from which the juice can be sipped. Tap water in Tanzania is often dodgy, and most travellers try to stick to mineral water, which comes in 1.5-litre bottles that cost a few hundred shillings in supermarkets in Arusha but are very overpriced at game lodges – it is advisable to stock up with a dozen bottles or so before your safari leaves Arusha.

The two main alcoholic drinks are beer and *konyagi*. Konyagi is a spirit made from sugar cane. It tastes a bit strange on its own, but it mixes well and is very cheap. The local Safari lager used to be appalling, but since the national brewery was taken over by South African Breweries a few years ago there has been a dramatic improvement not only in the quality of Safari, but also in the selection of other brands available. Around ten different lager beers are now available, of which Tusker, Castle, Kilimanjaro and Serengeti seem to be the most popular. All beers come in 500ml bottles and cost anything from US$1 at a local bar to US$5 at the most upmarket hotels, although some lodges also serves smaller 330ml cans. A variety of imported spirits are available in larger towns. A varied selection of wines, usually South African in origin, is available at most mid-range and upmarket lodges and hotels, and they generally quite reasonably priced by international standards.

PUBLIC HOLIDAYS

Tourists visiting Tanzania should take note of public holidays, since all banks, forex bureaux and government offices will be closed. In addition to Good Friday, Easter Monday, Idd-ul-Fitr, Islamic New Year and the Prophet's Birthday, which fall on different dates every year, the following public holidays are taken in Tanzania:

1 January	New Year's Day
12 January	Zanzibar Revolution Day
7 April	Karume Day (anniversary of the assassination of Vice President Abeid Amani Karume in 1972)
26 April	Union Day (anniversary of union between Tanganyika and Zanzibar)
1 May	International Workers' Day
7 July	Saba Saba (Peasants') Day
8 August	Nane Nane (Farmers') Day
14 October	Nyerere Memorial Day
9 December	Independence Day
25 December	Christmas Day
26 December	Boxing Day

SHOPPING

Until a few years ago it was difficult to buy anything much in Tanzania. One of my most vivid memories of Dar es Salaam in 1986 was walking into a general store where a lone shelf of teaspoons was the only stock. Things have improved greatly since then. In Dar es Salaam and most other large towns a fair range of imported goods is available, although prices are often inflated. If you have any very specific needs – unusual medications or slide film, for instance – bring them with you. Toilet roll, soap, toothpaste, pens, batteries and locally produced food are widely available. Shopping hours are normally 08.30 to 16.30, with a lunch break between 13.00 and 14.00, but *dukas*, the stalls you see around markets or lining roads, are cheaper than proper shops and stay open for longer hours.

CURIOS A variety of items specifically aimed at tourists is available: Makonde carvings, Tingatinga paintings (see box, page 119), batiks, musical instruments, wooden spoons and various soapstone and malachite knick-knacks. Arusha is the best place to shop for curios, as prices are competitive and the quality is good. Prices in shops are fixed, but you may be able to negotiate a discount. At curio stalls, haggling is necessary. Unless you are good at this, and know the going rate for the thing you want to buy, then expect to pay more than you would in a shop. The colourful *vitenge* (the singular of this is *kitenge*) worn by most Tanzanian women can be picked up cheaply at any market in the country.

MEDIA AND COMMUNICATIONS

NEWSPAPERS The English-language *Daily News*, *Citizen* and *Guardian*, available in all major towns, now carry a fair bit of syndicated international news, and the local news can also make for interesting reading. The Kenyan *Daily Nation*, available in Dar es Salaam, Arusha and Mwanza, is slightly better. The excellent *East African* is a weekly newspaper published in Kenya but distributed throughout the three countries to which it dedicates roughly equal coverage, ie: Kenya, Tanzania and Uganda. Stalls and vendors around the Clock Tower in Arusha sell *Time* and *Newsweek*, as well as a variety of European, British and American papers.

TELEPHONES
Phone calls If you want to make an international phone call or send a fax, a TCC Extelcomms centre can be found in most large towns. Calls are cheap by international standards, and some Extelcomms centres will receive as well as send faxes. The costlier but more convenient alternative is to phone directly from your lodge or hotel. If you are carrying a mobile phone that receives international calls, the satellite network is pretty good in and around towns but rather less so in more remote parts of the game reserves.

Mobile phones If you bring a mobile phone (commonly referred to as 'cell phone' in Tanzania), it's emphatically worth the minor investment in a Tanzanian SIM card (which costs around US$0.30 and gives you a local number) and airtime cards (available in a wide selection of units from Tsh500 to 50,000). International text messages are very cheap (US$1 will buy you around a dozen text messages to anywhere in the world) and international calls work out at around US$1 for three to four minutes. By contrast, you'll rack up a hefty bill if you use your home phone number for calls and/or messages, since in most instances these are charged at international rates out of your home country, even when you phone home. SIM and airtime cards can be bought at specialist Vodacom outlets (there are several in Arusha and Moshi) or at numerous other small shops displaying the ubiquitous Vodacom sticker. Network reception is increasingly widespread in northern Tanzania, even in the national parks. Many mobile numbers serve as fixed lines because the land lines are so bad in Tanzania – indeed, there are now more than 100 mobile phones in the country for every landline! Legally, you have to register a new SIM or the number may be deactivated after a few days. If you buy the SIM card direct from a Vodacom shop you can register it on the spot, provided you bring along your passport. Mobile money is getting bigger in East Africa, including for paying for flights. It's probably of marginal interest to tourists at this stage, but could potentially evolve into the tourist mainstream over the next few years

Internet and email The spread of internet use in Africa has been remarkable over the last decade, and the existence of email represents a real communications revolution on a continent where international lines tend to be unreliable and expensive. Internet and email have caught on particularly quickly in Tanzania, and internet cafés are prolific and affordable in most major urban tourist centres. The servers are usually quite fast, although not comparable to international broadband, and rates are very affordable. Internet access is not available in most game reserves and national parks, and the few game lodges that do offer browsing or email services tend to charge very high rates.

CULTURAL ETIQUETTE

Tanzania has perhaps the most egalitarian and tolerant mood of any African country that I've visited. As a generalisation, Tanzanians tend to treat visitors with a dignified reserve, something that many Westerners mistake for a stand-offish attitude, but in my opinion is more indicative of a respect both for our culture and their own. Granted, dignified probably won't be the adjective that leaps to mind if your first interaction with Tanzanians comes from the pestilence of touts that hang around bus stations in Arusha or Moshi, or somewhere similar. But then in most poor countries, you'll find that people who make a living on the fringe of the tourist industry tend to be pushy and occasionally confrontational in their dealings – from their perspective, they probably have to be in order to make a living. But I do think that anybody who spends time travelling in Tanzania will recognise the behaviour of touts to be wholly unrepresentative of what is essentially a conservative, unhurried and undemonstrative society.

On the whole, you would have to do something pretty outrageous to commit a serious faux pas in Tanzania. But, like any country, Tanzania does have its rules of etiquette, and while allowances will always be made for tourists, there is some value in ensuring that they are not made too frequently.

GENERAL CONDUCT Perhaps the most important single point of etiquette to be grasped by visitors to Tanzania is the social importance of formal greetings. Tanzanians tend to greet each other elaborately, and if you want to make a good impression on somebody who speaks English, whether they be a waiter or a shop assistant (and especially if they work in a government department), you would do well to follow suit. When you need to ask somebody directions, it is rude to blunder straight into interrogative mode without first exchanging greetings. With

3

Tanzanians who don't speak English, the greeting 'Jambo' delivered with a smile and a nod of the head will be adequate.

Whenever I visit Tanzania after travelling elsewhere in Africa, I am struck afresh by how readily people greet passing strangers, particularly in rural areas. In Tanzania, this greeting doesn't normally take the form of a shrieked 'Mzungu' (or whatever local term is used for a white person), or a 'Give me money', something that you become accustomed to in some African countries. On the contrary, in

EATING THE NEWS   Emma Thomson

In the same way that it is rude not to greet a Tanzanian with the standard 'Hujambo' or 'Mambo', no Maasai will encounter another without going through the amusing paces of a ritual known as 'eating the news'. It is basically a quick catch-up on the health of the family, state of the livestock, etc. The aim is to race through these formalities as fast as possible so you can continue with the rest of the conversation. Bizarrely, even if you are on your deathbed, you must reply that all is well to maintain the front of warrior strength integral to Maasai psychology. Give it a go and they will be bowled over!

Man:	Yeyio …	Mother …
Woman:	Eeu …	Yes …
Man:	Takwenya!	I greet you!
Woman:	Iko! Apaayia …	Hello! Warrior …
Man:	Ooe …	Yes …
Woman:	Supai!	I greet you!
Man:	Epa!	Hello!
Woman:	Ayia, koree indae?	Ok, how are you?
Man:	Kitii …	We are around …
Woman:	Ee	Uh-huh
Man:	Kira sedan	We are fine
Woman:	Ee	Uh-huh
Man:	Kira biot	We are healthy
Woman:	Ee	Uh-huh
Man:	Supat inkera	The children are well
Woman:	Ee	Uh-huh
Man:	Biot inkishu	The cattle are healthy
Woman:	Ee	Uh-huh
Man:	Metii endoki torono	There are no problems
Woman:	Ayia	OK
Woman:	Kira siyook …	As for us …
Man:	Ee	Uh-huh
Woman:	Mekimweyaa	We are not sick
Man:	Ee	Uh-huh
Woman:	Biot inkera	The children are healthy
Man:	Ee	Uh-huh
Woman:	Supat indare	The goats are well
Man:	Ee	Uh-huh
Woman:	Ayia	OK
Man:	Ayia, enda serian	OK, that's good news

Tanzania adults will normally greet tourists with a cheerful '*Jambo*', and children with a subdued '*Shikamu*' (a greeting reserved for elders). I find this to be a very charming quality in Tanzanian society, one that is worth reinforcing by learning a few simple Swahili greetings (see *Language*, page 413).

Among Tanzanians, it is considered poor taste to display certain emotions publicly. Affection is one such emotion: it is frowned upon for members of the opposite sex to hold hands publicly, and kissing or embracing would be seriously offensive. Oddly, it is quite normal for friends of the same sex to walk around hand in hand. Male travellers who get into a long discussion with a male Tanzanian shouldn't be surprised if that person clasps them by the hand and retains a firm grip on their hand for several minutes. This is a warm gesture, one particularly appropriate when the person wants to make a point with which you might disagree. On the subject of intra-gender relations, homosexuality is as good as taboo in Tanzania, to the extent that it would require some pretty overt behaviour for it to occur to anybody to take offence.

It is also considered bad form to show anger publicly. It is difficult to know where to draw the line here though because many touts positively invite an aggressive response, and I doubt that many people who travel independently in Tanzania will get by without the occasional display of impatience. Frankly, I doubt that many bystanders would take umbrage if you responded to a pushy tout with a display of anger, if only because the tout's behaviour itself goes against the grain of Tanzanian society. By contrast, losing your temper will almost certainly be counterproductive when dealing with obtuse officials, dopey waiters and hotel employees, or uncooperative safari drivers.

MUSLIM CUSTOMS Visitors should be aware of the strong Muslim element in Tanzania, particularly along the coast and in Zanzibar. In Muslim society, it is insulting to use your left hand to pass or receive something or when shaking hands. If you eat with your fingers, it is also customary to use the right hand only. Even those of us who are naturally right-handed will occasionally need to remind ourselves of this (it may happen, for instance, that you are carrying something in your right hand and so hand money to a shopkeeper with your left). For left-handed travellers, it will require a constant effort. In traditional Muslim societies it is offensive for women to expose their knees or shoulders, a custom that ought to be taken on board by female travellers, especially on parts of the coast where tourists remain a relative novelty.

TIPPING AND GUIDES The question of when to tip and when not to tip can be difficult in a foreign country. In Tanzania, it is customary to tip your guide at the end of a safari and/or a Kilimanjaro climb, as well as any cooks and porters who accompany you. A figure of roughly US$10 per day is the benchmark, although it is advisable to check this with your safari company in advance. I see no reason why you shouldn't give a bigger or smaller tip based on the quality of service. Bear in mind, however, that most guides, cooks and porters receive nominal salaries, which means that they are largely dependent on tips for their income. It would be mean not to leave a reasonable tip in any but the most exceptional of circumstances.

In some African countries, it is difficult to travel anywhere without being latched onto by a self-appointed guide, who will often expect a tip over and above any agreed fee. This sort of thing is comparatively unusual in Tanzania, but if you do take on a freelance guide, then it is advisable to clarify in advance that whatever price you agree is final and inclusive of a tip. By contrast, any guide who is given to you by a company should most definitely be tipped, as tips will probably be their main source of income. In Zanzibar and Arusha, a freelance guide may insist upon helping you find a hotel

3

room, in which case they will be given a commission by the hotel, so there is no reason for you to provide an additional tip. In any case, from the guide's point of view, finding you a room is merely the first step in trying to hook you for a safari or a spice tour, or something else that will earn a larger commission.

It is not customary to tip for service in local bars and *hotelis*, although you may sometimes want to leave a tip (in fact, given the difficulty of finding change in Tanzania, you may practically be forced into doing this in some circumstances). A tip of 5% would be very acceptable and 10% generous. Generally any restaurant that caters primarily to tourists and to wealthy Tanzanian residents will automatically add a service charge to the bill. Since the government claims the lion's share of any formal service charge, it would still be reasonable to reward good service with a genuine tip.

PHOTOGRAPHIC TIPS   *Ariadne Van Zandbergen*

EQUIPMENT Although with some thought and an eye for composition you can take reasonable photos with a 'point and shoot' camera, you need an SLR camera with one or more lenses if you are at all serious about photography. The most important component in a digital SLR is the sensor. There are two types of sensor: DX and FX. The FX is a full-size sensor identical to the old film size (36mm). The DX sensor is half size and produces lower quality. Your choice of lenses will be determined by whether you have a DX or FX sensor in your camera as the DX sensor introduces a 0.5x multiplication to the focal length. So a 300mm lens becomes in effect a 450mm lens. FX ('full frame') sensors are the future, so I will further refer to focal lengths appropriate to the FX sensor.

Always buy the best lens you can afford. Fixed fast lenses are ideal, but very costly. Zoom lenses make it easier to change composition without changing lenses the whole time. If you carry only one lens a 24–70mm or similar zoom should be ideal. For a second lens, a lightweight 80–200mm or 70–300mm or similar will be excellent for candid shots and varying your composition. Wildlife photography will be very frustrating if you don't have at least a 300mm lens. For a small loss of quality, teleconverters are a cheap and compact way to increase magnification: a 300 lens with a 1.4x converter becomes 420mm, and with a 2x it becomes 600mm. Note that 1.4x and 2x teleconverters reduce the speed of your lens by 1.4 and 2 stops respectively.

The resolution of digital cameras is improving all the time. For ordinary prints a 6-megapixel camera is fine. For better results and the possibility to enlarge images and for professional reproduction, higher resolution is available up to 21 megapixels.

It is important to have enough memory space when photographing on your holiday. The number of pictures you can fit on a card depends on the quality you choose. You should calculate how many pictures you can fit on a card and either take enough cards or take a storage drive onto which you can download the cards' content. You can obviously take a laptop, which gives the advantage that you can see your pictures properly at the end of each day and edit them and delete rejects. If you don't want the extra bulk and weight you can buy a storage device which can read memory cards. These drives come in a variety of different capacities.

Keep in mind that digital camera batteries, computers and other storage devices need charging. Make sure you have all the chargers, cables and converters with you. Most hotels/lodges have charging points, but it will be best to enquire

BARGAINING Tourists to Tanzania will sometimes need to bargain over prices, but generally this need exists only in reasonably predictable circumstances, for instance when chartering a private taxi, organising a guide, agreeing a price for a safari or mountain trek, or buying curios and to a lesser extent other market produce. Prices in hotels, restaurants and shops are generally fixed, and overcharging in such places is too unusual for it to be worth challenging a price unless it is blatantly ridiculous.

You may well be overcharged at some point in Tanzania, but it is important to keep this in perspective. After a couple of bad experiences, some travellers start to haggle with everybody from hotel owners to old women selling fruit by the side of the road, often accompanying their negotiations with aggressive accusations of dishonesty. Unfortunately, it is sometimes necessary to fall back on aggressive posturing in order

about this in advance. When camping you might have to rely on charging from the car battery.

DUST AND HEAT Dust and heat are often a problem. Keep your equipment in a sealed bag, and avoid exposing equipment to the sun when possible. Digital cameras are prone to collecting dust particles on the sensor which results in spots on the image. The dirt mostly enters the camera when changing lenses, so you should be careful when doing this. To some extent photos can be 'cleaned' up afterwards in Photoshop, but this is time-consuming. You can have your camera sensor professionally cleaned, or you can do this yourself with special brushes and swabs made for this purpose, but note that touching the sensor might cause damage and should only be done with the greatest care.

LIGHT The most striking outdoor photographs are often taken during the hour or two of 'golden light' after dawn and before sunset. Shooting in low light may enforce the use of very low shutter speeds, in which case a tripod/beanbag will be required to avoid camera shake. The most advanced digital SLRs have very little loss of quality on higher ISO settings, which allows you to shoot at lower light conditions. It is still recommended not to increase the ISO unless necessary.

With careful handling, side lighting and back lighting can produce stunning effects, especially in soft light and at sunrise or sunset. Generally, however, it is best to shoot with the sun behind you. When photographing animals or people in the harsh midday sun, images taken in light but even shade are likely to look nicer than those taken in direct sunlight or patchy shade, since the latter conditions create too much contrast.

PROTOCOL In some countries, it is unacceptable to photograph local people without permission, and many people will refuse to pose or will ask for a donation. In such circumstances, don't try to sneak photographs as you might get yourself into trouble. Even the most willing subject will often pose stiffly when a camera is pointed at them; relax them by making a joke, and take a few shots in quick succession to improve the odds of capturing a natural pose.

Ariadne Van Zandbergen is a professional travel and wildlife photographer specialising in Africa. She runs 'The Africa Image Library'. For photo requests, visit www.africaimagelibrary.com or contact her direct (e ariadne@hixnet.co.za)

Practical Information CULTURAL ETIQUETTE

3

STUFF YOUR RUCKSACK – AND MAKE A DIFFERENCE

www.stuffyourrucksack.com is a website set up by TV's Kate Humble which enables travellers to give direct help to small charities, schools or other organisations in the country they are visiting. Maybe a local school needs books, a map or pencils, or an orphanage needs children's clothes or toys – all things that can easily be 'stuffed in a rucksack' before departure. The charities get exactly what they need and travellers have the chance to meet local people and see how and where their gifts will be used.

The website describes organisations that need your help and lists the items they most need. Check what's needed in Tanzania, contact the organisation to say you're coming and bring not only the much-needed goods but an extra dimension to your travels and the knowledge that in a small way you have made a difference.

to determine a fair price, but such behaviour is also very unfair on those people who are forthright and honest in their dealings with tourists. It's a question of finding the right balance, or better still looking for other ways of dealing with the problem.

The main instance where bargaining is essential is when buying curios. What should be understood, however, is that the fact a curio seller is open to negotiation does not mean that you were initially being overcharged or ripped off. Curio sellers will generally quote a price knowing full well that you are going to bargain it down (they'd probably be startled if you didn't) and it is not necessary to respond aggressively or in an accusatory manner. It is impossible to say by how much you should bargain the initial price down. Some people say that you should offer half the asking price and be prepared to settle at around two-thirds, but my experience is that curio sellers are far more whimsical than such advice allows for. The sensible approach, if you want to get a feel for prices, is to ask the price of similar items at a few different stalls before you actually contemplate buying anything.

In fruit and vegetable markets and stalls, bargaining is the norm, even between locals, and the healthiest approach to this sort of haggling is to view it as an enjoyable part of the African experience. There will normally be an accepted price band for any particular commodity. To find out what it is, listen to what other people pay and try a few stalls. A ludicrously inflated price will always drop the moment you walk away. When buying fruit and vegetables, a good way to feel out the situation is to ask for a bulk discount or a few extra items thrown in. And bear in mind that when somebody is reluctant to bargain, it may be because they asked a fair price in the first place.

A final point to consider on the subject of overcharging and bargaining is that it is the fact of being overcharged that annoys; the amount itself is generally of little consequence in the wider context of a trip to Tanzania. Without for a moment wanting to suggest that travellers should routinely allow themselves to be overcharged, I do feel there are occasions when we should pause to look at the bigger picture. If you find yourself quibbling over a pittance with an old lady selling a few piles of fruit by the roadside, you might perhaps bear in mind that the notion of a fixed price is a very Western one. When somebody is desperate enough for money, or afraid that their perishable goods might not last another day, it may well be possible to push them down to a lower price than they would normally accept. In such circumstances, I see nothing wrong with erring on the side of generosity.

4

Health

with Dr Felicity Nicholson

Tanzania isn't a particularly unhealthy country for tourists. The most serious health threat to travellers is malaria, which is present in most parts of the country at most times of year, with the highest risk being along the coast and other low lying areas during the rainy season. All visitors should thus take preventative measures against malaria, regardless of their itinerary, and should also be alert to potential symptoms both during their trip and after they return home.

Other less common but genuine health threats include the usual array of sanitation-related diseases – giardia, dysentery, typhoid, cholera etc – associated with the tropics (although these seem to affect visitors to Africa less than they do travellers to Asia), and bilharzia, which can only be caught by swimming in freshwater habitats inhabited by the snail that carries the disease.

If you do get ill, bear in mind that the most likely culprit – as in most parts of the world – will be the common cold, flu or travellers' diarrhoea, none of which normally constitute a serious health threat. However, travellers with overt cold- or flu-like symptoms might not be allowed to track gorillas or chimpanzees, both of which are susceptible to infectious airborne human diseases and may lack our resistance.

Hospitals and clinics are listed under the relevant towns and cities in Part Two of this guide.

BEFORE YOU GO

IMMUNISATIONS Preparations to ensure a healthy trip require checks on your immunisation status: it is wise to make sure you are up to date on **tetanus**, **polio** and **diphtheria** (now given as an all-in-one vaccine, Revaxis, that lasts for ten years), and hepatitis A.

Immunisations against meningococcus and **rabies** may also be recommended. Proof of vaccination against **yellow fever** is needed for entry into Tanzania for all travellers over one year of age, if you are coming from a yellow fever area. The decision to vaccinate or not is a complex one as the actual risk of yellow fever in Tanzania is considered to be very low indeed. Having the vaccine – assuming that there were no contraindications – would only be warranted if you were spending time in another country where there is active disease. If the vaccine is not suitable for you and you are not at risk of disease then most healthcare professionals will issue an exemption certificate instead. Immunisation against cholera may also be recommended, particularly if there are any current known cases.

Hepatitis A vaccine (Havrix Monodose or Avaxim) comprises two injections given about a year apart. The course costs around £100, but in the UK may be available on the NHS; it protects for 25 years and can be administered even close to the time of departure. **Hepatitis B** vaccination should be considered for longer trips (two months or more) or for those working with children or in situations where contact with blood is likely. Three injections are needed for the best protection and can be given over a three-week period for those aged 16 or older if time is short. Longer schedules give more sustained protection and are therefore preferred if time allows and must be used for those under 16. Hepatitis A vaccine can also be given as a combination with hepatitis B as 'Twinrix', though two doses are needed at least seven days apart to be effective for the hepatitis A component, and three doses are needed for the hepatitis B. Again, this schedule can only be used by those aged 16 or over.

The newer injectable **typhoid** vaccines (eg: Typhim Vi) last for three years and are about 85% effective. Oral capsules (Vivotif) may also be available for those aged six and over. A dose of three capsules over five days lasts for approximately three years although in the UK it is only licensed for one year, but may be less effective than the injectable forms. They should be encouraged unless the traveller is leaving within a few days for a trip of a week or less, when the vaccine would not be effective in time. **Meningitis** vaccine containing strains A, C, W and Y is recommended for all travellers, especially those who will be in close contact with local people (see *Meningitis*, page 93). Vaccinations for rabies are ideally advised for everyone, but are especially important for travellers visiting more remote areas, especially if you are more than 24 hours from medical help and definitely if you will be working with animals (see *Rabies*, page 93).

Experts differ over whether a BCG vaccination against **tuberculosis** (TB) is useful in adults: discuss this with your travel clinic.

In addition to the various vaccinations recommended above, it is important that travellers should be properly protected against **malaria**. For detailed advice, see below. Ideally, you should visit your own doctor or a specialist travel clinic (see opposite) to discuss your requirements, if possible at least eight weeks before you plan to travel.

MALARIA PREVENTION Malaria is the greatest health risk to travellers in Tanzania and it is present in most parts of the region, with the notable exception of the Ngorongoro Crater rim. There is no vaccine against it, but using prophylactic drugs and preventing mosquito bites will considerably reduce the risk of contracting it. Seek professional advice to ascertain the preferred anti-malarial drugs for the country you are visiting at the time you travel. If mefloquine (Lariam) is suggested, start this 2½ weeks (three doses) before departure to check that it suits you; stop it immediately if it seems to cause depression or anxiety, visual or hearing disturbances, severe headaches, fits or changes in heart rhythm. Side effects such as nightmares or dizziness are not medical reasons for stopping unless they are sufficiently debilitating or annoying. Anyone who has been treated for depression or psychiatric problems, who has diabetes controlled by oral therapy or who is epileptic (or has suffered fits in the past) or has a close blood relative who is epileptic, should probably avoid mefloquine.

In the past doctors were nervous about prescribing mefloquine to pregnant women, but experience has shown that it is relatively safe and certainly safer than the risk of malaria. That said, there are other issues, so if you are travelling whilst pregnant, seek expert advice before departure.

Malarone (proguanil and atovaquone) is as effective as mefloquine. It has the advantage of having few side effects and need only be continued for one week after returning. However, it is expensive and because of this tends to be reserved for shorter trips. Malarone may not be suitable for everybody, so advice should be taken from a doctor. It can safely be used for up to a year though the cost may be prohibitive, and a paediatric form of tablet for children weighing 11kg or more is also available, prescribed on a weight basis.

Another alternative is the antibiotic doxycycline (100mg daily). Like Malarone it can be started one day before arrival. Unlike mefloquine, it may also be used by travellers with epilepsy, although certain anti-epileptic medication may make it less effective. In perhaps 1–3% of people there is the possibility of allergic skin reactions developing in sunlight; the drug should be stopped if this happens. It is also unsuitable during pregnancy or for children under 12 years.

Chloroquine and proguanil are no longer thought to be effective enough for most parts of Africa but may be considered as a last resort if nothing else is deemed suitable.

All tablets should be taken with or after the evening meal, washed down with plenty of fluid and, with the exception of Malarone, continued for four weeks after returning home.

In addition to prophylactic drugs, there is a case for carrying a treatment for malaria, in case you develop malarial symptoms when medical assistance is unavailable. The longer you are spending in Africa, the more the case for this strengthens, and it would certainly be recommended to anybody undertaking a long overland trip, or volunteering or working in a remote area, or who travels in Africa regularly. Whatever you decide, you should seek up-to-date advice to find out the most appropriate medication.

There is no malaria transmission above 3,000m; at intermediate altitudes (1,800–3,000m) the risk exists but is low. In addition to taking anti-malarial medicines, it is important to avoid mosquito bites between dusk and dawn, which is when the anopheles (malaria-carrying) mosquito is most active. Pack a **DEET-based insect repellent** (ideally containing 50–55% DEET), such as one of the Repel range, and take either a **permethrin-impregnated bed net** or a **permethrin spray** so that you can treat bed nets in hotels. Permethrin treatment makes even very tatty nets protective and mosquitoes are also unable to bite through the impregnated net when you roll against it. Putting on socks and long clothes (including long-sleeved shirts or blouses) at dusk reduces the risk of bites and the amount of repellent needed. Be aware, however, that malaria mosquitoes usually hunt at ankle level and their bite can penetrate through socks, so apply repellent to your feet and ankles whether or not you wear socks. Travel clinics usually sell a good range of nets, treatment kits and repellents. See *Insect bites* on page 89 for more information on how to avoid mosquito bites.

TRAVEL CLINICS AND HEALTH INFORMATION A full list of current travel clinic websites worldwide is available on www.istm.org. For other journey preparation information, consult www.nathnac.org/ds/map_world.aspx. Information about various medications may be found on www.netdoctor.co.uk/travel.

DEEP-VEIN THROMBOSIS (DVT) Prolonged immobility on long-haul flights can result in deep-vein thrombosis (DVT), which can be dangerous if the clot travels to the lungs to cause pulmonary embolus. The risk increases with age, and is higher in obese or pregnant travellers, heavy smokers, those taller than 6ft/1.8m or shorter than 5ft/1.5m, and anybody with a history of clots, recent major operation or varicose veins surgery, cancer, a stroke or heart disease. If any of these criteria apply, consult a doctor before you travel. Ensuring that you are well hydrated and trying to move around during long periods of travel can help to reduce the risk.

A minimal kit contains:

- A good drying antiseptic, eg: iodine or potassium permanganate (do not take antiseptic cream)
- A few small dressings (Band-Aids)
- Suncream
- Insect repellent; anti-malarial tablets including treatment for those going to remote places; impregnated bed net or permethrin spray
- Ibuprofen or paracetamol
- Antifungal cream (eg: Canesten)
- Ciprofloxacin or norfloxacin, for severe diarrhoea
- Tinidazole for giardia or amoebic dysentery
- Antibiotic eye drops, for sore, 'gritty', stuck-together eyes (conjunctivitis)
- A pair of fine pointed tweezers (to remove hairy caterpillar hairs, thorns, splinters, coral, etc)
- Alcohol-based hand rub or bar of soap in plastic box
- Condoms or femidoms
- A digital thermometer

TRAVEL INSURANCE Before you travel, make sure that you have adequate medical insurance – choose a policy with comprehensive cover for hospitalisation as well as for repatriation in an emergency. Nowadays the range of cover available is very wide – choose whatever suits your method of travel. Be aware, if you plan to use cycles or motorbike taxis, that not all policies cover you for this form of transport. Remember to take all the details with you, particularly your policy number and the telephone number that you have to contact in the event of a claim.

COMMON MEDICAL PROBLEMS IN TANZANIA

For those planning to climb Kilimanjaro, see the box in *Chapter 7, Kilimanjaro National Park*, page 166 for information on altitude sickness and hypothermia.

TRAVELLERS' DIARRHOEA At least half of those travelling to the tropics/developing world will experience a bout of travellers' diarrhoea during their trip; the newer you are to exotic travel, the more likely you will be to suffer. By taking precautions against travellers' diarrhoea you will also avoid typhoid, cholera, hepatitis, dysentery, worms, etc.

From food Travellers' diarrhoea and the other faecal-oral diseases come from getting other peoples' faeces in your mouth. This most often happens from cooks not washing their hands after a trip to the toilet, but even if the restaurant cook does not understand basic hygiene you will be safe if your food has been properly cooked and arrives piping hot. The maxim to remind you what you can safely eat is:

PEEL IT, BOIL IT, COOK IT OR FORGET IT.

This means that fruit you have washed and peeled yourself, and hot foods, should be safe, but raw foods, cold cooked foods, salads, fruit salads prepared by others, ice cream and ice are all risky, as are foods kept lukewarm in restaurant or hotel buffets. Self-service or buffet meals are safest to eat when the food is hot and freshly cooked – for example a late buffet lunch eaten in the mid-afternoon will have been sitting around a long while. If you do get travellers' diarrhoea, see box below for advice.

From water It is also possible to get ill from drinking contaminated water, so try to drink from safe sources. You must assume that tap water is risky wherever you are in Tanzania. To make risky water safe it should be brought to the boil (even at altitude it only needs to be brought to the boil), passed through a good bacteriological filter or purified with chlorine dioxide tablets. If you buy bottled water (which is widely available) make sure the seal is intact. Iodine is no longer recommended for anyone to use for purifying water.

INSECT BITES The prevalence of malaria means it is crucial to avoid mosquito bites between dusk and dawn, paying particular attention to your ankles, since **malaria-carrying mosquitoes** often hunt at ground level. As the sun is setting, don long clothes and socks, and apply repellent to your ankles (under or over your socks) and to any other exposed flesh. Ideally, sleep under a permethrin-treated bed net or in an air-conditioned room. If that is not possible, burning a mosquito coil or mat will hugely reduce mosquito activity, as will putting on a fan (mosquitoes dislike turbulent air). In areas where mosquitoes seem common, it is advisable to close all windows at night, or any time you have the lights on, to prevent them from infiltrating the room from outside.

Many budget hotels make no effort to control mosquito numbers, so rooms are

> ### TREATING TRAVELLERS' DIARRHOEA   *Dr Jane Wilson-Howarth*
>
> It is dehydration that makes you feel awful during a bout of diarrhoea and the most important part of treatment is drinking lots of clear fluids. Sachets of oral rehydration salts give the perfect biochemical mix to replace all that is pouring out of your bottom but they do not taste nice. Any dilute mixture of sugar and salt in water will do you good so if you like Coke or orange squash, drink that with a three-finger pinch of salt added to each glass. Otherwise make a solution of a four-finger scoop of sugar with a three-finger pinch of salt in a glass of water. Or add eight level teaspoons of sugar (18g) and one level teaspoon of salt (3g) to one litre (five cups) of safe water. A squeeze of lemon or orange juice improves the taste and adds potassium, which is also lost during a bout of diarrhoea. Drink two large glasses after every bowel action, and more if you are thirsty. If you are not eating, then you need to drink three litres a day plus the equivalent of whatever is pouring into the toilet. If you feel like eating, take a bland, high-carbohydrate diet. Heavy, greasy foods will probably give you cramps.
>
> If the diarrhoea is bad, or you are passing blood or slime, or you have a fever, you will probably need antibiotics in addition to fluid replacement. You should always seek medical treatment but if you are not near help then you may want to start some treatment *en route*. A three-day course of Ciprofloxacin 500mg twice daily (or Norfloxacin) may be appropriate treatment for dysentery and bad diarrhoea. If the diarrhoea is greasy and bulky and is accompanied by 'eggy' burps, the likely cause is giardia. This is best treated with Tinidazole (2g in one dose repeated seven days later if symptoms persist).

Health   COMMON MEDICAL PROBLEMS IN TANZANIA

4

89

Malaria usually begins with a fever, the first symptoms of which are often a general flu-like feeling of slight disorientation in the head or weakness in the legs. You may then feel cold, shivery, shaky and very sweaty. Headache, feeling sick and vomiting are common with malaria and you are also likely to experience muscle aches. The cycle of fever and sweating is repeated at intervals from daily, to alternate days to around three days with a fever-free period between. Some people develop jaundice (yellowing of the eyes and or skin). However, it is not necessary for all these symptoms to be present before suspecting malaria. The only consistent symptom is a fever of 38° C or more that lasts for more than a few hours.

While you are away, assume that any high fever lasting more than a few hours is malaria, regardless of other symptoms. Although the progression of malaria is variable and unpredictable, early diagnosis and treatment will greatly increase the likelihood it doesn't develop into a life-threatening condition, so seek medical help as soon as possible, or – if this is not possible – be prepared to self-diagnose and medicate. Remember that the symptoms of malaria may develop anything from seven days after entering a malarious area up to one year after leaving, so if symptoms appear after your return home tell a doctor immediately and mention that you have been in a malarious area.

often infested. If you suspect this to be the case, spray the room with a suitable aerosol insecticide before you go out for dinner, paying special attention to the dark corners where they rest up by day (under the bed or behind curtains or cupboards) and any en-suite bathroom. If you didn't bring an aerosol room spray with you, you should be able to buy one at larger supermarkets in most towns.

By day it is wise to wear long, loose (preferably 100% cotton) clothes if you are pushing through scrubby country; this will deter ticks as well as **tsetse** flies and day-biting **Aedes mosquitoes** that may spread dengue and yellow fever. Tsetse flies hurt when they bite and are attracted to the colour blue; locals will know where they are a problem and where they transmit sleeping sickness (see page 93).

Skin infections Any mosquito bite or small nick in the skin provides an opportunity for bacteria to foil the body's usually excellent defences; it will surprise many travellers how quickly skin infections start in warm humid climates and it is essential to clean and cover even the slightest wound. Creams are not as effective as a good drying antiseptic such as dilute iodine, potassium permanganate (a few crystals in half a cup of water), or crystal (or gentian) violet. One of these should be available in most towns. If the wound starts to throb, or becomes red and the redness starts to spread, or the wound oozes, and especially if you develop a fever, antibiotics will probably be needed: flucloxacillin (250mg four times a day) or cloxacillin (500mg four times a day). For those allergic to penicillin, erythromycin (500mg twice a day) for five days should help. See a doctor if the symptoms do not start to improve in 48 hours.

Fungal infections also get a hold easily in hot moist climates, so wear 100% cotton socks and underwear and shower frequently. An itchy rash in the groin or flaking between the toes is likely to be a fungal infection. This needs treatment with an antifungal cream such as Canesten (clotrimazole); if this is not available try

Whitfield's ointment (compound enzoic acid ointment) or crystal violet (although this will turn you purple!).

SUN AND HEAT Give some thought to packing suncream. The incidence of skin cancer is rocketing as Caucasians are travelling more and spending more time exposing themselves to the sun. Keep out of the sun during the middle of the day and, if you must expose yourself to the sun, build up gradually from 20 minutes per day. Be especially careful of exposure in the middle of the day and of sun reflected off water, and wear a T-shirt and lots of waterproof suncream (at least SPF20) when swimming. Sun exposure ages the skin, makes people prematurely wrinkly and increases the risk of skin cancer. Cover up with long, loose clothes and wear a hat when you can. The glare and the dust can be hard on the eyes, too, so bring UV-protecting sunglasses and, perhaps, a soothing eyebath.

Prickly heat A fine pimply rash on the torso is likely to be heat rash; cool showers, dabbing (not rubbing) dry, and talc will help; if it's bad you may need to check into an air-conditioned hotel room for a while. Slowing down to a relaxed schedule, wearing only loose, baggy 100% cotton clothes and sleeping naked under a fan reduce the problem.

EYE PROBLEMS The combination of **dust and glare** may create problems for those with sensitive eyes. Sunglasses afford some protection, and if you anticipate problems of this sort then don't forget to pack eye drops. Many people who wear contact lenses suffer in these dusty conditions, so it is a good idea to wear glasses on long drives, assuming that you have a pair.

OTHER DISEASES

SEXUALLY TRANSMITTED DISEASES Travel is a time when you may enjoy sexual adventures, especially when alcohol reduces inhibitions. Remember, however, that the risks of sexually transmitted infection are high, whether you sleep with fellow travellers or with locals. More than half of HIV infections in British heterosexuals

QUICK TICK REMOVAL

African ticks are not the prolific disease transmitters they are in the Americas, but they may occasionally spread disease. **Lyme disease**, which can have unpleasant after-effects, has now been recorded in Africa, and **tick-bite fever** also occurs. The latter is a mild, flu-like illness, but still worth avoiding. If you get the tick off whole and promptly, the chances of disease transmission are reduced to a minimum.

Manoeuvre your finger and thumb so that you can pinch the tick's mouthparts, as close to your skin as possible, and slowly and steadily pull away at right angles to your skin. This often hurts. Jerking or twisting will increase the chances of damaging the tick which in turn increases the chances of disease transmission, as well as leaving the mouthparts behind.

Once the tick is off, dowse the little wound with alcohol (local spirit, whisky or similar is excellent) or iodine. An area of spreading redness around the bite site, or a rash or fever coming on a few days or more after the bite, should stimulate a trip to a doctor.

are acquired abroad and AIDS is a serious problem in Tanzania. Use condoms or femidoms, preferably bearing the British kite mark and ideally bought before travel. If you notice any genital ulcers or discharge get treatment promptly.

BILHARZIA OR SCHISTOSOMIASIS (*with thanks to Dr Vaughan Southgate of the Natural History Museum, London, and Dr Dick Stockley, The Surgery, Kampala*) Bilharzia or schistosomiasis is a disease that commonly afflicts the rural poor of the tropics. Two types exist in sub-Saharan Africa – *Schistosoma mansoni* and *Schistosoma haematobium*. It is an unpleasant problem that is worth avoiding, although it can be treated if you do get it. The parasite is common in almost all water sources in Tanzania – even places advertised as 'bilharzia-free' – and the riskiest shores will be those close to places where infected people use water, wash clothes, etc.

It is easier to understand how to diagnose it, treat it and prevent it if you know a little about the life cycle. Contaminated faeces are washed into the lake, the eggs hatch and the larva infects certain species of snail. The snails then produce about 10,000 larvae (cercariae) a day for the rest of their lives. The parasites can digest their way through your skin when you wade, or bathe in infested fresh water.

Winds disperse the snails and cercariae. The snails in particular can drift a long way, especially on windblown weed, so nowhere is really safe. However, deep water and running water are safer, while shallow water presents the greatest risk. The cercariae penetrate intact skin, and find their way to the liver. There male and female meet and spend the rest of their lives in permanent copulation. No wonder you feel tired! Most finish up in the wall of the lower bowel, but others can get lost and can cause damage to many different organs. *Schistosoma haematobium* goes mostly to the bladder.

Although the adults do not cause any harm in themselves, after about four to six weeks they start to lay eggs, which cause an intense but usually ineffective immune reaction, including fever, cough, abdominal pain, and a fleeting, itching rash called 'safari itch'. The absence of early symptoms does not necessarily mean there is no infection. Later symptoms can be more localised and more severe, but the general symptoms settle down fairly quickly and eventually you are just tired. 'Tired all the time' is one of the most common symptoms among expats in Africa, and bilharzia, giardia, amoeba and intestinal yeast are the most common culprits.

Although bilharzia is difficult to diagnose, it can be tested for at specialist travel clinics. Ideally tests need to be done at least six weeks after likely exposure and will determine whether you need treatment. Fortunately it is easy to treat at present.

Avoiding bilharzia

- If you are bathing, swimming, paddling or wading in fresh water that you think may carry a bilharzia risk, try to get out of the water within ten minutes
- Avoid bathing or paddling on shores within 200m of villages or places where people use the water a great deal, especially reedy shores or where there is lots of water weed
- Dry off thoroughly with a towel; rub vigorously
- If your bathing water comes from a risky source try to ensure that the water is taken from the lake in the early morning and stored snail-free; otherwise it should be filtered or Dettol or Cresol should be added
- Bathing early in the morning is safer than bathing in the last half of the day
- Cover yourself with DEET insect repellent before swimming: it may offer some protection

DENGUE FEVER This mosquito-borne disease resembles malaria but there is no prophylactic available to prevent it. The mosquitoes that carry this virus bite during the daytime, so it is worth applying repellent if you see them around. Symptoms include strong headaches, rashes and excruciating joint and muscle pains with high fever. Dengue fever lasts for only a week or so and is not usually fatal if you have not previously been infected. Complete rest and paracetamol are the usual treatment; plenty of fluids also help. Some patients are given an intravenous drip to keep them from dehydrating. Dengue may be a serious illness particularly with repeated infections so it is best to avoid it in the first place.

MENINGITIS This is a particularly nasty disease as it can kill within hours of the first symptoms appearing. The telltale symptoms are a combination of a blinding headache (light sensitivity), a blotchy rash and a high fever. Immunisation with the newer tetravalent vaccine ACWY protects against the most serious bacterial form of meningitis and is usually recommended for longer-stay trips or if you are working closely with the local population – in particular with children. A single injection gives good protection for three years and also prevents carriage and therefore the possibility of bringing home the disease and giving it to family and friends. Other forms of meningitis exist (usually viral) but there are no vaccines for these. Local papers normally report outbreaks. If you experience symptoms go to a doctor immediately.

SLEEPING SICKNESS African trypanosomiasis, or sleeping sickness, is a parasitic infection transmitted by the tsetse fly. There are two sub-species; one predominates in East Africa and usually causes an acute infection, whereas the other predominates in central and west Africa and causes a slower progressive, chronic infection.

Tsetse flies are seasonally abundant in well-wooded areas such as Tarangire and the Western Corridor of the Serengeti, and are a common pest in many Tanzanian game reserves. Sleeping sickness is not a cause for serious concern, however, even though millions of Tanzanians live in tsetse areas. Fewer than 100 new cases of sleeping sickness are recorded in the country annually but the flies are sufficiently aggravating that it is worth applying insect repellent to your arms and legs before game drives (although this doesn't always deter tsetse flies) and avoiding the blue clothing that tends to attract them.

EBOLA Visitors to Africa often express concern about this deadly, very contagious and highly publicised disease. However, Ebola has never been diagnosed in Tanzania, and while outbreaks have occurred in neighbouring Uganda and Congo, these were highly localised and occurred a long distance from the border. In the unlikely event of an outbreak, protective measures will be taken and you should follow whatever local advice is given.

OTHER SANITARY DISEASES Travellers in Tanzania are at risk of suffering from a bout of the usual array of sanitation-related diseases – cholera, giardia, dysentery, typhoid, worms, etc – associated with the tropics. Preventative measures are the same as those for travellers' diarrhoea (see *Travellers' diarrhoea* on page 88).

DANGEROUS ANIMALS

RABIES Rabies can be carried by all mammals (beware village dogs and small monkeys in the parks) and is passed on to humans through a bite, scratch or a lick of an open wound; you must always assume any animal is rabid, and seek medical help as soon as possible.

Pre-exposure vaccinations for rabies are ideally advised for everyone, but are particularly important if you intend to have contact with animals and/or are likely to be more than 24 hours away from medical help. Ideally three doses should be taken over a minimum of 21 days as this will change and simplify the treatment course. Contrary to popular belief these vaccinations are relatively painless.

If you are bitten, scratched or an animal licks an open wound, find a reasonably clear-looking source of running water (ideally a tap or bottled or boiled water, but at this stage the quality of the water is not important), scrub the area with soap and then pour on iodine or a strong alcohol solution (gin, whisky or rum will do). This helps stop the rabies virus entering the body and will guard against wound infections, including tetanus. Post-exposure prophylaxis should be given as soon as possible, though it is never too late to seek help, as the incubation period for rabies can be very long. If you have been vaccinated against rabies, you will still need two post-bite rabies injections. Those who have not been immunised will need a full course of injections and in most cases the first dose of vaccine is given with a weight-determined injection of rabies immunoglobulin (RIG). This is expensive (around US$800) and may be very hard to come by – a good reason to have the rabies vaccination before you go if you have time.

And remember that, if you develop rabies, then mortality is virtually 100% and death from rabies is probably one of the worst ways to go.

SNAKEBITE Snakes rarely attack unless provoked and bites to travellers are unusual. You are less likely to be bitten if you wear stout shoes and long trousers when in the bush. Most snakes are harmless and even venomous species will only dispense venom in about half of their bites. If bitten, then, you are unlikely to have received venom; keeping this fact in mind may help you to stay calm. Many so-called first-aid techniques do more harm than good: cutting into the wound is harmful; tourniquets are dangerous; suction and electrical inactivation devices do not work. The only treatment is antivenom. In case of a bite that you fear may have been from a venomous snake:

- Try to keep calm – it is likely that no venom has been dispensed
- Prevent movement of the bitten limb by applying a splint
- Keep the bitten limb BELOW heart height to slow the spread of any venom
- If you have a crepe bandage, bind up as much of the bitten limb as you can, but release the bandage every half hour
- Evacuate to a hospital that has antivenom

And remember:

- NEVER give aspirin; you may offer paracetamol, which is safe
- NEVER cut or suck the wound
- DO NOT apply ice packs
- DO NOT apply potassium permanganate

If the offending snake can be captured without risk of someone else being bitten, take it to show to the doctor – but beware, since even a decapitated head is able to dispense venom in a reflex bite.

Part Two

THE GUIDE

5

Arusha and Around

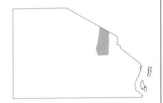

Set at an altitude of around 1,250m in the fertile southern foothills of Mount Meru, bustling Arusha, the fourth-largest city in Tanzania, is the most popular and convenient springboard from which to explore the country's legendary northern safari circuit. Less than 100km from the Kenyan border as the crow flies, this self-styled 'safari capital' is also an important gateway to Tanzania, not only for travellers driving across the border from Nairobi, but also for the growing number of tourists who arrive at nearby Kilimanjaro International Airport.

First impressions are that practically everything in Arusha revolves around the safari industry, a perception that is largely reinforced by more prolonged exposure. In the old town centre and backroads north of the stadium, it can feel like every second person you pass has something to sell, be it a safari, a batik or last week's edition of a foreign newspaper, while the roads are cluttered with 4x4s adorned with one or other safari company logo. And yet Arusha's rare economic vitality is buoyed by several other factors, among them its fertile surrounds, the tanzanite mining boom, and its role as capital of the East African Community.

Arusha is an attractively green town, with a northern skyline – weather permitting – dominated by the imposing hulk of Africa's fifth-highest mountain, the 4,556m Mount Meru. Situated in the mountain's rain-shadow, it also makes for a climatically temperate – and, during the rainy season, often downright soggy – introduction to tropical Africa. For first time visitors to Africa, the town centre is an agreeable introduction to urban Africa. It's neither as intimidating nor as sprawling as Nairobi or Dar es Salaam, and there are plenty of trendy bars, restaurants and cafés catering to expatriates, tourists and wealthier locals.

In most other respects, however, Arusha remains something of an African everytown, where low-rise, colonial-era buildings rub shoulders with a small but gradually increasing number of more modern structures. Indeed, it could be argued that the wealth generated by the safari industry serves to accentuate both the vast economic gulf between the haves and have-nots, and the spectrum of cultural influences that play havoc with visitors seeking to pigeonhole the 'Real Africa'. Which is it, then: the colourfully dressed Maasai and Arusha women who sell traditional beadwork on the pavement, the suited businessmen who scurry in and out of the International Conference Centre, or the swaggering, sunglass-shrouded wide-boys who scurry about offering cheap safaris, change money, marijuana …?

Paradoxically, while Arusha's status as northern Tanzania's safari capital is not in dispute, only a small proportion of fly-in safari-goers actually spend a night in town. This is because many people fly or drive straight into the parks and for those who do stop over in Arusha, the top accommodation options mostly lie out of town, along the main road to Moshi and Kilimanjaro International Airport, or in the vicinity of Arusha National Park. These out-of-town lodges tend to be more overtly African in character than their functional urban counterparts. Weather permitting, most of them also offer sterling views to Mount Meru and the more distant snow-capped peak of Kilimanjaro.

While many safari itineraries treat Arusha as little more than an overnight staging post *en route* to the great game reserves to its west, the surrounding area is well worth exploring in its own right. The main local attraction is undoubtedly Arusha National Park, an underrated conservation area that will amply pay back whatever time and effort you choose to invest in it – be it a quick afternoon game drive, a couple of nights at one of the lodges on its periphery, or the altogether more challenging ascent of the mighty Mount Meru. Also of interest is Lake Duluti, which lies within walking distance of the main road between Arusha town and the eponymous national park, while a number of low-key ecotourist programmes offer visitors the opportunity to interact with the local Maasai and Wa-Arusha in relatively non-contrived circumstances.

HISTORY

Little is known about the Arusha area prior to the 17th century, when the Bantu-speaking Meru people – migrants from the west with strong linguistic and cultural affinities to the Chagga of Kilimanjaro – settled and farmed the fertile and well-watered northern foothills of Mount Meru. In 1830 or thereabouts, the southern slopes of the mountain verging on the Maasai Steppes were settled by the Arusha, a Maasai subgroup who lost their cattle and territory in one of the internecine battles characteristic of this turbulent period in Maasailand. The Arusha people speak the same Maa language as the plains Maasai and share a similar social structure based around initiated age-sets, but when they settled in the Mount Meru area they forsook their pastoralist roots, turning instead to agriculture as a primary source of subsistence.

The Arusha economy was boosted by the trade in agricultural produce – in particular tobacco – with the closely affiliated Maasai of the plains. The Arusha also became known as reliable providers of food and other provisions for the Arab slave caravans that headed inland from the Pangani and Tanga area towards modern-day Kenya and Lake Victoria. Invigorated by this regular trade, the Arusha had, by 1880, cleared the forested slopes of Mount Meru to an altitude of around 1,600m to make way for cultivation. As their territory expanded, however, the Arusha people increasingly came into contact with their northern neighbours, the Meru, resulting in several territorial skirmishes and frequent cattle raids between the two tribes.

In 1881, prompted by the need to defend their combined territories against the Maasai and other potential attackers, the incumbent warrior age-sets of the Arusha and Meru united to form a formidable military force. Since they were settled on the well-watered slopes of Mount Meru, and their subsistence was not primarily dependent on livestock, the Arusha and Meru people were less affected than the plains pastoralists by the devastating series of droughts and rinderpest epidemics of the 1880s and early 1890s. As a result, the combined army, known as the Talala – the Expansionists – was able to exert considerable influence over neighbouring Maasai and Chagga territories.

The Talala staunchly resisted German attempts to settle in their territory, killing the first missionaries to arrive there and repelling an initial punitive attack by the colonial army. In October 1896, however, the Arusha and Meru were soundly defeated by a military expedition out of Moshi led by Karl Johannes and consisting of 100 German troopers supported by some 5,000 Chagga warriors. In the aftermath of this defeat, the Germans drove home the point by razing hundreds of Arusha and Meru smallholdings, killing the men, confiscating the cattle and repatriating women of Chagga origin to the Kilimanjaro area.

In 1889, the Germans established a permanent settlement – modern-day Arusha town – on the border of Arusha and Maasai territories, and used forced Arusha and Maasai labour to construct the Boma that can still be seen on the north end of Boma Road. Relations between the colonisers and their unwilling subjects remained tense, to say the least. During the construction of the fort, a minor dispute led to some 300 labourers being massacred while marching peacefully along present-day Boma Road, and several local chiefs from outlying areas were arbitrarily arrested and taken to Moshi to be hanged in the street.

Following the construction of the Boma, Arusha quickly developed into a significant trading and administrative centre, with about two dozen Indian and Arab shops clustered along what is today Boma Road. John Boyes, who visited Arusha in 1903, somewhat fancifully compared the Boma to 'an Aladdin's Palace transported from some fairyland and dropped down in the heart of the tropics'. The town, he wrote, was 'a real oasis in the wilderness' and 'spotlessly clean', while 'the streets [were] laid out with fine sidewalks, separated by the road from a stream of clear water flowing down a cemented gully'.

At the outbreak of World War I, the small German garrison town was of some significance as a local agricultural and trade centre, but it remained something of a backwater in comparison to Moshi, which lay a week's ox-wagon trek distant at the railhead of the Tanga line. Much of the area around Arusha was, however, settled by German farmers, who had forcibly displaced the original Arusha and Meru smallholders. In 1916, British troops captured Arusha and expelled the German farmers, resulting in some resettlement by indigenous farmers, but the German farmland was eventually re-allocated to British and Greek settlers. The British also set aside large tracts of land around Arusha for sisal plantations, which meant that by 1920, less than 20% of the land around Mount Meru was available to local farmers, most of it on dry foothills unsuited to cultivating the local staple of bananas.

Arusha grew steadily between the wars. The settler economy was boosted by the introduction of coffee, sisal and other export crops, and trade links were improved with the construction of road links to Moshi and Nairobi and the opening of the railway line to Moshi and the coast in 1929. Yet the land issues continued to simmer, eventually coming to a head after World War II, with the eviction of thousands of Meru farmers from north of Mount Meru to make way for a peanut production project overseen by 13 white farmers. The peanut project, aside from being a dismal and costly failure, resulted in the pivotal Meru Land Case, which not only caused great embarrassment to the UN Trusteeship Council, but also proved to be an important catalyst to the politicisation of the anti-colonial movement in Tanganyika.

Prior to independence, Arusha remained a relatively small town whose primary role was to service the surrounding agricultural lands. The official census of 1952 placed the urban population at fewer than 8,000 people, of which more than half were of Asian or European stock. All that changed in the post-independence era, when the town attracted, and continues to attract, large numbers of domestic migrants from surrounding rural areas and beyond. Indeed, by 1978 Arusha had become the ninth-largest town in Tanzania, supporting a population of 55,000, and it is the fourth-largest today, with a population of around 400,000 leaving it poised to pass Mwanza and Zanzibar to take second place in the course of the next decade.

Arusha's recent growth can be attributed to a number of factors, not least the town's location in the foothills of Mount Meru, whose drizzly sub-montane

5

microclimate nurtures the rich volcanic soil to agricultural profligacy. There is also its proximity to the Mererani Hills, the only known source of the increasingly popular gemstone tanzanite. A more ephemeral economic boost has been provided by the presence of UN and other NGO personnel linked to the Rwandan War Crimes Tribunal, which took up residence in the Arusha International Conference Centre in 1995 and is currently winding down towards its eventual planned closure in 2014. Arusha has also served as the main administrative base of the East African Community, a regionally significant international organisation comprising Tanzania, Kenya, Uganda, Burundi and Rwanda, since it was revived in 2000. The key to Arusha's modern economic growth, however, has undoubtedly been its role as the main urban pivot servicing a lucrative tourist industry focused on the likes of the Serengeti National Park, Ngorongoro Crater and lofty Mount Kilimanjaro.

GETTING THERE AND AWAY

BY AIR The main local point of entry is **Kilimanjaro International Airport** (often abbreviated to KIA, though the official airport code is JRO), which lies roughly two-thirds along the 80km asphalt road that runs eastward from Arusha to Moshi. Several international carriers now fly to KIA, among them Ethiopian Airlines, Air Kenya, Rwandair Express, KLM, Air France, SAS and Turkish Airlines, so that it is no longer necessary to travel to northern Tanzania via Nairobi or Dar es Salaam. Most new arrivals will be collected by their hotel or safari company, but charter taxis are also available at the airport, at a fixed price of US$60. Travellers with problematic flight times might think about booking into the excellent KIA Lodge (see *Where to stay*, page 131), which lies just 1km from the airport.

If you are flying to Arusha from within Tanzania, check your ticket carefully as most domestic flights now leave from and arrive at the smaller **Arusha Airport** (airport code ARK), which lies about 5km out of town along the Serengeti road. Daily flights connect this airport to all major airstrips on the northern Tanzania safari circuit, including Manyara, Ngorongoro, Seronera, Grumeti and Lobo, as well as to Dar es Salaam and Zanzibar. There are also regular scheduled flights to the likes of Mwanza, Rubondo Island, Mafia Island and the reserves of the southern safari circuit.

Most tourists flying around Tanzania will have made their flight arrangements in advance through a tour operator, and this is certainly the recommended way of going about things, but it is generally possible to buy tickets from Arusha to major destinations such as Dar es Salaam and Zanzibar at short notice.

Airlines The offices of the main airlines are mostly dotted along Boma Road in the old town centre. **Ethiopian Airlines** [113 C4] (✆ *027 250 7512; www.flyethiopian.com*) is immediately north of the New Safari Hotel, while **Precision Air** (✆ *027 250 3261; www.precisionairtz.com*) is only a door or two further south. **Coastal Aviation** [113 C5] (✆ *027 250 0087; www.coastal.cc*) is on the opposite side of Boma Road closer to the Clock Tower. **RwandAir** has an office on Swahili Street [115 H6] (m *0732 978558; www.rwandair.com*). The domestic airline offices are **Air Excel** (m *0754 211227; www.airexcelonline.com*) in Subzali Building on Goliondoi Road and **Fastjet** on India Road [113 B4] (✆ *068 568 0533; www.fastjet.com/tz*). The **Regional Air** office is out of town near the Arusha Coffee Lodge so it's best to call them at one of the following numbers: ✆027 250 4164/254 8536 or m 0753 500300/0784 285753. **KLM** no longer has an office in Arusha, but you can contact the Dar es Salaam office (✆ *022 213 9790; e reservations.daressalaam@klm.com*) for assistance.

BY ROAD There are now two main **bus stations** in Arusha. The old central station at the south end of Colonel Middleton Road [115 E4/5], facing the stadium, is the terminus of all minibuses and other dala-dalas, as well as most buses to relatively local destinations such as Moshi, Namanga and Babati. The newer Makao Mapya bus station [114 D2], often referred to as Dar Express after the best known operator there, consists of a row of perhaps two dozen coach company offices off Stadium Road about 300m west of the old bus station.

The old bus station can be somewhat chaotic and intimidating, thanks to the high density of 'flycatchers' and touts who to try to latch onto fresh arrivals (or to get in the middle of negotiations with travellers buying a ticket out of town). These guys can be annoyingly persistent, but they pose no serious threat, though it is definitely advisable to make it clear you don't want their services. By contrast, Makao Mapya is very orderly and quiet, and you can usually buy tickets at any of the offices there without hassle. For long hauls it is always advisable to buy a ticket the day before you want to travel.

The best coach service for Dar es Salaam and other destinations along the B1 is the **Dar Express** (m *0754 946155*), and buses depart every 30 minutes between 05.30 and 08.30, as well as at 10.00 and 14.30. Tickets costs US$18–20 depending on the type of coach, and the trip takes about 12 hours. Cheaper bus services between Arusha and Dar es Salaam are plentiful, but aren't really worth bothering with, as they are less comfortable and tend to stop at every town, taking around 15 hours to cover the same distance.

The quickest and most efficient road transport between Arusha and Nairobi are the **minibus shuttles** run by various operators. Among the most reliable of these is the Riverside Shuttle (m *0754 474968*), which costs US$25 for non-residents (it is, however, often possible to negotiate to pay the resident rate, equivalent to US$16) and which leaves from a parking area in front of the Mezzaluna Restaurant on Simeon Road [105 G6], although you can usually arrange to be picked up elsewhere. Departures in either direction are at 08.00 and 14.00 daily, and the trip takes four to five hours. In Nairobi, passengers are dropped and collected at the Parkside Hotel or at Jomo Kenyatta Airport, and the contact number is m +254 (0)722 826368 or (0)725 999121. Another recommended service is the Impala Shuttle (*www.impalashuttle.com*), which costs the same and leaves from the parking lot of the Impala Hotel [105 G7], at the same times. Tickets can be bought directly from the Impala Hotel (see page 109 for contact details), and the drop-off points in Nairobi are the Silver Springs or Parkside Hotel, or Jomo Kenyatta Airport.

A steady stream of minibuses and buses connect Moshi and Arusha. I would avoid using minibuses along this route due to the higher incidence of accidents, but they are generally quicker than buses. This trip usually takes between one and two hours. There are also regular buses to other relatively local destinations such as Mto wa Mbu, Karatu, Mbulu, Babati and Kondoa; the best company servicing these routes is Mtei (m *0755 717117*).

ORIENTATION

Unlike Dar es Salaam or Zanzibar's labyrinthine Stone Town, Arusha is not a difficult town to familiarise yourself with. Its most significant geographical features are the Naura and Goliondoi rivers, which run parallel to each other through the town centre, cutting it into two distinct parts. To the east of the rivers lies the 'old' town centre, a relatively smart area whose main north–south thoroughfares –

Boma, India and Goliondoi roads – are lined with upmarket hotels, tourist-friendly restaurants, safari companies, curio shops, banks, bookshops and tourist offices. Major landmarks in this part of town include the Clock Tower, the Old Boma (now a museum) and the Arusha International Conference Centre (AICC).

Connected to the old town centre by Sokoine Road in the south and Makongoro Road in the north, the more bustling modern town centre consists of a tight grid of roads west of the rivers centred on the market and the old central bus station south of the stadium. This area is well equipped with small budget hotels and affordable restaurants, but it boasts few facilities that approach international standards. Similar in feel, though more residential and less commercially orientated, is the suburb of Kaloleni immediately north of the stadium.

Another important suburb is Kijenge, which lies to the southeast of the old town centre, and is reached by following Sokoine Road across a bridge over the Themi River to become the Old Moshi Road. Kijenge has a spacious, leafy character and it is dotted with half-a-dozen relatively upmarket hotels and numerous good restaurants, as well as an increasing number of safari company offices.

GETTING AROUND

BY TAXI There are plenty of taxis in Arusha. Good places to pick them up include the market and bus station, the filling station on the junction of Goliondoi Road and the Old Moshi Road, and the open area at the north end of Boma and India roads. A taxi ride within the town centre should cost roughly US$4–6, though tourists are normally asked a slightly higher price. A taxi ride to somewhere outside the town centre will cost more.

ON PUBLIC TRANSPORT A good network of minibus dala-dalas services Arusha. A steady flow of these vehicles runs along the length of Sokoine Road, some of which continue west out of town past the Tanganyika Farmers' Association (TFA) centre, while others run east of the Clock Tower to the Impala Hotel and beyond. There are also regular dala-dalas between the town centre and the main Nairobi–Moshi bypass. Fares are nominal, and it's easy enough to hop on or off any passing dala-dala heading in your direction.

TOURIST INFORMATION

The **Tanzania Tourist Board** (TTB) office on Boma Road [113 C4] (✆ 027 250 3842; e ttbarusha@cybernet.co.tz; www.tanzaniatouristboard.com; ⊕ 08.00–16.00 Mon–Fri, 08.30–13.00 Sat) is refreshingly helpful and well informed. It stocks a useful colour road map of Tanzania as well as a great street plan of Arusha, both given free of charge to tourists (though this doesn't stop the book vendors out on the street from trying to sell the same maps at a very silly price). If you want to check out a safari company, the TTB office keeps a regularly updated list of all registered safari and trekking companies, as well as those that are blacklisted.

The TTB has been actively involved in the development of cultural tourism programmes in Ng'iresi, Mulala, Mkuru, Longido, Mto wa Mbu, Usambara, North Pare and South Pare, as well as several projects further afield. The Arusha office stocks informative pamphlets about these programmes, and can help out with information on prices and access. Details are also available at the **Cultural Tourism Program** office in the Old Boma (✆ 027 250 0025; e culturaltourism@habari.co.tz; www.tanzaniaculturaltourism.com).

The head office of **Tanzania National Parks** (Tanapa) is located in the Mwalimu J K Nyerere Conservation Centre about 3km out of town along the Serengeti road (✆ *027 250 3471/4082;* e *info@tanzaniaparks.com; www.tanzaniaparks.com*), roughly opposite the Cultural Heritage Centre.

The **Ngorongoro Conservation Authority** (NCA) has a helpful information office on Boma Road [113 C4] (✆ *027 253 7006; www.ngorongorocrater.org*) close to the tourist board office. In addition to some worthwhile displays on the conservation area, it sells a good range of books and booklets about the northern circuit.

The **Immigration Office** on Simeon Road [113 A2] (✆ *027 250 6565*) will normally extend visas on the spot.

SAFARI OPERATORS

The list given here is not definitive, but it provides a good cross-section of the sort of services that are on offer and, except where otherwise noted, it sticks to companies that have maintained high standards over the years. The listed companies generally specialise in northern circuit safaris, but most can also set up Kilimanjaro and Meru climbs, fly-in safaris on the southern safari circuit, and excursions to Zanzibar.

SAFETY

Arusha can be a daunting prospect on first contact, particularly if you arrive by bus. Competition between budget safari companies is fierce, and 'flycatchers' – the street touts who solicit custom for these companies – know that their best tactic is to hook travellers who don't have a pre-booked safari when they arrive. As a consequence, when you arrive in Arusha by bus you're likely to spend your first few minutes dodging the attention of a dozen yelling touts, all of who will claim to be able to offer you the cheapest safari and room in town. In most cases, the touts probably will show you to a decent room, but, unfortunately, by allowing them to get involved like this, you will open the door to your sense of obligation being exploited later in your stay.

Fortunately, once you've run the bus station gauntlet, things do calm down somewhat, though the flock of flycatchers, newspaper vendors and curio sellers who hang around the old town centre can be a nuisance. Unlike in some other parts of Africa, however, it is unusual for such an exchange to descend into something truly unpleasant: most touts here seem capable of taking a good-humoured 'No' for an answer, especially one spoken in Swahili, and they will usually back down at any show of genuine irritation. As for the dodgy money-changers that sometimes hang around with the touts, don't let the offer of a superior rate sucker you in – changing money on the street in Arusha as elsewhere in Tanzania is a definite no-no!

Such annoyances aside, Arusha is not an especially threatening city, though it is certainly not unheard of for tourists to be mugged after dark. The usual commonsense rules apply: avoid walking around singly or in pairs at night, especially on unlit roads and in parks, and avoid carrying valuables on your person or taking out significantly more money than you need for the evening. After dark, the dodgiest part of town for muggings is probably the area east of the Themi River, in particular the quiet, unlit roads between the Arusha Hotel, Impala Hotel and Mount Meru Hotel. On the whole, Arusha is very safe by day, but do be wary of bag-snatchers and pickpockets in the central market area.

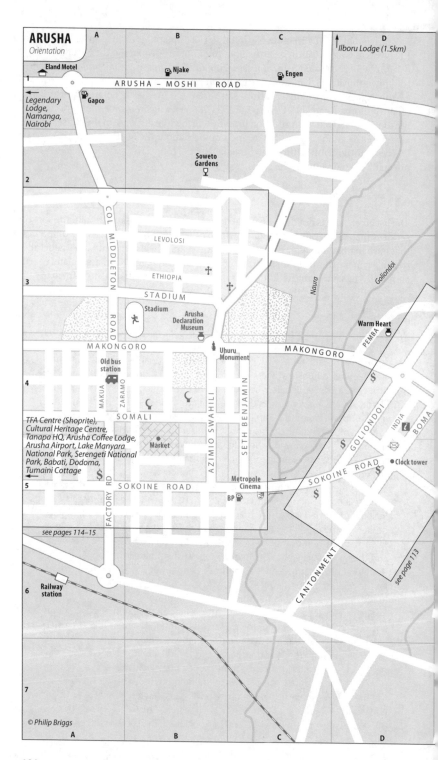

ARUSHA
Orientation

Eland Motel

Njake

Engen

↑ Ilboru Lodge (1.5km)

1   ARUSHA – MOSHI   ROAD

← Legendary Lodge, Namanga, Nairobi

Gapco

Soweto Gardens

2

COL MIDDLETON ROAD

LEVOLOSI

ETHIOPIA

Naura

Goliondoi

3   STADIUM

Stadium

Arusha Declaration Museum

Warm Heart

PEMBA

MAKONGORO

MAKONGORO

Uhuru Monument

Old bus station

MAKUA

ZARAMO

SOMALI

AZIMIO SWAHILI

SETH BENJAMIN

GOLIONDOI

INDIA

BOMA

4

SOKOINE ROAD

Clock tower

TFA Centre (Shoprite), Cultural Heritage Centre, Tanapa HQ, Arusha Coffee Lodge, Arusha Airport, Lake Manyara National Park, Serengeti National Park, Babati, Dodoma, Tumaini Cottage

Market

FACTORY RD

5   SOKOINE   ROAD

Metropole Cinema

BP

see pages 114–15

see page 113

CANTONMENT

6   Railway station

7

© Philip Briggs

A   B   C   D

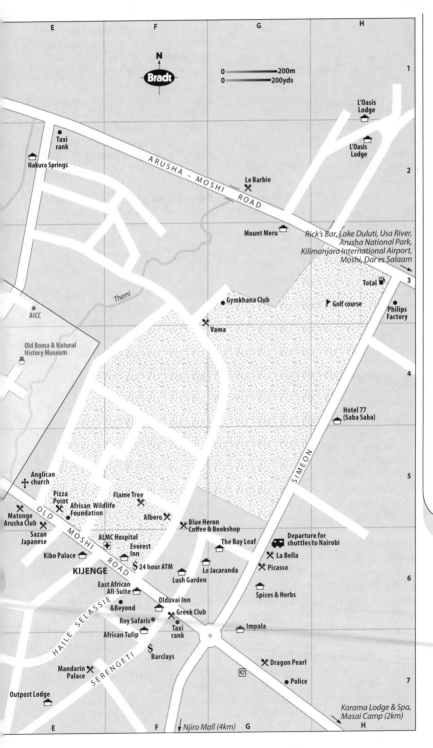

N

Bradt

0 ————— 200m
0 ————— 200yds

L'Oasis Lodge

L'Oasis Lodge

Taxi rank

Nakura Springs

ARUSHA – MOSHI ROAD

Le Barbie

Mount Meru

Rick's Bar, Lake Duluti, Usa River,
Arusha National Park,
Kilimanjaro International Airport,
Moshi, Dar es Salaam

Themi

Total

AICC

Gymkhana Club

Golf course

Philips Factory

Old Boma & Natural History Museum

Vama

Hotel 77 (Saba Saba)

SIMEON

Anglican church

Pizza Point

Flame Tree

African Wildlife Foundation

Albero

Blue Heron Coffee & Bookshop

Matonge Arusha Club

Sazan Japanese

ALMC Hospital

The Bay Leaf

Departure for shuttles to Nairobi

Kibo Palace

Everest Inn

24 hour ATM

La Bella

Picasso

KIJENGE

Le Jacaranda

OLD MOSHI ROAD

East African All-Suite

Lush Garden

Spices & Herbs

&Beyond

Olduvai Inn

Roy Safaris

Greek Club

African Tulip

Taxi rank

Impala

HAILE SELASSIE

SERENGETI

Barclays

Dragon Pearl

Mandarin Palace

Police

Outpost Lodge

Karama Lodge & Spa,
Masai Camp (2km)

↓ Njiro Mall (4km)

Africa Dream Safaris m 0752 225554 or (US toll free) 877 572 3274; e safari@africadreamsafaris.com; www.africadreamsafaris.com; see also advert on inside front cover. An award-winning outfit specialising in upmarket customised safaris for serious wildlife enthusiasts & photographers, using intimate tented camps & knowledgeable driver/guides who place strong emphasis on early morning & full-day game drives, avoiding circuits tsuffer from overcrowding.

Awaken to Africa m 1 732 271 8269 or (US toll free) 1 888 271 8269; e info@awakentoafrica.com; www.awakentoafrica.com; see also advert in colour section, page xviii. Managed by its enthusiastic & hands-on Tanzanian–US owners, this small new company specialises in tailor-made upmarket safaris using exclusive intimate camps. It has plenty of experience with, & is highly recommended to, dedicated photographers.

Fair Travel Tanzania m 0786 025886/8; e res@fairtraveltanzania.com; www.fairtravel.com; see also advert on page 171. This admirable new company is, as its name suggests, strongly committed to ecologically sound travel that pays fair wages to drivers & other staff, channels all profit into community projects, & still offers competitive rates to its clients (for further details, see the informative website). A recommended mid-range option.

Hoopoe Safaris [113 B4] 027 250 7011; e information@hoopoe.com; www.hoopoe.com. This long serving & highly regarded owner-managed safari company specialises in personalised luxury camping & lodge safaris. It owns tented camps outside Lake Manyara & Tarangire national parks, & is also a good contact for trekking & walking safaris in Natron, the Ngorongoro Highlands, & the game-rich Maasai Plains to the east of the Serengeti.

Kearsleys Travel 022 213 7713; e info@kearsleys.com; www.kearsleys.com; see also advert on page 96. Established in 1948, this is the oldest safari company in Tanzania, with dynamic management & staff, & well-maintained vehicles. Though it has traditionally focused on the more 'difficult' southern safari circuit, Kearsleys now has an office in Arusha (next to the Golden Rose Hotel) and is also a thoroughly reliable choice for safaris along the northern circuit.

Ker & Downey Tanzania 027 250 8917; m 0786 000510; e info@legendaryadventure.com; www.keranddowneytanzania.com. This established

operator specialises in ultra-exclusive photographic safaris centred on its private concessions bordering the Ngorongoro Conservation Area & Lake Natron, as well as a mobile camp following the migration through the Serengeti.

Leopard Tours 027 250 8441; e leopardtours@leopardtours.co.za; www.leopard-tours.com. This large-scale operator specialises in mid-range safaris concentrating on the larger lodges & more established game-viewing areas, & offers a highly reliable service to those who want to stick firmly to the beaten track.

Nature Discovery m 0754 400 003; e info@naturediscovery.com; www.naturediscovery.com. This eco-friendly operator is widely praised for its high-quality, top-end Kilimanjaro climbs, & it also arranges standard northern circuit safaris as well as trekking expeditions in the Ngorongoro Highlands & elsewhere.

Roy Safaris [105 F6] 027 250 2115/8081; e roysafaris@intafrica.com; www.roysafaris.com. This dynamic & efficient owner-managed company is recommended for reliable but reasonably priced budget & mid-range camping, semi-luxury camping safaris & lodge safaris.

Safari Makers m 0732 979195/0754 300817; e safarimakers@habari.co.tz; www.safarimakers.com. Owner-managed by a dynamic hands-on American–Tanzanian couple, Safari Makers runs competitively priced camping & lodge safaris, as well as arranging visits to various cultural programmes in communities outside Arusha, making it a recommended first contact at the budget to mid-range level.

Tanzania Adventure m 0786 013994; e info@tanzania-adventure.com; www.tanzania-adventure.com. This joint German–Tanzanian company offers a wide selection of safaris, including an extensive walking programme in the Ngorongoro Highlands & Serengeti border areas. It is especially recommended to German speakers.

Tropical Trails 027 250 0358; e info@tropicaltrails.com; www.tropicaltrails.com. Based at Masai Camp, this eco-friendly budget-oriented company arranges standard lodge-based & camping safaris, walking excursions on the fringes of the main national parks, & Kili climbs along the less usual routes.

TrueAfrica 0784 999738; e info@trueafrica.com; www.trueafrica.com. Strongly affiliated to the excellent Asilia chain of exclusive tented camps, this company specialises in tailor-made upmarket safaris at some of the country's top camps & lodges. **Wayo Africa** m 0784 203000; e info@ wayoafrica.com; www.wayoafrica.com; see also advert in colour section, page xvii. This environmentally minded operator can arrange safaris for most tastes & budgets, but its main speciality is walking safaris in wilderness areas within the Serengeti National Park, as well as bush camps set in more remote parts in the other parks. The standard of guiding can be exceptional, & it is highly recommended to active travellers seeking a genuine wilderness experience at reasonable rates. **Wild Frontiers** ☎ 027 250 2668; m (South Africa) +27 (0)72 927 7529; e reservations@wildfrontiers. com; www.wildfrontiers.com. Based in South Africa

but with its own ground operation in Arusha, this well-established & flexible company offers a varied range of motorised, walking & combination safaris using standard lodges or its own excellent tented camps. Recommended to those seeking a relatively unpackaged safari at a reasonable price. **&Beyond** [105 F6] ☎ (South Africa) +27 (0)11 809 4447; e safaris@andbeyond.com; www.andbeyond. com. Formerly known as CCAfrica, &Beyond operates some of the most sumptuous lodges in northern Tanzania, notable for their fine attention to detail, informal & personalised service, well-trained guides & rangers, & general air of exclusivity. It arranges fly-in, drive-in (or mixed) safaris throughout northern Tanzania, as well as mobile safaris using seasonal camps in the 'Under Canvas' brand.

WHERE TO STAY

This section concentrates on accommodation located within the city limits. It also includes a handful of individual hotels situated along the Old Moshi and Serengeti roads within 5km of the town centre, but excludes the ever-growing assortment of lodges that flank the Moshi road east of the Mount Meru Hotel. All hotels in the latter category are covered in *Around Arusha*, page 126, but it is worth noting that most would make a perfectly viable – and, on the whole, more aesthetically pleasing – alternative to staying in the town itself.

EXCLUSIVE

⌂ **Arusha Coffee Lodge** [104 A5] (30 rooms) ☎ 027 254 0630/9; e info@elewana.com, videar@

elewana.com; www.elewanacollection.com. Justifiably billed as 'the first truly 5-star hotel in Arusha' when it opened 10 years ago, the immaculate Arusha Coffee Lodge still ranks among the most luxurious options in the Arusha area. Accommodation is in standalone split-level chalets or suites distinguished by their elegant Victorian décor, hardwood floors, huge balconies & stunning fireplaces, & in-room percolators to provide the true aroma of the coffee estate. Designed around the original plantation houses, the excellent restaurant serves a spit-roasted lunchtime grill & a sumptuous à la carte dinner. Facilities include a swimming pool. It is situated about 5km out of the city alongside the Serengeti road, close to Arusha Airport, on what is reputedly the largest coffee estate in Tanzania, with a good view of Mount Meru. *US$375/500 en-suite sgl/dbl, or US$499/750 sgl/dbl suite, all B&B, with significantly discounted rates available Mar–May & Nov–mid Dec.*

🏠 **Legendary Lodge** [104 A1] (6 rooms) 📞027 250 8917; m 0786 000510. Arguably the plushest hotel anywhere in the Arusha area, Legendary Lodge is situated 3km west of the city centre on the Selari Coffee Estate, founded by the same family that established the Arusha Hotel in the 1980s. The lodge is centred upon the original early 20th-century estate house – which now serves as a common lounge & dining area complete with period décor – & is set in lush gardens teeming with birdlife (including what is most probably the most westerly breeding pair of the localised brown-throated barbet). The vast open-plan semi-detached cottages, decorated in understated contemporary classic style, consist of a sitting room with leather sofas, fireplace, minibar & flatscreen DSTV, a king-size bed with walk-in netting, & a spacious bathroom with tub & shower. The superb food is complemented by an excellent selection of house wines. *US$500 pp all-inc.*

UPMARKET

🏠 **The Arusha Hotel** [113 C5] (65 rooms) 📞027 250 7777/8870; e marketing@ thearushahotel.com; www.thearushahotel.com. Formerly the New Arusha Hotel, this stately old hotel is the smartest option in the city centre following a change of ownership & extensive renovations in 2004, & it is due for another round of refurbishments by early 2013. Situated right opposite the Clock Tower, it stands in large wooded grounds that run down towards the Themi River, & the décor has an Edwardian feel, befitting its status as the oldest hostelry in Arusha. The spacious

rooms & suites all come with DSTV, netting, in-room internet access, a smoke detector, electronic safes & tea-/coffee-making facilities. AC & non-smoking rooms are available. Facilities include 24-hr room service, a business centre, a craft shop, 24-hr satellite internet access, a heated swimming pool, 3 bars, 2 restaurants, a casino & an airport shuttle service. *US$200/240 sgl/dbl executive rooms B&B, or US$420/440 suite.*

🏠 **The African Tulip** [105 F7] (29 rooms) 📞027 254 3004/5; e info@theafricantulip.com; www.theafricantulip.com. Owned & managed by Roy Safaris, their office is next door, this chic service-oriented boutique hotel is set in a green suburban garden with a swimming pool. The rooms & suites are large & attractively decorated with Zanzibar-style wooden furnishing, & have good facilities including a safe, minibar, Wi-Fi, satellite TV & large en-suite bathroom with a choice of a tub or shower. There's a well-stocked gift shop on the ground floor, along with the aptly named Zanzibar Bar & promising Baobab Restaurant. *US$190/240 sgl/dbl B&B, or US$310/500 sgl/dbl suite.*

🏠 **The Bay Leaf Boutique Hotel** [105 G6] (5 rooms) 📞027 254 3035; e reservations@ thebayleafhotel.com. This stylish boutique hotel on leafy Vijana Road comprises just 5 individually decorated rooms, most with parquet floor, tasteful ethnically influenced décor, flatscreen DSTV, AC & spacious modern bathrooms. The ground floor restaurant offers one of the best fine dining experiences in Arusha. *US$245 dbl, or US$420 suite.*

🏠 **Mount Meru Hotel** (formerly The Arusha Hotel) [105 G3] (178 rooms) 📞027 254 5111; m 0757 557802/0756 411615; e info@ mountmeruhotel.com; www.mountmeruhotel. com. Recently reopened following privatisation & several years of renovations, this veteran 7-storey landmark stands in large green grounds bordering the golf course immediately northeast of the city centre. Geared more towards business travellers than tourists, it nevertheless offers some of the most comfortable accommodation & best facilities – 3 restaurants, a large swimming pool, a business centre, forex bureau & several onsite shops – within the city limits. Several types of en-suite room are available, all spacious & contemporary in feel, with minibar, free Wi-Fi, DSTV & pay-per-view movie channel, safe, AC, & tea-/coffee-making facilities. *US$180/210 standard sgl/dbl B&B, suites from US$250/280 sgl/dbl.*

🏠 **East African All-Suite Hotel** [105 F6] (40 rooms) 📞027 205 0075; m 0757 600110; e reservations@eastafricanhotel.com; www. eastafricanhotel.com. This slick hotel on the Old Moshi Road doesn't exactly evoke a safari atmosphere, but the accommodation is to a very high standard, consisting of large suites with varied facilities, including flat screen DSTV, king-size bed, safe, kitchen with stove & fridge, large bathroom with combination tub/shower, AC, & extensive leather furnishing that creates a slightly cluttered effect. The restaurant serves an imaginative selection of contemporary dishes & there's a swimming pool & cigar bar. Good value. *US$150/170 sgl/dbl suite, or US$230 presidential suite with 2 bedrooms.*

🏠 **Karama Lodge & Spa** [105 H7] (22 rooms) m 0754 475188/0732 971823; e info@karama-lodge.com; www.karama-lodge.com. Aptly named after the Swahili word for 'blessing', this fabulous eco-lodge possesses a genuine bush atmosphere, despite lying only 3km from central Arusha along the Old Moshi Road. Perched on the small but densely wooded Suye Hill, part of which is protected in a forest reserve, the wooded grounds harbour a wide range of Brachystegia-associated birds (brown-throated barbet prominent among them) as well as small nocturnal mammals such as bushbaby, genet & civet. Accommodation is in stilted wood-&-*makuti* units with Zanzibar-style beds draped in netting, en-suite shower & toilet, & private balcony facing Kilimanjaro. The restaurant serves tasty snacks & meals, & offers views to Kilimanjaro & Meru on a clear day. The highly rated spa offers massage, sauna, yoga & other treatments. Overall, it's a highly recommended & affordable alternative to the bland upmarket city hotels that characterise central Arusha, though the sloping grounds would make it a poor choice for disabled & elderly travellers. *US$95/135 sgl/dbl B&B, or US$ 129/203 sgl/dbl FB, with significant resident & low season discounts.*

MODERATE

🏠 **New Safari Hotel** [113 C4] (48 rooms) 📞027 250 3261/2; e newsafarihotel@habari.co.tz; www.thenewsafarihotel.com. This long-serving but recently renovated hotel on Boma Road, once popular with the hunting fraternity, now seems more geared towards business travellers, with its convenient – though potentially noisy – central location a few mins from the AICC & a number of government offices & restaurants. Facilities include a ground floor internet café & a good restaurant. The large, tiled en-suite rooms with digital satellite TV have a modern feel, & seem fair value. *US$95/115 sgl/dbl B&B, or US$200/220 suite.*

🏠 **Impala Hotel** [105 G7] (177 rooms) 📞027 254 3082/7; m 0754 678678/008448; e impala@impalahotel.com; www.impalahotel.com. The constantly expanding Impala Hotel, situated in Kijenge about 10 mins' walk from the city centre, is justifiably rated by many tour operators as the best-value hotel in the immediate vicinity of Arusha, & it's certainly one of the largest, busiest, smoothest running & most reasonably priced, despite being somewhat deficient in character. Facilities include 4 restaurants of which the Indian is strongly recommended, while the others specialise in more ordinary Italian, Chinese & continental cuisine. Other facilities include an internet café, a forex bureau offering good rates, a swimming pool, a gift shop, an inexpensive shuttle service to Nairobi as well as to Kilimanjaro International Airport, & an in-house safari operator. The newer rooms are comfortable & attractively decorated (the old ones are rather less so), & all have free Wi-Fi, satellite TV, hot showers & a fridge. *US$90/110 sgl/dbl B&B; US$150 executive dbl; US$250 dbl suite.*

🏠 **L'Oasis Lodge** [105 H2] (29 rooms) 📞027 250 7089; m 0757 557802/0756 411615; e info@loasislodge.com; www.loasistanzania.com. Set in large green grounds about 500m north of the Moshi road, along a side road signposted opposite the prominent Mount Meru Hotel, this pleasantly rustic lodge is one of the best-value options in its range. A variety of comfortable en-suite rooms are available, including some attractive stilted bungalows, while other facilities include a large bar alongside the swimming pool, & the wonderful Lounge at Oasis, whose funky but earthy décor is complemented by a cosmopolitan menu of light snacks, salads, wraps & full meals. *US$75/100 sgl/dbl B&B, or US$105/160 FB.*

🏠 **Outpost Lodge** [105 E7] (25 rooms) 37A Serengeti St; 📞027 250 8405; m 0715 430358; e outposttanzania@gmail.com; www.outposttanzania.net. The welcoming & homely Outpost, set in a suburban garden on Kijenge's

Serengeti Road, has proved to be consistently popular with travellers seeking its combination of affordability & comfort since it opened in 1990. Following extensive renovations in early 2012, the rooms in the main house & the garden bungalows all come with en-suite bathrooms, netting & DSTV. Outpost is also well equipped to care for disabled travellers, & has 1 dedicated, wheelchair-friendly room. Cheap & tasty lunches & dinners are available. *US$52/75 sgl/dbl.*

🏠 **Tumaini Cottage** [114 A6] (10 rooms) m 0784 588698; e info@tumainicottage.com; www.tumainicottage.com. This friendly new family-run lodge close to the African Heritage Centre has a relaxed atmosphere, a quiet out-of-town location, & good facilities inc free internet & a restaurant serving African & international cuisine. *US$50/60 en-suite sgl/dbl B&B, or US$120 for a family cottage.*

BUDGET

🏠 **Hotel Le Jacaranda** [105 G6] (23 rooms) ☎ 027 254 4624; m 0784 986116; e jacaranda@ tz2000.com; http://jacaranda.chez.com. Situated in the garden suburbs immediately east of the city centre, this converted colonial-era homestead ranks among the most characterful hotels in Arusha, & it's also exceptionally good value, set in pretty overgrown grounds with a mini-golf course & shady & highly rated restaurant/bar area. The individually styled en-suite rooms all have a 4-poster bed with netting & hot water. *US$45/55 sgl/dbl, dropping to US$40/45 in low season.*

🏠 **Natron Palace Hotel** [115 F4] (50 rooms) ☎ 027 254 4072; m 0769 646569; e info@ natronpalacehotel.com; www.natronpalacehotel. com. This modern 9-storey hotel overlooking the central bus station may somewhat lack character, but it has a useful location for early starts or late arrivals, & the comfortable en-suite rooms with DSTV, AC, minibar & private balcony are excellent value. *US$45/55 standard dbl, although it is worth asking about the much cheaper resident rate.*

🏠 **Arusha Naaz Hotel** [113 B6] (21 rooms) ☎ 027 250 2087; m 0754 282799; e arushanaaz@ yahoo.com; www.arushanaaz.net. Situated on Sokoine Road close to the Clock Tower, this clean, convenient & secure hotel has long been a favourite with budget travellers. There is a good, inexpensive Indian restaurant on the ground floor & an internet café & reliable car hire firm on the

premises. Unfortunately, the cramped en-suite rooms with net, fan, hot water & DSTV seem overpriced for what they are. *US$40/60 sgl/dbl.*

🏠 **Arusha Resort Centre** [113 C7] (33 rooms) m 0788 252760; e arusharesort@habari. co.tz; www.arusharesorttz.com. On a quiet back road only 2 mins' walk from the central Clock Tower, this is a comfortable & safe, albeit rather institutional, double-storey hotel offering clean & good-value accommodation in rooms or apts with negotiable discounts for long-stay visitors. Facilities include an internet café & an unexceptional but affordable restaurant. *US$40/50 en-suite sgl/dbl; US$60 for a dbl self-catering apt; US$100 for an apt sleeping 4.*

🏠 **Aba Hotel** [115 H5] (20 rooms) m 0776 989175/0785 969175; e reservations@ arushabudgethotels.com; www.abahotels-tanzania.blogspot.com. A few blocks east of the market & central bus station, this 4-storey hotel is one of the best budget deals in central Arusha, thanks largely to the switched-on & helpful owner-manager. The clean en-suite rooms have netting, a TV & telephone, & facilities include laundry, internet & a massage room. Great value. *US$15 pp B&B.*

🏠 **Golden Rose Hotel** [115 F2] (22 rooms) ☎ 027 250 7959; m 0744 588507; e goldenrose@habari.co.tz; http:// goldenrosehotel.tripod.com/goldenrosehotel. This well-known landmark on the western side of the city is close to both bus stations & is the most central departure point for the Riverside shuttle to/ from Nairobi. The small but comfortable en-suite rooms come with TV, fan, net & balcony, & though a little timeworn & gloomy are pretty good value following a recent drop in price. *US$30/40 sgl/dbl B&B, with a 35% discount to residents.*

🏠 **Olduvai Inn** [105 F6] (15 rooms) ☎ 027 254 3044; m 0754 761820. Set in large gardens on the junction of Serengeti & Old Moshi roads, this is a great little guesthouse offering clean & reasonably priced en-suite accommodation with nets, TV & hot shower. There's internet access onsite & plenty of choice of restaurants within a few hundred metres. *US$30/40 dbl/twin B&B.*

🏠 **Spices & Herbs** [105 G6] (12 rooms) m 0754 313162/0768 356191. Arusha's top Ethiopian restaurant offers accommodation in small but clean en-suite rooms within easy walking distance of the Riverside Shuttle. *US$35 sgl/dbl B&B.*

SHOESTRING AND CAMPING

Smile B&B [115 F2] (9 rooms) m 0754 263216. This good value new guesthouse, set in the backstreets behind the stadium, has clean twin rooms with fan, writing desk, tea-/coffee-making facilities & en-suite hot shower. *US$20 twin.*

Monje's Guesthouse [115 G2 & H1] m 0782 999011; e info@monjestz.com; www.monjestz.com. Long-serving favourites among the myriad guesthouses in the back roads north of the stadium, this quiet, family-run business now operates 4 guesthouses within a block or 2 of each other. All 4 places have clean rooms, friendly staff, hot showers & a vigorously enforced anti-flycatcher policy! Perhaps a touch overpriced. *US$18/25 en-suite sgl/dbl.*

Arusha Backpackers Hotel [114 D7] (34 rooms) m 0773 377795/0715 377795; e reservations@arushabackpackers.co.tz; www.arushabackpackers.co.tz. On Sokoine Road and within easy walking distance of the central bus station, this safe & reliable set-up is a favourite rendezvous for budget-conscious travellers. The small but clean rooms have a desk & fan, & the use of communal hot showers & toilets. *US$12/20 sgl/dbl B&B, or US$10 for a dorm bed.* Lunch & dinner an additional US$6 pp each.

Arusha By Night Annexe [115 F3] (22 rooms) m 0713 485237. This stalwart hotel close to the stadium & central bus station has unquestionably seen better days, but the one-price-for-all-comers policy means that the faded but spacious rooms with twin or dbl bed, TV, fan,

writing desk & en-suite hot shower feel like one of the best deals in this range. *US$12/13 sgl/dbl.*

Kitunda Guesthouse [115 F2] (40 rooms) m 0754 263216; e kgh2009@hotmail.com. Among the best of the innumerable little guesthouses scattered around the backstreets behind the stadium, this has a neat little restaurant at the front, & clean tiled rooms with a writing desk, net, TV & hot shower. *US$10/15 sgl/dbl using common showers, or US$15/20 en-suite sgl/dbl B&B.*

Masai Camp [105 H7] m 0754 507131; e masaicamp@africamail.com; www.masaicamptz.com. Situated about 2km out of the city along the Old Moshi Road, Masai Camp is one of the best campsites in Tanzania, & it also offers simple accommodation in huts. Facilities include an ablution block with hot water, a pool table, volleyball & a lively 24-hr bar, & an excellent safari company called Tropical Trails is onsite. The restaurant is well known for its pizzas. If you're without transport, you can get a taxi here for around US$3. *US$10 pp rooms; camping US$5 pp.*

YMCA [113 B4] 027 272 2544. This Arusha institution is looking pretty run down these days, but it has a conveniently central location on India Road, decent food, & feels like relatively good value. *US$10/13 sgl/dbl.*

Kilimanjaro Villa [115 G4] (8 rooms) m 0766 143709. A long-standing backpacker standby situated close to the market & central bus station, the Kilimanjaro Villa is nothing special but it's friendly, clean & reasonably priced. *US$7/10 sgl/dbl using common showers.*

WHERE TO EAT

Plenty of good restaurants are dotted around Arusha, with many international cuisines represented and most budgets catered for by a number of places. The following is an alphabetical selection of some long-standing favourites and interesting recent additions, but new places open and close frequently, so don't be afraid to try restaurants that aren't listed.

Eateries in the **old town centre** mostly cater to local business people and office workers at lunch, but generally stay open in the evening long enough for an early dinner. There are also decent restaurants at most central hotels, the pick being the à la carte eatery at the Arusha Hotel (see page 108), which also has a very pleasant bar.

The selection of restaurants listed in the **market area** section, below, are mainly limited to indifferent local eateries, but it does host two unpretentious but exceptional Indian restaurants, both open in the evenings.

There are several good places to eat in the **TFA (Shoprite) Shopping Centre** [114 A7], most tending to be at the higher end of the price spectrum.

The leafy suburb of **Kijenge** is the main centre of Arusha's dining scene, boasting a cosmopolitan selection of mostly quite upmarket restaurants concentrated within a few minutes' walk of each other.

OLD TOWN CENTRE

✗ Africafe [113 C4] Boma Rad ; m 0782 515634/0684 746892; e info@africafetanzania. com; www.africafetanzania.com; ⏰ 07.30–21.00 Mon–Sat, 08.00-21.00 Sun. This clean, modern restaurant serves good fresh coffee & juices, tasty muffins & other freshly baked good, as well as a long list of cooked b/fasts, burgers, salads, sandwiches & other meals. It is a popular spot for lunch, with most mains in the US$7–10 range.

✗ Arusha Masai Café [113 A2] Pemba Rd; m 0755 765 640; e julieroni@hotmail.com; www. letseat.at/arushamasaicafe; ⏰ 09.00–21.00 Mon-Sat, 11.00–20.00 Sun. One of the best new eateries in Arusha, this funky Italian garden restaurant, situated alongside the Warm Heart Art Gallery, specialises in pasta dishes, salads & (excellent) pizzas in the US$6–8 range.

✗ Bamboo Café [113 C4] Boma Rd; ☎027 250 6451; m 0754 317801; e bamboocafe2000@yahoo. com; ⏰ 07.00–20.00 daily. This homely restaurant serves decent coffee, fruit juices, sandwiches, pancakes & snacks, & full meals for around US$5–7. The lunch of the day is usually a bargain.

✗ Green Hut Burgers [115 H7] Sokoine Rd. Excellent & inexpensive burgers & other greasy fast-food staples & light meals. No alcohol.

✗ Hot Bread Shop [113 B6] Sokoine Rd; m 0754 302174; ⏰ 08.30–18.00 Mon–Sat, 08.30–14.00 Sun. This long-serving backpacker & volunteer hangout near the Clock Tower serves fresh bread, rolls & pastries, adequate light meals & fruit juice. Fast internet café attached.

✗ Milk & Honey Restaurant [113 B6] Sokoine Rd; ☎027 250 3014; m 0755 223202; ⏰ 07.00–20.00 Mon–Sat. This popular local lunch venue serves a variety of Tanzanian, Indian & Western dishes in the US$2–4 range.

✗ Via Via Restaurant [113 C2] Boma Rd; m 0753 492400; www.viaviacafe.com/en/arusha; ⏰ 09.30–22.00 daily, closing later Thu & Sat. This Belgian-owned garden restaurant-cum-bar tucked away behind the Old Boma has a relaxing suburban atmosphere & the most eclectic selection of music in Arusha. There is a lunchtime buffet for US$8 pp, & it also hosts occasional film evenings, live music & cultural events involving artistes from all of Africa.

MARKET AREA

✗ Big Bite [115 H5] Cnr Swahili & Somali Rd; m 0754 311474; ⏰ 12.00–14.30 & 18.00–22.00 Wed–Mon. This misleadingly named & rather low-key eatery near the market isn't a fast-food outlet but one of the oldest & best north Indian restaurants in Arusha. There is a good vegetarian selection, & alcohol is served. Expect to pay US$7–10 for a main plus rice or Indian bread.

✗ Dolly's Patisserie [115 F6] Sokoine Rd; ☎027 254 4013; ⏰ 09.00–18.00 Mon–Sat. This highly rated bakery sells fresh bread & cakes, along with tasty pastries & sandwiches to take away.

✗ Khan's Barbecue [115 G5] Mosque St; m 0754 652747; ⏰ 18.00–21.00. This singular eatery near the market is a motor spares shop by day & street BBQ in the evening. A mixed grill including beef, chicken & mutton kebabs, with a huge selection of salads, *naan* bread & the like, costs around US$5. No alcohol.

TFA CENTRE [114 A7]

✗ Michel's Brasserie m 0713 702806; ⏰ 12.00–23.00 Mon–Sat. With cuisine & background music reflecting the nationality of its French owner-manager, this classy but laid-back bistro specialises in fondues (US$10–15) & filled crepes (US$5–8) but it also has a good selection of meat & fish dishes. The wine list is exceptional.

✗ Msumbi Cafe m 0754 789603; ⏰ 08.00–19.00 daily. Excellent freshly brewed coffee, a varied selection of teas, & b/fasts & light lunches in the US$2–4 range are all on offer at this clean & modern looking patisserie.

✗ Stiggybucks Cafe m 0754 375535; ⏰ 09.00–17.00 Mon–Sat. This great owner-managed coffee shop has indoor & outdoor seating, & it serves a tempting selection of cakes, bagels, salads, sandwiches & light lunches, mostly for under US$5.

✗ Tigrae's Restaurant m 0754 895525; ⏰ 10.00–22.00 Mon–Sat. The best Thai restaurant in Arusha, Tigrae's serves a good selection of meat & vegetarian dishes, as well as being highly rated for steaks. Mains in the US$6–9 range.

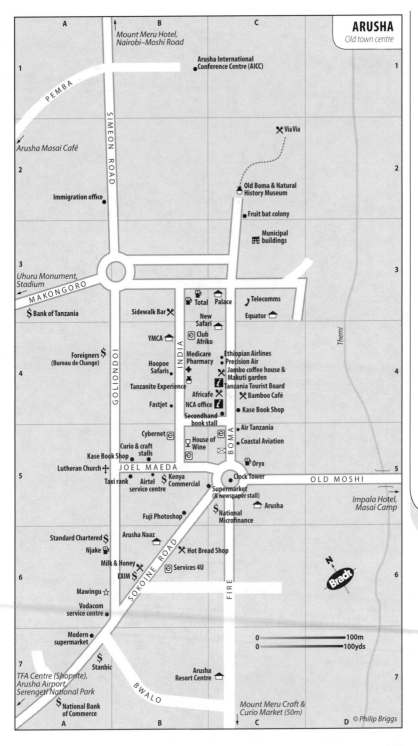

ARUSHA
Old town centre

Mount Meru Hotel,
Nairobi–Moshi Road

Arusha International
Conference Centre (AICC)

Via Via

Old Boma & Natural
History Museum

Fruit bat colony

Municipal
buildings

PEMBA

SIMEON ROAD

Arusha Masai Café

Immigration office

Uhuru Monument,
Stadium

MAKONGORO

Bank of Tanzania

Sidewalk Bar

Total Palace Telecomms

Equator

New
Safari

YMCA Club
Afriko

Foreigners
(Bureau de Change)

Hoopoe
Safaris

Medicare
Pharmacy

Ethiopian Airlines
Precision Air
Jambo coffee house &
Makuti garden
Tanzania Tourist Board

Tanzanite Experience

Fastjet

Africafe

NCA office

Bamboo Café

Kase Book Shop

Secondhand
book stall

Air Tanzania

Cybernet

House of
Wine

Coastal Aviation

Curio & craft
stalls

Kase Book Shop

Lutheran Church

Oryx

JOEL MAEDA

Taxi rank

Airtel
service centre

Kenya
Commercial

Clock Tower

OLD MOSHI

Supermarket
(& newspaper stall)

Arusha

Impala Hotel,
Masai Camp

Fuji Photoshop

National
Microfinance

Standard Chartered

Njake

Arusha Naaz

Milk & Honey

EXIM

Hot Bread Shop

Services 4U

Mawingu

Vodacom
service centre

Modern
supermarket

TFA Centre (Shoprite),
Arusha Airport,
Serengeti National Park

Stanbic

BWALO

Arusha
Resort Centre

National Bank
of Commerce

Mount Meru Craft &
Curio Market (50m)

GOLIONDOI

INDIA

BOMA

SOKOINE ROAD

FIRE

Themi

N
Bradt

0   100m
0   100yds

© Philip Briggs

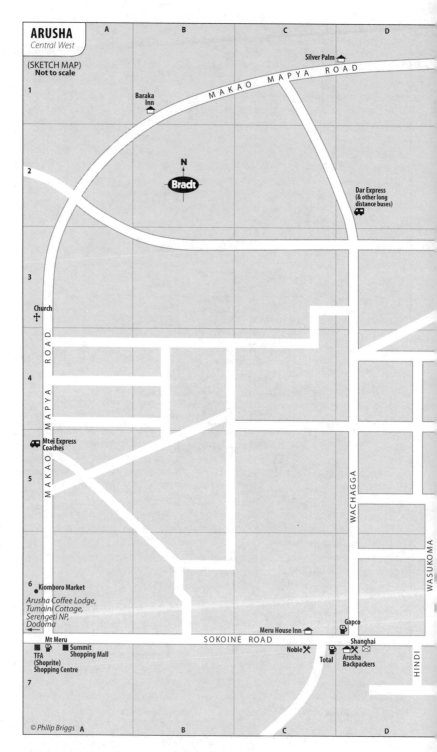

ARUSHA
Central West

(SKETCH MAP)
Not to scale

| | A | B | C | D |

Silver Palm

MAKAO MAPYA ROAD

1

Baraka
Inn

N
Bradt

2

Dar Express
(& other long
distance buses)

3

Church

MAKAO MAPYA ROAD

4

5

Mtei Express
Coaches

WACHAGGA

WASUKOMA

6 Kiomboro Market

Arusha Coffee Lodge,
Tumaini Cottage,
Serengeti NP,
Dodoma

Meru House Inn

Gapco

SOKOINE ROAD

Mt Meru
TFA
(Shoprite)
Shopping Centre

Summit
Shopping Mall

Noble

Total

Shanghai

Arusha
Backpackers

HINDI

7

© Philip Briggs A   B   C   D

114

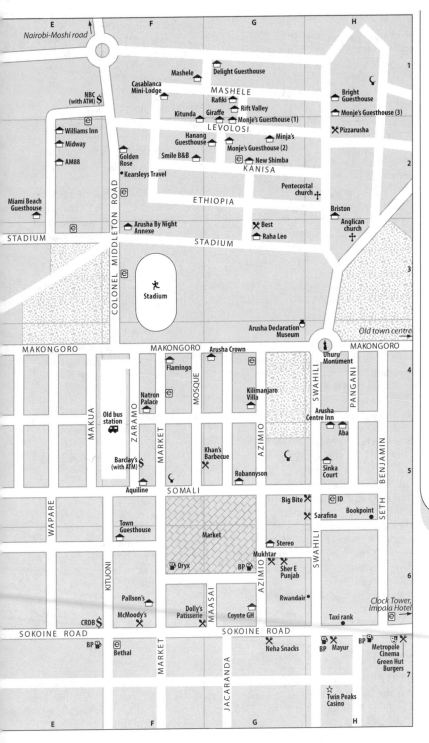

KIJENGE

✗ **Albero Restaurant** [105 F5] Haile Selassie Rd; ☎ 027 254 8987; m 0753 399145/0653 396529; ◷ 10.00–16.00 & 19.00–23.00 daily. This likeable open-air Italian restaurant has a pleasant setting in leafy suburbia & serves a varied selection of pasta dishes & pizzas in the US$5–8 range, while seafood & grills cost US$8–9.

✗ **Bay Leaf Fine Dining** [105 G6] ☎ 027 254 3035; e reservations@thebayleafhotel.com; www.thebayleafhotel.com; ◷ 12.00–15.00 & 18.00–22.00 daily. Widely regarded as one of the best fine dining restaurant experience in Arusha (& almost certainly the costliest), the Bayleaf specialises in inventive continental cuisine, with a good selection available for vegetarians. Lunchtime mains (including gourmet burgers) cost around US$10, while a 3-course dinner will set you back around US$20–30.

✗ **Blue Heron Coffee & Bookshop** [105 F5] Haile Selassie Rd; m 0783 885833; e theheron@ars.bol.co.tz; www.blue-heron-tanzania.com; ◷ 09.00–16.00 Mon–Thu, 09.00–22.00 Fri, 10.00–16.00 Sat. Combining classic colonial architecture with contemporary décor, this stylish coffee shop is a great spot for a relaxed open-air lunch, with seating on the veranda & in the green garden. Wholesome pasta dishes, salads & filled paninis cost around US$6–10, & there are also a selection of cheaper dishes & excellent coffee.

✗ **Dragon Pearl** [105 G7] ☎ 027 254 4107; ◷ 12.00–15.00 & 18.00–22.00 daily. Recently relocated to Kanisa Road, next to the Gymkhana Club, this is one of the best Chinese eateries in Arusha, with mains starting at around US$7–8.

✗ **Impala Hotel** [105 G7] Old Moshi Rd; ☎ 027 254 3082/7; www.impalahotel.com. The Indian restaurant in this large hotel is justifiably rated as one of the best in Arusha – & there are 3 other (lesser) specialist restaurants to choose from if Indian isn't your thing.

✗ **Picasso Café** [105 G6] Simeon Rd; m 0683 608636; ◷ 09.00–23.00 Mon–Sat, 09.00–17.00 Sun. This stylish café – which feels like it's been transplanted from Italy or France – serves a sumptuous selection of cakes & pastries, as well as an imaginative menu of filled crepes & salads for US$6–8. There are more substantial mains for around US$10, & the whole is complemented by good coffee & a great wine list.

✗ **Pizza Point** [105 E5] m 0754 294359; ◷ 08.00–22.00 daily. One of the more affordable options in this part of the city, this pleasant & unpretentious garden restaurant serves pizzas for around US$4–6, along with a selection of standard meat dishes for under US$4.

✗ **Sazan Japanese & Sushi Restaurant** [105 E5] Old Moshi Rd; m 0732 978624; ◷ lunch & dinner daily. Rated highly by many residents of Arusha despite its rather downmarket appearance, this quirky eatery, set in a converted container, serves good value platters of sushi, cooked seafood & other Japanese food in the US$4–8 range.

✗ **Spices & Herbs** [105 G6] Simeon Rd; m 0768 356191; ◷ lunch & dinner daily. The oldest & best Ethiopian restaurant in Arusha lies close to the Impala Hotel & serves the distinctive Ethiopian staples such as *kai wat* (a spicy meat or vegetarian stew) served with *injera* (flat round sour bread). There's occasional live music, & an internet café onsite. Vegetarian dishes are under US$5, other mains close to US$10.

✗ **Vama Restaurant** [105 F3] m 0784 326325; ◷ 12.00–14.30 & 19.00–22.00 daily. Now found close to the Gymkhana Club, Arusha's top Indian restaurant has a varied selection of meat & vegetarian dishes for around US$8–12.

OUT OF THE CITY

✗ **River House** m 0689 759067; e info@shanga.org; www.shanga.org; ◷ 10.00–14.30 daily. Situated at the Shanga craft workshop on the Burka Coffee Estate (signposted on the Serengeti Road near the Tanzania National Park headquarters), this excellent coffee shop provides healthy lunches, made mostly with homegrown ingredients, in shady pagodas overlooking a small river. Booking is necessary.

ENTERTAINMENT AND NIGHTLIFE

BARS AND NIGHTSPOTS There has been a notable increase in nightspots around Arusha in recent years. The liveliest upmarket venue for some years has been **Luxe Cocktail Club** (m *0786 575103*; ◷ *21.00–late*), which was known as the Colobus Club prior to reopening under new management in late 2011. It lies on the Old Moshi Road about 500m past the Impala Hotel, and comprises a sports lounge with pool tables and flatscreen TV, and a relaxed garden café, and has a cover charge of around US$3 on Fri and Sat nights, when there is also often live music or a name DJ.

There are several decent bars in the same area as the cluster of guesthouses behind the Golden Rose Hotel. The best place to drink in this part of the city is **Soweto Gardens** [104 B2], a relaxed but atmospheric garden bar that often hosts live bands over the weekends. Other good spots for live Tanzanian music include **Via Via** (see *Where to eat*, page 112) and **Rick's Bar** on the Moshi road. Further out of the city, **Masai Camp** (see *Where to stay*, page 111) on the Old Moshi Road is usually lively at night over weekends.

CINEMA The best cinema is the **Arusha Cinemax** [105 F7] (m *0732 102221/0755 102221; www.zoomtanzania.com/century-cinemax-arusha;* ⊕ *13.00 Tue–Sun*) in the out-of-town Njiro Mall, where the three screens show a varied selection of reasonably current Hollywood and Bollywood fare. Seats start at under US$5.

SHOPPING

BOOKS The best book shop by far is the branch of A Novel Idea next to the Barclays Bank in the TFA Centre [114 A7] (☏ *027 254 7333;* ⊕ *09.00-17.30 Mon–Fri*). This stocks a very good range of contemporary and classic novels, current bestsellers, guidebooks, field guides, and books about Tanzania. More central and also pretty good are the two branches of **Kase Book Shop** [113 C4] (☏ *027 250 2640;* ⊕ *09.00-17.00 Mon–Sat*), one of which lies on Boma Road next to Bamboo Café, and the other on Jael Marda Road more or less opposite the Kenya Commercial Bank. Both stock a good range of books about Tanzania and a more limited selection of contemporary bestsellers and novels. A few vendors usually hang around the Clock Tower selling maps and national park booklets at highly inflated prices, and most of the upmarket hotels also sell a limited selection of reading matter in their curio shops. To buy or exchange secondhand novels, there are a couple of stalls dotted around the city, one in the alley connecting Boma and India roads and several along Sokoine Road west of the market.

CRAFTS AND CURIOS Arusha is one of the best places in East Africa to buy Makonde carvings, Tingatinga paintings, batiks, Maasai jewellery and other souvenirs. The curio shops are far cheaper than those in Dar es Salaam and their quality and variety are excellent. Most of the curio shops are clustered between the Clock Tower and India Road, though be warned that the outdoor stalls can be full of hassle.

Two places stand out. The **Cultural Heritage Centre** (☏ *027 250 7496;* m *0741 510429;* ⊕ *09.00-17.00 Mon–Sat, 09.00-14.00 Sun*), about 3km out of the city on the main road towards the Serengeti, diagonally opposite the Tanzania National Parks headquarters, stocks the most vast collection of Tanzanian and other African crafts, ranging from towering carvings to colourful batiks and jewellery, and a useful selection of books about Tanzania. It's where the likes of King Harald of Norway and former South African and US presidents Thabo Mbeki and Bill Clinton did their curio shopping in Arusha, and an onsite branch of DHL can arrange shipping to anywhere in the world. It can be visited on the way back from a safari, or as a short taxi trip from Arusha.

Also on the Serengeti Road, where it is signposted just before the Tanzania National Parks headquarters, **Shanga** (see *River House* under *Where to eat*, opposite), named

5

The Makonde of the Tanzania–Mozambique border area are the finest traditional sculptors in East Africa. According to oral tradition the males of this matrilineal society have been practising this craft to woo their women for at least 300 years. Legend has it that the first person on earth, not yet male or female, living alone in the foothills of the Makonde Plateau, carved a piece of wood into the shape of a human figure. The carver left his creation outside his home overnight, and awoke to find it had been transformed into a living woman. Twice the woman conceived, but both times the child died after three days. Each time, the pair moved higher onto the plateau, believing this would bring them luck. The third child lived, and became the first true Makonde. The mother is regarded to be the spiritual ancestor of all the Makonde, and the legend is sometimes said to be a parable for the difficulty of creation.

In their purest form, the intricate, stylised carvings of the Makonde relate to this ancestral cult of womanhood, and are carried only by men, as a good-luck charm. Traditional carvings almost always depict a female figure, sometimes surrounded by children, and the style was practically unknown outside of Tanzania until a carving workshop was established at Mwenge in suburban Dar es Salaam during the 1950s. Subsequently, like any dynamic art form, Makonde sculpture has been responsive to external influences and subject to changes in fashion, with new styles of carvings becoming increasingly abstract and incorporating wider moral and social themes.

The most rustic of the new styles is the Binadamu sculpture, which depicts traditional scenes such as old men smoking pipes or women fetching water in a relatively naturalistic manner. Altogether more eerie and evocative is the Shetani style, in which grotesquely stylised human forms, sometimes with animal-like features, represent the impish and sometimes evil spirits for which the style is named. Many Makonde and other East Africans leave offerings for Shetani sculptures, believing them to be possessed by ancestral spirits. Most elaborate of all are the naturalistic Ujamaa sculptures, which depict many interlocking figures and relate to the collective social policy of Ujamaa fostered by the late President Nyerere. Also known as People Poles or Trees of Life, these statues sometimes incorporate several generations of the carver's family, rising in circular tiers to be up to 2m high. A newer style called Mawingu – the Swahili word for clouds – combines human figures with abstract shapes to represent intellectual or philosophical themes. Today, the finest examples of the genre fetch prices in excess of US$5,000 from international collectors.

The Makonde traditionally shape their creations exclusively from *Dalbergia Melanoxylon*, a hardwood tree known locally as *mpingo* and in English as African blackwood or (misleadingly) African ebony. The carver – always male – will first saw a block of wood to the required size, then create a rough outline by hacking away excess wood with an instrument called an adze. The carving is all done freehand, with hammers, chisels and rasps used to carve the fine detail, before the final sculpture is sanded and brushed for smoothness. A large Ujamaa sculpture can take several months to complete, with some of the carving – appropriately – being undertaken communally. Traditionally, the craft was more or less hereditary, with sons being apprenticed to their fathers from a young age, and different families tending to work specific subjects related to their own traditions.

for the Swahili word meaning 'bead', is an eco-friendly handicraft workshop founded in 2007 and now providing employment to more than 40 disabled craftsmen. It sells a variety of high quality handmade items combining colourful local beadwork and fabrics with recycled materials such as glass and aluminium.

Altogether different in atmosphere is **Mount Meru Craft & Curio Market** – more informally known as the Maasai Market – on Fire Road about 200m south of the Clock Tower [113 C5]. Here, some 50-plus stalls sell Maasai beadwork, Tingatinga and other local paintings, batiks, jewellery and pretty much any other ethno-artefact you might be interested in. Prices are lower than the Cultural Heritage Centre, and very negotiable, but the downside is that there is a bit more hassle, generally of a friendly rather than intimidating nature.

TINGATINGA PAINTINGS

The brightly coloured paintings of fabulous creatures you might notice at craft stalls in Arusha and elsewhere in the region are Tingatinga paintings, a school of painting that is unique to Tanzania and named after its founder Edward Tingatinga. The style arose in Dar es Salaam in the early 1960s, when Tingatinga fused the vibrant and popular work of Congolese immigrants with art traditions indigenous to his Makua homeland in the Mozambique border area (a region well known to aficionados of African art as the home of Makonde carving). When Tingatinga died in 1972, the accidental victim of a police shoot-out, his commercial success had already spawned a host of imitators, and shortly after that a Tingatinga art co-operative was formed with government backing.

In the early days, Tingatinga and his followers produced fairly simple paintings featuring a large, bold and often rather surreal two-dimensional image of one or another African creature on a monotone background. But as the paintings took off commercially, a greater variety of colours came into play, and a trend developed towards the more complex canvases you see today. Modern Tingatinga paintings typically depict a menagerie of stylised and imaginary birds, fish and mammals against a backdrop of natural features such as Kilimanjaro or an abstract panel of dots and whorls. An offshoot style, reputedly initiated by Tingatinga himself, can be seen in the larger, even more detailed canvases that depict a sequence of village or city scenes so busy you could look at them for an hour and still see something fresh.

Tingatinga painters have no pretensions to producing high art. On the contrary, the style has been commercially driven since its inception: even the largest canvases are produced over a matter of days and most painters work limited variations around favourite subjects. It would be missing the point altogether to talk of Tingatinga as traditional African art. With its bold, bright images – tending towards the anthropomorphic, often subtly humorous, always accessible and evocative – Tingatinga might more appropriately be tagged Africa's answer to Pop Art.

Labels aside, souvenir hunters will find Tingatinga paintings to be a lively, original and surprisingly affordable alternative to the identikit wooden animal carvings that are sold throughout East Africa (and, one suspects, left to gather dust in cupboards all over Europe). Take home a Tingatinga panel, and you'll have a quirky but enduring memento of your African trip, something to hang on your wall and derive pleasure from for years to come.

Shopping malls and supermarkets The biggest and best shopping mall, situated at the west end of Sokoine Road, is the **TFA Centre** [114 A7], also often referred to as the Shoprite Centre after the eponymous supermarket. The largest shop there is the **Shoprite Supermarket** (⤳ *027 254 4516; www.shoprite.co.za;* ⏱ *09.00–21.00 Mon–Fri, 09.00–17.00 Sat, 09.00–13.00 Sun*) a warehouse-sized representative of a major South African chain that stocks a huge range of imported and local goods (including South African wines at a third of the price charged by the hotels) as well as fresh meat, bread and vegetable, making it an excellent place to stock up with whatever goodies you need before you head out on safari. Also in the TFA Centre are half-a-dozen upmarket restaurants and coffee shops (see *Where to eat*, page 112), several safari outfitters and a good selection of other clothing and craft shops, hairdressers, banks with ATMs, internet cafés, etc. The more out-of-town **Njiro Mall** [105 F7], 4km south of the Impala Hotel, also boasts several eateries, and Arusha's best cinema (see page 117), as well as the excellent Village Supermarket, but the selection of shops is limited.

OTHER PRACTICALITIES

BANKS, ATMS AND FOREIGN EXCHANGE Various private and bank-related bureaux de change are dotted all around Arusha, and it is worth shopping around to find the best rate for US dollars cash. Many bureaux de change won't accept less widely used international currencies or travellers' cheques, but the **National Bank of Commerce** on Sokoine Road [113 A7] will, as will the bureau de change at the Impala Hotel [105 G7]. Whatever else you do, don't change money on the streets of Arusha, as you are sure to be ripped off. If you are desperate for local currency outside banking hours, **Foreigners Bureau de Change** on Goliondoi Road [113 A4] is open seven days a week from 07.00 to 18.30, and later than that you will probably have to ask a safari company or hotel to help you out with a small transaction.

There are now numerous ATMs where up to US$300 in local currency can be drawn against selected credit and debit cards. For Visa card holders, the ATMs at the **Standard Chartered Bank** on Goliondoi Road [113 A6] and the **Barclays Bank** on Serengeti Road [105 F7] offer a 24-hour withdrawal service, and there are also ATMs offering similar facilities in the **Njiro Mall** [105 F7] and **TFA Centre** [114 A7] on Sokoine Road. The ATMs at the two branches of the **Exim Bank**, one on the junction of Goliondoi and Sokoine Road [113 B6] and the other in the TFA Centre, also accept MasterCard. Travellers heading off on safari should be aware that Arusha will offer the first and last chance to reliably draw money against a credit card. ATM facilities are available in Mto wa Mbo and Karatu, but these cannot be relied upon 100%.

MEDIA AND COMMUNICATIONS
Internet and email There are numerous internet cafés dotted all over Arusha, generally asking less than US$1 per hour. One of the best is the **Telecom-run internet café** on the first floor of the post office building on Boma Road [113 C5]. Also good are the **Cybernet Centre** on India Road [113 B5] and the **Hot Bread Shop** on the east end of Sokoine Road [113 B6]. Many hotels also offer internet access, often for free to hotel residents. The **Damascus Restaurant** on Simeon Road offers free Wi-Fi to clients who eat or drink there.

Newspapers A selection of local newspapers is available on the day of publication, as is the *Nation*, a Kenyan paper which is generally stronger on international news. You won't need to look for these newspapers, because the vendors who sell them will find you quickly enough. The excellent weekly *East African* is available at several newspaper kiosks. The American weeklies *Time* and *Newsweek* are widely available in Arusha.

Post and telephone The main **post office** is on Boma Road facing the Clock Tower [113 C5]. The **telecommunications centre** further along Boma Road [113 C3] is a good place to make international phone calls and send faxes. If you want to buy a local SIM card for your mobile phone, the best and cheapest place to do so is the **Vodacom service centre** at the junction of Sokoine and Goliondoi roads [113 A6] – it should cost around Tsh300, though you'll need to buy some pay-as-you-go airtime (*Tsh500–50,000*) to activate it.

MEDICAL The **Arusha Lutheran Medical Centre** (ALMC) off Colonel Middleton Road ([105 F6] ✆ *027 254 8030/5118/5119; www.almc.habari.co.tz*) is generally regarded to be the best in Arusha. For other recommendations, consult your hotel reception or safari company.

SWIMMING The swimming pools at the **Ilboru Lodge** [104 D1] and **Impala Hotel** [105 G7] are open to non-residents for a small daily fee.

WHAT TO SEE AND DO

MUSEUMS Arusha is better known as a base for safaris and other excursions than as a sightseeing destination in its own right. However, a trio of museums dot central Arusha, none of which could be described as a 'must see', but all worth a passing look if you're in the area.

National Natural History Museum [113 C2] (*Boma Rd;* ✆ *027 250 7540; e nnmh@habari.co.tz;* ⏰ *09.00–18.00 daily; entrance US$5 non-resident adult, US$2 foreign student*) Housed in the old German Boma, this might more accurately be re-named the Archaeological or Palaeontological Museum. The limited displays – you can walk around the museum in one minute – include a selection of animal and hominid fossils unearthed at Olduvai and Laetoli in the Ngorongoro Conservation Area, as well as life-size models of *Australopithecus* hunter-gatherers at play.

Arusha Declaration Museum [115 G4] (*Uhuru Monument Circle;* ⏰ *08.30– 17.30; entrance US$5*) Dedicated primarily to 20th-century developments in Tanzania, this has some interesting displays on the colonial and post-independence Nyerere era. It also contains a few decent ethnographic displays, but seems overpriced for what it is.

The Tanzanite Experience [113 B4] (*3rd Floor, Blue Plaza Bldg, India Rd;* ✆ *027 250 5101; e info@tanzaniteexperience.com; www.tanzaniteexperience.com;* ⏰ *08.00–17.00 Mon–Fri, 09.00–13.00 Sat; no entrance fee*) Operated by TanzaniteOne, the world's largest tanzanite mining company, this modern museum provides a fascinating overview of the discovery and extraction of this exquisite blue gem, which occurs in Tanzania only. Imaginative multi-media displays and enthusiastic staff are complemented by many examples of rough and cut tanzanite (and other striking local rocks). There is also the chance to purchase certified gemstones direct from source, along with tanzanite and diamond jewellery.

Warm Heart Art Gallery [104 D3] (m *0754 672256;* e *what@warmheartart.com;* *www.warmheartart.com;* ⏰ *10.00–20.00 daily; no entrance fee*) This excellent little art gallery is well worth a look, especially if you're planning on grabbing lunch or a coffee at the adjacent Arusha Masai Cafe. The building also houses the Rock Art Conservation Centre (*www.racctz.org*), an NGO that is primarily dedicated to the preservation of the Kondoa Rock Art World Heritage Site, (see page 231), but that also offers weekend tours to the region, and is an excellent source of information for independent travellers wanting to see the rock art.

CULTURAL TOURS A number of cultural tourism programmes have been implemented around Arusha with the assistance of the Dutch agency SNV. Any one of these programmes makes for an excellent half- or full-day trip out of Arusha, offering tourists the opportunity to experience something of rural Africa away from the slick lodges and main safari circuit. You can ask your safari company to tag a visit to one of the cultural programmes onto your main safari, or can arrange a standalone day trip once you arrive in Arusha. Several of the programmes also offer the opportunity to spend a night in a village, although it should be stressed that accommodation of this sort is not up to accepted tourist-class standards. Of the various programmes, the one at Longido can easily be visited on public transport, but the rest are only realistically visited in a private vehicle. The TTB office on Boma Road and the Cultural Tourism Office in the Old Boma (see page 102), stock useful pamphlets about all the cultural programmes, and can advise you about current costs and accessibility.

Mkuru Camel Safari (m *0784 724498/472475;* e *info@mkurucamelsafari. com; www.mkurucamelsafari.com*) This most successful of the cultural tourism programmes around Arusha is based at Mkuru at the northern base of Mount Meru. It's a very well organised set-up, offering a selection of facilities and activities that seems to increase with every passing year, although these days it's pitched more at the mid-range market than budget travellers. The main attraction here is organised camelback trips, which range in duration from day outings and overnight trips into the wildlife-rich plains towards Longido to a week-long trek to Ol Doinyo Lengai and Lake Natron. In addition to camel rides, it offers a variety of day walks – a bird walk on the plain, a hike to the top of Ol Doinyo Landare, cultural visits to local healers and women's craft groups – for around US$20 per person. All activities are slightly cheaper as group sizes increase.

Activities run out of the down-to-earth and reasonably priced Mkuru Camel Camp, which is situated near the pyramidal Ol Doinyo Landare (literally 'Mountain of Goats') and Ngare Nanyuki (on the northern border of Arusha National Park) and it offers great views of Kilimanjaro and Meru. This solar-powered camp has comfortable accommodation in furnished standing tents, simple ground tents with beds, sleeping bags, sheets and towels – or you can pitch your own tent.

Longido (☎ *027 253 9209;* m *0787 855185;* e *touryman1@yahoo.com; www. tanzaniaculturaltourism.com*) This cultural tourism project run out of the overgrown village of Longido is one of the most accessible in the region for independent travellers, and it is an excellent place to visit for those who want to spend time among the Maasai. The original programme co-ordinator was a local Maasai who studied abroad as a sociologist before he was paralysed in a serious accident, and his successor can tell you anything you want to know about Maasai culture. Three different walking modules are on offer to tourists. On all modules, you can expect to see a variety of birds (including several colourful finches and barbets), and there is a fair amount of large game left in the area, notably gerenuk, lesser kudu, giraffe, Thomson's gazelle and black-backed jackal. It is worth trying to be in Longido on Wednesday, when a hectic cattle market is held on the outskirts of the village.

The first module is a half-day bird walk through the Maasai Plains, which also includes a visit to a rural Maasai *boma* (homestead), and a meal cooked by the local women's group. Then there is a full-day tour that follows the same route as the bird walk, before climbing to the top of the 2,637m Longido Mountain, an ascent of roughly 400m, offering views to Mount Meru and Kilimanjaro on a clear day, as well as over the Maasai Plains to Kenya. The two-day module follows the same route as the one-day walk, but involves camping out overnight in the green Kimokouwa Valley, before visiting a dense rainforest that still harbours a number of buffaloes as well as the usual birds and monkeys.

Longido straddles the main Namanga road roughly 100km from Arusha, so any of the regular minibuses and taxis that run between Arusha and Namanga can drop you there – these usually leave Arusha from the north end of the bus station opposite the stadium. The tourist project maintains a neat and inexpensive guesthouse about 100m from the main road, or you can arrange to pitch a tent at a Maasai boma for a small fee. A limited selection of cheap Tanzanian fare is available from one or two small restaurants that lie along the main road, and a couple of local bars (with pool table) serve cold beers and soft drinks.

Ng'iresi Village (m *0754 476079/0754 320966*; e *info@arusha-ngiresi.com; www. arusha-ngiresi.com*) Set on the slopes of Mount Meru some 7km from Arusha town, this cultural tourism programme based in the traditional Wa-Arusha village of Ng'iresi offers many insights into the local culture and agricultural practices. There are also some lovely walks in the surrounding Mount Meru foothills, an area characterised by fast-flowing streams, waterfalls and remnant forest patches. From Ng'iresi, it is possible to walk to Lekimana Hill, from where there are good views over the Maasai Steppes and on a clear day to Kilimanjaro. Another walk takes you to Kivesi Hill, an extinct volcano whose forested slopes support a variety of birds and small mammals.

Three different 'modules' are available at Ng'iresi, all inclusive of meals prepared by the Juhudu Women's Group and guided activities. There is no public transport to Ng'iresi, so you must either set up a visit through a safari company or make arrangements with a private vehicle.

Mulala Village (m *0784 378951/0784 747433*; e *agapetourism@yahoo.com; www.tanzaniaculturaltourism.com*). This is another cultural tourism programme situated in a village on the footslopes of Mount Meru. Mulala lies at an altitude of 1,450m, some 30km from Arusha, in a fertile agricultural area, which produces coffee, bananas and other fruit and vegetables. Several short walks can be undertaken in the surrounding hills, including one to the forested Marisha River, home to a variety of birds and primates, and to Mazungu Lake, where it is said that a *mzungu* was once lured to his death by a demon. Another local place of interest is Mama Anna's dairy, which supplies cheese to several upmarket hotels in Arusha. The tourist programme here is run in conjunction with the Agape Women's Group, which provides most of the guides as well as snacks and camping facilities.

Monduli Juu (m *0786 799688/0787 756299*; e *mpoyoni@yahoo.com, olejackson@ yahoo.com; www.monduli-juu.org*) The settlement of Monduli Juu (Upper Monduli) is situated some 50km west of Arusha in the Monduli Hills, a forested range that rises from the Rift Valley floor to an altitude of 2,660m, offering some superb views to other larger mountains such as Kilimanjaro, Meru and Ol Doinyo Lengai. Monduli Juu consists of a cluster of four Maasai villages, namely Emairete, Enguiki,

ALL THAT GLITTERS ...

In 1962, local legend tells, a Maasai cattle herder called Ali Juyawatu was walking through the Mererani Hills after a bush fire, and noticed some unusual blue crystals lying on the ground. Ali picked up the beautiful stones and took them to the nearby town of Arusha, from where they somehow made their way to the New York gemstone dealer Tiffany & Co, which had never seen anything like them before. In 1967, Tiffany launched the newly discovered gem on the market, naming it tanzanite in honour of its country of origin.

Tanzanite is by any standards a remarkable stone. A copper brown variety of zoisite, it is rather dull in its natural condition, but responds to gentle heating, transforming into a richly saturated dark-blue gem, with purple and violet undertones that have been compared among other things to the eyes of Elizabeth Taylor! Tanzanite comes only from Tanzania's Mererani Hills – rumours of a second deposit in Usangi, 75km from Arusha, have yet to be confirmed – and it is a thousand times rarer than diamonds. Despite its upstart status in the jewellery world, tanzanite has rocketed in popularity since its discovery. By 1997, 30 years after its launch, it had become the second most popular gemstone in the North American market, second to sapphires and ahead of rubies and emeralds, generating an annual trade worth US$300 million in the USA alone.

Remarkable, too, is the degree of controversy that the tanzanite trade has attracted in recent years. In the late 1990s, the Tanzanian government, comparing international tanzanite trade figures against their documented exports, realised that as much as 90% of the tanzanite sold in the USA was being smuggled out of Tanzania, resulting in a huge loss of potential government revenue in taxes and royalties. The ease with which the stones were being smuggled was clearly linked to the unregulated nature of the workings at Mererani, which consisted of more than 300 small claims operating in what has been described by more than one observer as a Wild West atmosphere. For the small claim holders, rather than distributing the stones they collected through legitimate sources, it was more profitable – and considerably more straightforward – to sell them for cash to illicit cross-border traders.

The lack of regulations at Mererani, or at least the lack of a body to enforce what regulations do exist, is also largely to blame for a series of tragedies that has dogged the workings in recent years. The greatest single catastrophe occurred during the El Niño rains of 1998, when one of the shafts at Block D flooded and at least 100 miners drowned. But it has been estimated that a similar number of miners died underground subsequent to this mass tragedy, as a result of suffocation, inept dynamite blasting, or periodic outbreaks of violent fighting over disputed claims. Aside from such incidents, it has long been rumoured that miners who are down on their luck will kidnap and sacrifice children from neighbouring villages, in the hope it will bring them good fortune and prosperity.

Eluwai and Mfereji, the first of which is set alongside a spectacular crater that betrays the mountains' volcanic origins and is still held sacred by locals.

The cultural programme at Monduli Juu offers several programmes, ranging from a few hours to several days in duration. For nature lovers, a recommended option is the hike to Monduli Peak, passing through patches of montane forest that support a large variety of monkeys, antelope, birds and butterflies as well as

In 1999, the Tanzanian government put out to tender a lease on Block C, the largest of the four mining blocks, accounting for about 75% of the known tanzanite deposit. The rights were acquired by a South African company – with a 25% Tanzanian stake – called African Gem Resources (AFGEM), which reputedly pumped US$20 million into establishing the mine with the intention of going online in early 2000. This goal proved to be highly optimistic, as local miners and stakeholders, understandably hostile to the corporate intrusion on their turf, not to mention the threat it posed to the illicit tanzanite trade, attempted to disrupt the new project and persuade AFGEM to withdraw.

The long-simmering tensions erupted in April 2001, when a bomb was set off in the new mining plant, killing nobody, but causing large-scale material damage nonetheless. Later in the same month, AFGEM security guards opened fire on a group of 300 irate miners who had invaded the plant, killing one trespasser and causing serious injury to nine. When the Minister for Energy and Minerals visited the scene a few days later, the trespassers claimed to have been protesting against AFGEM's alleged complicity in the alleged death of 20 miners who were buried alive. AFGEM refuted the claims as pure fabrication, part of a smear campaign designed to discredit them and protect the illicit tanzanite trade. The result of the official investigation into the incident has yet to be released.

The tanzanite plot took a new and wholly unexpected twist in late December 2001, when press reports linked four of the men convicted on charges relating to the 1998 US embassy bombings in Nairobi and Dar es Salaam with the illicit tanzanite trade. Amid wild speculation that the underground tanzanite trade was funding Osama bin Laden and his al-Qaeda organisation, three major US jewellery dealers announced a total boycott on the purchase or sale of the gem. Among them, ironically, was the retailer that had first placed it in the spotlight back in 1967. Tiffany & Co publicly conceded a lack of hard evidence supporting the bin Laden link, but announced that it 'troubled' them regardless. By the end of January 2002, the price of tanzanite dropped to a third of its 2001 level.

The Tanzanian government elected to suspend operations at Mererani until the claims were fully investigated. At a Tucson trade fair in February 2002, the American Gem Trade Association and the Tanzanian Minister of Energy and Minerals signed a protocol that placed several significant new controls on local access to the tanzanite mines. After the protocol was signed, the US State Department praised Tanzania for having 'done everything in its power to assist us in the war against terrorism' and declared it had 'seen no evidence that … any terrorist group is currently using tanzanite sales to finance its efforts or launder money'. Sales of the gem have since boomed, and many specialist stores line the streets of Arusha, while the opening of a museum called the Tanzanite Experience (see page 121) has raised the gem's profile higher. Prices remain volatile, ranging from US$100 to US$1,000 per carat, depending greatly on the size and quality of the individual gemstone.

relict populations of elephant and buffalo – an armed ranger is mandatory. Other attractions include visits to a traditional healer, Naramatu bead factory and general cultural programmes including a Maasai boma visit and a meat market.

A few local families in Monduli Juu offer camping sites. Meals – traditional or Western, as you like – can be prepared with a bit of notice.

AROUND ARUSHA

THE MOSHI ROAD With the exception of Lake Duluti and Arusha National Park, the Moshi road running eastward from Arusha boasts no tourist attractions of note. It's an attractive area, however – lush, fertile and bisected by numerous forest-fringed streams that rise on Mount Meru – and many tourists prefer to stay here instead of in the city. Certainly there is no shortage of accommodation along the stretch of road between Arusha and the small town of Usa River (near the turn-off for Arusha National Park), most of it in the mid-range to upmarket category, and set in large grounds with views to Mount Meru and Kilimanjaro.

Towards Lake Duluti The road between Arusha and Lake Duluti gives access to some of the most popular lodges in the Arusha area, including Moivaro, Machweo and Onsea House, and Kigongoni Lodge.

 Where to stay

Exclusive

⌂ **Machweo & Onsea House** (9 & 4 rooms) 📞 0784 833207; e info@onseahouse.com; www.onseahouse.com, www.machweo.com. These attractive & intimate boutique hotels, under the same Belgian owner-manager, are situated alongside each other on the slopes of Namasi Hill less than 10 mins' drive from central Arusha on the right side of the Moshi Road. The older & smaller Onsea House consists of just 4 rooms with funky but understated African décor, 2 of

which can be rented out as a separate house, while the offshoot Machweo offers the choice of 3 honeymoon suites or 6 semi-detached cottage suites decorated in simple classic contemporary style. All rooms have a minibar, walk-in netting, safe & flatscreen DSTV. There are 2 swimming pools on the combined property, as well as a highly rated wellness centre & spa, a games room with pool table, & a walking trail on the forested bird-rich hill behind the property. The complex is also home to arguably the top restaurant in Arusha, managed by the same Michelin trained Belgian chef since it opened in 2006, serving innovative European cuisine with an African twist (see *Where to eat*, below). *US$190/225 sgl/dbl B&B, or US$275/395 FB low season; US$255/310 B&B & US$340/430 FB high season.*

Upmarket

🏠 **Moivaro Coffee Plantation Lodge** (20 rooms) ☎ 027 250 6315; m 0754 324193; e marketing@moivaro.com; www.moivaro.com. This elegantly rustic lodge, set on a 16ha coffee estate 7km from central Arusha & 1.5km from the Moshi road, has been consistently popular since it opened in the late 1990s. The self-contained bungalows are set in a circular arrangement around a clean swimming pool & flowering lawns. The main dining & reception building has a large patio facing Mount Meru. Facilities include walking & jogging paths, internet & a massage room. *US$185/250 sgl/dbl B&B, or US$230/340 FB. Discounts Mar–Jun & Sep–mid Dec.*

🏠 **Kigongoni Lodge** (20 rooms) ☎ 027 255 3087; e assistant.managers@kigongoni.net; www.kigongoni.net. Set on a forested hilltop in a 70ha coffee plantation about 10km from Arusha along the Moshi road, this superb lodge consists of 20 large, airy & organic en-suite chalets, all of which come with a private balcony, 2 dbl beds with netting, hot shower & bath, & log fire. The countrified atmosphere of the accommodation is complemented by superb food & a good wine list, while other attractions include a swimming pool & plenty of monkeys & birds in the grounds. A significant portion of the profits is used to support Sibusiso, a home for disabled Tanzanian children situated on the same coffee estate. *US$172/244 sgl/dbl B&B, or US$209/318 FB. Discounts Mar–Jun & Sep–mid Dec.*

Moderate

🏠 **Songota Falls Lodge** (5 rooms) m 0754 095576; e info@songotafallslodge.com; www.songotafallslodge.com. Situated along a rough 1.5km dirt road that runs northward from the Moshi road, Songota Lodge consists of a few unfussy but clean en-suite bungalows overlooking the large green valley below the Songota Waterfall – to which guided walks are offered when underfoot conditions are reasonably dry. It's a refreshingly unpretentious set-up, owned & managed by a friendly Tanzanian woman with years of experience in the hotel trade, & likely to expand its facilities in due course, but as things stand it feels slightly overpriced for what you get. *US$60/70/96 sgl/dbl/tpl B&B, or US$80/108/165 FB.*

✗ Where to eat

✗ **Machweo Fine Dining** m 0787 112498; www.machweo.com; ⊕ lunch & dinner daily. Widely regarded as offering the top fine dining experience in Tanzania, this Belgian restaurant serves a different set menu every night, usually comprising 3 *amuses-bouche*, as well as soup, starter, main & dessert, optionally accompanied by wines selected to match the dishes. Bookings are mandatory for those not staying at the hotel.

Lake Duluti The small but attractive Lake Duluti lies roughly 10km east of Arusha and only 2km from the Moshi road near the busy little market town of Tenguru. Some 62ha in extent, 15m deep and fed by subterranean springs, the lake is nestled within an extinct volcanic crater whose formation was linked to that of Mount Meru. Although much of the surrounding area is cultivated and settled, the steep walls of the crater support a fringing gallery of riparian forest, while the lake itself is lined with beds of papyrus. The lake is of particular interest to birdwatchers, as it supports numerous diving and shore birds, as well as seven kingfisher species and breeding colonies of various weavers. An added attraction is the good views of Mount Meru and Kilimanjaro from the lakeshore on clear days.

The relatively developed northern lakeshore is open to the public, but the southern, eastern and western shores are now protected in the 19ha **Lake Duluti Forest Reserve** (☎ 027 250 9522; *entrance US$30 pp inc guided walk*). A 60- to 90-minute walking trail has been established in the reserve, offering the opportunity to see some of the 50-odd tree species, wildlife such as blue monkey, vervet monkey

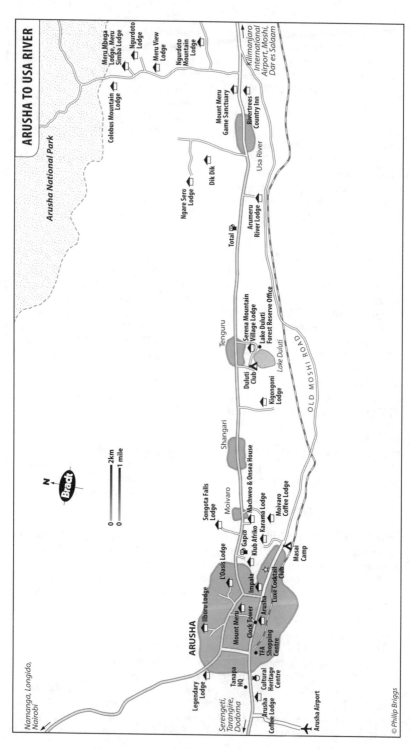

ARUSHA TO USA RIVER

Arusha National Park

Meru Mbega Lodge, Meru Simba Lodge
Ngurdoto Lodge
Meru View Lodge
Ngurdoto Mountain Lodge
Colobus Mountain Lodge

Mount Meru Game Sanctuary
Rivertrees Country Inn
Usa River

Dik Dik

Ngare Sero Lodge

Arumeru River Lodge

Total

Kilimanjaro International Airport, Moshi, Dar es Salaam

Tenguru

Serena Mountain Village Lodge
Lake Duluti Forest Reserve Office
Duluti Club
Kigongoni Lodge
Lake Duluti

OLD MOSHI ROAD

Shangari

Moivaro

Songota Falls Lodge
Machweo & Onsea House
Gapco
Klub Afriko
Karama Lodge
Moivaro Coffee Lodge
Masai Camp

N

0   2km
0   1 mile

Brandt

ARUSHA

Ilboru Lodge
L'Oasis Lodge
Impala
Mount Meru
Clock Tower
Arusha
Luxe Cocktail Club
TFA Shopping Centre

Legendary Lodge
Tanapa HQ
Cultural Heritage Centre
Arusha Coffee Lodge
Arusha Airport

Namanga, Longido, Nairobi

Serengeti, Tarangire, Dodoma

© Philip Briggs

128

and monitor lizard, and an interesting selection of forest birds including Hartlaub's turaco, crowned and silvery-cheeked hornbills, Narina trogon, brown-breasted and white-eared barbets, Africa broadbill, little greenbul, black-throated wattle-eye, paradise flycatcher, white-starred robin and black-breasted apalis. Canoe trips on the crater lake are operated by Wayo Africa (see *Safari operators*, page 107) out of the nearby Serena Mountain Village Lodge.

Getting there and away Lake Duluti lies about 2km south of the Arusha–Moshi road, and the side roads to Serena Mountain Village Lodge and the Duluti Club, both on the lakeshore, are signposted. On public transport, any vehicle heading from Arusha towards Moshi can drop you at the junction – hop off when you see a large carved wooden giraffe to your left coming from Arusha. The turn-off to Duluti Club is signposted to the right opposite this statue, and the turn-off to Mountain Village Lodge is another 200m or so towards Moshi. It's about 20 minutes' walk from the main road to the campsite. Entrance to the Lake Duluti Forest Reserve, on foot only, is via a manned entrance gate that lies along a rough road 1km east of the Duluti Club and 500m south of Serena Mountain Village Lodge.

 ### Where to stay
Upmarket
 Serena Mountain Village Lodge (42 rooms) ☏027 255 3313; **e** reservations@ serenahotels.com; www.serenahotels.com. With expansive green lawns verging on the northern shore of the gorgeous Lake Duluti, & fabulous views across to Mount Meru & Kilimanjaro, Mountain Village Lodge is easily one of the most attractive upmarket lodges in the greater Arusha area. The main building is a converted thatched farmhouse dating to the colonial era, & accommodation is in comfortable self-contained chalets. Subsequent to the lodge being taken over by the excellent Serena chain, the quality of service, meals & décor has been upgraded to match the atmospheric setting. *US$225/355 sgl/ dbl B&B. Low season discounts.*

Camping
Ⓐ Duluti Club **m** 0754 373977. The lovely & surprisingly little-used campsite at the Duluti Club is slightly rundown, but there's an ablution block with hot showers & the lakeshore setting is fabulous. Facilities include a cafeteria serving basic & reasonably priced meals & chilled drinks. *Camping US$6 pp.*

Usa River
The small and rather amorphous village of Usa River flanks the Moshi road about 20km east of Arusha near the turn-off to Arusha National Park. It is of interest to tourists primarily for a cluster of upmarket hotels, several of which rank as among the most attractive in the Arusha area, as well as being conveniently located for day safaris into the national park. If you're staying in the area, there are several good boutiques and adequate eateries in and around the Usa Mall, which also has an internet café and banking facilities.

Where to stay
Exclusive
Ngare Sero Lodge (15 rooms) **m** 0732 978931; **e** reservations@ngare-sero-lodge.com; www.ngare-sero-lodge.com. One of the most attractive places to stay anywhere near Arusha, particularly for those who enjoy outdoor pursuits, is this small, family-owned country-style lodge set on a forested 25ha estate dating to the German colonial era. As is implicit in the name Ngare Sero (Maasai for 'dappled water'), the estate is fed by several streams flowing from the higher slopes of Mount Meru, & a crystal clear reservoir below the lodge is stocked with barbel & trout, while also driving an electricity turbine. The forest & lake support an incredibly varied selection of birds & butterflies, while blue monkey & black-&-white colobus are both resident on the grounds. A superb range of activities & facilities includes horseback excursions, coffee

farm tours, boat rides on the lake, cultural visits to a nearby village, a swimming pool, internet access & massages in an old watchtower that presumably dates to WWI. The standard rooms, although set out in a rather tight row opposite the main building, are spacious & attractively decorated with Zanzibar-style king-size or twin beds and tiled en-suite bathrooms. Meals are taken in the original century-old farmhouse, which is furnished & decorated in period style. *US$250/340 sgl/dbl garden room; US$305/450 sgl/dbl suite; all rates FB. Substantial discounts for stays of 3 nights or longer.*

🏠 **Rivertrees Country Inn** (22 rooms) m 0713 339873; e info@rivertrees.com; www.rivertrees. com. Situated 300m from the main Moshi road facing the Mount Meru Game Sanctuary, this highly regarded lodge is set in magnificently shady green gardens on an old family estate offering great views of Mount Meru & Kilimanjaro, & bounded by a forest-fringed stretch of the Usa River. Centred on a rambling old farmhouse, the inn offers comfortable accommodation in spacious en-suite rooms with large wooden 4-poster beds, as well as a more exclusive river cottage & a stunning river house with 2 dbl bedrooms. Facilities include free internet access, a swimming pool & a highly rated restaurant serving hearty country food, while activities on offer include massage services, village tours, mountain biking & bird walks. *From US$198/243 sgl/dbl standard rooms B&B; from US$706 river house for up to 4 people.*

🏠 **Mount Meru Game Sanctuary** (17 rooms) ☎ 027 255 3643; e reservations@intimate-places. com; www.intimate-places.com. Established in 1959, about 1km east of Usa River immediately before the turn-off to Arusha National Park, this long-serving & highly recommended lodge has something of an *Out of Africa* ambience, consisting of a main stone building & a few semi-detached wooden cabins surrounded by bougainvillea-draped gardens. A large open enclosure in front of rooms 1 & 2 is stocked with various antelope, while naturally occurring blue monkeys make mischief

on the lawn, nicely setting the tone for your safari, & it is also the site of a papyrus heronry where hundreds of cattle egrets roost at dusk, alongside saddle-billed & yellow-billed storks. Rooms are stylishly decorated in classic Edwardian safari style. *US$188/264 sgl/dbl B&B, or US$226/340 FB. Huge discount in low season of Apr–Jun.*

Upmarket
🏠 **Dik Dik Hotel** (21 rooms) ☎ 027 255 3499; e dikdik@habari.co.tz; www.dikdik.ch. Owned & managed by the same Swiss family since it opened back in 1990, this attractive small hotel with comfortable, well-equipped en-suite chalets lies about 1km north of Kilala, a small village on the Arusha–Moshi road a few hundred metres west of Usa River. The thickly wooded 10ha grounds are bisected by an energetic stream, & contain a swimming pool, a small dam, a viewing tower offering clear views to Kilimanjaro, & a restaurant rated as one of the best in the Arusha area. Rooms 19 & 20 are particularly recommended for their view onto a riverine gallery forest inhabited by monkeys & numerous bird species. *US$160/220 sgl/dbl B&B, or US$210/320 FB. Low season discount Apr & May.*

🏠 **Arumeru River Lodge** (29 rooms) m 0732 979908; e info@arumerulodge.com; www. arumerulodge.com. This reasonably priced owner-managed lodge, set on a lushly vegetated 6ha plot bounded by 2 rivers, is centred upon a stunning open-sided thatch restaurant & reception area that overlooks a heated swimming pool, & serves top-notch continental cuisine. Some of the rooms face the river & associated swampland, which is home to 3 monkey species & a wide variety of birds. The tiled semi-detached standard rooms have a pleasing airy organic feel, & come with king-size bed & en-suite hot shower, & there are 6 newer junior suites with more contemporary décor & a larger bathroom. *US$140/210 sgl/dbl B&B, or US$185/300 FB standard room; or US$120/240 sgl/dbl B&B, or US$245/300 FB junior suite; rates work out to about US$35 pp cheaper out of season.*

Kilimanjaro International Airport
The only international airport serving northern Tanzania KIA, as it is often referred to locally, lies in almost total isolation roughly midway between Arusha and Moshi, making it a reasonably convenient point of access for both towns but absolutely ideal for neither. Most visitors arrange for their safari operator or hotel to meet them, or take a taxi. Another option for a one night stay in the area is to book into KIA Lodge, 1km from the airport.

Where to stay

KIA Lodge (20 rooms) 027 255 3243; e reservations@kialodge.com; www.kialodge. com. Under the same management as Moivaro Coffee Plantation Lodge, & similar in feel & quality, KIA Lodge is recommended to visitors with unusual or inconvenient flight times, as it lies just 1km from the airport & the staff are used to monitoring flight arrivals & departures for guests. It's an attractive set-up, with a good *makuti* restaurant & hilltop swimming pool, plenty of birdlife in the surrounding acacia scrub, & great views towards Kilimanjaro (the mountain, that is), but the noise from overhead flights makes it less than ideal for an extended stay. *US$185/250 sgl/dbl self-contained bungalows B&B, or US$230/340 FB. Substantially discounted Mar–Jun & Sep–mid Dec.*

ARUSHA NATIONAL PARK Only 45 minutes from Arusha town, this is the most accessible of northern Tanzania's national parks, but – after the remote Rubondo Island and recently created Mkomazi – it is also the one that has been most neglected by the safari industry, largely because it offers limited possibilities to see the so-called Big Five. And yet, this one perceived failing aside, Arusha National Park is a quite extraordinary conservation area, and thoroughly worth a visit.

Recently extended from 137km^2 to 542km^2, the park boasts a habitat diversity that spans everything from montane rainforest to moist savanna to alpine moorland, and its prodigious fauna includes some 400 bird species and many mammals. It is one of the best places in Tanzania to see forest primates such as the black-and-white colobus and blue monkey, while common large mammals include hippo, giraffe, zebra, buffalo and waterbuck (a population evidently intermediate to the Defassa and common races). You should also come across a few pairs of Kirk's dik-dik, an attractively marked small antelope that seems to be less skittish here than it is elsewhere in the country. Around 200 elephants are more-or-less resident in the park, but they tend to stick to the forest zone of Mount Meru, so sightings are relatively infrequent except along the road towards Meru Crater. The only large predators in the park are leopard and spotted hyena.

The most prominent landmark is Mount Meru, Africa's fifth-highest massif and a popular goal for dedicated hikers. The park also has much to offer non-hikers, including a cluster of attractive lakes, a spectacular extinct volcanic crater, and stirring views of Kilimanjaro looming large on the skyline, all of which can be seen in the course of a day trip out of Arusha Town or Usa River. A highly attractive alternative to game drives is the canoe trips run by Wayo Africa (see *Safari operators*, page 107).

A detailed booklet, *Arusha National Park*, containing information on every aspect of the park's ecology and wildlife, is widely available in Arusha, as is Giovanni Tombazzi's excellent map, which has useful details of the ascent of Mount Meru on the flip. Independent visitors should note that all fees – including the park entrance fee of US$35 per person per 24 hours, as well as camping or guide fees as applicable – must be paid with a Visa or MasterCard, or one of the Tanapa Cards that can be issued at any Exim Bank. No other cards are accepted, nor are travellers' cheques or cash (see box, page 71).

Getting there and away From Arusha, follow the surfaced Moshi road for about 20km to Usa River, then take the turn-off to the left signposted for Arusha National Park. After about 8km, this dirt road enters the park boundary, where park entrance fees are paid at the new main gate. The road reaches Hatari and Momella Lodges after another 15km or so, immediately outside the northern national park boundary. This road is in fair condition and can normally be driven in an ordinary saloon car, though a 4x4 may be necessary after rain.

Any safari company can arrange an overnight trip to the park or a day trip out of Arusha. Most companies can also organise a three-day climb up Meru. If you want to organise your own climb or spend some time exploring the park on foot, you will have to find your own way there. You could hire a taxi in Arusha, but it is cheaper to catch a bus or dala-dala along the Moshi road as far as the turn-off, from where 4x4 vehicles serve as dala-dalas to the village of Ngare Nanyuki about 3km past the northern boundary of the park, passing through the main entrance gate (where fees must be paid) *en route*.

Where to stay

Exclusive

⌂ **Hatari Lodge** (8 rooms) ☎027 255 3456; e marlies@theafricanembassy.com; www.hatarilodge.com. This characterful owner-managed lodge, situated in a patch of moist yellow fever woodland just outside the Momella Gate, is named after the 1961 film *Hatari!* (danger), & stands on a property formerly owned by Hardy Kruger, one of the film's co-stars. Accommodation is in large en-suite dbl chalets with king-size beds & tall *makuti* ceilings, while the individualistic décor is an imaginative, colourful blend of a classic African bush feel & a more 'retro' look dating back to the era of the film. The common areas – littered with *Hatari!* memorabilia – overlook a swampy area inhabited by buffalo, waterbuck, crowned crane & various other water birds. The food is excellent, the service is highly personalised, & there are also stirring views across to nearby Kilimanjaro & Meru. Activities on offer include game drives & walks, canoeing on the Momella Lakes & birdwatching excursions. *Rates on application.*

Upmarket

⌂ **Ngurdoto Lodge** (9 rooms) m 0784 419232; e info@africanview.co.tz; www.ngurdoto-lodge.com. This small lodge lies in large green grounds close to the southern national park boundary. Accommodation is in spacious, comfortable & earthily decorated twin or dbl cottages with large en-suite bathrooms. There is also a large swimming pool in the garden, while the main house consists of a good restaurant & a library/TV room with free internet access. *US$220/260 sgl/dbl B&B, or 255/330 FB. Low season specials offered Apr & May.*

⌂ **Ngurdoto Mountain Lodge** (188 rooms) ☎027 254 2217/26; m 0784 556162; e ngurdoto@thengurdotomountainlodge.com; www.thengurdotomountainlodge.com. Situated on a 70ha coffee plantation alongside the road

between Usa River & Arusha National Park, this large tourist village has exceptional facilities, including a 9-hole golf course, a gym, a 600-seat conference centre, a large swimming pool, 24-hr internet access, 2 restaurants & 2 bars. Given the hotel's size, the rooms – all en suite with king-size bed, fireplace & balcony – possess a surprising amount of character, making use of wrought iron & wood to create a contemporary ethnic look. *US$135/175 sgl/dbl standard rooms B&B; cottages US$160/200; executive rooms US$220/260. Additional meals US$15 pp.*

⌂ **Meru Simba Lodge** (8 rooms) m 0788 273278; e meru-simba-lodge@baobabvillage.com; www.meru-simba-lodge.com. Under the same management as the more established Meru Mbega Lodge (see below), & right next door to it, this consists of a row of comfortable & spacious en-suite cottages with private balconies facing the park boundary – which means that quite a bit of game comes past seasonally. Good value. *US$95/140 sgl/dbl B&B, or US$135/265 FB.*

Moderate

⌂ **Meru View Lodge** (15 rooms) m 0784 419232; e info@africanview.co.tz; www.meru-view-lodge.de. This small & very friendly lodge, owned & managed by a hands-on German/English couple, lies on the eastern side of the road from Usa River, about 1km south of where the road enters the national park. The en-suite rooms, dotted around flowering gardens & a large swimming pool, are very comfortable & reasonably priced. The owners are active mountain guides with plenty of experience setting up Kilimanjaro & Meru climbs. *US$90/130 sgl/dbl B&B, or US$115/180 FB.*

⌂ **Meru Mbega Lodge** (12 rooms) m 0732 978230/0788 273278; e mbegalodge@mt-meru.com; www.mt-meru.com. Part of a chain of affordable lodges run by Mbega,

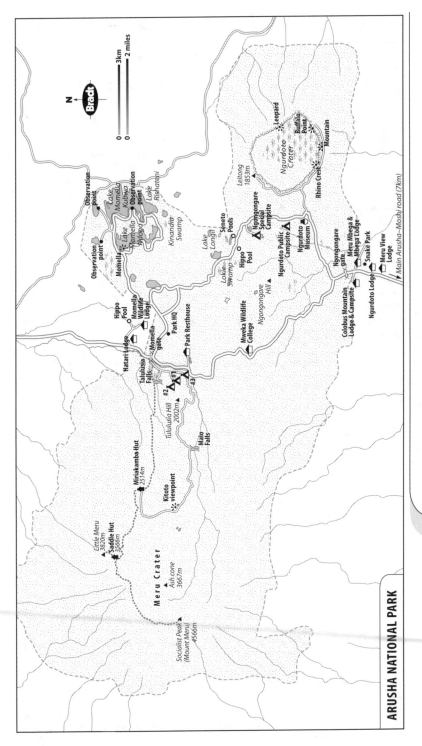

ARUSHA NATIONAL PARK

this unpretentious family-friendly set-up has comfortable en-suite accommodation with netted beds in double-storey buildings that offer views over a small pond towards Mount Meru. An attractive *makuti* structure serves as the bar & restaurant. It's a good place to arrange Meru climbs. *US$85/100/115/130 for 1/2/3/4 occupants B&B, or US$115/160/205/250 FB.*

⌂ **Kiboko Lodge** (19 rooms) m 0784 659809; e kibokolodge@watotofoundation.nl; www. kibokolodge.nl. Named for the solitary hippo ('*kiboko*') that lives in the swampy surrounds, this attractively rustic lodge bordering Arusha National Park offers great views of Mount Meru as well as excellent birding. Profits help fund the Watoto Foundation, a Dutch NGO dedicated to rehabilitating & educating former street children, & most of the staff are graduates of the school. Accommodation is in comfortable en-suite chalets reached via a wooden boardwalk over the swamp. Great value. *US$55/90 sgl/dbl B&B, or US$85/150 FB. Substantial discounts offered in low season.*

Camping

Ⓧ **National Park campsites** 3 sites lie at the foot of Tululusia Hill, 2km from Momella Gate, & 1 is situated in the forest near Ngurdoto Gate. All are scenically located close to a stream, have drop toilets & firewood. Note, however, that you may not walk between the campsites & the entrance gates without an armed ranger. *US$20 pp.*

Exploring Arusha National Park

Ngurdoto Crater Coming from Arusha, a good first goal is this fully intact 3km-wide, 400m-deep volcanic caldera, which has often been described as a mini-Ngorongoro. Tourists are not permitted to descend into the crater, but the views from the forest-fringed rim over the lush crater floor are fantastic. A large herd of buffalo is resident on the crater floor, and with binoculars it is normally possible to pick out other mammals, such as warthog, baboon and various antelope. Look out, too, for augur buzzard, Verreaux's eagle and other cliff-associated raptors soaring above the crater. The forest around the crater rim harbours many troops of black-and-white colobus and blue monkey, as well as a good variety of birds including several types of hornbill and the gorgeous Hartlaub's turaco and cinnamon-chested bee-eater.

Momella Lakes Another area worth exploring is the Momella Lakes, which lie to the north of Ngurdoto. Underground streams feed this group of shallow alkaline lakes, and each has a different mineral content and is slightly different in colour. In the late evening and early morning, it is often possible to stand at one of the viewpoints over the lakes and see Kilimanjaro on the eastern horizon and Mount Meru to the west. This is the best part of the park for large mammals such as buffalo and hippo, while a wide variety of water birds can be seen, including various herons, ducks (including the otherwise uncommon maccoa), waders, flamingos, pelicans and little grebe. It is on these lakes that Wayo Africa undertakes canoe safaris, a very tranquil way to enjoy the birdlife and scenery (see *Safari operators*, page 107).

Meru Crater Drive and Hike Best undertaken with a reasonably early start and a packed lunch, this half- to full-day outing will be a highlight of any visit to Arusha National Park, though an armed ranger (*US$20 per party*) must be collected at one of the entrance gates if you want to hike into the crater or drive further up the mountain than Kitoto. The first leg, about an hour's drive to Kitoto, climbs through a beautiful stretch of primary forest with lots of tall trees, ferns and epiphytes, a good place to look for elephant, black-and-white colobus monkeys, the raucous and very beautiful Hartlaub's turaco, and Harvey's red duiker (a small antelope associated with montane forests of the East African interior). At one point the road passes through the famous **Fig Tree Arch**, a natural formation at the base of an immense strangler fig large enough for a Land Cruiser to pass under (provided no heads are sticking out of the roof, take note).

From the car park at Kitoto, which lies at 2,500m, the guided hike through the crater takes at least two to three hours. The hike is not too demanding in terms of climbing, since the eastern wall of the crater has collapsed, but the scenery is truly spectacular, set below the 1,500m-high cliff that forms the western wall and peak of Mount Meru. Wildlife is scarce at this altitude, but you may well see klipspringers on the cliffs, as well as cliff-nesting raptors such as Verreaux's eagle, auger buzzard, and the scarce and eagerly sought lammergeyer (bearded vulture).

MBT Snake and Reptile Farm Signposted a short distance from the entrance to Arusha National Park, this long-serving private park has a good collection of reptiles and offers an intelligent guided tour. Creatures in residence include the Nile crocodile, various chameleon species and other lizards, and a fearsome collection of snakes, including spitting cobras, mambas, puff adders, Gabon viper, water snakes and some hefty pythons. It lies outside the national park so no park fees are payable but an entrance ticket inclusive of guided tour costs around US$4.

Mount Meru Arusha National Park's tallest landmark and most publicised attraction is Mount Meru, whose upper slopes and 4,566m peak lie within its boundaries. The product of the same volcanic activity that formed the Great Rift Valley 15 to 20 million years ago, Mount Meru attained a height similar to that of Kilimanjaro until 250,000 years ago, when a massive eruption tore out its eastern wall. Meru is regarded as a dormant volcano, since lava flowed from it as recently as 100 years ago, but there is no reason to suppose it will do anything dramatic in the foreseeable future. The Arusha and Meru people deify Mount Meru as a rain god, but it is unlikely that any local person actually reached the peak prior to Fritz Jaeger's pioneering ascent in 1904.

Often overlooked by tourists because it is 'only' the fifth-highest mountain in Africa, Meru is no substitute for Kilimanjaro for achievement-orientated travellers. On the other hand, those who climb both mountains invariably enjoy Meru more. Also going in its favour, Meru is less crowded than Kilimanjaro, considerably less expensive and – although steeper and almost as cold – less likely to engender the health problems associated with Kilimanjaro's greater altitude. Meru is just as interesting as Kilimanjaro from a biological point of view and, because comparatively few people climb it, you are more likely to see forest animals and plains game on the lower slopes.

Meru can technically be climbed in two days, but three days is normal, allowing time to explore Meru Crater and to look at wildlife and plants. Most people arrange a climb through a safari company in Arusha (see *Safari operators*, page 103). The going rate for a three-day hike is around US$300 per person, though this is bound to increase slightly when new park fees are implemented in July 2013. You can make direct arrangements with park officials at the gate, but won't save much money by doing this, and should check hut availability at the Tanapa office in Arusha (see page 103) in advance. The compulsory armed ranger/guide costs US$20 per day (*US$10 park fee & US$10 salary*), hut fees are US$20 per night, and there is the usual park entrance fee of US$35 per day. A rescue fee of US$20 per person covers the entire climb. The minimum cost for a three-day climb is therefore US$165 per person, with an additional US$60 to be divided between the climbers. Food and transport must be added to this, and porters cost an additional US$5 per day each.

Meru is very cold at night, and you will need to bring clothing adequate for alpine conditions. In the rainy season, mountain boots are necessary. At other times, good walking shoes will probably be adequate. The best time to climb is from October to February.

Day 1 The trail starts at Momella Gate (1,500m). From here it is a relatively gentle three-hour ascent to Miriakamba Hut (2,514m). On the way you pass through well-developed woodland where there is a good chance of seeing large animals such as giraffe. At an altitude of about 2,000m you enter the forest zone. If you leave Momella early, there will be ample time to explore Meru Crater in the afternoon. The 1,500m cliff rising to Meru Peak overlooks the crater. The 3,667m-high ash cone in the crater is an hour from Miriakamba Hut, and can be climbed.

Day 2 It is three hours to Saddle Hut (3,566m), a bit steeper than the previous day's walk. You initially pass through forest, where there is a good chance of seeing black-and-white colobus, then at about 3,000m you will enter a moorland zone similar to that on Kilimanjaro. It is not unusual to see Kilimanjaro peeking above the clouds from Saddle Hut. If you feel energetic, you can climb Little Meru (3,820m) in the afternoon. It takes about an hour each way from Saddle Hut.

Day 3 You will need to rise very early to ascend the 4,566m peak, probably at around 02.00. This ascent takes four to five hours. It is then an eight- to nine-hour walk back down the mountain to Momella Gate.

Some people prefer to climb from Miriakamba Hut to Saddle Hut and do the round trip from Saddle Hut to Meru Peak on the second day (*11 hrs altogether*), leaving only a five-hour walk to Momella on the third. Others climb all the way up to Saddle Hut on the first day (*6 hrs*), do the round trip to the peak on the second (*8 hrs*), and return to Momella from the Saddle Hut on the third (*5 hrs*).

WEST KILIMANJARO Also sometimes referred to as South Amboseli, this vaguely defined area is essentially the wedge of dry savanna country that divides the northwestern base of Kilimanjaro from the legendary Amboseli National Park in neighbouring Kenya. Some two to three hours' drive northeast of Arusha, it consists of several blocks of Maasai community land that recently amalgamated to form the 1,800km² **Enduimet Wildlife Management Area (EWMA)**, where local pastoralists live alongside the wildlife that ranges through this cross-border ecosystem. A major attraction here is the superb close-up view of Kilimanjaro, but the vast horizon is studded with several other notable peaks, including Mount Meru, Longido Mountain and Namanga Mountain (on the Kenyan side of the eponymous border crossing to Nairobi). The area also retains a genuine wilderness feel, since only one small (but utterly superb) permanent tented camp is situated within it, though it can also be explored on more rustic donkey camping safaris.

Despite being surrounded by dramatic peaks, much of West Kilimanjaro is composed of very flat land where the fine volcanic soil once formed the bed of Lake Amboseli (then twice as big as present-day Lake Manyara) before it started to dry up some 10,000 to 15,000 years ago. As the lake dried it left calcareous deposits that were later mined by the Germans in order to make the famous meerschaum tobacco pipes. The abandoned pits left behind by the open-cast mines are now an important part of the ecosystem, since they trap rainwater thereby providing drinking water for the Maasai cattle as well as the wildlife at the driest times of the year.

Ecologically, the EWMA supports a near-pristine cover of lightly wooded acacia savanna where Maasai herdsmen co-exist with a remarkable variety of wildlife, including wildebeest, zebra, eland, impala, Grant's gazelle, hartebeest and yellow baboon, as well as one of the few Tanzanian populations of the remarkable stretch-necked gerenuk. Predator densities are low, but cheetah and lion are still present and quite often observed. The area also forms part of a migration corridor used by the local elephant population – noted for its even temperament and the immense tusks of the bulls – to cross between the Kenyan part of the Amboseli ecosystem and the forested slopes of Kilimanjaro. Many impressive bulls are resident throughout the year, but numbers peak in June and July, after the rains, when the smaller family groups merge to form 100-strong herds. This also is when mating takes place, and irascible bulls follow the family herds accompanied by a fanfare of trumpeting.

Where to stay

Shu'mata Camp (5 tents) 027 255 3456; e marlies@theafricanembassy.com; www.shumatacamp.com. Under the same dynamic owner-management as Hatari Lodge, this small but luxurious camp sprawls across the eponymous hill, whose Maasai name translates as something close to 'heaven'. The camp has a lovely situation, offering panoramic views over the plains capped by Kilimanjaro to the southeast & Longido & Namanga to the northwest, marred only by the fierce winds that often blow in from the direction of Kilimanjaro. The large & stylish standing tents all have 2 dbl beds, a writing desk, colourful drapes & matting, a curvaceous adobe-style en-suite hot shower, & a private balcony. The camp has a flexible attitude to activities, which include game drives (night & day), guided walks (highly recommended) & visits to a local Maasai *boma*.

Game densities don't quite compare with the national parks & animals tend to be is a little more skittish than across the border in Kenya, but there is plenty of wildlife around & the sense of isolation & immersion in this wonderful tract of bush more than compensates. *Rates on application.*

West Kili Mobile Donkey Camp m 0784 203000; e reservations@wayoafrica.com; www.wayoafrica.com. This no-frills mobile camp, set up by request only, is aimed at active & adventurous travellers who want to combine wildlife viewing below Kilimanjaro with unforced interaction with the Maasai during the course of 2- to 4-day day hikes. The guests, guide, donkeys & other staff move together, with the entire camp being carried on donkey back, allowing the experienced armed guide to take a flexible approach to routes & camps. *US$300–350 pp all-inc.*

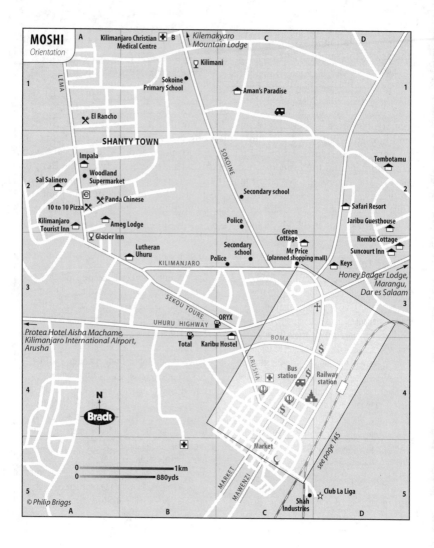

MOSHI
Orientation

Kilimanjaro Christian Medical Centre

Kilemakyaro Mountain Lodge

Kilimani

Sokoine Primary School

Aman's Paradise

El Rancho

SHANTY TOWN

Impala

Woodland Supermarket

Sal Salinero

Panda Chinese

10 to 10 Pizza

Kilimanjaro Tourist Inn

Ameg Lodge

Glacier Inn

Lutheran Uhuru

Secondary school

Police

Police

Secondary school

Green Cottage

Mr Price (planned shopping mall)

Tembotamu

Safari Resort

Jaribu Guesthouse

Rombo Cottage

Suncourt Inn

Keys

KILIMANJARO

SEKOU TOURE

UHURU HIGHWAY

ORYX

Total

Karibu Hostel

BOMA

*Protea Hotel Aisha Machame,
Kilimanjaro International Airport,
Arusha*

*Honey Badger Lodge,
Marangu,
Dar es Salaam*

SOKOINE

ARUSHA

Bus station

Railway station

Market

MARKET

MAWENZI

see page 145

Club La Liga

Shah Industries

N

Bradt

0 ————— 1km
0 ————— 880yds

© Philip Briggs

A   B   C   D

1

2

3

4

5

6

Moshi and Around

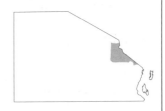

Situated at the heart of a major coffee-growing region about 80km east of Arusha, the smaller but not insubstantial town of Moshi – population 180,000 – is a likeable if intrinsically unremarkable commercial centre salvaged from anonymity by its spectacular location.

At dusk or dawn, when the great white-helmeted dome of Kilimanjaro is most likely to emerge from its customary blanket of cloud, Moshi can boast a backdrop as imposing and dramatic as any in Africa. And yet, the teasing proximity of that iconic snow-capped silhouette notwithstanding, Moshi is not the cool, breezy highland settlement you might expect it to be. Indeed, situated at an altitude of 810m, it is generally far hotter than Arusha, and not as drizzly, with a hint of stickiness in the air that recalls the coast.

Prior to the arrival of the Germans, Moshi was the capital of the area ruled by Rindi, who came to power in about 1860 and, largely through his diplomatic skills, became one of the most important chiefs in the area. By allying with the Maasai, Rindi extracted high taxes from passing caravans. He made a favourable impression on John Kirk, the British consul in Zanzibar, and signed a treaty with Carl Peters in 1885. When the first German colonial forces arrived at Kilimanjaro in 1891, Rindi assured them he ruled the whole area. At his insistence, they quelled his major rival, Sina of Kibosha.

Moshi is the Swahili word for smoke, but exactly when and why the town acquired that name is something of a mystery. Some sources suggest that it is because Moshi served as the terminus for the steam railway line from Tanga after 1911, but this seems unlikely given that the name pre-dates the arrival of the railway by many years. Equally improbable is the suggestion that the reference to smoke is due to the town lying at the base of a volcano, since Kilimanjaro hadn't displayed any significant activity for thousands of years when its present-day Bantu-speaking inhabitants arrived there.

Stirring views of Kilimanjaro aside, there is little to do or see in Moshi that you couldn't do or see in pretty much any similarly sized African market town. But it's a pleasant enough place to explore on foot, with an interesting central market area, and it comes across as far less tourist-oriented than Arusha, despite the inevitable attention paid to any visiting *mazungu* by a coterie of (mostly very affable) flycatchers offering relatively cheap 'n' dodgy Kilimanjaro climbs.

In terms of facilities, Moshi boasts an immense selection of decent budget to mid-range hotels, as well as several commendable and affordable restaurants. An ever increasing selection of smarter hotels is concentrated in the attractively leafy and somewhat misleadingly named suburb of Shantytown, a short walk north of the town centre and the Arusha Highway. There are also plenty of more upmarket options in the villages of Marangu and Machame on the Kilimanjaro footslopes, and the area can be explored from the lodges that run along the main road between Arusha and Usa River (see page 126).

GETTING THERE AND AWAY

BY AIR **Kilimanjaro International Airport** (often referred to locally as KIA, though the international code is JRO; *www.kilimanjaroairport.co.tz*) lies about 40km from Moshi town centre off the Arusha road. Several international carriers operate flights there, among them Ethiopian Airlines, Air Kenya, Rwandair Express, KLM, Air France, SAS and Turkish Airlines. It is also an important hub for domestic flights to the likes of Dar es Salaam and Zanzibar operated by Precision Air, Fastjet and other private airlines. A potential source of confusion for travellers booking their own flights is that flights to the Serengeti and other national parks on the northern safari circuit don't leave from KIA, but from **Arusha Airport** on the outskirts of Arusha.

Most tourists flying into KIA are met by their hotel or safari company. However, there are plenty of **taxis** waiting to meet all flights, and these usually charge around US$30 for a transfer to Moshi.

BY ROAD The town centre runs southward from the main surfaced road to Dar es Salaam some 80km east of Arusha. The driving time from Arusha in a **private vehicle** is about 60–90 minutes, and from Dar es Salaam at least seven hours. It is possible to drive from Nairobi (Kenya) to Moshi via Namanga and Arusha in about five hours.

Express coaches between Dar es Salaam and Moshi take roughly seven hours, with a 20-minute lunch break in Korogwe or Mombo. The best service is **Dar Express** [145 A3] (m *0754 286874*), which leaves at 11.00 daily from Boma Road opposite the Aroma Coffee House, and costs around US$18 per person. Alternatively, numerous cheaper and inferior bus services leave from the chaotic main bus station [145 C4], mostly in the morning.

There are also plenty of direct buses between Moshi and Tanga, which can drop you off at Same, Mombo, Muheza and other junction towns *en route*. In addition, a steady flow of **buses** and **dala-dalas** connects Arusha to Moshi, charging around US$3.50 and taking up to two hours, as well as to Marangu. There is no need to book ahead for these routes as vehicles will leave when they fill up, but be warned that there is a high incidence of accidents, particularly with minibuses.

Most **shuttle bus services** between Nairobi and Arusha continue on to Moshi, or start there, a total journey time of six to seven hours. The **Impala Shuttle** (\ *027 275 1786*; m *0754 293119*), based in an office on Kibo Road next to Chrisburgers [145 C2], runs two services daily, leaving at 06.30 and 11.30, while the **Riverside Shuttle** (\ *027 275 0093*) in the THB building on Boma Road [145 C3] operates one service daily, leaving at 11.30. Note that timings may change to fit in with departure and arrival times for Arusha.

RAIL All passenger trains to and from Moshi were suspended indefinitely in the 1990s and services are unlikely to resume.

TOURIST INFORMATION

There's no tourist information office in Moshi, the closest is in Arusha (see page 102). Most of the tour operators in town can provide local travel information, but this will not necessarily be impartial. A useful resource is the website www.kiliweb.com.

MOSHI CENTRE
Upmarket

Sal Salinero Hotel [138 A2] (30 rooms) 027 275 2240; m 0732 973864; e info@salsalinerohotel.com; www.salsalinerohotel.com. Set in compact palm-shaded gardens, this slightly pretentious hotel in Shantytown has large rooms with terracotta tiled floors, king-size beds, wooden ceilings, huge changing rooms & excellent facilities, including satellite TV, tea-/coffee-making facilities & a large en-suite bathroom with separate tub & shower. Unfortunately, the otherwise high quality of the accommodation is let down by the imposing décor. The gloomy public areas are similarly schizoid, with classy finishes set alongside some decidedly tacky touches. Far nicer are the restaurant & bar, with outdoor seating in a green garden. *US$90/120 sgl/dbl standard rooms B&B; suites US$180.*

Impala Hotel [138 A2] (11 rooms) 027 275 3443/4; m 0754 508503/0757 725944; e impala@kilinet.co.tz; www.impalahotel.com. Related to its namesake in Arusha, but smaller & plusher, the Impala Hotel lies on Lema Road in the leafy suburbia of Shantytown about 2km from the town centre. The large wood-panelled rooms with fan, hot bath & satellite TV are fair value, although standards vary a bit so ask to see a couple. Facilities include a swimming pool, internet café & forex bureau, & a good restaurant specialising in Indian dishes. *US$90/100 dbl/twin B&B.*

Keys Hotel [138 D3] (30 rooms) 027 275 2250/1875; m 0755 486377; e info@keys-hotel-tours.com; www.keys-hotel-tours.com. Situated in attractive suburban grounds about 1km from the Clock Tower, the Keys Hotel has offered good value for several years, & it remains, with justification, one of the most popular hotels within its price range. Visitors have the choice of a room in the double-storey main building or a *makuti*-roofed cottage in the gardens behind it. All rooms are en suite & have hot water, satellite TV & nets. There is a swimming pool & decent restaurant serving typical Tanzania hotel fare. Keys is also one of the more reliable places to organise climbs of Kilimanjaro, & while rates are a little higher than at some other places, they do include 1 night's HB accommodation at the hotel on either side of the climb. *US$78/91 sgl/dbl self-contained rooms B&B,* heavily discounted for Tanzanian residents; camping US$5 pp.

Ameg Lodge [138 A2] (20 rooms) 027 275 0175/0185; m 0744 058268; e info@ameglodge.com; www.ameglodge.com. This modern lodge, set in a 2ha plot in the leafy northern suburbs of Shantytown, is probably now the smartest hotel within the city limits, & certainly the best-value option in the mid- to upper price range. The large, airy en-suite rooms are unusually stylish, combining an ethnic feel with a contemporary touch, & they all come with digital satellite TV, fan & private balcony. Other facilities include the well-developed green gardens, a swimming pool with views of Kilimanjaro, a gym, free 24-hr Wi-Fi, & a good restaurant serving Indian & continental cuisine. *US$60/88 standard sgl/dbl B&B; US$94 deluxe dbl with walk-in dressing area; US$149 dbl suite with AC.*

Moderate

Bristol Cottages [145 B4] (17 rooms) 027 275 5083; e info@bristolcottages.com; www.bristolcottages.com. Located behind the Standard Chartered Bank close to the bus station, this neat lodge set in small, secure & peaceful manicured gardens is probably the pick in this range, as well as being very central. Accommodation is in spacious suites & cottages with AC & hot shower, satellite TV, nets, 2 beds & attractive modern décor. Facilities include secure parking, internet, email & secretarial services. The clean open-sided restaurant serves a variety of Asian & continental dishes. *US$60/70 sgl/dbl rooms in new wing B&B; suites & cottages US$65–130.*

Moshi Leopard Hotel [145 B7] (47 rooms) 027 275 0884/5134; m 0756 983311; e info@leopardhotel.com; www.leopardhotel.com. Among the most commodious options in the town centre, the multi-storey Leopard Hotel is clean, comfortable & thoroughly adequate without approaching the Kilimanjaro Crane Hotel in terms of quality or amenities. The smart, tiled en-suite rooms have AC, fan, TV, dbl or twin bed with netting, & a hot shower. *US$50/60 sgl/dbl B&B; US$80 dbl suite.*

Kilimanjaro Crane Hotel [145 C2] (30 rooms) 027 275 1114; e reservations@

kilimanjarocranehotels.com; www. kilimanjarocranehotels.com. This modern high-rise hotel has a useful central location on Kaunda Street, a block east of the Clock Tower. The en-suite rooms have large beds, DSTV, private balcony, netting, fan & hot bath. There's also a green garden, a welcome swimming pool, great views of Kilimanjaro from the rooftop, a good restaurant serving pizzas, Chinese & Indian cuisine, & a ground-floor souvenir shop stocking the most comprehensive selection of books in Moshi. Excellent value. *US$40/50 sgl/dbl B&B with fan, or US$50/60/65 sgl/dbl/tpl with AC; US$110 dbl suite.*

🏠 **Lutheran Uhuru Hotel** [138 B3] (72 rooms) 📞 027 275 4512; m 0753 037216; e reservations@uhuruhotel.org; www. uhuruhotel.org. Set in vast & pretty suburban gardens on Shantytown's Sekou Toure Road, this hostel used to be popular with tourists but the recent boom in hotel construction in & around Moshi seems to have reduced its custom, & it feels a touch overpriced for non-residents. The attached Bamboo Restaurant serves decent meals, but smoking & drinking are strictly prohibited. The hostel is about 3km out of town. *US$30/50 en-suite sgl/dbl with fan, or US$40/55 sgl/dbl with AC & TV. About 40% cheaper for residents.*

🏠 **Tembotamu** [138 D2] (4 rooms) m 0754 498690/0757 983007; e tembotamu@gmail.com; www.tembotamu.com. This highly praised & very reasonably priced B&B is owned & managed by a friendly New Zealand couple who also have a good reputation for organising reliable Kilimanjaro climbs. The spacious clean rooms are decorated in funky ethnic style, & there is a large tropical garden surrounded by local *shambas* & offering views of Kilimanjaro. Facilities include free internet access, a safe, vehicle storage, dinner by request, & free pick-up & drop-off in Moshi town on arrival & departure. Great value. *US$20 pp B&B, or US$35 pp HB.*

Budget

🏠 **Zebra Hotel** [145 C6] (72 rooms) 📞 027 275 0611; m 0754 951865; e zebrahotels@kilinet. co.tz. This smart 7-storey hotel, set around the corner from the Kindoroko, is exceptional value for money, partly because the lack of elevator access to the upper storeys has made it difficult to

market in the moderate category, where it would otherwise belong. The rooms are clean & spacious, & come with AC, fan, satellite TV & en-suite hot shower. A ground-floor restaurant is attached. *US$35/40 en-suite sgl/dbl B&B. A 40% discount for residents.*

🏠 **Kilimanjaro Tourist Inn** [138 A2] (8 rooms) 📞 027 275 3252; e kkkmarealle@yahoo.com; www. kiliweb.com/kti This converted colonial house set in a large suburban garden on Lema Road has a friendly, homely atmosphere that will appeal to travellers who avoid more institutionalised hotels. It's good value too, & all rooms come with net, fan & en-suite shower. *US$30 dbl or twin.*

🏠 **Kindoroko Hotel** [145 C6] (30 rooms) m 0715 377795/0753 377795; e reservations@ kindorokohotels.com; www.kindorokohotels. com. For some years the smartest of the cluster of popular budget hotels situated on & around Nyerere Road a couple of blocks south of the bus station, the 4-storey Kindoroko has maintained high standards & reasonable prices. The small but very clean rooms come with hot shower, fan, netting & digital satellite TV. Facilities include a lively courtyard bar, popular with both travellers & locals, a restaurant serving adequate meals, an onsite internet café & a massage centre. The hotel also arranges reliable Kilimanjaro climbs. *US$15/20/30 sgl/db/family B&B.*

🏠 **Buffalo Hotel** [145 C6] (35 rooms) 📞 027 275 0270; m 0754 018302; e buffalocompanyltd@ yahoo.com. This clean & perennially popular budget hotel is spacious with brightly tiled rooms with en-suite hot showers. The attached restaurant serves tasty & inexpensive Indian & Chinese meals. *US$16/20 sgl/dbl with fan, or US$23 exec dbl with AC; US$33 suite.*

Shoestring

🏠 **Haria Hotel** [145 B7] (8 rooms) m 0763 019395. Formerly a downmarket annexe to the Kindoroko Hotel opposite, this remains one of the best-value cheapies in Moshi, offering secure accommodation in large, clean rooms with tiled floors & nets. *US$13 for a twin using common showers, or US$17 for an en-suite twin with hot shower; dorm beds US$7 pp.*

🏠 **Hill Street Accommodation** [145 C5] (11 rooms) 📞 027 275 3919. This friendly hotel on Hill Street has a convenient location close to the bus station & several good eateries. All the rooms have tiled floors & en-suite hot showers, but no fan or netting. *US$13/20 en-suite sgl/dbl.*

🏠 **Karibu Hostel** [138 C4] (6 rooms) **m** (France) +33 (0)762 622315; **e** info@ borntolearntz.org; www.borntolearntz.org. Aimed at volunteers & backpackers, this pleasant & sociable hostel comprises a converted private house set in large secure gardens shaded by mango & banana trees on the Arusha Road, about 10 mins' walk from the town centre. There is a large terrace & a living room with TV & a selection of DVDs. All proceeds are used to fund the NGO Born To Learn (see website for details). Meals are available on request. *Dbl rooms & dorms €9 pp, or €12 B&B. Discounts for long-term volunteers.*

🏠 **Kilimanjaro Backpackers Hotel** [145 B7] (16 rooms) **m** 0715 377795; **e** reservations@ kilimanjarobackpackers.com; www. kilimanjarobackpackers.com. Situated 1 block south of the affiliated Kindoroko, the former Hotel Da Costa is perhaps the most popular cheapie in Moshi, offering accommodation in clean but no-frills tiled rooms & dormitories with net, fan & access to a common shower with a 24-hr hot-water supply. Fair value. *US$12/20 sgl/dbl B&B, or US$7 per dorm bed. Lunch & dinner an additional US$4 pp each.*

🏠 **YMCA Hostel** [145 C1] (47 rooms) 📞 027 275 1754; **e** ymcatanzania@gmail.com. On the opposite side of town to the above hotels, the YMCA is a perennial favourite with budget travellers, offering clean & secure accommodation in green grounds with a large swimming pool. *US$17/19 small sgl/dbl B&B using communal showers.*

OUT OF TOWN In addition to the two out-of-town options listed below (both excellent in their differing ways), there is plenty of accommodation in and around Marangu, the main starting point for Kilimanjaro hikes (see page 148).

Upmarket

🏠 **Protea Hotel Aisha Machame** [138 A4] (30 rooms) 📞 027 275 6941/8; **e** proteaaishareservations@satconet.com; www. proteahotels.com/protea-hotel-aishi-machame. html. Situated along the surfaced Machame road about 12km from Moshi & 27km from KIA, this smart rural hotel, managed by the South African Protea Hotels group, is easily the most upmarket option in the vicinity of Moshi. The motel-style en-suite rooms aren't exactly bursting with character but the property itself is lovely, with a large thatched dining room & bar area facing a patch of indigenous forest on the footslopes of the great mountain. The hotel specialises in Kilimanjaro climbs & has good equipment, but it also offers a variety of excursions to more sedentary guests, ranging from local cultural tours & horseback trips to day visits to Lake Chala, Arusha National Park & a short walk to the 30m-high Makoa Waterfall & bat-infested Matangalima Cave. The swimming pool is solar heated. *US$130/160 sgl/dbl B&B.*

Moderate and camping

🏠 **Honey Badger Lodge** [138 D4] (16 rooms) **m** 0787 730235; **e** info@honeybadgerlodge. com; www.honeybadgerlodge.com. Situated 6km out of town along the Dar es Salaam road, this is a friendly, owner-managed lodge that combines a rustic feel & an eco-friendly ethos with comfortable accommodation, good food & excellent facilities. It is a thoroughly refreshing low-key alternative to the budget hotels in town. It started life as a converted house & campsite set within a fenced green family compound, but has recently been expanded with the addition of a wonderful swimming pool area dotted with sunbeds & thatched gazebos, very comfortable en-suite rooms with hot showers, dormitories for large groups, & clean modern ablution blocks for campers. Traditional drumming performances & lessons can be arranged, along with traditional Chagga *ngoma* (drum) performances with songs, & acting depicting stories about marriage, harvesting time & initiation rites. Can also arrange day hikes on the Kilimanjaro foothills, as well as full Kilimanjaro climbs with experienced guides. All proceeds are channelled into the adjacent Second Chance Education Centre, which is run by the owner's mother & which provides secondary schooling to children who have slipped through the cracks of the normal education system. *US$20 pp dorm bed; US$35/40 small en-suite sgl/dbl; US$50/60 large en-suite sgl/dbl; US$10 pp camping. All rates are B&B, & about 20% cheaper in low season. A 3-course dinner costs US$10.*

Many of the places listed under *Where to stay* on pages 141–3 have restaurants. Otherwise, the majority of standalone restaurants are in the town centre but there are also several smarter options in the suburb of Shantytown to the north. The Shantytown restaurants are not accessible by public transport, so travellers staying more centrally will need to walk there and back (probably not a clever idea after dark) or arrange to be collected by taxi.

✖ **Abbasali Hot Bread Shop** [145 B3] ☏027 275 3099; ⏰ 08.00–17.00 Mon–Sat. This bakery on Boma Road sells the best bread in town, along with a selection of fresh pies, muffins & pastries.

✖ **Central Garden Café** [145 C3] ⏰ 07.00–18.30 daily. Located opposite the Clock Tower & close to the bus station, this is a convenient spot for a quick alfresco cold drink or greasy local meal. Meals & 'bitings' are in the US$2–4 range.

✖ **Chrisburgers** [145 C2] ⏰ 08.00–15.00 Mon–Sat. Cheap daytime snacks such as hamburgers, samosas & excellent fruit juice, opposite the Clock Tower.

✖ **The Coffee Shop** [145 B5] ☏027 275 2707; ✉ coffee-shop-moshi@yahoo.com; ⏰ 08.00–20.00 Mon–Fri, 08.00–18.00 Sat. Tucked away on Hill Street between the bus station & the market, this church-run institution offers an irresistible selection of homemade cakes, burgers, quiches, sandwiches, pies, snacks & light lunches, mostly at around US$2–4, served indoors or in a tranquil courtyard garden. It's also a good spot for b/fast.

✖ **Deli Chez Restaurant** [145 B5] ☏027 275 1144; m 0784 786241; ⏰ 10.00–22.00 Wed–Mon. This new deli on the corner of Hill & Market streets serves a great selection of Indian dishes, as well as a more limited selection of Chinese meals & fast food, & a sumptuous selection of milkshakes, sundaes & other desserts. No alcohol.

✖ **El Rancho** [138 A2] ☏027 275 5115; ⏰ 12.30–23.00 Tue–Sun. Top-notch Indian restaurant & bar in a converted old house & green garden close to the Impala Hotel in Shantytown. A broad selection of vegetarian mains is available for around US$5, while meat dishes are slightly more expensive. Highly recommended.

✖ **Indo-Italiano Restaurant** [145 C6] ☏027 275 2195; ⏰ 09.00–22.00 daily. This popular restaurant has a convenient location opposite the Buffalo Hotel & it serves a wide range of Indian & Italian dishes – tandoori grills & pizzas particularly recommended – in the US$6–10 range. Meals can be served indoors or on the wide veranda.

✖ **Milan's Restaurant** [145 C6] ☏027 275 1841; m 0754 269802; ⏰ 11.00–21.30 daily. As the name doesn't suggest, this low-key but thoroughly commendable eatery specialises in Indian vegetarian food, with around 40 dishes to choose from, but it also serves a limited Chinese selection & pizzas. Catering mostly to a local clientele, the décor is decidedly no-frills but the food is excellent value at around US$2–3 for a main. It also serves affordable lassis, fruit juices & milkshakes, but no alcohol.

✖ **Panda Chinese Restaurant** [138 A2] m 0754 838193/0784 875725; ⏰ 11.00–15.00 & 18.00–22.00 Mon–Fri, 11.00–22.00 Sat & Sun. This friendly & reliable Chinese eatery lies in pretty gardens just around the corner from the Ameg Lodge in Shantytown. It has the usual lengthy menu of meat, fish, chicken & vegetarian dishes, most at around US$6–8, although prawns are more expensive. Take-away available.

✖ **Salzburger Café** [145 A6] ☏027 275 0681; ⏰ 08.00–23.00 daily. Owned by a Tanzanian formerly resident in Austria, this unique restaurant on Kenyatta Road is a real gem, decorated with mementoes of the old European city to create an atmosphere of full-on kitsch. If the décor doesn't do it for you, then the food certainly should – US$5–6 for a variety of very good steak, chicken, vegetarian & spaghetti dishes, accompanied by mashed potato & salads in addition to the conventional chips & rice.

✖ **Sikh Club** [145 D6] ☏027 275 2473; ⏰ 10.30–15.00 & 18.00–23.00 Tue–Sun. This long-serving Indian eatery on Ghalla Street (near the old railway station) is as short on pretensions as it is long on value & it serves a great selection of tasty meat & vegetarian curries & tandoori grills, mostly for under US$5.

☕ **Aroma Coffee House** [145 A3] m 0754 363202; www.kiliweb.com/aroma; ⏰ 08.00–21.00 daily. This cosy café on Boma Road serves delicious Kilimanjaro coffee, light snacks, pastries & fresh juice.

☕ **Kilijava Coffee** [145 C3] ⏰ 08.30–20.30 daily. Found outside the Nakumatt Supermarket,

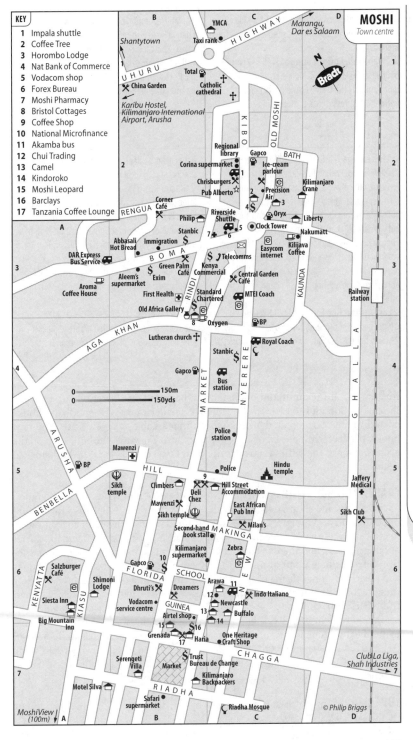

KEY

1 Impala shuttle
2 Coffee Tree
3 Horombo Lodge
4 Nat Bank of Commerce
5 Vodacom shop
6 Forex Bureau
7 Moshi Pharmacy
8 Bristol Cottages
9 Coffee Shop
10 National Microfinance
11 Akamba bus
12 Chui Trading
13 Camel
14 Kindoroko
15 Moshi Leopard
16 Barclays
17 Tanzania Coffee Lounge

MOSHI
Town centre

Marangu,
Dar es Salaam

YMCA
Taxi rank
HIGHWAY
Shantytown
UHURU
Total
China Garden
Karibu Hostel,
Kilimanjaro International
Airport, Arusha
Catholic
cathedral
KIBO
OLD MOSHI
BATH
Regional
library
Gapco
Corina supermarket
Ice-cream
parlour
Chrisburgers
Precision
Air
Kilimanjaro
Crane
Pub Alberto
Corner
Café
Liberty
Oryx
Philip
Riverside
Shuttle
Stanbic
Clock Tower
Nakumatt
Abbasali
Hot Bread
Immigration
Kilijava
Coffee
DAR Express
Bus Service
BOMA
Easycom
internet
Telecomms
Aleem's
supermarket
Green Palm
Café
Kenya
Commercial
Exim
RINDI
Central Garden
Café
Aroma
Coffee House
First Health
Standard
Chartered
MTEI Coach
Old Africa Gallery
Oxygen
BP
KAUNDA
Railway
station
Lutheran church
Royal Coach
AGA KHAN
MARKET
Stanbic
NYERERE
Gapco
Bus
station
GHALLA
Police
station
ARUSHA
Mawenzi
Police
Hindu
temple
BP
HILL
Jaffery
Medical
BENBELLA
Sikh
temple
Climbers
Coffee Shop
Hill Street
Accommodation
Mawenzi
Deli
Chez
East African
Pub Inn
Sikh Club
Sikh temple
Milan's
MAKINGA
Second-hand
book stall
Salzburger
Café
Kilimanjaro
supermarket
Zebra
KENYATTA
Shimoni
Lodge
Gapco
FLORIDA
SCHOOL
Arawa
Siesta Inn
KIASU
Dhruti's
Dreamers
Indo Italiano
Big Mountain
Inn
Vodacom
service centre
GUINEA
Newcastle
Buffalo
Airtel shop
Grenada
Hafia
One Heritage
Craft Shop
Serengeti
Villa
Market
Trust
Bureau de Change
CHAGGA
Club La Liga,
Shah Industries
MoshiView
(100m)
RIADHA
Kilimanjaro
Backpackers
Motel Silva
Safari
supermarket
Riadha Mosque
© Philip Briggs

RENGUA

0   150m
0   150yds

N

Bradt

this terrace café serves good coffee & fruit juice, plus a selection of sandwiches, snacks & salads for around US$2.

🍴**Tanzania Coffee Lounge** [145 B7] **m** 0754 610892; ⏲ 08.00–20.00 Mon–Sat, 10.00–17.00 Sun. Arguably the tastiest caffeine fix in Moshi, with filter, espresso, latte & cappuccino all

available at around US$1, this trendy little place on Chagga Road also serves great fruit juice, waffles, cakes & pastries, & the tasty lunchtime salads will satisfy those desperate for some fresh greens. Meals cost around US$3–6. There's a high-speed internet café at the back.

NIGHTLIFE

☆ **Club La Liga** [138 D5] **m** 0767 770022/0715 750076; ⏲ 18.00–late Tue–Sun; entrance US$5 Fri & Sat, but only US$2 for men & free for women on other nights. Moshi's premier nightclub lies about 500m from the town centre, among a row of old warehouses that can be reached by following Chagga Road eastward across the railway tracks, to where it becomes Viwanda Road. It usually has live music on Thu, while DJs play a selection of *bongo flava* (Tanzanian hip-hop) & other dance music on other nights.

🍷**East African Pub Inn** [145 C5] Nyerere Rd, 2 blocks north of the Kindoroko Hotel. This lively, 2-storey bar has a wooden roof, TV & loud music,

with cheap 'n' cheerful drink prices aimed at a predominantly local clientele.

🍷**Glacier Inn** [138 A3] **m** 0737 022764. Set in large jacaranda-shaded gardens on the corner of Lema & Kilimanjaro Rd, this is a great spot for a few outdoor drinks in suburban Shantytown. It also serves a varied selection of grills, Indian & Italian dishes in the US$4–5 range, & a selection of cheaper pub grub. A satellite TV ensures its popularity during major international sporting events.

☆ **Pub Alberto** [145 C2] ⏲ 18.00–04.00 Tue–Sun. Brightly decorated nightclub next to Chrisburgers. Good place for a last round.

SHOPPING

BOOKS A good **secondhand bookstall** can be found on Nyerere Road, between the bus station and the Newcastle Hotel. A smaller range of secondhand books is sold on the terrace of the otherwise unremarkable **Oxygen Cafe**. For new books, particularly material relating specifically to Tanzania, the bookshop on the ground floor of the **Kilimanjaro Crane Hotel** (see page 141) is the best stocked in town.

CRAFTS AND SOUVENIRS Although Moshi doesn't boast quite the proliferation of curio stalls and shops associated with Arusha, there are still plenty around, and prices tend to be a bit lower, as does the pushiness factor. The main concentration of craft shops in the town centre lies along Chagga Road close to the main cluster of budget hotels, and there's no better starting point here than the vast and hassle-free **One Heritage Craft Shop** [145 C7], which stocks a good selection of books and postcards alongside the usual carvings, paintings and other local crafts. Follow Chagga Road east across the railway tracks towards Club La Liga to visit **Shah Industries** [138 C6] (✆ 027 275 2414; e info@shahleather.com; www.shahleather. com), an excellent craft workshop specialising in leatherwork and staffed mainly by disabled Tanzanians. Another superior outlet is the **Old Africa Gallery** ([145 B4] **m** 0784 182208; ⏲ 09.00–18.00 Mon–Sat, 11.00–16.00 Sun), which sells some worthwhile West African masks and Makonde sculptures along with a fairly typical selection of Tanzanian paintings, carvings and beadwork.

SUPERMARKETS The best supermarket by far, the recently opened **Nakumatt** ([145 C3] ✆ 027 275 4501; ⏲ 08.30–22.00 Mon–Sat, 10.00–21.30 Sun) is part of a well-known Kenyan chain, and in addition to a wide range of local and imported manufactured goods, it sells a good selection of fresh baked goods, fresh vegetables and fruit, and frozen meat. Elsewhere, **Aleem's supermarket** on Boma Road (behind the post office) [145 B3] stocks a good range of imported goods and foods, while the **Carina supermarket** next to Chrisburgers [145 C2] is also very well stocked. There are also several good supermarkets on Nyerere Road between the bus station and the central market.

OTHER PRACTICALITIES

BANKS, ATMS AND FOREIGN EXCHANGE The National Bank of Commerce opposite the Clock Tower [145 C2] changes cash and cashes travellers' cheques at the usual rate of commission. Several forex bureaux are dotted around town, but while exchange rates are fairly good, you will generally get better in Arusha or Dar es Salaam. One exception, **Trust Bureau de Change**, on Chagga Road [145 B7] (⊕ *09.00–18.00 Mon–Sat, 09.00–14.00 Sun*) diagonally opposite the Kindoroko Hotel, offers good rates on US dollars or cash and charges no commission.

There are now several 24-hour ATMs where up to Tsh400,000 cash can be drawn daily with certain credit or debit cards. The ATMs at the **Standard Chartered Bank** [145 B3], **National Bank of Commerce** and **Barclays Bank** [145 B7] accept Visa, the one at the **Exim Bank** [145 B3] accepts MasterCard, while the one at **Stanbic** [145 B3] accepts both Visa and MasterCard. Other cards such as American Express are not accepted anywhere in Moshi.

MEDICAL The best place to head for in the case of a medical emergency is the **Kilimanjaro Christian Medical Centre (KCMC)** in Shantytown [138 A2] (☏ *027 275 4377/83; www.kcmc.ac.tz*) about 5km north of the town centre. More central options include the **First Health Hospital** on Rindi Road [145 B3] (☏ *027 275 4051*) alongside the Standard Chartered Bank, and **Jaffery Medical Services** [145 D5] (☏ *027 275 1843*) on Ghala Street.

IMMIGRATION Situated in Kibo House on Boma Road a few doors east of the Stanbic Bank, the immigration office in Moshi [145 B3] can process visa extensions on the spot during office hours (⊕ *08.00–15.00 Mon–Fri*).

MEDIA AND COMMUNICATIONS

Internet and email Numerous internet cafés are dotted around town. Most charge around Tsh500 per 30 minutes – the more expensive cafés generally provide a faster service – and stay open from around 08.00–20.00 daily, though some close on Sundays. In the Clock Tower area, **Twiga Communications**, on the Old Moshi Road [145 C2], is both speedy and helpful, as is **Easycom** in Twiga House on the main traffic circle [145 C3]. South of the bus station, **Fahari Cyber Centre** on Hill Street and the **Tanzania Coffee Lounge** on Chagga Road [145 B7] are both recommended.

SWIMMING Use of the swimming pool at the **YMCA** [145 C1] is free to hostel residents, but visitors must pay a daily entrance fee of Tsh3,000. The **Keys Hotel** [138 D4] charges a similar price to casual swimmers, but the pool is smaller and it is further out of town. You could also try the pool at the **Kilimanjaro Crane Hotel** [145 C2]. Another option, especially for those with time to kill and private transport, is the wonderful swimming pool at **Honey Badger Lodge**, 6km along the

Dar es Salaam road. Non-residents pay US$10 for a full three-course meal with use of the pool, or US$7 for pool usage only.

AROUND MOSHI

The most popular tourist destination in the vicinity of Moshi is of course Mount Kilimanjaro, the upper slopes and ascent of which are detailed in *Chapter 7, Mount Kilimanjaro National Park*, (page 160). Other lesser attractions in the region include the villages of Marangu and Machame; Chagga ecotourism projects in the Kilimanjaro foothills; a spectacular crater lake called Chala; the bird-rich shores of shallow Lake Jipe and the Nyumba ya Mungu Reservoir; the remote Mkomazi National Park; and the North and South Pare, the two northernmost Tanzanian ranges in the endemic-rich Eastern Arc Mountains.

MARANGU The village of Marangu, whose name derives from the local Chagga word meaning 'spring water', is situated on the lower slopes of Kilimanjaro about 40km from Moshi and 5km south of the main entrance gate to Mount Kilimanjaro National Park. Unlike lower-lying Moshi, Marangu has an appropriately alpine feel, surrounded as it is by lush vegetation and bisected by a babbling mountain stream, and it remains a popular springboard for Kilimanjaro ascents using the Marangu Route. For those who lack the time, inclination or money to climb Kilimanjaro, Marangu is a pleasant place to spend a night or a few days exploring the lower slopes of the great mountain, with several attractive waterfalls situated within easy striking distance.

Getting there and away The 40km drive from Moshi shouldn't take much longer than 30 minutes in a **private vehicle**. To get there, first head out along the Dar es Salaam road, bearing left after 23km as if heading towards Taveta, then turning left again after another 4km at the junction village of Himo. **Buses** and **dala-dalas** between Moshi and Marangu leave in either direction when they are full, normally at least once an hour, and generally take 45–60 minutes.

 Where to stay and eat

Upmarket

🏠 **Marangu Hotel** (26 rooms) ☎ 027 275 6591; m 0754 886092; e info@maranguhotel. com; www.maranguhotel.com. Unquestionably the top accommodation in the area, this stalwart family-run hotel, situated along the Moshi road 5km before Marangu, has an unpretentiously rustic feel, all ivy-draped walls & neat hedges that might have been transported straight from the English countryside. It also has a long-standing reputation for organising reliable Kilimanjaro climbs, whether you're looking at the standard all-inclusive package or the 'hard way' package aimed at budget travellers. Accommodation is in self-contained rooms, but camping is also available (see opposite). *US$90/130 sgl/dbl HB.*

🏠 **Capricorn Hotel** (70 rooms) ☎ 027 275 1309; m 0794 138571; e info@thecapricornhotels.com;

www.thecapricornhotels.com. Straggling over a steep hillside some 2km from Marangu along the road towards Kilimanjaro National Park's Marangu Entrance Gate, this is one of the newer hotels in the Marangu area but the en-suite rooms with satellite TV & minibar are rather variable in quality & the older ones are starting to look very frayed at the edges. Situated within the forest zone, the lushly wooded 2.5ha garden is teeming with birds. The restaurant has a mediocre reputation, but Kilimanjaro climbs arranged through the hotel are as reliable as it gets. *US$63/130 B&B for sgl/ dbl cottages in the old wing, or US$120/200 in the new wing.*

Moderate

🏠 **Nakara Hotel** (18 rooms) ☎ 027 275 6599; m 0754 277300; e info@nakarahotels.com; www.

nakarahotels.com. This smart but soulless high-rise lies about 3km past Marangu & around 2km before the eponymous entrance gate to Mount Kilimanjaro National Park. The self-contained twin rooms are small & rather lacking in character but are well maintained. Unfortunately, the rather cramped grounds lack the greenery & interest of other options in this price range, & on last inspection the staff was spectacularly inefficient. *US$60 pp B&B.*

🏠 **Kibo Hotel** (35 rooms) m 0754 038747; e kibohotel@myway.com. The venerable Kibo Hotel stands in attractive flowering gardens roughly 1km from the village centre towards the park entrance gate. Formerly on a par with the Marangu Hotel, the Kibo has emphatically seen better days – incredibly, lest it escape your attention, former US president Jimmy Carter stayed here in 1988 – but it has retained a winning air of faded dignity epitomised by the liberal wood panelling & creaky old verandas. If nothing else, following a recent change of management & sensible cut in rates, the large, self-contained rooms are good value. Facilities include a swimming pool, internet access, gift shop & a decent restaurant bursting with character, & the hotel makes a great base for casual rambling in the Kilimanjaro foothills. It has been arranging reliable Kilimanjaro climbs for decades. *US$40/70/80 sgl/ dbl/trpl B&B; camping US$5 pp per night.*

🏠 **Babylon Lodge** (25 rooms) ☎ 027 275 6355; m 0762 016016/0757 997799; e info@ babylonlodge.com; www.babylonlodge.com. Situated 500m from Marangu Post Office along the Mwika road, this former budget hotel has undergone a series of facelifts over the past decade. The en-suite rooms with combination tub/ shower & attractive ethnic décor are immaculately kept, but a touch on the cramped side. Overall, it's one of the best-value lodges in the Marangu area, especially when it comes to cleanliness & quality of service. *US$40/60/80 sgl/dbl/tpl B&B, another US$13 pp for lunch or dinner.*

Budget and camping It is also possible to camp at the Kibo Hotel.

🏠 **Coffee Tree Campsite** (8 rooms) ☎ 027 275 6604; e kilimanjaro@iwayafrica.com. Situated alongside the Nakara Hotel, this neatly laid-out site is a good place to arrange budget Kilimanjaro climbs, & while the simple rooms aren't great value, you won't find cheaper in Marangu. The camping seems a bit dear too, & even allowing for the above-average facilities (fridge, bar, BBQ, sauna & hot shower) the campsite at the Marangu or Kibo hotels seem infinitely better value. Tents & gas stoves are available for hire, various cultural tours can be arranged & there are onsite email & internet facilities. If you don't fancy self-catering, you could eat at the adjacent Nakara Hotel. *US$15 pp for a simple room; US$8 pp camping.*

⛺ **Marangu Hotel** ☎ 027 275 6591; m 0754 886092; e info@maranguhotel.com; www. maranguhotel.com. The large green campsite behind the main hotel buildings has a hot shower & is probably the best value for campers in the Marangu area. *Camping US$10 pp.*

Excursions from Marangu

Kinukamori Waterfall The most central tourist attraction in Marangu is the Kinukamori – 'Little Moon' – Waterfall. Situated about 20 minutes' walk from the town centre, from where it is signposted, this approximately 15m-high waterfall lies in a small park maintained by the district council (*entrance US$5*) as an ecotourism project in collaboration with two nearby villages. It's pretty enough without being an essential side trip, though the wooded banks of the Unna River above the waterfall harbour a variety of forest birds, and regularly attract troops of black-and-white colobus in the rainy season. A legend associated with Kinukamori relates to an unmarried girl called Makinuka, who discovered she was pregnant, a crime punishable by death in strict Chagga society, and decided to take her own life by jumping over the waterfall. When Makinuka arrived at the waterfall and looked over the edge, she changed her mind and turned to go home to plead for mercy. As she did so, however, she came face to face with a leopard and ran back screaming in fear, forgetting about the gorge behind her, to plunge to an accidental death. A statue of Makinuka and her nemesis stands above the waterfall. The waterfall can be visited independently, or by arrangement with your hotel as part of a longer sightseeing tour.

Kilasia Waterfall (m *0755 041040/252893;* e *kilasiawaterfalls@yahoo.com*) Clearly signposted to the left of the dirt road connecting the Kibo Hotel and Kilimanjaro Mountain Resort lies the rather spectacular Kilasia Waterfall, the centrepiece of a new ecotourist community that charges US$5 for a guided nature walk. Approximately 30m high, the waterfall tumbles into the base of a sheer-sided gorge before running through a set of violent rapids into a lovely pool that's said to be safe for swimming. The waterfall is at its most powerful during the rains, but it flows solidly throughout the year – the name Kilasia derives from a Chagga word meaning 'without end', reputedly a reference to its reliable flow. The path to the base of the falls, though no more than 500m long, is very steep and potentially dangerous when wet. The rocky gorge below the waterfall is lined with ferns and evergreen trees, and a troop of blue monkeys often passes through in the early morning and late afternoon. For further details, contact the community project manager.

LAKE CHALA Straddling the Kenyan border some 30km east of Moshi as the crow flies, this roughly circular crater lake, a full 3km wide yet invisible until you virtually topple over the rim, is one of northern Tanzania's true off-the-beaten-track scenic gems. The brilliant turquoise water, hemmed in by sheer cliffs draped in tropical greenery, is an arresting sight at any time, and utterly fantastic when Kilimanjaro emerges from the clouds to the immediate west. Not for the faint-hearted, a very steep footpath leads from the rim to the edge of the lake, its translucent waters plunging near-vertically to an undetermined depth from the rocky shore. Abundant birdlife aside, wildlife is in short supply, though Chala, in common with many other African crater lakes, is said locally to harbour its due quota of mysterious and malignant Nessie-like beasties. A more demonstrable cause for concern should you be nurturing any thoughts of dipping a toe in the water, however, is the presence of crocodiles, one of which killed a British volunteer off the Kenyan shore in March 2002.

Getting there For the time being, the only practical way to reach Chala is as an **organised day or overnight trip** out of Moshi, or in a **private 4x4 vehicle**. If you're driving, follow the Dar es Salaam road out of Moshi for 25km until you reach the junction at Himo, where a left turn leads to the Kenyan border at Taveta. About 7km along the Taveta road, turn left on to the rough road signposted for Kilimanjaro Mountain Lodge, which you must follow for about 40 minutes to reach the lake.

Where to stay

Ⱥ **Lake Chala Safari Camp** (10 units) m 0786 111177/0655 111377; e infolakechala@gmail.com, lakechala@gmail.com; www.lakechalasafaricamp.com. The only functional accommodation in the vicinity of Chala, this place opened on the crater rim in early 2010, initially as a campsite, bar & restaurant but upmarket standing tents are also under construction & are likely to open for business in 2013. *Camping US$10 pp, US$7 pp for residents, tent hire costs US$20–35 depending on the tent size.*

LAKE JIPE Shallow, narrow and enclosed by dense beds of tall papyrus, Lake Jipe runs for 10km along a natural sump on the Kenyan border between Kilimanjaro, the main source of its water, and the Mkomazi Game Reserve. It's an atmospheric

Hot air balloon rides in the Serengeti
are an unforgettable experience. Gliding
serenely above the trees as the sun rises
allows you to see the expansive plains
from a new and quite thrilling angle
page 299

top left **Leopard** (*Panthera pardus*)
page 24

top right **Common eland**
(*Taurotragus oryx*)
page 34

above left **African buffalo**
(*Syncerus caffer*)
page 37

above right **Warthog**
(*Phacochoreus africanus*)
page 38

right **Hippopotamus**
(*Hippopotamus amphibius*)
page 37

top left **Olive baboon**
(*Papio cynocephalus anubis*)
page 31

top right **Kirk's red colobus**
(*Procolobus kirkii*)
page 400

above left **Honey badger**
(*Mellivora capensis*)
page 29

above right **Spotted hyena**
(*Crocuta crocuta*)
page 28

left **Serval** (*Felis serval*)
page 25

left The Barabaig are dedicated cattle-herders who have steadfastly resisted pressure to forsake their semi-nomadic ways page 232

below The Maasai measure a man's wealth in terms of cattle and children rather than money page 270

bottom Numbering at around 1,000 individuals, the Hadza are Tanzania's only remaining tribe of true hunter-gatherers page 256

above   The Maasai traditionally worship a dualistic deity, Engai, who resides in the volcanic crater of Ol Doinyo Lengai pages 20 & 270

right   Colourfully dressed Shambaa women sell fresh fruit and vegetables at the vibrant Lushoto market page 173

below   The fishing industry continues to employ many local men in Zanzibar page 384

above **A cyclist overlooking Lake Manyara, Tanzania's finest spot for birdwatching** page 247

left **A kayaker along the mangroves and palm-lined beach in Pangani** page 205

below **Approximately 30m high, the spectacular Kilasia Waterfall flows solidly throughout the year** page 150 body of water with a fabulous setting: the Pare Mountains to the south, Chala crater rising from the flat plain to the east, and – when the clouds clear – Kilimanjaro hulking over the northeast skyline. Lake Jipe is seldom visited, and almost never from the Tanzanian side, but it is reasonably accessible, and there's quite a bit of wildlife around since part of the northern shore is protected within Kenya's unfenced Tsavo National Park. Gazelle and other antelope are likely to be seen in the arid country approaching the lake, and cheetah and lion are occasionally observed darting across the road. The lake itself is teeming with hippopotami and

CULTURAL TOURS AROUND MOSHI

Several cultural tourism projects operate in the Kilimanjaro foothills in association with local communities. In addition to offering insights into Chagga culture and the opportunity to limber up the limbs before a full-on ascent of Kilimanjaro, these cultural tours allow non-climbers to get a good look at the scenic Kilimanjaro foothills, with a chance of catching a glimpse of the snow-capped peak itself. In addition to the local telephone contacts given below, full details of the programmes can be obtained through the central website http://infojep.com/culturaltours.

MACHAME CULTURAL TOURISM PROGRAMME (*027 275 7033*) This programme is based at the village of Kyalia, close to the Machame Gate of Kilimanjaro National Park. A good day tour for those with a strong interest in scenery is the five-hour Sieny-Ngira Trail, which passes through the lush montane forest to a group of large sacred caves, a natural rock bridge over the Marire and Namwi rivers, and a nearby waterfall. For those with a greater interest in culture, the five-hour Nronga Tour, which visits a milk purification and processing co-operative run by women, is best done on Monday, market day in Kyalia village. Of similar duration, the Nkuu Tour focuses instead on agriculture, in particular coffee production. Longer excursions include the two-day Ng'uni Hike and three-day Lyamungo Tour. In a private vehicle, Kyalia can be reached by following the Arusha road out of Moshi for 12km, then following the turn-off signposted for Machame Gate and driving for another 14km. The road to Kyalia is surfaced in its entirety, and regular dala-dalas run to Kyalia from the junction on the Moshi–Arusha road.

MARANGU CULTURAL TOURISM PROGRAMME Geared primarily towards travellers staying in Marangu prior to a Kilimanjaro climb, this programme offers a variety of half-day trips taking in various natural and cultural sites on the surrounding slopes. Popular goals include any of three waterfalls, as well as the first coffee tree planted in Tanzania more than a century ago, and a traditional conical Chagga homestead. Few prospective climbers will be unmoved by the grave of the legendary Yohanu Lauwo, who guided Hans Meyer to the summit of Kilimanjaro back in 1889, continued working as a guide into his seventies, and reputedly lived to the remarkable age of 124! Other walks lead to nearby Mamba and Makundi, known for their traditional Chagga blacksmiths and woodcarvers, and for the Laka Caves, where women and children were hidden during the frequent 19th-century clashes with the Maasai of the surrounding plains. Guided tours can be arranged through any of the hotels in and around Marangu.

crocodiles, and the papyrus beds harbour several localised birds such as lesser jacana, African water rail, pygmy goose and black egret. Elephants regularly come to drink and bathe along the northern shore, especially during the dry season. Look out, too, for the lovely impala lily – this shrub-sized succulent, known for its bright pink and white flowers, is common in the dry acacia plains approaching the lake.

Although the papyrus that encloses Lake Jipe gives the lake much of its character, the rapid expansion of the plant over some 50% of the water in the last few decades is possibly symptomatic of a dying lake. Certainly, local fishermen, who now have to reach the open water along shallow canals cut through the crocodile-infested reeds, claim that the fish yield decreases every year along with the amount of open water. The probable explanation for the recent proliferation of papyrus – which can only grow at depths where it can take root in soil – is that the lake has gradually become shallower due to increased silt levels in the water that flows down from Kilimanjaro. In a chain of cause and effect, the infestation of papyrus on Jipe would thus appear to be a result of the extensive deforestation and a corresponding increase in erosion on Kilimanjaro's lower slopes over the last 50 years.

Whether or not this process will result in the lake drying up entirely is a matter of conjecture, but researchers have expressed serious concerns for its future. The loss of Jipe would be immense, not only to the thousands of villagers for whom the lake has traditionally formed a source of fresh water and protein, but also to the wildlife that is drawn to its water during the dry season. Measures that would contribute to the lake's future – and which are in any case ecologically sound – include an extensive reforestation programme on the Kilimanjaro footslopes, and an attempt to modernise traditional farming methods that tend to cause soil erosion as land pressure intensifies and the earth is worked harder.

There is no accommodation near Lake Jipe (at least not along the Tanzanian shore) but it is permitted to pitch a tent in Makayuni for a nominal fee. Aside from fish, no food is available locally, and you'll need to bring all drinking water with you, too. Mosquitoes (and occasionally lake flies) are prolific on the shore, so do cover up at dusk. Away from the lake, a few basic guesthouses can be found in Kifaru.

Getting there and onto the lake
The junction town for Lake Jipe, called Kifaru, straddles the B1 some 40km south of Moshi. At Kifaru, turn to the east along a reasonable dirt road towards Kiwakuku. After about 15km, turn onto a track running to the left, distinguished by a blue signpost reading 'Jipe' and, up ahead, a hill with a prominent bald boulder on top. Follow this track for about 2km, and you'll be in Makayuni on the lakeshore. In a **private vehicle**, the drive from Kifaru takes 30–45 minutes, depending on the condition of the road, so it would be feasible to visit Jipe as a day trip from Moshi. The only **public transport** from Kifaru is the daily bus to Kiwakuku. This generally leaves Kiwakuku at 04.00, passes the Makayuni junction at around 06.30 and arrives in Kifaru at 09.00 to start the return trip at around 14.00.

Once at Makayuni, it's straightforward enough to arrange to be poled onto the lake in a local **dugout canoe**, whether you want to fish, watch birds or just enjoy the lovely scenery and hope for glimpses of big game on the nearby Kenyan shore. Expect to pay around US$5–10 for a short excursion or US$15 for a full day on the lake. The best time to head onto the lake is in the early morning or late afternoon, when it's not too hot, game is more active and Kilimanjaro is most likely to be visible. Getting out onto the open water first involves a long pole through shallow papyrus marsh, with brightly coloured kingfishers darting in front of the boat and hippos grunting invisibly in the nearby reeds. This stretch can be quite difficult with two passengers weighing down the dugout, so it's best to take one per person.

NYUMBA YA MUNGU RESERVOIR Extending over 140km² after good rains, this relatively shallow and seasonally fluctuating reservoir was created in 1965 when the Nyerere administration constructed the Nyumba ya Mungu (House Of God) Dam on the Pangani River some 50km south of Moshi. Originally built as a source of hydro-electric power for newly independent Tanzania, Nyumba ya Mungu still helps light up Tanga, Moshi and several other small towns in between, as well as being an important source of protein, with an annual fish yield of up to 25,000 tonnes in a good year. Although the water is not piped out anywhere, it has encouraged agriculturist migration into what was formerly a rather arid extension of the Maasai Steppes, and several lakeshore settlements bear names that hint at the origin of their inhabitants – most memorable among them the tiny village of Banda, named by Malawian settlers after their former president.

Of interest primarily to birdwatchers, Nyumba ya Mungu can easily be explored in a private vehicle over a few hours, using a rough road loop that veers southwest from the B1 at Kifaru (40km south of Moshi, and also the junction village for Lake Jipe), and then follows the eastern lakeshore to the dam wall, from where a good dirt road leads back to the village of Kisangara on the B1.

Getting there Coming from Moshi, you need to turn right at Kifaru, immediately before the primary school, and then follow a rough track for about 12km to the village of Handeni, crossing a railway line at the 8km mark. From here you can drive along the floodplain for another 16km until you reach the village of Langata, passing an extensive area of riverine swamp that's teeming with birdlife. Among the more interesting species likely to be seen in the area are collared pratincole, African marsh harrier, open-billed stork, squacco heron, black egret, glossy ibis and a wide variety of kingfishers, waterfowl, plovers and waders including curlew sandpiper and bar-tailed godwit. Another 18km past Langata, you come out at the Kisangara road, where a right turn leads to the dam wall after 4km. There are no restrictions on visiting the dam, although you will need to sign in. The view from the wall over the forested Pangani River is rather attractive. Improbable as it sounds, the small village here is called Spiriway, a bastardisation of (and pronounced like) the English word 'Speedway', in reference to the waterfall-like plumes that crash through the overflow gates after heavy rain – or so they'll tell you locally!

A few (non-express) **minibuses** daily link Moshi to Spiriway, which boasts a couple of basic guesthouses if you feel like exploring the lake and its environs on foot.

USANGI AND THE NORTH PARE In tourist terms, the North Pare is the least developed of the mountain ranges in northeast Tanzania, despite lying a mere 35km southeast of Kilimanjaro. The high plateau of the range is extensively settled and ecologically degraded: only seven tracts of indigenous forest remain, isolated from each other by cultivated fields and *shambas*. The main base for exploring North Pare is the attractive small town of Usangi, which is ringed by 11 peaks and is particularly lively on Monday and Thursday market days.

At the cultural tourism office in Usangi's secondary school you can organise a number of excursions to nearby points of interest. A good half-day walk is the Mangatu Tour, which takes you through the Mbale Forest to a viewpoint facing nearby Kilimanjaro and Lake Jipe on the Kenya border. The half-day Goma Tour visits a set of caves that were dug by the Pare people in the 19th century as a hiding place from slave raiders. This tour can be extended to be a full-day walk to the upper slopes of the 2,112m-high Mount Kindoroko, which supports the largest relic forest patch in the range – around 900ha – and harbours a variety of monkeys and birds. Notable among these is Abbot's starling, a localised East African highland forest endemic at the most southern extension of its very limited range. Several other day walks are available to visitors, and it is possible to organise overnight hiking trails. All hikes cost around US$6 per group per day, with an additional village development and administration fee of US$3 per person per day.

Getting there Usangi lies roughly 25km east of the B1, along a good dirt road that branches off from the junction town of Mwanga, some 15km south of Kifaru. It is covered daily by a few **buses** and **dala-dalas**, and the journey from Mwanga takes around 90 minutes in either direction.

Where to stay There are a few guesthouses in Usangi, the best being the **Mhako Hostel** (◊ *027 275 7642; US$15/20 en-suite sgl/dbl*) or the more basic guesthouse and campsite at **Lomwe Secondary School**, which charges around US$5 per person for a room and US$2 to camp.

MBAGA AND THE SOUTH PARE The mountains that tower so impressively over the southeast horizon of Mkomazi National Park are the South Pare, a range separated from the Western Usambara by the Mkomazi River Valley. Named for their Pare inhabitants, the mountains boast a wealth of low-key cultural sites and natural attractions, most of which are accessible through a cultural tourism program that operates out of Hilltop Tona Lodge in Mbaga (or Manka).

Mbaga itself is an attractively wooded semi-urban sprawl that follows the main road along the northern slopes of the range. Its most striking feature, an oddly Bavarian apparition in these remote African hills, is the century-old church built by Jakob Dannholz (see box, overleaf). If you want to travel further afield, Hilltop Lodge can arrange visits to a highly respected traditional healer, who also happens to be a Seventh-Day Adventist, so don't bother visiting on a Saturday; to the Mghimbi Caves where the Pare hid from slave raiders in the 1860s; to Malameni Rock where children were sacrificed to appease evil spirits until the practice was outlawed in the 1930s; to the forested Ronzi Dam; and to the legendary 'Red Reservoir'.

Longer hikes include a three-day trip through Chome Forest Reserve, which lies on the slopes of the 2,462m Mount Shengena and is home to various monkeys and birds, including the endemic South Pare white-eye. Nominal guide fees must be paid for all activities.

Getting there and away The main springboard is Same on the Dar es Salaam road south of Moshi. The drive from Moshi to Same shouldn't take longer than 90 minutes in a private vehicle, and any public transport heading from Moshi to places further south can drop you off there.

With **private transport**, the most interesting route from Same skirts the boundary of Mkomazi National Park before passing through the small town of Kisiwani – an old slave-trading centre with a distinctly coastal feel and legendarily succulent mangoes – and ascending to Mbaga via a spectacular forest-fringed pass.

Using **public transport**, the 35km road from Same to Mbaga is traversed by at least one bus, and a couple of dala-dalas run daily. Normally, all transport out of Mbaga leaves before 07.00, and begins the return trip from Same at around 11.00. Sometimes there's a second run back and forth in the afternoon, but this is the exception rather than the rule. If you need to overnight in Same, see *Where to stay* under *Mkomazi National Park* for details, overleaf.

Where to stay
Hilltop Tona Lodge (11 rooms) m 0754 852010; e tona_lodge@hotmail.com; http:// tonalodge.org. This hub of tourist activity in South Pare consists of several en-suite cottages in a wonderful jungle setting with great views over the Mkomazi Plains. There is a natural swimming pool in the river below the lodge, & a restaurant serves reasonably priced meals & cold drinks. *US$15 pp for room with shared showers; camping US$10 pp.*

MKOMAZI NATIONAL PARK (*www.tanzaniaparks.com; entrance US$20 pp per 24hr period*) Gazetted as a game reserve in 1951 and upgraded to national park status in 2008, Mkomazi is effectively a southern extension of Kenya's vast Tsavo National Park, covering an area of 3,234km² to the east of Kilimanjaro and immediately north of the Pare Mountains. Together with Tsavo, it forms part of one of East Africa's most important savanna ecosystems, characterised by the semi-arid climatic conditions of the Sahel Arc, and housing a great many dry-country species rare or absent elsewhere in Tanzania.

In 1992, the Tanzanian government invited the Royal Geographical Society (RGS) to undertake a detailed ecological study of Mkomazi. Although mammal populations were very low, it was determined that most large mammal species present in Tsavo are either resident in Mkomazi or regularly migrate there from Kenya, including lion, cheetah, elephant, giraffe, buffalo, zebra, impala and Tanzania's most significant gerenuk population. African wild dogs were re-introduced into Mkomazi in the 1990s, as was a herd of black rhinos from South Africa, though neither is likely to be seen on an ordinary safari.

Mkomazi is listed as an Important Bird Area, with more than 400 species recorded, including several northern dry-country endemics that were newly added to the Tanzania list by the RGS – for instance three-streaked tchagra, Shelley's starling, Somali long-billed crombec, yellow-vented eremomella and the extremely localised Friedmann's lark. It is the only place in Tanzania where the lovely vulturine guineafowl, notable for its bright cobalt chest, is likely to be seen. Other conspicuous large ground birds include common ostrich, secretary bird, southern ground hornbill and various francolins and bustards.

Prior to becoming a national park, Mkomazi was practically undeveloped for tourism. It had also been subject to considerable pressure as the human population around its peripheries grew in number. As a result, wildlife is thinly distributed and skittish. This is likely to change, however, as animal populations benefit from the higher level of protection Mkomazi will be accorded as part of the national park system. It is also likely that the wildlife will become more habituated to safari vehicles as more people visit the park.

Although Mkomazi doesn't offer game viewing to compare with other reserves in northern Tanzania, this is compensated for by the wild scenery – mountains rise in all directions, with Kilimanjaro often visible to the northwest at dawn and dusk – and the near certainty of not seeing another tourist. The best game-viewing circuit runs for about 20km between Zange Entrance Gate and Dindera Dam, where topi, eland, giraffe, common zebra and gazelles are all quite likely to be seen. The thicker bush further east is a good place to see lesser kudu and gerenuk.

Getting there Mkomazi is among the most accessible of Tanzania's national parks. The gateway town is Same, a small but busy trading centre that straddles the main Dar es Salaam Highway about 105km southeast of Moshi. The drive from Moshi to Same shouldn't take longer than 90 minutes in a **private vehicle**, and any **public transport** heading from Moshi to places further south can drop you off there. From Same, a good 5km dirt road runs to the Zange Entrance Gate, where you need to pay the entrance fee.

Although Mkomazi is not often included on northern Tanzania safari itineraries, **Kanyambo Safaris** (m *0783 330046;* e *kanyambo.safaris@gmail.com; www. kanyambosafaris.com*) is a new specialist operator that runs general photographic and birding safaris to Mkomazi out of its base at Mambo View Lodge in the northern Usambara Mountains (only a couple of hours away by road). It also maintains an informative website about the park: www.mkomazi.info.

For budget travellers, the park could easily be visited as a day trip out of Same, where 4x4 and other vehicles are usually available for hire at a negotiable rate. Mkomazi is best avoided in the rainy season, due to the poor roads.

Where to stay and eat

Upmarket

🏠 **Babu's Camp** (5 tents) ☎027 250 3094; e babuscamp@bol.co.tz; www.babuscamp.com. This exclusive tented camp, situated 13km inside the park coming from Zange Entrance Gate, is spaciously laid out within a grove of gigantic baobabs & acacias, & it offers great views across the plains to the Pare Mountains & lower hills within the park. The spacious walk-in tents all have their own balcony & a private open roof shower & toilet out the back, offering fabulous views of the sparkling African night sky. It is usefully based for game drives, about 45 mins' drive from Dindera Dam. The birdlife around camp can be fabulous, & African wild dogs & other predators occasionally pass through. *From US$280 sgl/dbl FB.*

Budget

🏠 **Elephant Motel** (20 rooms) ☎027 275 8193; m 0754 839545; e elephantmotel@elct. org; www.elephantmotel.com. The smartest accommodation in the vicinity of Same is this motel set in large green grounds about 1.5km south of the town centre along the B1 to Dar es Salaam. It offers clean en-suite rooms with netting, TV & hot running water, & good Indian, Tanzanian & Western meals in the restaurant or garden cost around US$6–8. *US$35/40 sgl/dbl, with a 40% residents' discount likely to be offered to walk-in clients upon request.*

Shoestring

🏠 **Amani Lutheran Centre** (12 rooms) ☎027 275 8107. Situated on the main tar road through Same, about 200m uphill from the bus station, this clean & long-serving hostel consists of around a dozen rooms enclosing a small green courtyard. It's a friendly set-up, & facilities include an internet café, canteen & safe parking. *US$6/10 en-suite sgl/ dbl B&B, or US$12 suite.*

7

Mount Kilimanjaro National Park

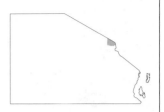

Reaching an altitude of 5,895m (19,340ft), Kilimanjaro is the highest mountain in Africa, and on the rare occasions when it is not veiled in clouds, its distinctive silhouette and snow-capped peak form one of the most breathtaking sights on the continent. There are, of course, higher peaks on other continents, but Kilimanjaro is effectively the world's largest single mountain, a free-standing entity that towers an incredible 5km above the surrounding plains. It is also the highest mountain anywhere that can be ascended by somebody without specialised mountaineering experience or equipment.

Kilimanjaro straddles the border with Kenya, but the peaks all fall within Tanzania and can only be climbed from within the country. There are several places on the lower slopes from where the mountain can be ascended, but most people use the Marangu Route (which begins at the eponymous village) because it is the cheapest option and has the best facilities. The less heavily trampled Machame Route, starting from the village of the same name, has grown in popularity in recent years. A number of more obscure routes can be used, though they are generally only available through specialist trekking companies. Most prospective climbers arrange their ascent of 'Kili' – as it is popularly called – well in advance, through an overseas tour operator or online with a local operator, but you can also shop around on the spot using specialist trekking companies based in Moshi, Marangu or even Arusha. Kilimanjaro can be climbed at any time of year, but the hike is more difficult in the rainy months, especially between March and May.

GEOLOGY

In geological terms, Kilimanjaro is a relatively young mountain. Like most other large mountains near the Rift Valley, it was formed by volcanic activity, first erupting about one million years ago. The 3,962m-high Shira Peak collapsed around half a million years ago, but the 5,895m-high Uhuru Peak on Mount Kibo (the higher of Kilimanjaro's two main peaks) and 5,149m-high Mawenzi Peak continued to grow until more recently. Shira plateau formed 360,000 years ago, when the caldera was filled by lava from Kibo after a particularly violent eruption. Kibo is now dormant, and nobody knows when it last displayed any serious volcanic activity. The Kilimanjaro National Park, gazetted in 1977, protects the entire Tanzanian part of the mountain above the 2,700m contour, an area of 756km².

HISTORY

Blessed by fertile volcanic soil and reliable rainfall, Kilimanjaro has probably always been a magnet for human settlement. Ancient stone tools of indeterminate age have

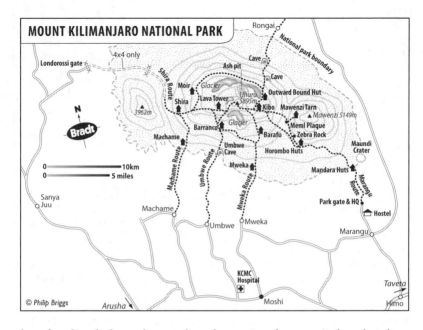

MOUNT KILIMANJARO NATIONAL PARK

Rongai

National park boundary

Londorossi gate

4x4 only

Cave

Ash pit

Cave

Moir

Glacier

Outward Bound Hut

Shira

Lava Tower

Uhuru 5895m

Kibo

Mawenzi Tarn

Mawenzi 5149m

3962m

Barranco

Glacier

Meml Plaque

Machame

Barafu

Zebra Rock

Maundi Crater

Umbwe Cave

Horombo Huts

Mweka

Mandara Huts

0   10km
0   5 miles

Sanya Juu

Machame

Park gate & HQ

Hostel

Umbwe

Mweka

Marangu

KCMC Hospital

Taveta

© Philip Briggs   Arusha   Moshi   Himo

N

Bradt

been found on the lower slopes, as have the remains of pottery artefacts thought to be at least 2,000 years old. Archaeological evidence suggests that, between 1,000 and 1,500 years ago, Kilimanjaro was the centre of an Iron Age culture spreading out to the coastal belt between Pangani and Mombasa. Before that, it's anybody's guess really, but references in Ptolemy's *Geography* and the *Periplus of the Erythraean Sea* suggest that the mountain was known to the early coastal traders, and might even have served as the terminus of a trade route starting at modern-day Pangani and following the eponymous river inland. Kilimanjaro is also alluded to in an account written by a 12th-century Chinese trader, and by 16th-century Spanish geographer Fernandes de Encisco.

These ancient allusions fired the curiosity of 19th-century geographers, who outdid each other in publishing wild speculations about the African interior. In 1848, locals told Johan Rebmann, a German missionary working in the Taita Hills, about a very large silver-capped mountain known to the Maasai as Ol Doinyo Naibor – White Mountain – and reputedly protected by evil spirits that froze anybody who tried to ascend it. When Rebmann visited the mountain, he immediately recognised the spirit-infested silver cap to be snow, but this observation, first published in 1849, was derided by European experts, who thought it ludicrous to claim there was snow so near the Equator. Only in 1861, when an experienced geologist, Von der Decken, saw and surveyed Kilimanjaro, was its existence and that of its snow-capped peaks accepted internationally. Oral tradition suggests that no local person had successfully climbed Kilimanjaro – or at least returned to tell the tale – before Hans Meyer and Ludwig Purtscheller reached the summit in 1889.

Kilimanjaro is home to the Chagga people, a group of Bantu-speaking agriculturists whose ancestors are said to have arrived in the area in the 15th century. This dating is contradicted by a Chagga legend describing an eruption of Kilimanjaro, which doesn't tally with the geological evidence for the past 500 years, so it's probable that the story was handed down by earlier inhabitants. The Chagga have no tradition of central leadership, and an estimated 100 small chieftaincies existed in the region in the mid 19th century. Today, the Chagga have a reputation for industriousness and are generally relatively well educated; for that reason you'll find that a high proportion of salaried workers and safari guides come from the Kilimanjaro region.

VEGETATION AND BIOLOGY

There are five vegetation zones on Kilimanjaro: the cultivated lower slopes; the forest; heath and moorland; alpine; and the barren arctic summit zone. Vegetation is sparse higher up due to lower temperatures and rainfall.

The **lower slopes** of the mountain were probably once forested, but are now mainly cultivated. The volcanic soils make them highly fertile and they support a dense human population. The most biologically interesting aspect of the lower slopes is the abundance of wild flowers, seen between Marangu and the park entrance gate.

The **montane forest zone** of the southern slopes lies between the altitudes of 1,800m and 3,000m. Receiving up to 2,000mm of rainfall annually, this zone displays a high biological diversity, and still supports a fair amount of wildlife. The most frequently seen mammals are the black-and-white colobus and blue monkeys, while typical forest antelope include three duiker species and the beautifully marked bushbuck. Leopard, bushpig and porcupine are fairly common but seldom encountered by hikers, while eland, buffalo and elephant are present in small numbers. The forest is home to many varieties of butterfly, including four endemic species. The forests of Kilimanjaro are less rich in birds (particularly endemics) than the more ancient forests of the Eastern Arc Mountains, but some 40 species peculiar to Afro-montane forest have been recorded. Most forest birds are quite difficult to observe, but trekkers should at least hear the raucous silvery-cheeked hornbill and beautiful Hartlaub's turaco.

The semi-alpine **moorland zone**, which lies between 3,000m and 4,000m, is characterised by heath-like vegetation and abundant wild flowers. As you climb into the moorland, two distinctive plants become common. These are *Lobelia deckenii*, which grows to 3m high, and the groundsel *Senecio kilimanjarin*, which grows up to 5m high and can be distinguished by a spike of yellow flowers. The moorland zone supports a low density of mammals, but pairs of klipspringer are quite common on rocky outcrops and several other species are recorded from time to time. Hill chat and scarlet-tufted malachite sunbird are two birds whose range is restricted to the moorland of large East African mountains. Other localised birds are lammergeyer and alpine swift. Because it is so open, the views from the moorland are stunning.

WHAT'S IN A NAME?

Nobody is sure about the meaning of the name Kilimanjaro, or even whether it is Swahili, Maasai or Chagga in origin. That the term 'kilima' is Swahili for little mountain (a joke?) is not in doubt. But 'njaro' could derive from the Chagga word for caravan (the mountain was an important landmark on the northern caravan route), or from the Maasai word 'ngare' meaning water (it is the source of most of the region's rivers), or the name of a Swahili demon of cold. Another unrelated version of the name's origin is that it's a bastardisation of the phrase 'kilemakyaro' (impossible journey), the initial Chagga response to European queries about trekking to the peak!

The **alpine zone** between 4,000m and 5,000m is classified as a semi-desert because it receives an annual rainfall of less than 250mm. The ground often freezes at night, but ground temperatures may soar to above 30°C by day. Few plants survive in these conditions; only 55 species are present, many of them lichens and grasses. Six species of moss are endemic to the higher reaches of Kilimanjaro. Large mammals have been recorded at this altitude, most commonly eland, but none is resident.

Approaching the summit, the **arctic zone** starts at an altitude of around 5,000m. This area receives virtually no rainfall, and supports little permanent life other than the odd lichen. Two remarkable records concern a frozen leopard discovered here in 1926, and a family of hunting dogs seen in 1962. The most notable natural features at the summit are the inner and outer craters of Kibo, surrounding a 120m-deep ash pit, and the Great Northern Glacier, which has retreated markedly since Hans Meyer and Ludwig Purtscheller first saw it in 1889. Indeed, since that historic ascent, it is thought that Kilimanjaro's distinctive snow cap has retreated by more than 80%, probably as a result of global warming, and some experts predict that it will vanish completely by 2020.

CLIMBING KILIMANJARO

As Africa's highest peak and most identifiable landmark, Kilimanjaro offers an irresistible challenge to many tourists. Dozens of visitors to Tanzania set off for Uhuru Peak every day, ranging from teenagers to pensioners, and those who make it generally regard the achievement to be the highlight of their time in the country. A major part of Kilimanjaro's attraction is that any reasonably fit person stands a fair chance of reaching the top. The ascent requires no special climbing skills or experience; on the contrary, it basically amounts to a long uphill slog over four (or more) days, followed by a more rapid descent.

The relative ease of climbing Kilimanjaro should not lull travellers into thinking of the ascent as some sort of prolonged Sunday stroll. It is a seriously tough hike, with potentially fatal penalties for those who are inadequately prepared or who belittle the health risks attached to being at an altitude of above 4,000m. It should also be recognised that there is no such thing as a cheap Kilimanjaro climb (see box, *Costing a climb*, page 171). A five-day Marangu climb generally costs at least

---

A ROYAL VISIT

An unsubstantiated legend holds that Emperor Menelik I of Ethiopia, the illegitimate son of King Solomon and the Queen of Sheba, visited Kilimanjaro about 3,000 years ago while returning from a successful military campaign in East Africa. The emperor camped on the saddle for a night, and then ascended Kibo, where he suddenly fell ill and died, possibly from exposure and/or altitude-related causes. Menelik's slaves buried the imperial corpse in the snowy crater, where the story says it remains to this day, together with a royal cache of jewels, religious scrolls and other treasures. An extension of this legend prophesies that a descendant of Menelik I will one day ascend Kibo, find the frozen body and claim the seal ring of Solomon worn by it, thereby endowing himself with the wisdom of Solomon and heroic spirit of Menelik. Pure apocrypha, as far as I can ascertain, is the story that the ancient Ethiopian emperor's 19th-century successor and namesake Menelik II once climbed Kilimanjaro in an unsuccessful bid to fulfil this centuries-old prophecy.

The names of Kilimanjaro's two main peaks, Kibo and Mawenzi, derive from local Chagga words respectively meaning 'cold' and 'jagged'. According to Chagga legend, the peaks are sisters and both were once as smoothly shaped as the perfect dome of Kibo is today. But the younger sister Mawenzi was habitually too lazy to collect her own firewood and kept borrowing from Kibo until one day the elder sister instructed her to go out and gather her own. When Mawenzi refused, the enraged Kibo reached into her woodpile, grabbed the largest log there, and started beating her over the head, resulting in the jagged shape of the younger sister today.

US$1,200 per person, depending to some extent on group size, while six-day climbs start at around US$1,400. People using high-quality operators and/or more obscure routes should expect to pay considerably more.

MARANGU ROUTE Starting at the Marangu Gate some 5km from the village of the same name, the so-called 'tourist route' is the most popular way to the top of Kilimanjaro, largely because it is less arduous than most of the alternatives, as well as having better facilities and being cheaper to climb. Marangu is also probably the safest route, due to the volume of other climbers and good rescue facilities relative to more obscure routes, and it offers a better chance of seeing some wildlife. It is the only route where you can sleep in proper huts throughout, with bathing water and bottled drinks normally available, too. The main drawback of the Marangu Route is that it is heavily trampled by comparison with other routes, for which reason many people complain that it can feel overcrowded.

Day 1: Marangu to Mandara Hut (*12km, 4hrs*) On an organised climb you will be dropped at the park entrance gate a few kilometres past Marangu. There is a high chance of rain in the afternoon, so it is wise to set off on this four-hour hike as early in the day as you can. Foot traffic is heavy along this stretch, which means that although you pass through thick forest, the shy animals that inhabit the forest are not likely to be seen. If your guide will go that way, use the parallel trail, which meets the main trail halfway between the gate and the hut. Mandara Hut (2,700m) is an attractive collection of buildings with room for 200 people.

Day 2: Mandara Hut to Horombo Hut (*15km, 6hrs*) You continue through forest for a short time before reaching the heather and moorland zone, from where there are good views of the peaks and Moshi. The walk takes up to six hours. Horombo Hut (3,720m) sleeps up to 120 people. It is in a valley and surrounded by giant lobelia and groundsel. If you do a six-day hike, you will spend a day at Horombo to acclimatise.

Day 3: Horombo Hut to Kibo Hut (*15km, 6–7hrs*) The vegetation thins out as you enter the desert-like alpine zone, and when you cross the saddle Kibo Peak comes into view. This six- to seven-hour walk should be done slowly: many people start to feel the effects of altitude. Kibo Hut (4,703m) is a stone construction that sleeps up to 120 people. Water must be carried from a stream above Horombo. You may find it difficult to sleep at this altitude, and as you will have to rise at around 01.00 the next morning, many people feel it is better not to bother trying.

Days 4 and 5: Kibo Hut to the summit to Marangu (*5km, 6 hours*) The best time to climb is during the night, as it is marginally easier to climb the scree slope to Gillman's Point on the crater rim when it is frozen. This ascent typically takes about six hours, so you need to get going between midnight and 01.00 to stand a chance of reaching the summit in time to catch the sunrise. From Gillman's Point it is a further two-hour round trip along the crater's edge to Uhuru Peak, the highest point in Africa. From the summit, it's a roughly seven-hour descent with a break at Kibo Hut to Horombo Hut, where you will spend your last night on the mountain. The final day's descent from Horombo to Marangu generally takes seven to eight hours, so you should arrive in Marangu in the mid-afternoon.

OTHER ROUTES Although the majority of trekkers stick to the Marangu Route, which is both the easiest and quickest ascent route up Kilimanjaro, with the best overnight facilities, an increasing proportion opt for one of five relatively off-the-beaten-track alternatives. While the merits and demerits of avoiding the Marangu Route are hotly debated, there is no doubt about two things: firstly that you'll see relatively few other tourists on the more obscure routes, and secondly that you'll pay considerably more for this privilege. Aesthetic and financial considerations aside, an unambiguous logistical disadvantage of the less-used routes is that, with the exception of Rongai, they are tougher going (though only the Umbwe is markedly so). Also, huts, where they exist, are virtually derelict, which enforces camping.

Machame Route In recent years, the Machame Route has grown greatly in popularity. It is widely regarded to be the most scenic viable ascent route, with great views across to Mount Meru, and as a whole it is relatively gradual, requiring at least six days for the full ascent and descent. Short sections are steeper and slightly more difficult than any part of the Marangu Route, but this is compensated for by the longer period for acclimatisation.

The route is named after the village of Machame, from where it is a two-hour walk to the park gate (1,950m). Most companies will provide transport as far as the gate (at least when the road is passable), and then it's a six- to eight-hour trek through thick forest to Machame Hut, which lies on the edge of the moorland zone at 2,890m. The Machame Hut is now a ruin, so camping is necessary, but water is available. The

---

CHAGGA HOME GARDENS *Emma Thomson*

For decades the Chagga have been making use of the fertile soil that lies at the foot of Kilimanjaro. Originally, the land was divided into family allotments or *shamba* (usually 0.68ha) and passed from father to son. Later on land was seized by the state, and re-allocated depending on the size of the family. These lush plots are used to grow coffee, plantain, bananas and medicinal herbs, allowing the Chagga to be self-sufficient. This cropping system remained stable for at least a century, and only recently has it come under pressure from rapid population growth, diminishing land resources, changes in dietary habits and economic pressures for improved housing and schooling. These pressing needs have forced the younger generations to travel into the towns in search of paid work. However, this migration of youngsters to urban areas not only leads to labour shortages on the farms but also disrupts the traditional transmission from one generation to the next of the knowledge and experience required for the successful management of the farms.

PORTER TREATMENT GUIDELINES

These guidelines are produced by the Kilimanjaro Porters Assistance Project (KPAP) (*Hill St, behind the Coffee Shop, Moshi;* m *0754 817615;* e *info@kiliporters.org; www.kiliporters.org*), an initiative of the International Mountain Explorers Connection, a non-profit organisation based in the United States.

Visit the website for further information, including a list of local and international operators that it regards to be committed to responsible treatment of porters, You can also drop into the office in Moshi to attend a 'Porter Briefing', obtain a free Swahili–English language card, purchase discounted maps, arrange for off-the-beaten-path trips and homestays that directly support the local people, report any instances of porter abuse, or make a donation of clothing, money or volunteer help.

1 Ensure your porters are adequately clothed with suitable footwear, socks, waterproof jackets and trousers, gloves, hats, sunglasses, etc. Clothing for loan is available at the KPAP office in Moshi.
2 Fair wages should be paid. Kilimanjaro National Park now recommends US$10 per day. Ask your company how much your porters are paid (and whether it includes food) to encourage fair treatment from operators and guides.
3 Porters should eat at least two meals a day and have access to water.
4 Check the weight of the loads. The recommended maximum of 25kg includes the porter's personal gear (assumed to be 5kg), so the load for the company should not exceed 20kg. If additional porters need to be hired make sure that the tour company is paying each porter their full wage when you return.
5 Count the number of porters every day: you are paying and tipping for them. Porters should not be sent down early as they will not receive their tips, and the other porters are then overloaded.
6 Make sure your porters are provided with proper shelter. Where no shelter is available, porters need proper sleeping accommodation that includes tents and sleeping bags. Sleeping in the mess tent means that the porters have to wait outside for climbers to finish their meals.
7 Ensure that each porter receives the intended tip. If you give tips to one individual you run the risk that they may not distribute the proper amount to the crew.
8 Take care of sick or injured porters. Porters deserve the same standard of treatment, care and rescue as their clients. Sick or injured porters need to be sent down with someone who speaks their language and understands the problem. If available, porters should also be provided with insurance.
9 Get to know your porters. Some porters speak English and will appreciate any effort to speak with them. Free Swahili-language cards are available at the KPAP office in Moshi. The word *pole* (which translates loosely as 'sorry') shows respect for porters after a long day carrying your bags. *Asante* means 'thank you'.
10 After your climb, report any instances of abuse or neglect by email or by visiting the office.

second day of this trail consists of a 9km, four- to six-hour hike through the moorland zone of Shira Plateau to Shira Hut (3,840m), which is near a stream. Once again, this hut has fallen into disuse, so the options are camping or sleeping in a nearby cave.

From Shira, a number of options exist: you could spend your third night at Lava Tower Hut (4,630m), four hours from Shira, but the ascent to the summit from here is tricky and only advisable if you are experienced and have good equipment. A less arduous option is to spend your third night at Barranco Campsite (3,950m), a tough 12km, six-hour hike from Shira, then to go on to Barafu Hut (4,600m) on the fourth day, a walk of approximately seven hours. From Barafu, it is normal to begin the steep seven- to eight-hour clamber to Stella Point (5,735m) at midnight, so that you arrive at sunrise, with the option of continuing on to Uhuru Peak, a two-hour round trip, before hiking back down to Mweka Hut via Barafu in the afternoon. This day can involve up to 16 hours of walking altogether. After spending your fifth night at Mweka Hut (3,100m), you will descend the mountain on the sixth day via the Mweka Route, a four- to six-hour walk.

The huts along this route are practically unusable, but any reliable operator will provide you with camping equipment and employ enough porters to carry the camp and set it up.

Mweka Route This is the steepest and fastest route to the summit. There are two huts along it – Mweka (3,100m) and Barafu (4,600m), each sleeping up to 16 people – though neither is reportedly habitable at the time of writing. There is water at Mweka but not at Barafu. This route starts at the Mweka Wildlife College, 12km from Moshi. From there it takes about eight hours to get to Mweka Hut, then a further eight hours to Barafu, from where it replicates the Machame Route. The Mweka Route is not recommended for ascending the mountain, since it is too short for proper acclimatisation, but is often used as a descent route by people climbing the Machame or Shira routes.

Shira Route Although this route could technically be covered in five days by driving to the high-altitude trailhead, this would allow you very little time to acclimatise, and greatly decrease the odds of reaching the summit. A minimum of six days is recommended, but better seven so that you can spend a full day at Shira Hut to acclimatise. The route starts at Londorossi Gate on the western side of the mountain, from where a 19km track leads to the trailhead at around 3,500m. It is possible to motor to the trailhead in a 4x4, but for reasons already mentioned it would be advisable to walk, with an overnight stop to camp outside Simba Cave, which lies in an area of moorland where elephants and buffalo are regularly encountered. From the trailhead, it's a straightforward 4km to the campsite at the disused Shira Hut. If you opt to spend two nights at Shira in order to acclimatise, there are some worthwhile day walks in the vicinity. From Shira Hut, the route is identical to the Machame Route, and it is normal to return along the Mweka Route.

Rongai Route The only route ascending Kilimanjaro from the northeast, the Rongai Route starts close to the Kenyan border and was closed for several years due to border sensitivity. In terms of gradients, it is probably less physically demanding than the Marangu Route, and the scenery, with views over the Tsavo Plains, is regarded to be as beautiful. The Rongai Route can be covered over five days, with equally good if not better conditions for acclimatisation than the Marangu Route, though as with Marangu the odds of reaching the summit improve if you opt for an additional day.

The route starts at the village of Nale Moru (2,000m) near the Kenyan border, from where a footpath leads through cultivated fields and plantation forest before entering the montane forest zone, where black-and-white colobus monkeys are frequently encountered. The first campsite is reached after three to five hours, and lies at about 2,700m on the frontier of the forest and moorland zones. On the five-day hike, the second day involves a gentle five- to six-hour ascent, through an area of moorland where elephants are sometimes seen, to Third Cave Campsite (3,500m). On the third day, it's a four- to five-hour walk to School Campsite (4,750m) at the base of Kibo, with the option of camping here or else continuing to the nearby Kibo Hut, which is more crowded but more commodious. The ascent from here is identical to the Marangu Route. A six-day variation on the above route involves spending the second night at Kikelewa Caves (*3,600m, 6–7hr walk*), a night at Mawenzi Tarn near the synonymous peak (*4,330m, 4hr walk*), then crossing the saddle between Mawenzi and Kibo to rejoin the five-day route at School Campsite.

Umbwe Route This short, steep route, possibly the most scenic of the lot, is not recommended as an ascent route as it is very steep in parts and involves one short stretch of genuine rock climbing. It is occasionally used as a descent route, and can be tied in with almost any of the ascent routes, though many operators understandably prefer not to take the risk, or charge a premium for using it. Umbwe Route descends from Barranco Hut, and comes out at the village of Umbwe. It is possible to sleep in two caves on the lower slopes along this route.

ARRANGING A CLIMB The only sensible way to go about climbing Kilimanjaro is through a reliable specialised operator. Readers who pre-book a climb through a known tour operator in their own country can be reasonably confident that they will be going with a reputable ground operator in Tanzania. Readers who want to make their arrangements online or after they arrive in Tanzania will find an almost infinite number of trekking companies operating out of Moshi, Arusha and to a lesser extent Marangu, and they should be able to negotiate a far better price by cutting out the middleman, but should also be circumspect about dealing with any company that lacks a verifiable pedigree. A list of respected operators is included in the box on page 168, and while such a list can never be close to comprehensive, it is reasonable to assume that anybody who can offer you a significantly cheaper package than the more budget-friendly companies on this list is not to be trusted.

Kilimanjaro climbs do not come cheaply (see box, *Costing a climb*, page 171). In 2012, five-day Marangu climbs with a reliable operator started at an all-inclusive price of around US$1,100 per person for two people. You may be able to negotiate the price down slightly, especially for a larger group, but when you are paying this sort of money, it strikes me as sensible to shop around for quality of service rather than a fractional saving. A reputable operator will provide good food, experienced guides and porters, and reliable equipment – all of which go a long way to ensuring not only that you reach the top, but also that you come back down alive. You can assume that the cost of any package with a reputable operator will include a registered guide, two porters per person, park fees, food, and transport to and from the gate. It is, however, advisable to check exactly what you are paying for, and (especially for larger parties) to ensure that one porter is also registered as a guide, so that if somebody has to turn back, the rest of the group can still continue their climb. It might also be worth pointing out the potential risk attached to forming an impromptu group with strangers merely to cut 5% or so off the price. If you hike on

Do not attempt to climb Kilimanjaro unless you are reasonably fit, or if you have heart or lung problems (although asthma sufferers should be all right). Bear in mind, however, that very fit people are more prone to altitude sickness because they ascend too fast.

Above 3,000m you may not feel hungry, but you should try to eat. Carbohydrates and fruit are recommended, whereas rich or fatty foods are harder to digest. You should drink plenty of liquids, at least three litres of water daily, and will need enough water bottles to carry this. Dehydration is one of the most common reasons for failing to complete the climb. If you dress in layers, you can take off clothes before you sweat too much, thereby reducing water loss.

Few people climb Kilimanjaro without feeling some of the symptoms of altitude sickness: headaches, nausea, fatigue, breathlessness, sleeplessness and swelling of the hands and feet. You can reduce these by allowing yourself time to acclimatise by taking an extra day over the ascent, eating and drinking properly, and trying not to push yourself. If you walk slowly and steadily, you will tire less quickly than if you try to rush each day's walk. Acetazolamide (Diamox) helps speed acclimatisation and many people find it useful; take 250mg twice a day for five days, starting two or three days before reaching 3,500m. However, the side effects from this drug may resemble altitude sickness and therefore it is advisable to try the medication for a couple of days about two weeks before the trip to see if it suits you.

Should symptoms become severe, and especially if they are clearly getting worse, then descend immediately. Even going down 500m is enough to start recovery. Sleeping high with significant symptoms is dangerous; if in doubt descend to sleep low.

Pulmonary and cerebral oedemas are altitude-related problems that can be rapidly fatal if you do not descend. Symptoms of the former include shortness of breath when at rest, coughing up frothy spit or even blood, and undue breathlessness compared with accompanying friends. Symptoms of high altitude cerebral oedema are headaches, poor co-ordination, staggering like a drunk, disorientation, poor judgement and even hallucinations. The danger is that the sufferer usually doesn't realise how sick he/she is and may argue against descending. The only treatment for altitude sickness is descent.

Altitude-related illness is also a potential problem on Mount Meru, and similar precautions should be taken. Other mountains in Tanzania are not high enough for it to be a cause for concern.

Hypothermia is a lowering of body temperature usually caused by a combination of cold and wet. Mild cases usually manifest themselves as uncontrollable shivering. Put on dry, warm clothes and get into a sleeping bag; this will normally raise your body temperature sufficiently. Severe hypothermia is potentially fatal: symptoms include disorientation, lethargy, mental confusion (including an inappropriate feeling of well-being and warmth!) and coma. In severe cases the rescue team should be summoned.

A US$20 rescue fee is paid by all climbers upon entering the national park. The rescue team ordinarily covers the Marangu Route only; if you use another route their services must be organised in advance.

your own or with people you know well, you can dictate your own pace and there is less danger of personality clashes developing mid-climb.

The standard duration of a climb on the Marangu Route is five days. Many people with repeated experience of Kilimanjaro recommend adding a sixth day to acclimatise at Horombo Hut. The majority opinion among operators and mountain experts is that this will improve the odds of reaching the summit by as much as 20%. However, other operators say that that the extra day makes little difference except that it adds a similar figure to the cost of the climb. No meaningful statistics are available to support one view or the other, but we would certainly recommend those can who afford it to take an extra day or two over the ascent.

In this context, it is worth noting that the exhaustion felt by almost all hikers as they approach the peak is not merely a function of altitude. On the Marangu Route, for instance, most people hike for six to eight hours on day three, and then after a minimal dose of sleep (if any at all) rise at around midnight to start the final five- to six-hour ascent to the peak. In other words, when they reach the peak, they will usually have been walking for up to 14 of the last 20-odd hours, without any significant sleep – something that would tire out most people even if they weren't facing an altitudinal increase of around 2,000m! On that basis alone, an extra night along the way would have some value in pure recuperative terms. And certainly, my firm impression is that travellers who spend six days on the mountain enjoy the climb far more than those who take five days, whether or not they reach the peak.

Of the less popular routes up Kilimanjaro, the one most frequently used by tourists, the Machame Route, requires a minimum of six days. Most operators will charge at least US$1,500 per person for this route, because it requires far more outlay on their part. The huts along the Machame Route are in such poor condition that tents and camping equipment must be provided, along with a coterie of porters to carry and set up the makeshift camp. The same problem exists on all routes except Marangu, so that any off-the-beaten-track climb will be considerably more costly than the standard one. Should you decide to use a route other than Marangu, it is critical that you work through an operator with experience of that route.

The dubious alternative to using a reputable company is to take your chances with a small operator or private individual who approaches you on the street. These people will offer climbs for around US$100 cheaper than an established operator, but the risks are greater and because they generally have no office there is little accountability on their side. A crucial point when comparing this

CHAGGA FAMILIES   *Emma Thomson*

Clan identity is highly important to the Chagga – to the extent that when individuals address each other, they will mention their clan name before revealing their first name or family name.

This sense of solidarity and membership is reinforced within the family unit, where every son is appointed a specific role. The first-born must protect and care for his grandmother, by visiting her at least once a month. The second son is raised to inherit the role of the father and must apply himself to his father's bidding. The third son must protect and cherish his mother.

Every year, between Christmas and the New Year, all family members must return to their home villages for at least three days, so they can be accounted for and to introduce new family members. If unable to attend, an absentee must provide a valid excuse, or from then on be considered an outsider.

situation with the similar one that surrounds arranging a safari out of Arusha is that you're not merely talking about losing a day through breakdown or a similar inconvenience. With Kilimanjaro, you could literally die on the mountain. I've heard several stories of climbers being supplied with inadequate equipment and food, even of travellers being abandoned by their guide mid-climb. The very least you can do, if you make arrangements of this sort, is to verify that your guide is registered; he should have a small wallet-like document to prove it, though even this can be faked.

OTHER PREPARATIONS Two climatic factors must be considered when preparing to climb Kilimanjaro. The obvious one is the cold. Bring plenty of warm clothes, a windproof jacket, a pair of gloves, a balaclava, a warm sleeping bag and an insulation mat. During the rainy season, a waterproof jacket and trousers will come in useful. A less obvious factor is the sun, which is fierce at high altitudes. Bring sunglasses, sunscreen and a hat.

Other essentials are water bottles, and solid shoes or preferably boots that have already been worn in. Most of these items can be hired in Moshi or at the park gate, or from the company you arrange to climb with. We've heard varying reports about the condition of locally hired items, but standards seem to be far higher than they were only a few years back.

KILIMANJARO: RECOMMENDED LOCAL OPERATORS

Almost any international agent selling safaris to Tanzania can also arrange a Kilimanjaro climb through a reliable local operator. However, travellers who want to book their climb direct through a local operator, whether they do it online or after arriving in Tanzania, will soon realise that there are a daunting number of options, ranging from costly quality operators with vast experience of the mountain through to small local operators offering cutthroat prices and similar services – and pretty much every gradation in between. It is impossible for a guidebook of this sort to attempt to assess every last operator in such a busy and competitive market, but the following companies can all be recommended as reputable and reliable.

MOSHI It is difficult to walk far in some parts of Moshi without having a local guide or self-styled tour operator trying to persuade you to arrange a climb. These guys may offer marginally cheaper rates than established operators, but they are notoriously unreliable. Our advice is to ignore anybody who approaches you on the street in favour of a proper travel agency, of which the following stand out.

Honey Badger m 0787 730235; e info@honeybadgerlodge.com; www.honeybadgerlodge.com. Based out of the lodge of the same name, this small ethically-minded operator is recommended both for its prices & socially conscious attitude to the treatment of porters & guides.
Keys Hotel 027 275 2250/1870; e info@keys-hotel-tours.com; www.keys-hotel-tours.com. Excellent & experienced operator based at one of the town's best hotels, & very reasonably priced.
Snow Cap Limited 027 275 0233; m 0784 451000; e snowcap@kilinet.co.tz; www.snowcap. co.tz. Another very experienced but reasonably priced operator known for its ethical treatment of porters & guides.
Zara Tours 027 275 4826; e zara@zaratours.com; www.zaratours.com. Situated on Rindi Lane diagonally opposite the Stanbic Bank, Zara Tours has been one of the most prominent & reliable budget/mid-range climb operators for decades.

First recorded ascent: Hans Meyer and Ludwig Purtscheller, 1889
Fastest ascent: Killan Jornet (Spain) in five hours 23 minutes, 2010
Fastest ascent and descent: Killan Jornet (Spain) in seven hours 14 minutes, 2010
Fastest ascent by a woman: Deborah Bachmann (Tanzania) in 11 hours, 51 minutes, 2011
Youngest to summit: Keats Boyd (USA), seven years old, 2008
Oldest person to summit: Bernice Buum (USA), 83 years old, 2010
Oldest man to summit: George Solt (UK), 82 years old, 2010

A good medical kit is essential, especially if you are climbing with a cheap company. You'll go through plenty of plasters if you acquire a few blisters (assume that you will), and can also expect to want headache tablets.

You might want to buy biscuits, chocolate, sweets, glucose powder and other energy-rich snacks to take with you up the mountain. No companies supply this sort of thing, and although they are sometimes available at the huts, you'll pay through the nose for them.

MARANGU The family-run **Marangu Hotel** has been taking people up Kilimanjaro for decades, and they have an impeccable reputation. The standard packages aren't the cheapest available, but they are pretty good value, and the standard of service and equipment is very high. The self-catering 'hard-way' climbs organised by the Marangu Hotel are probably the cheapest reliable deals you'll find anywhere in Tanzania. Also reliable are the **Kibo Hotel** and **Babylon Lodge**. Contact details for these hotels are found under *Where to stay* in Marangu, page 148.

ARUSHA Most safari companies in Arusha arrange Kilimanjaro climbs, but will generally work through a ground operator in Moshi or Marangu, which means that they have to charge slightly higher rates. Any of the Arusha-based safari companies listed in that section (see page 103) can be recommended, and short-stay visitors who are already going on safari with one of these companies will probably find that the ease and efficiency of arranging a Kilimanjaro climb through them outweighs the minor additional expenditure.

There are a few companies that arrange their own Kili climbs out of Arusha. **Hoopoe Safaris** has a long track record of organising ascents along the lesser-known routes, and is well worth contacting if you're prepared to pay a premium for top guides and equipment. So too is **Nature Discovery**, a highly regarded company that specialises in the more obscure routes up the mountain, and routinely sets up camp in the crater of Kibo, allowing you to explore the peaks area and ash cone at relative leisure. **Tropical Trails**, based at Masai Camp on the outskirts of Arusha, has an excellent reputation for Kili climbs. **Roy Safaris** also arranges its own trekking and climbing on Kilimanjaro, Mount Meru and elsewhere. **Fair Travel** is a new company that takes the novel approach of paying guides, cooks and porters around double the going rate rather than forcing them to be dependent on tips.

MAPS AND FURTHER READING Trekkers are not permitted on the mountain without a registered guide, and all sensible trekkers will make arrangements through a reliable operator, which means that there is no real need for detailed route descriptions once you're on the mountain. Nevertheless, many trekkers will benefit from the detailed practical advice and overview of route possibilities provided in a few specialist Kilimanjaro guidebooks. The pick of these is undoubtedly the 336-page *Kilimanjaro: The Trekking Guide to Africa's Highest Mountain* by Henry Stedman (Trailblazer Guides, 3rd edition 2009), which can be bought locally or ordered in advance through online bookshops such as abebooks.com, amazon.co.uk and amazon.com. Also recommended is *Kilimanjaro: A Complete Trekker's Guide* by Alexander Stewart (Cicerone Press, 2004).

More concerned with the overall geology and natural history of Kilimanjaro, making it a more useful companion to trekkers on organised hikes, *Kilimanjaro: Africa's Beacon* is one of a series of informative pocket-sized guides published by the Zimbabwe-based African Publishing Group in association with Tanapa. It is widely available in Arusha and Moshi for around US$8. Its predecessor, the 60-page national park handbook *Kilimanjaro National Park*, is arguably more informative but less attractively put together, and is still widely available in Arusha and Moshi.

Giovanni Tombazzi's *New Map of Kilimanjaro National Park*, sold in Arusha and Moshi, is arguably the best available map and certainly the most visually attractive. Current climbing tips are printed on the back, along with a close-scale map of the final ascent to Kibo, and day-by-day contour 'graphs' for the more popular routes.

Before you leave home – or as a memento when you get back – try to get hold of *Kilimanjaro* by John Reader (Elm Tree Books, London, 1982), which is long out of print but available cheaply secondhand through the likes of Amazon. Although it is superficially a coffee-table book, it offers a well-written and absorbing overview of

ABBOTT'S DUIKER

An antelope occasionally encountered by hikers on Kilimanjaro is Abbott's duiker (*Cephalophus spadix*), a montane forest species known as *minde* in Swahili. Formerly quite widespread in suitable East African habitats, the duiker is today endemic only to eastern Tanzania due to environmental loss and poaching elsewhere in its natural range. After Ader's duiker, a lowland species of the East African coastal belt, Abbott's is the most threatened of African duikers, categorised as Endangered in the International Union for Conservation of Nature (IUCN) Red Data list for 2008, but based on present trends it is likely to decline to a status of critically endangered in the foreseeable future. Abbott's duiker is today confined to five forested montane 'islands' in eastern Tanzania, namely Kilimanjaro, Usambara, Udzungwa, Uluguru and Rungwe. It is a notoriously secretive creature (the first photograph of one was taken in 2003) and the total population is unknown, but a 1998 estimate of 2,500 based on limited data is not implausible, and more recent estimates place the total at only 1,500. Either way, Udzungwa probably harbours the most substantial and secure single population, followed by Kilimanjaro. Should you be lucky enough to stumble across this rare antelope, it has a glossy, unmarked off-black torso, a paler head and a distinctive red forehead tuft. Its size alone should, however, be diagnostic: the shoulder height of up to 75cm is the third largest of any duiker species, and far exceeds that of other more diminutive duikers that occur in Tanzania.

COSTING A CLIMB

The reason why climbing Kilimanjaro is so expensive boils down to the prescribed park fees charged by Tanapa. The daily entrance fee is US$60 per person, then there's a hut or camping fee of US$50 per person per night, as well as a one-off rescue fee of US$20 per person per climb. This creates a fixed cost of US$520 per person for a five-day hike up Marangu, plus an additional US$110 per person per extra day, before any actual services are provided. On top of this, there are set fees of US$20 per guide and US$15 per cook per party per day, and US$10 per porter per day, which would for example add another US$187.50 per person for two people taking a five-day hike with two porters each, or US$112.50 per person for four people taking a six-day hike with one porter each. Or to put it another way, an operator charging US$1,200 per person for two people to climb via the Marangu Route will be forking out US$700 in fees and other fixed costs, even before budgeting for transportation, food, equipment, etc, as well as the general running costs attached to operating any business.

It is worth noting that hikers should set aside around 10% of the cost of their climb to tipping guides, cooks and porters at the end of the trip. Usual tipping guidelines per day per party are around US$10–20 per guide, US$8–15 per cook, and US$5–10 per porter.

the mountain's history and various ecosystems, far more so than any more recent book of its type. The photographs are good, too.

SOUTHERN CROSS SAFARIS

Connoisseur Safaris

5Y-SXS

Contact Us:
Direct line: 020-2434600/1/2
+254 720600200
Email: sales@southerncrosssafaris.com
www.southerncrosssafaris.com

8

The Usambara Mountains

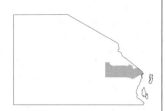

The series of forested mountain ranges rising to the east of the main road between Moshi and Tanga offers some of the most accessible, affordable and under-patronised opportunities for hiking and rambling anywhere in Tanzania. The largest of these ranges, and the most developed for tourism, is the Usambara, a single geological entity split into discrete eastern and western components by a deeply incised river valley. Both the Eastern and Western Usambara form part of the Eastern Arc formation, a sequence of isolated mountain ranges known for their rich biodiversity and high levels of endemism (see box, *An African Galápagos?* page 186).

The main regional tourist focus, situated near the southern end of the Western Usambara only 33km from the main road between Moshi and Dar es Salaam, is the low-key but attractive town of Lushoto, which forms an excellent base for relaxed day or overnight forays deeper into the same range. A more recent centre of tourist development is the Mambo Viewpoint EcoLodge, situated high on the northern escarpment of the Western Usambara, near the scenic village of Mtae. However, while both Lushoto and Mambo are great bases for walkers, the more alluring goal for dedicated nature lovers and birdwatchers, reached via an entirely separate access road closer to Tanga, is the forested Amani Nature Reserve in the Eastern Usambara.

LUSHOTO AND THE WESTERN USAMBARA

Set at an elevation of 1,400m (4,550ft), Lushoto is the principal town of the Western Usambara, the most densely populated and cultivated mountain range in northern Tanzania. The town peaked in significance during German colonial times, which may account for the slightly anachronistic aura that pervades it today. Many buildings on the main street date to the early 20th century, when Lushoto – then known as Wilhelmstal – provided weekend relief for German settlers farming the dry, dusty Maasai Steppes below. But if the main street of Lushoto dimly recalls an alpine village, the side roads are unambiguously African in architecture and spirit. So, too, is the vibrant market – busiest on Sunday and Thursday – where colourfully dressed Shambaa women sell fresh fruit and other agricultural produce grown on the surrounding slopes.

The vegetation around Lushoto is similarly dichotomous. Broad-leafed papaya and banana trees subvert neat rows of exotic pines and eucalyptus, which in turn are interspersed by patches of lush indigenous forest alive with the raucous squawking of silvery-cheeked hornbills and the banter of monkeys. These scenic highlands form superb walking country, riddled with small footpaths and winding roads, and studded with spectacular viewpoints over the low-lying plains below.

Less than an hour's drive from the main road between Moshi and Dar es Salaam, Lushoto has developed into the focal point of a travel scene that feels delightfully down-to-earth in comparison with the hype, hustle and extravagant prices associated with the likes of Arusha and Zanzibar. Indeed, a plethora of guides, community tourism projects and affordable guesthouses aimed at independent travellers makes it an ideal diversion for anybody interested in experiencing everyday Tanzanian culture away from the beach resorts and game reserves.

HISTORY The Shambaa of the Western Usambara are Bantu-speaking agriculturalists whose modern population totals around 200,000. Their origin is difficult to ascertain. Some clans claim they have always lived in the mountains, others that they moved there during times of drought, or in response to the 18th-century Maasai invasion of the plains. Quite possibly, these divergent accounts simply reflect divergent clan histories, since the ancestral Shambaa had a reputation for welcoming refugees, and the loosely structured political system that characterised the region until about 300 years ago would have encouraged the peaceful assimilation of newcomers. The notion that Shambaa identity was initially forged by physical proximity (rather than cultural affiliation or centralised leadership) is reinforced when you realise that their name derives from the geographical term used to describe the more moist upper reaches of the mountains, ie: Shambaai ('where the banana trees thrive').

Prior to the 18th century, the social structure of Shambaai was similar to the *ntemi* chieftaincies of western Tanzania. Each clan lived in a clearly defined territory with its own petty leadership of elders. A regional council of elders had the authority to settle disputes between different clans, and to approve marriages that would help cement inter-clan unity. According to tradition, the move towards centralised power – probably a response to the threat posed by the Maasai – was led by an outsider called Mbegha, the first Simba Mwene (Lion King) of Shambaai.

That Mbegha is a genuine historical figure is not in doubt, and the oral traditions of neighbouring tribes support the local story that he moved to the mountains from the plains below and became king after resolving a major crisis in Shambaai. Quite how Mbegha achieved his leonine coup is open to question. One – rather implausible – local tradition has it that, as a hunter of renown, Mbegha was called upon by a delegation of elders to rid the mountains of the bushpigs that were destroying all their crops, and was so effective in his campaign that he was appointed ruler of all Shambaai.

Mbegha went on to forge regional unity by taking a wife from each major clan and placing their firstborn son in charge of it. The Shambaa invested Mbegha and the Kilindi dynasty of Lion Kings that succeeded him with supernatural powers, believing among other things that they were able to control the elements. The dynasty consolidated power under the rule of Mbegha's grandson Kinyashi, who adopted a militaristic policy with the aim of forging the most important state between the coast and the great lake region. This ambition was realised by Kinyashi's son and successor, Kimweri, the greatest Simba Mwene of them all. Towards the end of his reign, Kimweri was held in sufficient esteem outside his kingdom that the explorer Richard Burton undertook the trek inland from Pangani to visit the Shambaa capital of Fuga (now more often called Vuga), close to modern-day Bumbuli (see box, *Portrait of a Lion King*, opposite).

Kimweri's death, a few years after Burton's visit, was the catalyst for the first major rift in Shambaa. Vuga was too deep in the mountains to have attracted regular contact with the Kilimanjaro-bound caravans. Not so the Shambaa town

Richard Burton's account of his 1857 visit to the Lion King of Shambaai, published in Volume 83 of *Blackwood's Edinburgh Magazine* in 1858, is probably the most revealing description of pre-colonial Shambaai ever printed. Some edited extracts follow:

Kimweri half rose from his cot as we entered, and motioned us to sit upon dwarf stools before him. He was an old, old man, emaciated by sickness. His head was shaved, his face beardless, and wrinkled like grandam's; his eyes were red, his jaws disfurnished, and his hands and feet were stained with leprous spots. The royal dress was a Surat cap, much the worse for wear, and a loinwrap as tattered. He was covered with a double cotton cloth, and he rested upon a Persian rug, apparently coeval with himself. The hut appeared that of a simple cultivator, but it was redolent of dignitaries, some fanning the Sultan, others chatting, and all holding long-stemmed pipes with small ebony bowls.

Kimweri, I was told, is the fourth of a dynasty ... originally from Nguru, a hilly region south of the river ... Kimweri, in youth a warrior of fame, ranked in the triumvirate of mountain kings above Bana Rongua of Chagga, and Bana Kizunga of the Wakuafy. In age he has lost ground [and] asserts kinghood but in one point: he has 300 wives, each surrounded by slaves, and portioned with a hut and a plantation. His little family amounts to between 80 and 90 sons, some of whom have Islamised, whilst their sire remains a 'pragmatical pagan'. The Lion [King]'s person is sacred; even a runaway slave saves life by touching royalty. Presently [Kimweri] will die, be wrapped up in matting, and placed sitting-wise under his deserted hut, a stick denoting the spot. Dogs will be slaughtered for the funeral-feast, and [Kimweri's son] Muigni Khatib will rule in his stead, and put to death all who dare, during the two months of mourning, to travel upon the king's highway.

Kimweri rules ... by selling his subjects – men, women, and children, young and old, gentle and simple, individually, or, when need lays down the law, by families and by villages ... Confiscation and sale are indigenous and frequent. None hold property without this despot's permission ... In a land where beads are small change, and sheeting and 'domestics' form the higher specie, revenue is thus collected. Cattle-breeders offer the first fruits of flocks and herds; elephant-hunters every second tusk; and traders a portion of their merchandise. Cultivators are rated annually at ten measures of grain ... The lion's share is reserved for the royal family; the crumbs are distributed to the councillors and [royal bodyguards].

Fuga, a heap of some 3000 souls, [is] defenceless, and composed of ... circular abodes [made with] frameworks of concentric wattles, wrapped with plantain-leaves ... fastened to little uprights, and plastered internally with mud ... The [people] ... file their teeth to points, and brand a circular beauty-spot in the mid-forehead; their heads are shaven, their feet bare, and, except talismans round the neck, wrists, and ankles, their only wear is a sheet over the shoulders, and a rag or hide round the loins. A knife is stuck in the waist-cord, and men walk abroad with pipe, bow, and quiverless arrows. The women are adorned with charm-bags; and collars of white beads – now in fashion throughout this region – from three to four pounds weight, encumber the shoulders of a 'distinguished person'. Their body-dress is the African sheet bound tightly under the arms, and falling to the ankles ...

of Mazinde, on what is now the main Moshi–Dar es Salaam road, whose chief Semboja exerted considerable influence over passing traders and was able to stockpile sufficient arms to overthrow Kimweri's successor at Vuga. This event split the Shambaa into several different splinter groups, and although Semboja retained nominal leadership of Shambaa, he controlled a far smaller area than Kimweri had before him.

Shambaa unity was further divided under German rule. Although the people of the Usambara played a leading role in the Abushiri Uprising of 1888–89, their resistance crumbled after Semboja's son and successor Mputa was hanged by the Germans in 1898. The Kilindi dynasty has, however, retained a strong symbolic role in modern Shambaa culture. Mputa's grandson Magogo, who took the throne in 1947, was one of the most respected traditional leaders in Tanzania prior to his death in 2000.

GETTING THERE AND AWAY Coming from Arusha, Moshi, Tanga, Dar es Salaam or almost anywhere else in Tanzania, the gateway to Lushoto is the small junction town of **Mombo**, which straddles the B1 on the plains below the Usambara massif (and shouldn't be confused with similarly named Mambo, higher up in the mountains). Mombo is connected to Lushoto by a surfaced 33km road that offers splendid views in all directions, passing *en route* through Soni with its famous waterfall, and the trip takes about 40-60 minutes by car, depending on how cowed the driver is by the precipitously steep drop-offs.

In a **private vehicle**, the driving time to Lushoto is about four hours from Arusha, three hours from Moshi, two hours from Tanga and four hours from Dar es Salaam. **Buses** usually take about 50% longer. There are direct buses along all these routes. Coming from Dar es Salaam, the best options are the Ibariki and Shambalai Luxury Coaches, which leave from Ubungo bus station at 06.00 and 12.00 respectively, take around six hours, and charge US$8 per person. From Arusha, a recommended service is Fasiha, which charges around US$10 per person, and leaves 06.30. Other buses tend to be slow and stop regularly to pick up or drop off passengers, so it is generally better to take an express service such as Dar Express or Kilimanjaro Express along the B1 and ask to be dropped off at Mombo, from where regular **minibuses** run through to Lushoto.

TOURIST INFORMATION AND TOUR OPERATORS The best source of tourist information in Lushoto, and to arrange a guided trip elsewhere in the mountains, is the TTB-endorsed tourist office run by the **Friends of Usambara** (⟨ *027 266 0132;* m *0787 094725/0784 449311;* e *info@usambaratravels.com; www.usambaratravels.com;* ⏲ *07.30–18.00 daily*). Prominently signposted opposite the park, this organisation stocks plenty of useful brochures, and the staff – most of whom double as guides – can arrange any walk or activity around Lushoto. They are also willing to dispense advice without being pushy about paid services. The fee structure is rather complex, but most guided day trips work out at around US$15–20 per person, while the daily rate for overnight excursions is about double that. The Friends of Usambara tourist office also arranges bicycle, tent, sleeping bag and roll-mat hire. All profits go towards the development of community projects.

Several other semi-official and private operators are dotted around Lushoto, distinguishing themselves from the Friends of Usambara mainly by having more of a hard sell approach. The most established and reputable of these, situated about 200m west of the bus station, is **Tayodea Tour Care** (m *0784 861969;* e *youthall2000@yahoo.com*), an offshoot of an NGO called the Tanga Youth

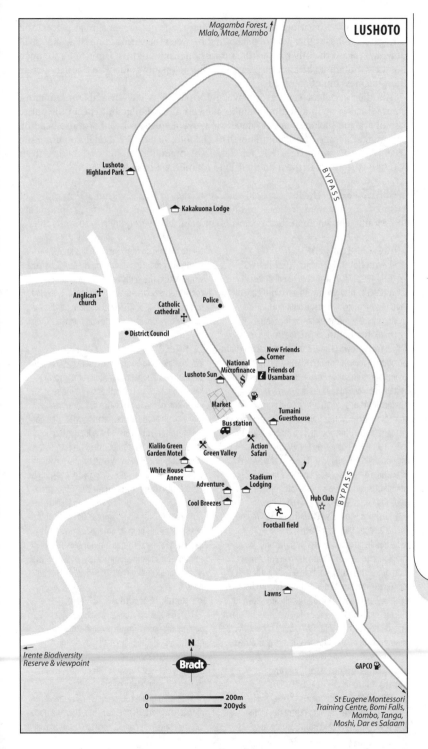

LUSHOTO

Magamba Forest,
Mlalo, Mtae, Mambo

BYPASS

Lushoto
Highland Park

Kakakuona Lodge

Anglican
church

Catholic
cathedral

Police

District Council

New Friends
Corner

National
Microfinance

Friends of
Usambara

Lushoto Sun

Market

Bus station

Tumaini
Guesthouse

Kialilo Green
Garden Motel

Green Valley

Action
Safari

White House
Annex

Adventure

Stadium
Lodging

Cool Breezes

Hub Club

Football field

BYPASS

Lawns

Irente Biodiversity
Reserve & viewpoint

N

Bradt

GAPCO

St Eugene Montessori
Training Centre, Bomi Falls,
Mombo, Tanga,
Moshi, Dar es Salaam

0 ——————— 200m
0 ——————— 200yds

Development Association that offers a similar range of tours at similar prices. You can expect to hear quite a bit of backbiting between the various tourist agencies, all of which regard the other as lacking professionalism, but this seems to be so much hot air – though do be circumspect about taking on any guide who doesn't operate their business out of an office.

Another excellent source of travel information is www.usambaramountains. com, which is maintained by Mambo Viewpoint EcoLodge but covers the entire Usambara and includes contact details for several guesthouses. For those heading through to Mambo, about 60km north of Lushoto, visit the EcoLodge's own website (see *Where to stay*, page 184) for details of organised biking and hiking from Mombo (the junction town on the B1) to Mambo via Lushoto.

WHERE TO STAY The listings below are restricted to places within a 3km radius of Lushoto. A great many other – and for the most part arguably better – options are to be found elsewhere in the Western Usambara, as covered later in this chapter.

Moderate and camping

⌂ **Lawns Hotel** (22 rooms) ☎027 264 0005; m 0784 420252/ 0744 464526; e enquiries@ lawnshotel.com; www.lawnshotel.com. Centred around a German homestead built *circa* 1900 & owned by the same Greek family for decades, the venerable Lawns Hotel, set in large gardens on a low hill above the town centre, is the most characterful accommodation option in Lushoto. The large rooms are all en suite with piping hot showers, the restaurant is one of the best in town, & there's a characterful bar decorated with banknotes & plates from around the world, & all sorts of other quirky paraphernalia. Other facilities include satellite TV, table tennis & a book swap library. The campsite is popular with overland tricks, so it can be a lively place for a drink. Rooms are variable in size & standard, so ask to see a few before you check in. *US$35/45 sgl/dbl B&B; camping US$9 pp.*

⌂ **Lushoto Highland Park Hotel** (21 rooms) ☎027 264 0001; m 0789 428 911; e lushotohighlandparkhotel@yahoo.com; www. highlandparktz.com. About 100m north of the main post office, this multi-storey hotel is the smartest option in town but it's decidedly lacking in character, & although it opened in 2009 it's already showing the first signs of wear & tear. The rooms are small but clean & tidy, & come with TV, en-suite hot shower, & in some cases a balcony. A decent café is attached. *US$30/40/50 sgl/dbl/suite B&B.*

⌂ **St Eugene Montessori Training Centre** (14 rooms) ☎027 264 0055; m 0784 523710; e steugenes_hostel@yahoo. com; . This modern training centre run by the Usambara Sisters is 2km from Lushoto town

centre at Ubiri on the Soni road. It is known locally for producing good jam, cheese, & banana wine. Within the landscaped grounds stands a comfortable & well-maintained hostel & a good restaurant. *US$25/45/54/60 en-suite sgl/dbl/tpl/ suite B&B. Lunch or dinner an additional US$7 pp.*

Budget

⌂ **Kakakuona Lodge** (10 rooms) ☎027 264 0273; e kakakuonainfo@yahoo.com; www. kakakuonatz.com. This rather smart lodge at the north end of the town centre has comfortable modern en-suite accommodation with tiled floors, pine furniture, dbl beds & TV. Added attractions include the onsite internet café & an excellent & reasonably priced balcony restaurant. Very good value. *US$16/20 en-suite sgl/dbl with hot shower.*

⌂ **Kialilo Green Garden Motel** (7 rooms) ☎027 266 6056; m 0715 237381; e kialilo24@ yahoo.co.uk. On a slope about 200m west of the bus station, this homely hotel has a pleasant garden, a rather cluttered interior & cramped comfortable en-suite rooms with hot water & TV. No food or alcohol served. *US$16/20/30 sgl/dbl/ twin.*

⌂ **Tumaini Guesthouse** (21 rooms) ☎027 264 0094; e tumaini@elct.org. This perennially popular church-run 2-storey guesthouse on the main road may be too institutional for some tastes, but otherwise it's arguably the best choice in this range – clean, secure, friendly & very central, with the bonus of a pleasant green courtyard with seating. All rooms have nets, showers are hot, there's a good internet café next door, & the restaurant is as good as it gets in the town centre (though no alcohol is served). *US$7 sgl using common showers, US$17 en-suite dbl, US$23 suite.*

Shoestring
⌂ **Lushoto Sun Hotel** (12 rooms) ☎ 027 264 0082; m 0748 471696. This established travellers' favourite has a usefully central location & welcoming atmosphere. The rooms are a little gloomy & tired but seem good value, with prices unchanged for several years now. An adequate

local restaurant is attached. *US$7/12/13 en-suite sgl/dbl/tpl with hot shower.*

⌂ **White House Annex** (10 rooms) m 0784 427471. This friendly local hotel less than 5 mins' walk from the bus station used to be a firm budget favourite, but standards have dropped & prices risen in recent years. Meals are excellent – a heaped plate of meat, roast potatoes & vegetables for around US$3. The small clean en-suite rooms are no better than adequate value. *US$10 twin, US$20 suite.*

✖ **WHERE TO EAT AND DRINK** The town is surprisingly short on decent, affordable eateries, although you can eat well – and cheaply – around the bus station and market. For lunch try the **Green Valley Café**, while in the evening street food such as beans and rice or *chipsi mayai* is sold by local women around the market. For a proper sit down meal, those listed below stand out.

There's not a lot of nightlife in Lushoto except on Saturday nights, when the **Hub Club** near the stadium hosts a disco from 21.00 until sunrise.

✖ **Kakakuona Lodge** ☎ 027 264 0273; e kakakuonainfo@yahoo.com; www.kakakuonatz. com. Our favourite eatery is this lodge's balcony restaurant, which overlooks a tree-fringed stream, & serves a great range of Western & Indian dishes in the US$3–4 bracket. Don't come here expecting a quick snack, though, as preparation of meat dishes takes at least an hour. It is one of the few eateries in Lushoto to serve alcohol.

✖ **Tumaini Café** ☎ 027 264 0094; e tumaini@ elct.org. Set on the ground floor of the guesthouse, this café serves a good selection of tasty pasta, seafood & curry dishes for US$3–5. No alcoholic beverages, & it has a rather canteen like feel, although you can eat on the balcony facing the main road.

PRACTICAL INFORMATION
Foreign exchange Foreign exchange is available at the **National Microfinance Bank**, which also has the only ATM, although it doesn't accept foreign cards. The internet café at **Tumaini Guesthouse** can exchange small amounts of hard currency cash.

Internet Your best option is the internet café in **Tumaini Guesthouse**, but a few other cafés are scattered around town. The services here are all quite slow and unreliable.

AROUND LUSHOTO A number of day and overnight trips can be undertaken in the Western Usambara, whether independently or with a guide provided by the Friends of Usambara tourist office in Lushoto. Popular day trips from Lushoto include Soni Falls, Irente Viewpoint and Magamba Forest. Worthwhile destinations further afield include Bumbuli and Mlalo. More remote still is the wonderfully scenic far north of the range, around the villages of Mambo and Mtae, an area covered under the separate heading Northern Usambara Escarpment (see page 183), along with the route there from Lushoto.

Irente Viewpoint and Biodiversity Reserve About 7km from Lushoto by road, Irente Viewpoint is the most popular day trip in the Usambara. It lies at the

8

western edge of the Usambara massif and offers a fantastic, vast view across the Maasai Steppes, 1,000m below. A second viewpoint at Yoghoi, about 1km further south, offers a very similar view encompassing the viewpoint at Irente. Either of the two viewpoints can be visited as a round trip from Lushoto, or you can loop between the two on foot.

A popular option is to combine the walk with a picnic lunch at the Irente Biodiversity Reserve, which consists of 6ha of former farmland re-planted with indigenous trees in the hope of recreating the original forest cover. Clearly signposted about 1.5km before you reach the viewpoint, the reserve lies on a 200ha working farm that started life as a German experimental coffee estate in 1896 and has been owned by the ELCT (Lutheran) Church since 1963. A delicious home-cooked lunch of rye bread, homemade cheese, organic vegetables, fruit juice and other farm produce can be provided between 10.00 and 14.00 Monday to Saturday for around US$4.50 per person, but do call in advance to make arrangements (see contact details under *Where to stay*, below). The farm shop at Irente (⏱ *08.00–16.00 daily*) also sells an array of local produce such as cheese for consumption off the premises, and the birding can be rewarding, with more than 80 species recorded in the area.

Getting there The road to Irente and Yoghoi leads eastward out of Lushoto from the Catholic Church. Once you're on it, there's no serious likelihood of getting lost. After about 3km, it passes through the village of Yoghoi and a large junction – keep going straight for Irente, or turn left for Yoghoi. By road, it's 4km from here to either viewpoint. There's no direct road between the viewpoints, but there is a clear footpath. It's perfectly possible to head out here alone, but most travellers arrange an official guide through the tourist office. The round trip takes around three hours.

⌂ Where to stay and eat

⌂ **Irente View Cliff Lodge & Campsite** (16 rooms) ☏027 264 0026; m 0784 866877; e info@ irenteview.com; www.irenteview.com. Ostensibly the most upmarket option in the Western Usambara, this new lodge looks the part initially, with its impressive thatched roof, modern décor, nice restaurant & stunning clifftop location. The en-suite rooms are also quite comfortable, but let down a little by poor quality fittings. A clifftop campsite with hot shower is attached. Good value. *US$50/65 standard sgl/dbl B&B; US$60/80 superior sgl/dbl B&B; camping US$5 pp.*

⌂ **Irente Biodiversity Reserve** (5 rooms) ☏027 264 0000; m 0784 502935; e info@ irentebiodiversityreserve.org; www. irentebiodiversityreserve.org. Set on Irente Farm, this reserve doubles as an orphanage & school for the blind funded partially by profits from the excellent home produce sold in its shop, as well as proceeds from the various accommodation options on the property. The latter includes Mkuyu Self-Catering Lodge, comprising 6 beds in 2 bedrooms, a kitchen with a gas stove & fridge, a sitting & dining room, & a private bathroom with hot shower. Other options are 1 trpl banda, 2 dbl bandas, & a campsite. Rooms at this pleasant retreat have self-catering facilities, but picnic lunches & simple home-cooked meals can be provided with a few hours warning. *Mkuyu Lodge US$80 per unit B&B for up to 6 people; bandas US$12–20 pp; camping US$4.50 pp.*

Soni Falls Straddling the surfaced road that connects Mombo to Lushoto, the small town of Soni is of interest primarily for the attractive but less than spectacular Soni Falls. This waterfall is visible from the main road to Lushoto, but to see it properly you need to stop in the town, from where a short, steep path leads to the rocky base. The quickest and best path to the waterfall, attracting a nominal fee, starts in the grounds of what was formerly the Soni Falls Hotel (established in 1930) but what is now the Soni Education Centre.

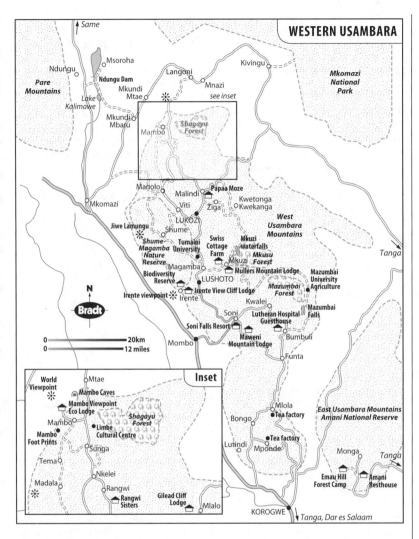

WESTERN USAMBARA

Getting there and away The drive between Lushoto and Soni takes no more than 30 minutes in either direction, using one of the regular **minibuses** that run back and forth to Mombo. If you visit Soni as a day trip, there is no reason to take a guide along. The Friends of Usambara tourist office in Lushoto organises a **half-day tour** out of Soni, taking in Kwa Mongo peak, known for its colourful butterflies, as well as the 300-year-old grave of the Shambaa King Mbegha and the so-called Magila 'Growing Rock' (whose base is exposed further every year as a result of soil erosion).

Where to stay and eat

Maweni Mountain Lodge (17 rooms) \027 264 0427; m 0784 297371; e info@ maweni.com; www.maweni.com. This rustic farm retreat lies 2km from Soni along a side road signposted from the Mombo–Lushoto road near

the junction with the Bumbuli road. Set in pretty gardens below a tall granite cliff, the main building consists of a 1920 farmhouse, & there's a more modern but dingier annexe & standing tents, too. *From €35/45 sgl/dbl HB.*

181

Soni Falls Resort (3 rooms) m 0784 384603/0715 364603. One of the most attractive lodges in the Usambara region, this Bavarian-style double-storey building originally dates to the German colonial era. Lovingly renovated & restored, it is set in well-wooded hilltop grounds, signposted to the right as you enter the village of Soni coming from Mombo. *US$30 dbl; US$50 family room sleeping 4. All rates B&B but other meals prepared by arrangement for around US$4pp.*

Bumbuli

Locally renowned for its old Lutheran Mission and associated hospital, Bumbuli lies 23km from Soni near the eastern rim of the Western Usambara, where King Mbegha reputedly entered the mountains some 300 years ago. A small waterfall can be found on the outskirts of the town, close to the Soni road, and the Saturday market is very colourful. The town lies in the shadow of Mazumbai Peak, whose upper slopes, covered in high montane forest, protect a variety of indigenous plants and rare birds. Bumbuli can be visited independently, but the Friends of Usambara tourist office in Lushoto also offers overnight hikes to the town and Mazumbai Forest, inclusive of guide, public transport and accommodation.

Getting there and away The 23km road between Soni and Bumbuli takes 45 minutes to cover in a **private vehicle**, passing through Mbelai, Kiboani and Kwahangara on the way. Using **public transport**, there are several direct buses daily between Bumbuli and Korogwe, Mombo and Lushoto. All these buses pass through Soni, so if no direct bus is about to leave, you could always catch one of the more frequent minibuses along the Mombo–Lushoto road, and hop off at Soni to board the next Bumbuli-bound vehicle.

Where to stay

Lutheran Hospital Guesthouse (8 rooms) Set in the mission grounds a 10min walk uphill from the town centre, this atmospheric restored colonial building has neat rooms with common hot shower & bath, as well as a lounge & self-catering kitchen. Cheap meals are also available. *US$10pp.*

Magamba Forest Reserve

Situated 15km from Lushoto, the most accessible indigenous forest in the Western Usambara covers the slopes of 2,230m Mount Magamba, the highest peak in the range. It is of great interest to birdwatchers, with the track to the old sawmill in particular offering a good chance of seeing Usambara weaver and Usambara akalat (both endemic to Western Usambara forests) and the localised red-capped forest warbler. A variety of mammals also live in this forest, although only black-and-white colobus and blue monkey are likely to be encountered by the casual visitor. It is also a stronghold for the endemic Western Usambara two-horned chameleon.

Guided day walks can be arranged through the tourist office in Lushoto, but it is possible to visit Magamba independently and explore it along a few self-guided trails. The most popular goal for day walks in the Magamba Forest is a small but pretty waterfall on the forest-fringed Mkuzu River about 2km from Migambo village. To reach this waterfall, take the right fork as you enter Migambo on the Magamba road. Follow this road downhill for about 20 minutes, passing a group of rocks in the river where local people wash their clothes, until you reach a bridge across the river. To your right, immediately before crossing the river, a footpath to the left follows the riverbank for about ten minutes to the waterfall.

Getting there Any vehicle heading north from Lushoto to Mtae, Mlalo or Mlola can drop you at the Magamba junction, 7km from Lushoto. The road heading to the right of this junction leads through the heart of the forest, following the course of the lushly vegetated Mkusu River for 7km to Migambo village. You could walk the length of this road in about 90 minutes in either direction, and it is also covered by a bus that runs daily between Lushoto and Mlola.

Where to stay and eat

⌂ **Muller's Mountain Lodge** \027 264 0204; m 0782 315666; e mullersmountainlodge@ yahoo.com, info@mullersmountainlodge.co.tz; www.mullersmountainlodge.co.tz. This family-run 1930s farm cottage, set in flowering gardens within the Magamba Forest, is arguably the most attractive place to stay anywhere in the Western Usambara, & an excellent base for birdwatchers. Home-cooked meals are available in the small restaurant or the gardens. Several day trails lead from the lodge; maps & directions can be supplied. It lies about 6km past Magamba junction on the Migambo road. A free transfer to/from Lushoto is offered to parties of 2 or more. *From US$38/48 B&B en-suite sgl/dbl; camping US$5 pp.*

⌂ **Swiss Cottage Farm** (2 rooms) \027 264 0155; m 0715 700813; info@swiss-farm-cottage. co.tz; www.swiss-farm-cottage.co.tz. This is another peaceful rustic retreat set on a working farm in the Magamba Forest area, & offering home-cooked lunch & dinners using organic farm produce. Coming from Magamba junction, the 1.5km turn-off to Swiss Farm Cottage lies to the left about 5km along the Migambo road, & 500m before the turn-off to Muller's. *US$35 dbl B&B.*

Mlalo This bizarre town sprawls over a large valley some 50km from Lushoto along a road that forks from the Mtae road at Malindi, 30km from Lushoto. Mlalo has an insular, almost otherworldly feel, epitomised by the unusual style of many of the buildings: two-storey mud houses whose intricately carved wooden balconies show German or Swahili influences.

Three buses run daily between Lushoto and Mlalo, leaving Lushoto in the early afternoon and Mlalo at around 07.00. The trip takes around two hours. Once there, accommodation options are limited to a few very basic guesthouses such as the **Afilex** and **Mlalo Motel**, both charging comfortably under US$5 for a room.

NORTHERN USAMBARA ESCARPMENT Though it traditionally sees less tourism than Lushoto, in part because it is more difficult to access, the most scenic part of the Western Usambara is undoubtedly the far north, where the high escarpment offers scintillating views across the expansive dry plains below to Lake Kalimawe, the Pare Mountains, Mkomazi National Park and Kilimanjaro, 250km distant but still a striking sight on a clear morning. Until recently, the only real travel base in the area was the small but idyllically sited village of Mtae, which boasts a few small and undistinguished guesthouses, and is largely undeveloped for tourism. That has changed, however, following the recent opening of the superb Mambo Viewpoint EcoLodge, which lies on the escarpment at Mambo village, about 5km from Mtae, and offers an exciting range of guided and unguided hikes as well as vehicle-based activities organised through its in-house tour operator. Highlights include Mtae itself (surely one of the most scenically located villages anywhere in Africa), as well as a variety of day walks along the escarpment and on the nearby forested slopes of Shagayu Mountain, as well as day or overnight camping trips to Lake Kalimawe and Mkomazi National Park

Getting there and away Mtae and Mambo lie about 65km north of Lushoto by road, a two-hour drive. If you are **driving** yourself, take the main road running north out of Lushoto, turn left at the junction shortly after the Lushoto Highland Park Hotel, then left again after 7km when you reach the junction for Magamba

8

Forest. When you reach Lukozi, the main road to Mtae and Mambo branches left in the small town centre, but if you are thinking of overnighting at Papaa Moze or the Rangwi Sisters (see *Where to stay*, below), then you need to keep going straight through town along a rough road that reconnects with the main road after about 20km at Nkelei. About 3km further on lies Sunga, from where it is about 10km without further diversions to Mtae, or a similar distance to Mambo, turning left at a signposted junction about 3km before Mtae. Using **public transport**, a few local buses connect Lushoto to Mtae and Mambo, usually leaving between 12.00 and 14.00, and charging around US$3.50 per person.

Coming from Arusha or Moshi in a **4x4** or on a **motorbike**, a scenic shortcut entails following the B1 towards Dar es Salaam for about an hour past Same to the village of Mkomazi (not to be confused with the eponymous national park), where a dirt road to the left is signposted for Mambo Viewpoint. Follow this road towards Mnazi, then after about one hour, turn right at Langoni (where there is another signpost for Mambo Viewpoint) and follow a clear diversion through a riverbed towards the base of the mountains, from where a steep but very striking scenic pass leads up the slopes to Mtae. This road should not be attempted after heavy rain, and a 4x4 is required in all conditions.

For **independent travellers**, it is also possible to do the trip between Mombo/ Lushoto and Mtae/Mambo in stages, stopping *en route* at small montane settlements such as Lukozi (which hosts a big Monday market), Malindi, Rangwi and Sunga. You could easily hike this yourself, or hop along using whatever public transport or lifts come your way, overnighting at some of the lodges listed below under the heading *En route from Lushoto*. Alternatively, Mambo Viewpoint EcoLodge has set out a few overnight hiking and mountain biking routes from Mombo or Lushoto, details of which are on their website.

Tour operators Kanyambo Safaris (m *0783 330046;* e *kanyambo.safaris@gmail. com; www.kanyambosafaris.com*) is a promising new operator based at Mambo Viewpoint EcoLodge run by a knowledgeable birdwatcher. It offers a variety of local excursions, including bird walks, village and other cultural visits, and walking excursions into the indigenous Shagayu Forest, as well as safaris to nearby Mkomazi National Park and further afield.

 Where to stay

En route from Lushoto

🏠 **Rangwi Sisters** m 0784 716529. Situated about 12km north of Lukozi, close to the junction village of Nkelei, this long-serving guesthouse, set on a Catholic Mission, offers the most comfortable accommodation *en route* from Lushoto to Mtae, & it also serves good home cooking. *US$16/20 en-suite sgl/dbl FB.*

🏠 **Papaa Moze Guesthouse** m 0784 599019; e lucasshem@yahoo.com. This small owner-managed guesthouse lies in the village of Malindi, about 4km north of Lukozi. It has a campsite, restaurant, bar & shop. *US$6/8 sgl/dbl.*

🏠 **Limbe Cultural Centre** (4 rooms) m 0786 887661. Situated on a smallholding on the right side of the main road 6km before Mtae & 3km past the village of Sunga, this rundown but friendly family-managed guesthouse has basic but clean rooms, & it can also serve meals upon request. *US$2/3 sgl/dbl.*

Mambo and Mtae

🏠 **Mambo Viewpoint EcoLodge** (5 cottages & 3 luxury tents) m 0785 272150/0774 272150; e info@mamboviewpoint.org; www. mamboviewpoint.org. Founded & managed by an environmentally & socially committed Dutch couple, this exemplarily eco-friendly lodge has a spectacular setting at an altitude of 1,900m on a stretch of escarpment offering stunning views to the Pare Mountains, the expansive plains of Mkomazi National Park & distant Kilimanjaro. It lies on the outskirts of Mambo, a village of 5,000, & is deeply committed to providing employment to locals & creating other grassroots economic opportunities through tourism. Accommodation is in a range of attractive individually styled cottages & en-suite luxury tents, & camping is also permitted. A wide range of guided & unguided activities is offered through the on-site operator Kanyambo Safaris (see opposite). It also offers a range of overnight hiking & biking trips to/ from other villages in & around the mountains, ranging from 1 to 6 nights in duration. The excellent website contains more details of these activities. Other attractions include the delicious home-cooked food, which is eaten communally, free Wi-Fi, & the opportunity to participate as a volunteer in local community projects. The grounds protect some interesting wildlife: the striking West Usambara 2-horned chameleon *Kinyongia multituberculata* is common (ask the staff to locate one for you) & the rare Taita falcon nests

on the cliffs below. *US$50/65 sgl/dbl B&B luxury tent; rooms from US$70/90 sgl/dbl B&B; camping US$8/10 sgl/dbl in your own tent, or US$15/20 in a hired tent. Lunch & dinner US$10 & US$15 pp respectively.*

⌂ **Mambo Cliff Inn** (5 rooms) m 0785 272150; e ndegec@gmail.com. Only 500m from Mambo Viewpoint & owned by its local manager, this clifftop lodge provides a relatively affordable alternative to its smarter neighbour. Accommodation is in neat little en-suite rooms with a balcony & a view, & a restaurant or bar is under construction. It is also possible to eat at Mambo Viewpoint & to participate in activities offered there. *US$10–30.*

⌂ **Mwivano I Guesthouse** The best of a few very basic local lodgings in Mtae, this guesthouse has a friendly owner, rooms with access to a communal cold shower, & an attached restaurant serving tasty, filling meals for next to nothing. *US$3 dbl.*

What to see

Mtae This small but sprawling village has perhaps the most spectacular location in the Western Usambara. Boasting several fine examples of traditional Shambaa mud houses, it runs for about 2km along what is in effect a dry peninsula, jutting out to the north of the range, and with a drop of several hundred metres on either side offering breathtaking views. The name Mtae translates as 'Place of Counting', a reference to its strategic importance to the Shambaa people during the 19th-century Maasai wars, when it was the site of several battles won by the Shambaa, who were able to see and count any raiding Maasai war party from afar.

The striking Lutheran church that stands in the middle of the town was built in the late 19th century on a site where, formerly, the most powerful ancestral spirits were believed to reside. The story is that the local chief showed this site to the missionaries, expecting them to flee in fear. Instead, the missionaries were unmoved, and the chief – concluding that they must be in touch with more powerful spirits – granted them permission to build a church there.

Mambo Several day hikes run from Mambo Viewpoint (see opposite) to sites on the nearby escarpment. The hike to the **Mambo Caves**, on the cliffs below the lodge, entails a 400m ascent and descent over 4km and takes around 3 hours, with a good chance of spotting cliff-nesting raptors, including the rare Taita falcon.

Another very scenic hike of similar length leads to the so-called **Mandala Hominid Footprints**, which some local sources reckon were imprinted in volcanic ash by early hominid inhabitants of the area perhaps a million years ago – an unlikely claim, given that the bedrock here is very ancient and non-volcanic in origin, and the impressions look a lot more like a function of weathering than they do footprints. Mambo Viewpoint can also arrange a cultural day tour encompassing a visit to a local healer, lunch with a local family, and meetings with local farmers.

AN AFRICAN GALÁPAGOS?

The phrase 'Eastern Arc' was coined by Dr Jon Lovett in the mid 1980s to describe a string of 13 physically isolated East African mountain ranges that share a very similar geomorphology and ecology. All but one of these crystalline ranges lies within Tanzania, forming a rough crescent that runs from Pare and Usambara in the north to Udzungwa and Mahenge in the south. Following a fault line that runs east of the more geologically recent Rift Valley, these are the oldest mountains in East Africa, having formed at least 100 million years ago, making them 50 times older than Kilimanjaro.

For the past 30 million years, the Eastern Arc has supported a cover of montane forest, one that flourished even during the drier and colder climatic conditions that have periodically affected the globe, thanks to a continuous westerly wind that blew in moisture from the Indian Ocean. It was during one such dry phase, ten million years ago, that these became isolated from the lowland rainforest of western and central Africa. More recently, each of the individual forested ranges became a discrete geographical entity, transforming the Eastern Arc into an archipelago of forested islands jutting out from an ocean of low-lying savanna. And as with true islands, these isolated ancient forests became veritable evolutionary hotspots.

The Eastern Arc Mountains host an assemblage of endemic races, species and genera with few peers anywhere in the world. In the two Usambara ranges alone, more than 2,850 plant species have been identified, a list that includes 680 types of tree, a greater tally than that of North America and Europe combined. At least 16 plant genera and 75 vertebrate species are endemic to the Eastern Arc forests. Their invertebrate wealth can be gauged by the fact that 265 invertebrate species are thus far known from just one of the 13 different ranges – an average of 20 endemics per range. Little wonder that the Eastern Arc is classified among the world's 20 top biodiversity hotspots, and is frequently referred to as the Galápagos of Africa.

Eastern Arc endemics fall into two broad categories: old endemics are modern relics of an ancient evolutionary lineage, while new endemics represent very recently evolved lineages. A clear example of a 'living fossil' falling into the former category are the giant elephant shrews of the suborder *Rhynchocyonidae*, whose four extant species are almost identical in structure to more widespread 20-million-year-old ancestral fossils. In many cases, these older, more stable endemics are affiliated to extant West African species from which they have become isolated: Abbott's duiker (see box, page 170) and the endemic monkey species of Udzungwa are cases in point.

The origins of new endemics are more variable. Some, such as the African violets, probably evolved from an ancestral stock blown across the ocean from Madagascar in a freak cyclone. Others, including many birds and flying insects, are local variants on similar species found in neighbouring savannas or in other forests in East Africa. The origin of several other Eastern Arc endemics is open to conjecture: four of the endemic birds show sufficient affiliations to Asian species to suggest they may have arrived there at a time when moister coastal vegetation formed a passage around the Arabian peninsula.

The forests of the Eastern Arc vary greatly in extent, biodiversity and the degree to which they have been studied and accorded official protection. A 1998 assessment by Newmark indicates that the Udzungwa range retains almost 2,000km² of natural forest, of which 20% has a closed canopy, while the forest cover on Kenya's Taita Hills is reduced to a mere 6km². The most significant forests in terms of biodiversity are probably Udzungwa, East Usambara and Uluguru. However, ranges such as Nguru and Rubeho remain little studied compared with the Usambara and Udzungwa, so they may host more endemics than is widely recognised.

The Eastern Arc forests are of great interest to birdwatchers as the core of the so-called Tanzania–Malawi Mountains Endemic Bird Area (EBA). This EBA includes roughly 30 forest pockets scattered across Malawi, Mozambique and Kenya, but these outlying forests cover a combined 500km^2 as compared with 7,200km^2 of qualifying forest in Tanzania. Of the 37 range-restricted bird species endemic to this EBA, all but five occur in Tanzania, and roughly half are confined to the country. In terms of avian diversity, the Udzungwa Mountains lead the pack with 23 regional endemics present, including several species found nowhere else or shared only with the inaccessible Rubeho Mountains. For first-time visitors, however, Amani Nature Reserve has the edge over Udzungwa in terms of ease of access to prime birding areas.

Distribution patterns of several range-restricted bird species within the EBA illuminate the mountains' pseudo-island ecology, with several species widespread on one particular range being absent from other apparently suitable ones. The Usambara akalat, for instance, is confined to the Western Usambara, while Loveridge's sunbird and the Uluguru bush-shrike are unique to the Uluguru. The most remarkable distribution pattern belongs to the long-billed tailorbird, a forest-fringe species confined to two ranges set an incredible 2,000km apart – the Eastern Usambara in northern Tanzania and Mount Namuli in central Mozambique. Stranger still is the case of the Udzungwa partridge: this evolutionary relic, discovered in 1991 and known only from Udzungwa and Rubeho, has stronger genetic affiliations to Asian hill partridges than to any other African bird.

The Eastern Arc has suffered extensive forest loss and fragmentation in the past century, primarily due to unprecedented land use pressure – the population of the Western Usambara, for instance, increased 20-fold in the 20th century. Of the 12 Eastern Arc ranges within Tanzania, only one – the inaccessible Rubeho massif – has retained more than half of its original forest cover, while five have lost between 75% and 90% of their forest in the last two centuries. Fortunately, none of Tanzania's Eastern Arc forests have yet approached the crisis point reached in Kenya's Taita Hills, where a mere 2% of the original forest remains.

Given that many Eastern Arc species are highly localised and that animal movement between forest patches is inhibited by fragmentation, it seems likely that 30% of Eastern Arc endemics have become extinct in the last century, or might well do so in the immediate future. True, the salvation of a few rare earthworm taxa might be dismissed as bunny-hugging esoterica, but the preservation of the Eastern Arc forests as water catchment areas is an issue of clear humanistic concern. Most of the extant Eastern Arc forests are now protected as forest reserves. The proclamation of a large part of the Udzungwa Mountains as a national park in 1992 is a further step in the right direction. Even more encouraging is the more recent creation of Amani Nature Reserve as part of a broader effort to introduce sustainable conservation and ecotourism with the involvement of local communities in the Eastern Usambara.

Anybody wishing to come to grips with the fascinating phenomenon of 'island' ecology in the Eastern Arc Mountains (and elsewhere on the African mainland) is pointed to Jonathon Kingdon's superb book *Island Africa*.

Shagayu Forest Reserve The second-largest indigenous forest in the Western Usambara, Shagayu extends over some 60km² along the slopes of the eponymous mountain, which rises to an altitude of 2,228m a few kilometres east of Mtae and Mambo. The forest here is thought to be in more pristine condition that the larger Magamba Forest Reserve, and it harbours a rich and varied forest birdlife, including the colourful Hartlaub's turaco, eagerly sought bar-tailed trogon, and Eastern Arc endemics such as Usambara akalat, Usambara double-collared sunbird, white-chested alethe and Usambara weaver. Visits to the forest can be arranged inexpensively through Mambo Viewpoint (see *Where to stay*, page 184). These include dedicated birding walks with knowledgeable guides, while non-birders can follow the scenic route to the **Kideghe Waterfall**, set deep in the forest, or undertake an overnight camping trip to the peak.

AMANI NATURE RESERVE AND THE EASTERN USAMBARA

The Eastern Usambara is one of the smallest of the Eastern Arc ranges, as well as one of the lowest, barely exceeding 1,500m in elevation. It is, however, one of the most important ecologically, receiving an annual rainfall of up to 2,000mm and covered in some of the most extensive and least degraded montane rainforest extant in Tanzania. In some places the indigenous vegetation has been replaced by tea plantations, while in others there has been more recent encroachment by subsistence farmers, but at least 400km² of natural forest remains. In common with the other montane forests of eastern Tanzania, the Eastern Usambara is cited as a biodiversity hotspot, characterised by a high level of endemism (see box, *An African Galápagos?* page 186). It is also a vital catchment area, providing fresh water to some 200,000 people, and the East Usambara Catchment Management Project (EUCAMP), funded by Finnish aid, has implemented a community-based conservation plan to protect the catchment forests.

The centrepiece of this project is the Amani Nature Reserve (*www.amaninature. org*), which formally opened in 1997 and protects almost 10,000ha of relatively undisturbed forest. Amani must rank close to being the most underrated reserve anywhere in northern Tanzania, offering the combination of excellent walking, beautiful forest scenery and a wealth of animal life. Although the nature reserve is a recent creation, Amani was settled by Germany as an agricultural research station in 1902, at which time the surrounding area was set aside to form what is reputedly still the second-largest botanical garden in the world. Lying at an elevation of roughly 900m, Amani remains a biological research station of some note, as well as an important centre for medical research. Most of the buildings date to the German and British colonial eras, giving it the genteel appearance of an English country village transplanted to the African jungle.

The development of Amani for ecotourism, with the emphasis on walking and hiking, has been a high priority over recent years. Nine trails have been demarcated at Amani, ranging in length from 3km to 12km, and leaflets with trail descriptions are available to visitors. The directions in the leaflets are reportedly not 100% accurate, so it might be worth hiking with a trained guide, who will also help you to spot birds and monkeys. The rehabilitated German stationmaster's house at Sigi (aka Kisiwani), some 7km from Amani on the Muheza road, doubles as an entrance gate and information centre, with an adjoining resthouse offering visitors a second, lower-elevation site from which to explore the forest.

For several years, a deterrent to visiting Amani Nature Reserve was the unrealistic and prohibitively high daily entrance fee charged to non-residents.

However, the good news is that as of January 2012 this fee was reduced to US$10 per person for all non-citizens, a one-off payment valid for the full duration of your stay, making the reserve a far more attractive prospect. Other fees include a daily vehicle entrance fee equivalent to around US$7 (or US$50 if the vehicle is foreign registered), a photography fee of US$50 per day, and an additional charge of US$15 per person per day for the services of a guide.

GETTING THERE AND AWAY The springboard for visits to Amani is the small town of **Muheza**, 40km west of Tanga on the main surfaced road to Moshi. There is plenty of **local transport** between Tanga and Muheza, and the trip takes less than two hours. Alternatively, any **bus** heading to Tanga from Arusha, Lushoto, Moshi

THE GENUS SAINTPAULIA

Without doubt the most familiar of the thousands of taxa that are endemic to the Eastern Arc Mountains is a small flowering plant first collected in the Eastern Usambara in 1892 by the District Commissioner of Tanga, Baron Walter von Saint Paul Illaire. Subsequently described as *Saintpaulia ionantha* in honour of its discoverer, the African violet (as it is more commonly known) was made commercially available in 1927, when ten different blue-flowered strains were put on the market. It is today one of the world's most popular perennial pot plants, with thousands of cultivated strains generating a global trade worth tens of millions of US dollars, and yet few enthusiasts realise that the wildflower is threatened within its natural range.

Although they vary greatly in shape and colour, most cultivated strains of African violet are hybrids of the original seeds collected by Baron Saint Paul, which belonged to two highly malleable races, *S. i. ionantha* and *S. i. grotei*. The specific taxonomy of the genus *Saintpaulia* is controversial: at one time more than 20 species were recognised but a 2006 study has reduced that number to six. The genus is unique to the Eastern Arc Mountains, and its main strongholds are the Eastern Usambara and Nguru Mountains.

Not affiliated to the true violets, *Saintpaulia* is a relatively recently evolved genus whose ancestral stock was most likely blown across from Madagascar in a cyclone (a flowering plant in the genus *Streptocarpus* has been cited as the probable ancestor). The wild *Saintpaulia* has probably never enjoyed a wide distribution or a high level of habitat tolerance. In the wild, as in the home, most species require continuous shade and humidity in order to flourish and because it depends on surface rather than underground moisture, *Saintpaulia* has an unusually shallow root system. It typically grows in moist cracks in porous rocks close to streams running through closed-canopy forest – though some specimens do lead an epiphytic existence on cycad trunks or the shady branches of palms.

The main threat to the wild *Saintpaulia* is the logging of tall trees, which creates breaks in the closed canopy. Researchers in the Eastern Usambara have come across dead or dying plants at several established *Saintpaulia* sites where the canopy has been broken due to logging. One of the many positive effects of the gazetting of Amani Nature Reserve in 1997 is that it should help secure the future of the genus – or at least those species that are resident within the reserve. Local guides will be able to show you the wildflowers on several of the established walking and driving trails.

BIRDING IN AMANI

Eastern Usambara takes second place to the Udzungwa as the most important avian site in the Eastern Arc Mountains, but it is still one of the most significant birding sites anywhere in East Africa. Amani in particular has several logistical advantages over the best birdwatching sites in the Udzungwa, namely relative ease of access, proximity to the established tourist circuit of northern Tanzania, and a superior tourist infrastructure and quality of guides. The Eastern Usambara's avifauna has received far more scientific attention than that of the other Eastern Arc ranges, dating from 1926 to 1948 when Amani was the home of the doyen of Tanzania ornithology, Reginald Moreau, credited with discovering and describing several new species including the long-billed tailorbird. This extensive study is reflected in a checklist of 340 bird species, including 12 that are globally threatened and 19 that are either endemic to the Eastern Arc Mountains or to the East African coastal biome.

The temptation on first arriving at Amani might be to rush off along one of the trails into the forest interior. In fact some of the most productive general birdwatching is to be had in the gardens and forest fringe around Amani village, slow exploration of which is likely to yield up to 50 forest-associated species including half-a-dozen genuine rarities. One of the more conspicuous and vocal residents around the resthouses is the green-headed oriole, a colourful bird that is restricted to a handful of montane forests between Tanzania and Mozambique. The flowering gardens are a good site for three of the four range-restricted sunbirds associated with the Eastern Usambara (ie: Amani, banded green and Uluguru violet-backed sunbird). The rare long-billed tailorbird has been discovered breeding at two sites in Amani village.

Having explored the resthouse area, the guided Turaco and Mbamole Hill trails are recommended for sighting further montane forest specials. Noteworthy birds resident in the forest around Amani include the Usambara eagle owl, southern banded snake eagle, silvery-cheeked hornbill, half-collared kingfisher, African green ibis, Fischer's turaco, African broadbill, East Coast akalat, white-chested alethe, Kenrick's and Waller's starlings, and several forest flycatchers. It is also worth noting that several of the more interesting Usambara specials are lowland forest species, more likely to be seen in and around Sigi than at Amani. Among the birds to look out for on the trails around Sigi are eastern green tinkerbird, African cuckoo-hawk, square-tailed drongo, bar-tailed trogon and chestnut-fronted helmet-shrike.

or Dar es Salaam can drop you there. Muheza is at its liveliest on the local market days of Thursday and Sunday, and there are numerous small guesthouses should you need to spend a night.

From Muheza, the road to Amani is clearly signposted, and the drive should take about 90 minutes, passing through the entrance gate at Sigi after an hour. Driving times will depend on the condition of the road, in particular the spectacular but steep 7km stretch between Sigi and Amani. Three buses daily run between Muheza and Sigi, leaving Muheza at around 12.30 and arriving about two hours later. One bus continues up the steep road to Amani, arriving an hour later. The bus from Amani to Muheza leaves at 06.30 and passes through Sigi at about 07.00.

WHERE TO STAY AND EAT Note that while camping is permitted in the reserve, the fee of US$35 per person per night for non-citizens makes it a somewhat uneconomic prospect when compared to staying in the resthouses or camping at Emau Hill, both of which are excellent value.

Moderate and camping
** Emau Hill Forest Camp** (6 rooms)
m 0782 656526; **e** emauhill@gmail.com; www.
emauhill.com. Situated about 3km from the park
headquarters at Amani, this environmentally
responsible new camp, operated by an NGO called
Takae, has accommodation in en-suite cottages
& standing tents, & it also has private campsites
for pitching a tent. The balcony offers fine views
into the forest: more than 130 bird species have
been seen from the dining banda & all the key
endemics are recorded in the immediate vicinity.
*US$110/160 sgl/dbl cottage FB, US$55-65 pp in
standing tent FB; camping US$7 pp.*

Budget
** Amani Resthouse** \ 027 254 0313;
e amaninaturereservetfs@yahoo.com; www.
amaninature.org. This well-maintained &
comfortable stone building set in the middle of the
research village dates to the colonial era. There is
a log fire in the lounge. Inexpensive meals can be
provided. *US$7.50 pp bed only.*
** Sigi Resthouse** \ 027 254 0313;
e amaninaturereservetfs@yahoo.com; www.
amaninature.org. The newer resthouse at Sigi is
similar in standard to the one at Amani, albeit with
a rather more modern feel. Inexpensive meals are
available. *US$7.50 pp bed only.*

WHAT TO SEE AND DO It is worth consulting with the reserve's guides about the trail most suited to your specific interest. The 10km **Konkoro Trail**, which can be covered on foot or in a vehicle, is good for African violets, and it cuts through several different forest types, as well as passing a viewpoint and terminating in an overnight campsite in the heart of the forest. The shorter **Turaco** and **Mbamole Hill** trails are recommended first options for birdwatchers. In addition to the prescribed walking trails, there is much to be seen along the roads and paths that lie within the research centre and botanical garden. Wandering around the forest-fringed village, you are likely to encounter a wide variety of birds, as well as black-and-white colobus and blue monkey – and you might even catch a glimpse of the bizarre and outsized Zanj elephant shrew.

Bradt Travel Guides

Claim 20% discount on your next Bradt book when you order from www.bradtguides.com quoting the code BRADT20

Africa

Africa Overland	£16.99
Algeria	£15.99
Angola	£18.99
Botswana	£16.99
Burkina Faso	£17.99
Cameroon	£15.99
Cape Verde	£15.99
Congo	£16.99
Eritrea	£15.99
Ethiopia	£17.99
Ethiopia Highlights	£15.99
Ghana	£15.99
Kenya Highlights	£15.99
Madagascar	£16.99
Madagascar Highlights	£15.99
Malawi	£15.99
Mali	£14.99
Mauritius, Rodrigues & Réunion	£16.99
Mozambique	£15.99
Namibia	£15.99
Nigeria	£17.99
North Africa: Roman Coast	£15.99
Rwanda	£16.99
São Tomé & Príncipe	£14.99
Seychelles	£16.99
Sierra Leone	£16.99
Somaliland	£15.99
South Africa Highlights	£15.99
Sudan	£16.99
Swaziland	£15.99
Tanzania Safari Guide	£17.99
Tanzania, Northern	£14.99
Uganda	£16.99
Zambia	£18.99
Zanzibar	£15.99
Zimbabwe	£15.99

The Americas and the Caribbean

Alaska	£15.99
Amazon Highlights	£15.99
Argentina	£16.99
Bahia	£14.99
Cayman Islands	£14.99
Chile Highlights	£15.99
Colombia	£17.99
Dominica	£15.99
Grenada, Carriacou & Petite Martinique	£15.99
Guyana	£15.99
Haiti	£16.99
Nova Scotia	£15.99
Panama	£14.99
Paraguay	£15.99
Peru Highlights	£15.99
Turks & Caicos Islands	£14.99
Uruguay	£15.99
USA by Rail	£15.99
Venezuela	£16.99
Yukon	£14.99

British Isles

Britain from the Rails	£14.99
Bus-Pass Britain	£15.99
Eccentric Britain	£16.99
Eccentric Cambridge	£9.99
Eccentric London	£14.99
Eccentric Oxford	£9.99
Sacred Britain	£16.99
Slow: Cornwall	£14.99
Slow: Cotswolds	£14.99
Slow: Devon & Exmoor	£14.99
Slow: Dorset	£14.99
Slow: New Forest	£9.99
Slow: Norfolk & Suffolk	£14.99
Slow: North Yorkshire	£14.99
Slow: Northumberland	£14.99
Slow: Sussex & South Downs National Park	£14.99

Europe

Abruzzo	£16.99
Albania	£16.99
Armenia	£15.99
Azores	£14.99
Belarus	£15.99
Bosnia & Herzegovina	£15.99
Bratislava	£9.99
Budapest	£9.99
Croatia	£15.99
Cross-Channel France: Nord-Pas de Calais	£13.99
Cyprus see North Cyprus	
Estonia	£14.99
Faroe Islands	£16.99
Flanders	£15.99
Georgia	£15.99
Greece: The Peloponnese	£14.99
Hungary	£15.99
Iceland	£15.99
Istria	£13.99
Kosovo	£15.99
Lapland	£15.99
Liguria	£15.99
Lille	£9.99
Lithuania	£14.99
Luxembourg	£14.99
Macedonia	£16.99
Malta & Gozo	£14.99
Montenegro	£14.99
North Cyprus	£13.99
Serbia	£15.99
Slovakia	£14.99
Slovenia	£13.99
Svalbard: Spitsbergen, Jan Mayen, Franz Jozef Land	£17.99
Switzerland Without a Car	£15.99
Transylvania	£15.99
Ukraine	£16.99

Middle East, Asia and Australasia

Bangladesh	£17.99
Borneo	£17.99
Eastern Turkey	£16.99
Iran	£15.99
Israel	£15.99
Jordan	£16.99
Kazakhstan	£16.99
Kyrgyzstan	£16.99
Lake Baikal	£15.99
Lebanon	£15.99
Maldives	£15.99
Mongolia	£16.99
North Korea	£14.99
Oman	£15.99
Palestine	£15.99
Shangri-La: A Travel Guide to the Himalayan Dream	£14.99
Sri Lanka	£15.99
Syria	£15.99
Taiwan	£16.99
Tajikistan	£15.99
Tibet	£17.99
Yemen	£14.99

Wildlife

Antarctica: A Guide to the Wildlife	£15.99
Arctic: A Guide to Coastal Wildlife	£16.99
Australian Wildlife	£14.99
East African Wildlife	£19.99
Galápagos Wildlife	£16.99
Madagascar Wildlife	£16.99
Pantanal Wildlife	£16.99
Southern African Wildlife	£19.99
Sri Lankan Wildlife	£15.99

Pictorials and other guides

100 Alien Invaders	£16.99
100 Animals to See Before They Die	£16.99
100 Bizarre Animals	£16.99
Eccentric Australia	£12.99
Northern Lights	£6.99
Swimming with Dolphins, Tracking Gorillas	£15.99
The Northwest Passage	£14.99
Tips on Tipping	£6.99
Total Solar Eclipse 2012 & 2013	£6.99
Wildlife & Conservation Volunteering: The Complete Guide	£13.99

Travel literature

A Glimpse of Eternal Snows	£11.99
A Tourist in the Arab Spring	£9.99
Connemara Mollie	£9.99
Fakirs, Feluccas and Femmes Fatales	£9.99
Madagascar: The Eighth Continent	£11.99
The Marsh Lions	£9.99
The Two-Year Mountain	£9.99
The Urban Circus	£9.99
Up the Creek	£9.99

9

Tanga and the North Coast

The beautiful and historic coastline running southward from the Kenya border towards Dar es Salaam, though reasonably well developed for visitors, is largely overlooked by the tourism industry. This is partly because it is eclipsed both in terms of reputation and facilities by the offshore island of Zanzibar, and partly because it is completely bypassed by the main trunk road between Moshi and Dar es Salaam. Nevertheless, the area does boast a wealth of little known travel possibilities to reward those with the time and initiative to explore. The principal town is Tanga, a somewhat time-warped port that briefly served as the capital of German East Africa before this role was usurped by Dar es Salaam. Also of interest, to the south of Tanga, is the traditional Swahili trading centre of Pangani and the lovely beaches that flank it, as well as the underutilised Saadani National Park.

The north coast has a typically sultry Indian Ocean climate, with hot and humid weather throughout the year. Travel conditions are most pleasant between June and September and least so during the hotter and wetter months of November to May. The main access road to the north coast is an excellent 71km stretch of asphalt that runs east from Segera (on the B1 from Moshi to Dar es Salaam) to Tanga. By contrast, the coastal road south of Tanga is mostly unsurfaced and parts of it are in poor condition. The stretch from Tanga to Pangani can usually be covered in any vehicle, but all roads south of Pangani may require a 4x4, and the road (shown on many maps) running south of Saadani to Bagamoyo and Dar es Salaam has been impassable for decades (although this may change following the planned reconstruction of a collapsed bridge north of Bagamoyo). As a result, there is currently no public transport running along the coast south of Pangani.

TANGA AND AROUND

Characterised by quiet, pot-holed avenues lined with timeworn pastel-shaded German and Asian buildings, Tanga's compact centre has a somnambulant aura belying the city's status as Tanzania's second busiest port and seventh-largest urban centre (population 250,000). This aura of semi-abandonment, reminiscent of much of Tanzania during its mid 1980s economic nadir, does reflect a genuine demise in Tanga's commercial fortunes over recent decades. As a barometer of this descent into backwater status, Tanga is the only Tanzanian city or town where fewer central hotel rooms are available today than was the case when the first edition of this guide was researched 20 years ago.

However, the unusually sedate atmosphere that characterises central Tanga also reflects the fact that the real hub of commercial activity has shifted gradually from the city centre to the grid of narrow streets that lie immediately inland of it. Far more lively and crowded than the city centre, the suburban roads around the bus station and market positively bustle with the sort of low-key entrepreneurial activity that is seldom seen in the city centre. Spend time exploring this area, and Tanga starts to look a lot more economically healthy than it might on first exposure.

Bypassed by the main northern highway, Tanga has never attracted a great number of travellers, and it practically dropped off the East African travel map in the late 1990s, following the termination of passenger train services to Moshi and Dar es Salaam. This is a shame because the old city centre certainly doesn't lack for character and it boasts a few intriguing architectural relicts, while the Ras Kazone Peninsula, immediately northeast of the city centre, is a quiet but well-preserved upmarket residential area, complete with a few decent hotels and a swimming beach. Tanga also offers a relaxed base for exploring the likes of the limestone Amboni Caves and medieval Tongoni Ruins.

HISTORY Tanga, despite its aura of faded prosperity, lacks the historical pedigree of smaller ports such as Pangani or Bagamoyo. The ruined mosques on Toten Island in Tanga Harbour indicate the presence of a small trading centre in the Omani and Shirazi eras, as do similar ruins within a 20km radius of the modern city. But while it can be assumed that some sort of

TANGA and surrounds

fishing settlement has existed here for millennia, there's no written or archaeological evidence of a more substantial settlement prior to the early 19th century. The name Tanga – 'sail' in Swahili – is probably derived from Mtangani, the original name for Tongoni, and it could well be that the foundation of modern Tanga was linked to the decline and eventual abandonment of that nearby ruined city.

By the mid 19th century, Tanga was a substantial ivory trade centre, neither as renowned as Pangani, nor as architecturally distinguished, but sufficiently profitable to be governed by an agent of the Sultan of Zanzibar. When the Sultan of Zanzibar leased the coastal strip to Germany in 1887, few would have predicted that Tanga would rise to prominence. Yet only two years after establishing its first headquarters at Bagamoyo, Germany relocated its administration to the deeper and better protected natural harbour at Tanga. Thus did Tanga become Germany's *ipso facto* East African capital, and although it relinquished this status to Dar es Salaam in 1891, its excellent harbour ensured that it was earmarked for colonial development. The first school in German East Africa was built at Tanga in 1893, and several other impressive buildings on the modern waterfront – notably the Regional Headquarters and Cliff Block – date back to the German era.

In 1911, the completion of a railway line to Moshi sealed Tanga's role as the country's second busiest seaport. No less significant was the introduction of sisal, which became Tanzania's most important agricultural export in the colonial era, and remains the most visible crop around Tanga to this day. Unfortunately, the city fell into economic decline following the collapse of the post-independence sisal boom and the widespread closure of local industries in the 1980s. It has been further sidelined in modern times by improvements to the national road infrastructure and a corresponding decline in the significance of rail, leaving the harbour somewhat without purpose.

TOURIST INFORMATION AND TOUR OPERATORS The semi-official **Tanga Tourism Network Association** has an office on Customs Road opposite the Exim Bank [199 H5] (m *0768 971166;* e *tangatourism@gmail.com; www.tangatourism. com*). It's a useful source of local travel advice and it usually stocks an excellent 100-page booklet covering the Tanga Region, which is also downloadable as a PDF from their website. The **Tanga Heritage Centre** (*www.urithitanga.org*) is a local organisation committed to the development and publicising of a variety of cultural projects and historical sites in and around Tanga. *Urithi*, the centre's quarterly newsletter, is well worth a look.

A recommended local tour operator is **Ilya Tours**, opposite the central market on the ground floor of the Ocean Breeze Hotel [199 F5] (m *0713 560569/0784 660569;* e *david@ilyatours.com; www.ilyatours.com*). It offers guided day trips to the Amboni Caves, Tongoni Ruins and Toten Island, for around US$35 per person. It also arranges all-inclusive overnight trips to Amani Nature Reserve (see *Chapter 8, The Usambara Mountains*, page 188). The staff are friendly and not at all pushy, so it is also a good place to pop into for more general travel advice.

GETTING THERE AND AWAY

Air Coastal Aviation (*www.coastal.cc*) operates daily flights connecting Tanga to Arusha (*US$210 one-way*), Dar es Salaam (*US$190*), Zanzibar (*US$120*) and Pemba (*US$95*). Flights can be booked online or through the Coastal Aviation office on

TANGA IN 1857

Richard Burton, who spent several days in Tanga in 1857, wrote in *Zanzibar and Two Months in East Africa* that:

Tanga ... is a patch of thatched pent-shaped huts, built upon a bank overlooking the sea, in a straggling grove of coconuts and calabash. The population numbers between 4,000 and 5,000 ... The citizens are a homely-looking race, chiefly occupied with commerce, and they send twice a-year, in June and November, after the great and little rains, trading parties to the Chagga and the Maasai countries. The imports are chiefly cotton-stuffs, brass and iron wires, and beads ... The returns consist of camels and asses, a few slaves, and ivory, of which I was told 70,000lb passes through Tanga. The citizens also trade with the coast savages, and manufacture hardware from imported metal ... Of late years Tanga has been spared the mortification of the Maasai, who have hunted and harried in this vicinity many a herd. It is now, comparatively speaking, thickly inhabited.

In late 1914, German Tanga was the setting of a tragically farcical British naval raid. Suffering from seasickness after a long voyage from India, 8,000 Asian recruits were instructed to leap ashore at Tanga, only to become bogged down in the mangroves, then stumble into a swarm of ferocious bees, and finally trigger off German trip-wires. The raid was eventually aborted, but not before 800 British troops lay dead, and a further 500 were wounded. In the confusion, 455 rifles, 16 machine guns and 600,000 rounds of ammunition were left on the shore – a major boon for the Germans. This battle forms a pivotal scene in William Boyd's excellent novel, *An Ice Cream War*. The Germans were eventually forced out of Tanga in 1916, when the British, better prepared this time, launched a land offensive from Moshi on the weakened German outpost.

Independence Avenue ([199 G5] \ *027 264 6548*; m *0713 376265*). The airport is about 3km west of the town centre.

Road A good surfaced 70km road connects Tanga to Segera, the junction town on the main road between Arusha and Dar es Salaam. The total driving distance to Tanga from Arusha is 435km, from Lushoto about 200km, and from Dar es Salaam 352km. In a **private vehicle**, expect to cover around 80–100km/h on any of these routes.

Regular **buses** run between Tanga and all the above towns, with the better companies being Simba and Raha Leo, although there is plenty of choice. Unfortunately, following the closure of Scandinavia Express, no proper luxury buses run to Tanga, but coming from Arusha or Dar Es Salaam, it would be possible to use a superior company such as Kilimanjaro or Dar Express as far as Segera, and then pick up local transport from there. Fares to/from Arusha or Dar es Salaam are around US$10.

All buses leave from and arrive at the main bus station, which lies about 500m from the city centre on the main road to Segera, as do numerous faster but more dangerous **dala-dalas**. Local buses and **minibuses** also connect Tanga to Lushoto (*around US$4*), Pangani (*US$1.50*), Muheza (*for Amani; US$1.50*) and Korogwe.

Rail Passenger train services were terminated in the late 1990s and are unlikely to resume in the foreseeable future.

Boat Intermittent **ferry** or **motorboat** services have connected Tanga to the islands of Pemba and Zanzibar in the past, but none has lasted for very long and nothing appears to be running at the time of writing. It may be possible to catch a fishing *dhow* between Tanga and Pemba, but it's dangerous, uncomfortable and (for tourists) illegal.

WHERE TO STAY
Tanga city centre
Upmarket

Tanga Beach Resort (46 rooms)
\ 027 264 5424/5; m 0785 171717; e info@
tangabeachresort.com; www.tangabeachresort.

com. Set in small lush gardens centred around a swimming pool, this is probably the most upmarket option in Tanga, albeit with all the character of a business hotel transplanted to the beach – or more accurately, to the edge of a mangrove swamp. The rooms are quite smart & come with AC, DSTV, balcony & fridge, but the distance both from the town centre & the nearest viable swimming beach suggests it is aimed more at the lucrative conference market than at tourists. *US$100/130 sgl/dbl B&B, or US$180/220 suite.*

🏠 **Majaba's B&B** [199 F3] (2 rooms) m 0786 395391; e graberh1@gmail.com. Situated opposite the Mkonge on the same property as the popular Pizzeria D'Amore, this small Swiss owner-managed B&B may lack a seafront location but it is only a short walk to the beach, & the rooms are easily the nicest in town – airy & spacious open-plan suites with king-size beds, AC, fan, flatscreen DSTV, fridge, tea-/coffee-making facilities & large en-suite bathrooms with hot shower. Good value. *US$100 B&B.*

🏠 **Mkonge Hotel** [199 F3] (49 rooms) 027 264 5440; m 0753 248611; e mkongehotel@ gmail.com; www.mkonge.com. Built in the 1950s, this former government hotel is the smartest in Tanga, set in large attractive gardens overlooking the harbour & Toten Island on Ras Kazone Peninsula. Now under a dynamic Swiss–Indian owner, it offers accommodation in characterful wooden-floored en-suite rooms with twin or king-size beds, AC, satellite TV & hot water. Facilities include a decent restaurant & a swimming pool. Good value. *US$70/80 sgl/dbl B&B, plus US$10 for sea view. Discount of around 20% for residents.*

Moderate

🏠 **CBA Hotel** [199 G2] (9 rooms) 027 264 5338; m 0689 444000; e cba.hotel@yahoo. com. Situated at the north end of the Ras Kazone Peninsula, this new hotel lies in large rather bare gardens that offer convenient access to the Tanga Yacht Club directly opposite. The spacious clean rooms all have AC, TV, & the restaurant serves decent meals for around US$5, although there is better food on offer at the Yacht Club. Fair value. *US$33 dbl.*

🏠 **Panori Hotel** [199 H3] (20 rooms) 027 264 6044; m 0655 769091; e panorihotel@yahoo. com; www.panorihotel.com. An isolated location on Ras Kazone Peninsula, some distance from any beach, makes this inconvenient for travellers without private transport. In all other respects, it's probably the best deal in this range, offering very

comfortable accommodation in large rooms with parquet floor, AC, TV & hot bath. The *makuti*-style restaurant, widely regarded as one of the best places to eat in Tanga, has a varied menu with most dishes around US$6–8. *US$23/30/40 sgl/ dbl/tpl.*

🏠 **Motel Seaview** [199 E5] (8 rooms) 027 264 5881; m 0713 383868/0784 441142; e motelseaviewtanga@hotmail.com. Following several years' closure, this stalwart of the Tanga accommodation scene, formerly the Bandarini Inn, reopened under a new name in 2011, & it once again looks to be the most characterful place to stay in the town centre. Set in a century-old seafront German building, it's been lovingly restored under new Indian management, & the spacious high-ceilinged, wooden-floored rooms mostly come with a king-size bed, net, DSTV & balcony. The terrace restaurant serves quality Indian cuisine & seafood. Good value. *US$23 en-suite dbl B&B.*

Budget and camping

🏠 **Inn by the Sea** [199 F3] 027 264 4614. Situated alongside the Mkonge Hotel, this has long been the only place to offer inexpensive seafront accommodation away from the town centre. It could do with a facelift, but the en-suite dbls with AC are more than adequate. No alcohol, bland food – you might well find yourself gravitating towards the adjoining Mkonge Hotel or Ras Kazone Swimming Club at meal times. *US$15 dbl.*

🏠 **Hotel Raskazone** [199 G3] (15 rooms) m 0713 670790. On the Ras Kazone Peninsula some 5 mins' walk from the Mkonge Hotel, this rambling & rather unassuming owner-managed hotel with its oddly landscaped front garden is a friendly budget choice. The large rooms are good value, & an OK restaurant & bar are attached. *US$10/15 en-suite dbl/twin with fan, or US$20 for a dbl with AC; camping US$5 pp.*

🏠 **Ocean Breeze Hotel** [199 F5] (40 rooms) 027 264 4545; m 0744 844337. The best budget lodging in the town centre is this well-maintained multi-storey block facing the main market square. Large clean rooms with net, fan, firm dbl bed, hot shower & balcony are great value. Some rooms have TV. An attached restaurant & beer garden serves reasonable Indian food for around Tsh5,000, as well as reliably cold beers & sodas. *US$10 en-suite dbl with fan, or US$13 with AC.*

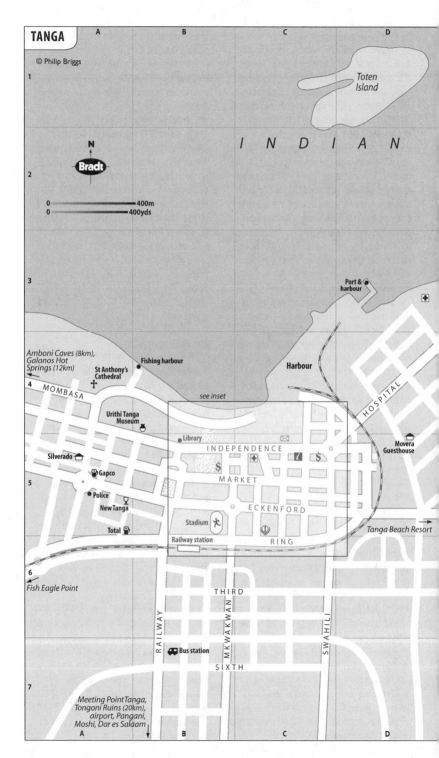

TANGA

© Philip Briggs

N

Bradt

0 —————— 400m
0 —————— 400yds

Toten Island

INDIAN

Port & harbour

Amboni Caves (8km), Galanos Hot Springs (12km)

Fishing harbour

St Anthony's Cathedral

Harbour

MOMBASA

see inset

HOSPITAL

Urithi Tanga Museum

Library

Movera Guesthouse

INDEPENDENCE

Silverado

Gapco

MARKET

Police

New Tanga

ECKENFORD

Total

Stadium

Tanga Beach Resort

Railway station

RING

Fish Eagle Point

THIRD

Bus station

SWAHILI

Meeting Point Tanga, Tongoni Ruins (20km), airport, Pangani, Moshi, Dar es Salaam

SIXTH

O C E A N

Ras Kazone Point

Tanga Yacht Club ✕   🏠 CBA Hotel

Ras Kazone
Swimming Club
Inn by the Sea 🏠 ✕
Mkonge 🏠
Majaba's &
Pizzeria D'Amore
Kiboko Restaurant
& campsite ✕
Football
field 🏃

O C E A N

B O M B O

O C E A N

Raskazone 🏠   🏠 Panori

Inset

Indian Ocean

0 ▬▬▬ 100m
0 ▬▬▬ 100yds

Library
Jamhuri
Park
Clock tower ●
Tanga Medicare ✉ Coastal
I N D E P E N D E N C E   Hospital   Aviation
Motel   Gapco   ➕   Usambara   ☆   Exim
✕ Ford's   Seaview 🏠 $ CRDB   Courthouse   💲   💲 Barclays
✕ Sea Access   Craft Supermarket   Club La ℹ
stalls   Casa Chica
National Bank   Ocean   Tanga
of Commerce   Covered   Breeze   Tourism
$ market   Network
M A R K E T   Food Palace   Shalimar
✕ ✕ Fast Food
Impala   TANESCO
🅴   Karibu Tanga 🅴   German
✕ Patwas   Le Café   ☕ Coffee Tree   war
Espresso   cemetery
Uhuru
Park   ⛴
E C K E N F O R D   E C K E N F O R D
Splendid View
🏃
Stadium   🐦 Oryx   ✕ Ice cream
parlour
Octopus Exotic ✕   ☬
Railway station   R I N G

Outside the city
Upmarket

🏠 **Fish Eagle Point** [198 A6] m 0784 346006; e out2explore@gmail.com; www.fisheaglepoint. com. This highly praised lodge, affiliated to the popular Outpost in Arusha, lies along the remote baobab-lined beach of Manza Bay, about an hours' drive north of Tanga; to get there, follow the main road towards Mombasa (Kenya) for 38km, then turn right along a signposted 10km turn-off. It has an idyllic unspoilt setting, far from any other beach resort, & snorkelling, fishing & coastal birding are all on offer. *From US$120/170 sgl/dbl FB. Significant discounts offered to residents.*

Moderate

🏠 **MeetingPoint Tanga** [198 B7] (20 rooms) m 0783 164495/0762 013902; e ellen@icctan. com, meetingpointtanga@gmail.com; www. meetingpointtanga.net. Also known as the TICC, this community-integrated centre is tucked away on the mangrove-lined shores of the Pemba Channel near Mwahako village, south of Tanga town. It offers socially conscious travellers something more than just your average beach holiday, since all profits are reinvested into local projects & guests are encouraged to 'make a difference' by sharing their knowledge & skills during their stay. The double & twin rooms have net, fan & writing desk, & some are en suite. Other facilities include an excellent restaurant, & bar, as well as local tours & boat trips. To get there from Tanga, follow the Pangani road south for 8km, then take a 4km dirt road signposted TICC to the left. By public transport, catch a dala-dala from the town centre marked 'Mwahako', then walk the last 4km. Admirable though the set-up is, it seems overpriced unless you qualify for the significant resident discounts. *US$44/66 sgl/twin using common showers, or US$55/75 en-suite sgl/dbl.*

✕ WHERE TO EAT

✕ **Food Palace** [199 G6] m 0715 418824; ⏲ 07.30–16.00 & 19.00–20.30 daily. This popular restaurant on Market Street has an extensive & sumptuous menu dominated by Indian dishes, most of which cost around US$4–5 inclusive of chips, rice or *naan* bread. The evening outdoor BBQ is good for chicken tikka & *mishkaki* (beef kebabs). No alcohol served, but a grocery opposite sells wine & beer, which you are allowed to drink on the balcony.

✕ **Patwas Restaurant** [199 F6] ⏲ 08.00– 20.00 Mon–Sat. This venerable café, situated around the corner from the market, is a genuine Tanga institution, having served delicious samosas, snacks & passion fruit juice, in the same seemingly unchanged & increasingly threadbare décor, since the 1980s.

✕ **Pizzeria D'Amore** [199 F3] m 0786 395391; ⏲ 11.30–14.00 & 18.30–23.00 Tue–Sun. Situated opposite the Mkonge Hotel, this Swiss owner- managed restaurant on the Ras Kazone Peninsula is generally rated Tanga's top eatery. As might be expected, pizzas are the main speciality, but it also serves good seafood & meat dishes, indoors or on the breezy makuti-shaded rooftop. Most mains are in the US$6–8 range.

✕ **Ras Kazone Swimming Club** [199 F3] Situated next to the Inn by the Sea, this is a good spot for a beachfront Indian-style meal. A nominal entrance fee of less than U$1 is charged, & mains are mostly around US$3–4.

✕ **Tanga Yacht Club** [199 G2] ☎ 027 264 4246; e tyctanga@gmail.com; www.tangayachtclub. com; ⏲ lunch & dinner daily. Boasting a prime seafront location on the Ras Kazone Peninsula, this friendly club has a good swimming beach & welcomes day visitors (who pay an entrance fee of around US$1.50). It also serves some of the best meals in town, with fish & meat dishes around US$5, & burgers & sandwiches for US$4.

ENTERTAINMENT AND NIGHTLIFE

Football Home matches are played at the central Mkwakwani Stadium [199 F7], usually on Wednesday and Saturday during March–August, with kick-off at 16.30. Ticket prices start at less than US$1.

Nightlife The long-standing **Club la Casa Chica** [199 G5], next to the Coastal Aviation office, is Tanga's top nightspot hosting regular discos ('ladies' are admitted for free, while 'gents' pay around US$2). Other popular drinking holes include the **New Tanga Hotel** [198 A5], where no rooms or meals are available, **Coffee Tree Restaurant** [199 G6], which is more of a bar than an eatery or coffee house, and the garden bar at the **Ocean Breeze Hotel** [199 F5], whch in spite of its name catches no significant breeze as it's in an enclosed courtyard.

Swimming The only swimming pools are at the **Mkonge Hotel** [199 F3] and **Tanga Beach Resort**. Technically they are open to hotel residents only, but when the hotels are quiet, visitors who stop in for a meal might be allowed to swim. If you fancy a dip in the ocean, try the small, sandy beach at the **Ras Kazone Swimming Club** next to the Inn by the Sea [199 F3] (*entrance US$0.65*). The **Tanga Yacht Club** [199 G2] (*entrance US$1.50*) also has a swimming beach. Both places have showers, and a bar and restaurant. There's also a swimming beach on **Toten Island** (see overleaf).

OTHER PRACTICALITIES
Banks, ATMs and foreign exchange Local currency can be drawn on Visa cards at ATMs outside the adjacent **Barclays** and **Exim** banks [199 H5] on Independence Avenue, or the **National Bank of Commerce (NBC)** [199 F6] on Market Street. The NBC also has full foreign exchange facilities for cash and travellers' cheques during normal banking hours. The normal 0.5% commission is charged to change travellers' cheques and they may ask to see proof of purchase. Surprisingly, there are no private forex bureaux in Tanga, which means that travellers who come from Kenya and expect to arrive in Tanga in the late afternoon or over the weekend ought to change sufficient cash into local currency at the border.

Internet Karibu Tanga [199 G6] (*Market St;* \ *027 264 2230; www.kaributanga. com;* ⊕ *09.00–21.00 daily, closed 12.00–14.00 Fri, & 14.00–16.00 Sat & Sun*), opposite the Food Palace, is very fast, keeps long hours and charges Tsh1,000 per hour. Several other internet cafés are dotted around town.

WHAT TO SEE
Urithi Tanga Museum [198 B4] (m *0784 440068; www.urithitanga.org;* ⊕ *09.00– 12.00 daily; nominal entrance fee*) Something of a work in progress at the time of writing, this new museum is housed in the so-called 'Second Boma', a handsome administrative building constructed by the Germans in 1890. Displays currently include a gallery of monochrome photographs of Tanga in the early 20th century, in some cases set alongside colour photographs taken a century later, all of which helps to make sense of the town centre's surprising but rather faded mishmash of German, English, Indian and Swahili architectural styles. Other displays, still under construction, include a collection of historical artefacts unearthed in the harbour and town centre.

Historical buildings and sights A wealth of colonial-era buildings line the leafy avenues of the town centre, including numerous early 20th-century two-storey residences that were built for Indian and Arabic merchants and would originally have doubled as shops. Notable for their intricately carved wooden balconies, thick pillars, large raised verandas, carved hardwood doors, small grilled windows and wooden shutters, these old residences are generally in a poor state of repair, but the Tanga Heritage Centre intends to restore some in the near future. The **Tanga School**, opposite the stadium on Eckenford Avenue, is the oldest school in the country, built in 1895 and currently used as a medical college. The current **railway station** on Ring Road was built by the British but the older German station, dating to 1896, can be found by following the railway line towards the port.

The main concentration of German administrative buildings lies between Independence Avenue and the waterfront. The old **German Boma** [198 B4], complete with underground bunkers and passages to the sea, now houses the **Urithi Tanga Museum**, and stands close to the gracious whitewashed **library** [199 E5] built during the British colonial era. Also along Independence Avenue you'll find the original **Clock Tower** [199 F5], dating to 1901. Nearby, the German-built **Usambara Courthouse** [199 G5] on Usambara Street is a beautiful two-storey building that has been fully restored by the Tanga Heritage Centre. Also of interest is the busy little dhow harbour and fishing market on Harbour Road below the Urithi Tanga Museum.

Less centrally, the partially disused **Cliff Block** on Hospital Road was the country's first hospital, built in the 1890s. Good examples of British architecture include the **Katani Building** and **Lead Memorial Hall** on Hospital Road, both dating to the early 1950s. There are two **World War I cemeteries**: the German Sakarani Cemetery on Swahili Street [199 H6], at the east end of Market Street, and the Commonwealth War Cemetery on Bombo Road. A **British War Memorial** in Usagara, near the Mkonge Hotel, consists of a plaque with illustrations and a brief history of the war.

Toten Island
Tiny and uninhabited, Toten Island, protected within Tanga Harbour, is dotted with overgrown relics of earlier Islamic settlements. On the west of the island, a large ruined mosque established in the 14th or 15th century and renovated during the late 18th century has a large east-facing balcony, a staircase leading to the roof and a well-preserved ornamental *mihrab* (the interior niche indicating the direction of Mecca), while a nearby cemetery contains inscribed Islamic tombs. A smaller and more ruinous mosque stands on the southern shore, and many ceramic artefacts and household objects from the 15th–18th centuries have been unearthed. No trace remains of a third mosque depicted on a German era map, or the large rectangular fort described by Burton, who visited the island in 1857, some 30 years before it was abandoned. There is also a German war cemetery, and a small swimming beach. The northern shore is the site of a recently implemented mangrove conservation project.

Toten Island can be reached by boat as a three- to four-hour round-trip excursion from Tanga. The most straightforward way to visit is with Ilya Tours (see *Tourist information and tour operators*, page 195), which charges around US$35 per person for a guided tour. Alternatively, you can negotiate with local boatmen at the harbour for a cheaper price using a traditional dhow. Best visit at low tide, when it is easier to walk on the beaches.

Amboni Caves
(*08.00–17.00 daily; the entrance fee, equivalent to US$13 pp, includes the services of the English-speaking caretaker/guide & use of a good torch, entering the caves without a guide would be extremely foolhardy as there is a real danger of getting lost or being injured*) The labyrinth of subterranean passages that runs through the 250km² limestone bed to the east of Tanga is probably the most extensive cave system in East Africa. Caves 3a and 3b, known less prosaically as the Amboni Caves, have been open to the public for years, and offer a combined 750m of accessible passages. Another two caves, 7 and 8, were opened in October 2000. The total network of caves is often said to be more than 200km long, and a

persistent rumour has it that one passage runs all the way to Fort Jesus in Mombasa. However, a comprehensive survey undertaken by a German–Turkish expedition in 1994 found the largest of ten caves studied to be less than 1km long.

The Amboni Caves make for a good day trip out of Tanga, even though their initial impact is diminished by the graffiti around the entrance – the handiwork of past visitors who couldn't resist the urge to paint their name for posterity. This unsightly roll call of buffoons doesn't extend far into the main cave, which opens into a magnificent 15m-high chamber overhung with large rippled stalactites. From this first chamber, the route leads through a succession of narrow passages and larger caverns, past natural sculptures including the so-called Madonna and Statue of Liberty. The caves support thousands upon thousands of bats, which can be seen streaming out of the entrance at dusk, and whose droppings feed a variety of cockroaches and weird invertebrates.

The entrance to the main cave lies on the north bank of the Mkulimuzi River, a beautiful clear stream that rises in the Usambara Mountains and is also fed locally by freshwater springs. The river is fringed by palms, and runs through one of the largest extant patches of coastal forest in northern Tanzania. A variety of localised birds inhabit the forest near the caves, as does a resident and regularly observed troop of black-and-white colobus monkeys. This is also a good place to look for the African violet in its wild state, but note that it is forbidden to pick or damage this protected flower.

To reach the Amboni Caves from Tanga, follow the Mombasa road for 5km and then turn left onto a dirt road signposted for 'Mohamed Enterprises'. About 100m along this dirt road turn left again, then continue more or less straight along a rough road through the *shambas* of Kiomoni village for 1.5km to the signposted entrance to the caves. There is no public transport to the caves, but dala-dalas

LEGENDS AND LOST DOG STORIES

The main Amboni Cave has long held a strong spiritual significance to the local Digo people, who refer to it as Mabavu. According to the caretaker, this translates as 'sacrifice', though most written sources suggest Mabavu is the name of a deity who lives within the cave. The chamber associated with this deity is called Mzimuni (Place of Spirits) and it contains a sacrificial altar that is normally scattered with bones, food and other gifts, left by pilgrims from all around East Africa. The cave's resident deity can reputedly alleviate all forms of illness and misfortune, but his speciality is making barren women fertile. The perceived powers of Amboni remain as strong today as ever – Tanga's football team reputedly slaughters a cow or goat at the altar before pivotal matches!

Amboni has attracted its fair share of modern legends. During the time of Kenya's Mau Mau rebellion, the main cave formed a hideout for the brave freedom fighter (or heinous bandit, depending on who's telling the tale) Osale Otango and his Tanzanian sidekick Paul Hamiso, at least until Otango was shot dead by the authorities in 1958. It is difficult to know what to make of another popular legend relating to two retired army officers who undertook a survey expedition of Amboni shortly after World War II. The men supposedly vanished without trace, but the dog that accompanied them into the caves turned up four months later at the entrance to another cave – on the lower slopes of distant Kilimanjaro.

between Tanga and Amboni village, which lies 2km further along the Mombasa road, will drop passengers at the first junction, from where it's a 20–30 minute walk. It is also possible to charter a taxi from Tanga, or to cycle there – local bikes are available to rent on the main market square. No accommodation or camping facilities are available at the caves.

Galanos Hot Springs Named after a Greek sisal plantation owner, the Galanos Hot Springs lie 8km from the Amboni Caves, and the two can be visited in conjunction. The clear, green water, which forms a large pool before flowing into a stream caked with lime deposits, is reputed to cure rheumatism, arthritis and other ailments. Locals bathe in the pool, but the sulphuric odour doesn't make this a very attractive prospect. A nominal entrance fee is charged, at least in theory, but there's seldom anybody there to collect it.

To reach the springs from Amboni, follow the main Tanga–Mombasa road north for 2km, where the road passes through Amboni village immediately before crossing a bridge over the Sigi River (where crocodiles are sometimes seen). About 1km past the bridge, turn right at an unsignposted junction on to a dirt track. After another 1km, you'll come to a fork in the road in front of a school building. The 2km track to the springs lies along the left fork. If you need to ask directions, the Swahili for hot springs is *maji moto*.

Tongoni Ruins (⊕ *08.00–17.00 daily; entrance US$7*) Tongoni means 'Place of Ruins', and the village of that name, situated alongside the Pangani road 20km south of Tanga, stands adjacent to the remains of an abandoned Swahili town known contemporaneously as Mtangata. Little is known about the early history of this settlement, but it must have been founded before the late 14th century (one unverifiable local tradition relates that it was founded at the same time as Kilwa, and by the same family). During its 15th-century commercial peak, Mtangata was the most prosperous trade centre for 100km in any direction.

Three Portuguese ships under the command of Vasco Da Gama ran aground at Mtangata in 1498, making it one of the first places in East Africa to be visited by Europeans. A year later, Da Gama spent two weeks at Mtangata, where he abandoned one of his ships due to a shortage of hands, and named the distant Usambara Mountains after São Raphael. Traditionally hostile to Mombasa, the rulers of Mtangata maintained a good relationship with the Portuguese, and the town evidently prospered until 1698, when the Portuguese were evicted from Mombasa. Thereafter Mtangata slid into obscurity, to be abandoned in about 1730. It enjoyed a minor 18th-century revival when settled and renamed Sitahabu (better here than there) by refugees from Kilwa. The new settlers never renovated the larger structures, but they did leave offerings in the *mihrab* of the abandoned mosque, and also appropriated the old cemetery.

Mtangata was long deserted in 1857, when Richard Burton stopped by *en route* to Tanga from Pangani. Burton, clearly affected by the ruinous apparition, wrote that:

> Moonlight would have tempered the view; it was a grisly spectacle in the gay and glowing shine of the sun. Shattered walls, the remnants of homesteads in times gone by, rose, choked with the luxuriant growth of decay, and sheltering in their desert shade the bat and the nightjar … I was shown the grave of a wali or saint – his very name had perished – covered with a cadjan roof, floored with stamped earth, cleanly swept, and garnished with a red and white flag. Near a spacious mosque, well built

with columns of cut coralline, and adorned with an elaborate prayer-niche, are several tall mausoleums of elegant construction, their dates denoting an antiquity of about two hundred years. Beyond the legend of the bay, none could give me information concerning the people that have passed away … [One particular engraved tile] was regarded with a superstitious reverence by the Swahili, who declared that Sultan Kimweri of Usambara had sent a party of bold men to bear it away; nineteen died mysterious deaths, and the tile was thereupon restored to its place.

Today, the ruins at Tongoni consist of one large mosque, several disused wells and walls, and a cemetery of 40 tombs. The ruined mosque, with a ground plan of 150m², is the only vaguely habitable structure, and aside from the ornate niche referred to by Burton, it is rather poorly preserved. However, the cemetery holds the largest known concentration of pillar tombs, a type of construction unique to the Swahili Coast. Most of the tombs have decorated borders and white plaster panels, and all except one has toppled over. Much of old Mtangata has been submerged through erosion, and it is feared that without adequate protection the cemetery may also eventually crumble into the ocean. In nearby Tongoni village stand the discrete ruins of a more recent mosque, dating from the Omani era. The surrounding area forms one of the successful mangrove conservation areas on the Tanga coast.

To reach the ruins from Tanga, follow the Pangani road south for 18km to Tongoni village, then turn left at the signposted junction and follow this motorable track for 1km. Any bus heading to Pangani can drop you at the junction, from where it is a ten-minute walk to the ruins. A return charter taxi from Tanga to Tongoni should cost around US$10–15.

PANGANI AND USHONGO

One of the most important 19th-century trade centres along the Swahili Coast, the estuarine port of Pangani has seen little subsequent development, and its waterfront is endowed with a number of crumbling old buildings dating to that distant heyday. Indeed, Pangani retains the most overtly traditional Swahili character of any town along the north coast, and is also perhaps the most attractively located, set on the north bank of the forest-fringed Pangani River mouth, from where a gorgeous beach stretches northward as far as the eye can see. And while the town itself remains little developed, the surrounding coast has witnessed an extraordinary mushrooming of beach resorts in recent years. The most accessible and affordable of these establishments line the Pangani–Tanga road, while a more attractive cluster of costlier resorts can be found some 12km south of Pangani at the attractive coastal village of Ushongo, whose fabulous and practically deserted beach ranks as one of the best-kept secrets on the Tanzanian coast.

PILLAR OF STONE

In the early days of Pangani, there was an important annual celebration day on which it was forbidden to swim in the ocean. One wealthy Arab woman decided to ignore this taboo and went in the ocean with her slave to wash her hair. When God saw this, he was so incensed that he punished both women by turning them into a stone, which stands in the water outside the town to this day.

9

Once settled into Pangani, there's plenty to keep you busy. The old town itself warrants a couple of hours' exploration, whether on a self-guided walking tour or with a guide from the tourist office on the waterfront. There's a good beach in front of the Pangadeco Beach Hotel, but you're advised against taking valuables. Other activities include a boat trip up the forested Pangani River, a snorkelling excursion to Maziwe Island, an agricultural walking tour of the hinterland or a trip to the Tongoni Ruins (see page 204).

GETTING THERE AND AWAY

Air The main airstrip in the area is Mashado, which lies to the south of the Pangani River between Pangani town and Ushongo. Until recently there were no scheduled flights here, but as of June 2012 **Coastal Aviation** has included Mashado as a scheduled stop on its existing daily flight network between Dar es Salaam,

PANGANI AND THE RIDDLE OF RHAPTA

Pangani has been cited by one historian as 'the Bagamoyo of the first eighteen centuries of the Christian era'. In a sense, this description is probably rather misleading. True, for much of the 19th century, Pangani was the main terminus for slave caravans heading to the Lake Victoria region, and probably the most important trading centre on the Tanzanian mainland after Bagamoyo and Kilwa Kivinje. But the town that now stands on the north bank of the Pangani River mouth is not particularly old, having been founded by Omani Arabs in the late 18th century and totally rebuilt in 1810 following a destructive flood.

It is possible, too, that the very name Pangani is of 19th century derivation – *panga* being a Swahili word for 'arrange', and Pangani the place where slaves from the interior were arranged into groups by their Arab captors. Other sources, however, suggest the name could be far older, alluding to the locally common *panga* shellfish or a type of boat known locally as *mtepe* but referred to by an English naval offer in 1608 as *pangaia*. Burton, meanwhile, translated Pangani as meaning 'in the hole'.

Pangani is a relatively modern settlement, possibly even a modern name, but it is equally true that the mouth and lower reaches of the Pangani River have played a major role in coastal trade for several centuries. Prior to the arrival of the Omani, the main settlement on the river mouth was Bweni, situated then, as it is now, on the southern bank facing the modern town. Prior to that, a larger trading post, Muhembo, was situated on Pangani Bay about 2km north of the present town. Local tradition dates Muhembo to the earliest Shirazi times, circa AD900, when the El Harth family, who reputedly founded Pangani, landed in the area. Archaeological excavations at Muhembo suggest that, aside from its impressive ruined mosque, the town was less built up than, and probably politically subservient to, the contemporary town of Mtangata at modern-day Tongoni. Muhembo suffered heavily in 1588 at the hands of the cannibalistic Zimba, and was razed in a punitive Portuguese raid in 1635, after which it was evidently abandoned.

The most intriguing historical question surrounding the lower Pangani River is whether it was the site of the ancient trade settlement referred to in the 1st-century *Periplus of the Erythraean Sea* and Ptolemy's 2nd-century *Geography* as Rhapta. The case for Pangani as Rhapta is compelling, if largely circumstantial. The anonymous author of the *Periplus* places Rhapta 'two days' sail' beyond a

Zanzibar, Arusha and Tanga. One-way tickets cost US$160 per person from Dar es Salaam, US$220 from Arusha and US$90 from Zanzibar.

Road Pangani is situated 53km south of Tanga. The dirt coastal road between the two is generally in reasonable condition, and can be covered in about 11/2 hours in a **private vehicle**. The beach resorts between Tanga and Pangani all lie within 1–2km of this road. **Buses** between Tanga and Pangani charge US$2.50 per person and take up to two hours. There are no minibuses along this route.

Heading to Ushongo and other points south of the Pangani River, note that no bridge crosses the river mouth but a **motor ferry** is in place to carry vehicles and passengers across on demand between 06.30 and 18.30 daily. The crossing from Pangani to Bweni, the small village on the south bank, takes five to ten minutes, and costs around US$3 per vehicle plus US$0.15 per person. Small local boats can take

'flat and wooded' island he calls Menouthesias, which itself lay 'slightly south of southwest after a voyage of two days and nights' from 'the Pyralaae Islands and the island called Diorux [the Channel]'. These vague directions lack any name that has survived into the modern era, and are open to interpretation, but they do seem to point to Menouthesias as either Pemba or Mafia Island, respectively making Pangani or the Rufiji Delta the most likely location of Rhapta.

Ptolemy's *Geography*, based on the firsthand and secondhand observations of three different sailors, talks of Rhapta as 'the metropolis of Barbaria, set back a little from the sea' on the river Rhapton, but – contradicting the *Periplus* – it places Menouthias Island (presumably the same as Menouthesias) considerably further south. More intriguingly, based on information gathered by a Greek merchant called Diogenes, Ptolemy talks of two snow-capped peaks and two large lakes lying 25 days' trek up the river Rhapton. The Pangani River has its source near Moshi, at the base of snow-capped Kilimanjaro.

No trace of an appropriately ancient settlement has ever been found near Pangani, which would not be entirely surprising had Rhapta been situated upriver and lacked the permanent stone structures of later mediaeval ports. Several other possible locations for Rhapta have been suggested, including Ras Kimbiji near Dar es Salaam and more plausibly the Rufiji Delta, the latter so vast and labyrinthine that the remains of a 2,000-year-old settlement would be difficult to locate and might well be submerged. To further complicate the picture, many historians regard it as unlikely that Rhapta was the local name for a port, since it appears to derive from *ploiaria rhapta*, the Greek name for a type of boat, which coincidentally was later referred to by an English navigator as *pangaia*. Furthermore, given that these two ancient documents were written centuries apart, and appear to contradict each other on several details, there's every chance that the Rhapta of the *Periplus* is a totally different port to the Rhapta described by Ptolemy's sources.

Whatever the truth of the matter, it does seem certain that the Pangani River has long formed an important route for exploration of the interior, largely because it provides a reliable source of fresh water as far inland as Moshi. It almost certainly served as an important trade inland corridor for Mtangata and Muhembo in the Shirazi era, and could as easily have done so 2,000 years ago. Ptolemy's information about the Rhapton River and the African interior, flawed and confusing as it may have been, seems too close to the truth to be dismissed as mere coincidence.

passengers without a vehicle for marginally less. Those without private transport should expect to pay around US$4–5 for a *pikipiki* (motorcycle-taxi) to any of the hotels around Ushongo.

From the south bank of the river, an erratic dirt road leads to Saadani village in the eponymous national park, an 80km drive that should take about two hours in dry conditions but might be impossible after heavy rain. The turn-off to Ushongo, accessible in any weather, is signposted about 10km along the Saadani road.

TOURIST INFORMATION AND TOURS The **Pangani Cultural Tourism Programme** [210 B2] (m *0784 916494/868499*), an ecotourism project developed in association with the Dutch SNV agency, has an office close to the ferry jetty in Pangani. Independent travellers can arrange most activities here, as well as hire bicycles. Travellers staying at the smarter beach lodges to the north and south of town should be able to arrange the same activities through their hotel.

WHERE TO STAY AND EAT
North of Pangani
Upmarket

🏠 **Mkoma Bay Tented Lodge** (8 tents)
📞027 263 0000; m 0786 434001/0784 283505;

e mkomabay@gmail.com; www.mkomabay.
com. This smart & reasonably priced tented
camp, owned & managed by a friendly Danish–
American couple, has a stunning location in

PANGANI IN 1857

The following edited extracts from Richard Burton's *Zanzibar and Two Months in East Africa*, originally published in 1858 in Blackwood's *Edinburgh Magazine* (vol 83), provide a vivid impression of Pangani in the mid 19th century, as well as its relationship with the kingdoms of the immediate interior:

Pangani ... and its smaller neighbour Kumba, hug the left bank of the river, upon a strip of shore bounded by the sea, and a hill range 10 or 11 miles distant. Opposite are Bweni and Mzimo Pia, villages built under yellow sandstone bluffs, impenetrably covered with wild trees ... Pangani boasts of 19 or 20 stone houses. The remainder is a mass of cadjan huts, each with its wide mat-encircled yard, wherein all the business of life is transacted ... Pangani, with the three other villages, may contain a total of 4,000 – Arabs, Muslim Swahili, and heathens. Of these, female slaves form a large proportion.

Pangani, I am told, exports annually 35,000lb of ivory, 1750lb of black rhinoceros horn, and 16lb of hippopotamus' teeth ... Twenty Banyans manage the lucrative ivory trade ... These merchants complain loudly of their pagazi, or porters, who receive 10 dollars for the journey, half paid down, the remainder upon return; and the proprietor congratulates himself if, after payment, only 15% run away. The Hindus' profits, however, must be enormous. I saw one man to whom 26,000 dollars were owed by the people. What part must interest and compound interest have played in making up such sum ...? Their only drawback is the inveterate beggary of the people. Here the very princes are mendicants; and the Banyan dare not refuse the seventy or eighty savages who every evening besiege his door with cries for grain, butter, or a little oil.

Coconuts ... and plantains grow about the town. Around are gardens of paw-paws, betel, and jamlis; and somewhat further, lie extensive plantations of ... maize ... and other grains. The clove flourishes, and as elsewhere upon the coast a little cotton is large, landscaped grounds that sprawl down to a swimming pool on a low cliff overlooking the deserted beach at Mkoma Bay. It lies 500m off the main road, along a side road signposted 49km from Tanga & 5km before Pangani. Accommodation is in 1 of 2 types of safari-style standing tents set on stilted platforms, all with king-size 4-poster bed with walk-in netting & fan. There is also an airy rambling 4-bedroom 'Swahili House' (min 4 guests) with a wide balcony offering memorable sea views framed by leafy tropical trees. It's a lovely spot to chill by the pool with a novel, or take long walks on the pristine beach running towards Pangani town, while organised activities include boat trips up the Pangani River & snorkelling excursions to Maziwe Island. The restaurant serves good continental meals & seafood. *US$80/150 sgl/dbl Selous tent, US$95/160 for a larger Savannah Tent; Swahili House US$75 pp, min 4 people. All rates B&B; add US$15 pp for a 3-course dinner.*

🏠 **Capricorn Beach Cottages** (3 rooms)
m 0784 632529; **e** capricornbeachcottages@gmail.com; www.capricornbeachcottages.com. This very welcoming owner-managed lodge, 33km south of Tanga off the Pangani road, lies in baobab-studded gardens sloping down to an attractive palm-lined beach. Accommodation is in smart, great value cottages with *makuti* roof, tiled floor, king-size bed with netting, fan, secluded balcony, well equipped kitchen & 24-hr internet access. Although technically self-catering, it operates an onsite pizzeria (see *Where to eat*, page 212), there's a small deli where self-caterers can purchase delicious gourmet items such as smoked fish & home-baked bread, & it also offers the choice of prepared or DIY BBQs in the evening for around US$10–15 pp. Also on the same property is a great little boutique, Capricorn Casuals (*www.capricorncasuals.com*), selling vibrantly coloured hand-woven clothes & beachwear made on site. *US$70/104 sgl/dbl B&B.*

cultivated for domestic use. Beasts are rare. Cows die after eating the grass; goats give no milk; and sheep are hardly procurable. But fish abounds. Poultry thrives, as it does all over Africa; and before the late feuds, clarified cow-butter, that 'one sauce' of the outer East, was cheap and well-flavoured … The wells produce heavy and brackish drink; but who, as the people say, will take the trouble to fetch sweeter? The climate is said to be healthy in the dry season, but the long and severe rains are rich in fatal bilious remittents.

The settlement is surrounded by a thorny jungle, which at times harbours a host of leopards. One of these beasts lately scaled the high terrace of our house, and seized upon a slave girl. Her master … who was sleeping by her side, gallantly caught up his sword, ran into the house, and bolted the door, heedless of the miserable cry, "Bwana, help me!" The wretch was carried to the jungle and devoured. The river is equally full of alligators [crocodiles], and whilst we were at Pangani a boy disappeared. When asked by strangers why they do not shoot their alligators, and burn their wood, the people reply that the former bring good-luck, and the latter is a fort to which they can fly in need.

Pangani and Bweni, like all settlements upon this coast, belong, by a right of succession, to the [Sultan] of Zanzibar, who confirms and invests the governors and diwans. At Pangani, however, these officials are *par congé d'elire* selected by Kimweri [the king of Usambara], whose ancestors received tribute and allegiance from para to the seaboard. On the other hand, Bweni is in the territory of the Wazegura, a violent and turbulent heathen race, inveterate slave-dealers, and thoughtlessly allowed by the Arabs to lay up goodly stores of muskets, powder, and ball. Of course the two tribes [Usambara and Wazegura] are deadly foes. Moreover, about a year ago, a violent intestine feud broke out amongst the Wazegura, who, at the time of our visit, were burning and murdering, kidnapping and slave-selling in all directions.

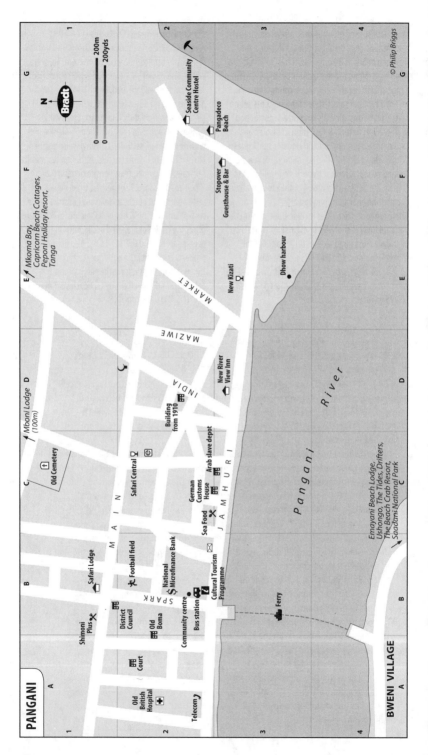

PANGANI

© Philip Briggs

Moderate and camping

⌂ **Bahari Pori Bandas** (8 rooms) m 0713 917754; e info@baharipori.com; www.baharipori. com. Boasting an attractive beachfront location 8km north of Pangani & 45km south of Tanga, this reasonably priced newcomer (opened in Dec 2010) offers accommodation in comfortable bandas with a canvas front & sides, makuti thatch roof, king-size or twin beds with walk-in netting, & an en-suite bathroom with hot shower. It lies on a mangrove beach with one clear opening where you can swim at high tide, & has a good restaurant serving seafood meals as well as pizzas from 12.00–22.00 on Fri, Sat & Sun. *US$55/80 sgl/dbl B&B; camping US$10 pp. Lunch & dinner an extra US$10 pp per meal.*

⌂ **Peponi Holiday Resort** [210 E1] m 0784 202962/0713 540139; e info@peponiresort.com; www.peponiresort.com. Owned & managed by long-term East Africa residents, this popular & friendly beachfront resort is clearly signposted a short distance off the Pangani road 30km south of Tanga. Accommodation is in rustic en-suite makuti bandas, & camping is also permitted. Facilities include clean ablution blocks, laundry service, & an attractive bar & restaurant serving good Western meals & seafood dishes. Dependent on tides, the beach in front of the resort is good for swimming & offers reasonable snorkelling. Local boats can be arranged for snorkelling or fishing excursions to the outer reefs or Maziwe Island. The owners are a reliable source of information about local tourist attractions. It's a very chilled spot, & readily accessible using public transport, or by charter taxi. *US$75/95 sgl/dbl HB; camping under shelters US$5 pp.*

Pangani and Bweni
Upmarket
⌂ **Mashado Beach Resort** (40 rooms) m 0717 512932; e mashadoresort@hotmail.com. Follies don't come much grander than this plush hotel in Bweni, constructed on a clifftop above the south bank of the Pangani River in the mid 1990s to cater to a mega-wealthy game fishing market that never existed on the scale envisaged. It has changed hands & closed several times since then, but was open again when this edition was researched in 2012. The immaculate grounds are centred around a swimming pool & offer a panoramic view over Pangani River & town, while the stylish rooms

boast imported materials & fittings. Problem is, there's no beach access, which – combined with its unfashionable location – ensures it's the most under-patronised hotel of comparable quality in the country. If that doesn't worry you, it's very good value. *US$75 pp FB.*

Moderate
⌂ **Seaside Community Centre Hostel** [210 G2] (8 rooms) ☏ 027 263 0318; m 0784 991449; e alcposs.spiritualcentre@yahoo.com. Run by Catholic nuns, this new purpose-built hostel & conference centre, surrounded by lovingly tended gardens that lead down to the beach, is by far the most attractive place to stay in Pangani town. Despite its slightly institutional feel, it has clean & comfortable tiled twin rooms (all with fans, nets & private balcony) & a huge thatched dining room with a fridge & basic cooking appliances for self-caterers. There's private access to a safe swimming beach. On the downside, it feels a little overpriced for what you get, & it's located alongside the noisy Pangadeco nightclub. *US$20/30 sgl/dbl B&B.*

Budget
⌂ **Mboni Lodge** [210 C1] (8 rooms) m 0717 727519/0657 019854; e hothotpetro@yahoo.com. This neat & reasonably priced new guesthouse on the northern outskirts of town has clean but cluttered en-suite rooms with tiled floor, TV, fan & the only AC in town. Rooms vary in size & quality but cost is uniform. *US$15 dbl.*

Shoestring
⌂ **New River View Inn** [210 D3] m 0784 530371. This long-serving guesthouse, set on the main waterfront road about 300m from where the buses stop, is the best of a dismal choice of cheap lodgings scattered around Pangani town. Though basic, it is quite clean with running water & electricity. *US$3.50 dbl with net, communal showers.*

Ushongo
Upmarket
⌂ **The Tides** [210 B4] (13 rooms) m 0784 225812/0713 325812; e info@thetideslodge. com; www.thetideslodge.com. This popular British-owned beachfront lodge is among the finest on the north coast, set on a superb

swimming beach in Ushongo, & noted for its excellent seafood. The laid-back atmosphere is ideal for those who just want to hang out on the beach (one of the few in Tanzania steep enough to swim at low tide) or the recently added swimming pool, but it also offers a wide selection of activities including deep-sea & in-shore fishing, snorkelling in Maziwe Marine Park, bicycle hire, kayaking in the mangrove-lined creeks nearby (a good place to see the localised mangrove kingfisher, beautiful malachite kingfisher & a host of waders & marine birds) & diving by arrangement for qualified divers. Road transfers from Tanga, Pangani, Saadani, Dar es Salaam or Arusha can be arranged, as can boat transfers to Zanzibar. Accommodation is in large en-suite chalets with an airy, classical interior of stone floors & whitewashed walls, king-size beds with walk-in nets, fans, en-suite hot showers, & private verandas & sunbathing areas. *US$300/330 dbl HB/FB, with a slight increase in Jul, Aug & over the Christmas period.*

Moderate

⌂ **Emayani Beach Lodge** [210 B4] (12 rooms) ☏ 027 264 0755; m 0782 457668; e info@emayanilodge.com; www.emayanilodge.com. This intimate beachfront resort, run by the owners of Tarangire Safari Lodge, consists of a dozen airy chalets made entirely from organic material & spaced out along a long, deserted stretch of sandy beach at Ushongo. It's a great place just to chill out with a beach towel & novel, but with the well-run Kasa Divers next door offering a range of activities (see opposite), there is plenty to keep more active visitors busy. The beach is good for swimming at high tide, while the exposed reefs & mudflats in front of the lodge offer decent snorkelling at low tide. Sea kayaks can be used to explore a mangrove-lined

creek 1km north of the lodge, & wind-surfers & a catamaran are also available. Good value. *US$80/120 sgl/dbl B&B, plus US$10 pp lunch & US$15pp dinner.*

Budget and camping

⌂ **The Beach Crab Resort** [210 B4] (14 rooms) m 0784 543700/0715 304455; e info@thebeachcrab.com; www.thebeachcrab.com. The cheapest resort at Ushongo, this very laid-back spot is the kind of place you visit for a couple of days & end up staying for a couple of weeks – or at the very least try to come up with reasons to return. Around 1km past The Tides, it's the closest thing to a backpackers on the north coast. There are 6 permanent safari-style tents with shared showers, as well as more comfortable en-suite bandas. The large thatched-roof beachside bar & restaurant offers a set daily menu with most meals around US$4. There are also plenty of activities on offer, including windsurfing, diving, snorkelling, mountain biking & beach volleyball. *US$80/120 sgl/dbl en-suite bandas HB; US$20/30 sgl/dbl safari tents B&B; camping US$3.50 pp. Meals are in the US$4–7 range.*

⌂ **Drifters** [210 B4] (14 rooms) ☏ 027 264 1071; m 0787 900869; e info@0714542909. This laid-back palm-shaded resort next to The Tides has a superb beach where you can swim at high or low tide, & it offers a variety of accommodation aimed at budget travellers. These range from family rooms sleeping up to 8, to en-suite dbl bandas with a fan, to simple wind-ventilated A-frame huts using common showers. There is also a good on-site restaurant/bar specialising in seafood. It offers fishing excursions as well as snorkelling trips to the islands. *US$140 family hut (sleeps 8); US$50/90 sgl/dbl en-suite banda HB; US$30pp A-frame HB; US$10 pp dorm bed.*

✗ **WHERE TO EAT** All the beach hotels listed above have onsite restaurants. For those seeking a casual meal, the following stand out.

Pangani and north of town

✗ **Capricorn Pizzeria** m 0784 632529; ⏱ 13.00–17.00 daily. Situated at Capricorn Cottages (see *Where to stay*, page 209), this attractive outdoor pizzeria serves great pizzas in the US$7–9 range, as well as freshly brewed coffee. The attached Capricorn Casuals boutique

& Capricorn Deli also offer some of the best retail therapy in this part of Tanzania.
✗ **Shimoni Plus Food & Drinks** [210 B1] The best eatery in central Pangani, this serves a decent local buffet lunch or dinner for around US$6, as well as the usual chilled beers and soft drinks.

OTHER PRACTICALITIES

Banks and foreign exchange Cash and travellers' cheques can be exchanged at the **National Microfinance Bank** [210 B2], though a hefty commission is levied on the latter.

Diving and watersports The only PADI registered operation in the vicinity of Pangani is **Kasa Divers** (m *0786 427645*; *www.kasadivers.com*), which is based in Ushongo next door to Emayani Lodge (see *Where to stay*, opposite). In addition to PADI dives and courses, it offers a range of activities including snorkelling, windsurfing, kayaking and fishing. Although it works most closely with Emayani, guests at other lodges are welcome to arrange dives through them.

Internet A small internet café a block back from Safari Central Bar [210 C2] offers unreliable connections for around US$0.30 per half hour.

ACTIVITIES AND EXCURSIONS IN AND AROUND PANGANI

Pangani town tour Strongly Swahili in mood, Pangani has seen little development in recent decades, and several buildings dating to the 19th and early 20th century are still standing. Guided tours of the old town can be arranged through the tourist office (see page 208), but it is equally possible to explore the town independently, following the walking tour described below.

The obvious place to start is the **ferry jetty** at the raised waterfront [210 B3], where an Omani trader erected a coral rag wall in 1810 after the town was destroyed by flooding. From here, walk a few metres up Spark Street, and to your left, surrounded by an open park-like area, stands the **Old Boma** [210 B2]. This rectangular two-storey building, the oldest in Pangani, was constructed in 1810 as the residence of the same wealthy Omani trader responsible for the waterfront wall. Legend has it that several slaves were buried alive under the pillars to ensure the building had strong foundations. The carved Zanzibar-style doors are thought to be the originals. The fortified roof is a later addition, dating to the early German era, when the building was appropriated to serve as an administrative centre (*boma*). The Old Boma has been maintained well: it was used as District Commissioner's Office in colonial times, and today houses an immigration office.

About 100m further west, behind the new telecommunications office, the **Former British Hospital** [210 A2] was built in 1918 as a 'native hospital' and subsequently served as a jail. A double-storey building with a creaky old balcony, it shows some Arabic influences in its architecture. It is currently a government office, but there is some talk of converting it to a resthouse. About 500m west of the hospital behind a football field stand several 17th-century **Portuguese graves** and 19th-century **German graves**, all quite difficult to locate in the dense bush.

Two significant adjacent buildings stand on the waterfront east of the ferry jetty. The older, built in the 1850s, is the castellated double-storey **Slave Depot** [210 C3], which supposedly opened into a subterranean tunnel through which slaves were taken to Bweni on the south bank. The building is derelict today, but the façade remains intact, and there is talk of restoring it as a tourist information centre and/or museum. The **German Customs House** [210 C3], constructed in the Hanseatic style with an impressive castellated front, is reminiscent of a fort or cathedral, though it has served as the customs house since its construction in 1910 to the modern day. Inland of these buildings, **India Street**, the main shopping drag through Pangani, is lined with old Indian residences. Dating to the late 19th century, these are typically double-storey buildings with ornate iron balconies, and the ground floors are used as shops.

Bweni, on the south side of the Pangani River, pre-dates the modern town by perhaps two centuries, though no significant historical relics can be seen there today. About 1km east of the ferry crossing at Bweni, however, stands the shell of a **German Fort** built in 1916 to repel British naval invasions. A further 1.5km along this stretch of coast, a tall **commemorative pillar** is dedicated to Christian Luutherborn, a Danish sisal estate director whose death in 1907 was probably linked to the Maji Maji Rebellion.

About 2km north of Pangani, accessible from the Tanga road, is the Shirazi mosque at **Muhembo**. This mosque was larger than its counterpart in Mtangani, but is more poorly preserved possibly as a result of damage sustained in the Portuguese raid of 1635.

Pangani River Trip Boat trips up the forested Pangani River are of interest primarily for the scenery and birds such as the mangrove kingfisher, though some large mammals still occur in the area, most visibly vervet monkeys. In the wet season, you can boat upriver to the base of the Pangani Falls, now swallowed by a hydro-electric plant, though pools at the base harbour crocodiles and hippos. Boat trips can be arranged through any of the beach resorts at Ushongo. The tourist office in Pangani charges around US$80 (for one to four people) to arrange the boat, plus the guide and development fees.

Maziwe and Fungu Islands These two small offshore islands south of Pangani form the centrepieces of a recently proclaimed marine park. Maziwe was once regarded as the most important nesting site on the Tanzanian coast for sea turtles, but it has been abandoned since the 1980s due to erosionof the beach, which causes

COCONUT PALMS

Industry and associated opportunities for formal employment are thin on the ground in Pangani, but the surrounding district is self-sufficient in food, thanks to its fertile soil and the rich bounty of the ocean. Cashew and sisal – the latter introduced by a German botanist in 1892 – form the region's main export crops, but Pangani is also known for its extensive coconut palm plantations. The coconut plantations around Pangani are significant employers (monthly salaries are equivalent to US$40), and also provide an estimated 50% of Tanzania's coconut yield.

Even on a casual stroll around Pangani, the ubiquity of coconuts is striking. Vendors selling young nuts provide travellers with a refreshing and nutritious alternative to bottled soft drinks. Near the harbour, you'll see large piles of drying husks, the debris of nuts shipped to other parts of the country. Women wander home from the market carrying their goods in palm fronds converted with a few deft strokes to disposable shopping baskets.

No part of the coconut palm goes unused. The flesh of the mature nut, harvested twice annually, is not only a popular snack, but also an important ingredient in Swahili cuisine, and a source of cooking oil. The fibrous husks surrounding the nut are twined to make rope and matting, or dried for fire fuel. Palm fronds form the basis of the makuti roofs characteristic of the Swahili coast, and are also used as brooms. The sap and flowers are brewed to make a popular local wine, and the timber is used for furniture. A multi-faceted resource indeed!

A FORGOTTEN REVOLUTIONARY

Pangani was the birthplace and home of Abushiri ibn Salim al-Harthi, the half-caste African–Arabic trader who masterminded the first and most successful indigenous uprising against German rule. On 20 September 1888, Abushiri's hastily assembled troops evicted the German East Africa Company from Pangani and several other minor German stations along the coast. On 22 September, Abushiri personally led a force of 8,000 men in an assault on Bagamoyo, at that time the German capital, and days of intense fighting resulted in the destruction of much of the town before a German Marine detachment of 260 men deflected Abushiri's army. Nevertheless, by the end of the month, only Bagamoyo and Dar es Salaam remained fully under German control, while Kilwa Kivinje was under permanent siege.

In the face of this onslaught, the trading company appealed to its government for support. A ragbag army of 21 German officers, 40 NCOs and 1,000 African mercenaries assembled by the German commander Hermann von Wissmann recaptured a number of the ports following naval bombardments that drove the occupying forces away, but the spirit of revolt remained high. The naval force was able to further secure the coast by setting up a blockade preventing arms and equipment from reaching the rebels. In May 1889, the Germans attacked Abushiri's fort at Jahazi (also called Nzole), between Pangani and Bagamoyo. Using artillery fire, Wissmann drove the defenders back from the 2m-high fortifications, and then led a charge in which more than 100 Arabs were killed and Jahazi was captured. Abushiri escaped, to launch a new series of mostly unsuccessful assaults assisted by Yao and Shambaa recruits.

Von Wissmann, realising he would not be able to wrest control of the hinterland while the revolution's leader remained at large, put a price of 10,000 rupees on Abushiri's head. This rich bounty persuaded a local chief who had been harbouring Abushiri to hand him over to the German commander. On 15 December 1889, Abushiri was taken to his hometown of Pangani, paraded through the streets clad in a skimpy loincloth, and hanged later the same day. The town bears no trace of the revolutionary's existence today.

it to be submerged at high tide. Today, the main attraction is the snorkelling on the offshore reefs, where the usual host of colourful reef fish can be observed. It is important to time a visit so you arrive at low tide, when the snorkelling is best. Boat trips to the islands can be arranged through the resorts at Ushongo, which generally charge US$35–40 per person for a minimum of three people to charter a large local dhow. The tourist office in Pangani arranges trips for US$120 (one to six people) inclusive of gear but excluding the development fees of US$6 per person. A nominal park entrance fee is levied.

SAADANI NATIONAL PARK

Protected as a game reserve since 1969, Saadani is the only wildlife sanctuary in East Africa with an Indian Ocean beachfront, and – having been run by Tanapa since 2001 – was officially gazetted as a national park in 2006, when it was expanded from 200km² to its present area of 1,062km². Until recently, Saadani was among the most obscure conservation areas in East Africa, lacking for tourist facilities and heavily affected by poaching. However, a concerted clampdown on poaching and an attempt to integrate adjacent villages into the conservation effort, initiated by the Department of Wildlife with assistance from Germany's GTZ agency in 1998, has changed all that. Saadani cannot yet bear comparison to Tanzania's finest game reserves, but it is a thoroughly worthwhile retreat, offering the hedonistic pleasures of a perfect sandy beach with wildlife viewing activities such as guided bush walks, game drives, and boat trips up the Wami River. It is the closest game-viewing destination to Zanzibar, and the two are now connected by daily flights.

Set within the reserve, the fishing village of Saadani, with a population estimated at 1,000, briefly rivalled Bagamoyo in stature during the 19th century. Its growth was inhibited by a defensive wall, however, built to protect against the warring Wadoe and Wazigua clans whose ongoing fighting also dissuaded caravans from passing through the Saadani hinterland. Saadani was briefly considered as a site for the London Missionary Society's first East African mission, but it was passed over in favour of Bagamoyo. A crumbling old German customs house and a clutch of late 19th-century German and British graves serve as reminders of those days.

FEES AND FURTHER INFORMATION Park entrance costs US$20 per person per 24 hours. The lodge – and effectively the park – is often forced to close in April and May when the black cotton soil roads tend to become waterlogged.

A few useful publications, including a full bird checklist for the park, and the booklet *Saadani: An Introduction to Tanzania's Future 13th National Park* by Dr Rolf Baldus, Doreen Broska and Kirsten Röttcher, can be downloaded for free from www.wildlife-programme.gtz.de/wildlife/tourism_saadani.html.

GETTING THERE AND AWAY

Air ZanAir (*www.zanair.com*) and Coastal Aviation (*www.coastal.com*) both currently operates a scheduled daily flight to the Saadani airstrip from Zanzibar and Dar es Salaam. Otherwise, air charters can be arranged through either of the lodges, as can road transfers from Dar es Salaam via Chalinze or boat transfers from Dar via Bagamoyo.

Road All roads to Saadani are unsurfaced and in poor condition at the time of writing, although that will undoubtedly change if plans to surface the entire road from Dar es Salaam to Tanga (and build a new bridge across the Wami River) come to pass by 2016, as expected. For now, however, while the shortest route (on paper) coming from Dar es Salaam is the coastal road via Bagamoyo, this has in fact been impassable for a decade, ever since the government ferry over the Wami River sank.

This means that the only viable route from the south is through Chalinze and Miono, a drive of roughly four hours that entails following the main surfaced road towards Morogoro west out of Dar es Salaam for 105km to the junction town of Chalinze, then turning right along the Moshi road. After 50km, the Moshi road crosses a bridge over the Wami River, and 1.5km further on you'll need to turn right onto a road that runs through Mandera, Miono (10km) and Mkange (27km), ignoring the signpost to your right for the WWF Forestry Centre (48km) and crossing a railway track (53km) until you reach the reserve entrance gate (58km). From the entrance gate, it's an 8km drive to Saadani village. Parts of this road are *very* rough, and can only be attempted in a good **4x4**. The road is sometimes impassable during April and May, so you are advised to ask about its current condition when you book. One very beat-up **bus** runs between Dar es Salaam's Ubungo station and Saadani daily. It would probably be a lot quicker to catch a fast bus heading in the direction of Moshi as far as the Miono junction, where you could hop on the Saadani bus or one of the occasional **pick-up trucks** that ply the route.

Coming from the north, the coastal road from Tanga through Pangani and Mkwaja is normally viable in a 4x4 vehicle, though it may become impassable after heavy rain. The drive from Pangani to Saadani generally takes about two hours. A daily bus connects Tanga to Mkwaja via Pangani, leaving Mkwaja at around 05.00 and Tanga at around 10.00, taking four hours in either direction. There is no public transport at all between Mkwaja and Saadani.

WHERE TO STAY
Upmarket

🏠 **Saadani Safari Lodge** (9 tents) 📞022 277 3294; m 0713 555678; e info@saadanilodge.com; www.saadanilodge.com. This small & intimate tented camp, which runs attractively along a palm-fringed beach about 1km north of Saadani village, has undergone a major facelift over the last couple of years, most notably with the addition of a swimming pool. Accommodation is in comfortable framed canvas tents with a *makuti* roof, en-suite facilities, solar electricity & twin or dbl bed, as well as a second netted bed on the balcony should you want to sleep outside. The open wooden bar & dining area is very peaceful, while a tree house overlooks a waterhole regularly visited by waterbuck, bushbuck, buffalo & various water birds – & very occasionally lion & elephant. Activities include game drives, guided walks with a ranger, & boat trips on the river. *US$290/490 sgl/dbl FB inc 1 activity per day.*

🏠 **Saadani River Lodge** (18 rooms) 📞022 277 3294; m 0713 555678; e info@saadaniriverlodge.com; www.saadaniriverlodge.com. The newest lodge in Saadani, this opened on the south bank of the Wami River in 2012, & is under the same management as the Saadani Safari Lodge. Accommodation is in luxurious stilted suites with hardwood floor, thatch roof & stylish furnishings including a king-size bed with walk-in netting.

It offers a similar range of activities as the Safari Lodge at similar prices, including guided walks, river cruises & game drives. *US$290/490 sgl/dbl FB inc 1 activity per day.*

🏠 **Tent With A View** (9 tents) 📞022 211 0507; m 0713 323318; e info@saadani.com; www.saadani.com. This small camp lies along a pretty beach some 30km north of Saadani village near Mkwaja, an area regarded as the best in the park for elephant sightings. The camp consists of 9 standing tents on stilted wooden platforms spaced out in the coastal scrub immediately behind the beach. It offers a similar range of guided activities to Saadani Safari Lodge, while several short self-guided walking trails emanate from the camp, & you can canoe in the nearby Mafuwe Creek. *From US$275/390 sgl/dbl FB; US$355/550 full game package.*

Budget and camping

🏠 **Saadani Resthouse & Bandas** (10 rooms) m 0785 555135/0754 730112; e saadani@tanzaniaparks.com; www.tanzaniaparks.com. This recently renovated TANAPA guesthouse can be found near the beach in Saadani village. Bookings are seldom necessary & camping is permitted. It is self-catering only, although you should be able to locate some food in the village. *US$40 pp for a room; US$20 pp camping.*

WHAT TO SEE Inland of its 20km coastline, Saadani supports a park-like cover of open grassland interspersed with stands of acacia trees and knotted coastal thicket. Along the coast, palm-lined beaches are separated by extensive mangrove stands, while the major watercourses are fringed by lush riparian woodland. Game densities are highest in January–February and June–August, when the plains hold more water. At all times, you can be reasonably confident of encountering giraffe, buffalo, warthog, common waterbuck, reedbuck, hartebeest and wildebeest, along with troops of yellow baboon and vervet monkey. Something of a Saadani special, the red duiker is a diminutive and normally very shy antelope found in coastal scrub and forest. Quite common, but less easily seen, are greater kudu and eland. Saadani also harbours a small population of Roosevelt's sable, an endangered race otherwise found in the Selous Game Reserve and Kenya's Shimba Hills. The elephant population is on the increase, with herds of up to 30 being sighted with increasing frequency, and lion are also making a solid comeback. Leopard, spotted hyena and black-backed jackal are also around, along with the usual small nocturnal predators.

In addition to game drives, guided walks offer a good chance of seeing various antelope and representatives of Saadani's rich variety of woodland birds. Best of all are boat trips on the Wami River, which hosts several pods of hippo, as well as crocodiles and a good selection of marine and riverine birds including mangrove kingfisher, Pel's fishing owl and various herons, storks and waders. The beaches in and around Saadani form one of the last major breeding sites for green turtles on mainland Tanzania.

10

Tarangire and the Central Rift Valley

The least celebrated of the quartet of reserves that comprises northern Tanzania's established safari circuit, Tarangire National Park is nevertheless a highly rewarding wildlife destination, especially during the latter half of the year, when it's a recommended inclusion on any safari itinerary of a week or longer. The park is best known for its density of baobab trees and year-round proliferation of elephants, but predators are also well represented, the birdlife is excellent, and from July until November large herds of migrant grazers are drawn to the perennial water of the Tarangire River.

Tarangire lies within the Central Rift Valley, a semi-arid region inhabited by various traditional pastoralists, most famously the Maasai, who live in the immediate vicinity of the national park, but also the Barabaig and other sub-groups of the Datoga further southwest. And although most tourists confine their exploration of the area to Tarangire itself, there is plenty else to see, ranging from the under-publicised Kondoa Rock Art (a UNESCO World Heritage Site) to pretty Lake Babati and little-known Mount Hanang, an isolated volcanic relic that towers from the Rift Valley floor near Katesh.

As with other game reserves on the northern circuit, Tarangire is serviced by a range of camps and lodges to suit most tastes, and is most easily explored as part of a road safari out of Arusha, though fly-in packages are available. At a push, the Kondoa Rock Art could be visited as a day trip out of Tarangire, but it's more realistic to make an overnight excursion of it. Lake Babati and Mount Hanang are accessible by public transport, and an excellent cultural tourism project in Babati town can arrange visits to both.

TARANGIRE NATIONAL PARK

The 2,850km² Tarangire National Park lies at the core of a vast ecosystem that also comprises the 585km² Tarangire Conservation Area (TCA) and around 5,000km² of unprotected land extending across the Maasai Steppes. In general, this region is drier than the Serengeti, and more densely vegetated, supporting a tangle of semi-arid acacia and mixed woodland. The park's dominant geographic feature is the Tarangire River, flanked by dense patches of elephant grass and a sporadic ribbon of riparian woodland dotted with the occasional palm tree. A striking feature of the park is the immensity and abundance of the baobabs that line the slopes away from the river.

It is difficult to put reliable figures on the wildlife populations currently associated with Tarangire, as the most recent census was completed more than 20 years ago, but there is no reason to suppose that the numbers recorded then – including 25,000 wildebeest, 30,000 zebra, 6,000 buffalo, 3,000 elephant, 2,700 giraffe, 5,500 eland, 30,000 impala and 2,000 warthog – have significantly changed.

As with Serengeti-Ngorongoro, the greater Tarangire ecosystem is characterised by a great deal of migratory movement. In contrast to the Serengeti, however, Tarangire National Park comes into its own during the dry season, between July and November, when elephant numbers can be little short of phenomenal and are boosted by large herds of zebra, wildebeest, antelope and other game attracted to the near-perennial waters of the Tarangire River. That isn't to say, however, that Tarangire is without merit at other times. True, a lot of wildlife disperses outside the park during the wetter months of December to June – wildebeest and zebra northwest to the Rift Valley floor between Manyara and Natron, other species across onto the Maasai Steppes – but the park is also greener and more scenic during the rains, and the birdlife is astounding. In addition, elephants have been less keen to range far from Tarangire during recent rainy seasons, presumably as a result of increased poaching outside the park boundaries. Also, against expectations, lions seem to be easier to locate than in the dry season, possibly because the tall grass makes then more inclined to walk and hunt along roads, and to rest up on them at night.

Abutting the park's northeastern border, the TCA comprises four contiguous tracts of land used for trophy hunting until the late 1990s when ownership was restored to the traditional Maasai inhabitants. The TCA now functions as a buffer to the national park, encompassing the main watershed for the Tarangire River, the wetlands around Gosuwa Swamp, and migration routes used by wildebeest and zebra to reach their breeding grounds near Lolkisale Mountain. The Maasai owners earn revenue from levies raised by tourist lodges set within the concessions, which differ from their counterparts within the national park in that game walks and night drives are permitted.

A more recent development is the opening of two exclusive private camps set in private concessions that form part of the historically important wildlife corridor between Tarangire and Lake Manyara National Parks, whose respective northern and southeastern tips lie only 20km apart but are separated by farmland and the surfaced Arusha–Dodoma Highway. Described in greater detail under the accommodation listings (see overleaf), these concessions are Manyara Ranch and Chem Chem, and they not only play an important role in reopening the migration route between the two national parks, but also offer visitors the opportunity to combine guided walks and drives within the concession with day trips to Tarangire (the closer park by road) and Lake Manyara.

A detailed booklet, *Tarangire National Park*, is widely available in Arusha and some of the park's lodges. The park entrance fee of US$45 per person per 24 hours can be paid by Visa, MasterCard or with a Tanapa Smartcard (issued at any Exim Bank). No other cards are accepted, nor are travellers' cheques or cash. For more details, see box, *Paying park fees*, page 71.

GETTING THERE AND AWAY Tarangire lies about 7km off the main Arusha–Dodoma road. Coming from Arusha, this road is tarred as far as the turn-off to the park, which is clearly signposted at Kwa Kuchinja, a small village situated about 100km south of Arusha and 25km past Makuyuni (the junction for Manyara and the Serengeti). Most people tag a visit to Tarangire onto a longer safari, but if your time or money is limited, a one- or two-day stand-alone safari would be a viable option.

WHERE TO STAY

Exclusive The lodges listed opposite are divided into those located in nearby concessions and those set within the national park or along its western border near the main entrance gate.

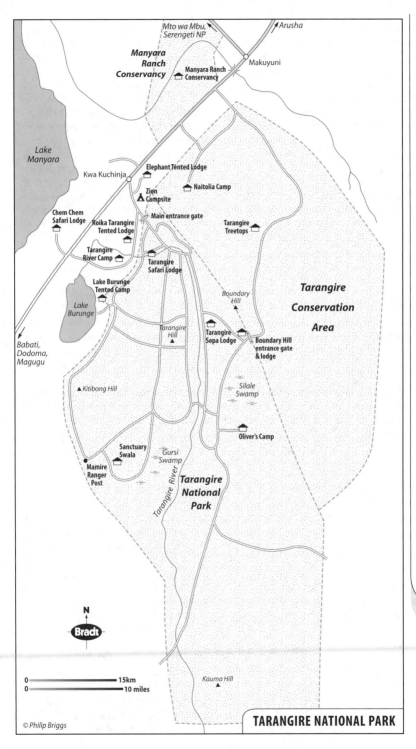

TARANGIRE NATIONAL PARK

© Philip Briggs

0 ——— 15km
0 ——— 10 miles

N

Bradt

Concession lodges

🏠 **Chem Chem Safari Lodge** (6 rooms)
📞 0718 139359; e reservations@chemchemsafari. com; www.chemchemsafari.com. This classy new owner-managed lodge lies on a 40km² concession running between the southeast shore of Lake Manyara & the main road west of the Burunge area of Tarangire. Accommodation is in ultra-spacious & earthily stylish cottages with canvas walls & roofs, each with king-size bed, walk-in nets, large bathroom with indoor tub & outdoor shower, & 2 private balconies. Long stilted wooden walkways link the cottages to the open-sided sitting & dining area, which overlooks a grassy floodplain, a line of borassus palms marking the distant shore of Manyara, & the tall escarpment above the lake. The unfenced concession forms part of a recently created Game Management Area in the important wildlife corridor connecting Tarangire to Lake Manyara, & plains wildlife – giraffe, zebra, various antelope – is already prolific, with a good likelihood that the Big Five will start to re-colonise the area in the near future. The main activity within the concession is guided walking safaris, which offer an opportunity to get close to plenty of wildlife. Walking is also the best way to experience the superb birdlife associated both with the tangled acacia scrub & the open floodplain of Manyara, a good site for coursers, pratincoles, storks, flamingos, avocets & other wading birds. The lodge is also a useful springboard for day trips into Tarangire National Park (it will be better still as and when the new Burunge Entrance Gate opens, which is likely to be during the lifespan of this edition) & to the little-visited southern end of Lake Manyara National Park, making it a great base for newly arrived safari-goers to settle in for a few days before heading further west to the Serengeti, etc. *US$1131/1560 sgl/dbl FB inc drinks, or US$1,380/1,840 sgl/dbl full game package. Seasonal discounts Mar, May & Nov.*

🏠 **Tarangire Treetops Lodge** (20 rooms)
📞 027 254 0630/9; e info@elewana.com, videar@ elewana.com; www.elewana.com. Situated within the TCA to the northeast of the national park, this architecturally innovative lodge consists of 20 spacious & luxurious stilted en-suite tree-houses sitting up in the canopy, where they offer great birding opportunities, soundtracked by a lively night chorus led by bushbabies. The tree-houses boast a floor area of 65m², as well as canvas sides, a wooden floor & deck, & an open-plan layout. The organic feel is complemented by the uncluttered minimalist décor, & they are so atmospheric & comfortable it almost seems a shame to leave them to go on a game drive! Because the lodge lies on private land, the usual diurnal game drives can be supplemented by other activities such as game walks, birding walks along a nearby watercourse, night drives & mountain-biking excursions. The quality of game viewing in the immediate vicinity varies seasonally, but it's only 45 mins by road to Boundary Hill Gate & the main road circuit in northern Tarangire. Ideal for honeymooners, this lodge is also a wonderful place to recover from jetlag at the start of a safari, or to stretch your legs at the end of one. A portion of the room rate funds community projects. *US$1,030/1,490 sgl/dbl FB, inc most drinks, laundry & transfer to/from Kuro airstrip. Seasonal discounts available Mar–May, Nov & early Dec. Full game package inc game drives an additional US$100 pp.*

🏠 **Manyara Ranch Conservancy** (6 tents)
📞 027 254 5284; m 0683 918888; e reservations@ manyararanch.com; www.manyararanch.com. Established as a cattle ranch during the colonial era, the 120km² Manyara Ranch was taken over by the African Wildlife Foundation in 2000, & it now doubles as a commercial ranch & part of an important wildlife corridor connecting the Natron/ Manyara region to Tarangire National Park. The emphasis here is strongly on game walks, which offer a good opportunity for close encounters with the likes of elephant, giraffe, wildebeest & zebra, as well as more localised antelope such as fringe-eared oryx, eland & lesser kudu. Night drives are also offered, with a chance of sighting lion, spotted hyena, & bat-eared fox. Birdlife is varied too, thanks to the wide variety of habitats ranging from open grassland to lush riparian forest. It is also a good base for day trips to Tarangire & Lake Manyara national parks, both of which lie a 30–45 min drive way. Accommodation comprises a wonderfully rustic & intimate tented camp space out in a shady acacia grove alive with birds & overlooking a floodplain that frequently attracts wildlife. The large screened tents are in the classic safari style, with hardwood floor, king-size bed, en-suite bathroom with hot shower, private balcony with camp chairs, & a great night chorus. Like Chem Chem, it's a great place to spend a few days at the start of a safari. *US$715/1,160 sgl/dbl FB inc drinks, guided walks & night drives. Closed Apr & May.*

☐ Boundary Hill Lodge (8 rooms) **m** 0787 293727; **e** simon@eastafricansafari.info; www. tarangireconservation.com. On a hilltop in the private Lolkisale concession, outside the Boundary Hill Entrance Gate, this new lodge is the first in Tanzania to have a local community shareholding, with the Maasai village of Lolkisale owning 50%. The 8 spacious suites, set among the rocky cliffs, are individually designed & lavishly decorated, & have private sitting areas & wide balconies offering spectacular views over the Silale & Gosuwa swamps, where elephant & buffalo are resident. En-suite facilities include cast-iron baths. In addition to daytime game drives into the national park, the lodge offers guided game walks with the local Maasai & night drives. The concession lies on a migration route & is particularly busy with wildlife from Nov–Mar. *From US$550 pp full game package.*

Lodges inside Tarangire
☐ Sanctuary Swala (12 tents) **** (UK) +44 (0)20 7190 7728; **e** info@sanctuaryretreats.com; www. sanctuaryretreats.com. Situated in the southern half of the park, this classic luxury tented camp stands in a grove of tall acacia trees overlooking the remote Gurusi Swamp, where it is wonderfully isolated from any other lodge or the more popular game-viewing circuits. The camp itself is something of a magnet for wildlife: the *swala* (antelope) for which it is named are much in evidence, especially a resident herd of impala, accompanied by a noisy entourage of vervet monkeys, guineafowl & various plovers,

Upmarket
☐ Tarangire Sopa Lodge (75 rooms) **** 027 250 0630-9; **e** info@sopalodges.com; www.sopalodges.com. Set in the heart of the national park, the Tarangire Sopa is the largest, most conventionally luxurious & least 'bush' of the lodges around Tarangire. The facilities & accommodation match the customary high standards of this chain, with smart self-contained suites & excellent food. The indifferent location, alongside a small & normally dry watercourse below a baobab-studded slope, is compensated for by the superb game viewing – the roads between here & Tarangire Safari Lodge are far & away the most rewarding in the park. *US$ 330/580 sgl/dbl FB; US$280/480 in Mar, Nov & early Dec, US$115/225 Apr–May.*

buffalo-weavers & starlings. The small waterhole in front of the camp attracts elephants in Jul & Aug, while a near-resident lion pride & the occasional leopard pass through with surprising regularity. The food is excellent, especially the bush dinners held in a grove of baobabs about 5 mins' drive from camp, & the quality of tented accommodation is in line with the best lodges of this type in southern Africa. *US$1,030/1,510 sgl/dbl inc meals, drinks & guided activities. Substantial discount Jan–Mar. Closed Apr & May.*

☐ Oliver's Camp (10 rooms) **** (South Africa) +27 (0)21 418 0468; **m** 0736 5005156; www. asiliaafrica.com. This excellent bush camp, overlooking Silale Swamp, lies within the park boundaries, far enough from the busy northern section that activities can usually be undertaken without seeing other tourists. The only location where walking safaris can be undertaken inside Tarangire, it offers 2-night stays incorporated into more wide-ranging safaris, as well as extended walking-oriented stays of 3 days or more, usually spending 1 or more nights at a mobile fly-camp. The lodge itself is unpretentious & comfortable rather than opulently luxurious, the guides are unusually personable & knowledgeable, & a superb library of natural history books underscores the emphasis on substance over style – strongly recommended to anybody seeking a genuinely holistic bush experience. *US$875/1,400 sgl/dbl inc all meals, drinks & activities Jul–Oct & 20 Dec–5 Jan; US$755/1160 all other times.*

☐ Lake Burunge Tented Camp (30 tents) **m** 0767 333223/0784 207727; **e** reservations@ tanganyikawildernesscamps.com; www. tanganyikawildernesscamps.com. Overlooking the seasonal Lake Burunge, this lodge lies some 10 mins' drive outside the park boundary, some distance south of the main Tarangire tourist circuit, in an area of dense bush known for its populations of dry-country antelope such as lesser kudu & gerenuk. Accommodation is in spacious & attractively rustic en-suite twin & dbl tents built on stilted platforms & shaded by *makuti* roofs. The camp is well positioned for game drives, & it also offers guided nature walks, along with canoe trips when the lake holds water. Under utilised & very good value. *US$230/330 sgl/dbl FB. Low season discount Apr–May.*

🏠 **Tarangire Safari Lodge** (40 tents)
📞 027 254 4752; m 0784 202777; e
bookings@tarangiresafarilodge.com; www.
tarangiresafarilodge.com. This comfortable &
unpretentious owner-managed lodge is the
oldest lodge in the park, & one of the most
characterful, boasting a sublime location on a
tall bluff overlooking the Tarangire River. Game
viewing from the veranda can be excellent, with
large herds of elephants, hippo, giraffe, etc coming
down to the river to drink. The grounds are also
highly attractive to birders, both for the habituated
hornbills, buffalo-weavers & starlings that parade
around the common areas, & for the host of more
secretive small birds resident in the acacia scrub.
The small but well-maintained standing tents
have en-suite hot showers & toilets, & private
balconies, & the restaurant serves great buffet
meals. Outstanding value & highly recommended.
US$225/360 sgl/dbl FB.

🏠 **Tarangire River Camp** (20 tents) m 0732
978879; e info@mbalimbali.com; www.mbalimbali.
com. Situated 3.5km outside the main gate as the
crow flies (but more like 15km by road) this tented
camp lies within a 250km² concession, set aside for
conservation by the Maasai community of Minjingu,
along the northwest boundary of the national park.
The camp is set below a massive old baobab on a
cliff overlooking the (normally dry) Minjingu River,
a tributary of the Tarangire, & wildlife can be quite
prolific in the vicinity seasonally, even though it is
not in the park. The lodge is centred on a vast stilted
thatch & timber structure composed of a main
lounge, a small library, & a dining & cocktail area,
offering sweeping views across the riverbed to the
Maasai Steppes. The large en-suite tents with private
balcony, 2 x 3/4 beds & 24-hr solar power are good
value. *US$225 pp FB.*

🏠 **Kirurumu Tarangire Lodge** (10 tents) 📞 027
250 7011/7541; e info@kirurumu.net; kirurumu@

kirurumu.net. Just 15 mins from the main park gate
overlooking a watering hole, this small bush camp
has just 10 spacious en-suite tents, all raised on
solid stone bases & suspended under thatch. Fairly
minimalistic in style & simple in design, they are
equipped with electricity & hot running water. The
small communal areas afford slightly more comfort
& luxury, with African fabrics lending a certain
rusticity to them. It's usual to gather around the
campfire for a pre-dinner drink & cross your fingers
for a sight of some thirsty animals coming down to
drink as the sun sets. As well as convenient access to
the park, guests can organise Maasai guided nature
walks, hire mountain bikes & arrange day treks in
the surrounding areas. The lodge is located alongside
a local village & $10 pp per night is put into a
community pot, which is in turn put to good use.
Guided visits can be arranged on request, although
the proximity to the village means it loses a little of
the wilderness feel some of the other camps enjoy.
*US$201/314 sgl/dbl FB, inc meals & guided walks.
Seasonal discounts available Mar–May, Nov & early
Dec. Full game package inc game drives, drinks &
transfers to nearest airstrip available at an extra cost.*

🏠 **Roika Tarangire Tented Lodge** (21 tents)
📞 027 250 9994; m 0754 001444/ 0787 005444;
e reservation@tarangireroikatentedlodge.com;
www.tarangireroikatentedlodge.com. Situated in
a stand of tangled acacia scrub about 5km from
the park entrance gate en route to Tarangire River
Lodge, Roika Tarangire offers accommodation
in large en-suite standing tents set on stilted
wooden platforms. Shaded by *makuti* roofs, the
tents are very comfortable, with 2 dbl beds each, &
decorated simply in safari style, though the rustic
mood is undermined somewhat by the tackily
sculpted animal-shaped baths. The main building
is thatched with open sides & overlooks a large
swimming pool. Good value. *US$200/320 pp FB.*

Camping For those on camping safaris, there are a couple of campsites within
Tarangire. These are strong on bush atmosphere but short on facilities, and rather
costly at the customary US$30 per person.

🏕 **Zion Campsite** m 0754 460539. This
small & very basic private camp is used by many
budget camping safaris. To get there, turn off the

Arusha–Dodoma road as if heading towards the
main entrance gate to Tarangire. The campsite is
immediately to the left after about 2km. *US$10 pp.*

EXPLORING TARANGIRE NATIONAL PARK Most people spend only one day in
Tarangire and thus concentrate on the game-viewing roads along its well-developed

northern circuit, which follows the river between the Tarangire Safari Lodge and Tarangire Sopa Lodge. And this is unambiguously the best game-viewing area, especially in the dry season, when wildebeest, zebra, buffalo, giraffe, impala, gazelle and warthog congregate along the river, the only source of water for many kilometres.

Tarangire is justifiably famous for the prolific elephant herds that congregate along the river during the dry season. It is likely that the population has grown significantly since the late 1980s, when 3,000 individuals were recorded in a census, although a recent growth in commercial poaching in the vicinity of Tarangire might yet reverse that trend. Still, in peak times, it is no exaggeration to say that you might see 500 elephants over the course of a day here. Tarangire's elephants used to be a lot more skittish than their counterparts in Manyara and Ngorongoro, but they are quite a lot more relaxed these days.

The full range of large predators is present on the main tourist road circuit too, but the dense vegetation can make it relatively difficult to pick up the likes of lion and leopard, even though they are quite common. Two localised antelope that occur in Tarangire are the fringe-eared oryx and gerenuk, although neither is seen with great regularity. Of the smaller mammals, the colonial dwarf mongoose is characteristic of the park, and is often seen on the termite hills where it breeds.

Tarangire is a great birdwatching site, with around 500 species recorded to date. A wide range of resident raptors includes bateleur, fish eagle and palmnut vulture, while the river supports saddle-billed and yellow-billed storks and several other water birds. Characteristic acacia birds are yellow-necked spurfowl, orange-bellied parrot, barefaced go-away bird, red-fronted barbet, and silverbird. A personal favourite is the red-and-yellow barbet, with its quaintly comical clockwork duet, typically performed on termite mounds.

Tarangire's location at the western limit of the Somali-Maasai biome means it harbours several dry-country bird species at the extremity of their range, among them vulturine guineafowl, Donaldson-Smith's nightjar, pink-breasted lark, northern pied babbler and mouse-coloured penduline tit. It is also the easiest place to observe a pair of bird species endemic to the dry heartland of central Tanzania: the lovely yellow-collared lovebird, and the somewhat drabber ashy starling, both of which are common locally.

For those with sufficient time to explore beyond the main tourist circuit, the Lake Burunge area offers the best chance of seeing bushbuck and lesser kudu, while the Kitibong Hill area is home to large herds of buffalo, and Lamarkau Swamp supports hippo and numerous water birds during the wet season. Further south, cheetahs favour the southern plains, while Mkungero Pools is a good place to look for buffalo, waterbuck and gerenuk.

BABATI

Set below the forested slopes of the 2,415m Mount Kwaraha, the bustling and fast-growing market town of Babati straddles the Arusha–Dodoma Road some 70km south of Kwa Kuchinja (the junction for the main gate to Tarangire National Park) and a similar distance north of Kondoa. It's a useful place to break up long bus journeys, and since it is situated at the junction for Katesh, a useful springboard for travel west to Mount Hanang. Further justification for stopping over in Babati is the eponymous lake on the town's southern outskirts, which is easily reached by walking along the Dodoma road for about ten minutes. The papyrus-fringed stretch of shore alongside the road supports a good selection of water birds – egrets, waders and storks – while flotillas of pelican sail pompously across the open water. Several pods of hippo are resident, and it's easy enough to negotiate with a local fisherman to take you out in search of them. Kahembe's Trekking & Cultural Tours, based in Babati, is a useful contact for arranging local excursions and Hanang climbs (see box opposite).

GETTING THERE AND AWAY Babati is 172km south of Arusha on what is now a good surfaced road. It shouldn't take longer than 21/2 hours to cover the full distance in a **private vehicle**. **Buses** in either direction leave throughout the day, taking three to four hours, and tickets cost around US$4.50. The best service is Mtei Express Coaches, hourly buses to from Arusha to Babati leave from their own station on Makao Mapya Road hourly between 06.00 and 16.00. There are also several buses daily to Katesh in the west, as well as to Kondoa via Kolo in the south.

WHERE TO STAY
Moderate
🏠 **Royal Beach Hotel** m 0784 395814/0785 125070; e meshakingomuo@yahoo.com. Boasting an idyllic situation on a small peninsula that juts out into Lake Babati, this is the most upmarket option in the Central Rift Valley. It forms an ideal base for visiting the Kondoa Rock Art, trekking Mount Hanang or cruising Lake Babati, activities that can all be arranged through the enthusiastic management. Accommodation is in comfortable concrete buildings with large beds, net, TV & en-suite toilet & shower. The restaurant is good & has lots of outdoor seating overlooking Lake Babati. *US$20 dbl chalet.*

Budget
🏠 **Kahembe's Modern Guesthouse** (8 rooms) m 0784 397477; e kahembeculture@yahoo.com; www.kahembeculturalsafaris.com. This pleasant guesthouse is less than 500m from the bus station, next door to the office of the affiliated Kahembe Trekking (see box opposite). It offers good quality en-suite accommodation, & a restaurant serving continental dishes is attached. *US$13/17/20 sgl/dbl/twin inc a good b/fast.*

Shoestring
🏠 **Motel Paapaa** ☎ 027 253 1111. This decent if slightly run-down hotel is about the smartest in town, & conveniently situated next to the bus stop. The restaurant serves large portions of reasonable

food. *US$8 en-suite dbl with cold water; or US$4 room & communal shower.*

✖ **WHERE TO EAT** Aside from the good restaurant at the **Motel Paapaa**, the **Dolphin** and **Ango** restaurants are decent and affordable local eateries, the latter with a pleasant outdoor sitting area.

This commendable Babati institution started life in the mid 1990s as a private ecotourism concern, and has since been formalised into an official cultural tourism project. It's an excellent point of contact for travellers who want to explore this little-known part of Tanzania in an organised manner, as Kahembe Trekking's overnight trips are well organised and informative (although not luxurious by any standard), and offer an unforgettable glimpse into African traditions without making you pay through the nose.

The most popular trips are the three-day and two-day Mount Hanang climbs out of Babati (several fixed departures weekly). Other possibilities range from a three-day Barabaig walking safari, to a couple of seven- and eight-day walking itineraries that visit several local bomas as well as incorporating walks on the game-rich verges of Lake Manyara and Tarangire National Parks. Day trips on Lake Babati and to local villages can also be arranged, and special requests and interests can be catered for with advance notice.

Contact them on m 0748 397477; e kahembeculture@yahoo.com; www.kahembeculturalsafaris.com.

MOUNT HANANG AND KATESH

Mount Hanang is Tanzania's fourth-highest mountain after Kilimanjaro, Meru and Lolomalasin in the Crater Highlands. Volcanic in origin, it is a product of the same geological process that sculpted the Rift Valley, and it is the only one of these mountains to actually stand within the rift. The dormant caldera towers to an elevation of 3,418m above the low-lying plains, and is visible from hundreds of kilometres away on a clear day. Not surprisingly, this imposing free-standing mountain is revered by the Barabaig who inhabit its lower slopes, and it features prominently in their myths. Hanang supports its own distinct microclimate and forms an important local watershed. Most of the rain falls on the northern and eastern slopes, where extensive forests still support elusive populations of bushbuck, duiker and various monkeys, as well as a wide range of forest birds.

Seldom visited by tourists, Hanang lies outside the national park system and forms a very affordable alternative montane hike to Kilimanjaro or Meru. The slopes support the usual range of montane forest and grassland habitats, and offer excellent views over a stretch of the Rift Valley studded with smaller volcanic cones and shallow lakes. The normal springboard for climbing Hanang is Katesh, which lies at its southern base 75km west of Babati. Further details of routes and costs are provided under the heading *Climbing Mount Hanang*, but travellers broadly have two options: placing themselves in the experienced hands of the cultural tourism programme in Babati (see box, *Kahembe Trekking*, above), or making their own arrangements out of Katesh.

The attractions of the Hanang area are not restricted to the mountain. On the contrary, the primal scenery of the surrounding plains is enhanced by the colourful presence of traditional pastoralists such as the Barabaig, people who have consciously retained their traditional way of life. Several substantial lakes also lie in the vicinity of Katesh, including the shallow and highly saline Lake Balangida, which is set at the base of the Rift Valley scarp immediately north of Mount Hanang. Finally, Katesh forms the starting point for an obscure but not unrewarding back route to Karatu and the Ngorongoro Crater Highlands via Basotu, Dongobesh and Mbulu.

10

GETTING THERE AND AWAY Katesh lies 250km from Arusha and 75km west of Babati. In a **private vehicle**, the drive from Arusha will take less than five hours, and the drive from Babati about 90 minutes. For those travellers dependent on **public transport**, buses run between Babati and Singida via Katesh throughout the day, taking two to three hours in either direction between Babati and Katesh. Several buses travel between Arusha and Singida via Katesh; the thrice-daily service operated by Mtei Express Coaches is recommended.

WHERE TO STAY AND EAT An established pick is the **Colt Guesthouse** (↳ *027 253 0030*), which lies near the main market and charges around US$3 for a double with use of communal showers and US$7 for a clean and spacious en-suite double with hot running water. Also recommended, the **Summit Hotel** (m *0787 242424*) near the municipal offices charges US$10/15 for a good en-suite single/double.

Decent eateries include **Mama Kabwogi's Hoteli** and the improbably named **Jesus Loves You Restaurant**.

AROUND KATESH

Climbing Mount Hanang Several ascent routes exist, but only two are suited to first-time climbers. The marginally easier **Jorodom** (or Katesh) **Route** starts at the eponymous village on the southern slopes 2km from Katesh, offering the best choice for those making their own arrangements. The **Giting Route** starts on the wetter eastern slopes 10km out of town, and is more densely forested, but also more slippery underfoot during the rains.

Hanang can be climbed as a full-day round trip out of Katesh, but this reduces the hike to something of an endurance test, with little opportunity to enjoy the scenery. What's more, while a very fit hiker could complete the full ascent and descent in 12 hours, others may struggle. An overnight climb is therefore recommended. There are several good places to pitch a tent, or you can sleep in the caves on the Giting Route (checking in advance that your guide knows their location). Either way, the upper slopes of Hanang get very chilly at night, so you'll need a good sleeping bag or thick blanket, and enough warm clothes.

The most straightforward option is to arrange a climb with Kahembe Trekking in Babati (see box, previous page). This costs around US$150 per person, inclusive of lodging in Katesh either side of the climb, forest reserve fees, food, porters, and an experienced English-speaking guide. You could lower the cost slightly by arranging your own climb, but you would still need to pay for your own accommodation, as well as the forest reserve fee of US$30 per person, the village fee of US$2 per person, guide and porter fees (around US$5–10 per day), and your own food. If you decide to do this, visit the Forestry Office (in Katesh's municipal offices near the Summit Hotel) to sort out fees and find out about a reliable guide (ideally one who speaks English). Porters can also usually be arranged here. No permanent water source exists on the mountain, so bring all the drinking water you'll require. This is an *absolute* daily minimum of four litres per climber, more during the hot, dry season. Bottled mineral water is available in Katesh, but not in Giting or Jorodom.

Climbers intending to use the Jorodom Route will need to walk the 2km from Katesh to Jorodom village. From Jorodom, the hike to a good campsite on the lower ridge takes about six hours. The upper ridge looks deceptively close at this point, but is in fact at least four hours distant. It is thus advisable to camp at the top of the lower ridge, then tackle the final ascent and full descent the next day.

To get to the trailhead for the Giting Route, follow the Babati road out of Katesh for 5km to Nangwa, then turn left on to a side road and continue for another 4km to the village of Giting. The Hanang Forestry Department has an office here where you can arrange a guide and porters at the same rate charged in Katesh or Jorodom. There's no accommodation in Giting, but you can camp in the Forestry Department compound.

Mount Hanang road loop A loop of rough road near Katesh circles around the north side of Mount Hanang, making for an interesting half-day drive for motorised travellers, or a worthwhile hike for backpackers who don't particularly want to climb the mountain or who want to explore the area without guides. The scenery along this road is lovely, passing through cultivated montane meadows and lower-lying acacia scrub, with the mountain looming to the south and Lake Balangida and the Rift Valley escarpment about 5km to the north. A diversion to the lake and its hinterland offers good birding and the opportunity to seek out some little-known rock paintings, as well as exposure to rustic Barabaig and Iraqw villages.

Leave Katesh along the Babati road, and after 5km you'll reach Nangwa, a small settlement noted locally for its Catholic church with impressive stained glass windows. A left turn at Nangwa leads you onto the loop road and, after about 4km, the semi-urban sprawl of Giting, also the trailhead for the Hanang ascent route of that name. From Giting, you'll probably need to ask somebody to point you in the right direction for Barjomet, which lies another 5–6km along the loop. The cultivated highlands between Giting and Barjomet buffer the forest zone of Hanang, and once you reach Barjomet, a small crater, clearly visible from the road, hosts a seasonal lake where local villagers bring cattle and sheep to drink. Moving on from Barjomet, the road deteriorates and becomes little more than a rough track as it descends into a hot valley, densely covered in acacia woodland. After about 5km and 10km respectively, it passes through the small traditional villages of Gendabi and Dawar, with fine views of Lake Balangida to the north. About 2km past Dawar, the loop road emerges on the main road between Katesh (to the left) and Basotu (to the right).

A worthwhile side trip from this loop, best undertaken in the company of a local guide and about 5km long in either direction, leads from Giting to Gidawira and the shore of Lake Balangida. This shallow body of water, far too saline to drink, is set in the sweltering depression that divides Hanang from the Rift Valley scarp, and it often harbours substantial concentrations of flamingos. In recent years, Balangida has often been reduced to a puddle, or has dried up entirely, during the dry season. When this happens, the extensive white flats are exposed, and the local Barabaig can be seen extracting coarse salt by the bucket load. Also of interest are some faded rock paintings, depicting both animals and people, which can be reached by scrambling up a rock face close to Gidawira. This is a hot walk, with no potable water to be found along the way, so do bring some bottled water with you.

Exploring this loop is straightforward enough in a private 4x4 vehicle, and it should take no longer than half a day allowing for stops and diversions. As for public transport, you'll have no problem finding transport along the Babati road as far as Nangwa, and may be able to pick something up from here to Giting. Unless you're very lucky, however, you'll probably have to cover the roughly 20km from Giting to the Basuto road on foot. With time and the right frame of mind, this is a far from an unattractive prospect, although covering the loop in its entirety in one day would be pretty tough going. Assuming you have a tent, it's permitted to camp at the Forestry Department Office at Giting, and it's unlikely you'd be stopped from camping elsewhere in the area, provided you asked permission from the local chief first. Even if you don't fancy covering the whole loop, you could consider camping at the Forestry Department in Giting and arranging a guide from there for a day trip to Lake Balangida.

Lake Basotu The little-known but very accessible Lake Basotu lies about 40km northwest of Katesh, and is reached via a scenic road that ascends the Rift Valley scarp north of Mount Hanang and Lake Balangida before passing through grassy highlands populated by Barabaig and Bulu pastoralists. Lake Basotu is a lovely, atmospheric spot, fringed by stands of papyrus and tall yellow fever trees, with Hanang towering on the eastern horizon. Large numbers of hippo are resident in the shallows, and troops of vervet monkey commandeer the wooded shore. The birdlife is fabulous, too, particularly on the far eastern shore, where a ghostly forest of waterlogged trunks supports a seasonal breeding colony of reed cormorant, pink-backed pelican and black-headed, grey and squacco herons.

TOWARDS LAKE VICTORIA

Katesh and Babati are the springboards for what is currently the shortest road route connecting Arusha to the Lake Victoria region without passing through any national parks. The two pivotal towns along this route are **Singida** and **Shinyanga**, both of which are well equipped little places with a good selection of lodgings and eateries, as well as banks with ATMs and internet cafés. Singida lies 350km from Arusha, and the two are connected by a thrice-daily nine-hour Mtei Express coach service via Katesh and Babati. Shinyanga lies another 320km northwest of Singida, 210km north of Tabora and 165km south of Mwanza, in all cases along good surfaced roads serviced by plenty of buses.

Singida, which lies 80km west of Katesh, is notable for the pair of Rift Valley lakes on its outskirts, in particular the shallow and hypersaline Lake Singida, a surreal apparition with eerie green waters offset by a shimmering white salt-encrusted shore and weird rock formations. Only 15 minutes' walk from the town centre, Lake Singida (together with the more distant Lake Kindai) is listed as an Important Bird Area, attracting thousands of lesser flamingo when the water level is suitable. The best place to stay (or eat) is the Stanley Hotel or one of its two annexes (*83 rooms;* m *0754 476785/844001;* e *info@stanleygroupofhotels.com; www.stanleygroupofhotels.com*), where en-suite rooms with DSTV, AC, hot shower and tea/coffee-making facilities start at US$15 for a double. Cheaper is the comfortable Lutheran Guesthouse (⟦ *026 250 2013*), where clean rooms using common showers cost around US$5 for a double.

Set on the dusty plains that slope towards Lake Victoria, **Shinyanga** is a more substantial town with a Wild West aura enhanced by the fabulous granite outcrops that dot the surrounds. The rundown colonial buildings in the town centre were built during its economic heyday, which was founded on a post-World War II cotton boom and nearby gold and diamond mines. Diamonds are still mined at nearby Mwadui, and several small dealerships are scattered around town, but otherwise it hosts little of interest to travellers. The usual abundance of cheap guesthouses are scattered around town, but the standout place to stay, right opposite the railway station, is the Shinyanga Hotel (⟦ *028 276 2369/2458*), a bright orange three-storey building with a pleasant garden bar and clean en-suite rooms with TV, hot water and balcony for US$15 (fan only) or US$20 (with AC).

The aforementioned heronry can be explored on foot at the point where the road from Katesh first skirts the eastern shore of the lake. This is also a favourite watering spot for traditionally attired Barabaig, Bulu and Maasai, who march their cattle here from many kilometres away. Directly opposite this stretch of shore, only 50m from the road but invisible until you stand on the wooded rim, is a small green crater lake with waters too saline to support any fish. The cattle herders who congregate here don't see many tourists and, based on our experience, are likely to be more than willing to show you the lake – ask for it by the Barabaig name of Gida Monyot (Salt Lake). Assuming you have a fair grasp of Swahili, you might also want to enquire about the folklore surrounding the lake. It is said that the local Barabaig used to throw their dead into it, because it is so deep, and also that when a woman had sexual intercourse outside of marriage she would undress and wade into the lake up to her shoulders to cleanse herself of wrongdoing.

After reaching the eastern part of Lake Basotu, the road from Katesh continues roughly parallel to the shore for about 3km before reaching the town of Basotu, which sprawls across a pretty peninsula on the southern shore of the lake. Today a sleepy and unexpectedly traditionalist small fishing town, though somewhat more bustling on Monday, the main market day, Basotu was the scene of the decisive battle in the German campaign to coerce the resistant Barabaig into their colony before World War I. The German garrisons at Singida and Mbulu marched into Barabaig territory, converging on Basotu, where after a short battle they hanged 12 leading elders and the most revered of the Barabaig medicine men, leaving the bodies dangling from the scaffold to discourage future resistance.

Whether in a private vehicle or on public transport, it is perfectly feasible to visit Basotu as a self-standing day trip out of Katesh. The drive takes about 60–90 minutes, following the Singida road for a few kilometres out of Katesh and then turning right at the first major intersection. A bus service runs between Katesh and Haidom (about 50km past Basotu) daily except for Sundays. This leaves from Katesh in the early morning, passes through Basotu two or three hours later, then passes through again in the early- to mid-afternoon on the return trip, allowing you a good four or five hours to explore the area. For details of approaching the lake from the north – or leaving it in that direction – see the box, *Katesh to Karatu via Mbulu*, page 235.

Should you choose to overnight in Basotu, there's at least one very basic guesthouse, and a couple of no-frills restaurants serve fresh fish from the lake.

KONDOA ROCK ART SITES

Inscribed as a UNESCO World Heritage Site in 2006, the prehistoric rock art that adorns the Maasai Escarpment south of Tarangire is the most intriguing outdoor gallery of its sort in East Africa, and among the most ancient and stylistically varied anywhere on the continent. Although it extends over an area of 2,350km², the best-known panels are centred around the blink-and-you'll-miss-it village of Kolo, which straddles the Arusha–Dodoma road between Kondoa and Babati.

The rock art around Kolo and Kondoa is the most prolific in equatorial Africa. This is partly due to the lay of the land. Like the equally rich uKhahlamba-Drakensberg region in South Africa, Kondoa is endowed with numerous granite outcrops tailor-made for painting. The major rock art panels here are generally sited within small caves or beneath overhangs aligned to an east–west axis, a propensity that might reflect the preferences of the artists, or might have provided the most favourable conditions for preservation against the elements. The age of the

The Barabaig are the most populous of a dozen closely related tribes, collectively known as the Datoga or Tatoga. At around 100,000, the Datoga are one of Tanzania's smaller ethno-linguistic groupings, but their territory, centred on Mount Hanang, extends into large semi-arid tracts within Arusha, Dodoma and Singida.

Superficially similar to, and frequently confused with, their Maasai neighbours by outsiders, the Barabaig are dedicated cattle-herders, speaking a Nilotic tongue, who have steadfastly resisted external pressure to forsake their semi-nomadic pastoralist ways. Unlike the Maasai, however, the Barabaig are representatives of the earliest known Nilotic migration into East Africa from southwest Ethiopia. Their forebears probably settled in western Kenya during the middle of the first millennium AD, splitting into two groups. One – the Kalenjin – stayed put. The other, the proto-Datoga, migrated south of Lake Natron 500 to 1,000 years ago to the highlands of Ngorongoro and Mbulu, and Rift Valley plains south towards Dodoma.

Datoga territory was greatest before 1600, thereafter being eroded by migrations of various Bantu-speaking peoples into northern and central Tanzania. The most significant incursion came in the early 19th century, with the arrival of the Maasai. Oral traditions indicate that several fierce territorial battles were fought between the two pastoralist groups, resulting in the Maasai taking over the Crater Highlands and Serengeti Plains, and the Datoga retreating to their modern homeland near Mount Hanang. The Lerai Forest in Ngorongoro Crater is said to mark the grave of a Datoga leader who fell in battle in about 1840, and the site is still visited by Datoga elders from the Lake Eyasi area. The Maasai call the Barabaig the 'Mangati' (feared enemies), and the Barabaig territory around Mount Hanang is sometimes referred to as the Mangati Plains.

The Barabaig used to move around the plains according to the feeding and watering requirements of their herds. They tend a variety of livestock, including goats, donkeys and chickens, but their culture and economy revolve around cattle, which are perceived to be a measure of wealth and prestige, and every part and product of the animal, including the dung, is ingested, or worn or used in rituals. In recent years, agriculture has played an increasingly significant support role in the subsistence of the Barabaig, which together with increased population pressures has more or less put paid to the nomadic lifestyle.

Barabaig territory receives an average annual rainfall of less than 500mm, which means that water is often in short supply. Although the area is dotted with numerous lakes, most are brackish and unsuitable to drink from. Barabaig women often walk kilometres every day to collect gourds of drinking water, much of which comes from boreholes dug with foreign aid. The cattle cannot drink from the lakes directly when water levels are low and salinity is high, but the Barabaig get around this by digging wells on the lakes' edges and allowing the water to filter through the soil. Even so, the herders won't let their cattle drink from these wells on successive days for fear that it will make them ill.

Barabaig social structure is not dissimilar to that of the Maasai, although it lacks the rigid division into hierarchical age-sets pivotal to Maasai and other East African pastoralist societies. The Barabaig do not recognise one centralised leader, but are divided into several hereditary clans, each answering to a chosen elder who sits on a tribal council. The central unit of society is the family homestead or *gheida*, dwelt in by one man, his wives and their unwed offspring. This consists of a tall outer protective wall, built of thorny acacia branches and shaped like a figure eight, with one outer gate entered through a narrow passage. Within this wall stand several small rectangular houses – low, thick-roofed constructions of wooden poles plastered with mud – and the all-important cattle stockade. Different huts are reserved for young men, young women, wives and elders. A number of gheida may be grouped together to create an informal community, and decisions are made communally rather than by a chief.

Patrilineal polygamy is actively encouraged. Elders accumulate four or more wives, up to three of which might share one hut, but marriage within any given clan is regarded to be incestuous. The concept of divorce is not recognised, but a woman may separate from her husband and return to her parents' home under some circumstances. The Barabaig openly regard extramarital sex to be normal, even desirable, although a great many taboos and conventions dictate just who may have intercourse with whom, and where they can perform the act. Traditionally, should a married woman bear a child whose biological father is other than her husband, the child remains the property of the husband – even when husband and wife are separated.

The appearance of the Barabaig is striking. The women wear heavy ochre-dyed goatskin or cowhide dresses, tasselled below the waist, and decorated with colourful yellow and orange beads. They adorn themselves with brass bracelets and neck-coils, tattoo circular patterns around their eyes, and some practise facial scarification. Men are less ornate, with a dyed cotton cloth draped over the shoulders and another around the waist. Traditionally, young men would prove themselves by killing a person (other than a Datoga) or an elephant, lion or buffalo, which might be used as the base of a ceremonial headdress along with the pelts of other animals they had killed.

The Barabaig are monotheists who believe in a universal creator whom they call Aseeta. The sun – to which they give the same name – is the all-seeing eye of Aseeta, who lives far away and has little involvement in their lives. Barabaig legend has it that they are descended from Aseeta's brother Salohog, whose eldest son Gumbandaing was the first true Datoga. Traditionally, most Barabaig elders can trace their lineage back over tens of generations to this founding father, and ancestral worship plays a greater role in their spiritual life than direct worship of God. Oddly, given the arid nature of their homeland, the Barabaig have a reputation as powerful rainmakers. It is said that only 1% of the Barabaig have abandoned their traditional beliefs in favour of exotic religions – a scenario which, judging by the number of internet sites devoted to the state of the Barabaig's souls, has spun quite a few evangelical types into a giddy froth.

The above statistic is indicative of the Barabaig's stubborn adherence to a traditional way of life. In the colonial era, the Barabaig refused to be co-opted into the migrant labour system, on the not unreasonable basis that they could sell one good bullock for more than the typical labourer would earn in a year. Other Tanzanians tend to view the Barabaig as embarrassingly primitive and ignorant – when the Nyerere government outlawed the wearing of traditional togas in favour of Westernised clothing, the Barabaig resolutely ignored them. Even today, few have much formal education or speak a word of English – it would, for that matter, be pretty unusual to meet a Barabaig who could hold a sustained conversation in Swahili.

paintings is tentatively placed at between 200 and 4,000 years, but their intent is a matter of speculation (see box *But what does it mean?*, page 242).

The pigments for the paintings were made with leaf extracts (yellow and green), powdered ochre and manganese (red and black) and possibly bird excrement (white), bound together by animal fat. Subjects and styles vary greatly. The most widely depicted animals are giraffe (26%) and eland (14%), which may have held mystical significance to the artists, or might simply have been their favoured prey. A large number of panels also contain human figures, generally highly stylised and often apparently engaged in ritual dances or ceremonies. At some sites, particularly those of the relatively recent and unformed 'late white' style, readily identifiable subjects are vastly outnumbered by abstract or geometric figures, the significance of which can only be guessed at. A common feature of the more elaborate panels is the jumbled superimposition of images, which is now widely thought to be a deliberate ploy to associate two or more significant images with each other.

The proposal to enshrine the Kondoa rock art as a UNESCO World Heritage Site stated that 'in terms of conservation, most of the sites are stable and relatively well preserved although there are a variety of problems including salt encrustation, erosion, water damage, and fading caused by sunlight'. Exposure to the elements notwithstanding, the rock art has been left undisturbed by locals in the past because it is regarded as sacred or taboo. In 1931, a government employee, A T Culwick, documented an example of one such taboo, so deeply ingrained that its source had evidently been forgotten. When Culwick needed to climb Ilongero Hill near Singida on official business, the chief of the village at the base warned him off, saying that the hill was inhabited by a demon. Culwick eventually persuaded the reluctant chief and entourage to accompany him on the ascent, where he discovered a large shelter covered with ancient rock art. The fear displayed by the villagers before climbing, combined with their startled reaction to the rock panel, left Culwick in no doubt that they had never suspected the existence of the paintings.

The erosion of traditional beliefs in recent years places the art at greater threat of local interference. Already, a few sites are partially defaced by graffiti or scratching, while other paintings are deteriorating as a result of unofficial guides splashing

A series of back roads leads northward from Katesh to Karatu (see page 269), which straddles the surfaced road connecting Lake Manyara National Park to the Ngorongoro Conservation Area. This route could, at a push, be driven in about five hours, or more comfortably over a full day allowing for a few stops. Using public transport, it would probably take two or three days to cover comfortably. Aside from its logistical significance in connecting the Hanang area to the northern safari circuit, this route passes through a varied and often very scenic landscape, ranging from the Rift Valley floor and escarpment, to several pretty lakes, to the wooded highlands around Mbulu. Roads in the Mbulu area are pretty good in the dry season, but they can become quite waterlogged during the rains.

Two alternatives exist. The shorter route involves heading northeast along the Babati road for about 50km to Ndareda, where a left turn leads directly via Dongobesh and Mbulu to Karatu. The second and more interesting option entails heading northwest to Lake Basuto, then continuing to Dongobesh to connect with the road to Mbulu. Using the second route, it should be noted that there is little or no direct public transport between Basuto and Mbulu, so you may need to board the daily Katesh–Basotu–Haidom bus service, then overnight at a guesthouse in Haidom before continuing towards Mbulu. At least one bus daily travels between Haidom and Arusha via Dongobesh, Mbulu and Karatu, and there is also some local transport along the Haidom–Dongobesh, Katesh–Dongobesh and Dongobesh–Mbulu stretches.

The road from Basuto converges with the road from Ndareda to Mbulu about 2km north of **Dongobesh**, a ramshackle traditional settlement set on the bank of a small seasonal river. Dongobesh is scarcely worth a conscious diversion, but it is the main public transport hub in the area and a couple of cheap local lodges are dotted around town.

Less than 500m west of the road between Dongobesh and Mbulu, alongside the village of Kwanzali, lies kidney-shaped **Lake Tlawi**. The reedy verges of this pretty lake support large numbers of birds, most visibly squacco heron and red-knobbed coot, but the localised maccoa duck and great crested grebe are also sometimes seen on the open water. Twali's resident hippo pod can often be seen walking to the shore closest to the road.

Far more substantial and attractive than Dongobesh, **Mbulu** is set in a moist wooded valley encircled by the tall mountains of the Mbulu Highlands, essentially a southern extension of the so-called Crater Highlands around Ngorongoro. The tallest of these mountains can be climbed as a day excursion from the town, offering great views across Lake Manyara and the Rift Valley, and passing through patches of montane forest rattling with birds. The town itself, an agricultural sprawl over leafy slopes emanating from a muddy central grid of roads, doesn't quite match its lovely setting, but it does possess a rustic small-town charm. The old German Boma, built in 1905, is still in use as an administrative office, and several other buildings appear to date to the British colonial era. Public transport runs from Mbulu to Karatu throughout the day, but if you want to spend the night, there's no shortage of undistinguished cheap guesthouses and local eateries dotted within a few hundred metres of the bus station.

Emma Thomson

To maintain the balance of power between the sexes, the Rangi people of Kondoa have devised an ingenious plan. From sunrise to sunset the men are in charge, but come sunset the rule of power shifts to the women, allowing them to reign supreme until daybreak.

This female empowerment was established following the legend of the cat, told to me by a village member one starry night near Kelema:

The cat was looking for a hero. While walking through the jungle one day he befriended a cheetah. 'This cheetah is surely the strongest and fastest animal in the forest – he will be my hero,' exclaimed the cat.

The next day, while walking with the cat through the undergrowth, the cheetah encountered a lion. They fought until the cheetah fell to the ground dead. 'The lion then must be the strongest and fiercest animal in the forest – he will be my new hero,' decided the cat.

The following day the two felines encountered an elephant foraging in the trees. Startled, the elephant charged, killing the lion. Bemused, the cat approached the elephant: 'You truly are the king of the jungle – will you be my hero?'

One day the elephant and cat were surprised by a man hunting. In fear the man killed the elephant and after cutting the meat from the body he turned for home. The cat decided to follow this beast that could defeat an animal without even touching it.

On arriving home the man approached his wife who took the elephant meat from him and set to work in the kitchen. The cat gasped: 'This woman surely must be the queen of all beasts – an animal that can take from another without fighting! She will forever be my hero.' From that day on, the cat is always to be found in the kitchen admiring its heroine.

water on them to bring out the colours, or through repeated exposure to flash photography, which damages sensitive organic pigments. More bizarrely, a local legend that the Germans buried a hoard of gold near one of the rock art sites during World War I has resulted in fortune-seekers manually excavating and dynamiting close to several rock sites. Under such circumstances, UNESCO's inscription of the rock art as a World Heritage Site is welcome indeed, although more formal protection is overdue.

VISITING THE SITES Although very few people do so, it is perfectly feasible to tag the Kondoa Rock Art Sites onto a standard northern circuit safari. One possibility is to visit as a day trip out of Tarangire National Park, a slightly pressured but by no means impossible foray, with the advantage to comfort-conscious travellers of allowing them to make use of one of the commodious lodges in and around Tarangire. For more adventurous or budget-conscious travellers, a better idea would be to bus to the area (several buses run daily between Arusha and Kondoa via Babati and Kolo) then to camp near Kolo or take a basic room there or in Kondoa, allowing you to see more sites in a less rushed manner.

For specialised visits, an excellent option is the **Rock Art Conservation Centre** (m *0754 672256*; e *what@warmheartart.com*; *www.racctz.org*) based in Arusha's Warm Heart Art Gallery (see Chapter 5, *Arusha and around*, page 122). Dedicated

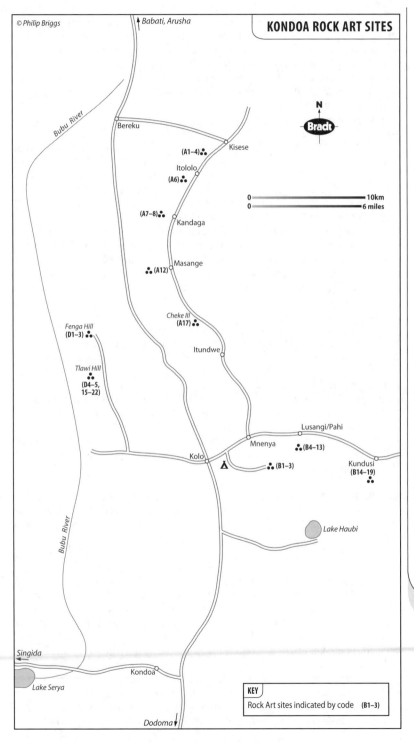

© Philip Briggs

Babati, Arusha

KONDOA ROCK ART SITES

N

Bradt

Bubu River

Bereku

(A1–4) Kisese

Itololo
(A6)

0 ——————————— 10km
0 ——————————— 6 miles

(A7–8) Kandaga

(A12) Masange

Fenga Hill
(D1–3)

Cheke III
(A17)

Itundwe

Tlawi Hill
(D4–5,
15–22)

Lusangi/Pahi

Mnenya (B4–13)

Kolo (B1–3)

Kundusi
(B14–19)

Bubu River

Lake Haubi

Singida

Lake Serya

Kondoa

Dodoma

KEY
Rock Art sites indicated by code (B1–3)

Tarangire and the Central Rift Valley   KONDOA ROCK ART SITES

10

to the preservation of Tanzania's rock art, this NGO also offers three-day trips to the region for US$170–270 per person depending on group size, inclusive of accommodation and meals. More locally, **Kahembe Trekking** in Babati (see box, page 227) and **Kondoa's Cultural Tourism Program** (m *0784 948858/0777 948858*; e *moshi@tanzaniaculturaltours.com; www.tanzaniaculturaltours.com*) both arrange tours for around US$60 per person per day inclusive of a knowledgeable guide but exclusive of transport.

Independent travellers take note that it is forbidden to explore the rock art without an official guide. Even if this were not the case, most sites would be very difficult to locate without one. For this reason, your first port of call locally should be the Kolo office of the **Department of Antiquities** (m *0752 575096*; ⊕ *07.00– 18.00*). This lies on the main junction in Kolo, about 20km north of Kondoa and 50km south of Babati, so any public transport heading between these two towns can drop you alongside it. Here you must pay an entrance fee equivalent to US$17, and collect a guide (free, but a tip will be appreciated).

Details on reaching the individual sites are provided on pages 239–44, but be aware that while distances between sites are relatively short, roads are very rough (**4x4 only**) and visiting most sites will entail some walking, often on steep slopes. For this reason, even motorised travellers will find it unrealistic to visit more than one cluster of sites in the space of one morning or afternoon, and a full three days would be required to explore the lot.

Travellers without private transport will find exploring the area trickier than those with vehicles or on tours. Several buses daily connect Kolo to Kondoa, Babati and Arusha, and it is possible to undertake the round trip from Kolo to the famous Mungomi wa Kolo site **on foot**, but this would take the best part of a day and you'd be expected to pay the guide a reasonable fee for walking, which way exceeds the bounds of duty. More accessible are Lusangi and Pahi, which are connected to Kolo by a few **dala-dalas** daily passing through Mnenya (Pahi also has a guesthouse). Some dala-dalas run daily between Kolo and Kisese via Mnenya. In both cases, however, you'd still need to cover the costs of a guide, and offer him a fair fee for his efforts. Another option would be to **hire a vehicle** for the day in Babati or Kondoa – since the distances involved would be relatively short, no more than 100km in all, this shouldn't be too costly.

WHERE TO STAY The closest proper hotels are situated in Kondoa town. The pick of these are the **New Planet Hotel** (☏ *026 236 1957*; m *0784 669322*) and the **Sunset Beach Hotel** (m *0784 948858*), both of which charge around US$10 for a no-frills en-suite room with net, fan and running water.

Accommodation options close to Kolo are very limited. It may be possible to arrange a **basic room** in Kolo for under US$10 through the Department of Antiquities, but ring first to make sure one is available (m *0752 575096*). Another option is the attractive **Mary Leakey Campsite** run by the Department of Antiquities on the banks of the seasonal Kolo River about 3km east of Kolo town in the direction of Mungomi wa Kolo and Mnenya. Water and toilet facilities are available at the campsite, but food and other drinks must be brought from Kolo. An even more attractive option, situated about 5km east of Kolo along the Pahi Road, is the **Amarula Tented Camp & Campsite** operated by the Rock Art Conservation Centre (m *0754 672256*; *what@ warmheartart.com; www.racctz.org*). They charge US$10 per person to pitch a tent, or US$20 per person to sleep in a standing tent, and rooms are planned.

There are a few **very basic local guesthouses** in Pahi and Masange, both of which lie below the Maasai Escarpment within walking distance of several good sites.

MAJOR ROCK ART SITES

Mungomi wa Kolo Most visitors with limited time are taken to the region's recognised showpiece, a cluster of ten sites scattered across the craggy upper slopes of Ichoi Hill about 10km from Kolo by road. Prosaically labelled B1–3, more evocatively known as Mungomi wa Kolo (The Dancers of Kolo), the three finest panels here provide a good overview of the region's rock art, and – aside from the last, very steep, foot ascent to the actual panels – it is easily reached in a 4x4 vehicle. To get there from Kolo, you need to follow the Mnenya road west for about 4km, crossing the normally dry Kolo River on the way, before turning right on to a rough 4x4 track that reaches the base of the hill after about 6km.

Probably the most intriguing of the panels is B2, which lies in a tall overhang right at the top of the hill. This panel includes more than 150 figures, including several fine, but very faded, paintings of animals (giraffe, leopard, zebra and rhino), as well as some abstract designs and numerous humanoid forms. Richard Leakey regarded this site as representing a particularly wide variety of superimposed styles and periods, and it must surely have been worked over hundreds if not thousands of years. One striking scene, which Mary Leakey dubbed 'The Abduction', depicts five rather ant-like humanoid forms with stick bodies, spindly limbs and distended heads. The two figures on the right have elongated heads, while the two on the left have round heads, as does the central figure, which also appears to have breasts and whose arms are being held by the flanking figures. Leakey interpreted the painting as a depiction of an attempted abduction, with the central female figure being tugged at by two masked people on the right, while friends or family try to hold on to her from the left. Of course, a scene such as this is open to numerous interpretations, and it could as easily depict a ritual dance as an abduction. And why stop there? I recently stumbled across a web page that makes an oddly compelling case for this haunting scene, and other paintings in Kondoa, providing evidence of extraterrestrial visits to Kondoa region in the distant past. If this sort of speculation tickles you, the long-snouted figures to the right, according to this interpretation, are alien abductors, while a separate scene to the right shows another alien standing in a hot air balloon!

Panel B1, also in an overhang, is even larger and more elaborate, though most of the paintings have been partially obliterated by termite activity. Prominent among several animal portraits are those of elephants and various antelope. The most striking scene consists of three reposed humanoid figures with what appear to be wild, frizzy hairstyles (some form of headdress?) and hands clutching a vertical bar. A small cave in front of the panel is used for ceremonial purposes by local rainmakers, and sacrifices are still sometimes left outside the shelter. Finally, near the base of the mountain, the most accessible of the three main panels, B3, depicts the animated humanoids that gave rise to the local name, along with a few faded animal figures, including a cheetah and buffalo.

Pahi, Lusangi and Kinyasi Panels B4–13 all lie close to the base of the escarpment near the twin villages of Lusangi and Pahi, about 12km from Kolo. To reach them from Kolo, follow the same road you would to get to Mungomi wa Kolo, but instead of turning right after crossing the river, keep straight on the main road, passing through Mnenya until you reach Lusangi. This site is normally accessible in any vehicle, though a 4x4 may be useful after rain. Lusangi can be reached by dala-dala from Kolo, and there is a guesthouse about 1km away in Pahi. A 1km *piste* leads from the main road to the base of the escarpment, from where a flat 100m footpath leads to three shelters about 20m apart.

10

Outside attention was first drawn to the rock art of Kondoa District in the 1920s, although it would be several decades before the full extent of its riches was grasped. In 1923, District Commissioner Bagshawe visited and described the two main shelters at Mungomi wa Kolo, and six years later several of the sites on and around Twali Hill were visited by Dr T Nash. In the early 1930s, the eminent archaeologists Louis and Mary Leakey explored a handful of new sites, notably Cheke III, on which was based Louis Leakey's formative attempt at stylistic categorisation and relative chronology, published in his 1936 book *Stone Age Africa*.

By the late 1940s, enthusiasts and archaeologists had located 75 sites in the Kondoa region, and their discoveries led to the publication in 1950 of a unique special edition of *Tanganyika Notes and Records* dedicated solely to the rock art. The first intensive survey of the region was undertaken in 1951 by Mary Leakey, who boosted the tally of known panels for A sector alone from 17 panels to 186, of which one-third were sufficiently well preserved to be studied. Leakey traced and redrew 1,600 figures and scenes, an undertaking that formed the basis of her 1983 book *Africa's Vanishing Art: The Rock Paintings of Tanzania*. Leakey said of her time in the Kondoa region, 'No amounts of stone and bone could yield the kinds of information that the paintings gave so freely ... here were scenes of life, of men and women hunting, dancing, singing and playing music'.

The two works mentioned above are out of print, but Mary Leakey's book is freely available on abeboks.com or abebooks.co.uk and difficult to locate. Worth the small asking price, however, is the National Museums of Tanzania's Occasional Paper No 5 *The Rock Art of Kondoa and Singida*, written by Fidelis Masao and available at the National Museum in Dar es Salaam. A newer book with detailed coverage of the Kondoa rock art placed within a broader African context, is *African Rock Art: Paintings and Engravings on Stone* by David Coulson and Alec Campbell, published by Harry N Abrams in 2001.

The art at Lusangi is not as impressive as that at Mungomi wa Kolo, but it is probably a more suitable goal for those unwilling or unable to climb steep footpaths. Several figures do stand out, however, the most notable being a 70cm-high outlined giraffe superimposed on a very old painting of a rhino. Below this, a red and yellow figure of an eland-like antelope with a disproportionately small head is regarded by archaeologists as one of the very oldest paintings known in Kondoa region. Only a couple of clear humanoid figures are found at these sites, and several of the panels are dominated by bold, childlike patterns in the 'late white' style and are often superimposed over older and more finely executed portraits. From Pahi it is possible to drive another 12km to Kinyasi, where sites B14–19 are situated in a valley below the 1,000m high Kome Mountain. The most interesting of these sites is a 1m² panel of small, finely executed antelope, which also includes one of the few known examples of a painting depicting a homestead.

Mnenya to Kisese Sites A1–18 all lie along the stretch of the Maasai Escarpment that runs immediately east of the reasonable dirt road connecting Mnenya to Kisese. This road itself runs roughly parallel to, and about 10km east of, the Great North Road, and is connected to it by a roughly 8km road between Kolo and

Mnenya in the south and about a 15km road between Bereko and Kisese in the north. Ideally, travellers driving southwards from Babati or Arusha along the Great North Road would explore sites A1–18 by turning on to the Kisese road at Bereku, then following the Mnenya road south and returning to the Great North Road at Kolo. Unfortunately, however, it is mandatory to pass through Kolo first to pay fees and collect a guide, which will enforce quite a bit of backtracking for southbound travellers (but makes no real difference to travellers driving north from Kondoa). There isn't much public transport on the Mnenya–Kisese road, but a few dala-dalas run along it daily, and there is basic accommodation in Masange.

Running northwards from Mnenya, the direction in which regulations practically force you to travel, the first major site is A17 or Cheke III, which lies about 5km along the Kisese road. This extensive, intricate panel contains at least 330 figures, is rich in superimposition, and is studded with various animals as well as surreal humanoids with circular heads and pincer legs and a couple of unusually robust human figures seemingly draped in robes. The shelter is dominated by the so-called Dance of the Elephant, a red painting of a solitary elephant surrounded by perhaps a dozen people – who might as easily be worshipping or hunting the elephant as dancing around it. Getting to Cheke III involves following a 2km track west of the main road, followed by a short but steep ascent to the actual panel.

About 5km further along the road, you arrive at Masange village, from where a roughly 1km-long side road leads to the base of the escarpment, and another five to ten minutes' climb brings you to sites A12–14. The most compelling panel in this cluster is A13, another elaborately decorated overhang with numerous superimposed paintings, but A14 is of interest for its solitary painting of ten faded human figures in a row. Most of the sites between Masange and Kisese lie some distance from the main road, but site A9 or Kandaga III, 6km past Masange, consisting of a series of geometric representations in the 'late white' style first described in 1931 by Julian Huxley, is particularly recommended to serious enthusiasts. The excellent and well preserved site dubbed Kisese II or A4 lies another 8km past Kandaga on a tall rock no more than ten minutes' walk from the road.

Bubu River Sites Unlike the other rock art sites within the proposed reserve, this cluster lies to the west of the Great North Road, overlooking the Bubu River about 12km from Kolo. Short of walking there and back from Kolo, this is the one cluster that cannot easily be reached without private transport, ideally a 4x4. It is, nevertheless, perhaps the best cluster of them all, with several panels in close proximity and in a particularly good state of preservation.

Of the three panels D1–3 situated on Fenga Hill, the most worthwhile is D3, sometimes referred to as the Trapped Elephants. Covered in a jumble of superimposed red features, including several slim humanoid figures with distended heads and headdresses, this panel is named for the central painting of two elephants surrounded by a stencilled oblong line. Some experts believe that this depicts an elephant trap, a theory supported by three fronds below the elephants that might well represent branches used to camouflage a pit. Others believe that it might have a more mystical purpose, placing the elephants in a kind of magic circle. A trickle of circles dripping from the left base of the picture could be blood, or the elephants' spoor.

About 3km south of Fenga Hill, the immediate vicinity around Twali Hill hosts at least ten panels, numbered D4–5 and D15–22. A dedicated enthusiast could easily devote half a day to this cluster of very different sites. Panel D19 is notable for an almost life-size and unusually naturalistic attempt to paint a human figure in a

There is a strangely eerie sensation attached to emerging from a remote and nondescript tract of bush to be confronted by an isolated panel of primitive paintings executed by an artist or artists unknown, hundreds or maybe thousands of years before the time of Christ. Faded as many of the panels are, and lacking the perspective to which modern eyes are accustomed, you can still hardly fail to be impressed by the fine detail of many of the animal portraits, or to wonder at the surrealistic distortion of form that characterises the human figures. And, almost invariably, first exposure to these charismatic works of ancient art prompts three questions: how old are they, who were the artists and what was their intent?

When, who and why? The simple answers are that nobody really knows. The broadest time frame, induced from the absence of any representations of extinct species in the rock galleries of Kondoa, places the paintings at less than 20,000 years old. The absence of a plausible tradition of attribution among the existing inhabitants of the area – a Gogo claim that the paintings were the work of the Portuguese can safely be discounted – makes it unlikely that even the most modern paintings are less than 200 years old. Furthermore, experts have noted a clear progression from the simplest early styles to more complex, expressive works of art, and a subsequent regression to the clumsy graffiti-like finger painting of the 'late white' phase, indicating that the paintings were created over a substantial period of time.

Early attempts at dating the Kondoa rock art concentrated on categorising it chronologically based on the sequence of superimposition of different styles on busy panels. The results were inconclusive, even contradictory, probably because the superimposition of images was an integral part of the art, so that a foreground image might be roughly contemporaneous with an image underneath it. It is also difficult to know the extent to which regional style, or even individual style, might be of greater significance than chronological variation. The most useful clue to the age of the paintings is the stratified organic debris deposited alongside red ochre 'pencils' at several sites. Carbon dating of a handful of sites where such deposits have been found suggests that the artists were most active about 3,000 years ago, though many individual paintings are undoubtedly much older. The crude 'late white' paintings, on the other hand, are widely agreed to be hundreds rather than thousands of years old, and there is evidence to suggest that some underwent ritual restoration by local people who held them sacred into historical times.

The identity of the artists is another imponderable. In the first half of the 20th century, the rock art of southern Africa was solely attributed to 'Bushmen' hunter-gatherers, a people whose click-based Khoisan tongue is unrelated to Bantu and who are of vastly different ethnic stock from any Bantu speakers. True, the Bushmen are the only people who practised the craft in historical times, but much of the rock art of southern Africa (like that of eastern Africa) dates back thousands of years. Coincidentally, two of East Africa's few remaining click-tongued hunter-gatherers, the Sandawe and the Hadzabe, both live in close proximity to the main concentration of Tanzanian rock art, but neither has a tradition relating to the paintings.

Given that the archaeological record indicates east-southern Africa was populated entirely by hunter-gatherers when the paintings were probably executed, furthermore that a succession of human migrations has subsequently passed through the region, postulating an ancestral link between the artists of

Kondoa and modern hunter-gatherers would be tenuous in the extreme. If anything, the probable chronology of the rock art points in the opposite direction. Assuming that creative activity peaked some 3,000 years ago, it preceded the single most important known migration into East Africa, the mass invasion of the Bantu-speakers who today comprise the vast majority of Tanzania's population. Most probable, then, that a Bantu- or perhaps Nilotic-speaking group, or another group forced to migrate locally as a ripple effect of the Bantu invasion, moved into the Kondoa region and conquered or assimilated the culture responsible for the rock art, resulting in the gradual stylistic regression noted by archaeologists. All that can be said about the artists with reasonable certainty is that they were hunter-gatherers whose culture, were it not for the painted testament left behind on the granite faces of Kondoa, would have vanished without trace.

The most haunting of the questions surrounding the rock art of Kondoa is the intent of its creators. In determining the answer to this, one obstacle is that nobody knows just how representative the surviving legacy might be. Most extant rock art in Kondoa is located in caves or overhangs, but the small number of faded paintings that survive on more open sites must be a random subset of similarly exposed panels that have been wiped clean by the elements. We have no record, either, of whether the artists dabbled on canvases less durable than rock, but unless one assumes that posterity was a conscious goal, it seems wholly presumptuous to think otherwise. The long and short of it, then, is that the extant galleries might indeed represent a sufficiently complete record to form a reliable basis for any hypothesis, but they might just as easily represent a fraction of a percentage of the art executed at the time. Furthermore, there is no way of telling whether rocks were only painted in specific circumstances – it is conceivable that the rock art would maker greater sense viewed in conjunction with other types of painting that have not survived.

Two broad schools of thought surround the interpretation of Africa's ancient rock art. The first has it that the paintings were essentially recreational, documentary and/or expressive in intent – art for art's sake, if you like – while the second regards them to be mystical works of ritual significance. It is quite possible that the truth of the matter lies between these poles of opinion. A striking feature of the rock art of Kondoa is the almost uniform discrepancy in the styles used to depict human and non-human subjects. Animals are sometimes painted in stencil form, sometimes filled with bold white or red paint, but – allowing for varying degrees of artistic competence – the presentation is always naturalistic. The people, by contrast, are almost invariably heavily stylised in form, with elongated stick-like bodies and disproportionately round heads topped by a forest of unkempt hair. Some such paintings are so downright bizarre that they might be more reasonably described as humanoid than human (a phenomenon that has not gone unnoticed by UFO theorists searching for prehistoric evidence of extraterrestrial visits, see page 239).

The discrepancy between the naturalistic style favoured for animals and highly stylised presentation of humans has attracted numerous theoretical explanations. Most crumble under detailed examination of the evidence, but all incline towards supporting the mystical or ritualistic school of interpretation. Ultimately, however, for every tentative answer we can provide, these enigmatic ancient works pose a dozen more questions. It is an integral part of their charisma that we can speculate to our heart's content, but will never know the whole truth.

crouched or seated position, and it also contains some finely executed paintings of animals, including a buffalo head and a giraffe leaning forward. Directly opposite this panel, site D20 depicts several seated human figures, while 500m further away site D22 is also known as the Red Lion for the striking painting of a lion, with a stencilled black outline and red fill, that dominates the shelter.

Five minutes' walk along the same ridge towards the Bubu River brings you to a pair of shelters called D17 or The Hunter, for a rare action painting of a hunter killing a large antelope – presumably an eland – with his bow and arrow. Several other interesting human figures are found on these twin shelters. Another 10–20 minutes' walk downhill towards the river stand two large rock faces, D4 and D5, respectively known as The Rhino and The Prancing Giraffe. The former is named for the 60cm-long portrait of a rhino with a rather narrow head, and it also depicts what appears to be a herd of antelope fleeing from human pursuers. The nominated painting at site D5 is a strikingly lifelike depiction of a giraffe with its front legs raised as if cantering or rearing, but no less interesting is a tall pair of very detailed, shaggy-headed human figures sometimes referred to as The Dancers.

DODOMA

Situated at an elevation of 1,135m on the windswept, drought-prone plains of the central plateau, Dodoma is the principal town of the Gogo people. It was an important stopover on the 19th-century caravan route between the coast and Lake Tanganyika, and it became a regional administration centre after Germany built a railway station there in 1910. As the country's most central town, it was chosen as the designate capital of Tanzania in 1974, a role that was formalised in 1996 when parliament relocated there (though most government offices stayed in Dar es Salaam and are still there today).

The name Dodoma is derived from the Gogo word *idodomya*, which means 'place of sinking'. The most widely accepted explanation for this name is that it was coined by a group of villagers who came down to a stream to collect water, to find an elephant stuck irretrievably in the muddy bank. Another version of events is that a local clan stole some cattle from a neighbouring settlement, slaughtered and ate the stolen beasts, then placed their dismembered tails in a patch of swamp. When a search party arrived, the thieves claimed that the lost animals had sunk in the mud. Whether or not anybody actually believed this unlikely story goes unrecorded!

Since becoming the capital, Dodoma has experienced a high influx of people from surrounding rural areas, but it remains unremittingly small-town in atmosphere and of no specific interest to tourists (unless perhaps there are those who collect capital cities as others collect passport stamps). Dodoma is also the focal point of Tanzania's low-key viniculture industry, founded by an Italian priest in 1957, though the product is as readily available in Arusha and other tourist centres.

GETTING THERE AND AWAY Dodoma lies about 450km inland of Dar es Salaam. The road is surfaced in its entirety and shouldn't take longer than six hours to cover in a **private vehicle**. It is also serviced by a steady stream of **buses**, which generally leave before midday and take around seven hours, stopping briefly in Morogoro.

The main roads heading to Dodoma from Iringa in the south and Arusha in the north are in poor condition, though it is rumoured this is soon going to change. For now, however, any itinerary that involves bussing through Dodoma purely because the distance looks shorter than the main road between the north and south is best reconsidered!

All **trains** on the central railway from Dar es Salaam to Tabora and Kigoma stop at Dodoma, often for several hours. Westbound scheduled trains leave Dar es Salaam at 17.00 every Tuesday and Friday, typically passing through Dodoma shortly after sunrise the next morning, while eastbound trains leave Kigoma at 17.00 on Sunday and Thursday, usually passing through Dodoma about 24 hours later.

WHERE TO STAY

New Dodoma Hotel (96 rooms) ☎026 232 1641; e info@newdodomahotel.com; www. newdodomahotel.com. The top place to stay, conveniently located opposite the railway station, this stalwart hotel has a gym, swimming pool, health club, internet café, hair salon & 2 good restaurants serving Indian, Chinese & continental dishes, & comfortable en-suite rooms with AC & DSTV. *Starting at US$45/65 sgl/dbl.*

Christian Council of Tanzania (CCT) Hostel m 0756 090816/0713 475741; e director@ cct-centre.org; www.cct-centre.org. There's no shortage of cheap guesthouses dotted around the town centre, but the pick remains this long-serving hostel, which is only 300m from the railway station. *US$6/8 en-suite sgl/dbl.*

11

Lake Manyara and the Northern Rift Valley

The main road initially running southwest from Arusha towards the Ngorongoro Highlands and Serengeti passes through a dramatic stretch of the Rift Valley where the semi-arid, acacia-studded floor supports a chain of shallow mineral-rich lakes hemmed in by a sheer escarpment to the west. The largest of these lakes, Manyara, Eyasi and Natron, are all prone to substantial cyclic fluctuations in level, dependent to some extent on local rainfall patterns, but each of them reaches a length of 50km or greater when full.

The most accessible and popular tourist attraction in this region is Lake Manyara National Park, which protects the northwestern shores of the eponymous lake, a compact but ecologically varied area known for its dense elephant population, tree-climbing lions and prodigious birdlife. Only two hours' drive from Arusha on a good asphalt road, Lake Manyara forms an obvious first port of call on any northern Tanzanian safari. It is serviced by several upmarket lodges, most of which run along the escarpment above the lake, while a selection of cheaper lodgings and campsites is centred on the village of Mto wa Mbu near the entrance gate.

The other two lakes, though considerably more remote and visited by relatively few tourists, are both recommended as off-the-beaten-track deviations from a standard northern safari itinerary. Eyasi, the largest of these Rift Valley lakes, is of interest primarily for the Hadzabe hunter-gatherers and Datoga pastoralists who inhabit its dry hinterland. Connected to the outside world by just one rough road running southwest from the small town of Karatu, Eyasi is something of a travel cul-de-sac, but a few basic campsites and mid-range tented camps can be found in the vicinity, and it is easy to arrange visits to Hadzabe and Datoga encampments.

More remote and inhospitable still, Lake Natron – which nudges up to the border with Kenya – is the site of a legendarily inaccessible flamingo breeding ground and is overlooked by Ol Doinyo Lengai, a majestic (and, if you're up to it, climbable) active volcano whose Maasai name translates as God's Mountain. Two mid-range lodges and a few more basic campsites service Lake Natron, which can be visited along an alternative route connecting the northern Serengeti to Mto Wa Mbu and Manyara.

LAKE MANYARA NATIONAL PARK

Lake Manyara is a shallow, alkaline lake set at the base of a sheer stretch of the Western Rift Valley escarpment. The northwestern lakeshore and its hinterland are protected in a scenic national park whose diversity of terrestrial habitats – grassy floodplain, rocky escarpment, acacia woodland and lush groundwater forest – seems all the more remarkable given that up to two-thirds of its surface area of 330km^2 (prior to the recent incorporation of the Marang Forest above the escarpment) comprises water. And this habitat diversity is reflected in Manyara's varied mammalian fauna, with buffalo, giraffe, olive baboon, blue monkey and various antelopes likely to be seen in the course of any game drive. The park is also renowned for its tree-climbing lions (see box, page 254), which are still seen in arboreal action from time to time – we had an excellent encounter as recently as May 2012 – but these days this behaviour is actually more likely to be seen in parts of the Serengeti than in Manyara.

The elephants of Manyara were immortalised by Iain Douglas-Hamilton, author of *Amongst the Elephants*, in the 1970s, and while the population suffered a slight decline in the 1980s due to poaching, this was not as severe as in many larger parks in southern Tanzania. By the 1990s, the Manyara population had recovered fully, and its elephants were generally well endowed on the tusk front, and very relaxed around vehicles, making for great viewing. Sadly, this situation has changed in recent years following a fresh spate of poaching; indeed, on the research trip for this edition, we were struck by how skittish and bad-tempered Manyara's elephants have become, and how few large tuskers we observed.

Manyara, despite its small size, is a great birding reserve, with around 400 species recorded. As Duncan Butchart, writing in the &Beyond *Ecological Journal*, has noted, 'If a first-time birdwatcher to Africa had the time to visit only a single reserve in Tanzania, then Manyara must surely be it.' It's perfectly feasible for a casual birder to see 100 species here in a day, ranging from a variety of colourful bee-eaters, barbets, kingfishers and rollers to the gigantic ground hornbill and white-backed pelican. Substantial flocks of flamingo are also present when the water level is suitable. In rainy years, the trees around the entrance gate often support large and pungent breeding colonies of the handsome yellow-billed stork and pink-backed pelican between February and June.

A remarkable 51 diurnal raptor species are known from the park, of which 28 are resident or regular. Two unusual species worth looking out for are crowned eagle, which is commonly observed in the forests close to the entrance gate, and African hawk-eagle, which often rests up on rocks and stumps immediately south of the hot springs. Also common is the African fish eagle and superficially similar palm-nut vulture, the latter often associated with doum palms. In addition, six species of owl are regularly recorded.

Manyara's well-defined game-viewing circuit kicks off a high proportion of safaris through northern Tanzania. And while visitors with limited time might reasonably elect to forsake Manyara's more subtle attractions in favour of additional time in the Serengeti, the park is a valuable addition to a longer safari, offering the opportunity to see several species less common or shyer elsewhere on the northern circuit. Morning game drives tend to be most enjoyable, as the compact circuit of roads close to the entrance gate can get uncomfortably busy in the afternoon. Better still, if your budget runs to it, stay at one of the handful of camps in the southern part of the park, an area that sees very few day visitors.

Shortly before going to print, it was confirmed that a long-mooted plan to incorporate the 250km² Marang Forest Reserve into Lake Manyara National Park has gone ahead. Aside from expanding the park's area by almost 80%, this move will also help secure an ancient elephant migration corridor connecting Manyara to the highlands to its west. It will also greatly expand the already impressive bird checklist for this small national park, as Marang – though relatively unexplored – hosts a similar selection of highland forest species to similar habitats in the Crater Highlands. Access to the forest is limited at the time of writing, but by the time you read this, Wayo Africa (see page 107) should be running adventure hikes in the area.

Several locally published booklets, providing detailed coverage of the park's flora and fauna, can be bought from street vendors and shops in Arusha and elsewhere on the northern safari circuit. The park entrance fee of US$35 per person per 24 hours is set to increase to US$45 in July 2013. The fee can be paid by MasterCard, Visa or Tanapa Smartcard only. No other cards are accepted, and neither are travellers' cheques or cash. For more details, see box, *Paying park fees*, page 71.

GETTING THERE AND AWAY The main entrance gate, used by at least 99% of visitors to Lake Manyara, lies at the northern end of the park on the outskirts of Mto wa Mbu. The 120km drive from Arusha follows the Dodoma road as far as the junction village of Makuyuni, where you need to turn right for Mto wa Mbu. The road is surfaced in its entirety and the drive usually takes less than two hours. A second and very little used entrance gate lies in the far south of the park, close to Lake Manyara Tree Lodge.

WHERE TO STAY AND EAT The only permanent accommodation set within the park boundaries is &Beyond Lake Manyara Tree Lodge, which functions almost as a private concession in the far south, a long way from the busy northern circuit near Mto mw Mbu. Also situated within the park is the semi-permanent Lemala Manyara tented camp, and a number of special campsites favoured as sites for temporary camps by operators offering a true bush experience. Otherwise, most of the accommodation servicing Manyara lies outside the park, including a string of upmarket and mid-range and lodges along the Rift Valley escarpment overlooking the lake, and a large choice of more budget-oriented hotels and campsites dotted in and around the small town of Mto wa Mbu outside the main entrance gate. Other good bases for exploring the park are Chem Chem and Manyara Ranch, both of which lie in the wildlife corridor connecting Tarangire and Lake Manyara National Parks (see *Tarangire National Park, Where to stay*, page 222).

Exclusive

&Beyond Lake Manyara Tree Lodge
(10 rooms) (South Africa) +27 (0)11 809 4441; e safaris@andbeyond.com; www.lakemanyara. com. Offering the ultimate Manyara experience, Tree Lodge is a small & very exclusive property operated by &Beyond deep in a mahogany forest about 20 mins' drive south of the hot springs at Maji Moto & 45km south of the main entrance gate. Accommodation is in 10 tree-house-like hardwood suites with banana leaf roofs, large en-suite bathrooms with indoor tub & outdoor shower, & private decks offering intimate views into the forest. The surrounding forest supports a wealth of birds & monkeys, & is frequently visited by large tuskers, while bushbabies call throughout the night. Important features of the lodge are the exceptional standard of guiding & the feeling of having this beautiful park pretty much to yourself, as very few day trippers make it this far south & those that do tend to be there around midday rather than during prime game viewing hours.

Night drives, village visits & exclusive lakeshore sundowners are also offered, while facilities include a swimming pool, the usual superb &Beyond food, & personal butler service. *US$2,410 dbl inc all meals, drinks & activities. Substantial discounts in Mar, May, Nov & early Dec. Closed Apr.*

Lemala Manyara (10 tents) 027 254 8966; e res@lemalacamp.com; www.lemalacamp. com. The only semi-permanent tented camp in Manyara, Lemala is located close to the Endabash River & lakeshore about 30km south of the main entrance gate, a location almost as remote as Tree Lodge. Accommodation is in classic safari tents with a wooden floor, solar powered lights & heating, twin or dbl beds, small private veranda, & en-suite toilet & shower. This is probably the most full-on bush experience on offer in the Manyara area, not luxurious but genuinely exclusive thanks to its isolation from the main tourist circuit. *US$895/1,240 sgl/dbl game package inc meals, drinks & activities, or US$750/950 sgl/dbl FB inc drinks. Low season discounts available Mar, Jun & Nov. Closed Apr & May.*

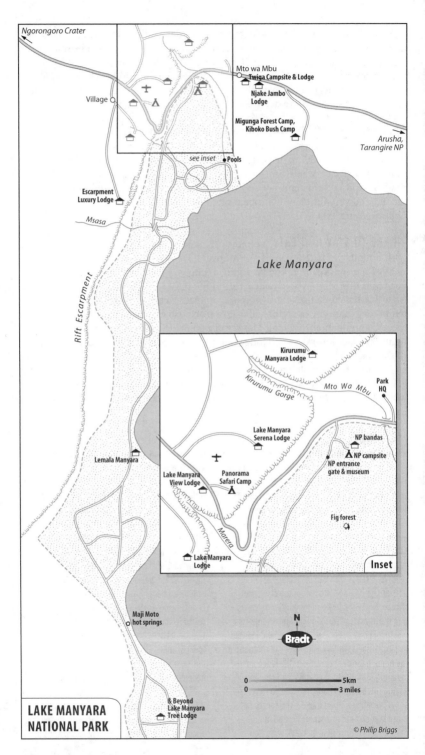

Ngorongoro Crater

Mto wa Mbu
Twiga Campsite & Lodge

Village

Njake Jambo
Lodge

Migunga Forest Camp,
Kiboko Bush Camp

Arusha,
Tarangire NP

see inset • Pools

Escarpment
Luxury Lodge

Msasa

Lake Manyara

Rift Escarpment

Kirurumu
Manyara Lodge

Park
HQ

Kirurumu Gorge

Mto Wa Mbu

Lake Manyara
Serena Lodge

NP bandas

NP campsite

Lemala Manyara

NP entrance
gate & museum

Lake Manyara
View Lodge

Panorama
Safari Camp

Marera

Fig forest

Lake Manyara
Lodge

Inset

Maji Moto
hot springs

N

Bradt

0   5km
0   3 miles

LAKE MANYARA
NATIONAL PARK

& Beyond
Lake Manyara
Tree Lodge

© Philip Briggs

☗ **Escarpment Luxury Lodge** (16 rooms)
m 0762 605778/0767 804856; **e** info@
escarpmentlodge.co.tz; www.escarpmentlodge.
co.tz. The most stylish & exclusive of the lodges on
the escarpment above Manyara, this has received
plenty of praise from operators & safari-goers since
it opened in Jul 2011. A swimming pool set in lush
bush on the escarpment edge offers stunning views
over the national park, & the funky but organic
interiors create a contemporary African feel. The
state-of-the-art suites are large & very comfortable,
& come with wooden floor, fan, AC, internet access,
king-size bed with walk-in netting, large bathroom
with indoor tub & outdoor shower, & private deck
with a view. In addition to game drives in the park,
activities on offer include cycling, bird walks &
village visits. The introductory rate is great value,
the all-inclusive rate less so unless you plan to wreak
havoc with the bar stock! *US$295/446 sgl/dbl FB, or
US$850/950 sgl/dbl all inc.*

Upmarket
☗ **Lake Manyara Serena Safari Lodge**
(67 rooms) ☏ 027 254 5555; **e** lakemanyara@
serena.co.tz; www.serenahotels.com. This smart &
popular upmarket lodge is situated on the edge of
the escarpment overlooking the lake & its environs.
Like other lodges in the Serena chain, it is a very
appealing set-up, run through by a small wooded
stream that attracts a wide range of birds including
chattering flocks of breeding weavers. Adventure
activities such as abseiling & mountain biking are
offered by Serena Active, a company based at the
lodge. Accommodation is in attractively furnished
ethnic-looking *rondawels* with private balconies.
The buffet food is generally very good. *US$315/515
sgl/dbl FB. Substantial discounts Mar–May, Nov &
early Dec.*
☗ **Kirurumu Manyara Lodge** (31 tents)
☏ 027 250 2417/8907; **e** info@kirirumu.net;
www.kirurumu.net. Owned & managed by
Hoopoe Adventure Tours, this popular tented
lodge is perched on the rift escarpment to the
north of the Serena, from where it offers a grand
view across the plains of the Rift Valley to the
north of Lake Manyara. The unpretentious rustic
atmosphere contrasts strongly with other more
built-up lodges on the Rift escarpment, & it
will be far more attractive to people who want
a real bush experience. There's plenty of small
wildlife around, ranging from bush squirrels to

foot-long yellow-speckled plated lizards by day
to hedgehogs & bushbabies by night – plus a
wide variety of birds. The food is adequate & the
service friendly & efficient. Accommodation is
in comfortable & secluded en-suite dbl tents,
each of which has a private veranda. *US$256/358
sgl/dbl B&B, or US$256/414 FB in high season,
US$114 pp FB low season*.

Moderate
☗ **Migunga Forest Camp** (19 tents) ☏ 027
250 6315; **m** 0754 324193; **e** reservations@
moivaro.com; www.moivaro.com. This well-
established but little-known Moivaro camp shares
many assets with Kirurumu, but is considerably
more downmarket in feel & priced accordingly.
Migunga has a winning location in a yellow fever
forest about 2km by road from Mto wa Mbu, &
within walking distance of the lake when water
levels are high. Accommodation is in comfortable
dbl standing tents with en-suite hot showers.
Though a little frayed at the edges, it's an excellent
compromise between price & comfort, with
the added bonus of a real bush feel. Reedbuck,
bushbuck & buffalo sometimes pass through,
vervet monkeys & banded mongoose are resident,
bushbabies are often heard at night, & 70-odd
acacia-associated bird species have been recorded
in camp. *US$206/247 sgl/dbl FB Mar, Jun & Sep to
early Dec; US$241/287 sgl/dbl FB other months.
Low-season discount in Apr & May.*
☗ **Lake Manyara View Lodge** (70 rooms)
m 0784 653911; **e** info@njake.com. This relatively
new lodge rises above the Rift Valley escarpment
alongside the main asphalt road between Mto
wa Mbu & Karatu. In common with other lodges
along the escarpment, it offers stunning views
over Lake Manyara & the Rift Valley floor, but its
enormous potential is totally undermined by the
unfinished look of the common areas (including a
still unfinished swimming pool) & general aura of
operating with all lights dimmed. There's nothing
wrong with the en-suite rooms, but otherwise it's
a second rate option, although quite reasonably
priced. *US$120/135 sgl/dbl B&B, or US$145/220
FB Jan, Feb, Jul, Aug & Oct, with slight discounts at
other times.*
☗ **Kiboko Bush Camp** (12 tents) ☏ 027
253 9152; **m** 0754 476861 **e** kibokotz@yahoo.
co.uk. Situated a few hundred metres away from
Migunga, but with a more nondescript setting,

this unpretentious & rather under-staffed camp provides adequate accommodation in en-suite standing tents set on a stilted wooden platform with a small private veranda. Once again, it's good value. *US$110/180 sgl/dbl FB.*

Budget and camping

🏠 **Njake Jambo Lodge & Campsite**
(16 rooms) ✆ 027 250 1329; e info@njake.com; www.njake.com. Set in the heart of Mto wa Mbu, this quality budget lodge offers accommodation in 4 double-storey blocks each containing 4 smart en-suite rooms with 2 4-poster beds with netting, satellite TV, fridge, phone & tiled bathroom with hot shower. The large green gardens also host a restaurant, bar & large swimming pool area, as well as a shady campsite. It lacks the bush atmosphere of many other lodges around Manyara, & it would seem overpriced almost anywhere else, but it seems like fair value in context. *US$90/120 sgl/dbl B&B, or US$120/160 FB; camping US$10 pp in your own tent or US$20 pp in theirs.*

🏠 **Twiga Campsite & Lodge** (34 rooms) ✆ 025 253 9101; m 0713 334297; e twigacampsite@ yahoo.com; www.twigacampsite.com. Probably the pick of several locally run lodges in Mto wa Mbu, Twiga lies in neatly cropped gardens centred upon a good restaurant & internet café, & a large clean swimming pool. The spacious campsite is justifiably popular with budget safari operators, & there are also several blocks of large self-contained dbl rooms, variable in size & facilities, but all with hot water & nets, & as good value as you'll find in the vicinity of Manyara. *From US$40 B&B for an ordinary dbl to US$130 en-suite FB exec dbl with DSTV, fan, desk & fridge; camping US$10 pp.*

🏠 **National Park Bandas & Campsite**
✆ 027 250 3471/4082; e info@tanzaniaparks. com; www.tanzaniaparks.com. Situated in a lovely forest glade immediately outside the national park entrance gate, this is easily the most inherently attractive place to stay in this price category, & comparatively good value, too. Clean self-contained brick bandas have hot water but no net – the latter a serious omission in Mto wa Mbu. Facilities include

---

MTO WA MBU

This village, which lies close to the Lake Manyara entrance gate, sees a large volume of tourist traffic and is said locally to be the only place in Tanzania where representatives of 120 Tanzanian tribes are resident. Mto wa Mbu is the normal base for budget safaris visiting Lake Manyara, and even if you aren't staying in the village or visiting Lake Manyara, your safari driver will probably stop at the huge curio market in the hope of picking up a commission. Mto wa Mbu (pronounced as one word, mtowambu) means River of Mosquitoes, and if you do spend the night here, then you'll be in no doubt about how it got its name. By day, the curio dealers who will swarm around you the moment you leave your vehicle might draw an obvious analogy.

A clutch of inexpensive walking tours out of Mto wa Mbu have been set up as part of a cultural tourism programme with the assistance of SNV (Stichting Nederlandse Vrijwilligers [Foundation of Netherlands Volunteers]). One of the most interesting of these walks is the papyrus lake tour, which takes you to the Miwaleni waterfall, as well as to a papyrus lake where Rangi people collect basket- and mat-weaving material, and to the homesteads of Sandawe hunter-gatherers. Other tours take you to Balaa Hill, which boasts excellent views over the village and lake, and to Chagga farms and Maasai bomas.

The tourism programme is run out of the Red Banana Restaurant in the centre of Mto wa Mbu. This is where you must pay your fees, arrange a guide and (if you like) rent a bicycle, as well as paying the mandatory village development fee. For more details, visit the website http:// mtoculturalprogramme.tripod.com or contact the guides at ✆ 027 253 9303; m 0748 606654; e mtoculturalprogramme@hotmail.com.

a kitchen & dining area, & an elevated tree-house looking into the forest canopy. *US$20 pp banda accommodation for non-residents; camping US$30 pp.* **⋏ Migunga Campsite** ✆ 027 250 6315; **m** 0754 324193; **e** reservations@moivaro. com; www.moivaro.com. Situated alongside the eponymous tented camp & under the same management (see page 251), this campsite boasts a stunning setting amid the yellow fever trees, & facilities include hot showers – highly recommended. *US$8 pp.*

⋏ Panorama Safari Camp **m** 0765 379641/0784 118541. Boasting a prime location on the escarpment overlooking the lake, this campsite set only 500m from the main asphalt road towards Karatu forms an attractively located alternative to the more mundane cheapies in town. There's a clean shower & toilet block with running hot water, & other facilities include a bar & restaurant. *US$7 pp large standing tent with bedding & towel provided.*

EXPLORING LAKE MANYARA

Game drives For logistical reasons, most safari operators visit the national park in the afternoon but there's much to be said for doing an additional morning game drive, starting as soon as possible after the entrance gate opens at 06.30. Manyara is wonderfully and unexpectedly peaceful in the morning, and you'll probably see fewer other vehicles over two or three hours than you would in five minutes in the late afternoon. By being the first car through the gate, you also stand a chance of disturbing one of the park's plentiful but skittish leopards before it vanishes into the thickets for the day.

Unless you are staying overnight in the park, all game drives start at the entrance gate, which lies on the northern boundary near Mto wa Mbu. From here, the main road winds for several kilometres through a cool, lush, mature groundwater forest dominated by large ficus trees and a tangle of green epiphytes. With appropriate jungle noises supplied by outsized silvery-cheeked hornbills, this is one part of the northern safari circuit that might conjure up images of Tarzan swinging into view. It's a good place to see olive baboons (Manyara supports a density of 2,500 baboons in 100km²), which plonk themselves down alongside the road, often in the company of the smaller and more beautiful blue monkey, which is also common in the forest. The shy bushbuck might also be encountered here, but otherwise the main point of faunal interest is the diversity of birds and butterflies.

The road emerges from the forest onto the northern floodplain, where a series of small pools on the Mto wa Mbu River supports a wide variety of birds, notably giant kingfisher and African and painted snipe. This is a lovely spot, too, with the Rift Valley escarpment rising to the west, and the sparsely vegetated floodplain of Lake Manyara stretching to the south. Giraffes are common in this area, many of them so dark in colour that they appear to be almost melanistic. The nearby hippo pool was submerged for several years following the El Niño floods of 1997/98, causing the hippos to relocate to the main lake, but it has since re-emerged and harbours several dozen soaking, yawning hippos, as well as an impressive selection of water birds. An ongoing relic of the El Niño floods is the ghost forest of dead tree stumps lining the floodplain between the fig forest and the lakeshore.

For large mammals, the best road runs inland of the lake to the Maji Moto (literally 'Hot Water') springs in the south. The tangled acacia woodland here – quite dry for most of the year, but spectacularly lush after the rains – offers views across the floodplain, where you should see large herds of zebra and wildebeest, and the occasional warthog, impala, Kirk's dik-dik and giraffe. The acacia woodland is the place to look out for the famous tree-climbing lions of Manyara (see box, overleaf), although on an afternoon game drive the safari driver grapevine is bound to ensure that you know about any arboreal lions long before you encounter them. As you head further south, several large seasonal waterfalls tumble over the escarpment, most visibly during the rainy season. The marshy area around the hot springs reliably harbours waterbuck and plenty of buffaloes, while several pairs of klipspringer are resident on the rocky escarpment base towards the southern end of the park.

Other activities An exciting aspect of Lake Manyara is a varied selection of mild adventure activities operated exclusively by Wayo Africa, which is based out of the Manyara Serena Lodge (see *Where to stay*, page 251) but takes on guests staying at other lodges in the area. These activities offer safari-goers tired of bouncing around dusty roads within the confines of a vehicle the opportunity to stretch their legs or arms in natural surrounds.

The most popular of these activities is **mountain biking** down the Rift Valley escarpment, with a variety of different itineraries available. Also offered is an

THE TREE-CLIMBING LIONS OF MANYARA

Lake Manyara National Park is famous for its tree-climbing lions, which habitually rest up in the branches for most of the day, to the excitement of those lucky tourists who chance upon them. But while the tree-climbing phenomenon is well documented, the explanation behind it remains largely a matter of conjecture.

In the 1960s, Stephen Makacha undertook research into lion behaviour at Manyara to compare with similar studies being conducted by George Schaller in the Serengeti. In Schaller's book, *The Serengeti Lion: A Study of Predator–Prey Relations*, he noted that:

> The lions in the Lake Manyara National Park climbed trees far more often than those in the Serengeti. They were resting in trees on two-thirds of the occasions on which we encountered them during the day. The reason why Manyara lions rest in trees so often is unknown. Fosbrooke noted that lions in the Ngorongoro Crater ascended trees during an epidemic of biting flies, but this is an unusual situation … and the vegetation in the various parks is in many respects so similar that no correlation between it and tree climbing is evident. The Manyara lions sometimes escaped from buffalo and elephant by climbing trees, but there would seem to be no reason for lions to remain in them all day because of the remote chance that they might have to climb one. I think that the behaviour represents a habit, one that may have been initiated by for example, a prolonged fly epidemic, and has since been transmitted culturally.

Schaller's suggestion that the lions were climbing trees to avoid flies made the most sense to me, but I had also heard that the lions climbed to enjoy the cool breezes that came off the lake, and to keep a lookout for prey and threats. So I decided to make notes whenever I saw the lions in order to explore these theories. For every sighting, I noted whether flies were present on the ground or in the trees; the temperature and breeze conditions; whether buffalo or elephant were in the vicinity; how high up the tree the lions were and the view it afforded; and the species of tree.

In the 1960s, Iain Douglas-Hamilton noted that on 80% of the occasions when tree-climbing lions were observed, they were in one of just 17 individual trees. These favoured trees were so well known to park guides at the time that they were given particular names and – to protect them from debarking and destruction by elephants – wrapped in coils of wire mesh. My observations indicated a similar afternoon walk through the groundwater forest in the Kirurumu Gorge outside the national park entrance, and a village walk with a local guide through agricultural areas around Mto wa Mbu with a local lunch on a banana plantation. It also used to offer canoeing on Lake Manyara, which may one day be resumed if the water level is sufficiently high.

Most of these activities cost around US$50–70 per person. No experience is required, and all equipment is supplied at no extra cost. The latest addition to Wayo Africa's Manyara menu is three-day hiking expeditions into the little-known Marang Forest, which lies on the escarpment above the lake. There trips are aimed at fit and adventurous travellers wanting a genuinely off-the-beaten-track wilderness experience, since all equipment needs to be carried into the forest by guests, and sleeping is in lightweight tents or expedition hammocks. Expect to pay US$350–400 per person per day including all park fees.

pattern. Lions were found to be resting in trees on about half of the times they were sighted, and although six different tree species were used, three – *Acacia tortilis*, *Kigelia africana* and *Balanites aegyptiaca* – accounted for 90% of sightings. Specific trees were usually favoured, and the lions often moved a considerable distance to reach them.

In most cases the lions were seen to be resting during the heat of the day, and they would usually come down at dusk. Only 5% of sightings coincided with hot weather and breezy conditions, and at most sightings there was no significant breeze, so it seems unlikely that the lions climb to escape the heat. Although buffalo have been documented killing lions at Manyara, there was never any sign of the lions taking to trees to avoid harassment. Most of the time the lions were found to be resting approximately 5–6m above the ground, which afforded them a better view of their surroundings, but since the trees were normally in densely vegetated areas, it would have been difficult for them to observe any potential prey or threat.

My conclusions were similar to those of Makacha and Schaller. Although lions that I found resting on the ground were apparently not greatly concerned by biting flies, lions observed in trees were surrounded by flies in only 10% of cases, when flies were present on the ground below them about 60% of the time. Because the lions generally rested above 5m and flies were seldom encountered at this height, it seems likely that the behaviour was originally initiated during a fly epidemic, and it has since been passed on culturally. I observed the cubs of the Maji pride begin their attempts to climb up to the adults when they were about seven or eight months old. It seemed definitely to be a case of 'lion see, lion do', as there was no apparent reason as to why they should have climbed. Once they had mastered climbing, they too spent a lot of time playing and climbing up and down the trees. More thorough research would be required to fully understand the reasons for this unusual and fascinating behaviour.

Edited from Notes on Tree-climbing Lions of Manyara by Kevin Pretorius, a former manager of Maji Moto Lodge, as originally published in the &Beyond Ecological Journal, volume 2:79–81 (2000). Interestingly, since it was written, tree climbing has become less frequent among the lions of Manyara, and more frequent in the Serengeti, particularly during the rains, evidently confirming the behaviour is essentially cultural and habitual.

11

On-the-spot enquiries about activities are welcomed, but bookings can be made through any safari operator or by contacting **Wayo Africa** (m *0782 627667/0784 203000*; e reservations@wayoafrica.com, *info@wayoafrica.com; www.wayoafrica.com*).

LAKE EYASI AND THE YAEDA VALLEY

The vast Lake Eyasi verges on the remote southern border of the Ngorongoro Conservation Area, and lies at the base of the 800m Eyasi Escarpment, part of the Western Rift Valley wall. In years of plentiful rain, this shallow soda lake can extend

THE LAST HUNTER-GATHERERS

The Hadza (or Hadzabe) of the Lake Eyasi hinterland, which lies to the east of Karatu, represent a unique – and increasingly fragile – link between modern East Africa and the most ancient of the region's human lifestyles and languages. Numbering at most 1,000 individuals, the Hadza are Tanzania's only remaining tribe of true hunter-gatherers, and their Hadzame language is one of only two in the country to be classified in the Khoisan family, a group of click-based tongues that also includes the San (Bushmen) of southern Africa.

The Hadza live in nomadic family bands, typically numbering about 20 adults and a coterie of children. Their rudimentary encampments of light grass shelters are erected in the space of a couple of hours, and might be used as a base for anything from ten days to one month before the inhabitants move on. These movements, though often rather whimsical, might be influenced by changes in the weather or local game distribution, and a band will also often relocate close to a fresh kill that is sufficiently large to sustain them for several days. The Hadza are fairly indiscriminate about what meat they eat – anything from mice to giraffe are fair game, and we once saw a family roasting a feral cat, fur and all, on their campfire – but baboons are regarded to be the ultimate delicacy and reptiles are generally avoided. Hunting with poisoned arrows and honey gathering are generally male activities, while women and children collect roots, seeds, tubers and fruit – vegetarian fodder actually accounts for about 80% of the food intake.

The Hadza have a reputation for living for the present and they care little for conserving food resources, probably because their lifestyle inherently places very little stress on the environment. This philosophy is epitomised in a popular game of chance, which Hadza men will often play – and gamble valuable possessions on – to while away a quiet afternoon. A large master disc is made from baobab bark, and each participant makes a smaller personal disc, with all discs possessing distinct rough and smooth faces. The discs are stacked and thrown in the air, an action that is repeated until only one of the small discs lands with the same face up as the large disc, deciding the winner.

Many Hadza people still dress in the traditional attire of animal skins – women favour impala hide, men the furry coat of a small predator or baboon – which are often decorated with shells and beads. Hadza social groupings are neither permanent nor strongly hierarchical: individuals and couples are free to move between bands, and there is no concept of territorial possession. In order to be eligible for marriage, a Hadza man must kill five baboons to prove his worth. Once married, a couple might stay together for several decades or a lifetime, but there is no taboo against separation and either partner can terminate the union at any time by physically abandoning the other partner.

for 80km from north to south, but in drier periods it sometimes dries out altogether to form an expansive white crust. Most of the time, it falls somewhere between the two extremes: an eerily bleak and windswept body of water surrounded by a muddy white soda crust and tangled dry acacia scrub. In the middle of the day, it can have a rather desolate appearance but it is very beautiful in the softer light of early morning and late afternoon, especially when the sun sets dramatically behind the tall escarpment that hems it in.

Also known as the Yaeda Valley (after the eponymous river), the Eyasi area was very sparsely inhabited in prehistoric times, since it was unsuited to cultivation,

The Hadza might reasonably be regarded as a sociological and anthropological equivalent of a living fossil, since they are one of the very few remaining adherents to the hunter-gatherer lifestyle that sustained the entire human population of the planet for 98% of its history. In both the colonial and post-independence eras, the Hadza have resolutely refused to allow the government to coerce them into following a more settled agricultural or pastoral way of life. The last concerted attempt to modernise Hadza society took place in the 1960s, under the Nyerere government, when a settlement of brick houses with piped water, schools and a clinic was constructed for them alongside an agricultural scheme. Within ten years, the model settlement had been all but abandoned as the Hadza returned to their preferred lifestyle of hunting and gathering. The government, admirably, has since tacitly accepted the right of the Hadza to lead the life of their choice; a large tract of communal land fringing Lake Eyasi has been set aside for their use and they remain the only people in Tanzania automatically exempt from taxes!

Classified as part of the Khoisan language group on account of its click-based sounds, the Hadza tongue has no close modern affiliates, but is thought to be an isolated relic of a linguistic family that possibly dominated eastern and southern Africa until perhaps 3,000 years ago. As Bantu-speaking agriculturists and pastoralists swept into the region from the northwest, however, the Khoisan-speaking hunter-gatherer communities were killed or assimilated into Bantu-speaking communities or forced to retreat into arid and montane territories ill-suited to herding and cultivation. This slow but steady marginalising process has continued into historical times: it has been estimated that of around 100 documented Khoisan languages only 30 are still in use today, and that the total Khoisan-speaking population of Africa now stands at less than 200,000.

That most Khoisan languages, if not already extinct, are headed that way, takes on an added poignancy if, as a minority of linguists suggested throughout the 20th century, the unique click sounds are a preserved element of the very earliest human language. In order to investigate this possibility, the anthropological geneticists Alec Knight and Joanna Mountain analysed the chromosome content of samples taken from the geographically diverse San and Hadza, and concluded that they 'are as genetically distant from one another as two populations could be'. Discounting the somewhat improbable scenario that the clicking noises of the Hadza and San languages arose independently, this wide genetic gulf would imply a very ancient common linguistic root indeed. Several linguists dispute Knight and Mountain's conclusion, but if it is correct, then Hadzame, along with Africa's other dying Khoisan languages, might represent one last fading echo of the first human voices to have carried across the African savanna.

11

and tsetse flies made it unattractive to livestock farmers. Back then, the region's only semi-permanent inhabitants were the Hadza, hunter-gatherers who still inhabit the area today, and practice a largely traditional lifestyle (see box, *The last hunter-gatherers*, page 256), despite several more recent human influxes, most significantly the Datoga, a pastoralist people with many cultural affinities to the Maasai (see box, *The Barabaig*, page 232) . In addition, thanks to an irrigation scheme dating to the colonial era, the Yaeda Valley is now the most important onion-growing area in East Africa, and the main supplier to both Nairobi and Arusha. Eyasi is also an important source of fish for Arusha. Indeed, during the wet season, when the water is highest, the shores often hold temporary encampments populated by fishermen from all over northern Tanzania.

Lake Eyasi supports large seasonal concentrations of water birds, including hundreds of thousands of flamingos at some times of year. Otherwise, little wildlife is resident, and most of what is around – a list that includes lesser kudu, Kirk's dik-dik and olive baboon – tends to be rather shy. Overall, Lake Eyasi is less of interest for its wildlife than the opportunities for cultural interaction. Guided visits to Datoga homesteads and Hadza encampments are easily arranged through the tourist office in Mang'ola, an overgrown village that qualifies as the most important settlement in the area, and it is also possible to go hunting with the Hadza or visit an onion farm.

GETTING THERE AND AWAY The gateway town to the Yaeda Valley is Karatu, which lies in the Ngorongoro Highlands along the surfaced road connecting Lake Manyara National Park to the Ngorongoro Conservation area (see *Chapter 12*, page 269). **Mang'ola** lies about one hour's drive on dirt from Karatu, and can be reached by following the Ngorongoro road out of town for about 5km, then taking a left turn towards the lake. Once at Mang'ola, it's easy enough to locate the guides and arrange a visit to a Hadza encampment. Most visitors stay in the area overnight, but it could be visited as a full- or half-day trip out of Karatu. It would be difficult to explore Eyasi using public transport

TOURIST INFORMATION The centre of tourist activity is the **Lake Eyasi Cultural Tourism Programme** (*LECTP*; m *0753 808601*; e *eyasiculturaltourismprogramme@yahoo.com*), which was founded in 2011 to regulate tourism in the area. It operates a tourist office at the road barrier where you enter Mang'ola coming from Karatu. You'll need to stop here to pay the mandatory entrance fee of US$20 per vehicle, and it is also where all activities and guides must be arranged.

WHERE TO STAY

Upmarket

Kisima Ngeda (7 tents) ◊027 254 8715; m 0782 101101; e reservations@kisimangeda.com; www.kisimangeda.com. This remote owner-managed tented camp is set in a shady grove of doum palms near the eastern shore of Lake Eyasi, with magnificent views across to the kilometre-tall western Rift Valley escarpment, the Ngorongoro Highlands & the Oldeani Mountains. It makes an excellent base for visiting a Hadzabe encampment or exploring the arid lake hinterland. The accommodation is comfortable but simple rather than luxurious, & the structures around the en-suite tents are made entirely from organic local materials. The excellent food includes fresh tilapia from the lake. *US$360/500 sgl/dbl FB.*

Moderate

Tindiga Tented Camp (10 tents) ◊027 250 6315; m 0754 324193; e reservations@moivaro.com; www.moivaro.com. Set on a bushy slope about 10 mins' drive from Mang'ola & the tourist office, this comfortable & welcoming camp consists of large no-frills standing tents with twin beds, nets, en-suite hot shower, & a dining room bar that serves adequate meals & a limited selection of alcoholic & other drinks. It's nothing fancy, but it's good value & the staff can arrange Hadza hunts & other activities around Mang'ola. *US$175/250 sgl/dbl FB Mar, Jun & Sep to early Dec; US$195/270 sgl/dbl FB other months. Low-season discount in Apr & May.*

Camping

Å Lake Eyasi Bush Camp m 0753 178241/0756 712801; e eyasibushcamp@yahoo. com. Situated a few hundred metres from Tindiga, this spacious & little-used campsite has a pleasant location in a glade of acacias, & facilities include a small ablution block with old showers & a cooking area. *US$15pp.*

WHAT TO SEE AND DO All cultural activities in the area must be arranged through the tourist office operated by the Lake Eyasi Cultural Tourism Programme. This offers a number of guided activities, including Hadza hunts and visits, Datoga village visits, and visits to a Datoga blacksmith (who makes copper and tin jewellery from recycled car parts, broken padlocks and other junk). All activities cost US$20 for a party of up to ten, plus a guide fee of US$30 per party covering all activities undertaken.

The definite must-do here is a visit to a Hadza encampment. The people struck us as being very warm and unaffected, and going on an actual hunt is a primal and exciting experience – though do be warned that a temporary conversion to vegetarianism might be in order should you come back with a baboon or another large mammal and be offered the greatest delicacy, which is the raw liver. It might be expected that regular exposure to tourists could erode the traditional lifestyle of certain Hadza bands, but we have seen no sign of this over repeated visits, perhaps because the Hadza have chosen their nomadic lifestyle despite the attempts by successive governments to settle them.

NORTH OF MANYARA

The vast majority of Serengeti safaris head directly west from Manyara along the asphalt road that climbs the Rift Valley escarpment into the Ngorongoro Highlands, and then return to Arusha exactly the same way. An offbeat alternative to this well-trodden route, one that will transform your safari itinerary into a genuine loop, is the spine-jarring 250km road that connects Mto wa Mbu to the northern Serengeti via the parched stretch of the Rift Valley abutting the border with Kenya. This is not, it should be stressed, a route that should instil any great enthusiasm in anybody who nurses a dodgy back or chronic agoraphobia, or who has limited tolerance for simple travel conditions. But equally this half-forgotten corner of northern Tanzania also possesses some genuinely alluring off-the-beaten-track landmarks in the form of the ruined city of Engaruka, the brooding Lake Natron, and above all perhaps the fiery volcanic majesty of Ol Doinyo Lengai.

Most experienced safari operators can arrange trips to the northern Rift Valley, taking Lake Natron as their focal point, but many will also discourage you from visiting the area as it is rough on vehicles and has been prone to outbursts of banditry in the past. Technically, it is possible to travel between Mto wa Mbu and the northern Serengeti via Natron in nine to ten hours of flat driving, but it would make for a very long day and would rather defeat the point of the exercise. More realistic is to split the drive over two days, stopping for a night at the lakeshore village of Engaresero, or two nights if you intend to climb Ol Doinyo Lengai or undertake any other exploration of the region. It is common practice to tag this area onto the end of a safari, but there is a strong case for slotting it in between the

11

Tarangire/Manyara and Ngorongoro/Serengeti legs of your itinerary, if for no other reason than it will break up the vehicle-bound regime of game drives with a decent leg-stretch – whether you opt for a gentle stroll around the Engaruka ruins or the southern shore of Natron, the slightly more demanding hike to the Engaresero Waterfall in the escarpment west of Natron, or the decidedly challenging nocturnal ascent of Ol Doinyo Lengai.

If you visit this area in your own vehicle, treat it as you would any wilderness trip: carry adequate supplies of food, water and fuel. If you go with a safari company, avoid those at the lower end of the price scale, or you risk getting stuck in the middle of nowhere in a battered vehicle. Note, also, that while no entrance fee is formally charged for visiting the Natron area, a trio of roadblocks has been established along the road from Mto wa Mbu by Engaruka, Longido and Ngorongoro District Councils, and each currently levies a toll fee of US$10–15 per person to all non-Tanzanian passengers. The legitimacy of these barriers is such that they have been

PHOTOGRAPHING THE MAASAI

A surprisingly frequent cause of friction on safaris is the somewhat entrepreneurial Maasai attitude to being photographed by tourists. It's an issue that frequently leads visitors to conclude that the Maasai are 'too commercialised', a misguided allegation that reflects Western misconceptions and prejudices about Africa far more than it does any aspect of modern Maasai culture.

The root cause of this misunderstanding is a Western tendency to distinguish between 'authentic' traditional practices and more cosmopolitan influences, rather than recognising both as equally valid components in the ever-evolving hybrid that is modern African culture. To give one clearly identifiable example, you'll find that most Africans are devout Christians or Muslims, yet many also simultaneously adhere to an apparently conflicting traditional belief system. On the streets of Arusha, suited businessmen yapping into mobile phones and trendy safari guides brush past traditional Maasai street hawkers, a co-existence of modernity and traditionalism that seems contradictory to outsiders but is unremarkable to the country's inhabitants. What's more, the same slick businessmen or casually dressed safari guides might well visit traditional healers on occasion, or return home for tribal ceremonies dressed in traditional attire, to all outward purposes indistinguishable from less 'Westernised' relatives who always dress that way.

The point is that the Maasai, like us, are living in the 21st century, and a variety of external factors – among them, population growth, the gazetting of traditional grazing land as national parks, exposure to other Tanzanian cultures and exotic religions, the creation of a cash economy – have combined to ensure that their culture is not a static museum piece, but a dynamic, modern entity.

Another point of confusion is the *only* direct exposure to Maasai culture experienced by most visitors takes place in 'cultural villages' where tourists wander around as they please and photograph whomever they like after paying a fixed fee. There is nothing wrong with these villages, and much that is commendable about them, but they should be approached with realistic expectations – essentially, as cottage industries whose inhabitants derive a substantial portion of their living from tourist visits. And most such villages are longstanding Maasai settlements whose inhabitants live a largely traditional lifestyle. Indeed, it is we, the tourists, who are the distorting factor in their behaviour.

pulled down several times by police or other officials (only to be restored again within days), but still you are highly unlikely to talk your way past them, and prolonged debate might even result in you being charged a higher toll. If you are stopped at the barriers, at least ensure you obtain a receipt for any payment so it doesn't go straight into the pocket of the person at the gate.

ENGARUKA RUINS Situated below the Rift Valley escarpment about 65km north of Manyara, Engaruka is the Maasai name for the extensive ruins of a mysterious terraced city and irrigation system constructed at least 500 years ago by a late Iron Age culture in the eastern foothills of Mount Empakaai. Nobody knows for sure who built the city: some say it was the Mbulu, who inhabited the area immediately before the Maasai arrived there; others that it was built by Datoga settlers from the north. Locally, the city is said to have been home to forebears of the Sukuma, whose greeting 'Mwanga lukwa' was later bastardised to Engaruka by the Maasai – more

Make no mistake, were you to wander off into a Maasai boma that doesn't routinely deal with tourists, the odds are that its inhabitants would simply refuse to be photographed no matter what payment you offered. What's more, you might well find a spear dangling from the end of your lens if you don't respect their wishes. So concluding that the Maasai are 'too commercialised' on the basis of an inherently contrived form of interaction is as daft as walking into a London shop and concluding that the English are 'too commercialised' because the assistant expects you to pay for the items you select.

There is a deeper irony to this cultural misunderstanding. Here we have well-off visitors from media-obsessed, materialistic Europe or North America fiddling with their Blackberries and video cameras, straightening their custom-bought safari outfits, and planning the diet they'll go on back home to compensate for the endless lodge buffets. They are confronted by a culture as resilient, non-materialistic and ascetic as that of the Maasai, and they accuse it with a straight face of being 'commercialised'. This genuinely concerns me: are we so culture bound, so riddled with romantic expectations about how the Maasai should behave, that any slight deviation from these preconceptions prevents us from seeing things for what they are?

So let's start again. The Maasai are proud and dramatically attired pastoralists who adhere almost entirely to the traditions of their forefathers. They fascinate us, but being the bunch of gadget-obsessed wazungu we are, our response is not to absorb their presence or to try to communicate with them, but to run around thrusting cameras in their faces. And this, I would imagine, irritates the hell out of those Maasai who happen to live along main tourist circuits, so they decide not to let tourists photograph them except for a fee or in the context of an organised tourist village. In theory, everybody should be happy. In practice, we somehow construe this reasonable attempt by relatively poor people to make a bit of honest money as rampant commercialism. Okay, I recognise this is a bit simplistic, but we create the demand, the Maasai satisfy it, and if we pay to do so, that's just good capitalism, something the West has always been keen to encourage in Africa. If you don't like it, save space on your memory card and buy a postcard – in all honesty, you'll probably get a lot more from meeting these charismatic people if you leave your camera behind and enjoy the moment!

likely, however, is that the name of this well-watered spot has roots in the Maasai word 'ngare' (water).

The discovery of the ruins by outsiders is generally credited to Dr Fischer, who followed the base of the Rift Valley through Maasailand in 1883, and wrote how: 'peculiar masses of stone became suddenly apparent, rising from the plain to heights up to ten feet. Partly they looked like mouldering tree trunks, partly like the tumbled down walls of ancient castles.' An older reference to Engaruka can be found on the so-called Slug Map drawn up by the missionaries Krapf and Erhardt in 1855. The first person to excavate the site was Hans Reck in the early 20th century, followed by the legendary Louis Leakey, who reckoned it consisted of seven large villages containing roughly 1,000 homes apiece and thought the total population must have exceeded 30,000.

The ruined villages overlook a complex stone-block irrigation system that extends over some 25km² and is fed by the perennial Engaruka River. This highly specialised and integrated agricultural community was abandoned in the 18th century, probably due to a combination of changes in the local hydrology and the immigration of more militaristic pastoralist tribes from the north. Yet Engaruka is unique only in scale, since a number of smaller deserted sites in the vicinity form part of the same cultural and agricultural complex, and radiocarbon dating suggests it might be older than has been assumed in the past – possibly as old as the 4th century AD, which would make it a likely precursor to the great centralised empires that thrived in pre-colonial Uganda and Rwanda.

Guided tours of the ruins can be arranged easily through the **Engaruka Cultural Tourism Office** (m 0787 228653/0754 507939; e engaruka@yahoo.com), which is based at Engaruka Ruins Campsite (see *Where to stay*, opposite). An entrance fee equivalent to around US$7 is payable here, while your guides will expect to be paid around US$5–10 per party. Without a local guide, it's debatable whether the ruins would convey anything much to the average tourist. However, the floor plan of the main village is still quite clear, and a few of the circular stone houses remain more or less intact to around waist level, their floors strewn with shards of broken earthenware. Substantial sections of the irrigation canal are still in place, as are some old burial mounds that might or might not be related to the war with the Maasai that caused the village to be abandoned.

Getting there and away
The feeder road to the ruins runs westward from Engaruka Chini, a junction village situated on the dirt road between Mto wa Mbu and Engaresero. The junction lies about 50km from Mto wa Mbu along a good stretch of dirt road that can be covered in under an hour, and 40km from Engaresero along a much more erratic road that takes more like 1½ hours. From Engaruka Chini, the feeder road continues through a semi-urban sprawl for about 5km before reaching Engaruka Juu, site of the Jerusalem Campsite, from where it is a ten-minute walk to the nearest ruined village.

Using **public transport**, at least one bus connects Arusha to Engaruka via Mto wa Mbu daily, charging around US$5 for a journey in either direction. It leaves Engaruka Chini from the station next to the Engaruka Ruins Campsite at 06.00, passes through Mto Wa Mbu about two hours later, and usually arrives in Arusha by 12.00 before turning around again to make the return trip. However, it tends to be very slow and crowded, so there is much to be said for bussing directly to Mto wa Mbu and then picking up local transport, which is most prolific on Monday and Wednesday, respectively the main market days in Engaruka Juu and Engaruka Chini.

Where to stay

Ⅹ **Engaruka Ruins Campsite** m 0787 228653/0754 507939; e engaruka@yahoo.com. Set in compact green grounds next to the bus station, this friendly campsite has the best facilities in town, including hot running water, electricity, flush toilets, simple standing tents (at no extra change), a bar & a restaurant. It also houses the Engaruka Cultural Tourism Office, which arranges guided tours of the ruins, as well as visits to local Maasai bomas, traditional dancing displays & ascents of Ol Doinyo Lengai. *US$10 pp*.

Ⅹ **Jerusalem Campsite** Set alongside the Lutheran Church in a pretty grove close to the ruins, this site has no facilities other than toilets, making it more suitable for groups than for independent travellers. *US$5 pp*.

LAKE NATRON There are but a handful of places where the Rift Valley evokes its geologically violent origins with graphic immediacy. Ethiopia's Danakil Desert is one such spot; the volcanic Virunga Range in the Albertine Rift is another. And so too is the most northerly landmark in the Tanzanian Rift Valley, the low-lying Lake Natron, a shallow sliver of exceptionally alkaline water that extends southward from the Kenya border near Mount Shompole for 58km. The Natron skyline is dominated by the textbook volcanic silhouette of Ol Doinyo Lengai, which rises more than 2km above the surrounding Rift Valley floor to an altitude of 2,960m, its harsh black contours softened by an icing of white ash that glistens brightly below the sun, as if in parody of Kilimanjaro's snows. Then there is the lake itself, a thrillingly primordial phenomenon whose caustic waters are enclosed by a crust of sodden grey volcanic ash and desiccated salt, punctuated by isolated patches of steamy, reed-lined swamp where the hot springs that sustain the lake bubble to the surface.

Thought to be about 1.5 million years old, Natron is a product of the same tectonic activity that formed the Ngorongoro Highlands and Mount Gelai, the latter being a 2,941m-high extinct volcano that rises from the eastern lakeshore. Nowhere more than 50cm deep, it has changed shape significantly since that time, largely as a result of volcanic activity associated with the creation of Ol Doinyo Lengai to its immediate south. It lies at an altitude of 610m in an unusually arid stretch of the rift floor, receiving an average of 400mm of rainfall annually, and it would have probably dried out centuries ago were it not also fed by the freshwater Ewaso Ngiro River, which has its catchment in the central Kenyan Highlands, and the hot springs that rise below its floor. The alkaline level has also increased drastically over the millennia, partially because of the high salinity of ash and lava deposits from Lengai, partially because the lake's only known outlet is evaporation. Today, depending on recent rainfall, the viscous water has an average pH of 9–11, making it almost as caustic as ammonia when the level is very low, and it can reach a temperature of up to 60°C in extreme circumstances.

Natron's hyper-salinity makes it incapable of sustaining any but the most specialised life forms. The only resident vertebrate is the endemic white-lipped tilapia *Oreochromis alcalica*, a 10cm-long fish that congregates near hot spring inlets where the water temperature is around 36–40°C. The microbiology of the lake is dominated by halophytic (salt-loving) organisms such as spirulina, a form of blue-green algae whose red pigments make the salt-encrusted flats in the centre of the lake look bright red when seen from the air. Natron is also the only known breeding ground for East Africa's 2.5 million lesser flamingos, which usually congregate there between August and October, feeding on the abundant algae (whose pigments are responsible for the birds' trademark pink hue). The breeding ground's inhospitality to potential predators makes it an ideal flamingo nursery, but it also makes it difficult for human visitors to access – situated in the centre of the lake, it was discovered as recently as the 1950s and it can only be seen from the air today. In addition to the flamingos, Natron attracts up to 100,000 migrant water birds during the European winter.

The area around Lake Natron supports a thin population of large mammals typical of the Rift Valley, including wildebeest, zebra, fringe-eared oryx, Grant's and Thomson's gazelle, and even the odd lion and cheetah. The main game-viewing destination in the vicinity is the **Natron Game Controlled Area (NGCA)**, a 4,000km² tract of dry low-lying Maasailand that runs east from the lakeshore towards the main Namanga–Arusha road. The NGCA is leased by local Maasai communities to Ker & Downey Tanzania, who effectively operate it as a private game reserve that is most easily explored out of Tandala Tented Camp (see *Where to stay*, below).

Getting there and away The centre of tourist activity on Natron is the small lakeshore village of **Engaresero** (also spelled Ngare Sero), bisected by the wooded Mikuyu River from whence derives its Maasai name ('black water', 'clear water', 'dappled water' or 'forest of water', depending on who does the translating). Engaresero lies about 90km north of Mto wa Mbu along an erratic road that usually takes about 2½ hours to cover in its entirety, though this might improve as and when proper bridges are built across the larger watercourses north of Engaruka. Coming to/from the northern Serengeti, Engaresero is about 160km from Klein's Gate, a drive that takes five to six hours without stops, and involves a spectacular ascent/descent of the rift escarpment to the west of the lake.

The only **public transport** to Engaresero is a bus that connects Arusha to Loliondo most days. This usually leaves Arusha in the early morning from the central bus station, and takes around five to six hours to get to Engaresero. However, it is known to be quite unreliable and it may not run at all when under repair. An alternative would be to catch a bus as far as Mto Wa Mbu, then take one of the **4x4s** that serve as occasional public transport from there. Or you could bus to Engaruka, and hire a 4x4 to Natron and/or Lengai from the Engaruka Ruins Campsite (see *Where to stay*, page 263).

Where to stay

Exclusive

Tandala Tented Camp (6 tents)
027 250 8917; **m** 0786 000510; **e** www.keranddowneytanzania.com. Operated by Ker & Downey Tanzania, this stunning tented camp straddles a rocky kopje alive with birdlife & hyrax activity, & offering great views across the plains of Maasailand to nearby Mount Gelai & the more distant Lengai volcano. It has sole traversing rights to the vast NGCA, & only hosts one party at a time, making it an excellent option for family & other parties wanting a totally exclusive all-inclusive safari experience. Game viewing in the area is slower than in the national parks, but there is plenty of wildlife around, & it has a thrilling wilderness feel, amplified by the striking scenery in this remote corner of the Rift Valley. It is a good place to look for relatively scarce dry-country species such as lesser kudu, gerenuk & fringe-eared oryx, & along with small populations of cheetah & lion, a semi-resident pack of wild dogs is sometimes seen along the dry watercourses. Birders will enjoy the varied selection of dry acacia woodland species (many that are more typically associated with Kenya than Tanzania). It is emphatically worth taking a day trip to the eastern lakeshore to see the hot springs, numerous flamingos & shorebirds, & the always impressive ash-strewn outline of Lengai on the opposite shore. This part of the lakeshore is so remote that many of the local Maasai don't recognise the most basic of Swahili greetings (the equivalent of a Welsh-speaker in the UK not understanding the phrase 'Good morning'). The stilted tents are very spacious, coming with king-size bed, en-suite hot shower & private wooden balcony, & are complemented by the excellent service, food & drinks selection. *US$800 pp (min rate for 4 guests) inc meals, drinks, activities, & all park & camp fees.*

Upmarket

⌂ **Lake Natron Camp** (8 tents) m 0732 978931/0764 305435; e reservations@ngare-sero-lodge.com, ngaresero@gmail.com; www.ngare-sero-lodge.com/lake-natron-camp. Set around a spring-fed oasis in a 315ha Maasai concession on the soda flats that hem in the southern lakeshore, this old-style eco-friendly bush camp doesn't offer the sort of under-canvas luxury you associate with Tanzania's top tented camps, but it will appeal greatly to those seeking an isolated wilderness experience in arguably the most spectacular stretch of the Tanzanian Rift Valley. Accommodation, likely to be revamped within the lifespan of this edition, consists of standing safari tents not much larger than the queen-size beds (with walk-in nets) they contain, & private (but not en suite) toilets & showers. The stylish net-shaded dining area, bar & lounge is surprisingly cool during the heat of the day, & while there is no swimming pool, it is great fun to swim in the clear & rather soapy spring-fed stream that runs in front of the sleeping tents. The camp offers superb views of Mount Lengai & Gelai, wonderful star-studded night skies, & day outings to some of the oldest hominid footprints yet discovered (*What to see and do*, overleaf) as well as to a section of the lakeshore rich in flamingos & other birds. The camp also offers Lengai climbs using the standard northern ascent route or the safer & less known southeastern route. *US$365/600 sgl/dbl FB.*

Moderate

⌂ **Natron Tented Camp** (9 rooms) ☎027 250 6315; m 0754 324193; e reservations@moivaro.com; www.moivaro.com. Established in 1989, this low-key camp is in wooded grounds on the southern outskirts of Engaresero. It has a spectacular position some 4km from the southern lakeshore, & offers great views across the floodplain to Mount Gelai. Though it has a somewhat no-frills feel compared to most tented camps & lodges in Tanzania, this is in keeping with the austere surrounds, & it does have a welcoming swimming pool & pleasant restaurant & bar area. Accommodation is in en-suite tents or chalets with twin or dbl beds, netting & hot water. Inexpensive organised guided climbs of nearby Ol Doinyo Lengai are offered, too. *US$275/330 sgl/dbl FB Jan, Feb, Jul, Aug & late Dec; US$240/300 Mar, Jun & Sep–early Dec. Low-season discount Apr & May.*

⌂ **Natron River Camp** (6 tents) m 0754 371650/0682 819855; e info@wildlandssafaris.com; www.wildlandssafaris.com. Situated alongside the Mikuyu River, on the southern edge of Engaresero, this pleasant little camp lies in tree-shaded grounds with a plunge pool, makuti-shaded dining room/bar & great views towards Lengai. Accommodation is in neat standing tents with dbl beds, nets & en-suite hot showers. *US$110 pp FB.*

Camping

⋏ **Mikuyu River Campsite** This no-frills campsite is set in large shady grounds alongside Natron River Camp. Facilities include a bar, but campers unequipped for self-catering will need to eat at one of the handful of small local eateries running along the main road through Engaresero. *US$10 pp.*

⋏ **Waterfall Campsite** Situated about 2km out of town close to the starting point for the walk to Engaresero Waterfall, this basic campsite has a great location but facilities are limited to basic toilets. *US$10 pp.*

What to see and do Most activities can be arranged through the various camps and campsites in the area, but you can also make arrangements for Lengai climbs and other activities directly with the **Engaresero Tourist Office** (☎ 027 205 0025; e engaraserotourism@gmail.com, mengoru2006@yahoo.com; www.tanzaniaculturaltourism.com; ⏲ 08.00–18.00 daily), which lies on the east side of the main road about 500m north of the village itself (look for the compound signposted *Engaresero Maasai Pastoralist Heritage Area*).

Southern lakeshore To reach the southern lakeshore from Engaresero, you need to drive for around 5km to an unofficial parking spot about 1km from the water's edge, then walk for about ten minutes across salt-encrusted flats to a series of pockmarked black volcanic protrusions that serve as vantage points over the water. It's a lovely spot with Lengai looming in the background, and it hosts a profusion of water birds, most visibly large flocks of the pink-tinged lesser flamingo but also various pelicans, egrets, herons and waders. Wildebeest and zebra are also often seen in the area. If your driver doesn't know the way to the lakeshore – it's a rather obscure track – then ask for a local guide at one of the campsites. Whatever else you do, don't let the driver take the vehicle beyond the tracks left behind by his predecessors, or you run a serious risk of getting stuck in the treacherously narrow saline crust that surrounds the lake.

Engaresero Human Footprints One of the most important sites of its type in the world, this set of 58 human footprints is embedded in a layer of tuff-like compressed ash close to the southern shore of Natron. Although much older hominid fossil footprints have been discovered elsewhere in East Africa, these might well be the earliest known ones associated with *Homo sapiens*. The prints were discovered by a Maasai herder in 1998 but only investigated properly by scientists about ten years later. It is thought that they were made by a party of 18 adults and children as they traipsed through a field of muddy ash when Lengai erupted around 120,000 years ago. The footprints are remarkably clear (although they can be obscured below a layer of fine dust) and their presence here only goes to underscore the prehistoric feel of this vast volcanic stretch of the Rift Valley. The site lies on the concession operated by Lake Natron Camp, about 15 minutes walk from the camp itself. The site is open to visitors from elsewhere – arrangements can be made through the Engaresero Tourist Office – but the camp management asks that outsiders first pop into the camp to introduce themselves and to pick up a guide there.

Engaresero Waterfall The Engaresero River forms a series of pretty waterfalls as it descends from the Nguruman Escarpment west of Lake Natron, a kilometre or two south of the village of Engaresero. The lowest two falls can be reached by driving out to Waterfall Campsite, and then following the river upstream on foot for 45–60 minutes through the gorge it has carved into the escarpment wall. If you are not already sufficiently doused by the time you reach the second waterfall, there's a chilly natural swimming pool below it. There is no clear footpath through the gorge: you will need to wade across the river several times (potentially dangerous after heavy rain) and can also expect to do a fair bit of clambering along ledges and rocks. This walk can only be recommended to reasonably fit and agile travellers, and it's advisable to take somebody who knows the way to help you navigate a couple of tricky stretches – a guide can be arranged at any of the camps listed on pages 264–5, or through the Engaresero Tourist Office.

Ol Doinyo Lengai Estimated to be around 350,000–400,000 years old, Ol Doinyo Lengai – the Maasai 'Mountain of God' – is one of the youngest volcanoes in East Africa and possibly the most active. Its crater is known to have experienced almost continuous low-key activity since 1883, when Dr Fischer, the first European to pass through this part of Maasailand, observed smoke rising from the summit and was told secondhand that the mountain regularly emitted rumbling noises. At least a dozen minor or major eruptions have occurred since then. An interesting feature of Lengai is that it is the only active volcano known to emit carbonate lava, a form of molten rock that contains almost no silicon, is about 50% cooler than other forms of lava at around 500°C, and is also exceptionally fluid, with a viscosity comparable to water.

During an eruption in 2004, plumes in the crater could be seen from as far away as Engaresero and many local Maasai herdsmen moved their livestock out of the area. The mountain once again experienced a high level of volcanic activity between July 2007 and June 2008. On 18 July 2007, tremors emanating from the mountain measured 6.0 on the Richter scale and were felt as far away as Nairobi city. Ol Doinyo Lengai erupted spectacularly on 4 September 2007, emanating an ashen steamy plume almost 20km downwind and sending fresh lava flows along the north and west flanks. Eruptions continued intermittently into mid 2008, with further eruptions occurring in March, April and August. At the time of writing. Lengai has been more or less dormant since early 2009, but obviously that might change at any time.

Climbing Ol Doinyo Lengai The ascent of Lengai is a popular hike with adventurous travellers, and it forms an excellent budget alternative to climbing Kilimanjaro, at least when the volcano is sufficiently placid. The ascent passes through some magnificently arid scenery and offers spectacular views back towards the Rift Valley, before leading to the bleakly visceral lunar landscape of the crater, studded with ash cones, lava pools, steam vents and other evidence of volcanic activity. Suitable only for reasonably fit and agile travellers, the normal northern ascent route to the top

THE 1966 ERUPTION

The most impressive eruption of Ol Doinyo Lengai in recorded history occurred in the latter part of 1966, when ash fall was reported as far away as Seronera, more than 100km to the west, as well as at Loliondo and Shombole, both some 70km further north. It is believed that the otherwise inexplicable death of large numbers of game around Empakaai Crater in that year was a result of an ash fall that coated the grass up to 2cm deep, though it is unclear whether the animals starved to death or they succumbed to a toxin within the ash. The effect on Maasai livestock was also devastating according to Tepilit Ole Saitoti, who recalled the incident as follows in his excellent book *Worlds of a Maasai Warrior*:

In the year 1966, God, who my people believe dwells in this holy mountain, unleashed Her fury unsparingly. The mountain thunder shook the earth, and the volcanic flame, which came from deep down in the earth's crust, was like a continuous flash of lightning. During days when the eruption was most powerful, clouds of smoke and steam appeared. Many cattle died and still more would die. Poisonous volcanic ash spewed all over the land as far as a hundred miles away, completely covering the pastures and the leaves of trees. Cattle swallowed ash each time they tried to graze and were weakened. They could not wake up without human assistance. We had to carry long wooden staffs to put under the fallen animals to lift them up. There must have been more than enough reason for God to have unleashed Her anger on us, and all we could do was pray for mercy. My pastoral people stubbornly braved the gusting warm winds as they approached the flaming mountain to pray. Women and men dressed in their best walked in stately lines towards God, singing. The mountain was unappeased and cattle died in the thousands. Just before the people started dying too, my father decided to move; as he put it: 'We must move while we still have children, or else we will all lose them'.

11

of Lengai is very steep, climbing in altitude from around 800m to around 2,900m, while the descent on loose scree can be very tough on knees and ankles. The climb normally takes five to six hours along slopes practically bereft of shade, for which reason many locals recommend leaving late at night (around 23.00–24.00) to avoid the intense heat and to reach the crater rim in time for sunrise. If you ascend by day a 05.00 start is advised, and precautions should be taken against dehydration and sunstroke. Either way, the descent takes about two hours.

Most adventure safari operators in Arusha offer guided Lengai climbs (see *Chapter 5, Arusha*, page 103), but it is also possible to arrange a one-day climb locally, either at the Engaresero Tourist Office or at one of the camps dotted around Engaresero village. The mountain lies outside any conservation area so no park fees are charged, but a fixed guide fee of US$100 per party of up to five, or US$190 for larger parties, is levied. Alternatively, overnight hikes using the little-known southeast route can be arranged through Lake Natron Camp, listed on page 265, at US$225/250 for one/two people.

All hikers should be aware that the cones on the crater floor can easily collapse under pressure and they often cover deadly lava lakes. Under no circumstances should you climb on a cone, or walk inside a partially collapsed cone. It is inadvisable (and may be forbidden) to climb the mountain during periods of high activity. For further information on the Ol Doinyo Lengai, check out this excellent website http://blogs.stlawu.edu/lengai, which has detailed background and practical information.

12

Ngorongoro and the Crater Highlands

Immediately west of Lake Manyara, the surfaced B144 – the main access road to the Serengeti – switchbacks up a spectacular stretch of the Rift Valley escarpment to the fertile moist slopes of the Crater Highlands. Rising to a maximum altitude of 3,648m, these volcanically created highlands are pockmarked with dormant and extinct calderas, most famously the wondrous Ngorongoro Crater, the region's main tourist focus.

Much of Crater Highlands are protected within Ngorongoro Conservation Area (NCA), a vast biosphere reserve where the iconic Maasai people live alongside a bewildering diversity of wildlife, which ranges from the lions and elephants that strut fearlessly across the Ngorongoro Crater floor to the secretive forest birds that flit through the jungle-like tangle of greenery that swathes the crater's rim and outer slopes.

Coming from Arusha or Manyara, the gateway to the Crater Highlands is the small town of Karatu, which straddles the B144 below the eastern slopes of Ngorongoro Crater 8km before the main entrance to the NCA. An important agricultural centre, Karatu and its immediate environs also support an ever-growing number of hotels, lodges and campsites designed to supplement the relatively limited options situated within the NCA itself.

KARATU

Set at an altitude of 1,500m along the road between Lake Manyara and Ngorongoro Crater, Karatu, despite its bland and unprepossessing appearance, vies with Mto wa Mbu as the most populous settlement *en route* between Arusha and the Serengeti. And while most tourists pass through in the blink of an eye on their way to the more glamorous wildlife reserves to its west, it's worth knowing that the town boasts a fair selection of tourist facilities, including several restaurants, guesthouses, filling stations, internet cafés and adequately stocked supermarkets. It also hosts a branch of the National Bank of Commerce with foreign exchange facilities and an ATM where local currency can be drawn against Visa cards, while the CRDB branch here is the closest place to the Ngorongoro Conservation Area where entrance fees can be paid (see box, *Ngorongoro entrance fees*, page 274).

Karatu's local nickname of 'safari junction' refers mainly to its tourist facilities. Nevertheless, it is a route focus of sorts, situated close to the junction of the roads running south to Lake Eyasi and Katesh via Mbulu (see *Chapter 11, Lake Manyara and the Northern Rift Valley*, page 256). Both the town itself and the farmland to its west host an ever-growing number of campsites and lodges built to supplement the limited bed space in the NCA. These lodges are routinely used as bases for game drives in the Ngorongoro Crater, Note, however, that sleeping outside the NCA precludes the sort of very early start that allows you to get the most from a trip into Ngorongoro Crater.

GETTING THERE AND AWAY Karatu lies about 30km from Mto wa Mbu along a good surfaced road that can easily be covered in 30 minutes. Coming directly

THE MAASAI

The northern safari circuit is the homeland of the Nilotic-speaking Maasai, whose reputation as fearsome warriors ensured that the 19th-century slave caravans studiously avoided their territory, which was one of the last parts of East Africa ventured into by Europeans. The Maasai today remain the most familiar of African people to outsiders, a reputation that rests as much on their continued adherence to a traditional lifestyle as on past exploits. Instantly identifiable, Maasai men drape themselves in toga-like red blankets, carry long wooden poles, and often dye their hair with red ochre and style it in a manner that has been compared to a Roman helmet. And while the women dress similarly to many other Tanzanian women, their extensive use of beaded jewellery is highly distinctive, too.

The Maasai are often regarded to be the archetypal East African pastoralists, but are in fact relatively recent arrivals to the area. Their language Maa (Maasai literally means 'Maa-speakers') is affiliated to those languages spoken by the Nuer of southwest Ethiopia and the Bari of southern Sudan, and oral traditions suggest that the proto-Maasai started to migrate southward from the lower Nile area in the 15th century. They arrived in their present territory in the 17th or 18th century, forcefully displacing earlier inhabitants such as the Datoga and Chagga, who respectively migrated south to the Hanang area and east to the Kilimanjaro foothills. The Maasai territory reached its greatest extent in the mid 19th century, when it covered most of the Rift Valley from Marsabit (Kenya) south to Dodoma. Over the 1880s/90s, the Maasai were hit by a series of disasters linked to the arrival of Europeans – rinderpest and smallpox epidemics exacerbated by a severe drought and a bloody secession dispute – and much of their former territory was re-colonised by tribes whom they had displaced a century earlier. During the colonial era, a further 50% of their land was lost to game reserves and settler farms. These territorial incursions notwithstanding, the Maasai today have one of the most extensive territories of any Tanzanian tribe, ranging across the vast Maasai Steppes to the Ngorongoro Highlands and Serengeti Plains.

The Maasai are monotheists whose belief in a single deity with a dualistic nature – the benevolent Engai Narok (Black God) and vengeful Engai Nanyokie (Red God) – has some overtones of the Judaic faith. They believe that Engai, who resides in the volcano Ol Doinyo Lengai, made them the rightful owners of all the cattle in the world, a view that has occasionally made life difficult for neighbouring herders. Traditionally, this arrogance does not merely extend to cattle: agriculturist and fish-eating peoples are scorned, while Europeans' uptight style of clothing earned them the Maasai name Iloredaa Enjekat – Fart Smotherers! Today, the Maasai co-exist peacefully with their non-Maasai compatriots, but while their tolerance for their neighbours' idiosyncrasies has increased in recent decades, they show little interest in changing their own lifestyle.

The Maasai measure a man's wealth in terms of cattle and children rather than money – a herd of about 50 cattle is respectable, the more children the better, and from Arusha, the 140km drive takes about two hours. There is plenty of **public transport**: minibus-taxis depart from Arusha throughout the day and cost around US$5, while the best of several slightly cheaper bus services is probably Dar Express, which leaves Arusha from the new bus terminus a few hundred metres west of the central bus station (see *Chapter 5, Arusha*, page 101).

a man who has plenty of one but not the other is regarded as poor. Traditionally, the Maasai will not hunt or eat vegetable matter or fish, but feed almost exclusively off their cattle. The main diet is a blend of cow's milk and blood, the latter drained – it is said painlessly – from a strategic nick in the animal's jugular vein. Because the cows are more valuable to them alive than dead, they are generally slaughtered only on special occasions. Meat and milk are never eaten on the same day, because it is insulting to the cattle to feed off the living and the dead at the same time. Despite the apparent hardship of their chosen lifestyle, many Maasai are wealthy by any standards. On one safari, our driver pointed out a not unusually large herd of cattle that would fetch the market equivalent of three new Land Rovers.

The central unit of Maasai society is the age-set. Every 15 years or so, a new and individually named generation of warriors or Ilmoran will be initiated, consisting of all the young men who have reached puberty and are not part of a previous age-set – most boys aged between 12 and 25. Every boy must undergo the Emorata (circumcision ceremony) before he is accepted as a warrior. If he cries out during the five-minute operation, which is performed without any anaesthetic, the post-circumcision ceremony will be cancelled, the parents spat on for raising a coward, and the initiate taunted by his peers for several years before he is forgiven. When a new generation of warriors is initiated, the existing Ilmoran graduate to become junior elders, who are responsible for all political and legislative decisions until they in turn graduate to become senior elders. All political decisions are made democratically, and the role of the chief elder or Laibon is essentially that of a spiritual and moral leader.

Maasai girls are permitted to marry as soon as they have been initiated, but warriors must wait until their age-set has graduated to elder status, which will be 15 years later, when a fresh warrior age-set has been initiated. This arrangement ties in with the polygamous nature of Maasai society: in days past, most elders would typically have acquired between three and ten wives by the time they reached old age. Marriages are generally arranged, sometimes even before the female party is born, as a man may 'book' the next daughter produced by a friend to be his son's wife. Marriage is evidently viewed as a straightforward, child-producing business arrangement: it is normal for married men and women to have sleeping partners other than their spouse, provided that those partners are of an appropriate age-set. Should a woman become pregnant by another lover, the prestige attached to having many children outweighs any minor concerns about infidelity, and the husband will still bring up the child as his own. By contrast, although sex before marriage is condoned, an unmarried girl who falls pregnant brings disgrace on her family, and in former times would have been fed to the hyenas.

For further details about Maasai society and beliefs, get hold of the coffee-table book *Maasai*, by the photographer Carol Beckwith and Maasai historian Tepilit Ole Saitoti (Harry N Abrams, New York, reprinted 1993).

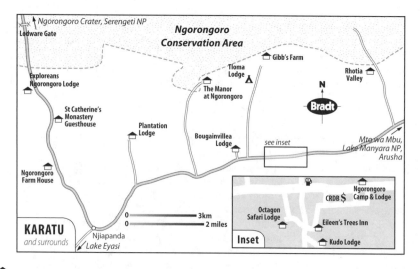

Ngorongoro Conservation Area

Ngorongoro Crater, Serengeti NP
Lodware Gate

Gibb's Farm

Tloma Lodge

Rhotia Valley

Exploreans Ngorongoro Lodge

The Manor at Ngorongoro

N
Bradt

St Catherine's Monastery Guesthouse

Plantation Lodge

Bougainvillea Lodge

see inset

Mto wa Mbu, Lake Manyara NP, Arusha

Ngorongoro Farm House

0 — 3km
0 — 2 miles

KARATU *and surrounds*
Njiapanda
Lake Eyasi

Inset

CRDB $

Ngorongoro Camp & Lodge

Octagon Safari Lodge

Eileen's Trees Inn

Kudo Lodge

WHERE TO STAY The choice of accommodation in and around Karatu is enormous. It includes several upmarket lodges dotted around the slopes west of town, some of which actually border the NCA, along with a number of more moderate options within the town itself. In all cases, the lodges' *raison d'être* is as a base for day trips to the popular Ngorongoro Crater, and to supplement the limited accommodation within the NCA. In most cases, the lodges around Karatu are inherently better value than their counterparts within the NCA, and they tend to have greater room availability in high seasons. The negative is that they lack the spectacular views and sense of immediacy associated with sleeping on the crater rim, while entrance gate opening times preclude their guests from getting the early start required to make the best of the crater.

Exclusive

The Manor at Ngorongoro (20 rooms) 027 254 0630/9; e info@elewana.com, videar@ elewana.com; www.elewana.com. Boasting a magnificent hilltop setting on a coffee estate running along the forested border of the NCA, this handsome new lodge with its whitewashed exteriors, tall gables, slate tiled roofs & neatly tended gardens is architecturally reminiscent of the Cape Dutch style associated with the wine estates of South Africa. Though purpose built, the main building, comprising several dining & sitting areas, recalls a 19th-century manor house, with hardwood floors, muted period décor & furnishings, & a wide shaded balcony. Accommodation is in semi-detached cottages, each containing 2 large split-level open-plan suites with king-size or twin beds, a comfortable sitting area, fireplace, large windows, & a en-suite bathroom with old fashioned tub & shower. Excellent service & top quality food makes this

one of the top picks in the Ngorongoro area. *US$1,067/1,490 sgl/dbl FB inc most drinks, & laundry. Seasonal discounts available Mar–May, Nov & early Dec. Full game package inc game drives an additional US$100 pp.*

Gibb's Farm (22 rooms) 027 253 4397; e reservations@gibbsfarm.net; www.gibbsfarm. net. This long-serving hotel, set on a family-run farm on the eastern border of the NCA, was transformed into one of Tanzania's most sumptuously exclusive boutique lodges by radical renovations in 2008. Situated 6km from Karatu along a rough dirt road, it lies on an active coffee estate bordering an extensive patch of indigenous forest on the Ngorongoro footslopes. The main building, a converted 1920s farmhouse, retains a strong period feel with its red polished cement floor, tall bay windows, hearty home-style 4-course meals, & leather & wood furnishing, & its colonial ambience is far removed from the relative uniformity that characterises so many upmarket lodges in northern Tanzania. The exquisite guest cottages combine a more contemporary feel with farmhouse rusticity, & are seriously spacious, with 2 dbl beds in each bedroom, varnished wood floors, comfy armchairs, lovely views from the balcony, & the choice of indoor or outdoor shower. Activities include bird walks with the resident naturalist, cultural & farm excursions, a 2hr hike to a waterfall & cave made by elephants on the forested slopes of the crater, & a massage room & spa (traditional Maasai treatments from a Maasai elder). There is no TV or swimming pool. *US$535/762 sgl/dbl FB.*

🏠 **Exploreans Ngorongoro Lodge** (20 rooms) m 0736 502496; e info.ngoro@exploreans.com; www.exploreans.com. Opened in Jun 2012, this plush, new all-suite lodge literally borders the NCA & lies only 2km by road from the Lodware Entrance Gate. Accommodation is in spacious, airy & uncluttered standalone cottages with makuti thatch roof, wooden floor, lounge with fireplace & stylish hardwood furniture, large bedroom with king-size or twin 3/4 beds in a walk-in net, spacious private balcony with forest view, Wi-Fi, safe, minibar & en-suite bathroom with tub or shower. Facilities include a good à la carte restaurant, a large swimming pool with a great view, & a spa. Service is superb. Although part of the Italian Planhotel Group, it doesn't feel like a chain hotel in the slightest. *From around US$470/690 sgl/dbl all inc. Check the website for low season & late booking specials.*

Upmarket

🏠 **Plantation Lodge** (16 rooms) ☎ 027 253 4405; m 0784 260799; e info@plantation-lodge. com; www.plantation-lodge.com. This popular German-owned lodge is set in flowering grounds only 2km from the Ngorongoro road & a few kilometres out of Karatu. It has a classic whitewash & thatch exterior, complemented by the stylish décor of the spacious self-contained rooms, making for a refreshingly individualistic contrast to the chain lodges that characterise the northern circuit, while also forming a good base for day trips to Ngorongoro Crater. *From US$255/380 sgl/dbl FB.*

🏠 **Ngorongoro Farm House** (50 rooms) m 0767 333223/0784 207727; e reservations@ tanganyikawildernesscamps.com; www. tanganyikawildernesscamps.com. Situated on a large coffee farm about halfway between Karatu &

the NCA, this stylish lodge offers luxurious en-suite accommodation in 3 separate camps of large semi-detached thatched cottages with views across what may one day be a 9-hole golf course to the forested slopes of Ngorongoro. There's a very pleasant swimming pool area & the restaurant serves good country-style cooking. In terms of location, it doesn't quite match up to the lodges on the crater rim, but it's much smaller & has a less packaged feel than most lodges set within the NCA. Guided nature walks, mountain biking & other leg-stretching activities are on offer, too. *US$230/335 sgl/dbl FB. Substantial discounts Apr & May.*

🏠 **Tloma Lodge** (34 rooms) m 0767 333223/0784 207727; e reservations@ tanganyikawildernesscamps.com; www. tanganyikawildernesscamps.com. Situated about 1km from Gibb's Farm & sharing a similarly lovely view over the forested Ngorongoro footslopes, this attractive lodge is set in spacious grounds that lead down to a wooden deck enclosing a large swimming pool. Accommodation is in large, cosy earth-coloured cottages with colonial-style green corrugated iron roofs, screed floors, wood ceilings, fireplaces, 4-poster king-size or twin beds, & a large bathroom with shower. The food is excellent, & facilities include birdwatching tours, massage, village walks, internet, coffee plantation demonstrations & the obligatory day tours to Ngorongoro Crater. *US$230/335 sgl/dbl FB. Substantial discounts Apr & May.*

🏠 **Rhotia Valley Tented Lodge** (15 tents) m 0784 446579; e rhotiavalley@gmail.com; www.rhotiavalley.com. This low-key hilltop lodge abuts the NCA, but lies 30–45 mins' drive away from the Lodware Entrance Gate, since the clearly signposted 10km access road is actually on the Mto Wa Mbu side of Karatu. A significant portion of proceeds go to support the affiliated Rhotia Valley Children's Home, a Dutch-run NGO set on the same property. Accommodation is in comfortable en-suite standing tents, & the home-cooked meals, made largely from organic ingredients grown on site, are a treat. Several nature trails run through the scenic property. *From US$180/300 sgl/dbl FB.*

Moderate

🏠 **Bougainvillea Lodge** (24 rooms) ☎ 027 253 4083; e bougainvillea@habari.co.tz; www. bougainvillealodge.net. This small lodge lies in large but characterless gardens about 300m from the main road towards NCA just outside Karatu. For budget-conscious tourists it's a decent compromise between quality & cost, offering unpretentious accommodation in neat & comfortably decorated tiled cottages set in a circle around the swimming pool area. All cottages have twin or king-size beds with netting, a fan, a fireplace, a sitting area with cane furniture & a private balcony facing the pool. The lodge serves good meals & has a gift shop specialising in local Iraqw beadwork, & it's a useful base for excursions to Eyasi & Ngorongoro. Good value. *US$120/230 sgl/dbl FB.*

⌂ **Octagon Lodge** (15 rooms) m 0787 858485/0784 650324; e sales@ octagonlodge.com, octagonlodgetz@gmail. com; www.octagonlodge.com; see also advert on page 287. Set in compact green gardens in the backstreets of Karatu close to Eileen's, this is another modest & reasonably priced set-up

offering en-suite accommodation in airy wooden cottages with queen-size or twin beds, walk-in nets, colourful but earthy décor & private balcony. Buffet style meals are served & the characterful 'Irish Bar' actually has more of an African feel with its thatched roof. Good value, especially for singles. *US$87 pp FB.*

⌂ **Eileen's Trees Inn** (9 rooms) m 0732 971949/0783 379526/0785 186572; e eafocus@ habari.co.tz; www.eileenstrees.com. This appealing owner-managed lodge is 500m from the main road through Karatu, in quiet leafy grounds that feature an inviting swimming pool & a homely stilted restaurant/bar with wooden floor & makuti roof. The large rooms are stylishly decorated & come with king-size or 2 3/4 beds, en-suite hot shower & private balcony. Probably the best value in town. *US$85/120 sgl/dbl FB. Substantial discounts Apr–Jun, cheaper resident rates.*

NGORONGORO ENTRANCE FEES

The entrance fee to NCA, currently US$50 per person per 24 hours for non-residents (but likely to increase during the lifespan of this edition), is payable by all who enter the conservation area, even if they are only in transit to or from Serengeti National Park. A vehicle fee of Tsh10,000 (around US$7) per 24 hours is also payable for all Tanzanian-registered vehicles (as well as privately registered vehicles from elsewhere in East Africa) with a tare weight up to 2,000kg. Foreign-registered vehicles with a similar tare weight pay US$40 per 24 hours. Heavier vehicles pay more, as detailed on the website www.ngorongorocrater.org.

The above fees cover entry to the NCA but not to the Ngorongoro Crater, which attracts an additional Crater Service Fee (CSF) of US$200 per vehicle for each and every game drive there. At one point, the authorities threatened to impose a six-hour limit on visits to the crater. This ruling has never been implemented, but it is sometimes quoted by budget operators as a pretext to limit game drives to six hours and save on fuel costs.

Visitors on organised safaris will almost invariably find that the NCA fees are included in the price, and won't have to concern themselves with the logistics of payment. However, self-drive or other independent travellers, who will need to deal with it themselves, should – at the time of writing – be prepared for several complications.

Primary among these is that neither credit cards nor travellers' cheques nor cash in any currency are accepted at any entrance gate. Instead, fees must be paid in advance (with US dollars cash or a Visa or MasterCard) at a branch of Barclays Bank (represented in Arusha and Mwanza) or the CRDB (in both these towns as well as Karatu). The bank will then issue a receipt for presentation at the entrance gate, where the sum paid will be loaded on to a temporary NCA smartcard. This smartcard is then swiped through a machine upon entering or exiting the conservation area (at Lodware Gate in the east or Naabi Hill Gate in the west) until the funds are depleted, after which it will be reclaimed by the NCA authorities.

Budget and camping

⌂ **Ngorongoro Camp & Lodge** (31 rooms)
☏ 025 253 4287. This well-established but utterly characterless complex in Karatu offers accommodation in comfortable self-contained rooms, as well as camping in a neat well-maintained site. The attached supermarket, though not cheap, is the best in Karatu, & the restaurant serves a good range of tasty Indian & continental dishes. Other facilities include 4x4 rental, heated swimming pool, internet café, filling station & a large bar with satellite TV. A good set up, though perhaps a little overpriced for what it is. *US$87/140 sgl/dbl B&B; camping US$10 pp.*

⌂ **St Catherine's Monastery Guesthouse**
(15 rooms) m 0784 372808/0753 497886;
e stelamatutina2002@yahoo.com; www.
safaringorongoro.com/inglese/convent.html.
Situated 5 mins from the Lodware Gate alongside the road running back to Karatu, this Benedictine monastery run by Italian- and English-speaking nuns has 15 spacious en-suite rooms with hot showers. Lunch & dinner with a strong Italian influence served by arrangement. *US$40/50 sgl/dbl B&B.*

NGORONGORO CONSERVATION AREA

An eastern annex to Serengeti National Park, the 8,292km² Ngorongoro Conservation Area (NCA) is named after Ngorongoro Crater, the world's largest intact volcanic caldera, and a shoo-in contender for any global shortlist of natural wonders – not only for its inherent geological magnificence, but also because its

This byzantine system enforces independent visitors to calculate their exact fee requirements in advance, eliminating any possibility of spontaneous plan changes once past Karatu. It is vital to get the sums right, as entry will be refused unless sufficient funds are loaded, but unused money is not refunded. So, in addition to individual and vehicle entrance fees and the CSF mentioned opposite, you will need to add on any camping fees (*US$30 pp per night*) as well as guide fees (*US$20 per party for any walking safaris, inc a visit to Empakaai Crater*).

Furthermore, if the plan is to enter the NCA from the east, cross the Serengeti at Naabi Hill, and then travel back through the NCA on your return leg to Arusha, you must allow for this second transit in your calculations (otherwise you risk being turned away at Naabi Hill Gate and having to drive all the way back to Mwanza). And it is imperative that you swipe your NCA smartcard when you exit the conservation area, otherwise the system will continue to deduct fees while you are in the Serengeti, depleting your funds before you return.

Another potential complication is that the CRDB and Barclays only operate during normal banking hours (⊕ *08.00–15.00 Mon–Fri, 09.00–12.00 Sat*), which means that fees cannot be paid in the late afternoon or on Sundays or public holidays. Also, be aware that the CSF can be processed against your smartcard only at Lodware Gate during opening hours (⊕ *06.00–18.00*) or at the administrative headquarters near Ngorongoro Crater Lodge during office hours (⊕ *08.00–16.00*). If you try to descend into the crater without a permit issued at one of the above offices, you will simply be turned back at the entry barrier. And if you plan on an early morning start, it's best to sort out your CSF the afternoon before you want to enter the crater.

On a discordantly simple note, neither credit cards nor NCA smartcards can be used to pay the entrance fee for Oldupai Gorge, currently set at Tsh 27,000 (about US$16). This fee is payable in cash only, at the museum.

12

verdant floor serves as a quite extraordinary natural sanctuary for some of Africa's densest large mammal populations. The rest of the NCA can be divided into two broad ecological zones. In the east lie the Crater Highlands, a sprawling volcanic massif studded with craggy peaks (notably the 3,648m-high Lolmalasin, the third-highest mountain in Tanzania after Kilimanjaro and Meru) and more than a dozen calderas, among them Ngorongoro itself. By contrast, the sparsely wooded western plains of the NCA are essentially a continuation of the Serengeti ecosystem, supporting a cover of short grass that attracts immense concentrations of grazers during the rainy season.

Coming from the direction of Arusha, the road ascent of Ngorongoro Crater is a sensational scene setter, switchbacking through densely forested slopes to Heroes Point, where most visitors will catch their first breathtaking view from the rim to the 260km² crater floor 600m below. Even at this distance, it is often possible to pick out hundred- or even thousand-strong ant-like formations foraging across the crater floor – in fact, herds of wildebeest, zebra and buffalo – and with binoculars you might even see some of the elephants that haunt the fringes of Lerai Forest. The drive along the crater rim to your lodge will be equally riveting: patches of forest interspersed with sweeping views back across to patchwork of farmland around Karatu, and the possibility of encountering buffalo, zebra, bushbuck, elephant and even the occasional leopard.

The Ngorongoro Crater is the main focal point of tourist activity in the NCA but those who have the time can explore any number of less publicised natural features further afield. Oldupai Gorge, for instance, is the site of some of Africa's most important hominid fossil finds, and can easily be visited *en route* from the crater rim to the Serengeti. Other highlights include the Empakaai Crater and (to a lesser extent) Olmoti Crater in the northern NCA, while the crater rim is highly rewarding for montane forest birds.

The official NCA website www.ngorongorocrater.org is a useful source of up-to-date information. Also worthwhile, the 84-page booklet *Ngorongoro Conservation Area*, similar in style to the national park booklets, is readily available in Arusha and has good information on the crater and Oldupai Gorge. For a more detailed overview of the NCA, Veronica Roodt's excellent *Tourist Travel & Field Guide to the Ngorongoro Conservation Area* is widely available at hotel gift shops and craft shops in Arusha and elsewhere in northern Tanzania.

The fee situation with NCA is rather complicated; see box *Ngorongoro Entrance Fees*, page 274. Note, too, that the crater rim gets very cold at night, and is often blanketed in mist in the early morning, so you will need a jumper or two, and possibly a windbreaker if you are camping.

GETTING THERE AND AWAY The road from Arusha to Lodware, the only entrance gate along the eastern border of the NCA, runs via Makuyuni, Mto wa Mbu and Karatu. The road can comfortably be covered in less than three hours, with another 30–60 minutes required to get from Lodware Gate to any of the lodges on the crater rim. All roads within the NCA are unsurfaced, and a decent **4x4** is required to reach the crater floor. Most tourists visit Ngorongoro as part of a longer safari, but those with time or budgetary restrictions could think about visiting the crater as a self-contained one-night safari out of Arusha.

⌂ **WHERE TO STAY AND EAT** No accommodation or camping facilities exist within Ngorongoro Crater, but a handful of upmarket lodges and camps are perched on the rim, most offering superb views to the crater floor, as does the public campsite

With an altitudinal span of 1,230m to 3,648m, the NCA is among the most geologically spectacular reserves in Africa, comprising flat short-grass plains in the southwest and low rocky mountains in the northwest, while the west is dominated by the so-called Crater Highlands, a tall breezy plateau studded with standalone mountains. The mountains of the NCA date from two periods. The Gol Range, to the north of the main road to the Serengeti, is an exposed granite block that formed some 500 million years ago. Somewhat less antiquated, at least in geological terms, the Crater Highlands and associated free-standing mountains of the eastern NCA are volcanic in origin, their formation linked to the same fracturing process that created the Rift Valley 15–20 million years ago.

Ngorongoro Crater itself is the relic of an immense volcanic mountain that attained a similar height to that of Kilimanjaro before it imploded violently some two to three million years ago. It is the world's sixth-largest caldera, and the largest with an unbroken wall. Eight smaller craters in the NCA, most notably Olmoti and Empakaai, are the product of similar eruptions. The Crater Highlands are no longer volcanically active, but the free-standing Ol Doinyo Lengai immediately northeast of the main highland block is among the world's most active volcanoes, having last erupted between 2007 and 2008.

Based on fossil evidence unearthed at Oldupai Gorge in the western NCA, it is known that various species of hominid have occupied this area for at least three million years. It was the domain of hunter-gatherers until a few thousand years ago, when pastoralists moved in. The fate of these early pastoralists is unknown, because a succession of immigrants replaced them: the ancestors of the Cushitic-speaking Mbulu some 2,000 years ago and those of the Nilotic-speaking Datoga about 300 years ago. A century later the militaristic Maasai drove both of these groups out of what is now the NCA: the Datoga to the Eyasi Basin and the Mbulu to the highlands near Manyara. Most place names in the area are Maasai, and although several explanations for the name Ngorongoro are floating around, the most credible is that it is named after a type of Maasai bowl.

Europeans settled in the NCA around the turn of the 20th century. Two German brothers farmed on the crater floor until the outbreak of World War I. One of their old farmhouses is still used by researchers, and a few sisal plants dating to this time can be seen in the northeast of the crater. Tourism began in the 1930s when the original Ngorongoro Crater Lodge was built on the crater rim. The NCA formed part of the original Serengeti National Park as gazetted in 1951, but Maasai protests at being denied access to such a huge tract of their grazing land led to it being split off from the national park in 1959 and downgraded to a multi-use conservation area. The NCA was inscribed as a UNESCO World Heritage Site in 1979, and two years later it was declared an International Biosphere Reserve, together with the neighbouring Serengeti.

there. The crater is often visited as a day trip from one of the lodges in and around Karatu (see *Karatu, Where to stay*, page 272), but staying outside the NCA does mean you miss out on the stirring view over the crater at dusk, and the possibility of a dawn game drive on the crater floor. The anomalous Ndutu Lodge, though set inside the western border of the NCA, is not a realistic base from which to explore

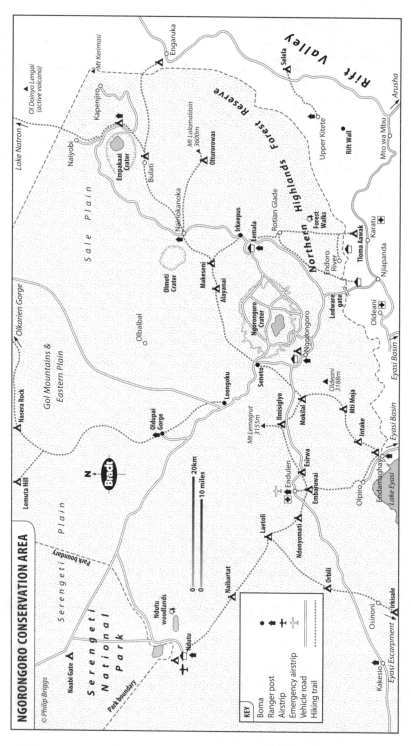

NGORONGORO CONSERVATION AREA

KEY

- Boma
- Ranger post
- Airstrip
- Emergency airstrip
- Vehicle road
- Hiking trail

© Philip Briggs

Rift Valley

Northern Highlands Forest Reserve

Gol Mountains & Eastern Plain

Serengeti Plain

Serengeti National Park

Sale Plain

Ol Doinyo Lengai (active volcano)
Lake Natron
Mt Kerimasi
Engaruka
Kapenjiro
Naiyobi
Empakaai Crater
Bulati
Mt Lolomalasin 3600m
Olturorowas
Nairokanoka
Irkeepus
Lemala
Rotian Glade
Selela
Upper Kitete
Rift Wall
Mto wa Mbu
Arusha
Olkarien Gorge
Nasera Rock
Olmoti Crater
Makeseni
Alayanai
Olbalbal
Ngorongoro Crater
Endoro River
Forest Walks
Tloma Aawak
Karatu
Njapanda
Oldeani
Eyasi Basin
Lemuta Hill
Oltupai Gorge
Loongoku
Seneto
Mt Lemagrut 3155m
Ilmisigiyo
Ngongoro
Oldeani 3188m
Mokilai
Mti Moja
Intake
Eyasi Basin
Naibartat
Laetoli
Ndonyomati
Endulen
Esirwa
Embartuwai
Olpiro
Orbili
Endamaghay
Lake Eyasi
Osinoni
Kakesio
Eyasi Escarpment
Inkisale
Eyasi Basin
Ndutu woodlands
Ndutu
Naabi Gate
Park boundary
Lodware gate

N

Bradt

0   10 miles
0   20km

Ngorongoro Crater, so it is covered in the chapter on the Serengeti, to which it has closer ecological affiliations.

Exclusive

⌂ &Beyond Ngorongoro Crater Lodge

(40 rooms) ☎ (South Africa) +27 (0)11 809 4441; e safaris@andbeyond.com; www. ngorongorocrater.com. This unique top-of-the-range lodge, which started life in 1934 as a private hunting lodge with a commanding view over the crater, was converted to a hotel shortly after independence in 1961. Acquired & rebuilt from scratch by &Beyond in 1995, it is a truly fantastic & architecturally innovative creation that largely lives up to its billing as 'the finest safari lodge in Africa'. Each individual suite consists of 2 adjoining round structures that resemble oversized Maasai huts, but are distorted in an almost Dadaist style. The large interiors combine elements of baroque, classical, African & colonial décor to create an effect as ostentatious as it is eclectic. As might be expected of such a trend-flaunting lodge, it does divide opinion (the defiantly non-'bush' atmosphere often irks safari purists, though to be fair a traditional tented camp would be a seriously chilly prospect at this sort of altitude) but it is difficult to fault in terms of ambition & originality. For all its architectural flourishes the lodge literally never loses sight of its spectacular location – it is designed in such a way that the crater is almost constantly in sight, & even the baths & the toilets have a view. Likewise, the in-house guides are immensely experienced & knowledgeable both about the crater & wildlife in general. The food is world-class, too – from the sumptuous packed b/fasts taken on early morning drives into the crater to the mouth-watering homemade chocolate in the room – as is the butler service & overall ambience. *US$1,550 pp, dropping to US$1,000 Mar–May; rate inc all meals, most drinks & game drives. No sgl supplement.*

⌂ Lemala Camp

(9 tents) ☎ 027 254 8966; e res@lemalacamp.com; www.lemalacamp. com. Opened in Dec 2007, this is the only semi-permanent luxury tented camp on the crater rim, situated in a wonderful stand of lichen-stained flat-topped red-thorn acacias immediately inside the Lemala Gate (the start of the same road used to descend into & ascend from the crater rim from Ngorongoro Sopa Lodge). The views from the camp are great, it has an outdoor atmosphere lacking from all other camps on the rim, & it also has a peerless location for early-morning game drives into the crater itself. The tents are very spacious & decorated in classic safari style, with a wooden floor & canvas top, & all have twin or king-size beds, solar powered lighting & hot water. It's not cheap, but must rank as the 1st choice of accommodation for anybody seeking to experience Ngorongoro in a real bush atmosphere. *US$1,324/1,480 sgl/dbl FB. Low season discounts Mar, Jun, Nov & early Dec. Closed Apr–May.*

Upmarket

⌂ Ngorongoro Serena Safari Lodge

(75 rooms) ☎ 027 254 5555; e reservations@serena.co.tz; www.serenahotels.com. Meeting the usual high Serena standards, this is arguably the pick of the more conventional lodges on the crater rim, receiving consistent praise from tourists & from within the safari industry. It lies on the western crater rim along the road towards Seronera, several kilometres past the park headquarters & Crater Lodge. It is the closest of the lodges to the main descent road into the crater, a decided advantage for those who want to get to the crater floor as early as possible. The setting is a secluded wooded valley rustling with birdlife & offering a good view over the crater. Serena Active, which operates out of the lodge, offers a good range of afternoon & full-day walks ranging from a gentle stroll through the grassy highlands to a rather more challenging ascent of Olmoti Crater. The facilities, food & service are all of a high standard, & rooms are centrally heated. *US$375/615 sgl/dbl FB. Low season discounts Mar–May, Nov & early Dec.*

⌂ Ngorongoro Sopa Lodge

(96 rooms) ☎ 027 250 0630–9; e info@sopalodges.com; www. sopalodges.com. Situated on the forested eastern edge of the crater rim some 20km distant from the headquarters & main cluster of lodges, this attractive modern hotel is similar in standard to the Serena & arguably nudges ahead of it on the basis of location. Accommodation is in vast semi-detached suites, each with 2 double beds, a heater, a large bathroom, a fridge, & a wide bay window facing the crater & Ol Mokarot Mountain. There is a swimming pool in front of the bar, & the food & service are

excellent. One thing that stands out about this lodge is the large, forested grounds, a good place to look for characteristic montane forest birds, with sunbirds (tacazze, golden-winged & eastern double-collared) well represented & a variety of weavers, seedeaters & robins present. Another is that it lies close to what, in effect, is a private road that can be used both to ascend from & descend into the crater, which greatly reduces the driving time either side of game drives – particularly useful for an early morning start. *US$ 330/580 sgl/dbl FB; US$280/480 in Mar, Nov & early Dec; US$115/225 Apr–May.*

⌂ **Ngorongoro Wildlife Lodge** (72 rooms) \027 254 4595; e res@hotelsandlodges-tanzania. com; www.hotelsandlodges-tanzania.com. Situated roughly 2km away from &Beyond Ngorongoro Crater Lodge, this former government hotel is one of the oldest on the crater rim & it shows its antiquity in the rather monolithic architecture. Despite a minor facelift following privatisation in 2008, the décor, service & food remain a little substandard. This is compensated for by the finest location of all the crater rim lodges, directly above the yellow fevers of Lerai Forest. Rooms are comfortably functional, with piping hot baths & windows facing the crater. The grounds support a fair range of forest birds. *US$340/460 FB.*

Moderate

⌂ **Rhino Lodge** (24 rooms) m 0762 359055; e rhino@ngorongoro.cc; www.ngorongoro.cc.

Formerly the home of the first conservator of NCA & later managed as a guesthouse by the conservation authorities, this modest low-rise lodge had been closed for the best part of a decade prior to being leased to the Dar es Salaam-based operator Coastal Aviation, who undertook extensive renovations prior to reopening it in 2007. It is far & away the most affordable lodge on the crater rim, & though it lacks a direct crater view, the surrounding mist-swathed forest has a charm of its own, & the location is very convenient for game drives. Accommodation is in simple but comfortable ground-floor rooms with twin or dbl beds & en-suite hot shower, & rates include good buffet meals in the cosy dining room, which comes complete with log fire. Superb value. *US$135/240 sgl/dbl FB.*

Camping

⋏ Simba Campsite Situated about 2km from the park headquarters, this is the only place where you can pitch a tent on the crater rim, & it's hardly great value given that facilities are limited to basic latrines, cold showers & a rubbish pit. Still, the wonderful view makes it a preferable option to camping in Karatu, assuming you place a greater priority on the experience than creature comforts. The village near the headquarters has a few basic bars & shops, & there is nothing preventing you from dropping into nearby Ngorongoro Wildlife Lodge for a drink or snack. *US$30 pp.*

WHAT TO SEE AND DO

Ngorongoro Crater Floor The opportunity of spending a day on the crater floor is simply not to be missed. There are few places where you can so reliably see such large concentrations of wildlife all year round, and your game viewing (and photography) will only be enhanced by the striking backdrop of the 600m-high crater wall. The crater is also excellent Big Five territory: lion, elephant and buffalo are all but guaranteed, rhino are regularly seen, and a leopard is chanced upon from time to time. The official road down to the crater descends from Malanja Depression to the western shore of Lake Magadi, while the official road up starts near Lerai Forest and reaches the rim on the stretch of road between Wildlife and Crater lodges. There is a third road into the crater, which starts near the Sopa Lodge, and this can be used either to ascend or to descend.

There are several notable physical features within the crater. **Lerai Forest** consists almost entirely of yellow fever trees, large acacias noted for their jaundiced bark (it was once thought that this tree, which is often associated with marsh and lake fringes, the breeding ground for mosquitoes, was the cause of yellow fever and malaria). To the north of this forest, **Lake Magadi** is a shallow soda lake that varies greatly in extent depending on the season. Standing close to the lakeshore is a cluster of **burial cairns** that show some similarities with the tombs at the Engaruka

Ruins further east, and are presumably a relic of the Datoga occupation of the crater prior to the arrival of the Maasai. To the south and east of this, the **Gorigor Swamp** also varies in extent seasonally, but it generally supports some water. There is a permanent hippo pool at the **Ngoitokitok Springs** at the eastern end of the swamp. The northern half of the crater is generally drier, though it is bisected by the **Munge River**, which is lined by thickets and forms a seasonally substantial area of swamp to the immediate north of Lake Magadi.

The open grassland that covers most of the crater floor supports large concentrations of wildebeest and zebra (the population of these species is estimated at 10,000 and 5,000 respectively), and smaller numbers of buffalo, tsessebe, and Thomson's and Grant's gazelle. The vicinity of Lerai Forest is the best area in which to see waterbuck, bushbuck and eland. The forest and adjoining Gorigor Swamp are the main haunt of the crater's elephant population, which typically stands at around 70. All the elephants resident in the crater are old males (although females and families sometimes pass through the area), and you stand a good chance of seeing big tuskers of the sort that have been poached away elsewhere in East Africa. Two curious absentees from the crater floor are impala and giraffe, both of which are common in the surrounding plains. Some researchers attribute the absence of giraffe to a lack of suitable browsing fodder, others to their presumed inability to descend the steep crater walls. Quite why there are no impala in the crater is a mystery.

The crater floor reputedly supports the densest concentration of predators in Africa. The resident lion population has fluctuated greatly ever since records were maintained, partly as a result of migration in and out of the crater, but primarily because of the vulnerability of the concentrated and rather closed population to epidemics. Over the course of 1962, the lion population dropped from an estimated 90 to about 15 due to an outbreak of disease spread by biting flies, but it had recovered to about 70 within a decade. In recent years, the pattern of fluctuation saw the population estimated at 80 in 1995, 35 in 1998, and 55 divided into four main prides and a few nomadic males in 2000. The crater's lions might be encountered just about anywhere, and are generally very relaxed around vehicles. The most populous large predator is the spotted hyena, the population of which is estimated at around 400. You won't spend long in the crater without seeing a hyena: they often rest up on the eastern shore of Lake Magadi during the day, sometimes trying – and mostly failing – to sneak up on the flamingos in the hope of a quick snack.

In the 1990s, no cheetahs were resident within the crater, surprising given that the open grassland is textbook cheetah habitat but probably due to the high density of competing predators. However, two different female cheetahs colonised the crater floor in 2000, and a small population has been present – and regularly sighted – ever since. Leopards are resident, particularly in swampy areas, but they are not often seen. Other common predators are the golden and black-backed jackals, with the former being more frequently encountered due to its relatively diurnal habits.

The crater floor offers some great birding. Lake Magadi normally harbours large flocks of flamingo, giving its edges a pinkish tinge when seen from a distance. The pools at the **Mandusi Swamp** can be excellent for water birds, with all manner of waders, storks, ducks and herons present. The grassland is a good place to see a number of striking ground birds. One very common resident is the kori bustard, reputedly the world's heaviest flying bird, and spectacular if you catch it during a mating dance. Ostrich are also common, along with the gorgeously garish crowned crane, and (in the rainy season) huge flocks of migrant storks. Less prominent, but common, and of great interest to more dedicated birders, is the lovely rosy-throated

12

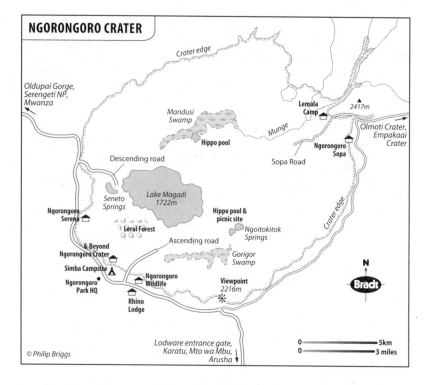

NGORONGORO CRATER

Crater edge

Oldupai Gorge,
Serengeti NP,
Mwanza

Mandusi
Swamp

Hippo pool

Lemala
Camp

2417m

Munge

Olmoti Crater,
Empakaai
Crater

Ngorongoro
Sopa

Sopa Road

Descending road

Seneto
Springs

Lake Magadi
1722m

Ngorongoro
Serena

Lerai Forest

Hippo pool &
picnic site

Ngoitokitok
Springs

Ascending road

Gorigor
Swamp

Crater edge

N

Bradt

& Beyond
Ngorongoro Crater

Simba Campsite

Ngorongoro
Park HQ

Ngorongoro
Wildlife

Viewpoint
2216m

Rhino
Lodge

© Philip Briggs

Lodware entrance gate,
Karatu, Mto wa Mbu,
Arusha ▼

0 ——— 5km
0 ——— 3 miles

longclaw. Two of the most striking and visible birds of prey are the augur buzzard, sometimes seen here in its unusual melanistic form, and the foppish long-crested eagle. The localised Egyptian vulture – whose ability to crack open ostrich eggs by holding a stone in its beak makes it the only bird that arguably uses tools – is sometimes seen in the vicinity of Mungu Stream.

There are a few hippo pools in the crater, but the one most often visited is Ngoitokitok Springs, a popular picnic spot where lunch is enlivened by a flock of black kites that have become adept at swooping down on tourists and snatching the food from their hands.

The authorities rigidly forbid tourists from entering the crater before 07.00, and they must be out of the crater before 18.00. This is a frustrating ruling for photographers, since it means that you miss out on the best light of the day, and it has encouraged a situation where most safari drivers suggest that their clients take breakfast before going on a game drive, and carry a picnic lunch. This programme is difficult to avoid on a group safari, but for those on a private safari it is well worth getting down to the crater as early as permitted. Photography aside, this is the one time of the day when you might have the crater to yourself, the one time, in other words, when you can really experience the Ngorongoro Crater of television documentary land. Note that it is forbidden to descend to the floor after 16.00, and that a 'crater service fee' of US$200 per vehicle is payable every time you enter the crater.

Empakaai and Olmoti craters The NCA also protects two major craters other than Ngorongoro, both relics of the volcanic activity that shaped the Crater Highlands over the past ten million years or so. These are the Empakaai and

Olmoti craters, and while both are dwarfed in size and reputation by the peerless Ngorongoro, they are also well worth a visit, offering a welcome opportunity to break the typical safari regime of twice-daily game drives with a stiff steep walk in lovely mountain scenery. Furthermore, the view from the rim of Empakaai has to rank among the most spectacular in East Africa.

The most alluring of the two craters is Empakaai, which is around 540m deep and has a diameter of almost 8km. The crater floor, enclosed by sheer forested cliffs, supports a sparkling soda lake that covers about half of its area and has a depth of

NOT A ZOO

You won't spend long in northern Tanzania before you hear somebody complain that Ngorongoro Crater is 'like a zoo'. It's a common allegation, but one as facile as it is nonsensical. The defining quality of a typical zoo is surely its total artificiality: the captive inmates have been placed there by people largely for entertainment, a high proportion are exotic to the zoo's location, they are invariably confined within enclosures of some sort (with different species, particularly predator and prey, normally kept apart), and most are fed manually like pets.

Ngorongoro Crater could scarcely be more different to a typical zoo. The wildlife you see in the crater is neither caged nor artificially fed. Indeed, with the exception of a few reintroduced black rhinos, it is all 100% indigenous and free to come and go as it pleases, forming part of the same cohesive ecosystem that includes the Serengeti and Masai Mara.

The only respect in which the crater is faintly zoo-like is that the wildlife mostly seems very relaxed. But that doesn't mean it is tame, merely habituated to vehicles (in the same way that the mountain gorillas of Rwanda or the chimps at Mahale are habituated to pedestrian visits). This creates superb opportunities to observe wildlife interaction and behaviour at close quarters – trust me, an infinitely more satisfying experience than travelling through a reserve where the wildlife is so skittish that most sightings amount to little more than a rump disappearing into the bush.

Perhaps the notion of Ngorongoro as a glorified zoo stems from something else entirely. Namely, the high volume of tourist traffic, a factor that does tend to dilute the crater's wilderness character and has some potential for environmental damage, but is of questionable impact on the animals. In fact, the wildlife of Ngorongoro is clearly less affected by the presence of vehicles than, say, the elephants and giraffes in the Selous, which regularly display clear signs of distress at the approach of a vehicle.

So, no, Ngorongoro Crater is not a zoo. It's nothing like one. But the high tourist volume within its confines can jar against our sense of aesthetics – especially when game spotting entails looking for a group of vehicles clustered together in the distance rather than looking for an actual animal! Personally, I feel that the scenery and abundance of animals more than makes up for the mild congestion, but if crowds put you off then there are other places to visit in Tanzania. Instead of adding to the tourist traffic and then moaning about it, why not give the crater a miss? Or better still, make the effort to be in the crater first thing in the morning when, for a brief hour or so before the post-breakfast crowds descend, it really does live up to every expectation of untrammelled beauty.

12

THE RHINOS OF NGORONGORO

Ngorongoro Crater has always been noted for its density of black rhinos. Back in 1892, Dr Oscar Baumann, the first European to visit the area, remarked on the large numbers of rhino, particularly around Lerai Forest – and he shot seven of the unfortunate beasts to prove his point. More recently, the biologist John Goddard estimated the resident population at greater than 100 in 1964. By 1992, poaching had reduced the crater's rhino population to no more than ten individuals, although this number had increased to 18 by 1998, including a mother and calf relocated from South Africa's Addo National Park to boost the local genetic pool. Sadly, five of these rhinos died soon after, one taken by a lion and the remainder thought to be victims of a tick-borne disease linked to the low rainfall of 2000/01. Since then, numbers have gradually recovered: the population resident in the crater stood at around 20 individuals in 2008 and it has increased to 33 in 2012. The crater's rhinos all have a tracking device implanted in their horns, to discourage poachers and to enable the rangers to monitor movements.

Despite the overall decline in numbers over recent decades, Ngorongoro is today the only accessible part of the northern safari circuit where these endangered animals are seen with any regularity. For many visitors to the crater, therefore, rhino sightings are a very high priority, and fortunately the chances are pretty good. In the wet season, the rhinos are often seen in the vicinity of the Ngoitokitok Springs and the Sopa road. For most of the year, however, they range between the Lerai Forest by night and Lake Magadi by day.

The crater's rhinos display a couple of local quirks. The black rhino (unlike its 'white' cousin) is normally a diurnal browser, which makes it rather odd to see them spending most of the day in open grassland, but the story is that they mostly feed by night while they are in the forest. Baumann noted that the crater's rhinos were unusually pale in colour, a phenomenon that is still observed today and is due to their predilection for bathing and rolling in the saline lake and fringing salt flats.

around 60m. The emerald lake's shallows are frequently tinged pink with thousands of flamingos, and a variety of other aquatic birds are common, too. As for mammals, elephant and leopard are still present in the area, but bushbuck, buffalo and blue monkey are more likely to be seen, especially on the crater rim.

The drive from Ngorongoro to Empakaai takes around 90 minutes, leaving from the crater rim close to the Sopa Lodge. A 4x4 is required, and if you want to hike to the crater floor you need to stop *en route* at Nainokanoka village to pick up a mandatory armed ranger for US$20. Past Nainokanoka, the road descends to the grassy bowl of the Embulbul Depression, which dips to a low point of 2,325m at the bases of the 3,260m Mount Losirua and 3,648m Lolmalasin (the highest point in the Crater Highlands, and third-highest peak in Tanzania). The road then climbs Empakaai's outer slopes, passing through alpine moorland and lush Afro-montane forest, before reaching the rim and its fantastic views over the crater to Ol Doinyo Lengai and, on very clear days, Kilimanjaro and Lake Natron.

A road circles part of the forested rim, which reaches an elevation of 3,200m in the east. An excellent footpath to the crater floor was constructed in 2008 – a steep but wonderful walk that takes around 45 minutes each way, longer if you're looking out for the (plentiful) forest birds – which definitely requires decent walking shoes.

There is a campsite with rustic ablution facilities on the crater rim a few metres from the start of the footpath, but no other accommodation in the area.

If that walk hasn't sapped your energy, the smaller and less dramatic Olmoti Crater, a sunken caldera situated close to Nainokanoka, is worth a stop on the way back to Ngorongoro. A motorable track leads from Nainokanoka to a ranger post further west, from where the crater rim can only be reached on foot, following a footpath through montane forest that takes about 30 minutes up and 20 minutes back down. From the ranger post it is a half-hour walk to the rim. This is a shallow crater, covered in grass and bisected by a river valley, and it offers good grazing for Maasai cattle and also sometimes supports a few antelope. From the viewpoint at the rim, you're bound to see pairs of augur buzzard cartwheeling high in the sky, and might also catch a glimpse of the mighty cliff-loving Verreaux's eagle. On a clear day, the viewpoint also offers glimpses of the distant southern wall of Ngorongoro Crater, and you can follow a short footpath to the seasonal Munge Waterfall, where the eponymous river leaves the crater.

Oldupai Gorge It's difficult to believe today perhaps, but for much of the past two million years the seasonally parched plains around Oldupai – the Maasai name for the sisal plant, often but incorrectly transcribed as Olduvai – were submerged beneath a lake that formed an important watering hole for local animals and our hominid ancestors. This was a fluctuating body of water, at times expansive, at other times drying up altogether, creating a high level of stratification accentuated by sporadic deposits of fine ash from the volcanoes that surrounded it. Then, tens of thousands of years ago, volcanic activity associated with the rifting process caused the land to tilt, and a new lake formed to the east. The river that flowed out of this new lake gradually incised a gorge through the former lakebed, exposing layers of stratification up to 100m deep. Oldupai Gorge thus cuts through a chronological sequence of rock beds preserving a practically continuous archaeological and fossil record of life on the plains over the past two million years.

The significance of Oldupai Gorge was first recognised by the German entomologist Professor Katwinkle, who stumbled across it in 1911 while searching for insect specimens. Two years later, Katwinkle led an archaeological expedition to the gorge, and unearthed a number of animal fossils before the excavations were abandoned at the outbreak of World War I. In 1931, the palaeontologist Louis Leakey visited the long-abandoned diggings and realised that the site provided ideal conditions for following the hominid fossil record back to its beginnings. Leakey found ample evidence demonstrating that ancient hominids had occupied the site, but lacking for financial backing, his investigations went slowly and frustratingly refused to yield any truly ancient fossilised hominid remains.

The pay-off for the long years of searching came in 1959 when Mary Leakey – Louis's wife, and a more than accomplished archaeologist in her own right – discovered a heavy fossilised cranium whose jawbone displayed unambiguous human affinities but was also clearly unlike any other fossil documented at the time. Nicknamed 'nutcracker man' in reference to its bulk, the cranium proved to belong to a robust Australopithecine that lived and died on the ancient lakeshore around 1.75 million years earlier (palaeontological taxonomy being a somewhat fluid science, the Leakeys named their discovery *Zinjanthropus boisei*, but it was later designated as *Australopithecus boisei*, and is now usually known as *Paranthropus boisei*). And while 'nutcracker man' would later be superseded by more ancient fossils unearthed elsewhere in East Africa, it was nevertheless a critical landmark in the history of palaeontology: the first conclusive evidence

Because the NCA lies outside the national park system, it is permissible to walk and hike along a number of trails covering most main points of interest (but not the crater floor) in the company of an authorised guide. Indeed, you could theoretically spend a fortnight exploring the NCA along a trail network that connects Lake Eyasi in the south to Lake Natron in the north, as well as running west across the plains towards Laetoli and Lake Ndutu and northwest to Oldupai Gorge. Other possible targets for hikers include the Olmoti and Empakaai craters, Mount Lolmalasin (the third-highest in Tanzania), and the remote Gol Mountains. Any safari operator can advise you about routes and arrange hikes with the NCA authorities, but it is advisable to work through an operator with specialist trekking experience.

It would also be possible to set up a trekking trip directly with the NCA authorities, bussing to the crater rim from Arusha. Were you to attempt something like this, you would have to organise food yourself, to clarify arrangements for a tent, sleeping bag and other equipment, and to take warm clothes since parts of the NCA are very chilly at night. At least five different one-day hiking trails from the crater rim can be arranged at very short notice. Some of the longer hikes and trekking routes require 30 days' notice to set up, so you will need to make advance contact.

The best place to make initial enquiries and arrangements is the NCA Information Centre, whose office on Boma Road in Arusha (027 254 4625; e www.ngorongorocrater.org/email.php; www.ngorongorocrater.org; for more details see *Chapter 5*, page 103). A useful map and brochure showing all hiking routes in the NCA is downloadable at www.ngorongorocrater.org/downloads/pdf/walking_safaris.pdf.

that hominid evolution stretched back over more than a million years and had been enacted on the plains of East Africa.

This important breakthrough shot the Leakeys' work to international prominence, and with proper funding at their disposal, a series of exciting new discoveries followed, including the first fossilised remains of *Homo habilis*, a direct ancestor of modern man that would have dwelt on the lakeshore contemporaneously with its Australopithecine cousin. After Louis's death in 1972, Mary Leakey continued working in the area until she retired in 1984. In 1976, at the nearby site of Laetoli, she discovered footprints created more than three million years ago by a party of early hominids that had walked through a bed of freshly deposited volcanic ash – still the most ancient hominid footprints ever found.

Today, the original diggings may only be explored with a guide, and – since all fossils are removed upon discovery – they are probably of greater immediate geological than archaeological interest. Not so the excellent **site museum**, however, which displays replicas of some of the more interesting hominid fossils unearthed at the site as well as the Laetoli footprints. Also on display are genuine fossils of some of the extinct animals that used to roam the plains: pygmy and short-necked giraffes, giant swine, river elephant, various equines and a bizarre antelope with long de-curved horns.

Oldupai Gorge lies within the conservation area about 3km north of the main road between Ngorongoro Crater and the Serengeti, and is a popular and worthwhile place to stop for a picnic lunch. Outside the museum, evolutionary diversity is represented by the variety of colourful – and very alive – dry-country birds that hop around the picnic area: red-and-yellow barbet, slaty-coloured boubou, rufous chatterer, speckle-fronted weaver and purple grenadier are practically guaranteed. There is no charge to stop at the site for a picnic, but in order to enter the museum or explore the diggings, you need to pay the entrance fee, which was recently hiked up to Tsh27,000 (equivalent to US$16).

Lake Ndutu This alkaline lake lies south of the B144 on the Ngorongoro–Serengeti border. When it is full, Maasai use it to water their cattle. In the rainy season it supports large numbers of animals, so Ndutu Safari Lodge (see *Chapter 13, Serengeti National Park, Where to stay*, page 300) is a good base for game drives. The acacia woodland around the lake supports different birds from those in surrounding areas. The campsite on the lakeshore costs US$40 per person.

13

Serengeti National Park

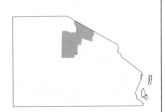

Tanzania's oldest, largest and most famous national park, the Serengeti is a strong contender for the accolade of the continent's finest game-viewing destination. Home to dense populations of lions and other predators, and renowned for an annual migration comprising millions of wildebeest and other plains grazers, this is the sort of place that's been so heavily hyped you might reasonably brace yourself for disappointment when you actually get to visit it. Fear not though, the Serengeti truly is all it is cracked up to be – notable both for the sheer variety and volume of the wildlife that inhabits its vast plains and for the liberating sense of space attached to exploring them.

Extending over 14,763km², the Serengeti National Park is the centrepiece of a twice-larger cross-border ecosystem that also includes the Ngorongoro Conservation Area, Kenya's Maasai Mara National Reserve, and a number of smaller game reserves and private protected areas. Much of the national park comprises open grassland, but other areas support a denser cover of acacia woodland, and the region as a whole is studded with isolated granite hillocks known as *koppies* (a Dutch or Afrikaans word literally meaning 'little heads'). There is little permanent water aside from a few perennial rivers, notably the Mara and Grumeti, so animal migration within the ecosystem is linked strongly to rainfall patterns.

Several guides to the park are available locally. They include the official 72-page booklet *Serengeti National Park*, with good maps and introductory information, and the newer and glossier *Serengeti* published by African Publishing House. Far more detailed is Veronica Roodt's *Tourist Travel & Field Guide to the Serengeti*, which is strong on maps, photographs and information.

The park entrance fee of US$50 per person per 24 hours is set to increase to US$60 in July 2013. It can be paid only by MasterCard, Visa or Tanapa Smartcard. No other cards are accepted, and neither are travellers' cheques or cash. For more details, see box, *Paying park fees*, page 71.

HISTORY

Prior to becoming a national park, the Serengeti was inhabited by the Maasai, who migrated into the area in the 17th century, when they forcefully displaced the Datoga pastoralists. The name Serengeti derives from the Maa word *serengit*, meaning 'Endless Plain', and it most properly refers to the short-grass plains of the southeast rather than the whole park. Partly because it lay within the territory of the then inhospitable Maasai, the Serengeti area was little known to outsiders until after World War I, when the first European hunters moved in to bag its plentiful wildlife.

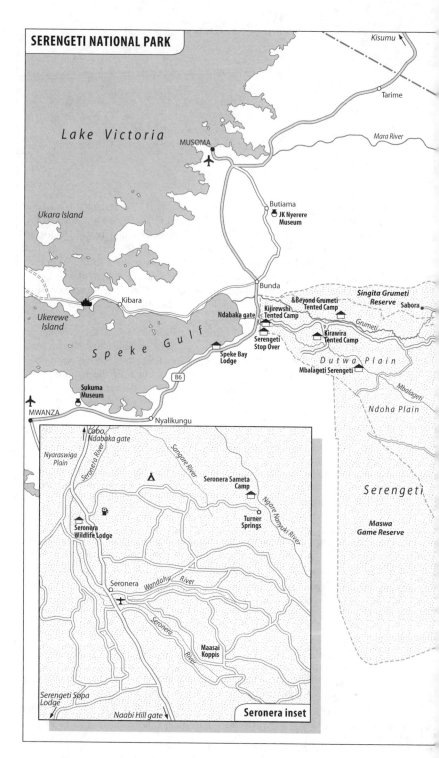

SERENGETI NATIONAL PARK

Kisumu

Tarime

Lake Victoria

MUSOMA

Mara River

Butiama
JK Nyerere Museum

Ukara Island

Bunda

&Beyond Grumeti Tented Camp

Singita Grumeti Reserve

Sabora

Kibara

Ndabaka gate

Kijirewshi Tented Camp

Grumeti

Ukerewe Island

Serengeti Stop Over

Kirawira Tented Camp

S p e k e   G u l f

Speke Bay Lodge

D u t w a   P l a i n

Mbalageti Serengeti

Mbalageti

Sukuma Museum

B6

Ndoha Plain

MWANZA

Nyalikungu

Lobo, Ndabaka gate

Nyaraswiga Plain

Seronera River

Sangare River

Seronera Sameta Camp

S e r e n g e t i

Maswa Game Reserve

Seronera Wildlife Lodge

Turner Springs

Ngare Nanuki River

Seronera

Wandahu River

Seronera River

Maasai Koppis

Serengeti Sopa Lodge

Naabi Hill gate

Seronera inset

K E N Y A

Maasai Mara
Game Reserve

Mara River Causeway
(may close after heavy rain)
& Kogatende Ranger Post
Sayari
Camp

Lemala Serengeti
(Jun–Nov)
Lamai Serengeti

Bologonja
gate

Klein's Camp,
&Beyond Buffalo
Luxury Camp

Tabora 'B'
gate

Bwanauke
Hills

Klein's gate

Mapito Tented
Camp & Ikoma
Bush Camp

Migration
Camp

Lobo
Hills

Grumeti

Fort Ikoma gate

see inset right

Retima
Hippo Pool

Mbuzi Mawe
Tented Camp

Orangi River

Nyabogati River

Serengeti
Serena
Lodge

Seronera

Ngare Nanyuki River

see inset left

Serengeti
Sopa Lodge

Lake
Magadi

Gol
Koppis

Moru
Koppis

Simba
Koppis

Naabi Hill gate

Ngorongoro
Conservation Area

Plains

L Kaslya   L Ngorano

Oldupai Gorge

Ndutu
Safari Lodge

Lake Ndutu

Ndutu

Sanctuary
Kusini Camp

Ngorongoro
Conservation Area

Kanatu,
Lake Manyara NP,
Arusha

Lake Eyasi

Lake Manyara

Lobo inset

Klein's
gate

Grumeti River

Lobo
Hills

Springs

Ngare Naronja
Springs

Lobo
Wildlife Lodge

Gabott River

Bo'olodi River

Lake Natron

N

Bradt

0   50km
0   30 miles

© Philip Briggs

Serengeti National Park was gazetted in 1951 and originally covered the present-day national park along with what is now the Ngorongoro Conservation Area (NCA). The park's Maasai residents were threatened with forceful eviction, leading to widespread protests and eventually a compromise was reached wherein the NCA was split off from the park and the Maasai were allowed to stay there. The Maasai are no longer allowed to graze their cattle in the national park, but evidence of their previous occupation can be seen in the form of well-preserved rock paintings at Moru Koppies. The Serengeti became famous through the work of Professor Bernard Grzimek (pronounced 'Jimek'), author of *Serengeti Shall Not Die*. Grzimek's son Michael died in an aeroplane crash over the Serengeti aged just 24, and is buried at Heroes Point on the Ngorongoro Crater rim.

THE GREAT MIGRATION

The annual migration of at least two million ungulates – predominantly wildebeest but also large concentrations of zebra and lesser numbers of Thomson's gazelle, Grant's gazelle and eland – through the greater Serengeti ecosystem is the greatest spectacle of its type in Africa. Dictated by local rainfall patterns, the Serengeti migration does follow a reasonably predictable annual cycle, although there is also a fair amount of variation from one year to the next, dependent mainly on the precise timing of the rainy seasons. The cycle breaks up into the following main periods:

DECEMBER–APRIL The plains that stretch southeast from Seronera into the Ngorongoro Conservation Area form the Serengeti's main wildebeest calving grounds, centred on the Ndutu area of the NCA–Serengeti border. The wildebeest typically disperse into this area during the short rains, which fall in late November or early December, and stay put until the end of the long rains, generally in early May. These southeastern plains are the most accessible part of the park, particularly for those on a budget safari, and this is a fantastic time to be on safari in the Serengeti. True, you won't see the big herds on the move, but it's not uncommon to see herds of 10,000 animals, and the scenery is lush and green. The optimum time to visit this area is the peak calving season (late January into February) when hundreds, even thousands, of calves are dropped daily, and predator concentrations are also at their peak.

MAY–JULY Usually towards the end of April, the wildebeest and their entourage start to congregate on the southern plains in preparation for the 800km northward migration. The actual migration, regularly delayed in recent years due to late rain, might start any time from late April to early June, with a herd of more than a million migrating animals marching in a braying column of up to 40km long, one of the most impressive spectacles in the world. The major obstacle faced by the wildebeest on this migration is the crossing of the Grumeti River through the Western Corridor, which typically occurs from June into early July. A great many animals die in the crossing, many of them taken by the Grumeti's ravenous and prolific population of outsized crocodiles, and the first herds to cross are generally at the greatest risk. For this reason, it can take up to two weeks from when the first wildebeest arrive at the southern bank of the river for the actual crossing to begin, by which time thousands upon thousands of wildebeest are congregated in the Western Corridor.

WILDLIFE

The most recent full census figures for the Serengeti Ecosystem date to the 1980s and indicate that the commonest large herbivore species are wildebeest (1,300,000), Thomson's gazelle (250,000), Burchell's zebra (200,000), impala (70,000), topi (50,000), Grant's gazelle (30,000), kongoni (15,000) and eland (10,000). Anecdotal sources and more recent partial surveys indicate that these figures are now on the low side for several species. The current population of wildebeest, for instance, could be as high as two million, while the total number of zebras probably stands at 500,000, with the two species often encountered together in immense mixed herds.

Other antelope species include Kirk's dik-dik, klipspringer, and small numbers of roan, oryx, oribi and waterbuck. There are significant numbers of buffalo, giraffe

AUGUST–NOVEMBER Following the great northward sweep across the Grumeti, the ungulates usually cross the Mara River in August, before dispersing across the plains of the northwest. Conventional wisdom has it that August–October is a bad time to visit the Serengeti, because the wildebeest have crossed the Kenya border into the Maasai Mara National Reserve. In reality, however, about half of the wildebeest stay in the northwest Serengeti over these months, and game viewing can be excellent, assuming that you can afford to base yourself at one of the exclusive tented camps in the Mara River area. Here, relatively small herds of wildebeest – typically between 500 and a few thousand – frequently travel back and forth between the northern and southern banks of the Mara River in response to changes in the local rainfall pattern, a truly spectacular event. In October, sometimes earlier, the animals generally cross the Mara River one last time and start to plod back southward to the short-grass plains of the southeast, and there is a good chance of catching the southward migration in the Lobo area between late October and mid November. The wildebeest usually reach the short-grass plains around Ndutu in late November, when the cycle starts all over again.

Whether it is worth planning your safari dates around the migration is a matter of choice. With the best will in the world, it would be practically impossible to ensure that a few days in the Serengeti will coincide with the exact date of a river crossing, which is the most spectacular event in the migration calendar. On the other hand, if you choose the right part of the Serengeti – the southeast from December–May, the Western Corridor from May–July, the Mara River area from July–October, and the Lobo area from October–November – large herds of grazers should be easy enough to locate and there's a fair chance of witnessing a more spectacular migrational movement or river crossing.

On the other hand, bearing in mind that most predators and ungulate species other than zebra and wildebeest are strongly territorial and do not stray far from their core territory over the course of any given year, there is a lot to be said for avoiding the migration. Most of the lodges now charge considerably lower rates during April and May, with a knock-on effect on the rates offered by safari companies that suddenly become hungry for business. Furthermore, the safari circuit as a whole is far less crowded outside of peak seasons, and in our experience the Serengeti, irrespective of season, will still offer game viewing to equal that of any game reserve in Africa.

13

and warthog. Elephants used be scarce on the open plains, but they are quite common today, and are more numerous in the north and west. The park's black rhino population today stands at around 30 individuals, as compared to 700 in the mid 1970s, and is restricted to the vicinity of the Moru Koppies in the far southeast, and the Mara River area in the far north. The most common and widespread diurnal primates are the olive baboon and vervet monkey, but an isolated and seldom seen population of patas monkey is resident in the west, and a few troops of black-and-white colobus haunt the riparian woodland along the Grumeti River through the Western Corridor.

Ultimately, the success of most first-time safaris lies in the number and quality of the big cat encounters. There is something infinitely compelling about these animals, a fascination that seems to affect even the most jaded of safari drivers – many of whom are leopard obsessives, content to drive up and down the Seronera Valley all day in the search for a tell-tale tail dangling from a tree. And when it comes to big cats, the Serengeti rarely disappoints. Lions are a practical certainty: the Tanzania side of the greater Serengeti ecosystem supports an estimated 2,500–3,000 individuals, which is probably the largest single population anywhere in Africa, and hundreds of resident lions stalk the plains around Seronera, with the main concentration centred on Simba, Moru and Gol koppies close to the main Ngorongoro road. Here, it's normal to see two or three prides in the course of one game drive. Sociable, languid and deceptively pussycat-like, lions are most often seen lying low in the grass or basking on rocks. The challenge is to see a lion exert itself beyond a half-interested movement of the head when a vehicle stops nearby.

AVOIDING THE CROWDS

Many visitors whose experience of the Serengeti is limited to the Seronera area complain that the park is uncomfortably crowded, and that any worthwhile sighting attracts a gaggle of safari vehicles within a few minutes. To some extent, this reputation is justified: Seronera is the most accessible part of the park, coming from the direction of Arusha, and it boasts the highest concentration of camping and lodge facilities, so that game-viewing roads within a 5–10km radius tend to carry an uncharacteristically high level of vehicular traffic.

This situation is exacerbated by the tendency of the budget safari companies that favour Seronera to impose heavy budgetary restrictions on drivers, discouraging them from burning excess fuel to explore further afield. Furthermore, some of the safari industry's obsession with the Big Five and large predators has created a mindset where drivers tend to rely heavily on radio messages from other drivers to locate the animals they think their clients most want to see. As a result, all vehicles within radio earshot tend to congregate on any such sighting within minutes. Sadly, this all goes to create the common misperception that one of Africa's wildest and most wonderful parks is far more crowded with tourists than is actually the case.

What can you do about this? Well, for one, assuming that you can afford it, arrange your safari through a company that specialises in more offbeat areas of the park and whose budget incorporates unlimited mileage. If you work with a cheaper company, try to avoid being based at Seronera. True, this area does usually offer the best wildlife viewing in the park, but many other parts of the Serengeti are almost as good, whilst carrying a significantly lower tourist volume. Failing that, should your itinerary include Seronera, speak to the safari company about what, if any, fuel restrictions they impose on drivers and try to reach an understanding in advance.

Leopard numbers are unknown, due to their secrecy, but they are probably quite common throughout the park, and are very often seen in the Seronera Valley. Cheetahs, too, are very common: the park's estimated population of 500–600 is densest in the open grasslands around Seronera and further east towards Ndutu. In direct contrast to their more languid cousins, these streamlined, solitary creatures are most normally seen pacing the plains with the air of an agitated greyhound.

Of the other predators which can be seen in the Serengeti, spotted hyenas are very common, perhaps more numerous than lions. Golden jackals and bat-eared foxes appear to be the most abundant canid species on the plains around Seronera, while black-backed jackals are reasonably common in the thicker vegetation towards Lobo. Driving at dusk or dawn, you stand the best chance of seeing nocturnal predators such as civet, serval, genet and African wildcat. The real rarity among the larger predators is the African wild dog, which was very common in the area until the 1970s, before the population dwindled to local extinction as a result of canid-borne diseases and persecution by farmers living on the park's periphery. Fortunately, wild dogs are very mobile and wide-ranging animals, and sightings have been reported with increased frequency over recent years, particularly in the far north and the adjacent Loliondo concessions.

SERONERA, NDUTU AND THE SOUTHERN PLAINS

The short-grass plains stretching southeast from Seronera towards Lake Ndutu on the border with the NCA might be termed the 'classic' Serengeti: a vast open

It's also worth bearing in mind that roads around Seronera tend to be busiest during peak game viewing hours of 07.30–10.00 and 14.00–16.30. So instead of breakfasting in camp, take a packed breakfast and head out as early as possible – game drives are permitted from 06.00 onwards, and even if you ignore the crowding issue, the first hour of daylight is the best time to see predators on the move. Also, bearing in mind that drivers tend to place emphasis on seeking out big cats because they think it's what their clients want, travellers with different priorities should talk them through with the driver – more radically, ask him to switch off his radio, stop worrying about what everybody else might be seeing, and just enjoy what animals you happen to chance upon.

WALKING SAFARIS Wayo Africa (*www.wayoafrica.com*) now offers multi-day walking safaris in designated wilderness sectors of the Serengeti that are all but inaccessible to other tourists. These safaris usually take place out of a simple but well-equipped mobile camp – dome tents with mattresses and bedding, safari-style hot bucket shower, mess tent with food cooked by a trained chef – which serve as a base for long morning hikes and shorter afternoon walks with an experienced armed guide. Alternatively, they can also set up more elaborate itineraries using a moveable camp that relocates every night or two. Close-up encounters with the Big Five are commonplace, and it is a great for birding, not to mention dazzling night skies, but the biggest attraction is the opportunity to experience Africa's greatest national park at its most raw and untrammelled, far away from the crowding that often characterises the busier road circuits.

expanse teeming with all manner of wild creatures ranging from the endearing bat-eared fox to the imperious lion, from flocks of habitually panicked ostrich to strutting pairs of secretary birds, and from the gigantic eland antelope to the diminutive mongooses. Densely populated with wildlife all year through, these southern plains are especially rewarding between December and May, when the rains act as a magnet to the migrant herds of wildebeest and zebra. At this time of year, the prime game viewing area is usually around Lake Ndutu, which lies at the epicentre of the wildebeest dispersal, and offers truly dramatic game viewing during and after the calving season.

Otherwise, the main focal point of the southern plains – indeed of the entire national park – is the park headquarters at Seronera, which is also the site of the oldest lodge in the Serengeti, as well as a cluster of public and special campsites, the staff village and various research projects. The **visitor information centre** at Seronera is well worth a visit: facilities include a small site museum, as well as a picnic area and coffee shop, while an elevated wooden walkway leads through an informative open-air display.

The southern plains are interspersed with several clusters of rocky hills known as koppies, each of which forms a microhabitat inhabited by non-plains wildlife such as klipspringer, rock hyrax, leopard, rock agama, rock thrushes, mocking chat and various cliff-nesting raptors. As the name suggests, **Simba Koppies**, which straddles the main road between the NCA and Seronera, is particularly good for lion, while the grassland around the more easterly **Gol Koppies** is excellent for cheetah and lion. About 25km south of Seronera, the **Moru Koppies** area can also provide good lion and cheetah sightings, and it's home to around 25 black rhinos, descended from a herd of seven that migrated across from the NCA in the mid 1990s.

A striking feature of this part of the Serengeti is the paucity of trees, which flourish only at the sides of koppies and along the riparian belts that follow the Mbalageti and Seronera rivers. The most likely explanation for this quirk is that the soil, which consists of volcanic deposits from an ancient eruption of Ngorongoro, is too hard for most roots to penetrate, except where it has been eroded by flowing water. Paradoxically, one consequence of this is that the thin strip of sausage trees and camelthorn acacias that follows the course of the Seronera River Valley ranks among the best places in Africa to search for leopards – there are simply too few tall trees for these normally elusive creatures to be as well hidden as they tend to be in dense woodland. More surprisingly, the lion prides resident along

MAASAI ROCK ART

An unusual relic of the Serengeti's former Maasai inhabitants is to be found at Moru Koppies in the form of some well-preserved rock paintings of animals, shields and other traditional military regalia near the base of a small koppie. This is one of the few such sites associated with the Maasai, and the paintings, which are mostly red, black and white, may well have been inspired by the more ancient and more accomplished rock art of the Kondoa area – although it's anybody's guess whether they possess some sort of ritual significance, or are purely decorative. On another koppie not far from the rock paintings is an ancient rock gong thought to have been used by the Datoga predecessors of the Maasai – a short but steep scramble up a large boulder leads to the rock gong, which also makes for a good picnic spot.

the Seronera River have taken to the trees with increasingly regularity in recent years, particularly during the rains, when arboreal lion sightings are possibly more frequent than terrestrial ones.

Aside from the two perennial rivers, both of which might be described as streams in another context, there is little permanent standing water in this part of the Serengeti. One exception is the small, saline **Lake Magadi** (a common name for lakes as 'magadi' just means soda or salt), which is fed by the Mbalageti River immediately northeast of Moru Koppies and supports large numbers of aquatic birds, including thousands of flamingos when the water level is suitable. A small hippo pool lies on the Seronera River about 5km south of Seronera along the road back towards the NCA. Far more impressive, however, is the **Retima Hippo Pool**, where up to a hundred of these aquatic animals can be seen basking near the confluence of the Seronera and Grumeti rivers about 15km north of the park headquarters.

The most central base for exploring this region is Seronera Wildlife Lodge, or one of the nearby campsites at the park headquarters. Two of the other three large lodges in the Serengeti – respectively part of the Serena and Sopa chains – are also well positioned for exploring the southern plains, and have far better facilities. Many safari companies also set up seasonal or semi-permanent tented camps at one or another of the myriad special campsites in the vicinity of Seronera. Of the smaller lodges in the national park, the underrated Ndutu Safari Lodge (which actually lies within the NCA) and the wonderfully remote Sanctuary Kusini Camp are both well sited for exploring the southern plains, and remote from the perennially busy road circuit in the immediate vicinity of Seronera.

🏠 **WHERE TO STAY** It may cause some confusion that the listings below include all lodges and seasonal camps based in the Ndutu area, even though some of these technically lie within Ngorongoro Conservation Area. This is because the Ndutu area is an ecological extension of the southern Serengeti Plains, and the experience it offers is essentially a 'Serengeti' one of open plains and large wildebeest herds (especially between December and April). Indeed, despite lying within the NCA, Ndutu isn't well positioned for visiting Ngorongoro Crater. It should be noted, however, that if you stay at a lodge on the NCA side of the border, then crossing over to the Serengeti will attract a separate national park entrance fee.

Exclusive

🏠 **Sanctuary Kusini Camp** (14 tents) ☎ (UK) +44 (0)20 7190 7728; e info@sanctuaryretreats. com; www.sanctuaryretreats.com. With its fantastic location among a set of tall black boulders some 40km south of the Moru Koppies, this spaciously laid-out camp is the most remote & exclusive place to stay in the southern Serengeti, especially in Mar when the area hosts immense herds of wildebeest & zebra. At other times of the year, elephant, giraffe & buffalo are quite common in the surrounding acacia woodland. The best goal for game drives out of Kusini is Moru Koppies, where lion are plentiful & rhino present but seldom seen. There are plenty of birds around, including the striking secretary bird for which the camp is named. *US$1,105/1,730 sgl/*

dbl full game package 16 Dec–Mar; US$785/1,090 Jun–16 Dec. Closed Apr & May.

🏠 **Serengeti Safari Camp** (6 tents) ☎ 027 254 3281; m 0784 734490; e info@nomad-tanzania. com; www.nomad-tanzania.com. The oldest mobile camp in the Serengeti, established in the early 1990s, this small & exclusive old-style camp offers an authentic bush experience in comfortable standing tents with double beds, a small dressing area, eco-flush toilets & safari-style bucket showers. The emphasis is on tracking the migration, so it relocates seasonally in accordance with the predicted movements of the wildebeest, but it is generally located close to Seronera or Ndutu from Dec–May. *US$1,045/1,590 sgl/dbl, dropping to US$805/,1260 15 Mar–May & Nov–19 Dec.*

13

🏠 **Olakira Camp** (9 tents) 🔧(South Africa) +27 (0)21 418 0468; m 0736 5005156; www. asiliaafrica.com. This wonderful mobile camp moves seasonally between the northern & southern Serengeti. It is in the south from Dec–Mar, usually to the east of Ndutu, for wildebeest calving season. It has a classic safari ambience & décor, consisting of attractively furnished standing tents with king-size or twin beds, private veranda & en-suite flush toilet & hot shower. *US$870/1,400 sgl/dbl full game package late Dec–Feb; US$725/1,240 early Dec & Mar.*

🏠 **Serengeti Legendary Camp** (8 tents) 🔧(0)27 250 8917; m 0786 000510; www. keranddowneytanzania.com. Operated by Ker & Downey Tanzania, this is about as luxurious as a mobile tented camp gets, & it only hosts 1 party at a time, making it an excellent option for families & other parties wanting a totally exclusive safari experience. It moves several times annually, using special campsites that offer a combination of good seasonal game viewing & a reasonably remote location. It is usually in the southern Serengeti from Dec–Apr. Service, food & the drinks selection are all out of the top drawer, & the exclusivity means that the clients get to dictate game drive hours & other aspects of the daily schedule. *US$850 pp (min rate for 4 guests) inc meals, drinks, activities & all park & camp fees.*

🏠 **Lemala Ndutu** (9 tents) 🔧027 254 8966; e res@lemalacamp.com; www.lemalacamp.com. This luxury mobile tented camp, described under Lemala Mara on page 310, relocates to a beautiful site in the NCA about 5km from Ndutu Airstrip from Dec–Mar, when it is well positioned to catch the migration as it disperses in the southeast for the calving season. *US$815/1,080 sgl/dbl FB late Dec–Feb; US$547/994 early Dec & Mar. Full game packages inc activities an additional US$80pp.*

🏠 **Mwiba Ranch** (8 tents) 🔧027 250 8917; m 0786 000510; www.keranddowneytanzania. com. Operated by Ker & Downey Tanzania, this exclusive tented camp lies in a 200km² chunk of former Maasai land bordering the NCA & Maswa Game Reserve on the Eyasi escarpment south of the Serengeti. The tented camp only hosts 1 party at a time, & it has exclusive traversing rights of the surrounding ranch, making it ideal for families & other parties wanting an exclusive & holistic safari experience, rather than just ticking off the Big Five as quickly as possible. The ranch consists mainly of thick acacia woodland, but there are areas of more open grassland, as well as more than 30 permanent springs that attract large numbers of wildlife during the dry season. Most species associated with the Serengeti are present, although resident populations are less dense, & wildlife tends to be shyer as a result of hunting in the neighbouring Maswa Game Reserve. In addition to more widespread species such as buffalo, elephant & zebra, it is the best place in northern Tanzania to see the greater kudu, the male of which is arguably the most handsome of all African antelope. Because it lies outside the national parks, standard game drives are supplemented by expertly guided night drives & game walks, the latter being a particularly enjoyable feature of the Mwiba experience. As with other camps operated by this company, the service, food & the drinks selection are all excellent, & the exclusivity means that the clients get to dictate the timing & duration of activities. *US$800 pp (min rate for 4 guests) inc meals, drinks, activities & all park & camp fees.*

🏠 **Seronera Sametu Camp** (6 tents) 🔧(USA) +1 877 572-3274; e info@seronerasametucamp. com; www.seronerasametucamp.com. This new semi-permanent tented camp has a wonderfully isolated location overlooking the seasonal Ngare Nanyuki River about an hour's drive east of Seronera & 30 mins from the Maasai Koppies. It has a very exclusive atmosphere, comprising only 6 comfortable en-suite tents strung out along a wooded ridge, as well as a mess tent & lounge. A big plus with this camp is that its proximity to Seronera allows you to do some game drives in this wildlife-rich but sometimes over-touristed area, but equally you can opt to stick to the more off-the-beaten-track circuit of roads around Moru Koppies, an area that is also good for big cats but tends to attracts low tourist numbers. *US$645/950 sgl/dbl FB.*

Upmarket
🏠 **Serengeti & Ndutu Wilderness Camps** (10 tents each) 🔧(South Africa) +27 (0)11 7092 2035; m 0786 642466/0754 842466; e reservations@wildfrontiers.com; www.wildfrontiers.com. These down-to-earth & reasonably priced tented camps are run by the highly regarded operator Wild Frontiers, & each comprise 10 en-suite tents with solar lighting, eco-friendly toilets & comfortable but

SERENGETI BALLOON SAFARIS

Serengeti Balloon Safaris is – no prizes for guessing – the name of the company that runs balloon safaris daily at 06.00 from two launch sites in the national park: one close to Seronera Wildlife Lodge and the other in the Western Corridor. Although not cheap, a balloon safari is definitely worth the expense if you can afford it. Gliding serenely above the trees as the sun rises allows you to see the expansive plains from a new and quite thrilling angle. It also offers the chance to see secretive species such as bushbuck and reedbuck, and, because you leave so early in the morning, you are likely to spot a few nocturnal predators (we saw hyenas in abundance, civet twice and had a rare glimpse of an African wildcat). That said, any images you have of sweeping above innumerable wildebeest and zebra may prove a little removed from reality; you can only be confident of seeing large herds of ungulates if you're fortunate enough to be around during the exact week or two when animals concentrate immediately around Seronera.

The safari culminates with a champagne breakfast in the bush, set up at a different site every day, depending on which way the balloons are blown. The meal is presented with some flourish: the immaculately uniformed waiters in particular conjure up images of the safaris of old. Our particular mad-hatters' breakfast party was enlivened by the arrival of three male lions, who strolled past less than 100m from the table apparently oblivious to the unusual apparition of 24 people eating scrambled eggs and sausages at a starched tablecloth in the bush. This sort of thing doesn't happen every day, whether you're a lion or a human!

The package, which costs US$499 per person, includes the transfer to the balloon site, a balloon trip of roughly one hour's duration and the champagne breakfast. Be prepared for a very early start (the transfer from Seronera leaves at 05.30 and from the other lodges at around 04.30). There is a booking desk for the Seronera launch site at the Seronera Wildlife, Serengeti Sopa and Serengeti Serena. Balloon safaris can also be arranged through most other lodges and camps in the central Serengeti and Western Corridor. If you want to be certain of a place, however, it is advisable to book in advance, particularly during high season. Reservations can be made through any safari company, or directly through Serengeti Balloon Safaris (027 254 8967; e info@balloonsafaris.com; www.balloonsafaris.com).

unpretentious furnishings. Serengeti Wilderness Camp is semi-permanent with a central location that offers good game viewing all year round; in addition to game drives with expert guides, it is one of the few camps in the Serengeti to offer daily guided walks, & it can be used as a base for multi-day wilderness trails. *Ndutu Wilderness Camp, set on the NCA side of Lake Ndutu, is open Dec–Mar only. US$450/600 sgl/dbl FB.*

🏠 **Serengeti Serena Lodge** (66 rooms) 027 254 5555; e reservations@serena.co.tz; www. serenahotels.com. Situated on a hilltop roughly 20km west of Seronera, this is probably the most comfortable of the larger lodges in this part of the Serengeti. Accommodation is in a village-like cluster of Maasai-style double-storey rondawels (round African-style huts), built with slate, wood & thatch to create a pleasing organic feel. The spacious self-contained rooms each have 1 sgl & 1 king-size bed, nets & fans, & hot showers. There is a swimming pool, & the buffet meals are far superior to those in most East African safari lodges. The one negative is that game viewing in the thick scrub around the lodge is poor except for when the migration passes through, & it's a good half-hour drive before you reach the main game-viewing circuit east of

13

Seronera Wildlife Lodge. *US$375/615 sgl/dbl FB. Low season discounts Mar–May, Nov & early Dec.*

🏠 **Serengeti Sopa Lodge** (73 rooms) ☎ 027 250 0630–9; e info@sopalodges.com; www.sopalodges.com. This large ostentatious lodge lies about 30 mins' drive south of Seronera, on the side of a hill near the Moru Koppies. The rooms here are practically suites: each has 2 double beds, a small sitting room, a large bathroom, a private balcony & a large window giving a grandstand view over the plains below, perfectly appointed to catch the sunset. Following extensive renovations between 2005 & 2006, the formerly rather ostentatious & jarring interior has been supplanted by a more attractive & distinctively African look. The food is excellent & facilities include a swimming pool & internet café. Game viewing in the surrounding area is generally very good, with a high chance of encountering tree-climbing lions on the road north to Seronera, & there's much less traffic in the immediate vicinity than there is around the park HQ. *US$330/580 sgl/dbl FB; US$280/480 in Mar, Nov & early Dec; US$115/225 Apr–May.*

🏠 **Seronera Wildlife Lodge** (100 rooms) ☎ 027 254 4595; e res@hotelsandlodges-tanzania.com; www.hotelsandlodges-tanzania.com. The most central lodge in the Serengeti, Seronera Wildlife Lodge is situated only a couple of kilometres from the park HQ & boasts an unbeatable location for game drives. It was built around a granite koppie in the early 1970s, & utilises the natural features to create an individual & unmistakably African character. The bar, frequented by bats & rock hyraxes, is reached through a narrow corridor between 2 boulders, while the natural rock walls of the cavernous restaurant are decorated with traditionally styled paintings. In common with other former government lodges, however, the service, food & facilities have long lagged behind those of most newer lodges, & the outmoded fittings just feel rather tacky after 3 decades of service. Rooms are compact but comfortable, with en-suite bathrooms & large windows facing the surrounding bush. The best reason to select this lodge is simply its brilliant location, at the heart of the superlative (but sometimes rather overcrowded – see page 295) Seronera game-viewing circuit. *US$340/460 sgl/dbl FB.*

🏠 **Ndutu Safari Lodge** (35 rooms) ☎ 027 253 7015; m 0736 501045/6; e bookings@ndutu.com; www.ndutu.com. Set within the NCA, this low-key & underrated family-owned retreat lies in thick acacia woodland overlooking the seasonal Lake Ndutu. It has a distinct 'bush' atmosphere lacking from other comparably priced lodges in the Serengeti ecosystem. The rooms are in small, unfussy stone chalets & have netting & hot water. The bar & restaurant are open-sided stone & thatch structures frequented by a legion of genets by

---

MEANINGS OF THE MAASAI BEADS   *Emma Thomson*

Maasai jewellery beads are composed of nine main colours. It's a common misconception that the colours are blended to create complex messages. In fact, while the colours carry meaning, the combinations are randomly selected, mainly for beauty. It's often possible to tell the age of some necklaces according to the fashionable arrangement of colours that vary from year to year. Tendons extracted from the meat consumed originally served as string to hold these intricate designs together but these have now been replaced with shredded plastic bags.

The meanings for each colour vary from area to area but in general they mean the following:

black	God/rain	orange	rainbow
blue	water	red	warrior/blood/bravery
dark blue	God in the sky	white	milk/peace
gold	ground water	yellow	sun
green	life/spring (rainy season)		

night. This is an excellent place to stay if you want to avoid the crowds, & the surrounding plains offer good general game viewing, particularly during the wet season when they are teeming with wildebeest. It is also excellent value. *US$287/474 sgl/dbl FB Dec–Apr; US$174/299 May–Nov.*

🏠 **Serengeti Savannah Camps**
(12 tents) 📞 027 254 7066; 📧 bookings@ serengetisavannahcamps.com; www. serengetisavannahcamps.com. This small, mobile

tented camp, one of the few in northern Tanzania that's not part of a chain, aims to offer safari-goers a genuine bush experience at a reasonable price. It moves between 2 locations, 1 in the Seronera area from Jun–Nov & 1 near Ndutu between Dec–Mar to catch the calving season. The tents are simply but comfortably furnished & all have a private veranda, chemical toilet & starlight shower. *US$260/410 sgl/ dbl FB. Hefty discounts for East African residents.*

Budget and camping Situated at the Seronera park headquarters, the **Tanapa Resthouse** (*3 rooms;* 📞 *028 262 1510/5;* 📧 *serengeti@tanzaniaparks.com*) charges US$30 per person B&B, and there is also a hostel with bunk accommodation at US$20 per person B&B. A cluster of seven **campsites** lies about 5km from Seronera Wildlife Lodge. Camping costs the usual US$30 per person. Facilities are limited to long-drop toilets and a rubbish pit. You may be able to organise a shower and fill up water containers for a small fee at the lodge. There is a good chance of seeing nocturnal scavengers such as hyena and genet – even, rather disconcertingly, the occasional lion pride – pass through the campsites after dark.

THE WESTERN CORRIDOR

The relatively narrow arm of the Serengeti that stretches westward from Seronera almost as far as the shore of Lake Victoria is generally flatter than the more northerly parts of the park but moister and more densely vegetated than the southern plains. Aside from a few small isolated mountain ranges, the dominant geographic feature of the Western Corridor is a pair of rivers, the Grumeti and Mbalageti, whose near-parallel west-flowing courses, which run less than 20km apart, support tall ribbons of riparian forest before eventually they exit the national park to empty into Lake Victoria. The characteristic vegetation of the Western Corridor is park-like woodland, interspersed with areas of open grassland and dense stands of the ghostly grey 'whistling thorn' *Acacia drepanolobrium*.

Game viewing is pretty good there throughout the year. The broken savanna to the south of the Grumeti River supports substantial resident populations of lion, giraffe, elephant, wildebeest, zebra and other typical plains animals, while the little-visited vistas of open grassland north of the river are especially good for cheetah. The riverine forest along the two rivers harbours a few troops of the exquisite black-and-white colobus monkey, and the Grumeti is also home to plenty of hippos, crocodiles and water-associated birds. The side road to Mbalageti Serengeti is a good place to look for the localised kongoni antelope, and the acacia woodland around the junction with the main road is the one place in Tanzania where the localised patas monkey is regularly seen.

Few camping safaris make it this far west, and permanent accommodation is limited to a handful of smallish lodges and camps, so tourist traffic tends to be low. The exception is from late May to July when the migration usually passes through the Western Corridor (although it may stick further east in years of heavy rain) and several mobile camps set up in the vicinity. The crossing of the Grumeti River, usually in late June or early July, is one of the most dramatic sequences in the annual wildebeest migration, and a positive bonanza for a dense population of gargantuan crocodiles.

Exclusive

🏠 **&Beyond Grumeti Serengeti Tented Camp** (10 tents) ☏ (South Africa) +27 (0)11 809 4441; e safaris@andbeyond.com; www.grumeti. com. Overlooking a small pool near the Grumeti River, this archetypal bush camp easily ranks as one of our favourite lodges in the Serengeti. The mood here is pure in-your-face Africa: the pool in front of the bar supports a resident pod of hippos & attracts a steady stream of other large mammals coming to drink, while birdlife is prolific both at the water's edge & in the surrounding thickets. At night, the place comes alive with a steady chorus of insects & frogs, & hippos & buffaloes grazing noisily around the tents. This place isn't for the faint-hearted, & you shouldn't even think about walking around at night without an armed escort, as the buffaloes have been known to charge. Facilities include an outdoor *boma*, where evening meals are served (except when it rains), & a circular swimming pool from where you can watch hippos bathing while you do the same thing. Accommodation consists of 10 stylish tents, each of which has a netted king-size bed, & en-suite

---

MODERN–DAY MAASAI *Emma Thomson*

The future of the Maasai seems an uncertain one. The Tanzanian government regards them as primitive and criticises them for 'holding the country back'. They are banned from wearing their distinctive *rubega/shuka* (robes) on public transport and in order to attend primary or secondary school the children are forced to remove their elaborate bead jewellery, and dress in Western-style clothes, while boys must shave off their long hair. All this follows a scheme launched by the government in the 1960s named the 'official national ideology of development', whose unspoken aims were to integrate the Maasai forcibly into mainstream society and settle them so the government could implement taxation.

Originally transhumant pastoralists, alternating the movement of their cattle between established wet- and dry-season pastures, the Maasai have now lost these latter areas to commercial farmers and wildlife conservation. Increasingly unpredictable rains leave grass and cattle dehydrated, and freak outbreaks of rinderpest and east coast fever (brought by explorers in the early 19th century) combine to often wipe out herds all together.

Squeezed into this bottleneck of depleted herds and land, the Maasai have had to overcome one of their greatest taboos – the ban on 'breaking the ground' and destroying grass, believed to have been sent by the Creator as sacred food for the cattle – in order to grow crops. Skills were acquired from nearby neighbours, the Chagga and Meru, and the latest studies show that now 40–45% of Maasai in East Africa trade meat for beans and maize, with only 50% living purely on the traditional diet of milk, blood and meat.

Unfortunately, when farming fails as a result of nutrient-poor soil, members of the family come back into the towns in search of paid work to supplement the unavoidable financial needs of providing for their families in the modern world. Men often find employment as nightwatchmen, while the women may have to resort to petty trading, beer brewing and, increasingly, prostitution.

However, the Maasai are both resourceful and resilient and the developing tourist industry brings new opportunities. Gemma EnoLengila, co-founder of the NGO Serian UK, stresses that 'the real challenge lies in creating sustainable projects that are developed in partnership with (traditional) communities, in a way that empowers rather than oppresses them'.

toilets & showers whose earthy adobe & wood architecture recalls Dogon structures from West Africa. The atmosphere is very informal, the good food is complemented by excellent house wines, & the service & guiding are world class. *US$1,205 pp Jun–Aug & late Dec, inc meals, drinks & activities; US$755 all other months. Closed Apr.*

🏠 **Singita Grumeti Reserves** (24 rooms/tents across 3 lodges) ☎ (South Africa) +27 (0)21 683 3424; e enquiries@singita.com; www.singita.com. The legendary South African lodge operator Singita has exclusive traversing rights across the 1,400km² Grumeti Game Reserve, a northern extension of the Western Corridor, where it operates a trio of luxury upmarket lodges aimed at seriously affluent travellers seeking an exclusive safari experience. The flagship Sasakwa Lodge on the eponymous hill offers dramatic elevated views across the verdant plains of the Western Corridor, while the chic, minimalist Faru Faru Lodge lies in a wooded area noted for its high mammal & bird diversity, & the more earthy Sabora Camp is a tented camp set in the open plains. The wildlife in this formerly undeveloped corner of the greater Serengeti is similar to other parts of the vast ecosystem, but notable population increases have been recorded since 2003. The enterprise employs 600 people, mostly from surrounding communities, & it offers cultural visits to nearby villages. Although wildlife viewing is good all year through, it peaks during Jul–Sep, when the migration is in the area. *From US$1,190 pp, rising to US$1,700 Jun–Aug & 16 Dec–16 Jan. Rates inc all meals, drinks & activities.*

🏠 **Serengeti Legendary Camp** See page 298. This exclusive Ker & Downey mobile tented camp takes up residence in the Western Corridor, using a remote campsite north of the Grumeti River, from May to Jul in anticipation of the migration. *US$850 pp (min rate for 4 guests) inc meals, drinks, activities & all park & camp fees.*

🏠 **Kirawira Tented Camp** (25 tents) ☎ 027 254 5555; e reservations@serena.co.tz; www.serenahotels.com. This plush tented camp, set on a small acacia-covered hill offering sweeping views over the Western Corridor, has Edwardian décor that gives it a distinct *Out of Africa* feel. The atmosphere is neither as intimate nor as 'bush' as other camps in this range, but it will probably appeal more to nervous safari-goers who prefer not to have hippo & buffalo chomping around their tent. The standing tents are all set on a raised platform & comfortably

decorated, with a netted king-size bed & en-suite shower & toilet. Facilities include a large swimming pool & some of the best food in the Serengeti. *US$730/1,055 sgl/dbl FB. Huge low season discounts Jan–May, Nov & early Dec.*

Upmarket

🏠 **Mbalageti Serengeti** (40 rooms) ☎ 255 27 254 8632; e info@mbalageti.com; www.mbalageti.com. Located in the Western Corridor, Mbalageti is perched on the northwestern slopes of Mwamnevi Hill, which lies 16km south of the main road through the Western Corridor, crossing the game-rich seasonal Dutwa floodplain & the Mbalageti River *en route*. Accommodation is in stunning thatch, wood, stone & canvas cottages, all of which are secluded in the evergreen woodland running along the ridge of the hill, & come with large wooden decks offering a superb view over the river to the Dutwa Plains from the outdoor bath. The dining area & bar are centred on a swimming pool, also offering panoramic views, & the food – different theme buffets every night – is excellent. Overall, it's a very comfortable & relatively affordable alternative to the more exclusive lodges in the Western Corridor. *US$352/673 tented chalets 21 Dec–7 Jan & Jun–Aug, US$277/513 Feb–Mar & Sep–Oct & the rest of Dec & Jan, US$219/398 Apr, May & Nov. US$212/385 lodge rooms sgl/dbl. All rates FB.*

Moderate

🏠 **Mapito Tented Camp** (10 tents) m 0732 975210/0765 379949; e info@mapito-camp-serengeti.com; www.mapito-camp-serengeti.com. Similar in style & feel to Ikoma Bush Camp & situated outside the same entrance gate, this likeable & reasonably priced tented camp has a bush feel, plenty of avian & mammal activity in the immediate vicinity, & a variety of activities on offer, including guided walks & night drives. Set on stone platforms, the standing tents come with twin or king-size beds, are furnished with a strong African touch, & have a private veranda & en-suite toilets & showers. The solar-lit mess tent serves hearty home-style meals. *US$290/480 sgl/dbl FB; US$280/450 low season. Closed for 2 weeks mid April.*

🏠 **Ikoma Bush Camp** (17 tents) ☎ 027 255 3243/250 6315; e reservations@moivaro.com; www.moivaro.com. This refreshingly unpretentious camp is situated on a concession immediately outside of the national park, roughly 3km from Ikoma Gate by road, & about 40km northwest of Seronera. The concession has been granted to the lodge by the nearby village of Robanda, which is paid a fee (used to fund the local school, water pump & clinic) in exchange for use of the land & assistance with anti-poaching patrols. Set in a glade of acacias, accommodation is in old-style no-frills dbl & twin tents with en-suite showers & small verandas facing out towards the bush. Because it lies outside the park, guided game walks are on offer, as are night drives, which come with a chance of encountering the likes of leopard, genet & more occasionally the secretive aardvark. It's a great base at any time of year, but especially in Jun when the migration passes through, & still quite reasonably priced. *US$286/357 sgl/dbl FB; US$251/314 Mar, Jun, Sep–mid Dec; US$168/210 Apr & May.*

🏠 **Speke Bay Lodge** (8 rooms, 12 tents) 📞 028 262 1236; e info@spekebay.com; www. spekebay.com. This lovely beachfront lodge, in the hands of the same Dutch owner-managers since it was founded in the mid 1990s, forms an excellent overnight stop for those coming to the Serengeti from western Kenya or the Lake Victoria region, as well as offering an opportunity for those on lengthy safaris to take a day or two's break from bouncing through the dusty bush to enjoy the moister environment alongside Africa's largest lake. Only 15 mins' drive outside the Ndabaka Entrance Gate, the lodge lies in 40ha of lakeshore woodland close to the Mbalageti River mouth. It offers good birdwatching (250 species recorded, including red-chested sunbird, swamp flycatcher, black-headed gonolek, slender-billed weaver & other lake specials unlikely to be seen in the Serengeti proper) as well as cultural visits by dugout to a nearby fishing village. The en-suite cottages have a thatched roof, stone floor, king-size bed, lake-facing balcony & high quality hardwood & wrought iron furnishing & finishes,

SERENGETI BIRDS

The Serengeti National Park, although popularly associated with grassland and open savanna, is in fact a reasonably ecologically varied entity. The western part of the national park consists of broken savanna, interspersed with impenetrable stands of whistling thorns and other acacias, and run through by the perennial Grumeti River and an attendant ribbon of riparian forest. The north, abutting Kenya's Maasai Mara National Reserve, is unexpectedly hilly, particularly around Lobo, and it supports a variety of more or less wooded savanna habitats. So, while the actual Serengeti Plains in the southeast of the park do support the relatively limited avifauna you tend to associate with open grassland, the national park ranks with the best of them in terms of avian variety. A working Serengeti checklist compiled by Schmidt in the 1980s tallied 505 species, and a further 30 species have been added since 1990.

The Serengeti-Mara ecosystem is one of Africa's Endemic Bird Areas, hosting five bird species found nowhere else, some of which are confined to the Tanzanian portion of the ecosystem. These 'Serengeti specials' are easy to locate and identify within their restricted range. The grey-throated spurfowl, a common roadside bird around the park headquarters at Seronera, is easily distinguished from the similar red-throated spurfowl by the white stripe below its red mask. In areas of woodland, parties of exquisite Fischer's lovebird draw attention to themselves by their incessant screeching and squawking as they flap energetically between trees. If the endemic spurfowl and lovebird are essentially local variations on a more widespread generic type, not so the rufous-tailed weaver, a fascinating bird placed in its own genus, but with nesting habits that indicate an affiliation to the sparrow-weavers. The rufous-tailed weaver is significantly larger and more sturdily built than most African ploceids, and its scaly feathering, pale eyes and habit of bouncing around boisterously in small but there are also cheaper & more basic standing tents using common showers. *US$230/350 sgl/dbl en-suite thatched bungalow FB; US$110/200 sgl/dbl safari tent with common showers & toilets FB.*

Budget and camping

🏠 **Serengeti Stop Over** (10 rooms) 📞028 262 2273; 📱 0784 406996/422359; 📧 info@ serengetistopover.com; www.serengetistopover. com. This excellent budget lodge lies alongside the main Mwanza–Musoma road, about 1km south of the Ndabaka Entrance Gate & 18km south of Bunda. The lodge consists of 10 bandas & a campsite with hot showers & cooking shades. A great advantage of staying here for motorised

travellers coming from Kenya or Mwanza is that park fees are only payable once you enter the park. The lodge can arrange safaris to Serengeti National Park, which will work out cheaper than a safari out of Arusha, if only because the lodge is a mere 1km from the entrance gate & 135km from Seronera so an overnight or day trip is a realistic possibility. The cost of a vehicle to carry up to 5 people for a day trip into the park is US$130. Other activities on offer include a walking safari to Lake Victoria at US$18 per trip pp, traditional & game fishing trips, a visit to the Nyerere Museum, & dancing & other cultural activities. *US$35/60 sgl/dbl banda B&B; camping US$10 tent hire plus US$5 pp.*

LOBO, LOLIONDO AND THE NORTH-CENTRAL SERENGETI

Wildly beautiful, and refreshingly untrammelled by comparison to the southern Serengeti, the plains that stretch northwards from Seronera towards the Lobo Hills are characterised by green undulating hills capped by some spectacular

flocks could lead to it being mistaken for a type of babbler – albeit one with an unusually large bill!

Of the two other Serengeti-Mara EBA endemics, the most visible and widespread is the Usambiro barbet, a close relative of the slightly smaller D'Arnaud's barbet, with which it is sometimes considered conspecific. Altogether more elusive is the grey-crested helmet-shrike, which strongly resembles the white helmet-shrike but is larger, has a more upright grey crest, and lacks an eye wattle. Although this striking bird indulges in typically conspicuous helmet-shrike behaviour, with small parties streaming noisily from one tree to the next, it is absent from the southern Serengeti, and thinly distributed in the north, where it is often associated with stands of whistling thorns.

Endemic chasing will be a priority of any serious birding visit to the Serengeti, but the mixed woodland and grassland offers consistently good birdwatching, including many species that will delight non-birders. The massive ostrich is common, as are other primarily terrestrial giants such as the kori bustard, secretary bird and southern ground hornbill. Perhaps the most distinctive of the smaller birds is the lilac-breasted roller, often seen perched on trees alongside the road. Highlights are inevitably subjective, but include a breeding colony of Jackson's golden-backed weaver at &Beyond Grumeti Serengeti Tented Camp, the magnificent black eagle soaring above the cliffs at Lobo, and up to six different vulture species squabbling over a kill. And there is always the chance of an exciting 'first'. Recent additions to the Tanzanian bird list from Serengeti include European turtledove (1997), short-eared owl (1998), long-tailed nightjar, black-backed cisticola and swallow-tailed kite (2000). In 2001, close to Grumeti River, we were fortunate enough to see (and photograph) the first golden pipit ever recorded in the national park.

13

granite outcrops, particularly in the vicinity of Lobo itself. A cover of dense acacia woodland is interspersed with tracts of more open grassland, bisected by the ribbons of lush riparian woodland that enclose the eastern Grumeti River and its various tributaries. Partially due to the relatively dense foliage, the area doesn't generally match up to the far south in terms of game viewing, but it is also relatively untrammelled by tourism, so much so that it's still possible to do an entire game drive without seeing another vehicle.

Wildlife viewing in the Lobo area generally comes into its own during September and October, when the wildebeest pass through the area on the southward migration from Kenya to the Serengeti Plains. It also sometimes hosts large numbers of wildebeest in July, normally in wetter years when the northward migration tends to use a more easterly route than normal. But even at other times of year, there is plenty to see. This area supports most of the park's elephant population, and the Lobo Hills are known for hosting several large lion prides. Cheetah, leopard, spotted hyena and bat-eared fox are also quite common, as is the exquisite serval, a small spotted cat most often seen darting through open grassland shortly after sunrise.

Extending over 4,000km² along the northeastern border of the Serengeti and northern border of the NCA, the **Loliondo Game Controlled Area (LGCA)**, reached via Klein's Gate 20km north of Lobo, is an integral part of the wildebeest migration route through the Greater Serengeti. Inhabited by the pastoralist Maasai, it effectively functions as a buffer zone to the national park, where cattle herds are frequently seen grazing alongside wild animals. Several lodges lie within the LGCA, on concessions that range in extent from a few dozen to a few thousand hectares. The largest and best of these concessions – indeed, one of the finest game viewing destinations anywhere in Tanzania – is Klein's Camp, which effectively functions as a exclusive private reserve, and offers superb game viewing as well as optional extras such as night drives and game walks.

⌂ WHERE TO STAY
Exclusive

⌂ **&Beyond Klein's Camp** (10 rooms) ☏(South Africa) +27 (0)11 809 4441; e safaris@ andbeyond.com; www.kleinscamp.com. Set within the LGCA on a hilly private concession bordered by the Serengeti National Park & Grumeti River, this wonderful &Beyond lodge offers some of the finest & most exclusive wildlife viewing in northern Tanzania, with a maximum of 20 guests & 5 4x4s patrolling its 100km² of acacia-strewn grassland. Because it lies outside the national park, there are no restrictions prohibiting night drives or off-road driving, both of which add an extra dimension to a safari. The range of wildlife is similar to the neighbouring part of the Serengeti, with at least 1 pride of around 20 lions resident, & a good chance of encountering 1 of several very relaxed leopards. The camp has a stunning location, comprising 10 en-suite bandas with hot shower, king-size beds with walk-in nets & a private balcony strung along a hilltop offering panoramic views in all directions.

Facilities include a swimming pool, a computer with internet access, & a well stocked gift shop. Food, service & guiding are all to the highest standard. US$1,205 pp Jan–Feb, Jun–Oct & late Dec, inc meals, drinks & activities; US$995 Nov & early Dec; US$755 all other months.

⌂ **Nduara Loliondo** (6 tents) ☏027 254 3281; m 0784 734490; e info@nomad-tanzania. com; www.nomad-tanzania.com. This most singular mobile camp, which moves seasonally between the south & north of the LGCA, replaces the standard safari tent with circular bamboo-&-canvas structures based on the wood-framed yurts built by Turkic nomads on the steppes of central Asia. The imaginative & colourful décor celebrates nomadic lifestyles from all over the world – in particular Mongolians, Navajo & of course the Maasai – & all units have a king-size bed, scatter rugs & skins, & an en-suite bathroom yurt with eco-flush toilets & hot bucket showers. Meals are served in a separate dining yurt & there is also a library/lounge tent. The location allows visitors to choose between game drives in the national park or around the camp, & guided walks, night drives & Maasai cultural visits are also available. *US$1,045/1,590 sgl/dbl; US$805/1,260 15 Mar–12 Apr, 19 May–30 Jun & 1 Nov–19 Dec.*

🏠 **Serengeti Migration Camp** (20 rooms) ☎027 254 0630-9; e info@elewana.com; www. elewanacollection.com. Set in the Ndasiata Hills about 20km from Lobo, this now ranks as one of the most exclusive lodges within the Serengeti National Park. Accommodation is in spacious en-suite luxury 'tents' made of canvas & wood, complemented by stylish wooden décor evoking the Edwardian era, & with large balconies facing the perennial Grumeti River. The lushly wooded grounds are rustling with birds & lizards, & there is a hippo pool on the river, with larger mammals often passing through camp. The surrounding area supports resident populations of lion, leopard, elephant & buffalo, & is fantastic when the migration passes through. Facilities include a swimming pool, jacuzzi, cocktail bar, library & lounge. An unusual feature of the camp is that short, guided game walks can be undertaken along several trails leading out from it. *US$1,030/1,490 sgl/dbl FB, inc most drinks, laundry & transfer to/from Kuro airstrip. Seasonal discounts available Mar–May, Nov & early Dec. Full game package inc game drives an additional US$100 pp.*

Upmarket
🏠 **Buffalo Luxury Camp** (20 tents) m 0753 888555; e info@buffaloluxurycamp.com; www. buffaloluxurycamp.com. Situated within the LGCA about 4km from Klein's Gate, this pleasant tented camp offers good access for game drives in the Serengeti's Lobo Hills, & guided walks & night drives can be undertaken within the confines of the 30ha concession. The spacious accommodation

is in canvas-sided suites with a split level hardwood floor, king-size bed, sitting room, & large en-suite hot showers. *US$880/1,230 sgl/dbl suite, or US$635/1,040 sgl/dbl in a smaller tent FB, with an extra US$30 pp charged for a full game package. Low season discount Feb–Apr.*

🏠 **Lobo Wildlife Lodge** (75 rooms) ☎027 254 4595; e sales@hotelsandlodges-tanzania. com; www.hotelsandlodges-tanzania.com. As with several other former government hotels in this chain, Lobo boasts a wonderful setting & interesting architecture compromised by inferior service & maintenance, & fittings that betray its age. It was built between 1968 & 1970, when most tourism to the Serengeti came directly from Kenya, & has waned in popularity now that visitors to the Serengeti come through Arusha. It is built around a koppie, spanning 4 floors & with a fantastic view over the plains. The surrounding hills can offer some wonderful game viewing & the grounds are crawling with hyraxes & colourful agama lizards. *US$340/460 sgl/dbl FB.*

🏠 **Mbuzi Mawe Tented Camp** (16 tents) ☎027 254 5555; e reservations@serena.co.tz; www.serenahotels.com. This tented camp is set among a group of ancient granite koppies overlooking the Tagora Plains, roughly 45km northeast of Seronera & 30km southwest of Lobo. The lodge's central location makes it a useful base from which to explore most of the key game-viewing areas in the Serengeti, & there is quite a bit of wildlife resident in the immediate vicinity (including the rock-dwelling klipspringer for which it is named), supplemented by the migration as it heads southwards in Nov or Dec. Accommodation is in large, earthily decorated en-suite standing tents, each of which contains 2 double beds & has a private stone patio with a view towards the rocks. *US$415/660 sgl/dbl FB. Significant discounts Jan–May & Nov–early Dec.*

Camping The campsite immediately outside the Lobo Wildlife Lodge is little used compared to those at Seronera and it also costs US$30 per person. Facilities are limited to a toilet and a rubbish pit. If you decide to stay, you can pop into the neighbouring lodge for a drink or meal.

THE MARA RIVER AND FAR NORTHWEST

The one part of the northern Serengeti to match the southern plains for general game viewing is the northwestern wedge of sloping grassland that divides the Mara River from the Kenyan border. Accessed from the south via a concrete causeway near Kogatende Rangers Post, this extension of the legendary Maasai Mara National Reserve supports prodigious herds of elephant, eland, topi, gazelle, zebra, wildebeest, buffalo, etc throughout the year, as well as significant numbers of lion and cheetah, and a small but regularly seen population of black rhino.

Game viewing along the Mara River can be little short of mind-boggling when the migration moves into the vicinity between July and September. During this time, large herds of wildebeest frequently gather on one or other side of the river, sometimes milling around for hours, even days, before one brave or foolish individual initiates a sudden river crossing, often for no apparent reason – indeed, it's not unusual for the same group of wildebeest to cross back in the opposite direction within hours of the initial crossing, suggesting that these slow-witted beasts are firm adherents to the maxim that the grass is always greener on the other side.

Back in the days when most safaris entered the park from Kenya, the far north of the Serengeti was quite busy with tourist traffic. However, the closure of the border between the Serengeti and Masai Mara to non-residents in the late 1970s led to a long lull in casual tourism to the region, partly due to its remoteness from any lodge, and partly due to a period of regular banditry and poaching. The area effectively reopened to tourism with the arrival of Sayari Camp in 2005, and it is now serviced by quite a number of small camps and lodges, most of which lie to the south of the Mara River near Kogatende and the causeway. Though not quite as remote in feel as it was ten years ago, it remains perhaps the most untrammelled and exciting part of the Serengeti, and particularly during the migration season it makes for a highly recommended (albeit rather expensive) addition to any Tanzanian safari itinerary.

 WHERE TO STAY

Exclusive

⌂ **Lamai Serengeti** (12 rooms) ☎ 027 254 3281; m 0784 734490; e info@nomad-tanzania.com; www.nomad-tanzania.com. Currently the most luxurious permanent lodge in the northern Serengeti, Lamai is situated on the lushly wooded slope of the Kogakuria Kopjes, about 25km south of the Kogatende Rangers Post & Mara Causeway. There are grandstand views in all directions, & the camp itself supports plenty of gaudy agama lizards, hyraxes, & plentiful birds including several localised barbet species. The game viewing circuit immediately around the camp passes through an impressive group of koppies, where a large pride of lions is often seen sprawled out on the granite boulders. It is also well placed to explore the network of roads around the Mara River, home to a resident group of black rhino & site of frequent

---

OLOIBONI   *Emma Thomson*

The *oloiboni* acts as a spiritual psychiatrist within Maasai communities, using stones to divine past, present and future events. Members of the homestead are able to consult him about family or mental and physical health problems, the answers to which come to the oloiboni in dreams. A reading involves the patient sitting cross-legged before him, spitting on the stones to infuse them with his/her spirit, and waiting for the results.

The skills are only passed on through the patrilineal line, and even then sons are not permitted to practise their powers of mediation until their twentieth birthday.

Intriguingly, two oloibonis are forbidden to meet each other, so if a neighbouring spiritual leader appears to be stealing business or enjoying good trade, villagers will claim that their oloiboni will send lions to attack the offending culprit.

The most controversial conservation issue to afflict East Africa in recent years is a proposal by the Tanzanian government to commence construction of a new road linking Arusha to the Lake Victoria region via the northern Serengeti in 2012. The proposal came into being as a result of President Kikwete's 2005 election promise to stimulate economic development in the isolated and impoverished region between the national park and the lake. The proposed road would follow the Rift Valley north from Mto wa Mbu to Lake Natron, then ascend westward into the Loliondo Game Controlled Area, crossing through the Serengeti for about 53km between Klein's Gate and Tabora B Gate, before connecting with the main road along the east shore of Lake Victoria close to Musoma. But while an asphalt road might indeed help uplift communities living outside the park, well-informed local sources suggest that better transport links to the site of a proposed soda-ash mine (mooted for Lake Natron) is likely to be a bigger factor behind this proposal. Regardless of the proponent's motivations, the proposal has been roundly and universally condemned by ecologists and the tourism sector.

There are two main arguments against the road's construction. The first is that it would bisect the northward and southward routes followed by the annual wildebeest migration, thereby disrupting this unique natural phenomenon. The second is that, if the existing asphalt road through Mikumi National Park serves as an indicator, regular truck traffic through the park would result in a huge number of road kills. Other concerns are that the road would improve access for poachers, provide an avenue for the spread of diseases and invasive weeds, and impact negatively on a globally important carbon sink through disruption to grazing patterns. It would also jeopardise the Serengeti's status as a UNESCO World Heritage site, while a decrease in tourism to not only the Serengeti but to Tanzania as a whole would cause a great loss of revenue and employment.

The current status of the proposal is difficult to ascertain. In June 2011, Tanzania's Minister for Natural Resources and Tourism wrote a letter to the UNESCO World Heritage Centre stating that if the proposed northern route did go ahead, the stretch running through the Loliondo Game Controlled Area and the Serengeti National Park would remain unpaved. Furthermore, the latter would continue to be managed by Tanapa, which imposes strict speed limits on all roads in national parks, and also forbids driving at night (when wildlife is at most risk of being killed in collisions).

Rather ambiguously, the same letter also stated that the government was considering an alternative southern route between Arusha and the Lake Victoria region. This alternative route, originally proposed by lobbyists against the Serengeti Highway, would run south of lakes Manyara and Eyasi and then veer north to connect with the existing Lake Victoria road near Bunda. It would have less potential for high profile ecological damage, since it would bypass the Serengeti ecosystem entirely, but it would also be longer and probably more costly to construct, and would have less direct economic impact on communities living to the west of the park. As far as we can establish, no definitive decision has been made at the time of writing, but regular updates are posted on the website www.savetheserengeti.org.

Serengeti National Park   THE MARA RIVER AND FAR NORTHWEST

13

wildebeest crossings in migration season. The luxurious & well lit chalets, all attractive pastel shades & minimalist décor, have king-size beds with walk-in netting, massive en-suite bathrooms, & large balconies offering great in-house birding. The food & service are superb, & the large swimming pool is a welcome luxury on hot days. *US$1,045/1,590 sgl/dbl, dropping to US$760/1,180 sgl/dbl 15 Mar–12 Apr, 19 May–30 Jun & 1 Nov–19 Dec.*

Sayari Camp (15 tents) (South Africa) +27 (0)21 418 0468; m 0736 5005156; www. asiliaafrica.com. Established in 2005, this wonderful, remote tented camp lies close to the south bank of the Mara River close to Kogatende, offering excellent access to the Mara Triangle, as well as being ideally placed to catch wildebeest crossings in migration season. It is divided into a 9-unit & 6-unit wing, each with its own sitting area & mess serving imaginative & tasty food. Both wings offer accommodation in stylishly decorated tents with hardwood floors, walk-in netted king-size beds, private balconies & hot showers. But the main attraction of Sayari is the genuine wilderness atmosphere, the remoteness from other lodges & the high quality guiding typical of Asilia. *US$925/1,540 sgl/dbl FB, or US$1,025/1,700 full game package. Low-season discount of around 20%.*

Olakira Camp (9 tents) See page 298. This wonderful mobile camp relocates from the southern Serengeti north to Mukutano along the Mara River from Jun–Nov. *US$870/1,400 sgl/dbl full game package.*

Lemala Mara (9 tents) 027 254 8966; e res@lemalacamp.com; www.lemalacamp. com. This luxury, mobile tented camp relocates from Ndutu to the Mara River area from Jun–Oct, when it is close to 2 major crossing points. The tents are very spacious & decorated in classic safari style, with a wooden floor & canvas top, & all have twin or king-size beds, solar powered lighting & hot water. *US$815/1,080 sgl/dbl FB. Full game packages inc activities an additional US$80 pp.*

Upmarket
Serengeti North Wilderness Camp (10 tents) (South Africa) +27 (0)11 7092 2035; m 0786 642466/0754 842466; e reservations@ wildfrontiers.com; www.wildfrontiers.com. This down-to-earth & reasonably priced mobile camp moves from Ndutu to a location north of the Mara River from Jul–Oct. The en-suite tents have solar lighting, eco-friendly toilets & comfortable but unpretentious furnishings. *US$ 450/600 FB.*

Find **accommodation, safaris** and **information** at:
www.mwanza-guide.com

above Reaching an altitude of 5,895m, Kilimanjaro is the highest mountain in Africa, and on the rare occasions when it is not veiled in clouds, its distinctive silhouette and snow-capped peak form one of the most breathtaking sights on the continent page 157

below Ol Doinyo Lengai is estimated to be around 350,000 – 400,000 years old and is East Africa's most active volcano page 266

14

Lake Victoria

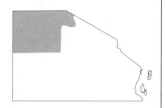

Straddling the borders with Kenya and Uganda, Lake Victoria extends over almost 70,000km² – an area comparable to Ireland – making it the second-largest freshwater body in the world after North America's Lake Superior. Some 51% of the lake's surface area falls within Tanzania, and the largest ports on the Tanzanian part of the lake are Mwanza, Musoma and Bukoba. Other important ports include Kisumu in Kenya, and Port Bell, Entebbe and Jinja in Uganda. Some 30 million people across the three countries are dependent on Lake Victoria as a primary source of water and/or food.

Lake Victoria fills an elevated depression between the two major forks of the Rift Valley. Nowhere more than 75m deep, it's very shallow by comparison with lakes Tanganyika and Nyasa, both of which hold a greater volume of water. Much of the shoreline is shallow and marshy, while the open water laps four of the world's 20 largest freshwater islands (including Ukerewe and Rubondo). The water level has fluctuated little in historical times, but the lake dried up entirely some 10,000–15,000 years ago. The Kagera River, rising in the highlands of Rwanda and emptying into Lake Victoria near Bukoba, is the most remote source of the Nile, the world's longest river, which exits the lake near Jinja in Uganda.

Lake Victoria practically borders the Western Serengeti but it has never featured prominently on Tanzania's tourist circuit. The one nascent upmarket tourist attraction in the region is the pedestrian-friendly Rubondo Island National Park. Mwanza, the largest Tanzanian port on the lake, is the main regional route focus and public transport hub. Away from the few largest towns, most of the people who live around Lake Victoria are fishermen, whose livelihood is increasingly threatened by the recent proliferation of introduced Nile perch and other ecological threats mentioned in greater detail in the box, *A Dying Lake*, on page 330.

For those who just want to take a quick look at Africa's largest lake, as an extension of a Serengeti safari, a recommended option (covered in the accommodation listings for the Western Corridor of Serengeti National Park; see page 304) is an overnight stay at Speke Bay Lodge. With its beautiful lakeshore location about 15 minutes from Ndabaka Gate (the most westerly point of entry to the Serengeti), this owner-managed lodge makes for a great break from the usual safari regime, and the large wooded grounds also supports a varied selection of birds associated with the lake but not with the Serengeti itself.

MWANZA AND AROUND

Updated by Hans Kristoffersen, Editor of the online Mwanza Guide

Once the second-largest city on mainland Tanzania, Mwanza now ranks fourth on that list, with a population variously estimated at between 220,000 and 350,000. It sprawls across the undulating and rocky southwest shore of Lake Victoria,

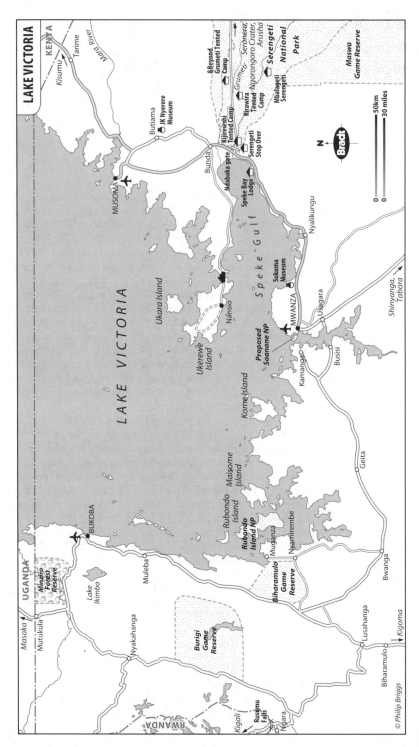

LAKE VICTORIA

© Philip Briggs

below the small hill where Speke reputedly arrived in 1858. The name Mwanza is a bastardisation of the Sukuma word *nyanza*, which simply means 'lake', and there's no reason to suppose that any settlement of significance existed on the site prior to 1890, when the modern city was founded as a German administrative outpost and the surrounding area was developed for cotton production.

Captured by Britain in July 1916, Mwanza received two economic boosts in the 1920s. The first was the discovery of significant gold deposits in Mwanza and Musoma districts. The second was the completion of the railway line from Dar es Salaam in 1928, which liberated Mwanza from dependence on the coastal rail link from Kisumu on the Kenyan shore of Lake Victoria. By the late 1930s, gold mined in the Lake Victoria region had become Tanganyika's second most profitable export after sisal. Production dried up in the post-independence era – a mere 2kg of gold was sold in 1975 – largely due to the depletion of established mines. The Mwanza area remains rich in minerals, however, and several gold veins discovered in the 1990s are currently being mined, notably at Geita. In addition, the cotton and textile industries remain important economic mainstays for the Mwanza region, as does the expanding fisheries sector. The region as a whole, however, is dominated by smallholder agriculture, which accounts for about 85% of employment.

Mwanza's main significance to travellers today is as a transport hub, it being the most important air, rail, road and lake terminal in northwest Tanzania. The city centre, with its recent rash of new modern buildings standing jarringly alongside decaying colonial-era structures, is nothing very special, but it does have a likeable and quite lively atmosphere – and travellers arriving from the sticks will doubtless enjoy the proliferation of reasonably priced lodgings, restaurants, bars and internet facilities. The best-known local landmark is Bismarck Rock, a precariously balanced granite formation – named after the German Chancellor Otto von Bismarck – that lies within the main harbour, but several similarly impressive outcrops can be seen by wandering along Station Road on the peninsula to the south of the city centre. For a good view over the lake from the city centre, clamber up the rocky green hills above Station Road. The rocks are crawling with colourful agama lizards and surprisingly, given the urban location, the trees still harbour a small troop of vervet monkeys. Further afield, worthwhile day or overnight trips from Mwanza include the Sukuma Museum at Bajoro, the proposed Saanane National Park, and Ukerewe Island at the heart of the lake.

GETTING THERE AND AWAY Mwanza is the main transport hub on Lake Victoria, and is likely to be passed through at some point by any traveller exploring the northwest of Tanzania, or travelling between Tanzania and Uganda or Rwanda.

By air Mwanza airport is situated on the lakeshore about 12km north of the city centre. **Precision Air** (✆ 028 250 0046; *www.precisionairtz.com*) runs daily flights to Mwanza from Dar es Salaam and Kilimanjaro International Airport (Arusha). There are daily flights to Nairobi, Kenya, by Precision Air, too. **Coastal Aviation** (m 0784 520949; *www.coastal.cc*) flies daily between Arusha and Mwanza with some flights connecting via Grumeti in the western Serengeti. A budget airline called **Fastjet** started flying from Dar to Mwanza in November 2012. There are also occasional services to Rubondo Island National Park.

The taxis that hang around in the airport car park generally ask around US$8 for a ride to the city centre, but regular minibuses to the city leave from the main road, about 500m from the airport.

14

By road The surfaced road running east of the lake via the turn-off to Serengeti National Park, leading to Musoma and the Kenyan port of Kisumu, is quite good by East African standards. The drive from Mwanza to Musoma should take just under two hours in a **private vehicle** and three hours by bus. Note that **buses** to Musoma and other easterly destinations do not depart from the central bus station near the market, but from the **Buzuruga terminal** (Nyakato) about 5km (*a US$3 taxi ride*) from the city centre. Regular minibuses run between the two bus stations. Mohammed Trans runs four services daily from Mwanza to Musoma.

All buses heading south now depart from the **Nyegezi bus terminal**, about 10km south of Mwanza on the road to Shinyanga (*a US$6 taxi ride*). That said, many bus companies still start or end their services from either their offices in the city centre or the central bus station, so confirm with the company when purchasing your ticket. As above, regular minibuses run from the centre to the bus station. We strongly advise against catching buses heading south towards Dodoma or Dar es Salaam, or west to Kigoma for that matter. While the roads are steadily being upgraded they are still in terrible condition, and the trip is normally measured in days rather than hours. The one exception is Tabora, which now only has roughly around 150km of unpaved road. Muhammad Trans runs two buses daily from Mwanza to Tabora via Shinyanga, departing at 06.00 and 13.00, taking seven hours and costing Tsh14,000.

Several buses run daily between Mwanza and Dar es Salaam (taking 15–16 hours). The only company that can be recommended is Sumry High Class, which charges around US$25 one-way. Buses leave Dar es Salaam from the Ubongo Terminal at 06.00 daily, and Mwanza from the Nyegezi Station at the same time. Check also www.mwanza-guide.com/howtoget/domestic.htm for updates.

By train Trains between Mwanza and Dar es Salaam – which used to run twice weekly and take around 40 hours one-way – had been suspended at the time of writing. Check www.mwanza-guide.com/howtoget/train.htm for updates on the service's status (see also advert on page 310).

By ferry The **Tanzania Railway Corporation** (TRC; ☏ 022 211 7833; e ccm_cserv@trctz.com; www.trctz.com) runs ferries connecting Mwanza to Bukoba and Ukerewe Island. The boats are in good condition, and first- and second-class cabins offer a comfort level matched in East Africa only by the Nairobi– Mombasa railway in Kenya, but third class tends to be overcrowded and there is a real risk of theft. The restaurants serve good, inexpensive meals and chilled beers and sodas. Timetables change regularly, since one or the other boat is almost always in dry dock, but current schedules and fares are listed below.

The MV *Victoria*, which does a 12-hour overnight run between Mwanza and Bukoba, is quite old but meets all safety standards. It departs from Mwanza at 21.00 on Tuesday, Thursday and Sunday, and from Bukoba at the same time on Monday, Wednesday and Friday. One-way fares work out to around US$19 for a first-class cabin, US$14 for second-class sleeping, US$11 for second-class sitting and US$10 third class.

For Ukerewe Island, the MV *Summary* and MV *Nyehunge* set sail for Nansio on alternate days, departing from Mwanza at 09.00 and 14.00 on weekdays, and at 16.00 on Saturday and 14.00 on Sunday. The trip takes about three hours and costs less than US$5 whether you travel first class or public class. Check-in is one hour before departure.

For anyone driving westwards to Geita, the most direct route is via the northern ferry crossing between Kamanga and Mwanza. The MV *Nansio* and MV *Orion*, operated by **Kamanga Ferry Ltd** [316 B2] (◊ *0784 626337; www.kamangaferry. com*), depart every hour or so from the southern port just off Nasser Road with the 30-minute ride costing less than US$1 per person and around US$2 per vehicle. Other details for travelling west to Geita, Biharamulo and the Rwanda border are included on our website, http://bradttanzania.wordpress.com.

TOURIST INFORMATION There is no tourist information office in Mwanza. However, the informative website www.mwanza-guide.com is well worth checking out for the latest hotel recommendations and other travel tips – and the webmaster is very helpful when it comes to answering queries (e *qanda@mwanza-guide.com*; see also advert on page 310).

TOUR OPERATORS For flights and other bookings, the best bet is generally thought to be **Fourways Travel** [352 D4] (◊ *028 250 2273/250 2620;* m *0741 230620/0748 230620;* e *fourways@fourwaystravel.net; www.fourwaystravel.net*), based in the NCU Hostel Building at the intersection of Kenyatta and Station roads. For budget travellers, a day or overnight safari to the Serengeti National Park from the Mwanza side will be far cheaper than a full northern circuit safari out of Arusha. A good contact for affordable Serengeti excursions is Serengeti Stop Over near the national park's Ndabaka Entrance Gate (see page 305). In Mwanza, you could try **Masumin Tours and Safaris** (◊ *028 250 0192/3292;* e *info@masumintours.com; www.masumintours. com*) or **Serengeti Services & Tours** (◊ *028 250 0061/0754; www.serengetiservices. com, www.serengetiservices.com*), which both deal with car hire and Serengeti safaris.

WHERE TO STAY

Exclusive

🏠 **Wag Hill Lodge** [316 A7] (3 rooms) ◊028 250 2445; m 0754 917974/777086; e waghill-admin@mwanza.org; www.waghill.com. Situated on a 17ha stand on a forested stretch of lakeshore a few mins by boat from central Mwanza, this small & exclusive lodge is particularly suited to keen anglers & birdwatchers, or anybody else who just wants to get away from it all. Rates inc meals, drinks & 10.00 pick-up by boat from the Mwanza Yacht Club. *US$425 pp.*

Upmarket

🏠 **Malaika Beach Resort** [316 D1] (32 rooms) ◊028 2561111/2222; m 0754 441222; e info@malaikabeachresort.com; www. malaikabeachresort.com. The closest thing to a 5-star resort near Mwanza, this all-suite hotel stands on an imposing rock formation with stunning views over Lake Victoria, 8km from the city centre along the airport road. The non-smoking suites have AC, king-size beds, satellite flat-screen TV, in-room safe, coffee-/tea-maker & impressive bathrooms – some even with a jacuzzi. Facilities include swimming pool (with a pool bar), a top-end restaurant, Wi-Fi, bar, children's

playground, secure off-street parking, pool tables & airport shuttle from/to Mwanza Airport. *US$120/150 sgl/dbl deluxe suite, or US$150/180 executive suite.*

🏠 **Hotel Tilapia** [316 A7] (40 rooms) ◊028 250 0517/617; e tilapia@mwanza-online.com, info@tilapiahotel.com; www.hoteltilapia.com. This comfortable hotel, 1km from the city centre along Station Road, has an attractive lakeshore position adjacent to the Saanane jetty. There are large chalets with satellite flat-screen TV & AC, luxury berths on the docked *African Queen*, & a selection of suites. Facilities include swimming pool, car hire, business centre, Japanese, Thai & Indian restaurants, & an attractive wooden bar & patio overlooking the lake. *US$90/110 sgl/dbl B&B; suites US$140 upwards.*

🏠 **Gold Crest Hotel** [316 D3] (86 rooms) ◊028 250 6058; e info@goldcresthotel.com; www.goldcresthotel.com. One of the newest hotels in Mwanza, having opened in mid 2011, the business-oriented Gold Crest Hotel has spacious suites with modern amenities & striking views of the downtown area. Centrally located, it offers 4 suite types, all with Wi-Fi, & is a popular conference venue. *From US$83/115 sgl/dbl.*

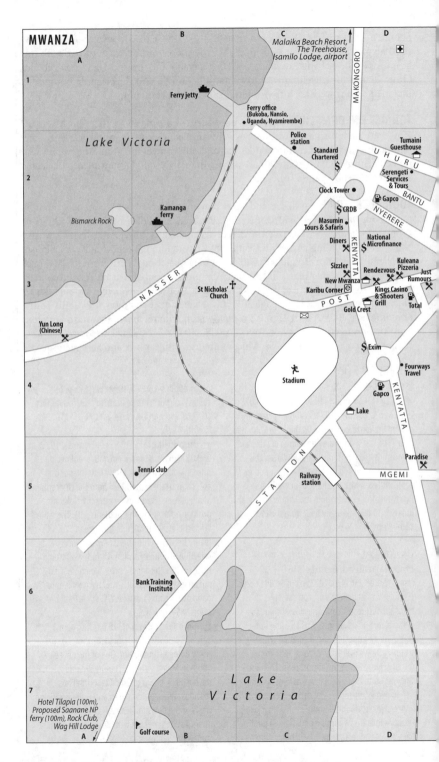

MWANZA

A B C D

Malaika Beach Resort,
The Treehouse,
Isamilo Lodge, airport

MAKONGORO

Ferry jetty

Ferry office
(Bukoba, Nansio,
Uganda, Nyamirembe)

Lake Victoria

Police
station

Standard
Chartered

Tumaini
Guesthouse

U H U R U

Clock Tower

Serengeti
Services
& Tours

Gapco

BANTU

Kamanga
ferry

CRDB

NYERERE

Bismarck Rock

Masumin
Tours & Safaris

National
Microfinance

Diners

KENYATTA

NASSER

Sizzler

Kuleana
Pizzeria

Rendezvous

Just
Rumours

St Nicholas'
Church

New Mwanza

Karibu Corner

Kings Casino
& Shooters
Grill

POST

Gold Crest

Total

Yun Long
(Chinese)

Exim

Fourways
Travel

Stadium

Gapco

KENYATTA

Lake

Tennis club

STATION

Paradise

MGEMI

Railway
station

Bank Training
Institute

Hotel Tilapia (100m),
Proposed Saanane NP
ferry (100m), Rock Club,
Wag Hill Lodge

Golf course

Lake
Victoria

B C D

316

Bariadi Guesthouse

Deluxe

Salma Cone

Worldlink travel & tours

Rafiki Guesthouse

National Bank of Commerce

Stanbic

BP

Uhuru Monument

Shinyanga Guesthouse

Market

Bus station

Oryx

Christmas Tree

G&G

Buzuruga bus terminal, Bujora Sukoma Museum, Musoma, Serengeti

Hotel Ramada

Busigasolwe Guesthouse

New Pentagon

N

Bradt

Gapco

Nyegezi bus terminal, Shinyanga, Tabora, Bukoba

NKRUMAH

UHURU

NKOMO

STATION

NYERERE

TEMPLE

LUMUMBA

LIBERTY

MARKET

RWEGASORE

MGEMI

MITI   MEREFU

NYERERE

PAMBA

KENYATTA

0   200m
0   200yds

14

🛏 **Isamilo Lodge** [316 D1] (25 rooms)
☎ 028 254 1627/8; e info@isamilolodge.com;
www.isamilolodge.com. Carved into the hillside
overlooking the city, this impressive lodge is
reputedly located in the exact spot where Speke
first saw Lake Victoria. It caters mostly to local
business travellers, & all rooms have AC, Wi-Fi,
satellite TV, phone & tiled en-suite bathrooms. Two
good restaurants serve continental, Indian & Asian
dishes, & there's a very pleasant terrace bar with
fabulous panoramic lake views. It's in the Isamilo
area, 3km from the city centre & 8km from the
airport (the junction is signposted on the left as
you enter Mwanza from the airport). *US$70/100
standard en-suite sgl/dbl; suites US$150. Hefty
resident discounts available.*

🛏 **New Mwanza Hotel** [316 D3] (55 rooms)
☎ 028 250 2583; m 0784 503511/0783 431985;
e gm@mwanzahotel.com, newmwanzahotel@
gmail.com; www.newmwanzahotel.com. This
former government hotel on Post Road is similar
in standard to the Tilapia, with the advantages
of a more central location & cheaper rates, &
disadvantages of a blander atmosphere & the
absence of a lake view. A business centre, coffee
shop, restaurant, casino & shopping arcade are
within the hotel building. From *US$50/70 sgl/dbl
B&B with AC & satellite TV.*

Moderate
🛏 **The Treehouse** [316 D1] (5 rooms) ☎ 028
254 1160; e treehouse@streetwise-africa.org;
www.streetwise-africa.org. This great homely
B&B, located around 600m from Isamilo Lodge,
is perfect for travellers interested in contributing
to the community. Run by the charity group

Streetwise Africa, all profits help to fund
programmes supporting street kids in Mwanza.
All rooms have 24-hr internet access & include
delicious homemade b/fast. Discounts available
for backpackers & volunteers. *US$30 comfy sgls
with shared bath; US$50/60 en-suite dbls; US$112
family banda.*

🛏 **G&G Hotel** [317 H5] (40 rooms) ☎ 028
254 2351; e hotelgandg@yahoo.com; www.
gnghotel.com. This welcoming, reasonably priced
& convenient hotel lies in the heart of the city
opposite the Aga Khan School on Miti Merefu
Road. The comfortable en-suite rooms with AC,
satellite TV & Wi-Fi are very good value & the hotel
is also wheelchair friendly. *From US$25 dbl; royal &
honeymoon suites (each with 2 en-suite bedrooms)
US$50.*

Budget
🛏 **Christmas Tree Hotel** [317 E5] ☎ 028 250
2001. This likeable high-rise hotel lies a short
distance from the bus station, within a 5 min walk
of the better restaurants & shops in the city centre.
Clean en-suite rooms come with large dbl bed, net,
fan, satellite TV & running hot water. Good value.
US$10/12 sgl/dbl B&B.

Shoestring
🛏 **Deluxe Hotel** [317 E2] This has been
justifiably popular with travellers for years, &
remains a good compromise between comfort &
price. The clean but rather worn en-suite rooms
with nets & running water are good value. A
restaurant & 2 bars are on the ground floor, along
with a noisy disco at w/ends. *Around US$5 dbl.*

✖ WHERE TO EAT AND DRINK
✖ **Diners** [316 D3] Situated roughly opposite
the New Mwanza Hotel, this excellent Asian eatery
serves a huge variety of Indian & Chinese dishes for
around US$6 with rice or naan bread.

✖ **Gold Crest Hotel** [316 D3] ⏱ 06.30–24.00.
This new hotel has an open-air restaurant &
swimming pool with a fantastic view of the city
from the 8th floor. There is occasional live music,
& good mains are in the US$7–15 range. The 1st
floor restaurant serves an 'all you can eat' buffet
lunch for US$7.

✖ **Hotel Tilapia** [316 A7] With 4 themed
restaurants, including Teppanyaki, Mwanza's only

Japanese restaurant, where you can cook your own
dishes on an iron griddle in the middle of your
table, & Domo Domo which offers a selection of
continental, Indian & Thai cuisine, the Tilapia offers
plenty of choice. Meals US$6–10.

✖ **Kuleana Pizzeria** [316 D3] ☎ 028 256 0566;
⏱ 08.30–17.00. Run by a charity for street
children, this popular pizzeria serves good pizzas &
a selection of other snacks & sandwiches. Prices are
in the US$3–5 range. Fresh brown bread is usually
available to take away.

✖ **Malaika Beach Resort** [316 D1] ☎ 028
2561111/2222. The restaurant at the out-of-town

Malaika – open 24 hrs a day – is the priciest in the Mwanza area & also probably the best, it's worth it if you feel like splashing out. The eclectic menu includes fresh tilapia & a variety of Asian & continental dishes.

✕ Sizzler Restaurant [316 D3] ⏲ lunch & dinner daily. A couple of doors down from Diners, & not quite in the same class, the Sizzler is nevertheless a very good Indian restaurant, & meals are about half the price. In the evenings, an outdoor BBQ does mishkaki, chicken tikka & fresh chapatis & roti bread. No alcohol.

✕ Yun Long Chinese Restaurant [316 A4] m 0784 821723; ⏲ lunch & dinner daily. About 5 mins walk from the city centre, this lovely outdoor bar & restaurant is probably unique for Mwanza in that it actually has a view over the lake & Bismarck Rock. It's a great spot for sundowners, but the restaurant also serves excellent, though pricey, Chinese food as well as a few continental dishes for US$5–12.

⊵ Salma Cone [317 E2] Great ice cream sundaes & fresh popcorn at reasonable prices.

OTHER PRACTICALITIES

Banks, ATMs and foreign exchange All the main banks are represented and have foreign exchange facilities, with the **National Bank of Commerce** [317 G4] usually offering the best rates and the fastest service. The **ATM** outside this bank allows you to draw local currency (max Tsh300,000/400,000 per transaction) against Visa cards, as does the one at the **Standard Chartered Bank** [316 D2], while the **Exim Bank** on Kenyatta Road [316 D4] accepts both Visa and MasterCard. The banks are mostly clustered close to the roundabout at the junction of Makongoro and Nyerere roads, or in the vicinity of the Clock Tower at the other end of Nyerere Road. The best place to change cash and travellers' cheques is at the bureau de change at Serengeti Services & Tours [316 D2] on Post Street.

Internet There's no shortage of internet cafés dotted around Mwanza city centre, charging a fairly uniform rate of Tsh800 per 30 minutes. The best and most central is **Karibu Corner Café** [316 D3] (opposite the New Mwanza Hotel). It charges Tsh1,500 per hour and is open from 08.00 Monday to Saturday and from 09.00 on Sunday.

Swimming There is no public swimming pool in Mwanza but it is often possible to use the swimming pool at the Hotel Tilapia for a small fee. Ask the front desk or call ✆ 028 250 0517/617 in advance. Swimming in the lake around the city is emphatically not recommended due to the high risk of contracting bilharzia – as well as the huge crocodiles!

EXCURSIONS FROM MWANZA

Saanane Island This small, rocky island in Lake Victoria, likely to be gazetted as a national park during the lifespan of this edition, once served as a rather dispiriting zoo, but thankfully all the captive animals have been relocated elsewhere. It also supports a selection of naturally occurring wildlife. Gaudy agama lizards bask on the rocks, monitor lizards crash gracelessly through the undergrowth, and a profusion of birds includes fish eagle, pied kingfisher and white-bellied cormorant near the shore, and more localised species such as swamp flycatcher, yellow-throated leaflove, grey kestrel and slender-billed weaver in the forest. The rock hyrax is the most visible naturally occurring mammal, and a reintroduced impala herd grazes the grassy shore.

Saanane once made for a worthwhile and affordable day trip out of Mwanza, but a recent entrance fee hike to US$30 per non-resident adult (plus a similar amount for the return boat trip) seems wildly disproportionate to its rather low-key attractions. If you want to visit, however, it lies about five minutes from the mainland using a

14

motorboat service that leaves from the jetty next to the Hotel Tilapia, ten minutes' walk from Mwanza city centre along Station Road.

Bujora Sukuma Museum (*http://philip.greenspun.com/sukuma;* ⏱ *08.00–17.00 Mon–Sat, 10.00–17.00 Sun; entrance US$7 pp*) The excellent Sukuma Museum, situated within the Bujora parish grounds about 20km east of Mwanza, is dedicated to the culture and history of the Sukuma, Tanzania's most populous tribe (see box, *The dancers of Usukuma*, below). The museum was established in the 1950s by Father David Clement (whose local nickname Fumbuka means 'Unexpected'), and designed in collaboration with a local Sukuma committee with the primary intent of preserving this culture for local Sukuma visitors.

The museum consists of five discrete pavilions or buildings, each devoted to a particular aspect of Sukuma culture. First up is the Sukuma homestead, which

THE DANCERS OF USUKUMA

Usukuma – literally 'Northern Land' – lies to the immediate south and east of Lake Victoria, and is home to the Bantu-speaking Sukuma, the largest tribe in Tanzania, comprising approximately 13% of the national population. The Sukuma are thought to have migrated into their present homeland prior to the 17th century, possibly from elsewhere in the Lake Victoria hinterland. Pre-colonial Usukuma differed from the centralised states that characterised areas to the north and west of the lake in that it was comprised of about 50 affiliated but autonomous local chieftaincies. Historically, culturally and linguistically, the Sukuma are strongly affiliated to the Nyamwezi of the Tabora area. It may well be that no marked division between the local chieftaincies of the two groups existed until the latter half of the 19th century, when the militant aspirations of Mirambo, who forged the more centralised Nyamwezi state, would have enforced a greater degree of political unity among the Sukuma.

The traditional political structure of Usukuma is typical of the *ntemi* chieftaincies of central Tanzania. Chiefs are part of a royal line, and are invested with mystical and religious qualities as well as political power. However, any autocratic tendencies are curbed by the necessity for a chief to be elected by a committee of princes and elders, which also has the ability to remove any chief whose actions are unpopular or inappropriate. The chief is thought to be mystically linked to the supreme being, who is regarded by the Sukuma as having many of the attributes of the sun. Ancestor worship plays as important a role in Sukuma religion as direct worship of the creator, since the spirits of the dead are seen to occupy a realm close to God. Although most Sukuma today are practising Christians or Muslims, many adhere concurrently to the traditional religion, and particularly in rural areas it is normal to leave offerings to the ancestors in the hope that they will bring rain, health and prosperity.

The Sukuma have the reputation within Tanzania of being snake charmers, and are also known for their varied and spectacular traditional dances, disciplines that combine in a ritual dance called the Bugobogobo. The dancers coil a live python around their body and then writhe to a frenetic drumbeat, alternately pretending to embrace the gigantic snake and to fight with it. The dance becomes more frenzied as the drumbeat speeds up and the snake becomes increasingly excited or agitated, often causing the audience to scatter in all directions. Bugobogobo dances are sometimes held at the Bujora Sukuma Museum (see above) on Saturday afternoons.

contains traditional household items such as cooking utensils, religious objects and agricultural tools. The blacksmith's house is a low circular thatched hut containing cowhide bellows and other implements used to forge metal, as well as metal tools and spearheads made by the blacksmith. The concrete house of the *Iduku* (traditional healer) contains medicinal calabashes, divination tools, various charms and other traditional medical paraphernalia. The Dance Society Pavilion concentrates on the history and costumes of the Bagika and Bagalu, the competing dance societies of the Sukuma. Most impressive of all is the Royal Pavilion, a two-storey building designed in the shape of a royal throne. This section houses a vast collection of royal Sukuma thrones and crowns, while a wall display delineates the area and name of each of the 52 Sukuma chiefdoms, as well as lineages for the more important ones. The second storey of the pavilion houses royal drums donated by some local chiefs. The colourful Bujora Church, on a

Traditionally, most Sukuma people under the age of 30 will belong to one of several dance societies, of which the largest and oldest are the Bagika and Bagalu. According to oral tradition the two societies were founded about 150 years ago by Ngika and Gumha, rival dancers and traditional healers who held regular competitions to determine who had the most potent medicine. The two would dance alongside each other, using magic charms to attract spectators and induce errors in their rival's routine, and the winner was the one who eventually attracted the largest crowd.

A similar format is followed in modern dance competitions held by the rival societies, with the two troupes dancing concurrently and attempting to outdo each other in order to attract the greater number of spectators. The dancers mostly base their performances around traditional routines, but innovative and outrageous stunts – masks, props, costumes or fresh steps – are encouraged, and may well be decisive in attracting the crowd required in order to win the competition.

Until recent times, the dancing societies of Sukuma were important spiritual entities with somewhat Masonic overtones. Members of any given society would wear a distinctive tattoo. The Bagika favour a diagonal double incision running from one shoulder to the opposite side of the waist, and sometimes a series of arrow-shaped incisions on one cheek. The Bagalu used circular rather than linear incisions, sometimes around the left eye or breast, sometimes around the torso. Today, the dance competitions are held mainly as entertainment, but a large element of mysticism is still attached to the societies. The leader of a troupe will consult traditional spiritual leaders prior to the competition, and cover his body in a paste made from a powdered dance medicine called *samba* when dancing. Some dancers even build ancestral shrines on the dance ground.

Dance competitions take place throughout Usukuma after the end of the harvest season, starting in June and running through to August, with particularly impressive festivals likely to be held on the public holidays of 7 July and 8 August. If you're in the area at the time, ask around about where competitions are being held. For more information about the Sukuma dancers and other aspects of Sukuma culture, take a look at Sukuma Museum's website, www.sukumamuseum. org, which covers most aspects of Sukuma culture and history.

14

The first European to see Lake Victoria was John Hanning Speke, who marched from Tabora to the site of present-day Mwanza in 1858 following his joint 'discovery' of Lake Tanganyika with Richard Burton the previous year. Speke named the lake for Queen Victoria, but prior to that Arab slave traders called it Ukerewe (still the name of its largest island). It is unclear what name was in local use, since the only one used by Speke is Nyanza, which simply means lake.

A major goal of the Burton–Speke expedition had been to solve the great geographical enigma of the age, the source of the White Nile. Speke, based on his brief glimpse of the southeast corner of Lake Victoria, somewhat whimsically proclaimed his 'discovery' to be the answer to that riddle. Burton, with a comparable lack of compelling evidence, was convinced that the great river flowed out of Lake Tanganyika. The dispute between the former travelling companions erupted bitterly on their return to Britain, where Burton – the more persuasive writer and respected traveller – gained the backing of the scientific establishment.

Over 1862–63, Speke and Captain James Grant returned to Lake Victoria, hoping to prove Speke's theory correct. They looped inland around the western shore of the lake, arriving at the court of King Mutesa of Buganda, then continued east to the site of present-day Jinja, where a substantial river flowed out of the lake after tumbling over the cataract that Speke named Ripon Falls. From here, the two explorers headed north, sporadically crossing paths with the river throughout what is today Uganda, before following the Nile to Khartoum and Cairo.

Speke's declaration that 'The Nile is settled' met with mixed support back home. Burton and other sceptics pointed out that Speke had bypassed the entire western shore of his purported great lake, had visited only a couple of points on the northern shore, and had not attempted to explore the east. Nor, for that matter, had he followed the course of the Nile in its entirety. Speke, claimed his detractors, had seen several different lakes and different stretches of river, connected only in Speke's deluded mind. The sceptics had a point, but Speke had nevertheless gathered sufficient geographical evidence to render his claim highly plausible, and his notion of one great lake, far from being mere whimsy, was backed by anecdotal information gathered from local sources along the way.

Matters were scheduled to reach a head on 16 September 1864, when an eagerly awaited debate between Burton and Speke – in the words of the former, 'what silly tongues called the "Nile Duel"' – was due to take place at the Royal Geographic Society (RGS). And reach a head they did, but in circumstances more tragic than anybody could have anticipated. On the afternoon of the debate, Speke went out shooting with a cousin, only to stumble while crossing a wall, in the process discharging a barrel of his shotgun into his heart. The subsequent inquest recorded a verdict of accidental death, but it has often been suggested – purely on the basis of the curious timing – that Speke deliberately took his life rather than face up to Burton in public. Burton, who had seen Speke less than three hours earlier, was by all accounts deeply troubled by Speke's death, and years later he was quoted as stating 'the uncharitable [say] that I shot him' – an accusation that seems to have been aired only in Burton's imagination.

Speke was dead, but the 'Nile debate' would keep kicking for several years. In 1864, Sir Stanley and Lady Baker were the first Europeans to reach Lake Albert and nearby Murchison Falls in present-day Uganda. The Bakers, much to the delight of the anti-Speke lobby, were convinced that this newly named lake was a source of the Nile, although they openly admitted it might not be the only one. Following the Bakers' announcement, Burton put forward a revised theory, namely that the most remote source of the Nile was the Rusizi River, which he believed flowed out of the northern head of Lake Tanganyika and emptied into Lake Albert.

In 1865, the RGS followed up on Burton's theory by sending Dr David Livingstone to Lake Tanganyika. Livingstone, however, was of the opinion that the Nile's source lay further south than Burton supposed, and so he struck out towards the lake along a previously unexplored route. Leaving from Mikindani in the far south of present-day Tanzania, Livingstone followed the Rovuma River inland, continuing westward to the southern tip of Lake Tanganyika. From there, he ranged southward into present day Zambia, where he came across a new candidate for the source of the Nile, the swampy Lake Bangweulu and its major outlet, the Lualaba River. It was only after his famous meeting with Henry Stanley at Ujiji, in November 1871, that Livingstone (in the company of Stanley) visited the north of Lake Tanganyika and Burton's cherished Rusizi River, which, it transpired, flowed *into* the lake. Burton, nevertheless, still regarded Lake Tanganyika to be the most likely source of the Nile, while Livingstone was convinced that the answer lay with the Lualaba River. In August 1872, Livingstone headed back to the Lake Bangweulu region, where he fell ill and died six months later, the great question still unanswered.

In August 1874, ten years after Speke's death, Stanley embarked on a three-year expedition every bit as remarkable and arduous as those undertaken by his predecessors, yet one whose significance is often overlooked. Partly, this is because Stanley cuts such an unsympathetic figure, the grim caricature of the murderous pre-colonial White Man blasting and blustering his way through territories where Burton, Speke and Livingstone had relied largely on diplomacy. It is also the case, however, that Stanley set out with no intention of seeking out headline-making fresh discoveries. Instead, he determined to test out the various theories that had been advocated by Speke, Burton and Livingstone about the Nile's source. First, Stanley sailed around the circumference of Lake Victoria, establishing that it was indeed as vast as Speke had claimed. Stanley's next step was to circumnavigate Lake Tanganyika, which, contrary to Burton's long-held theories, clearly boasted no outlet sufficiently large to be the source of the Nile. Finally, and most remarkably, Stanley took a boat along Livingstone's Lualaba River to its confluence with an even larger river, which he followed for months with no idea as to where he might end up.

When, exactly 999 days after he left Zanzibar, Stanley emerged at the Congo mouth, the shortlist of plausible theories relating to the source of the Nile had been reduced to one. Clearly, the Nile did flow out of Lake Victoria at Ripon Falls, before entering and exiting Lake Albert at its northern tip to start its long course through the sands of the Sahara. Stanley's achievement in putting to rest decades of speculation about how the main rivers and lakes of East Africa linked together is estimable indeed. He was nevertheless generous enough to concede that: 'Speke now has the full glory of having discovered the largest inland sea on the continent of Africa, also its principal affluent as well as its outlet. I must also give him credit for having understood the geography of the countries we travelled through far better than any of us who so persistently opposed his hypothesis.'

hilltop overlooking the museum, is also worth a look around, since it incorporates large elements of Sukuma royal symbolism into its design, for instance an altar shaped like a traditional throne.

The Sukuma Museum is a short walk from Kisesa on the Mwanza–Musoma road. Any bus to Musoma can drop you off there at the junction. The best day to visit is Saturday, when the Sukuma Snake Dance is sometimes performed with a live python. Traditional performances can be arranged for Tsh60,000 per person. An inexpensive campsite and a few rooms are available for travellers who want to stay the night.

Ukerewe Island The 530km² Ukerewe is the largest island in Lake Victoria or for trivia lovers, the sixth-largest lake-bound landmass in the world. It is also the most accessible substantial island on the Tanzanian part of the lake.

Ukerewe Island can be visited by ferry (see page 314) and the trip is a good way to see some of Africa's largest lake, but it is also connected to Bunda on the main Mwanza–Musoma road by a causeway and occasional dala-dalas.

The port of Nansio is a rather scruffy little place but the island itself is very pretty, boasting some attractive sandy beaches and plenty of possibilities for casual rambling. If you visit the island as a day trip from Mwanza you'll only have an hour or so to explore, so it's worth staying overnight. There are several local guesthouses in Nansio, of which the **La Bima Bar** and **Island Inn** are about the best.

Butiama This otherwise undistinguished small town is of note as the birthplace of former President Julius Nyerere, and it is also where he is buried. The **Mwalimu Julius K Nyerere Memorial Museum** (✆ *028 262 1338;* ⏱ *09.30–18.00 daily; entrance US$7 pp*) was officially opened here in July 1999, and contains a variety of exhibits about Tanzania's first president, including various personal possessions and gifts presented to him on his inauguration and retirement, as well as about the local Zanaki culture. Nyerere's grave and those of his parents can also be visited. Butiama lies off the main road along a 30–40km side road branching from Bunda. The drive from Bunda takes less than an hour in a private vehicle, and there is some public transport.

MUSOMA

On the eastern shores of Lake Victoria, Musoma is the administrative centre of the Mara Region, and a reasonably substantial town with a population estimated at just over 120,000. The compact town centre shares with Mwanza and Bukoba a likeable combination of run-down colonial architecture – the Old Boma on Mkendo Hill dates to the German period – and friendly African bustle. And its setting, on a narrow, rocky peninsula, is the equal of any port on Lake Victoria, terminating in an impressive granite outcrop covered in clucking cormorants and offering an almost 360° vantage point for sunsets over the lake. Unfortunately, however, because it is tucked up so close to the Kenyan border, Musoma is something of a dead end in terms of travel within Tanzania, and it would be difficult to justify a special diversion here. For travellers heading between Mwanza and the Kenyan port of Kisumu, however, this remote but hospitable port is likely to prove a more than agreeable place to break up the trip. Two possible water excursions from Musoma are to Lukuba Island, known for its impressive breeding bird colonies, and to the crocodile-infested Mara River mouth. The Nyerere Museum in Butiama also makes for an easy day trip out of Musoma.

MUSOMA

© Philip Briggs

Rocky Peninsula

Lake Victoria

N

Bradt

Lake Victoria

Silver Sand

Tembo Beach

Football field

0 — 200m
0 — 200yds

German Boma

Immigration

Roman Catholic Hostel

BP

TANESCO

Fishing harbour

Market

see inset

Football field

Mwanza, Kenya

New Peninsula

Inset

0 — 100m
0 — 100yds

Fishing Harbour

Police station

Barclays

GHANDI

CRDB

Matvilla

Precision Air

KUSAGA

Salamander

KAHAWA

Afrilux

NYERERE

MUKENDO

Market

Bus station

Gapco

BP

Total

Gapco

Embassy Lodge

Orange Tree

Masero Inn

National Bank of Commerce

GETTING THERE AND AWAY

By air There is an airstrip [325 C5] on the outskirts of central Musoma, between the Catholic Hostel and the Peninsula Hotel. **Precision Air** [325 B6] (📞 *028 250 0046; www.precisionairtz.com*) flies here a few times a week from Dar es Salaam.

By road Musoma lies about 180km from Mwanza along an 18km-long side road branching west from the main road towards the Kenyan border. The road between Mwanza and Musoma is surfaced and in pretty good nick for most of its length. The drive takes around two hours in a **private vehicle**. Regular **buses** run along the road, taking about four hours one-way; the most reliable is Mohammed Trans, which runs three services daily, departing Musoma at 06.00, 09.00 and 13.30. Small and very regular **minibuses** cover the stretch between Musoma and Bunda, but don't seem to operate any further south towards Mwanza. Coming from the Kenya side, direct buses between Kisumu and Mwanza run past the junction to Musoma, but generally bypass the town itself. If you need to get out at the junction, you'll have no difficulty finding transport on to Musoma.

GETTING AROUND If you're staying at one of the beach hotels, the standard fare for a taxi from town is around US$1.50.

🏠 WHERE TO STAY AND EAT

Exclusive

🏠 **Lukuba Island Lodge** (5 rooms) 📞 027 254 8840; e inquiries@lukuba.com; www.lukuba. com. Set on a small island a 45 min boat ride from Musoma, this peaceful retreat is ideally suited to keen birdwatchers, with more than 70 species recorded, & it's also home to spotted-necked otters, vervet monkeys & agama lizards, while anglers have the prospect of hooking Nile perches that clock in at up to 80kg. Accommodation is in 5 stone bungalows with thatch roofs & verandas offering idyllic lake views. *US$320/590 sgl/dbl FB.*

Upmarket

🏠 **New Peninsula Hotel** [325 A5] m 0787 679620. The former government Lake Hotel, now privatised, revamped & renamed, is a well-maintained & atmospheric wood & whitewash set-up on a somewhat sterile stretch of lakeshore about 500m west of the town centre. Coming from elsewhere in Tanzania, it seems a little pricey, however. Rooms have satellite TV, AC, fridge & en-suite bathrooms. The open-sided restaurant on the ground floor serves a variety of Western & Indian dishes for around Tsh5,000. *US$20/40 en-suite sgl/ dbl; US$55 suites.*

Moderate

🏠 **Afrilux Hotel** [325 C6] 📞 028 262 0031/0534; e afriluxhotel@nyatwalibeach.co.tz;

www.afriluxhotel.nyatwalibeach.co.tz. This smart, modern 4-storey hotel is situated right in the town centre, 500m from the bus station. The clean en-suite rooms with satellite TV, fan & running hot water are all you could possibly ask for at this price. The restaurant & garden bar serves decent continental & Indian meals for around Tsh4,000. *US$18/25 sgl/dbl.*

Budget and camping

🏠 **Tembo Beach Hotel** [325 B3] (7 rooms) 📞 028 262 2887; e tembobeach@yahoo.com. Set on a small strip of beach around 500m from the centre of town, Tembo Beach is a popular stop-off on the overland route. The rooms, with their fabulous retro 70s ski lodge appeal – loads of wood panelling & some with loft beds – seem optimistically priced. There's a campsite, & a friendly bar & restaurant serves meals for around US$4–6. Bike hire is also available & boat trips on the Mara River can be arranged. *US$30 B&B en-suite dbl with fan; camping US$10 pp.*

Shoestring

🏠 **Orange Tree Hotel** [325 C7] 📞 028 262 2353. This long-established budget hotel has seen better days, but it remains a friendly, sensibly priced option. *US$7/10 en-suite sgl/dbl.*

🏠 **Roman Catholic Conference Centre & Hostel** [325 C4] (30 rooms) 📞 028 262 0168. This is the best budget option in town, about 200m from the bus station along the road towards the airport, & consisting of 30 clean dbls with netting (but no fan). A canteen serves inexpensive local meals. *US$6 dbl*.

RUBONDO ISLAND NATIONAL PARK

The only bona fide tourist attraction on Lake Victoria, Rubondo Island National Park, gazetted in 1977, lies in its far southwest corner, some 200km west of the Serengeti as the crow flies, where it forms a potentially very different extension to a standard northern Tanzania safari package. That so few tourists do actually make it to Rubondo is in some part because the island's attractions are more low-key and esoteric than those of Tanzania's high-profile savanna reserves. A greater factor in Rubondo's obscurity is quite simply, however, that the park long lacked for the sort of tourist infrastructure and ease of access that would have made it a realistic goal for any but the most intrepid or wealthy of travellers.

This is a real shame, because Rubondo is a lovely retreat, offering the combination of a near-perfect climate, atmospheric jungle-fringed beaches, some unusual wildlife viewing, and the opportunity to explore it all on foot or by boat. Rubondo may not be to everybody's taste, but the island can be recommended without reservation to anybody with a strong interest in birds, walking or game fishing – or simply a yen to escape to an uncrowded and blissfully peaceful tropical paradise. It is to be hoped, however, that the recent acquisition of Rubondo's only private camp by the highly regarded Asilia group, and the likely reintroduction of scheduled flights from the Serengeti, will attract renewed interest in this unheralded gem of a park.

Rubondo has a remarkably pleasant climate all year round, with temperatures rarely falling outside a range of 20–25ºC by day or by night. The average annual rainfall is around 1,200mm, with the driest months being June to September, and January and February. These dry months are the perfect time to visit Rubondo, but the park and lodge are open all year, and there is no serious obstacle to visiting during the rains. The entrance fee of US$20 per 24 hours must be paid in hard currency. A national park fishing licence valid for three days costs US$50.

GEOGRAPHY AND VEGETATION The 457km² national park is dominated by the green and undulating 240km² island for which it is named, but it does protect another 11 islets, none much larger than 2km², and there is talk of extending the boundary eastward to incorporate the forested west of Maisome Island. Rubondo Island itself essentially consists of a partially submerged rift of four volcanically formed hills, linked by three flatter isthmuses. It measures 28km from north to south but is nowhere more than 10km wide. The highest point on Rubondo is the Msasa Hills in the far south, which reach an elevation of 1,486m (350m above the level of the lake). The park headquarters, airstrip and various accommodation facilities lie within 2km of one another at Kageye, on the central isthmus, about 10km from the northern tip at the narrowest part of the island.

The dominant vegetation type is closed-canopy lowland forest, which covers about 80% of the island's surface area. This is interspersed with patches of open grassland and, all but restricted to the Lukaya area, acacia woodland. The eastern lakeshore is characterised by rocky areas and sandy beaches (such as those in front of the lodge and camp), while the western shore supports extensive papyrus swamps, often lined with wild date palms. Between December and March, an estimated 40 terrestrial and epiphytic orchid species come into bloom, as do gloriosa and fireball lilies. The red coral tree, which flowers almost all year round, is also a spectacular sight.

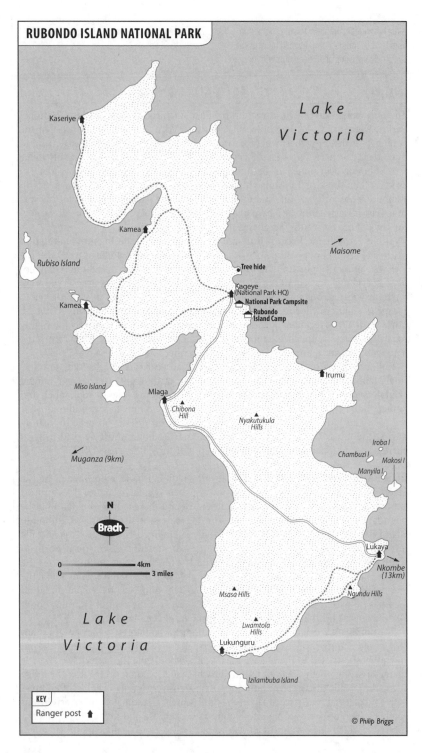

RUBONDO ISLAND NATIONAL PARK

Lake Victoria

Kaseriye

Kamea

Rubiso Island

Kamea

Miso Island

Maisome

Tree hide

Kageye
(National Park HQ)
National Park Campsite
Rubondo Island Camp

Mlaga

Chibona Hill

Nyakutukula Hills

Irumu

Muganza (9km)

Iroba I

Chambuzi I

Makosi I

Manyila I

N

Bradt

0   4km
0   3 miles

Lukaya

Nkombe (13km)

Msasa Hills

Ngundu Hills

Lwamtola Hills

Lukunguru

Lake Victoria

Izilambuba Island

KEY
Ranger post

© Philip Briggs

WILDLIFE Rubondo's wildlife doesn't offer the easy thrills of many savanna reserves, but many large mammals are present, most alluring perhaps the introduced populations of chimpanzee and elephant (see box, *The floating zoo*, page 332). However, the presence of these glamour boys shouldn't shift the focus away from the island's interesting assemblage of naturally occurring residents, including the aquatic sitatunga antelope, hippopotamus, crocodile and water monitor.

Vervet monkeys are numerous and easily seen all over Rubondo, but no other primate species occurs here naturally. This is difficult to explain, given the variety of primates that are present in similar island habitats on the Ugandan part of the lake, and given that the lake dried up fully in the biologically recent past, which would have allowed a free flow of species between the island and mainland forests.

There is no better place in Africa to observe the spot-necked otter, a widespread but elusive diurnal predator that feeds mainly on fish and frogs. A few pairs of otter are resident in the rocky bay around the lodge and camp – they regularly swim past camp, and the den can sometimes be seen through binoculars during the breeding season. The only terrestrial predators that occur on the island are the marsh mongoose and large-spotted genet, the latter regularly coming to feed around the lodge at dinnertime.

Birds With its combination of aquatic and forested habitats, Rubondo Island is an alluring destination for birdwatchers, especially as it can so easily be explored on foot. Oddly, the park's avifauna has never been properly studied, with the result that the only checklist, compiled from reported sightings by the Frankfurt Zoological Society and available at the Rubondo Island Camp, tallies up at a relatively low 225 species. It is likely that a substantial number of forest species that are resident on the island, or regular visitors, have thus far gone unrecorded.

The main avian attraction for casual visitors will be the concentrations of large water birds that occur along the island's swampy shores. Rubondo hosts Lake

STALKING THE SITATUNGA

Two closely related antelope species occur naturally on the Rubondo Island, the swamp-dwelling sitatunga and forest-dwelling bushbuck. Of these, the more interesting is the sitatunga – a widespread but localised species with uniquely splayed hooves that allow it to manoeuvre through swampy habitats – since Rubondo is one of only two East African parks where it is easily observed. The males of both these antelopes are very handsome, with large spiralled horns, but the sitatunga is larger, shaggier in appearance, and grey where the bushbuck is chestnut brown. The females of both species are smaller and less striking, but easily distinguished from one another, since the bushbuck is striped on its sides, whereas the sitatunga is unmarked.

Rubondo's sitatunga population probably exceeds ten individuals per km², and is not so habitat-specific as elsewhere, apparently – and unexpectedly – outnumbering bushbuck even in the forest. Researchers have noted that the sitatunga of Rubondo's forests are more diurnal than is normally the case, and have less-splayed feet and darker coats than those resident in the swamps – whether this is genetically influenced, or a function of wear and sun bleaching, is difficult to say. A possible explanation for this anomalous situation is that sitatunga colonised the island and expanded into forested habitats before there were any bushbuck around.

Lake Victoria has been afflicted by a series of manmade ecological disasters over the past century. The degradation started in the early colonial era, with the clearing of large tracts of indigenous vegetation and drainage of natural swamps to make way for plantations of tea, coffee and sugar. One result of this was an increase in the amount of topsoil washed into the lake, so that the water became progressively muddier and murkier during the 20th century. More serious was the wash-off of toxic pesticides and other agricultural chemicals, which in addition to polluting the water contain nutrients that promote algae growth, in turn tending to decrease oxygenation levels. The foundation of several large lakeshore cities and plantations attracted migrant labourers from around the region, many of whom settled at the lake, leading to a disproportionate population increase and – exacerbated by more sophisticated trapping tools introduced by the colonials – heavy overfishing.

By the early 1950s, the above factors had conspired to create a noticeable drop in yields of popular indigenous fish, in particular the Lake Victoria tilapia (*ngege*), which had been fished close to extinction. The colonial authorities introduced the similar Nile tilapia, which restored the diminishing yield without seriously affecting the ecological balance of the lake. More disastrous, however, was the gradual infiltration of the Nile perch, a voracious predator that feeds almost exclusively on smaller fish, and frequently reaches a length of 2m and a weight exceeding 100kg. How the perch initially ended up in Lake Victoria is a matter of conjecture – game fishermen might have introduced some perch, while others possibly swam downriver from Uganda's Lake Kyoga, where they had been introduced in the mid 1950s. But, however they first arrived in Lake Victoria, Nile perch regularly turned up in fishermen's nets from the late 1950s. The authorities, who favoured large eating fish over the smaller tilapia and cichlids, decided to ensure the survival of the alien predators with an active programme of introductions in the early 1960s.

It would be 20 years before the full impact of this misguided policy hit home. In a UN survey undertaken in 1971, the indigenous haplochromine cichlids still constituted their traditional 80% percentage of the lake's fish biomass, while the introduced perch and tilapia had effectively displaced the indigenous tilapia without otherwise altering the ecology of the lake. A similar survey undertaken ten years later revealed that the perch population had exploded to constitute 80% of the lake's fish biomass, while the haplochromine cichlids – the favoured prey of the perch – now accounted for a mere 1%. Lake Victoria's estimated 150–300 endemic cichlid species, all of which have evolved from a mere five ancestral species since the lake dried out 10,000–15,000 years ago, are regarded as representing the most recent comparable explosion of vertebrate adaptive radiation in the world. Ironically, these fish are also currently undergoing what Boston University's Les Kauffman has described as 'the greatest vertebrate mass extinction in recorded history'.

For all this, the introduction of perch could be considered a superficial success within its own terms. The perch now form the basis of the lake's thriving fishing industry, with up to 500 tonnes of fish meat being exported from the lake annually, at a value of more than US$300 million, by commercial fishing concerns in the three lakeshore countries. The tanned perch hide is used as a substitute for leather to make shoes, belts and purses, and the dried swim bladders, used to filter beer and make fish stock, are exported at a rate of around US$10 per kg. The flip side of this is that as fish exports increase local fishing communities are forced to compete against large commercial companies with better equipment and more economic clout. Furthermore, since the perch is too large to roast on a fire and too fatty to dry in the sun, it does not really meet local needs.

The introduction of perch is not the only damaging factor to have affected Lake Victoria's ecology. It is estimated that the amount of agricultural chemicals being washed into the lake has more than doubled since the 1950s. Tanzania alone is currently pumping two million litres of untreated sewage and industrial waste into the lake daily, and while legal controls on industrial dumping are tighter in Kenya and Uganda, they are not effectively enforced. The agricultural wash-off and industrial dumping has led to a further increase in the volume of chemical nutrients in the lake, promoting the growth of plankton and algae. At the same time, the cichlids that once fed on these microscopic organisms have been severely depleted in number by the predatory perch.

The lake's algae levels have increased fivefold in the last four decades, with a corresponding decrease in oxygen levels. The lower level of the lake now consists of dead water – lacking any oxygenation or fish activity below about 30m – and the quality of the water closer to the surface has deteriorated markedly since the 1960s. Long-term residents of the Mwanza area say that the water was once so clear that you could see the lake floor from the surface to depths of 6m or more; today visibility near the surface is more like 1m.

A clear indicator of this deterioration has been the rapid spread of water hyacinth, which thrives in polluted conditions, leading to high phosphate and nitrogen levels, and then tends to further deplete oxygen levels by forming an impenetrable mat over the water's surface. An exotic South American species, the water hyacinth was introduced to East Africa by expatriates in Rwanda, and made its way down to Lake Victoria via the Kagera River. Unknown on the lake prior to 1989, it has subsequently colonised vast tracts of the lake surface and clogged up several harbours, where it is barely kept under control by constant harvesting. To complete this grim vicious circle, Nile perch, arguably the main cause of the problem, are known to be vulnerable to the conditions created by hyacinth matting, high algae levels and decreased oxygenation in the water.

As is so often the case with ecological issues, what might at first be dismissed by some as an esoteric concern for bunny-huggers in fact has wider implications for the estimated 20–30 million people resident in the Lake Victoria basin. The infestation of hyacinth and rapid decrease in indigenous snail-eating fish has led to a rapid growth in the number of bilharzia-carrying snails. The deterioration in water quality, exacerbated by the pumping of sewage, has increased the risk of sanitary-related diseases such as cholera spreading around the lake. The change in the fish biomass has encouraged commercial fishing for export outside of the region, in the process depressing the local semi-subsistence fishing economy, leading to an increase in unemployment and in protein deficiency. And there is an ever-growing risk that Africa's largest lake will eventually be reduced to a vast expanse of dead water, with no fish in it at all – with ecological, economic and humanitarian ramifications that scarcely bear thinking about.

14

Victoria's densest fish eagle population – 638 individuals were recorded in a 1995 census – as well as large numbers of open-billed and yellow-billed storks. An excellent spot for varied water birds (as well as aquatic mammals and reptiles) is Mlaga Bay on the western side of the island, where some of the more prominent species are Goliath, purple and squacco heron, long-toed plover, blue-headed coucal, swamp flycatcher and various weavers. Of interest less for their variety than for their high number of birds are the so-called Bird Islands, a pair of tiny rocky islets that lie about 1km off the southeast shore of Rubondo, and support breeding colonies of various cormorants, egrets and ibises.

Dedicated birders are likely to be more interested in the forest and other terrestrial species. Two common birds on the island – Vieillot's black weaver and black-and-white casqued hornbill – are Guinea–Congo biome species with a very limited range in Tanzania. The lodge grounds and adjacent road and forest loop – where it is permitted to walk unguided – are as good a place as any to seek out other forest birds. Among the more interesting species recorded in this area are the blue-breasted kingfisher, grey-winged akalat, snowy-headed robin-chat, paradise flycatcher, common wattle-eye and green twinspot. The area around the lodge is also the main stomping – and screeching – ground for the recently introduced flock of African grey parrots.

THE FLOATING ZOO

Rubondo Island is unique among Tanzania's national parks not only in its aquatic location, but also in that it was conceived less as a game reserve than as a sort of 'floating zoo'. Proclaimed a forest reserve in German times, the island was upgraded to a game reserve in 1966, at the behest of Professor Bernhard Grzimek of the Frankfurt Zoological Society. Grzimek, best known for his tireless efforts to protect the Serengeti, believed that the forested island would make an ideal sanctuary for the breeding and protection of introduced populations of endangered Congolese rainforest species such as golden cat, okapi, bongo and lowland gorilla.

This plan never quite attained fruition, even though several chimpanzees were introduced to the island along with small numbers of elephant, giraffe, roan antelope, suni, black-and-white colobus monkey and black rhinoceros – most of which would not normally be regarded as forest-specific species. This arbitrary introduction programme was abandoned in 1973, only to be resurrected briefly in July 2000, when a flock of 37 grey parrots – captured in Cameroon for sale in Asia and confiscated in transit at Nairobi – were released on to the island.

Not all of the mammal re-introductions were a success. The 16 black rhinoceros that were relocated from the Serengeti in 1965 were poached in the 1970s, while the five roan antelope introduced in 1967 evidently died of natural causes before producing any offspring. By contrast, the six sub-adult elephants that were released on to the island between 1972 and 1973 have bred up to a population of greater than 40, with the larger herds concentrated in the south and lone bulls ranging all over the island – they are quite regularly seen around the park headquarters and lodge. Some concern has been expressed that an overpopulation of elephants could lead to the destruction of the natural forest, but the herd would probably need to grow to 200 before this became a real threat, and contraception can be used to keep numbers in check.

The introduced black-and-white colobus also occasionally roam close to the lodge, but the main population of about 30 is concentrated in the far south of the

GETTING THERE AND AWAY The easiest way to get to Rubondo is by air, and the only company that flies there is **Auric Air** (m *0783 233334; www.auricair.com*) at a cost of US$185 per person from Mwanza. However, Asilia is currently negotiating with other airlines to provide a scheduled flight service from the Serengeti, Arusha and other points on the northern safari circuit.

WHERE TO STAY
Upmarket

Rubondo Island Camp (8 rooms) (South Africa) +27 (0)21 418 0468; m 0736 5005156; www.asiliaafrica.com. Acquired by Asilia in late 2012 & set to reopen in June 2013 following major renovations, this attractive & immensely tranquil tented lodge will comprise 8 luxury suites similar in standard to Asilia's other Tanzanian camps & lodges. Unchanged will be the truly fabulous location, with a tall forest gallery rising high behind & a sandy palm-lined beach fringed by rocky outcrops directly in front. The open-sided communal areas stand on one of the rocky outcrops, offering a pretty view over the lake. This leads down to a secluded beachfront platform where a variety of large water birds have taken up more or less permanent residence. Pied & malachite kingfishers hawk for food, paradise flycatchers flutter in the trees & the occasional pair of otters swims past. The swimming pool is built in a natural rock outcrop. A good selection of boat & foot excursions is offered, along with fishing trips. *US$875/1,400 sgl/dbl inc all meals, drinks & activities Jul–Oct & 20 Dec–28 Feb; US$755/1160 all other times.*

island, and their normal territory can be reached by boat or car, followed by a ten-minute walk. The giraffe herd, estimated at around 100 individuals, is most likely to be encountered in the restricted area of acacia woodland around Lukaya, some distance south of the lodge and park headquarters. The suni are the most elusive of the introduced species, because they are so small, and secretive by nature.

Between 1966 and 1969, eight male and nine female chimpanzees were released on to the island, all of them born wild in the Guinean rainforest belt but captured when young to be taken to European zoos and circuses. Some had been held in good zoos where they had the company of other chimpanzees, while others were caged inadequately or in solitary confinement. Several individuals were regarded as troublesome and had regularly attacked or bitten their keepers, and two of the males were shot after their release because they had attacked people living on the island. The others appeared to settle down quickly. Two newborn chimps were observed in 1968, and it is now estimated that the total community numbers around 40, most of them at least second generation, but it is possible though unlikely that a couple of the original individuals survive. The chimps are normally resident in the central and northern parts of the island, near the Kamea and Irumu ranger posts, which respectively lie about 5km northwest and a similar distance southeast of the park headquarters at Kageye.

The chimp community on Rubondo is currently being habituated by researchers, with the long-term aim of offering visitors a tracking experience comparable to Mahale or Gombe. However, this aim is some way from being realised, so at this stage it would not be realistic to visit Rubondo with the primary aim of seeing chimps. That said, forest walks do go through areas inhabited by chimps, so you might well see nests and other evidence of their existence, or even hear or catch a fleeting glimpse of them.

14

Budget and camping

🏠 **National Park Campsite & bandas** The national park banda & camping site lies on a lovely forest-fringed beach about 1km north of Rubondo Island Camp, & a similar distance from park headquarters. No meals are available, & it's advisable to bring most of what you will need with you, but a shop in the park headquarters does sell a few basic foodstuffs (essentially what the national park staff would eat), as well as warm beers & sodas. A cook can be arranged on request. *US$20 pp rather grotty bandas with common showers; US$50 pp smarter self-contained chalets; camping US$20 pp.*

WHAT TO SEE A wide variety of activities can be arranged either through Rubondo Island Camp or through the national park headquarters. A good, inexpensive introduction to the park, taking two to four hours depending on how often you stop, is the **guided trail** to Pongo Viewpoint and Nhoze Hide, the latter a good place to see sitatunga, a variety of birds and – very occasionally – elephant. Another popular activity is **a forest walk** from either Kamea or Irumu ranger posts (ask at headquarters which of the two currently offers the better chance of seeing chimpanzees). This generally takes about six hours, and it costs US$25 per person inclusive of a guide and transport to the ranger post. Other options include **boat trips** to the swampy Mlaga Bay or Bird Island, **fishing expeditions** (the record catch is a 108kg Nile perch), and **walks** on more remote parts of the island to look for colobus monkeys or giraffes.

As for unguided activities, quite a bit of wildlife and lots of birds can be seen in the grounds of Rubondo Island Camp and the national park campsite, while the roughly 1km footpath and road between the two can be walked unaccompanied as a loop. **Swimming** is reputedly safe, at least at the beaches in front of the lodge and camp. The lake water is regularly tested for bilharzia, thus far always with a negative result, and – bearing in mind that human beings form an integral part of the bacteria's life cycle – all residents of the island take the bilharzia cure as a precautionary routine every six months. Do be aware that crocs occasionally swim past the beaches, so far without incident – still, you might want to look before you leap in!

BUKOBA AND AROUND

Updated with assistance from William Rutta (Kiroyera Tours)
Founded as a German administrative centre by the Emin Pasha in 1890, Bukoba is the regional headquarters of Kagera Region. The second largest port on the Tanzanian part of Lake Victoria, its population of around 100,000 is far smaller than that of Musoma. Bukoba is situated about 50km south of the Ugandan border on a lush, moist and hilly stretch of lakeshore that supports a thriving coffee industry as well as recently discovered deposits of nickel and cobalt that are likely to be exploited in the near future. The main food crop and dietary staple of the Bukoba area, as in Uganda, is *batoke* (or *matoke*), a large green banana that is roasted or steamed, and eaten in much the same manner as *ugali* elsewhere in Tanzania.

Bukoba's flat, compact town centre is dominated by several mid 20th-century Asian buildings – most in a poor state of repair – and lies about 1km inland of the lakeshore. At the lake end of leafy Jamhuri Road, near the Lake View Hotel, stands a cluster of old German buildings, including the Old Boma and Magistrate's Court, the original post office, the German cemetery, and the first general store, known locally as *duka kubwa* (big shop). The main port and ferry terminal is situated on a separate part of the lakeshore, about 3km from the town centre along Government Road.

There is little in the way of sightseeing in Bukoba, but it is an agreeable place. Points of interest include the impressive Catholic Cathedral built by Bishop Hirth between 1893 and 1904, and the marshy area between the town and the lake, which supports a surprisingly large variety of water birds. Further afield, Musira Island, which lies a short distance from the shore and is accessible by boat, has a small fishing village and is enjoyable to visit. Nyamukazi is a picturesque fishing village about 20 minutes' walk from town, on the other side of the airport. More remote excursions from Bukoba include the bird-rich Minziro Forest Reserve and Bwanjai Rock Art.

GETTING THERE AND AWAY

By air The airport is on Aerodrome Road alongside the lake. **Precision Air** [336 A2] (*www.precisionairtz.com*) currently operates daily flights between Bukoba and Mwanza, with connections to Arusha, Dar es Salaam and Nairobi. Flights can be booked through Precision Air's website, Kiroyera Tours (see below) or Bukoba Machinery (⟨ 028 2220545). In addition, **Auric Air** (m 0783 233334; *www.auricair. com*) operates a daily charter flight to/from Mwanza for US$100 one-way.

By bus The main bus stand is in the centre of town. For **long-haul buses**, Mohammed Trans, Sumry High Class, RS Bus and Osaka Raha run coaches directly to Dar es Salaam (*24 hrs; US$35 pp*). Mohammed Trans, Bunda and Bukoba Coaches all run daily buses to/from Mwanza (*7 hrs; US$13*). Tickets can be booked in advance at the nearby bus offices, but it's much simpler to book through **Kiroyera Tours** [336 B2]. Other buses go to Kigoma, Kasulu and Kibondo.

Dala-dalas run to smaller towns such Muleba, Nshamba, Rubya and Karagwe for Tsh4,000–5,000. They leave when full, which can often involve a very long wait, and are very crowded. **Taxis** can be found at the market, near the bus stand and at the port, and charge at least Tsh3,000 for a charter trip in town.

Travellers who visit Bukoba by land generally do so on their way to or from Uganda. Friends Coach and Jaguar run daily buses between Kampala and Bukoba (*5–6 hrs; US$10*) via Masaka and the Mutukula border post. It is also possible to do the trip in hops, using minibus-taxis from Kampala to Masaka and on to Mutukula, then local transport between the border and Bukoba, but this takes a lot longer and won't cost significantly less.

By ferry The MV *Victoria* sails overnight between Mwanza and Bukoba three times a week in either direction. It leaves from Mwanza at 21.00 every Tuesday, Thursday and Sunday and from Bukoba at the same time every Monday, Wednesday and Friday. The trip takes about 12 hours in either direction. One-way fares work out at around US$19 for a first-class cabin, US$14 for second-class sleeping, US$11 for second-class sitting and US$10 third class. Kiroyera Tours can book and reserve tickets in advance for an extra US$3.

TOURIST INFORMATION AND TOUR OPERATOR The dynamic award-winning **Kiroyera Tours** [336 B2] (⟨ 028 222 0203; m 0784 568276; e info@kiroyeratours. com; *www.kiroyeratours.com*; see also advert on page 340) is an excellent source of local information. It can arrange a wide variety of inexpensive guided tours to local attractions such as the Kagera Museum, Musila Island, Minziro Forest, Rubale Forest and various waterfalls, caves, rock art shelters and sites relating to Bahaya history and culture. Kiroyera can also organise short safaris to Rubondo Island, and serve as a booking agent for Precision Air, the ferry to Mwanza, and most long-haul bus services.

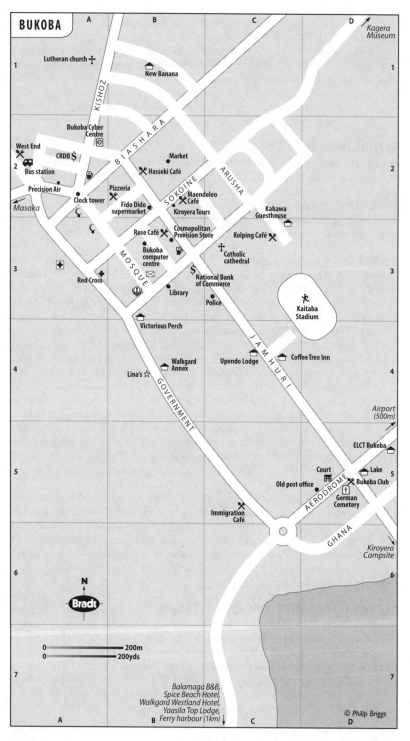

BUKOBA

A B C D

Kagera Museum

Lutheran church

New Banana

KISHOZ

BIASHARA

Bukoba Cyber Centre

West End
CRDB
Bus station

Precision Air

Clock tower

Pizzeria

Fido Dido supermarket

Market

Hasseki Café

SOKOINE

ARUSHA

Maendeleo Café

Kiroyera Tours

Kahawa Guesthouse

MOSQUE

Rose Café

Bukoba computer centre

Cosmopolitan Provision Store

Kolping Café

Catholic cathedral

Red Cross

Library

National Bank of Commerce

Police

Kaitaba Stadium

Victorious Perch

JAMHURI

Walkgard Annex

Lina's

Upendo Lodge

Coffee Tree Inn

GOVERNMENT

Airport (500m)

ELCT Bukoba

Court

Old post office

AERODROME

Lake

Bukoba Club

German Cemetery

Immigration Café

GHANA

Kiroyera Campsite

N

Bradt

0 ——— 200m
0 ——— 200yds

*Balamaga B&B,
Spice Beach Hotel,
Walkgard Westland Hotel,
Yaasila Top Lodge,
Ferry harbour (1km)*

© Philip Briggs

A B C D

WHERE TO STAY

Upmarket

Walkgard Westland Hotel [336 C7] (30 rooms) 028 222 0935; **m** 0713 482423; **e** support@walkgard.com; www.walkgard. com. Situated on breezy Balamaga Hill 3km from the town centre, this is easily the smartest accommodation option in Bukoba, with a grandstand position overlooking the port & good facilities including a swimming pool. Rooms are en suite & have AC, DSTV & hot water. *US$35/45 en-suite sgl/dbl; US$75 suites.*

Moderate

Balamaga B&B [336 C7] (4 rooms) **m** 0787 757289; **e** bbb_bukoba@yahoo.co.uk; www.balamagabb.com. Further up the same hill as the Walkgard, this lovely little B&B, boasting great views & an idyllic garden setting, is a refreshing alternative to the bland, run-of-the-mill hotel rooms offered elsewhere in Bukoba. Accommodation is in 4 bright, airy rooms with satellite TV – 2 with dbl bed & en suite, 2 with twin beds & shared bathroom. Meals are also available. *From US$27/42 en-suite sgl/dbl.*

ELCT Bukoba Hotel [336 D5] (22 rooms) 028 222 3121; **m** 0754 415404; **e** info@ elctbukobahotel.com; www.elctbukobahotel.com. Situated close to the Lake Hotel & within walking distance of the airport, this efficient church-run hostel has comfortable, clean AC rooms, a small restaurant serving inexpensive meals, & a curio shop, internet café & communal TV room. No alcohol. *From US$35 en-suite dbl.*

Victorious Perch Hotel [336 B3] (20 rooms) 028 222 0115; **m** 0756 189475; **e** info@victoriousperchhotel.com; www. victoriousperchhotel.com. This new hotel is strategically located in the centre of Bukoba

town. Comfortable en-suite rooms have modern furnishings & amenities. *From US$30 dbl.*

Budget

Yaasila Top Lodge [336 C7] 028 222 1251. This evergreen hotel has a lovely beachfront location near to the port & large en-suite rooms with king-size bed, lake-facing balcony, fridge, TV, AC & telephone. It's a good place to eat or drink while you wait to board the ferry. *US$15/25 en-suite.*

Lake Hotel [336 D5] (14 rooms) **m** 0754 767964. Boasting a scenic location at the lakeshore end of Jamhuri Avenue, & overhung with an aura of fading colonial charm, this rambling old hotel has drab but spacious en-suite dbls with TV, fan & net. There's a lovely outdoor garden & restaurant. *US$8–15, depending on size.*

Shoestring and camping

Kiroyera Campsite [336 D6] (5 rooms) 028 222 0203; **e** info@kiroyeratours.com; www.kiroyeratours.com. Right on the beach overlooking Lake Victoria & only a few mins' walk from the centre of town, this perfectly positioned campsite operated by Kiroyera Tours is a great choice for budget travellers. There are clean facilities, hammocks to laze in & a volleyball court if you're feeling active, as well as a lively beach bar & restaurant. There's a nightly bonfire, & cold drinks. *US$10 pp traditional banda; camping US$4 pp with own tent, or US$5 pp to rent a tent.*

Spice Beach Hotel [336 C7] 028 222 0142. This pleasant beach hotel near the Yasila Hotel & ferry jetty has inexpensive food & beer, & en-suite rooms with TV, hot water & AC. *US$10 dbl.*

WHERE TO EAT AND DRINK Recommended for cheap lunches and snacks is the **Rose Café** [336 B3], which serves matoke, beans, samosas, fruit juice, etc and is popular with volunteers working in and around Bukoba. The **Kolping Café** [336 C3] opposite the Kahawa Guest House near the cathedral dishes up inexpensive fish, meat, rice and matoke and has a TV.

For evening meals, the **Lake Hotel** [336 D5] is recommended for its view of the lake and good variety of food and drink. The satellite TV and outdoor beer garden make it a popular mzungu hangout, particularly on Friday nights. Also recommended is the restaurant at the **Yaasila Top Lodge** [336 C7], which serves a good variety of food and has a nice location, with two pool tables, darts and TV. Cheaper options include the lakeshore **Bukoba Club** (opposite the Lake Hotel)

14

[336 D5] and **Spice Beach Hotel** [336 C7]. **Kiroyera Campsite** [336 D6] has a restaurant that serves tasty pizzas and large plates of fish, chicken and chips.

If you're self-catering, or want to stock up on packaged goods before visiting Minziro Forest or catching the ferry, the **Fido Dido supermarket** [336 B2] and **Cosmopolitan Provision Store** [336 B3] stock packaged and refrigerated imported goods, including bread and many types of biscuits and drinks.

The top spot in town for after hours entertainment is the effervescent **Lina's Nightclub** [336 B4] which is open 24 hours, with a DJ on Friday, Saturday and Sunday nights. If you are nervous about clubbing alone, Kiroyera Tours or campsite can arrange an escort.

OTHER PRACTICALITIES

Banks, ATMs and foreign exchange The National Bank of Commerce near the Catholic Cathedral [336 B3] has an ATM that accepts foreign Visa and MasterCard, and it has foreign exchange facilities but doesn't exchange Ugandan Shillings – you're best off trading any excess Ugandan money for Tanzanian currency at the border post. The **CRDB** next to Bukoba Cyber Centre also accepts Visa and MasterCard.

Internet The best options are the **Bukoba Cyber Centre** [336 A2] (near the CRDB) and the **Post Office Internet Café** [336 B3]. Both stay open until 20.00 except on Sunday. There is also a reliable internet café at the **ELCT Bukoba Hotel** [336 D5].

Sporting facilities The **Bukoba Club** [336 D5] has tennis, snooker, table tennis and darts. The **Kaitaba Stadium** [336 C4] hosts football matches and other events, including concerts and the annual celebration of Farmers Day on 8 August. The **Red Cross** [336 A3] has a basketball court and volleyball net.

Swimming There is no swimming pool in town, but you can swim at the **Walkgard Westland Hotel** [336 C7] for a daily entrance fee of around US$2. A number of nearby **beaches**, including Bunena, lie within easy walking distance of town. The lake is infested with bilharzia, however, so swimming anywhere carries an element of risk.

WHAT TO SEE IN AND AROUND BUKOBA

Kagera Museum [336 D1] (✆ 028 222 0203; e info@kiroyeratours.com; ⊕ 09.30–18.00 daily; entrance US$2 pp) This small museum houses a superb collection of wildlife photographs taken by Danish wildlife photographer Dick Persson – whose work is also displayed at the National Museum in Dar es Salaam – as well as a small exhibit of traditional tools and artefacts. The quickest way to get there is to walk east along the lakeshore past the airstrip, then turn left and follow the signs. While this is the route promoted by the museum, it cannot be recommended, as you're not in fact allowed to walk over the airstrip. The longer route follows Sokoine Street northeast as it rambles its way around the top end of the airstrip, from where the museum is again signed. Alternatively, you can arrange a guided walking tour with Kiroyera Tours (see page 335), which cost US$5 per person excluding entrance fee.

Katuruka Heritage Site (⊕ 09.00–16.30 Wed–Mon; entrance US$7 inc informative guided tour) Only 12km south of Bukoba, this recently established heritage site protects the remains of one of the most ancient and important Iron Age settlements in this part of East Africa. It was the location of the 17th-century palace of King Rugomora Mahe, and is still the site of an important shrine called Kaiija, dedicated to an ancient rain god called Mugasha. Two massive fig trees within the palace boundaries mark a far more ancient landmark, an iron smelter that appears to have been active circa 500BC, the oldest evidence of Iron Age activity in this part of Africa. Katuruka is about 30 minutes from Bukoba by dala-dala.

Bwanjai Rock Art Half-a-dozen ancient rock art sites are dotted around northern Kagera, of which the most impressive is a large rock shelter at the village of Bwanjai, about 25km northwest of Bukoba, and linked to it by erratic dala-dalas. Unlike the better-known Kondoa rock art sites, there are no naturalistic efforts on the Bwanjai panel, nor any animal portraits, although a few heavily stylised human figures are present. The panel is otherwise dominated by blocks of red dots, and a cluster of strange symbols that look a bit like a tripod with antennae at the top. What these symbols might signify is anybody's guess, since local people have no tradition relating to the paintings except that they have always been there. It has been suggested the Bwanjai paintings are relatively recent, possibly the work of Bantu-speakers living in the area prior to the 16th-century formation of the Karagwe Empire.

Minziro Forest Reserve This 250km^2 reserve abuts the Uganda border some 20km inland of Lake Victoria, where it is bounded to the east by the Kagera River. One of the largest forest reserves anywhere in Tanzania, Minziro is essentially a southern extension of Uganda's Malabigambo Forest, which runs northwards to Sango Bay. The topography of the reserve is generally flat, but dotted with small rocky hills, and most areas below 1,150m are subject to seasonal flooding from the Kagera between October and May. Roughly three-quarters of the reserve is comprised of groundwater forest, with a tree composition divided about equally between western lowland and eastern montane species, while the remainder is predominantly open grassland, with extensive papyrus beds running along the riverbanks.

There are no local guesthouses at Minziro, so visitors wishing to overnight in the forest reserve must camp out, after first obtaining the necessary permit from the Forestry Office in Bukoba (☎ +255 28 222 2052).

Wildlife Minziro is unique within Tanzania for the predominantly west African affinities of its fauna. This is perhaps most evident in the birdlife, which had received little attention prior to a pioneering ornithological trip undertaken by Neil and Liz Baker in 1984. This and subsequent expeditions have produced a formative bird checklist of approximately 250 species, of which 56 are restricted to the Guinea–Congo biome and unknown elsewhere else in Tanzania – representing about 5% of the national checklist. It should be noted that this is essentially a political rather than a biological phenomenon – had the boundaries drawn up by the European colonists been slightly different, Minziro might lie within Uganda, where most of its Guinea–Congo biome species are common.

Nevertheless, Minziro is an extremely alluring birding destination. A long list of birds recorded nowhere else in Tanzania includes forest francolin, great blue turaco, white-bellied kingfisher, shining blue kingfisher, yellow-crested woodpecker, orange-throated forest robin, lowland akalat, blue-shouldered robin-chat, fire-crested alethe, white-tailed ant thrush, chestnut wattle-eye, red-headed bluebill, and at least half-a-dozen greenbuls. In addition to this, the grasslands of the

Minziro–Sango Bay area have been recently confirmed as an important wintering ground for the endangered blue swallow, a migrant from further south, and the papyrus swamps along the Kagera River harbour the globally threatened (and very beautiful) papyrus gonolek.

Another indication of Minziro's biodiversity is a tally of at least 500 butterfly species. Large mammals are more poorly represented, probably partially the result of local subsistence poaching, but the forest's western affiliations are manifested in three monkey species (Angola colobus, grey-cheeked mangabey and red-tailed monkey), as well as red-legged sun squirrel, western tree hyrax (vociferous at night) and Peter's Duiker. Buffalo and elephant visit the reserve seasonally, the bushbuck is common in the forest, and hippopotami are present but rare along the river, which also supports a substantial population of crocodiles and monitor lizards.

Getting there and away The village of Minziro, within the forest reserve, lies approximately 90km from Bukoba, a drive of less than two hours in dry conditions. To get there, first follow the road towards the Uganda border inland for 55km to the small town of Kyaka, crossing a bridge over the Kagera River, then passing though the Kyaka checkpoint where you must turn right onto the district road to Minziro. This road passes through some eucalyptus plantations and then through the banana plots of the local Haya people, approaching a small hill known locally as Kele, which is a dominant topographical feature. From there on the road traverses the forest reserve, passing through grassland and a block of the forest proper, emerging again into grassland before eventually climbing rising ground into Minziro village. From the track up to the church on top of the hill above the village you can obtain a good view of the extent of the forest on both sides of the cleared strip marking the Uganda border.

The road to Minziro is in good condition and accessible to normal two-wheel drive vehicles, but 4×4 and good ground clearance is necessary for off-road excursions, which are advisable only from July to September when the swampy ground has dried out.

15

Zanzibar

Chris and Susan McIntyre

Zanzibar is one of those magical travel names, richly evocative even to the many Westerners who would have no idea where to start looking for it on a global map. Steeped in history, and blessed with a sultry tropical climate – Zanzibar has a typical coastal climate, warm to hot all year round and often very humid; it receives more rainfall and is windier than the mainland – and a multitude of idyllic beaches, Zanzibar is also that rare travel destination that genuinely does live up to every expectation. Whether it's a quick cultural fix you're after, scintillating diving, or just a palm-lined beach where you can laze away the day, some time on Zanzibar is the perfect way to round off a dusty safari on the Tanzanian mainland.

A separate state within Tanzania, Zanzibar consists of two large islands, Unguja or Zanzibar Island and Pemba, plus several smaller islets. Zanzibar Island is about 85km long and between 20km and 30km wide; Pemba is about 75km long and between 15km and 20km wide. Both are flat and low-lying, surrounded by coasts of rocky inlets or sandy beaches, with lagoons and mangrove swamps, and coral reefs beyond the shoreline. Farming and fishing are the main occupations, and most people live in small villages. Cloves are a major export, along with coconut products and other spices. The capital, and by far the largest settlement, is Zanzibar Town (usually known as Stone Town) on the west coast.

Zanzibar used to be hard to reach, and had a reputation for being expensive and unfriendly. Not any more. The island now positively welcomes tourists, and it offers facilities suitable to all tastes and budgets, though unrestricted development in some areas, especially around Nungwi, is becoming an issue.

For many, the highlight of a stay is the old Stone Town, with its traditional Swahili atmosphere and wealth of fascinating buildings. For others, it is the sea and the coral reefs, which offer diving, snorkelling and game fishing to compare with anywhere in East Africa. And then there are the clove and coconut plantations that cover the interior of the 'Spice Island'; the dolphins of Kizimkazi; the colobus monkeys of Jozani; and the giant sea turtles of Nungwi. And above all, some will say, those seemingly endless tropical beaches.

For a dedicated guide to Zanzibar and Pemba, see our comprehensive *Zanzibar, Pemba & Mafia: The Bradt Travel Guide* (8th edition), 2013. An extensive range of literature about Zanzibar, mainly coffee-table style books, is stocked at The Gallery on Gizenga Street in Zanzibar Town (e *gallery@swahilicoast.com*). The Zanzibar Travel Network can be contacted at e info@zanzibar.net, see also www.zanzibar.net.

HISTORY

Zanzibar has been trading with ships from Persia, Arabia and India for approximately 2,000 years. From about the 10th century AD, groups of immigrants

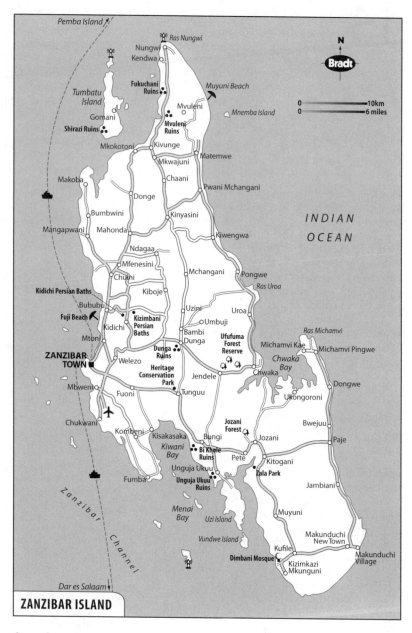

ZANZIBAR ISLAND

from Shiraz (Persia) settled in Zanzibar and mingled with the local Swahili. The Portuguese established a trading station on the site of Zanzibar Town in the early 16th century. At the end of the 17th century, the Sultan of Oman's navy ousted the Portuguese from the island.

In 1840, Sultan Said of Oman relocated his capital in Muscat to Zanzibar. Many Omani Arabs settled on Zanzibar as rulers and landowners, forming an elite group, while Indian settlers formed a merchant class. The island became an Arab state, an important centre of regional politics, and the focus of a booming slave trade. Britain had interests in Zanzibar throughout the 19th century; explorers such as Livingstone, Speke and Burton began their expeditions into the African interior from there. In 1890 Zanzibar became a British protectorate.

Zanzibar gained independence from Britain in December 1963. In 1964, the sultan was overthrown in a revolution and nearly all Arabs and Indians were expelled. Later the same year, Zanzibar and Tanganyika combined to form the United Republic of Tanzania.

Today, the distinctions between Shirazi and Swahili are often blurred. The islanders fall into three groups: the Hadimu of southern and central Zanzibar, the Tumbatu of Tumbatu Island and northern Zanzibar, and the Pemba of Pemba Island. Many people of mainland origin live on Zanzibar, some the descendants of freed slaves, others more recent immigrants. Many of the Arab, Asian and Goan people expelled in 1964 have since returned.

GETTING THERE AND AWAY

BY AIR An ever-increasing number of airlines offer direct flights between Zanzibar and Dar es Salaam, a 30-minute trip that costs around US$80. There are also regular flights to Zanzibar from Kilimanjaro International Airport (between Moshi and Arusha), some of which are direct, taking roughly one hour, while others require a change of plane at Dar and might take three to four hours depending on your connection. The main established airlines covering these routes are **Air Tanzania**, **Precision Air**, **ZanAir** and **Coastal Aviation**, all of which offer a range of other domestic flights, while some also fly to Kenya, so the best choice will depend largely on your other travel plans. Any reliable tour operator will be able to advise you about this.

Airlines

✈ **Air Tanzania** (ATC) ATC Bldg, Ohio St/Garden St, Dar es Salaam; ☎ 022 211 8411; m 0782 737732 (Dar Airport); e info@airtanzania.com; www.airtanzania.co.tz
✈ **Coastal Aviation** 107 Upanga Rd, Dar es Salaam; ☎ 022 211 7959 or 022 284 2700/1 (Dar Airport) or 024 223 3112, m 0713 670815 (Zanzibar Airport); e safari@coastal.cc; www.coastal.cc

✈ **Precision Air Flight Services** NIC Building, Samora/Pamba Rd, Dar es Salaam; ☎ 022 2168000; m 0748 550022 (Dar) or ☎ 024 223 5126 (Zanzibar); e contactcentre@precisionairtz.com; www.precisionairtz.com
✈ **ZanAir Limited** Malawi Rd, Zanzibar Town; ☎ 024 223 3670/3768; branch office, Zanzibar Airport; ☎ 024 223 3670; e reservations@zanair.com; www.zanair.com

BY BOAT A number of hydrofoils and catamarans run daily between Dar es Salaam and Zanzibar, with prices determined largely by the efficiency and speed of the service. The booking kiosks for all these boats are clustered together at the ports on Zanzibar and in Dar. There's a lot to be said for asking around before you make any firm arrangements, or for using a tour operator to make your booking (this won't cost much more and saves a lot of hassle). Do be wary of the hustlers who hang around both ports – many are con artists and some are thieves. Tickets must be paid for in hard currency, as must the port tax of US$5. There have been two major ferry disasters in recent years, resulting in several hundred deaths, so it is imperative that you choose your carrier carefully. The website www.usizame.com - meaning 'don't drown' – offers reliable, free text updates on capacity, vessel safety and weather conditions, as well as allowing you to register as a passenger.

Note that it is both unsafe and illegal to travel between Zanzibar and the mainland by fishing *dhow*.

Boats and ferry companies

Fast Ferries (*Sea Express I & Sea Express II*) 024 223 4690; m 0754 278692 (Zanzibar); 022 213 7049 (Dar); e info@fastferriestz.com; www.fastferriestz.com. *Sea Express I* is a large hydrofoil, with a capacity of 150 passengers, which travels between Dar & Zanzibar twice daily in each direction. The journey takes 2–2.5hrs. Departures from Dar are at 09.00 & 11.30, arriving Zanzibar around 11.30 & 14.00; departing Zanzibar at 07.00 & 15.00 to head back to Dar. This boat looks significantly more attractive than some, though it is sometimes reported to be unsteady in rough seas. There is limited deck space but comfortable airline-style seating is provided inside. *Sea Express II*, the company's newest vessel, travels a circuit between Dar, Zanzibar Island & Pemba; it's worth checking locally or online for the current schedule. At the time of writing, Fast Ferries were departing Zanzibar at 12.00 daily for the 3hr crossing to Pemba, and returning from Pemba to Zanzibar at 11.00 daily. One-way fares for non-residents are Dar–Zanzibar US$35/40 economy/first, with child fares reduced by 30%. Fast Ferries have an excellent & clear website, which has timetables, tariffs & an online booking facility (collect tickets at port).

MV *Flying Horse* 022 212 4507 (Dar); m 0784 472497/606177 (Zanzibar); e asc@raha.com. This large catamaran has a capacity of more than 400. The daytime service from Dar to Zanzibar departs at 12.30 daily & arrives at 15.30. The return trip from Zanzibar departs at 21.00 daily, but does not arrive in Dar until 06.00 the following day. The boat runs deliberately slowly on this overnight journey so passengers don't have to disembark in the middle of the night. The seating areas have AC & an 'in-flight' video is usually shown. The ship also has a small bar & restaurant. It's possible to travel on the deck, which has a few seats & an awning to keep off the sun but little else. Some travellers view this as a very pleasant way to travel, especially when leaving Zanzibar port at sunset, & for budget travellers it is a good way to save on a night's accommodation. US$25pp inc a mattress for overnight.

Sea Bus & Kilimanjaro 024 223 1655 (Zanzibar), 022 212 3324 (Dar); m 0777 334347; e azam@cats-net.com; www.azammarine.com. These 2 large Sea Bus vessels are Australian-built high-speed boats owned by Azam Marine Company, & both run once daily in either direction between Zanzibar & Dar es Salaam, taking about 2hrs to make the crossing. *Sea Bus I* departs Dar at 10.30 & starts the return trip from Zanzibar at 13.00, *Sea Bus II* departs Zanzibar at 10.00 & starts the return trip from Dar at 16.00. In addition, there are a trio of catamarans named *Kilimanjaro I, II & III*, & a new state of the art catamaran, *The Pride of Tanzania*, currently under construction & expected to be in service by mid 2013. Between them, the Kilimanjaro ferries sail 4 times daily each way between Dar & Zanzibar (07.00, 09.30, 12.30 & 15.30). On Mon, Thu & Sat, there are is also a service running from Dar to Pemba, with a 30min transit in Zanzibar (depart Zanzibar 09.30 & 16.00 respectively). First-class tickets US$40, second class US$35, children US$20, & all can be booked online (collect tickets at port 24hrs in advance) as well as portside.

Sea Star Services Ltd 024 223 4768; m 0777 411505. This large catamaran is also among the most efficient services between Dar es Salaam & Zanzibar. Tickets can be bought for the once-daily departure to Dar es Salaam from the grand-looking (relative to the beach hut-style offices occupied by others) green marble booking office at the port. Departs Zanzibar for Dar at 07.00, 2hr crossing. First class US$35, second class US$45.

ORGANISED TOURS Most international tour operators (see *Chapter 3, Practical information,* page 59) offering safaris to Tanzania can append a flight to Zanzibar (or a full travel package on the island) to your safari arrangements. Likewise, most safari companies based in Arusha are able to set up excursions to Zanzibar. If you are booking a safari in advance, there is probably a lot to be said for making all your travel arrangements in Tanzania through one company.

ARRIVAL AND DEPARTURE Visitors who fly in to Zanzibar from mainland Tanzania do not need to complete an immigration card or show their passport and visa, but they may still be asked to produce a yellow fever certificate. All documentation must be shown, however, and an immigration card completed if you arrive at the port by ferry from the mainland.

Travellers flying into Zanzibar from outside Tanzania can now buy a **visa on arrival** at the airport. A visa costs between US$20 and US$100 depending on your nationality and should be paid for in US dollar cash (travellers' cheques and local currency are not accepted, though either can be converted into cash at a bureau de change at a poor rate; and while cash in most other hard currencies is accepted, it will be at a highly unfavourable rate). The **airport tax** of US$20 for international flights out of Zanzibar should be incorporated into the price of a ticket but, if not, it must also be paid in US dollar cash (not by credit card or travellers' cheque). Flights within Tanzania attract a US$9 airport tax, payable in local currency.

If you lose your passport while on Zanzibar, you will need to have an Emergency Travel Document issued at the Ministry of Home Affairs (*Kilimani/Miembeni, Zanzibar Town;* \024 223 9148). This will allow you to travel back to the mainland (where nationals of most countries will find diplomatic representation in Dar es Salaam) or directly to your home country.

GETTING AROUND

PUBLIC MINIBUSES AND DALA-DALAS Local minibuses and small converted trucks called *dala-dalas* cover many routes around Zanzibar Island. These are faster than buses and fares are cheap, typically about US$0.50 around Zanzibar Town and a few dollars to cross the island.

Dala-dalas have standardised route numbers, destinations and frequencies. Buses and dala-dalas from outlying villages heading for Zanzibar Town tend to leave very early in the morning but, apart from that, most vehicles simply leave when they're full. Be aware that the last buses to some coastal villages will leave Zanzibar Town by mid-afternoon.

There are three **main terminals** in Zanzibar Town: Darajani Station on Creek Road (opposite the market), Mwembe Ladu, and Mwana Kwerekwe. The latter two locations are a few kilometres from town and are best accessed by a short hop on a dala-dala from Darajani.

The most useful dala-dala routes and times are in the box overleaf; the name in brackets is the destination as written on the front of the vehicle.

BUSES It is possible to reach many parts of Zanzibar Island by public bus, although most visitors use tourist minibuses or dala-dalas. All buses leave from **Darajani Bus Station**, on Creek Road in Zanzibar Town. Generally you can expect to pay only a few dollars to travel half the length of the island between Zanzibar Town and Bwejuu. Note, though, that journeys can be very slow.

On most routes, especially the longer ones, there is only one bus each day. It leaves Zanzibar Town around midday, in order to reach its destination in the evening and return in time for the morning market. Always check that the bus is going to the destination you think it should be.

Some of the bus routes are also covered by public minibuses or dala-dalas (see overleaf). These are usually slightly more expensive than the buses, but also tend to be quicker.

The bus route numbers, destinations and frequencies are given in the box overleaf.

DALA-DALA ROUTES AND FREQUENCY

Dala-dala number	Departs	To	No per day	First	Last
AROUND ZNZ TOWN					
502	Darajani	Bububu, via Maruhubi & Mtoni	Lots	06.00	21.00
505	Darajani	Airport (U/Ndege)	Lots	06.00	21.00
510	Darajani	Mwana Kwerekwe (M/Kwerekwe)	Lots	06.00	21.00
511	Darajani	Kidichi Spice (K/Spice), via Kidichi Persian Baths	Lots	06.00	21.00
NORTH					
101	Creek Rd	Mkokotoni	15	05.30	21.00
102	Darajani	Bumbwini, via Mangapwani	5	10.00	16.00
116	Creek Rd	Nungwi	25	05.30	21.00
121	Darajani	Donge & Mahonda	5	10.00	18.00
NORTHEAST					
117	Creek Rd	Kiwengwa, some continue to Pwani Mchangani	9	06.00	19.00
118	Creek Rd	Matemwe	10	06.00	19.00
206	Darajani or Mwembe Ladu	Chwaka, via Dunga Palace	10	06.00	18.00
209	Mwembe Ladu	Pongwe	3	07.00	16.00
214	Mwembe Ladu	Uroa, via Dunga Palace	7	06.00	18.00
SOUTHEAST					
309	Darajani or Mwana Kwerekwe	Jambiani, via Jozani	5	07.30	16.00
310	Darajani	Makunduchi, via Jozani	10	06.30	21.00
324	Darajani	Bwejuu, via Jozani, Paje & Kae Michamvi	Lots	09.00	14.00
SOUTHWEST					
308	Mwembe Ladu or Mwana Kwerekwe	Unguja Ukuu	4	08.00	15.00
336	Darajani or Mwana Kwerekwe	Kibondeni	Lots	06.00	20.00
326	Darajani or Mwana Kwerekwe	Kizimkazi, via Zala Park	5	07.00	16.00

CAR HIRE To hire a car (in reality, probably a Suzuki 'jeep') or scooter, contact one of the island's tour operators (see list on page 350). A jeep for a day will cost US$50–100, and is unlikely to have much, if any, fuel in the tank when you hire it. **Insurance cover** is in theory comprehensive, but check this thoroughly. Note that driving standards on Zanzibar are not good, and the roads can be pot-holed, so think carefully before hiring a car. You should be aware that, unlike on the mainland, you need an **international driving licence** and **local permit** to drive a vehicle on Zanzibar. Your tour operator can help organise a local permit, and insist that they do to avoid roadside police fines. Petrol is available (usually, but not with total reliability) island-wide nowadays, and prices here, as in the rest of the world, are increasing.

TAXIS Taxis are fairly widely available. A short hop within Zanzibar Town costs just over US$3, while the trip to Mtoni costs around US$7–10 one way; to Jozani or the east coast US$20–25 one way or US$30–35 return. The going rate for transfers between the airport and Zanzibar Town is US$10–15.

BICYCLE HIRE Most of the tour operators in Zanzibar Town can arrange bicycle hire. The current rate for a heavy Chinese bike is from US$10 per day, while mountain bikes go for around US$15.

ZANZIBAR TOWN

Zanzibar's old quarter, usually called Stone Town, is a fascinating maze of narrow streets and alleyways that lead the visitor past numerous old houses and mosques, ornate palaces, and shops and bazaars. Many buildings in Stone Town date from the 19th-century slave boom. Houses reflect their builder's wealth: Arab houses have plain outer walls and large front doors leading to an inner courtyard; Indian

BUS ROUTES AND FREQUENCY

Route number	To	No per day	First	Last
NORTH				
1	Mkokotoni (sometimes continuing to Nungwi)	15	05.30	20.00
2	Bumbwini & Makoba, via Mangapwani	3	05.30	18.00
14	Nungwi, via Mahonda, Kinyasini & Chaani	7	07.00	18.00
NORTHEAST				
6	Chwaka (some continue to Uroa & Pongwe)	5	07.00	16.00
13	Uroa	5	08.00	16.00
15	Kiwengwa	5	08.00	18.00
16	Matemwe	6	07.00	18.00
SOUTHEAST				
9	Paje, sometimes to Bwejuu & Jambiani	7	06.00	17.00
10	Makunduchi, via Tunguu, Pete & Munyuni	4	07.00	16.00
SOUTHWEST				
7	Fumba, via Kombeni	4	06.00	16.00
8	Unguja Ukuu	4	06.00	16.00
CENTRAL				
3	Kidichi & Kizimbani, via Welezo	7	06.00	18.00
4	Mchangani, via Dunga, Bambi & Uzini	5	06.00	17.00
5	Ndagaa, via Kiboje	4	06.00	16.00
11	Fuoni, via Tungu & Binguni	10	07.00	18.00
12	Dunga, then north to Bambi	5	07.00	17.00

houses have a more open façade and large balconies decorated with railings and balustrades. Most are still occupied.

A striking feature of many houses is the brass-studded doors with their elaborately carved frames. The size of a door and the intricacy of its design was an indication of the owner's wealth and status. The use of studs probably originated in Persia or India, where they helped prevent doors being knocked down by war-elephants. In Zanzibar, studs were purely decorative.

The area outside Stone Town used to be called Ng'ambo ('The Other Side'), and is still often referred to as such, though its official name is actually Michenzani (New City). Attempts have been made to modernise it and at the centre of Michenzani are some ugly apartment blocks, built by East German engineers as part of an international aid scheme.

GETTING AROUND Walking is the easiest way to get around Zanzibar Town. Buses, dala-dalas and taxis are available, and you can also hire bikes or scooters.

TOURIST INFORMATION The head office of the Zanzibar Tourist Corporation (ZTC) is in Livingstone House, about 1km from the town centre along the Bububu road, but for general information, the **ZTC office** on Creek Road will probably be more clued up and helpful. Alternatively, ask at your hotel or one of the better tour companies, such as **Eco+Culture**, **Sama Tours** or **Zanzibar Different**. The information desk at the Arab Fort has details of local musical, cultural and sporting events, and the noticeboard at the Fort's open-air restaurant is another good source of information.

TOUR OPERATORS A number of tour companies operate out of Zanzibar Town, offering tours, as well as transfers to the east coast and Nungwi. The better companies can set up bespoke trips to anywhere on the island, as well as make hotel reservations and other travel arrangements. For straightforward day trips and transfers, there is no real need to make bookings before you arrive in Zanzibar, as they can easily be set up at the last minute. If, however, you want to have all your travel arrangements organised in advance through one company, or you have severe time restrictions, then it would be sensible to make advance contact with one of the companies with good international connections, such as those shortlisted on page 59.

While prices vary greatly depending on standard of service, season and group size, typical costs per person for the most popular outings are US$20 for a Stone Town tour, US$25 for a Prison Island tour, US$25 for a spice tour, US$25 for a trip to Jozani Forest and US$35 for a Kizimkazi dolphin tour. These are based on four to eight people sharing, and will be substantially higher for smaller groups. That said, prices are negotiable, particularly out of season, but do be wary of unregistered companies offering sub-standard trips at very low rates.

It's possible to arrange many of the standard tours more cheaply through taxi drivers or independent guides (nicknamed *papaasi* after a type of insect). With spice tours, this may often turn out to be a false economy, in that the guide will lack botanical knowledge and may cut the excursion short, rendering the whole exercise somewhat pointless. One taxi driver who has been consistently recommended by travellers over many years is **Mr Mitu** (024 223 4636). His spice tours leave every morning from in front of the Ciné Afrique [349 C2], though these days they are so popular that you might find yourself joining a fleet of minibuses rather than hopping into Mr Mitu's own vehicle! It makes little difference if you use *papaasi* to set up trips to the islands, because specialist knowledge isn't required, and you can agree in advance how long you want to spend on any given island.

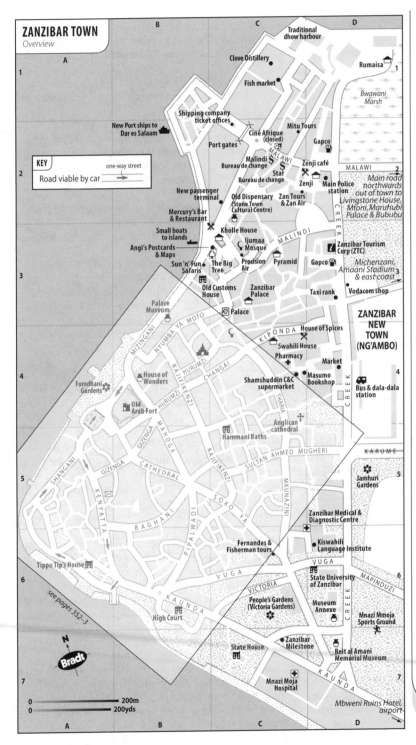

ZANZIBAR TOWN
Overview

Traditional dhow harbour

Clove Distillery

Rumaisa

Fish market

Bwawani Marsh

Shipping company ticket offices

New Port ships to Dar es Salaam

Ciné Afrique (closed)

Mitu Tours

Gapco

Port gates

MALAWI

KEY
one-way street
Road viable by car →

Malindi Bureau de change

Zenji café

Bureau de change

Star

Zenji

MALAWI

New passenger terminal

Old Dispensary (Stone Town Cultural Centre)

Zan Tours & Zan Air

Main Police station

Main road northwards out of town to Livingstone House, Mtoni, Maruhubi Palace & Bububu

Mercury's Bar & Restaurant

Kholle House

MALINDI

CREEK

Small boats to islands

Ijumaa Mosque

Precision Air

Zanzibar Tourism Corp (ZTC)

Angi's Postcards & Maps

Sun 'n' Fun Safaris

The Big Tree

Pyramid

Gapco

Michenzani, Amaani Stadium & east coast

Old Customs House

Zanzibar Palace

Taxi rank

Vodacom shop

Palace Museum

Palace

ZANZIBAR NEW TOWN (NG'AMBO)

MZINGANI

NYUMBA YA MOTO

KIPONDA

House of Spices

Swahili House

Pharmacy

Market

House of Wonders

KAJIFIKENZI

HURUMZI

CHANGAI

Shamshuddin C&C supermarket

Masumo Bookshop

CREEK

Bus & dala-dala station

Forodhani Gardens

Old Arab Fort

GIZENGA

MAHOGA

THARIA

Hammani Baths

Anglican cathedral

KARUME

SHANGANI

KENYATTA

GIZENGA

CATHEDRAL

BAGHANI

KAJIFIKENZI

SOKO YA

SULTAN AHMED MUGHERI

MKUNAZINI

Jamhuri Gardens

Zanzibar Medical & Diagnostic Centre

PIPALWADI

Fernandes & Fisherman tours

Kiswahili Language Institute

VUGA

Tippu Tip's House

VUGA

State University of Zanzibar

MAPINDUZI

CREEK

VICTORIA

People's Gardens (Victoria Gardens)

Museum Annexe

Mnazi Mmoja Sports Ground

KAUNDA

High Court

Zanzibar Milestone

Beit al Amani Memorial Museum

State House

KAUNDA

Mnazi Moja Hospital

Mbweni Ruins Hotel, airport

see pages 352–3

N

Bradt

0   200m
0   200yds

Zanzibar ZANZIBAR TOWN

15

349

You can assume that any tour operator working through one of the upmarket hotels will be reliable and accountable, but bear in mind that they deal primarily with a captive, big-spending clientele and therefore their costs may be somewhat inflated.

A list of a few recommended and well-established tour companies follows. Most of them offer a pretty similar selection of trips at reasonably uniform prices, and can also make flight, ferry and hotel bookings.

Eco+Culture Tours [352 C1] Hurumzi St; ☏ 024 223 3731; m 0777 410873/462665; e ecoculture@gmx.net, ecoculturetours@gmail.com; www.ecoculture-zanzibar.org. A respected, ethically minded operator offering slightly more expensive, but excellent, day trips for those who want to avoid the more established circuits & contribute to community development.

Island Express Safaris & Tours ☏ 024 223 4375/64; m 0774 111222/111888; e info@islandexpress.co.tz; www.islandexpress.co.tz. A smart, efficient operation offering a more personal service than most operators. Tours & transfers are never for groups, but are only ever arranged on a private basis. This does make them slightly more expensive, though not prohibitively so, & of course gives complete flexibility for your trip.

Sama Tours [352 C3] Gizenga St; m 0713 608576/0777 430385/0777 431665; e samatours@zitec.org; www.samatours.com. Trips include 'special' spice tours with a knowledgeable local naturalist, plus boat trips & tailor-made tours, with guides who speak English, French, German or Italian.

ZanTours [349 C2] ☏ 024 223 3042/3116; m 0777 417279; e zantoursinfo@zantours.com; www.zantours.com. Largest operator on Zanzibar, linked to ZanAir, with efficient staff, a fleet of clean vehicles & an impressive range of tours, transfers, excursions & safaris.

Zanzibar Different ☏ 0777 430177; m 0779 226 966; e info@zanzibardifferent.com; www.zanzibardifferent.com Owned by the delightful Stefanie Schoetz of Mrembo Traditional Spa (see box, page 365) & creator of the Princess Salme Tour (see box, page 368), this ethical operation has put a new spin on some classic Zanzibari tours, as well as adding original offerings in music, cookery & the arts, including fabulously atmospheric dinner concerts at Mtoni Palace (usually Fri). Very flexible, all tours can be adapted for children.

🏠 **WHERE TO STAY** The last decade has seen a mushrooming of new hotels in Zanzibar Town, as well as around the island, and there are now numerous options at every level, from basic guesthouses to smart upmarket hotels. As a rule, room rates on Zanzibar are quoted in US dollars, and at the top end of the range the management will probably insist that you pay in hard currency. Hotels at the lower end of the price bracket generally accept local currency at an exchange rate similar to those given at forex bureaux.

Most prices include breakfast, though at budget hotels this may amount to little more than a slice of stale bread and a banana. The rates quoted in this guide are high season only; most upmarket hotels will offer a discount out of season. At the lower end of the price range, rates may be negotiable depending on how busy the hotel is and the intended duration of your stay. It is advisable to make an advance reservation for any upmarket or moderate hotel, particularly during peak seasons, but this shouldn't be necessary for cheaper lodgings.

Travellers who arrive on Zanzibar by boat can expect to be met by a group of hotel touts. Some are quite aggressive and likely to take you to whichever hotel gives them the largest commission, while others are friendly and will find you a suitable hotel if you tell them what you want. Either way, the service shouldn't cost you anything, since the tout will get a commission from the hotel, and it may save a lot of walking in the confusing alleys of Stone Town. Given the difficulty of getting past the touts and the general aura of chaos around the ferry port, there is probably a lot to be said for taking the path of least resistance when you first arrive. Should you not like the place to which you are first directed, you can always look around yourself once your bags are securely locked away, and change hotel the next day.

However you arrive, many of the hotels in Stone Town cannot be reached by taxi. You are liable to get lost if you strike out on foot without a guide, though we found that people were always very helpful when it came to being pointed in the right direction (bearing in mind that the right direction may change every few paces). Most taxi drivers will be prepared to walk you to the hotel of your choice, but they will expect a decent tip.

Upmarket

🏠 **Emerson Spice** [352 D1] (6 rooms) `024 223 2776; m 0774 483483; e reservation@ emersonspice.com; www.emersonspice.com. This exotic, newly opened hotel has striking theatrical rooms, each with a colourful twist on traditional Swahili design. Ceilings are immense; vibrant colours adorn the walls, & potted plants, stained-glass windows & intricately carved wooden doors add to the atmosphere. Rooms are kitted out with open-plan en suites, fans & AC, fridges & mosquito nets, & some even have dramatic hand-painted murals. There's an interior courtyard complete with twinkling blue pool reminiscent of a Moroccan riad, & a terrific rooftop restaurant (see *Where to eat*, page 356) offering a nightly 5-course tasting experience. One of the best choices for an atmospheric stay in Stone Town. *US$225 dbl, B&B.*

🏠 **Maru Maru** [352 C3] (44 rooms) `024 223 8516/7/8; e info@marumaruzanzibar.com; www. marumaruzanzibar.com. On the site of an old Hindu temple, Maru Maru opened in 2012 after extensive renovation of 2 adjoining buildings. It's a spotless, well-finished & bright hotel. Enthusiastic & organised manager Paolo heads the well-trained & incredibly polite staff. The modern rooms all have en suites (some with traditional hammam baths), powerful AC, Wi–Fi, fridge & a safe. In-room tea & coffee facilities are provided as well as a flat screen TV. There's a choice of 2 dining areas – the Fountain Restaurant, in the courtyard, for snacks & afternoon teas, & the rooftop Terrace Restaurant, popular for sunset laughter & cocktails, followed by spicy Indian suppers. One of the few hotels in Stone Town with a lift. Parking provided. *US$119–175 dbl, B&B.*

🏠 **Jafferji House & Spa** [352 C4] (10 rooms) 170 Gizenga St; m 0774 078442/1; e info@ jafferjihouse.net; www.jafferjihouse.net. This hotel has the wow factor: an artistic blend of old & new. Zanzibari doors, old wall clocks & gramophones

are reminiscent of days gone by, while warm colours & a top-quality finish give a modern feel. The 8 suites & 2 standard rooms all have AC, baths, exquisite furniture & traditional fabrics. Up on the rooftop is a tiny but gorgeous outpost of Cinnamon Spa. Downstairs, the Mistress of Spices restaurant offers freshly prepared international food from an à la carte menu. There's also an internet café & TV room. Despite all the opulence, the hotel still feels warm & welcoming, like a home, albeit a stylish one! *US$160–590 dbl, B&B.*

🏠 **Kholle House** [349 C3] (10 rooms) m 0779 898200; e info@khollehouse.com; www. khollehouse.com. Opened in Feb 2011, Kholle is already a hit with those seeking a traditionally inspired boutique bolthole. It's beautiful, & much thought has gone into the high quality furnishings, with antique chests, French ceramics, glass lanterns & Zanzibari beds complementing a warm ochre colour scheme. Rooms are split into 3 categories, varying in size, but all with Zanzibari beds, mosquito nets, fans & AC. B/fast is à la carte overlooking the small garden, where loungers & cushions surround the swimming pool – a precious rarity in Stone Town & a welcome relief after a hot day's sightseeing. If arriving by taxi, ask your driver for 'Holy House' (the Swahili pronunciation). *US$160–210 dbl, B&B.*

🏠 **Mashariki Palace Hotel** [352 B2] (18 rooms) `024 223 7232/3; m 0776 775774; e info@masharikipalacehotel.com; www. masharikipalacehotel.com. Once the home of the religious councillor to the sultan, Mashariki Palace was completely renovated before opening as a fashionable boutique hotel in early 2011. While some original features remain, the décor leans towards a more modern style, with soaring ceilings & bare white walls bringing a sense of space & calm. The contemporary rooms offer AC, tea & coffee facilities, a TV & a fridge. Outside is a pretty little courtyard with a couple of photos of the hotel's restoration, while upstairs the breezy terrace offers

Creek

G

La Taverna ✖

St Monica's Hostel ▯

SULTAN AHMED MUGHERI

Anglican cathedral ✝ (& old slave mkt)

F

MKUNAZINI

SOKO YA

Jambo Guesthouse ✖ Green Garden

SULTAN AHMED MUGHERI

KAJIFIKENZI

SOKO YA

E

Zanzibar Coffee House ▯

THARIA

Hammani Baths ▦

MAHOGA

CATHEDRAL

Membo Spa ●

D

Emerson Spice ▯

C

Aga Khan Mosque

CHANGAI

236 Hurumzi ▯

Moto Shop ●

Sama Tours ●

Maru Maru ▯

HURUMZI

IZWNUAH

GIZENGA

Sasik ●

Gallery Tours ●

Jafferji House & Spa ●

Gallery Bookshop

Eco+Culture Tours ▮

HURUMZI

IZWNUAH

KAJIFIKENZI

Suraka Gallery & Bookshop ●

B

Kiponda ▯

Seyyida ▯

NYUMBA YA MOTO

Mashariki Palace ▯

KAJIFIKENZI

House of Wonders ▯

MAHOGA

Arab Fort, Fort Resaurant & Keramica shop ▦

Keramica ●

People's Bank of Zanzibar

Orphanage

Palace Museum ▯

Taxi rank ●

MIZINGANI

🚗 🚗 🚗

🚗

🚗

🚗

Forodhani Gardens

A

N

Brad!

1

2

3

4

1

2

3

4

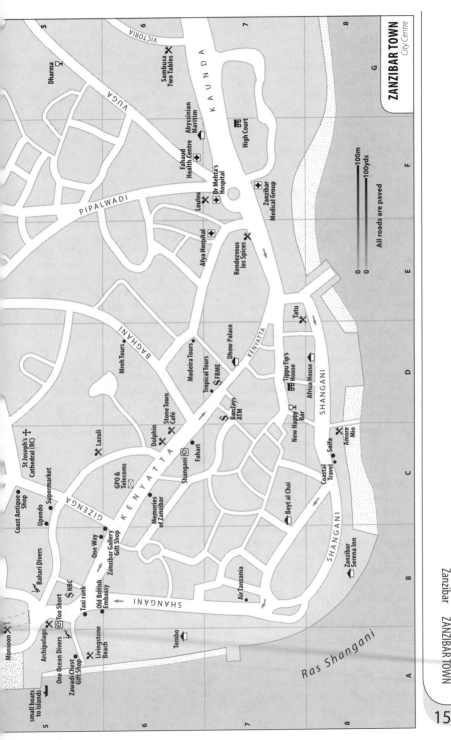

ZANZIBAR TOWN
City Centre

0 — 100m
0 — 100yds

All roads are paved

Monsoon

small boats to islands

Ras Shangani

Archipelago
One Ocean Divers
Zawadi Chest Gift Shop
Livingstone Beach
Taxi rank
Too Short
NBC
Old British Embassy
Bahari Divers
Zanzibar Gallery Gift Shop
One Way
Coast Antique Shop
Upendo
Supermarket
St Joseph's Cathedral (RC)
Lazuli
Dharma

Tembo
Memories of Zanzibar
GPO & Telecoms
Fahari
Shangani
Dolphin
Stone Town Café

Air Tanzania
Beyt al Chai
Barclays ATM

Zanzibar Serena Inn
Coastal Travel
Saifa
Amore Mio
New Happy Bar
Africa House
Tippu Tip's House

Mreh Tours
Madeira Tours
Tropical Tours
FBME
Dhow Palace

Tatu

Rendezvous les Spices
Afya Hospital
Loulou
Dr Mehta's Hospital
Zanzibar Medical Group
Fahaud Health Centre
Abyssinian Maritim
High Court

Sambusa Two Tables

PIPALWADI
VUGA
VICTORIA
KAUNDA
BAGHANI
KENYATTA
GIZENGA
SHANGANI
SHANGANI
SHANGANI

Zanzibar   ZANZIBAR TOWN

15

353

rooftop and distant sea views from the well-stocked bar & restaurant. *US$220–475 dbl, B&B.*

⌂ **The Seyyida** [352 B1] (17 rooms) \024 2235462; **m** 0776 247744; **e** info@ theseyyidazanzibar.com; www.theseyyidazanzibar. com. In the heart of Stone Town's alleys, The Seyyida is a cool & quiet haven from the heat & bustle outside. The spacious rooms are set around a verdant linear courtyard, & vary in size & view from the window. All are equipped with various mod-cons including satellite TV, minibar fridge, an internet connection & very effective AC. The décor is a mixture of modern & Zanzibari style, with attractive wooden furniture & billowing gold curtains. At the top of the building, Lulu is a cheerful rooftop bar & restaurant whose sweeping sea & harbour views are some of the best in town. *US$160, B&B.*

⌂ **Zanzibar Serena Inn** [353 B8] (51 rooms) \024 223 2306; **e** zserena@zanzinet.com; www. serenahotels.com. This large, impressive hotel, converted from 2 historic buildings, overlooks the sea in the Shangani area. The staff are excellent & the hotel boasts all the in-room & public facilities that you would expect of an international-class establishment, including inviting pool, 2 excellent restaurants (or a porter escort to the public food market), coffee shop, AC, Wi–Fi, satellite TV & reasonably priced, in-house massage treatments. *US$150–900 dbl, B&B.*

⌂ **236 Hurumzi** [352 C1] (22 rooms) \024 223 2784 **m** 0777 423266; **e** 236hurumzibookings@ zanlink.com; www.emerson-green.com. This hotel sprawls across 2 restored buildings dating from 1840–70, decorated with antique Zanzibari furniture & carpets. Each room is different, but each, very deliberately, is without phone, TV or fridge. Some have AC, others natural cooling – shutters, shades, deep balconies & a sea breeze. The hotel's Tower Top Restaurant, the second-highest building in Zanzibar Town, has fine views, but standards at dinner (US$25 pp, reservations essential) are not always up to scratch. *US$160–250 dbl, B&B.*

⌂ **Beyt al Chai** [353 C7] (5 rooms) **m** 0777 444111; **e** reservations@stonetowninn.com; www.stonetowninn.com. With its thick walls & antique shuttered windows, the peaceful & friendly Beyt al Chai was a private home until 2005 & it continues to offer relaxed hospitality & home comforts. Large, en-suite rooms are full of character with authentic Zanzibari furniture &

vibrant fabrics; the Princess room is the only one without a view over the square. The restaurant is one of Zanzibar Town's culinary hotspots &, though relatively expensive, good value for money. *US$150–330 dbl, B&B.*

⌂ **The Swahili House** [349 C4] (20 rooms) **m** 0777 510209 **e** info@theswahilihouse.com; www.theswahilihouse.com. This towering 19th-century Indian merchant's house, built around a central roofed courtyard, it is today a traditionally elegant hotel with an authentic Zanzibari feel & good management. The rooms are decked out in locally produced furniture & antiques, with polished stone floors, narrow wooden balconies (some rooms) & a touch of modernity thrown in in the form of AC & fans. Spread over 4 floors, rooms nearest the top offer excellent views of Stone Town's alleyways. But for the best panorama head for the rooftop restaurant, with its long bar, cushion covered benches and even a jacuzzi. *US$240–325 dbl, B&B.*

⌂ **Zanzibar Palace Hotel** [349 C3] (9 rooms) \024 223 2230; **m** 0773 079222; **e** info@zanzibarpalacehotel.com; www. zanzibarpalacehotel.com. One of the best boutique hotels in Stone Town, this place has a distinctly Zanzibari feel, with steep staircases, handcrafted wooden furniture & antique Arab *objets d'art*, yet modern creature comforts abound: AC throughout, DVD library & in-room player, & Wi–Fi. Helpful staff are on hand for travel tips, & the small bar serves cold drinks throughout the day. *US$160–315 dbl, B&B.*

Moderate

⌂ **Tembo Hotel** [353 A6] (36 rooms) Shangani Rd; \024 223 3005/2069; **e** tembo@ zitec.org; www.tembohotel.com. In a great location just west of Forodhani Gardens, Tembo combines a grand old house & a more recent extension, both quite Indian in décor. Rooms are en suite, including mosaic bath, with heavily carved furniture, AC, fridge & TV; most have a sea view or overlook the pool. There's a beachfront restaurant under a row of almond trees (non-residents welcome; no alcohol served). On the beach itself, expect a degree of hassle from touts, & note that swimming is not advisable. *US$105 dbl, B&B.*

⌂ **Dhow Palace Hotel** [353 D7] (30 rooms) \024 223 3012; **e** dhowpalace@zanlink.com; www.dhowpalace-hotel.com. This excellent hotel in the Shangani area is a renovated old house built around 2 central courtyards. Newer rooms have private balconies, while larger original rooms access a private section of shared balcony; all are en suite (complete with Persian baths), & are furnished with Zanzibari beds & antiques, plus mod-cons including AC. The stylised Indian restaurant overlooks the city's rooftops (no alcohol served). All is spotlessly clean, the staff are friendly & the atmosphere tranquil. *US$110–170 dbl, B&B.*

△ **Rumaisa Hotel** [349 D1] (7 rooms) m 0777 410695; e inforumaisa@yahoo.com; www.rumaisahotel.blogspot.com. This funky little place opened in Nov 2011 & trendy travellers have been recommending it ever since. Located in the Funguni area of Stone Town, it's quite a walk from the centre but prices are lower than they otherwise would be for the room standard. Simple rooms are well-finished & furnished in different vivid colours in Zanzibar style. The decoration is pretty, with Indian furniture giving a homely feel. Staff are helpful & friendly. The blustery rooftop bar is filled with music in the evenings, when the owner's father plays the guitar & drums for guests. At the front, a communal balcony has a sea view with Prison Island in the distance. There are plans to add a further 14 rooms at some point in the future. *US$35 dbl , B&B.*

△ **Stone Town Café & Bed & Breakfast** [353 C6] (8 rooms) m 0778 373737; baraka@ zanlink.com; www.stonetowncafe.com Above the bustling Stone Town Café (see *Where to eat*, page 358) on Kenyatta Road, the family-owned & run Stone Town B&B offers delightful modern rooms with dbl polished wooden Zanzibari beds, AC, fans & fridges. Each room has a small seating area with a TV, & en-suite shower rooms with hot water are standard. Cool floors & warm colours make this a cosy place to spend a night or 2, while high quality accessories & sturdy furniture raise the standard above the average Stone Town B&B. B/fast is included at the café downstairs, where guests can order what they want from the menu up to a value of $7, with anything over this costing extra. *US$80 dbl, B&B.*

△ **Zanzibar Coffee House** [352 D1] (8 rooms) ☏ 024 2239319; m 0773 061532; e coffeehouse@ zanlink.com; www.riftvalley-zanzibar.com. Housed in an 1885 Arabic home, this unpretentious haven is above the excellent café of the same name. Most of the rooms, with traditional Zanzibari 4-poster beds & AC, are en suite, though a few share facilities. Gracious staff provide a friendly service, the tower-top terrace offers one of Stone Town's best b/fast views, & rates remain great value. *US$135–150 dbl, B&B*

△ **Zenji Hotel** [349 C2] (9 rooms) m 0774 276468/0776 705592; info@zenjihotel.com; www. zenjihotel.com. This Dutch–Zanzibari hotel is a haven of calm & tranquillity with the hustle & bustle of Malawi road literally on its doorstep. In fact, it is only the noisy location that lets down this quirky little place, a real find among the shabbier options near the port. The 9 cosy rooms are each priced differently depending on facilities. All have AC, fans & hot water, but not all are en suite or have balconies. Kitted out in handcrafted furniture, with colour-trim mosquito nets, pastel walls & tie-dye sheets, the rooms are full of charm & light. A tasty buffet b/fast is served up on the little roof, while caffeine fiends enjoy cappuccinos & espressos from Zenji Café (see *Where to eat*, page 358), included in the room price. Wi–Fi is free, & the hotel has laptops that guests can borrow. Zenji is also conscious of giving back to the community & there's a great fair-trade curio shop on site. *US$50–70 dbl, B&B.*

△ **Kiponda Hotel** [352 B1] (15 rooms) Nyumba ya Moto St; ☏ 024 2233052; m 0777 431665; e info@kiponda.com; www.kiponda.com. Formerly a sultan's harem, this quiet, friendly hotel has been renovated in local style & retains the original carved wooden door. Rooms are fastidiously clean, with simple furnishings & efficient fans. After b/fast, the airy restaurant with clear sea views mutates into a casual coffee bar, serving cold drinks & beer (⏰ 11.00–18.00). *US$20–40.*

Shoestring

△ **Jambo Guesthouse** [352 F3] (9 rooms) ☏ 024 223 3779; m 0777 496571; e info@ jamboguest.com; www.zanzibar.net/hotels/ jambo_guest_house. In a quiet quarter of the Mkunazini area, near the Anglican Cathedral, this good-value place has been justifiably popular with backpackers for years. Its simple rooms, all sharing facilities, have mosquito nets & ceiling fans, & 2 have AC. Extras include free luggage store, free tea & coffee, & cheap internet. With advance bookings it's possible to arrange free pick-up from the port or airport. The shady café opposite is a pleasant outdoor hang-out, too. *US$30 dbl, B&B.*

🏠 **Pyramid Hotel** [349 C3] (11 rooms) Kokoni St; 📞 024 223 3000; m 0777 461451/0784 255525; e pyramidhotel@yahoo.com. Between the Malindi & Kiponda areas, this old hotel is a short walk from the seafront. A budget travellers' favourite for many years, & deservedly so, it gets its name from the very steep & narrow staircases (almost ladders) that lead to the upper floors. Rooms have netting, fan & hot water, but some are large & bright, & others small & dark, so choose carefully. The manager & his staff are friendly, the rooftop restaurant does great b/fast, & there's a book-swap service. Free pick-up from the airport or port. *US$35 dbl.*

🏠 **St Monica's Hostel** [352 F1] (16 rooms) Sultan Ahmed Mugheiri Rd; 📞 024 223 0773 e monicaszanzibar@hotmail.com; www. stmonicahostelzanzibar.s5.com. Built in the 1890s to house workers at the UMCA mission, St Monica's now welcomes both church guests & younger backpackers. Cool thick walls, wide staircases & Arabesque arches form the backdrop for simple & very clean rooms with wide balconies overlooking the cathedral or gardens. The restaurant, run by the Mother's Union, offers fresh Swahili cuisine (no alcohol); there's also an art shop & an airy lounge area. *US$20–35 dbl.*

✖ **WHERE TO EAT AND DRINK** The dining experience in Stone Town has recently taken a dramatic turn for the better, with some stylish evening eateries opening, a burgeoning selection of cool cafés, & even a great new street food area for Forodhani Gardens' traditional night dining. There are now dozens of restaurants catering specifically to tourists, and the following serves as an introduction only.

There are numerous more affordable options listed in the *Moderate* section opposite, with main courses around US$8. We have only listed a selection; there are plenty more to choose from, and the level of competition for custom means that standards are generally reflected by prices. Quality is highly variable, and any one place can go up or down, so do ask reliable local sources for the current hot spots.

The cheapest place to eat in Stone Town is at Forodhani Gardens [352 A4], along the seafront, where dozens of vendors serve freshly grilled meat, chicken, fish, calamari and prawns with salad and chips or *naan* bread. This is far and away the best street food we've come across anywhere in southern and East Africa, and offers excellent value. The stalls cater primarily to locals and travellers, and many return night after night. Even if you aren't hungry or an adventurous eater, it's worth visiting for the spectacle. We have listed the current cheap and cheerful hotspots in the *Budget* section opposite:

Upmarket Top-end options, with main courses from around US$10, include:

✖ **Abyssinian Maritim** [353 F6] 📞 0772 940556/0713 359054/0752 940556; ⏰ 11.00–14.00 for lunch & 18.00–23.00 for dinner daily. In 2011, this great little place opened on the corner opposite the High Court in Vuga. A traditional Ethiopian restaurant, it serves authentic cuisine, great coffee & *shisha* pipes amid a north African décor. Already gaining popularity with Zanzibari expats & visitors who've stumbled across its entrance, this culinary departure from Swahili curries is a very welcome addition to the restaurant scene. *US$3–12.*

✖ **Baharia** [353 B8] Zanzibar Serena Inn, Shangani Rd; 📞 024 223 3587. Less flamboyant than better rooftop experiences, the Baharia is nonetheless a good-quality place. The food is a mix of Asian, African & European. In the hotel's coffee shop & patisserie, snacks & light meals start from around *US$5.*

✖ **Beyt al Chai** [353 C7] Kelele Sq; m 0777 444111; www.stonetowninn.com. At one of Zanzibar Town's culinary hot-spots, succulent prawn curries (*US$10*), grilled line fish (*US$10–15*) & crisp vegetables are matched with a tempting wine list. Service is friendly & polite, if sometimes a little slow &, though prices are relatively high, the food & sophisticated atmosphere combine to make it good value for money & highly recommended.

✖ **Emerson Spice Rooftop Tea House** [352 D1] 📞 024 223 2776; m 0775 046395; e reservation@ emersonspice.com; www.emersonspice.com;

⏲ 17.30–23.00 daily. On the rooftop of Emerson Spice, this intimate dining experience offers a lovely bird's-eye vista over town, a buzzing atmosphere & an impressive 5-course degustation menu. Open every night for a single sitting (cocktails from 17.30; dinner 19.00), the US$25 pp set menu is excellent value, consistently delicious and worth booking to avoid disappointment. It's highly personal & often overseen by the charismatic owner. For special occasions, traditional music or dancing may also be arranged, & is a real treat for diners.

Moderate

✘ **Archipelago Restaurant** [353 B5] Shangani Rd; ✆ 024 223 5668. Come here for curries, seafood & burgers around US$7–8.

✘ **House of Spices** [349 C4] Kiponda St; ✆ 024 223 1264; m 0773 573727; e info@houseofspiceszanzibar.com; www. houseofspiceszanzibar.com. Offering tempting fusions of local & Mediterranean cuisine from the top floor of an attentively renovated Zanzibari house, House of Spices is justifiably popular. Most diners sit up on the lantern-lit roof terrace, where there's also a bar, while on the ground floor is a small spice shop selling tea & coffee. The varied menu includes curries & salads (*US$6–9*), as well as tapas & pizza (*US$8.50*).

✘ **La Taverna** [352 G1] ✆ 0776 650301; ⏲ 11.00–23.00 daily. A little off the main tourist trail, towards the market, this is a gem of a restaurant with a host of happy regular customers, delightful young Italian owners & consistently tasty, homemade pasta/pizza. Wine is inexpensive and free-flowing, which adds to the relaxed, casual vibe.

✘ **Lazuli** [353 C5] Off Kenyatta Rd; ✆ 0776 266679; e bonita_zanzibar@yahoo.com; ⏲ 11.00–21.00 Mon–Sat. This small, cheerful café is a highlight for casual dining. With a simple, unassuming exterior, it's cheery inside & the menu boasts probably the most refreshing drinks in town & a consistently excellent selection of vitamin-packed smoothies (*US$2*), fresh fruity cocktails (non-alcoholic) & iced coffees, & a tempting selection of pancakes, wraps, tempura, burgers & creative salads (*US$6–10*). Service here *is* slow; don't come in a rush, everything is made fresh to order & will be delicious when it eventually arrives. No toilet facilities.

✘ **Livingstone Beach Restaurant** [353 A5] m 0773 164939. Large, uncluttered & attractively decorated dining room leading out to a private beach where you can dine with your toes trailing in the sand. The restaurant has a decidedly upmarket ambience & the (mostly seafood) menu is priced accordingly; a children's menu & shisha pipes are also available.

✘ **Loulou** [353 F7] ✆ 024 224 0170; e info@ loulouzanzibar.com; www.loulouzanzibar. com; ⏲ 11.00–22.00 daily. Loulou is a swish, contemporary Belgian-run restaurant. In the sleek white-&-orange interior, tantalise your taste buds with such delights as puffed crab pancake with béchamel sauce (*US$9*) or handmade *bilingani* (pasta with aubergine, plum tomato, cashew nuts, olive oil & herbs; *US$8*), but do leave room for the signature decadent Belgian chocolate mousse (*US$6*). Don't confuse this place with the similar sounding Lulu at the Seyyida Hotel; also pleasant. Cash only. Highly recommended.

✘ **Mercury's Bar & Restaurant** [349 C3] Mizingani Rd; ✆ 024 223 3076; m 0777 416666; ⏲ daily. Named after Zanzibar's most famous son, this has a fine setting on the bay & is perennially popular. The menu unashamedly cashes in on the former Queen singer's apparent dietary preferences – Freddie's Favourite Salad (*US$6.50*). Despite this corniness, the food is reliably good, & there's a baffling range of cocktails. Happy 'hour' is 17.00–20.00, & there's live music Fri–Sun nights (from 19.30).

✘ **Monsoon Restaurant** [353 A5] m 0777 410410. Facing Forodhani Gardens, this is a good place for traditional Zanzibari & Mediterranean food (*US$6–15*), accompanied by live *taarab* music on Wed & Sat nights. Aside from its bar, & a shady terrace with tables, Monsoon is a place to lounge around, *kasbah* style. Thick walls & good ventilation mean it's always cool, & so are most of the clients. You can even enjoy a shisha pipe with your Arabic coffee or cocktail (*US$5*).

✘ **Old Fort Restaurant** (Ngome Kongwe) [352 B4] Mizingani Rd; m 0744 278737/0713 630206; ⏲ 08.00–20.00 lunch & dinner daily. Opposite the Forodhani Gardens, Zanzibar's old Arab Fort was renovated in the early 1990s & now incorporates a shady outdoor café-restaurant. There's a good selection of snacks for around US$2, local dishes such as chicken & *ugali* (maize meal) or octopus & chips for around US$3, plus coffees, beers & chilled

15

wine. Every Tue, Thu & Sat, there's live entertainment & a BBQ (*US$9*); booking is advised.

✗ **Rendezvous les Spices** [353 E7] Kenyatta Rd; m 0777 410707. With what is arguably the best Indian food on the island & some strikingly colourful murals, this restaurant buzzes most evenings & is reasonably priced too, with main courses such as crab masala, chicken tikka, lamb biriyani or various tandooris for US$7–8. No credit cards.

✗ **Sambusa Two Tables** [353 G6] Victoria St; 024 223 1979. This small place on the balcony of a private house really does have only 2 tables (although 1 seats about 8 people). It's a family affair, so phone or visit to book a table at least in the afternoon of the day to allow time for shopping & preparation. A full meal of spiced rice, curries & numerous local delacacies costs about US$10.

✗ **Tatu** [353 E7] www.tatuzanzibar.com. Meaning 3 in Swahili, 'tatu' is a reference to the three-storey building that's home to this relatively new bar/restaurant. The 1st floor is a social little pub area, complete with free Wi–Fi & a satellite TV; the 2nd floor is a reasonably good restaurant open for lunch & dinner (*US$6–10*); whilst the top floor is a fine, open-sided cigar & whisky bar serving super snacks & serious nightcaps. Tatu is currently a hit with residents & tourists alike, making it a fun evening hangout.

Budget

✗ **Cafés of Forodhani Gardens** [353 A4] In the revamped Forodhani Gardens, there are now 3 small waterfront cafés, including **Café Foro** (nearest the children's playground) & **Zenji Forodhani Garden Café** (*www.zenjiforodhani. com*). Each has an identical pavilion building by the sea & shaded outdoor seating. Selling a selection of cold drinks & with varying menus of fish, burgers, wraps, salads & sweet treats, they

are all open for b/fast, lunch & snacks, & offer a very pleasant sense of calm & green space during a day's sightseeing in Stone Town's narrow alleys.

✗ **Green Garden Restaurant** [352 F3] Off Mkunazini St; ⏱ 11.00–22.00 daily. A delightfully chilled, open-air eatery, set on raised terraces under tall palms. Food ranges from tapas-style dishes (hummous & warm pitta US$3) to the more substantial (king prawn platter US$10), with refreshing snacks (tropical fruit salad US$1.50) & wood fired pizza (*US$7*). Free Wi-Fi for paying customers.

✗ **Stone Town Café** [353 C6] Off Kenyatta Rd; 0773 861313; www.stonetowncafe.com; ⏱ 08.00–22.00. The scents of spiced tea & falafel waft from this buzzing Aussie–Zanzibari run café. Marked out by lush potted plants, passers by queue for unfussy, tasty dishes served by friendly staff. All day b/fasts for US$5, cheesy pizzas (*US$6*), fresh fruit shakes & smoothies, & tasty teatime treats are recommended.

✗ **Zanzibar Coffee House Café** [352 D1] ⏱ 08.00–18.00 daily. This friendly café behind Creek Rd market is an excellent place for a strong cup of freshly ground coffee & a light snack – the glass cabinet boasts a deliciously tempting array of fresh cakes, pies, pastries, croissants & sandwiches. The café is filled with heavy wooden kitchen-style tables that are perfect for gossiping groups, as well as intimate tables for 2.

✗ **Zenji Café** [349 C2] m 0777 247243; www. zenjicafeboutique.com. Despite its busy roadside location, this is a great café, whipping up a selection of milkshakes, ice creams, smoothies & coffees (*US$2–5*). The Dutch–Zanzibari owners claim to bake the best brownies in Zanzibar – and they could well be right. The small, adjoining boutique sells gifts made by Tanzanian craft workers.

ENTERTAINMENT AND NIGHTLIFE Although a largely Muslim island, most tourist restaurants serve African beers and many of the larger hotels have separate bars. Their atmosphere and quality vary considerably. The current pick of the bunch are The **Seyyida rooftop bar** [352 B1] and **Tatu** [353 A7] for a tantalising combination of well-made cocktails and brilliant sunsets. Tatu also boasts a dazzling array of single malt whiskies to tempt late-night revellers. There's also **Mercury's** [349 C3] (*Mizingani Rd*), with its perennially popular happy hour that, out of high season, is a generous 17.00–20.00; and the once must-visit **Africa House Hotel** [353 D8] terrace bar, which has sadly become a little tired and over-priced.

There is live taarab music at the **Monsoon Restaurant** [353 A5] on Wednesday and Saturday nights, and local musicians – from traditional taarab to afro-pop and rap – often perform at bars such as **Mercury's**. The **Arab Fort** [352 B4] is a great venue for live music – mostly traditional musicians and dancers, but sometimes contemporary performances, too, so check their noticeboard for what's on during your stay. A couple of times each week a 'night at the fort' evening is organised, which includes at least two performances plus a barbecue dinner. For a beautifully atmospheric and authentic musical night, **Mtoni Palace Ruins** (see *What to see and do*, page 369) organises taarab orchestra concerts amid the crumbling palace pillars.

SHOPPING Zanzibar Town is something of an Aladdin's cave for shoppers, with a vast array of shops catering for the ever-growing tourist influx. A selection of both favourites and perennials are listed here, though particularly worth checking out are those mentioned in the box, *Made in Zanzibar* (see overleaf); aside from their positive credentials, their products are some of the best quality and most original around.

In the larger tourist shops, prices are fixed and payable in Tanzanian shillings or US dollars, or by credit card (surcharges are usual), but in the market and at smaller, locally run outlets, cash is necessary and bargaining is part of the experience. There are no hard and fast rules to the latter, and sensible judgement is required, but a basic rule of thumb is to start negotiations at half the asking price; if you ultimately pay around 75% of the initial price, then it's likely that both parties will walk away happy.

One of the best places to start a shopping trip is the **Zanzibar Gallery** [353 B6] on Kenyatta Road. This shop sells an excellent range of carvings, paintings, jewellery, materials, maps, clothes, rugs, postcards, antiques and real pieces of art from all over Africa. You can also buy local spices, herbs, pickles and honey, and locally made oils. It also has a very good selection of books. The shop is run by local photographer and publisher Javed Jafferji, whose own books (signed) are sold here, plus illustrated diaries and address books featuring photos from Zanzibar and Tanzania.

Also on Kenyatta Road is **Memories of Zanzibar** [353 C6], opposite the post office, selling everything from beaded flip-flops and silver bracelets to carpets and gourd-lamps, as well as a good selection of books about Zanzibar, and African music CDs. At the seafront end of the same road is **Zawadi Chest** [353 A5]. It has a particularly good display of *kikois (sarong)*, metalwork from the Dar es Salaam charity Wonder Welders, and an excellent selection of swimwear.

SAUTI ZA BUSARA – ZANZIBAR'S ANNUAL MUSIC FESTIVAL

If you're heading to Stone Town in early February, be sure to buy tickets for Sauti Za Busara, Zanzibar's annual music festival. Centred on Stone Town's atmospheric Old Fort, this four-day extravaganza celebrates the best of African music, traditional and modern. Over 200 musicians & artists take to the stage during this highly successful festival, which also includes screenings of documentaries and music videos. An electric atmosphere of African beats, friendly festivalgoers from all over the world, plus a variety of souvenirs and street food, make this eclectic festival one of Africa's best. Tickets can be purchased through the festival's website www.busaramusic.org, or bought on the door, but expect to queue. Do bear in mind that city accommodation sells out fast around festival time, so book early for a guaranteed room.

15

Another place for good-quality crafts is **Hurumzi Art & Craft Gallery**, next to the 236 Hurumzi Hotel on Hurumzi Street [352 C2]. There are many more shops along these streets, and on Changa Bazaar Road. You'll also find pavement traders here offering carvings, paintings and beaded trinkets. Tingatinga paintings on canvas or wooden trays, assorted gold, silver and stone jewellery, packets of spices, and mobiles made from coconut shells in the shapes of dolphins, dhows or tropical fish are readily available at every turn.

Antiques Around Zanzibar Town several shops sell antiques from Arabia and India, dating from Omani and British colonial times. **Coast Antique Shop** on Gizenga Street has a particularly good selection of Zanzibar clocks. There are several more antique shops on the street between St Joseph's Cathedral and Soko Muhogo crossroads.

Art and local crafts Places to buy paintings and pieces of art include the outlets inside **Old Fort** [352 B4], where the resident artists deliberately concentrate on watercolours and batik-like works 'painted' with different-coloured candle wax. Alternatively, for original, slightly more contemporary products, **Keramica** [349 B4], in the shadow of the amphitheatre, is worth a look.

Nearby, beside the House of Wonders [352 B3], Tingatinga painting salesmen hang their works on the railings, and you can also watch some of the artists (all men) working here. In the same area, local weavers (all women) make mats and baskets from grass and palm leaves. Local craftwork can also be found in the Orphanage Shop on Mizingani Road [352 B4] near the fort, where blind craft-workers weave a good range of baskets, rugs and other items. The orphanage is a large building, with a tunnel passing right through the middle of it; the shop is on the side nearest the sea.

Tailors and clothes On Gizenga Street, the tailor at **Mnazi Boutique** can copy any shirt, skirt or pair of trousers you like, from material you buy in the shop or elsewhere in town. Prices start at US$10, and go up to US$25 for a complicated dress. If you prefer traditional African clothing, consider a *kanga* or a *kikoi*. On Kenyatta Road, the smart **One Way** boutique [353 B5] specialises in T-shirts

MADE IN ZANZIBAR – FAIR-TRADE AND HIGH QUALITY

There has been a welcome trend recently towards training members of the local community, especially women, to produce high-quality, well-designed clothing and accessories for sale to tourists. The women benefit from a new skill and a fair price for their efforts. Several of the brands belong to the 'Made in Zanzibar' producers' network. Founded in 2008, the collective hopes to cross-promote quality products from Zanzibar to support the local 'economy', and provide an identifiable brand for visitors. A little more information is available online at www.madeinzanzibar.com. Currently, the best projects, products and shopping outlets are: **Fahari** (*opposite Stone Town Café*) for stylish leatherwork; **Dada** for wholesome tropical preserves and cosmetics; **Moto** (*Hurumzi St, & outside Jozani Forest*) for basketry; funky fashion from **Malkia** (several hotel shops); **Sasik** on Gizenga Street for applique; **Surti & Sons** for leather sandals; **Upendo Means Love** for gorgeous island kidswear; and **Zenji Boutique** for a pan-African craft selection.

embroidered with Kenyan and Tanzanian slogans and logos, whilst **Saifa**, along from the Serena Inn, has fair-trade cotton T-shirts.

Postcards and books For postcards you can't go wrong at **Angi's Postcards & Maps**, on Mizingani Road [349 C3], near the Big Tree; there's a truly massive selection here, all at good prices. Books – coffee-table, fact and fiction – can be purchased from the well-stocked **Gallery Bookshop** [353 C5] (*Gizenga St;* ⏱ *09.00–19.00 Mon–Sat, 09.00–14.00 Sun*).

Jewellery If a more precious purchase is what you're after, **Eddy G at Hassan Jewellers** (*Mkunazini St;* ☎ *027 223 1242*), close to the market, is reliable and reputable. He stocks a good range of tanzanite and is able to supply authentication certificates. Be aware that tanzanite is a soft stone that scratches easily; better to have it set as earrings or in a necklace than as a ring.

OTHER PRACTICALITIES
Banks and money changing A number of banks and forex bureaux are dotted around the Stone Town, offering similar exchange rates against cash to their mainland counterparts. The only place that exchanges travellers' cheques is the first-floor 'Foreign Trade Dept' at the National Bank of Commerce on Kenyatta Road [353 B5]. You can draw cash against Visa cards at the ATM outside the same bank, but the only place where you can draw against MasterCard is the ATM at Barclays Bank, a couple of kilometres out of town along the road towards the north coast. There are additional Barclays ATMs in Shangani, near the Creek Road market and at Mwana Kwerekwe. Most upmarket hotels accept major credit cards.

These days, there isn't much to choose between banks and private bureaux in terms of rates, but you'll generally find the transaction takes a minute or two at a private bureau whereas changing money at banks often involves long queues and plenty of paperwork. Good private bureaux de change include the **Shangani Bureau de Change** (*at the northern end of Kenyatta Road, near the Tembo Hotel*) and **Malindi Bureau de Change** [349 C2] (*next to the ZanAir office, east of the port gates*). Most large hotels will also change money, although some deal only with their own guests, and they often offer poor rates.

Communications The main post office lies outside the Stone Town towards the stadium, but the old post office on Kenyatta Road [353 C6] in the Shangani area is the most convenient for tourists, and is also the place to collect *poste restante* mail addressed to Zanzibar. A better place from which to make international phone calls lies next door at the **Tanzanian Telecommunications office** [353 C6]. Rates here are generally similar to those at some of the private bureaux around town, though it's as well to ask around. Purchasing a local SIM card may be a better bet if you're here for a while. You will need to register the SIM – try the Zantel office at Vuga roundabout – or else it will only last for a few days.

Numerous internet cafés have sprung up in Zanzibar Town over the past few years, charging a fairly uniform US$1/hr. These include **Palace Internet** [349 C3] (*Forodhani Rd*), **Sanjay Internet Café** (*off Gizenga St nr House of Wonders*), **Shangani Internet Café** [353 C6] (*Kenyatta Rd*) and **Too Short Internet Café** [353 B5] (*Shangani St*).

Maps Aside from those in this book, the most accurate and attractive map of Stone Town is Giovanni Tombazzi's *Map of Zanzibar Stone Town*, which also has a good map of the island on the flip side.

Medical facilities Zanzibar's private medical clinics, where staff speak English and drugs are more readily available, are usually a better option for visitors than the public Mnazi Mmoja General Hospital. There are pharmacies at the medical centres as well as in Stone Town; the pharmacist at the outfit opposite the Shamshuddin Cash & Carry Supermarket near the market [349 C4] is recommended.

✚ **Afya Medical Hospital** [353 E7] Off Vuga Rd at the southern end of Stone Town; ☎ 024 223 1228; 📱 0777 411934. Afya is large & well stocked, with friendly staff. Consultations cost US$2, blood or urine tests are available, & there's also a pharmacy.

✚ **Dr Mehta's Hospital** [353 F7] On Vuga Rd; ☎ 024 223 0194; 📱 0741 612889.
✚ **Fahaud Health Centre** Near St Joseph's Cathedral, this very basic centre offers consultations for US$3, whilst a malaria blood test is US$2. Should your test prove positive, they also sell FansiDar at US$1 per tablet.

Swahili lessons The **Institute of KiSwahili and Foreign Languages** [349 D6] (*Vuga Rd;* ☎ *024 223 0724/3337;* e *takiluki@zanlink.com; www.glcom.com/hassan/ takiluki.html*) offers week-long courses for US$80 and half-day classes (*US$4/ hr*). Another option is **KIU** (*657 Kokoni St;* ☎ *0777 422499/773;* e *zanzibar@ swahilicourses.com; www.swahilicourses.com*) which offers in-depth two-week courses for US$220 as well as individual or group courses from US$5–10 per hour depending on numbers.

Swimming pool The pool at the **Dhow Palace Hotel** [353 D7] is open to non-residents for Tsh3,000 per person. Out of town, there's the option to swim at **Maruhubi Beach Villas** for US$5 per day, and children of diners can swim at **Mtoni Marine** (see *Around Zanzibar Town, Where to stay and eat*, page 368, for details of both).

WHAT TO SEE AND DO

Spice tours and other excursions The one organised trip that practically all visitors to Zanzibar undertake is a 'spice tour', something that would be logistically difficult to set up independently, and which relies heavily on the local knowledge of a guide. In addition to visiting a few spice plantations, most spice tours include a walk around a cultivated rural homestead, as well as a visit to one of the island's ruins and a traditional Swahili lunch. The Princess Salme tour operated from Mtoni Palace (see box, page 369) is a particularly good example at around US$55 per person.

Several other short excursions can be undertaken out of Zanzibar Town. Although many visitors prefer to do their exploring in the form of an organised day tour, most places of interest on the island can be visited independently. Popular excursions from Stone Town include a boat trip to one or more of the nearby islands, a visit to the dolphins at Kizimkazi, and a trip to Jozani Forest to see the endemic Kirk's red colobus. Also easily explored from Zanzibar is the 10km of coastline stretching northwards to the small seaside settlement of Bububu, that boasts a number of interesting ruins, while Fuji Beach at Bububu is the closest public swimming beach to the Stone Town. In fact, the only parts of Zanzibar which are more often visited for a few nights than as a day trip are Nungwi and Mnemba Island in the north, and the several beach villages that line the east coast of the island.

Stone Town walking tour You can spend many idle hours getting lost in the fascinating labyrinth of narrow streets and alleys of the old Stone Town, and will almost inevitably hit most of the main landmarks within a couple of days of arriving. However, the following roughly circular walking tour through the Stone Town will allow those with limited time to do their sightseeing in a reasonably organised manner (though they are still bound to get lost), and should help those with more time to orientate themselves before they head out to explore the Stone Town without a map or guidebook in hand.

The obvious starting point for any exploration of Zanzibar Town is **Forodhani Gardens** [352 A4] (see box below), the open park between Mizingani Road and the main sea wall. Laid out in 1936 to mark the silver jubilee of Sultan Khalifa, the gardens are a popular eating and meeting point in the evening, and the staircase rising from the gardens to the arched bridge to the south offers a good view over the old town.

Three of the most significant buildings in the Stone Town lie alongside each other overlooking the seafront behind the Forodhani Gardens. The **Palace Museum** [352 A1] (⊕ *09.00–18.00 daily; admission US$3 pp*) is the most northerly of these, a large white building with castellated battlements dating from the late 1890s. The palace was

FORODHANI GARDENS

The Forodhani Gardens (Jamituri Gardens on some maps) are between the Arab Fort and the sea, overlooked by the House of Wonders. They were first laid out in 1936 to commemorate the Silver Jubilee of Sultan Khalifa (who ruled 1911–60), and were called Jubilee Gardens until the 1964 revolution. In the centre stands a podium where the band of the sultan's army used to play for the public. Nearer the sea is a white concrete arabesque arch, built in 1956 for the visit of Princess Margaret (sister of Queen Elizabeth II of Britain), but never officially used as the princess arrived at the dhow harbour instead. She did visit the gardens, however, and planted a large tree, which can still be seen today.

Forodhani has long been a popular place for local people and visitors in the evenings, lured by the waterfront gathering of stalls serving drinks and hot snacks. Years of excessive overuse and poor maintenance took its toll, though, and for several years 'gardens' was a euphemism for an unattractive, parched wasteland.

Wonderfully, things have changed. On 17 January 2008, the Aga Khan Trust for Culture, with approval from the Zanzibar government, finally began a major rehabilitation of the gardens. They had been in discussion about the project with the government since 2002 when the organisation first proposed comprehensive seafront rehabilitation. The aims of the project were to improve the infrastructure and to restore and preserve the civic components of the gardens, none of which had happened in the past as a result of overuse, disrepair and limited private refurbishment.

The project was completed in 2010, and the changes are plain to see. Everyone agrees that the new Forodhani Gardens are a vast improvement, with the practical introduction of wheelie bins, lighting and waste collections, a new sea wall of salvaged stone, an organised foodcourt for the evening stall holders, three inviting cafés, a bandstand, a dhow-shaped adventure playground and tropical planting amid manicured lawns. We, like the Aga Khan, hope that this project will prove a catalyst for urban upgrading and economic opportunity, as well as aesthetically improving the remaining waterfront area.

the official residence of the Sultan of Zanzibar from 1911 until the 1964 revolution, after which it was renamed the People's Palace. For many years after this, it served as a government office and was closed to the public. Since 1994, however, it has housed an excellent museum, with a variety of displays relating to the early days of the sultanate, including a room devoted to artefacts belonging to Princess Salme. The graves of all the early sultans of Zanzibar are in the palace garden.

Next to the Palace Museum, the **House of Wonders** [352 B3] is a square, multi-storey building surrounded by tiers of impressive balconies and topped by a clocktower. It was built as a ceremonial palace in 1883, and was the first building on Zanzibar to have electric lights. Local people called it Beit el Ajaib, meaning the House of Wonders. Until recently it was the CCM party headquarters, and it has recently opened to tourists as the Museum of History and Culture (*admission US$3*), which houses about half of the eight planned permanent exhibitions (dedicated to the history of the Swahili Coast, and Zanzibar in particular). Sadly, it's crumbling more as the years go by and suffered a partial balcony collapse in late 2012. It is still an interesting diversion, but without better upkeep and curating its appeal is waning.

Directly facing Forodhani Gardens, the **Old Arab Fort** [352 B4] (*admission free, donations welcome*) is probably the oldest extant building in Stone Town, built by Omani Arabs between 1698 and 1701 over the site of a Portuguese church constructed a century before that, remnants of which can still be seen in the inner wall. A large, squarish, brown building with castellated battlements, the fort ceased to serve any meaningful military role in the 19th century, since when it has served variously as prison, railway depot and women's tennis club. The interior of the fort is open to visitors, who can climb to the top of the battlements and enter some of the towers. There is a restaurant serving cold drinks, and traditional dancing shows take place there at least three evenings every week (see *Entertainment and nightlife*, page 359).

Heading southwest from the fort, under an arched bridge, the fork to your right is **Shangani Road**, the site of notable important buildings. Just before following this fork, to your left, the **Upimaji Building** was the home of the German merchant Heinrich Ruete (later the husband of Princess Salme) in the 1860s. To the left of the fork is a block of government offices which served as the **British Consulate** [353 B5] from 1841 until 1874, and next to that the **Tembo Hotel** [353 A6], a restored 19th-century building. As you follow Shangani Road around a curve, you'll come out to a leafy green square, where the Zanzibar Shipping Corporation Building, dating to around 1850, stands to your left and the **Zanzibar Serena Inn** [353 B8], formerly Extelcoms House, to your right.

Perhaps 100m past the Serena Inn, to your left, you'll see the rear of **Tippu Tip's House** [353 D7], a tall brown building that once served as the residence of Tippu Tip, the influential 19th-century slave trader who helped explorers such as Livingstone and Stanley with supplies and route planning. The building is privately owned and is closed to visitors, but if you follow the alley around the rear of the house, you can see its huge carved front door from the streetResidents will sometimes show visitors around, although some 'guides' here are heroin addicts and visitors are advised to exercise caution. From here, wander up another 50m past the former New Happy Bar, and you'll pass the **Africa House Hotel** [353 D8], which served as the English Club from 1888 onwards, and is a good place to punctuate your walk with a cold drink on the attractively positioned balcony.

From the Africa House Hotel a small alley leads to **Kenyatta Road**, an important thoroughfare dotted with hotels, shops and restaurants, as well as a number of old buildings with traditional Zanzibari doors. Follow Kenyatta Road eastwards for about 300m, passing the somewhat unkempt **People's Gardens** [349 C6], originally laid out under Sultan Barghash for the use of his harem, until you reach the **Zanzibar Milestone** [349 C7]. This octagonal marble pillar shows the distance from Zanzibar Town to various settlements on the island and further afield.

Cross the gardens in front of the milestone to the distinctive **Beit el Amani (House of Peace) Memorial Museum** [349 D7] (⏱ *08.30–19.00 Mon–Fri, 08.30–15.00 Sat & Sun; small entrance charge*), which, despite its name, is now little more than a library; most of its exhibits have been shifted to the rapidly developing museum in the House of Wonders. The Zanzibari door at the back of the building is reputedly the oldest in existence.

From the museum, follow Creek Road northwards for about 400m, and to your left you'll easily pick out the imposing **Anglican Cathedral** [352 F1] built by the Universities' Mission in Central Africa (UMCA) over the former slave market between 1873 and 1880. Tradition has it that the altar stands on the site of the market's whipping block, and the cellar of the nearby **St Monica's Guesthouse**

MREMBO TRADITIONAL SPA

Recently, a number of 'spas' have sprung up around Zanzibar as the Western craze for 'wellness' treatments has descended on the island. Many are little more than a massage table, some lemongrass oil and a friendly, if untrained, local masseuse; a few, in the larger hotels, are more sophisticated and professional. All can prove an enjoyable distraction, but the most engaging and original by far is Mrembo Traditional Spa [352 D4] (*Cathedral St & Mtoni Marine;* ☏ *0777 430117;* e *mrembo@zanzibar.cc*).

In an old antique store close to St Joseph's Cathedral, Mrembo is a small, wonderfully unassuming place offering the finest traditional treatments from Zanzibar and Pemba. Their flagship treatment, Singo, is a natural exfoliating scrub traditionally used when preparing Zanzibari girls for marriage. Prepared by hand with a pestle and mortar (*kinu*), the fresh jasmine, ylang ylang, rose petals, *mpompia* (geranium), *mrehani* (sweet basil) and *liwa* (sandalwood) combine to create the most wonderfully aromatic blend. For men, the clove-based scrub Vidonge is said by Pembans to increase libido and stamina, and is even offered in souvenir packages. Hot sand massages, authentic henna painting and beauty treatments are available too, with all the herbal products coming from the owner's garden and skilfully prepared in front of you.

Although not its *raison d'être*, Mrembo is also an impressively inclusive community project. Two of the four local therapists are disabled: one deaf, Ali, and one blind, Asha. Trained in therapeutic massage by professional therapists from The African Touch (a Canadian-funded, community-based organisation in Kenya), they have both benefited enormously in confidence and social standing from their practical education and employment. Each has an able-bodied assistant at Mrembo to ease understanding, though Ali will cheerfully encourage you to try a little KiSwahili sign-language, using the alphabet poster for guidance.

For a lazy afternoon, or a simple massage or manicure whilst the sun's at its peak, Mrembo Traditional Spa is a great place. It is a true oasis of calm in the centre of Stone Town, and an experience not to be hurried. Alternatively, you can visit its sister spa at Mtoni Marine hotel (page 368) and enjoy the hotel restaurants afterwards.

[352 G1] is said to be the remains of a pit where slaves were kept before being sold. Sultan Barghash, who closed the slave market, is reputed to have asked Bishop Steere, leader of the mission, not to build the cathedral tower higher than the House of Wonders. When the bishop agreed, the sultan presented the cathedral with its clock. The foundation of the UMCA was inspired by Livingstone: a window is dedicated to his memory, and the church's crucifix is made from the tree under which his heart was buried in present-day Zambia. Several other missionaries are remembered on plaques around the cathedral wall, as are sailors killed fighting the slave trade and servicemen who died in action in East Africa during World War I. The cathedral is open to visitors for a nominal fee, which also covers entrance to the dungeon below the guesthouse.

A short distance further along Creek Road lies the **covered market** [349 D4], built at around the turn of the 20th century, and worth a visit even if you don't want to buy anything. It's a vibrant place where you can buy anything from fish and bread to sewing machines and secondhand car spares. Once you've taken a look around the market, follow Creek Road back southwards for 100m or so, passing the cathedral, then turn into the first wide road to your right. This is New Mkunazini Road, and if you follow it until its end, then turn right into Kajificheni Street and right again into Hammani Street, you'll come out at the **Hammani Baths** [352 D3] – one of the most elaborate Persian baths on Zanzibar, built for Sultan Barghash; the caretaker will show you around for a small fee.

Barely 200m from the baths, on Cathedral Street, **St Joseph's Catholic Cathedral** [353 C5] is notable for its prominent twin spires, and was built between 1896 and 1898 by French missionaries and local converts. There are now few Catholics on Zanzibar, and the cathedral is infrequently used, but visitors are welcome when the doors are open. The best way to get here from the baths is to retrace your steps along Kajificheni Street, then turn right into the first alley (which boasts several good examples of traditional Zanzibari carved doors) until you reach an open area where several roads and alleys meet – Cathedral Street among them. If you're in this area, or indeed if you fancy some serious pampering, consider making an appointment at the nearby Mrembo Traditional Spa [352 D4] (see box, page 365).

From the cathedral, continue northwards along Cathedral Street for perhaps 50m, then turn right into Gizenga Street, a good place to check out the work of **local Tingatinga artists** and other curios at any of numerous small shops. If you follow Gizenga Street until you see the old Arab Fort to your left, you can conclude your walk by wandering back out to Forodhani Gardens. Alternatively, if you want to keep going, turn right opposite the fort into Hurumzi Street and, after continuing straight for about 300m, you'll come to the open square close to the Zanzibar Coffee House [352 D1] (a good place to take a break for a tasty snack and a drink). A left turn as you enter this square takes you past the Ismaili Jamat Khan Mosque and on to Jamatini Road, which after about 200m will bring you out at the seafront opposite the **Big Tree** [349 C3]. Known locally as Mtini, this well-known landmark was planted in 1911 by Sultan Khalifa and now provides shade for traditional dhow builders.

On Mizingani Road, next to the Big Tree, the **Old Customs House** [349 B3], a large, relatively plain building dating to the late 19th century, is where Sultan Hamoud was proclaimed sultan in 1896. Next to this is another large old building, formerly Le Grand Hotel, which is being renovated and likely to reopen as a hotel again.

From the open area next to the Big Tree, a left turn along Mizingani Road will take you back to the Arab Fort, passing the above-mentioned buildings. Turn right into Mizingani Road, however, and after about 100m you'll pass the **Old Dispensary** [349 C2], an ornate three-storey building built in the 1890s. Restored to its former glory by the Aga Khan, the dispensary now also contains a small exhibition hall of old monochrome photographs of the Stone Town. You can continue for a few hundred metres further, past the port gates, to the **traditional dhow harbour** [349 C1], though based on our experience you are unlikely to be allowed inside.

If the above directions seem too complicated, or you want further insight into the historical buildings of the Stone Town, most tour operators can arrange a guided city tour for around US$15–20 (see *Tour operators*, page 350, for listings).

AROUND ZANZIBAR TOWN

North of Zanzibar Town, the small town of Bububu served as the terminus for a 10km stretch of 36-inch gauge track to connect the north coast to the Arab Fort, constructed in 1904 and used until 1928. The springs outside Bububu supply most of Zanzibar Town's fresh water, and the name of the town presumably derives from the bubbling sound that they make. For most tourists, Bububu's main attraction is Fuji Beach, the closest swimming beach to town, no more than 500m to your left when you disembark from the dala-dala at the main crossroads at Bububu.

Of interest in Bububu is a small, centuries-old mosque about 200m from the main crossroads, along the road back towards Zanzibar Town. There is a little-known but large double-storey ruin on the beachfront about 500m north from where you arrive at the Fuji Beach. Complete with Arabic frescoes, this house must date to the early 19th century, and it could well have been the Bububu residence of Princess Salme in the 1850s, as described in her autobiography (see overleaf).

Between Zanzibar Town and Bububu lie the ruined palaces of Maruhubi and Mtoni, and Bububu is also the closest substantial settlement to the Persian baths at Kidichi and Kizimbani.

GETTING AROUND Although some of the places mentioned below might be included in your spice tour, it is easy to visit most of them independently, using a combination of dala-dala No 502 (with frequent services to Bububu from the bus station on Creek Road) and your legs. Another possibility is to hire a motor scooter or bicycle from one of the tour operators (see *Tour operators*, page 349).

WHERE TO STAY AND EAT

Mbweni Ruins Hotel (13 rooms) \024 223 5478/9; e hotel@mbweni.com; www.mbweni.com. This small hotel in the grounds of the Mbweni Ruins is rated as one of the best of its type in & around Zanzibar Town. Comfortable en-suite rooms with AC & private balconies are a short hop to the pool or beach. It's a relaxing spot, with a spa & waterside bar, & a popular restaurant (lunch US$10–20; dinner US$10–35). The staff can advise visitors on local natural history. There's a free shuttle service to & from town, & port/airport transfers cost US$15 for 4 people. *US$200–265 dbl, B&B.*

Imani Beach Villa (9 rooms) \024 225 0050; m 0773 903983; e info@imani-zanzibar. com; www.imani-zanzibar.com. About 9km from Stone Town, clearly signposted off the main road, this delightful home from home is tucked away

down a bumpy track by the sea. En suite rooms, with enormous Zanzibari beds, offer a superb sea view, while in the tropical garden are an Arab-style bar & restaurant, with meals (around US$20) taken seated on piles of cushions & Persian carpets at low tables. The British management offer good personal service & have buckets of enthusiasm. Bikes are free for guest use. *US$90–120 dbl, B&B.*

Mangrove Lodge (10 rooms) m 0777 436954 e info@mangrovelodge.com; www. mangrovelodge.com. Mangrove Lodge is a peaceful, leafy & relaxed seaside retreat on a pretty slice of mangrove beach. The Zanzibari–Italian owners have taken admirable measures to reduce the environmental impact of the lodge: no energy-devouring AC, cooking over fire, locally sourced construction materials, furnishings by local tailors. Now, sandy pathways through tropical gardens & lawns link the 10 pretty thatched bungalows, each with either a dbl or a sgl bed & a kitchenette. It's peaceful here – butterflies flutter around the orchard gardens, the restaurant looks over fishing boats bobbing on the bay, & sunbathers can choose between 2 secluded beaches. *US$79–90 dbl, B&B.*

🏠 **Mtoni Marine** (43 rooms) ✆024 2250140; m 0777 486214; e mtoni@ zanzibar.cc; www. mtoni.com. Between the palaces of Maruhubi & Mtoni, about 5min drive north of Zanzibar Town,

this highly recommended, friendly hotel is set in tropical gardens overlooking the bay & a large sandy beach. Rooms are cool & comfortable with high ceilings & a raft of mod-cons. There's plenty of choice at mealtimes, with the Zansushibar on the beach particularly popular, as well as a casual bistro with sports TV & a candlelit restaurant. The hotel has a spa, swimming pool & a great playhouse/climbing frame for children. Sunset (US$15 pp) & all-day (US$40 pp) dhow cruises are offered, & tours can be arranged, including The Princess Salme tour (see box below). *US$90–185 dbl, B&B.*

WHAT TO SEE AND DO Most people visit this area as a day trip from Zanzibar Town, but it is perfectly possible to explore using Bububu as a base.

Maruhubi Palace This palace (*admission US$0.30*) is probably the most impressive ruin on this part of the coast, built in 1882 for the concubines of Sultan Barghash. At one time he kept around 100 women here. The palace was destroyed by fire in 1899, and all that remains are the great pillars that supported the upper storey, and the Persian-style bathhouse. You can also see the separate bathrooms for the women, the large bath used by the sultan, and the original water tanks, now overgrown with lilies. Sadly, local authorities have been using the site as an overflow dumping ground for rubbish in recent years, so the atmosphere and environment are pretty unpleasant these days. If you're still keen to visit, the palace is signposted about 200m from the Bububu road, roughly 3km from the Stone Town. Traditional dhow builders can be seen at work on the beach in front of the palace.

THE PRINCESS SALME TOUR

Created by the team at Mtoni Palace Conservation Project (✆ *024 225 0140; m 0777 430117; e mtoni@zanzibar.cc; www.mtoni.com*), this day trip combines a number of historical palaces and traditional ceremonies with an informative spice tour and delicious Swahili lunch. Escorted by a guide from the conservation project, small groups (*approximately 4–6*) are taken by boat from the evocative ruins of Mtoni Palace, Princess Salme's birthplace, to Bububu for a traditional coffee ceremony with tasty local treats (*kashata* – peanut brittle – and candy-like *halua*). After a short walk, perhaps into the grounds of Salme's cousin's home, visitors are transported by donkey and cart, Salme-style, to the Kidichi plantation area, where Mzee Yussuf guides a tour of his spice farm before his wife serves a deliciously fresh, homemade meal. Heading back down the hillside after lunch, there are great views towards the Indian Ocean and Stone Town before the cart arrives at the Persian Baths, originally built in 1850 for Sultan Said's second wife Scheherazade. From here, visitors are whisked back to Mtoni Marine by minibus for a chilled drink in the bar. Thoroughly original and enjoyable.

Departs Mtoni Marine 08.30, return 14.00; cost US$55 per person, plus US$5 per person supplement for fewer than three people, including entrance fees, lunch, and a US$5 donation to Mtoni Palace Conservation Project. Reservations one day in advance essential.

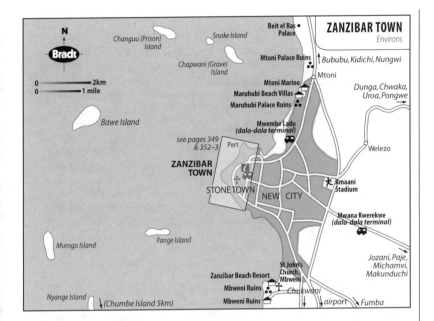

Mtoni Palace The ruins of Mtoni Palace lie a short distance north of Maruhubi, and can be reached along the beach. The oldest palace on Zanzibar, Mtoni was built for Sultan Said in the 1840s. A book written by his daughter Salme describes the palace in the 1850s. At one end of the house was a large bathhouse, at the other the quarters where Said lived with his principal wife. Gazelles and peacocks wandered around the large courtyard until Mtoni was abandoned around 1885. Now, only the main walls, roof and bathhouses remain, but members of the resident Mtoni Palace Conservation Project are working hard to restore significant sections and offer interesting guided tours. The palace was used as a warehouse in World War I, with evidence of this alteration still visible.

Kidichi and Kizimbani Persian baths The Kidichi baths were built in 1850 for Said's wife, Binte Irich Mirza, the granddaughter of the Shah of Persia, and were decorated with Persian-style stucco. You can enter the bathhouse and see the bathing pool and toilets, but there is mould growing on much of the stucco.

The baths lie about 3km east of Bububu; from the main crossroads follow the road heading inland (ie: turn right coming from Zanzibar Town) and you'll see the baths to your right after a walk of around 30 minutes. The Kizimbani baths are less attractive and less accessible on foot, lying a further 3km or so inland. The surrounding Kizimbani clove plantation, which is visited by many spice tours, was founded in the early 19th century by Saleh bin Haramil, the Arab trader who imported the first cloves to Zanzibar.

Mangapwani Slave Chamber Near the village of Mangapwani, some 10km north of Bububu, are a large natural cavern and a manmade slave chamber. This square cell cut into the coral was apparently built to hold slaves by one Muhammad bin Nassor Al-Alwi, an important slave trader. Boats from the mainland would unload their human cargo on the nearby beach, and the slaves would be kept here before being taken to Zanzibar Town for resale, or to plantations on the island. It is

Princess Salme was born at Mtoni Palace, on the coast about 8km outside Zanzibar Town. The daughter of Seyyid Said, Sultan of Oman and Zanzibar, she had around 36 brothers and sisters, almost all of different mothers, and some of whom were old enough to be her grandparents. Her own mother, one of around 75 'wives' or *sarari*, owned by the sultan, was a Circassian by birth, but had been abducted by bandits as a child from her home near the Black Sea.

It was at Mtoni Palace that Salme spent her early years, playing with her brothers and sisters, floating toy boats on the river. Hers was an idyllic childhood, surrounded by love and attention, and wanting for nothing. Much of the palace social life was centred on the numerous bathing houses, where people would spend several hours each day, praying, working, reading or even taking their meals. In spite of the restrictions of traditional 19th-century Muslim society, members of the household had considerable freedom and Salme and her sisters were encouraged to be active. Twice a day, children over five years of age were given riding lessons. While the boys rode on horseback, the girls were given much-valued white donkeys. Unusually for a woman, Salme was also taught to read and write.

Salme's father had several properties on the island, many by the sea, some in the city and others on his 45 plantations. At the age of seven, Salme and her mother reluctantly moved with an elder brother into the town at Beit el Watoro. As her brothers Barghash and Majid grew older, petty jealousies surfaced, and at around the time of her father's death, when she was nine, such jealousies turned to intrigue and feuds. Three years later, after a cholera epidemic carried off Salme's mother, the princess became entangled in a web of conspiracy as Barghash, supported by Salme, sought to overthrow his brother. Although Majid defeated the rebellion, Salme claims that he continued to maintain a good relationship with his younger sister.

It was shortly after this that Salme found herself living next door to a young German who worked for a Hamburg mercantile firm. Although their friendship was known to Salme's family, the prospect of a Christian marriage would not have been acceptable, and the two planned their escape so that they could marry in a Christian church. With the help of the British vice-consul, Salme boarded a British man-of-war, the *Highflier*, and headed north to Aden. Here she was baptised, taking the name Emily, and shortly after this the two were married. They spent just three years together in Germany before Emily was widowed, left alone in a strange country with three young children. Nevertheless, she made her home in Germany, and later in London; it was 19 years before she was to set foot once again on Zanzibar soil.

Emily Ruete's *Memoirs of an Arabian Princess from Zanzibar* is published by Markus Wiener.

---

thought that some time after 1873, when slavery was officially abolished, the cave was used as a place to hide slaves, as an illicit trade continued for many years.

To get there from Zanzibar Town, take bus route 2 or a No 102 dala-dala. Coming by dala-dala, disembark at Mangapwani, where a road forks left towards the coast. About 2km past the village this road ends and a small track branches off to the right. Follow this for 1km to reach the slave chamber. About halfway between Mangapwani and the track to the slave chamber, a narrow track to the left leads to the cavern, which has a narrow entrance and a pool of fresh water at its lowest point.

ISLANDS CLOSE TO ZANZIBAR TOWN

Several small islands lie between 2km and 6km offshore of Zanzibar, many of them within view of Zanzibar Town and easily visited from there as a day trip. Boat transport to Chumbe arranged with an independent guide will cost around US$20, but you will pay more to go on an organised tour (see page 348 for tour operators). To cut the individual cost, it is worth getting a group together. Despite their individual attractions, these islands are quiet yet close to main shipping routes, so are not ideal overnight stays for those in search of either total isolation or entertainment and nightlife. Note that crossing to or from Zanzibar Town in an unlit boat at night is dangerous.

CHUMBE ISLAND The coral island of Chumbe, along with several surrounding reefs, is gazetted as a nature reserve under the title of Chumbe Island Coral Park (CHICOP). The area is in near-pristine condition because it served as a military base for many years and visitors were not permitted. Snorkelling here is as good as anywhere around Zanzibar, with more than 350 reef fishes recorded, as well as dolphins and turtles. A walking trail circumnavigates the island, passing rock pools haunted by starfish, and beaches marched upon by legions of hermit crabs. Look out, too, for the giant coconut crab, an endangered nocturnal creature that weighs up to 4kg. Some 60 species of bird have been recorded on the island, including breeding pairs of the rare roseate tern, and the localised Ader's duiker, hunted out in the 1950s, has been re-introduced. Of historical interest are an ancient Swahili mosque and a British lighthouse built in 1904.

Day trips to the island (*US$95 pp, inc transfers, guides, snorkelling equipment & lunch*) can be arranged only through reputable tour operators or from the Mbweni Ruins Hotel (see *Around Zanzibar Town, Where to stay and eat*, page 367). Alternatively visitors can stay overnight.

Where to stay

⌂ **Chumbe Island Lodge** (7 rooms) ☎024 223 1040; m 0777 413582; e chumbe@zitec. org; www.chumbeisland.com; ⊕ mid Jun–mid Apr. Bungalows here are simple but clean, very comfortable & genuinely ecologically sensitive, with solar electricity, composting toilets & funnelled roofs designed to collect rainwater. Made mostly from local materials, each has 2 storeys, with an open-fronted lounge-terrace & a bathroom below, & upstairs, a mattress laid on the floor, shrouded in a mosquito net, with a stunning view. An ingenious main *boma* houses the dining room (good seafood), education centre, snorkelling equipment room & lounge/bar. Chumbe is highly recommended to those with a strong interest in wildlife & conservation & has won numerous global awards for ecotourism.

CHANGUU (PRISON) ISLAND Changuu was originally owned by a wealthy Arab, who used it as a detention centre for disobedient slaves. A prison was built there in 1893, but never used; today it houses a café, library and boutique. A path circles the island (about an hour's stroll). There is a small beach, a secluded hotel and a restaurant, and snorkelling equipment can be hired. The island is home to several giant tortoises, probably brought from the Seychelles in the 18th century, which spend much of their time mating, a long and noisy process though numbers remain severely threatened. An entrance fee of US$5 per person must be paid in hard currency.

Where to stay

Changuu Private Island Paradise

(27 rooms) m 0773 333241/2; e info.changuu@
privateislands-zanzibar.com; www.privateislands-
zanzibar.com. The restoration & conversion of
many of the crumbling buildings on the island, &
construction of individual beachfront cottages, has
resulted in spacious & colourful rooms, the latter
in the 'deluxe' category & with greater privacy.
There is no mains electricity (& thus no AC), &
it's worth taking a good torch for evening beach
walks. The restaurant, in a restored 19th-century
home, serves extensive 4-course dinners & a good
(predominantly seafood) lunch menu. Facilities
include swimming pool & floodlit tennis court, &
there's a pleasant beach – though it's important
to be careful when swimming as these are busy
shipping waters. While guests have free run of
the island, day visitors are confined to the ruins &
tortoise sanctuary.

CHAPWANI (GRAVE) ISLAND This long, narrow and very pretty island has been
the site of a Christian cemetery since 1879. Most of the graves belong to British
sailors who were killed tackling Arab slave ships, while others date from World
War I, when the British ship *Pegasus* was sunk in Zanzibar harbour. The island also
has a small swimming beach – good at low and high tide – and faces Snake Island,
where thousands of egrets roost overnight. The indigenous forest supports about
100 duikers, large numbers of fruit bats, and various coastal scrub birds. The giant
coconut crab is often seen along the shore.

Where to stay

Chapwani Private Island (10 rooms)

⏰ mid Jun–mid Apr e info@ houseofwonders.
com; www.chapwaniisland.com. Rooms in 5 small,
semi-detached bungalows are on the sandy beach;
all are en suite with Zanzibari beds, mosquito nets
& a timber-decked terrace. Power is by generator,
so there's no AC, & don't forget a torch. There's a
nice pool tucked among the trees or, for a more
natural dip, a tidal outlet in a coral crevasse on the
northeast of the island makes a pleasant place to
swim at high tide. At low tide, the exposed reef
offers coral, starfish & barnacle-clad rock pools to
explore.

BAWE ISLAND About 6km due west of Zanzibar Town, Bawe has broad sandy
beaches and a densely vegetated centre. In 1879, it was given to the Eastern
Telegraph Company by Sultan Barghash to be used as the operations station for
the underwater telegraphic cable linking Cape Town with Zanzibar, the Seychelles
and Aden in Yemen. A second line was run from Bawe Island to the External
Telecommunications building in the Shangani area of Zanzibar Town. The old
'Extelcoms' building has now been converted into the Serena Inn, but the original
phone line is largely redundant.

Lovely as the beach may be, it is firmly on the busy shipping route to Zanzibar
Town and isn't visited as frequently as Changuu. In theory, it's possible to combine
trips here with the tortoise excursions or simply arrange an out-and-back voyage
with a boat captain in Zanzibar Town, though access prices do tend to be higher
than those to Changuu.

Where to stay

Bawe Tropical Island (15 rooms) m 0773

333241/2; e info.bawe@privateislands-zanzibar.
com; www.privateislands-zanzibar.com. With
the arrival of this new lodge, sister to the one on
Changuu Island, visitors can retreat to this pretty
beach spot from the frenzy of Zanzibar Town.
Thatched cottages, with en-suite bathrooms &
colourful interiors, line the sand, just a stone's
throw from the warm, shallow sea – though a
good awareness of the shipping traffic is important
if you plan to swim. Otherwise there is little more
to do than sit on the beach & relax.

The large fishing village of Nungwi, situated on the northern end of the island, is the centre of Zanzibar's traditional dhow-building industry. It has also emerged over the last decade as probably the most popular tourist retreat on Zanzibar, thanks to a lovely beach lined with palm and casuarina trees, good snorkelling and diving in the surrounding waters, and a profusion of cheaper hotel options. That said, recent years have seen almost unbridled tourist development in this area, with a twofold increase in hotel beds in just two years, so it's important to choose your accommodation carefully to avoid disappointment; many travellers find that the bustling atmosphere that characterises Nungwi is not to their taste.

On the west coast, about 4km south of Nungwi, is the tiny village of Kendwa, and a beautiful beach that doesn't suffer the vast tidal changes of the east coast. It has seen plenty of tourist development since the mid 1990s, when it was the site of a solitary backpacker lodge and campsite, but it remained relatively serene (most of the time) until 2005. The arrival of La Gemma dell'Est heralded the first of a new style of development, yet it's the growing beach party scene that's potentially off-putting for some. By day though, the main beach remains relatively peaceful, with some well-spaced places to stay, a clutch of beach bars, and two dive schools. Things do liven up in the evenings, with bonfires, barbecues and full-moon beach parties, but hopefully these will be kept somewhat in check.

GETTING THERE AND AWAY An erratic handful of dala-dalas connect Zanzibar Town to Nungwi daily, while the local bus (No 14) operates from north to south between 07.00 and 18.00. That said, the vast majority of travellers prefer to be transferred by private minibus, which can cost up to US$15 per person depending on group size and your negotiating skills. The ideal is to get a group together in Zanzibar Town when you want to head out to Nungwi, then organise a transfer through a *papaasi*, a taxi driver or a tour company. Unless you have very rigid timings, there is no need to organise your transfer back to Zanzibar Town in advance, since several vehicles can be found waiting around for passengers in Nungwi, especially mid-morning.

WHERE TO STAY The number of hotels and guesthouses in this area has mushroomed in recent years, with the busiest beach that to the southwest of the peninsula. We are aware of a number of new properties currently under construction in Kendwa, many taking over from existing low-level budget options. While there's no shortage of accommodation – new or old – finding something that is both good quality and good value is more of a challenge.

If you plan to walk along the beach in **Kendwa**, make sure you know the tide times before setting off, or you could be cut off. Note, too, that it's not advisable to walk alone between Baobab Beach Bungalows and La Gemma dell'Est, where there have been reports of robbery.

Nungwi
Upmarket

Essque Zalu Zanzibar (40 rooms, 9 villas) m 0778 683960; e reservations@essquehotels. com; www.essquehotels.com. Essque Zalu is difficult to miss with its imposing makuti roof visible from quite a distance, & vaguely reminiscent of Sydney Opera House. Opened in 2011, the spacious suites and vast villas are set in lush landscaped gardens & boast countless mod-cons & stylish interiors. The resort is centred on the huge, saltwater pool, which comes complete with a whirlpool, water jets & multi-coloured lighting – ecological awareness is not a priority here. There are the 2 restaurants: the deli-style Market Kitchen & the upmarket A La Carte (7 courses

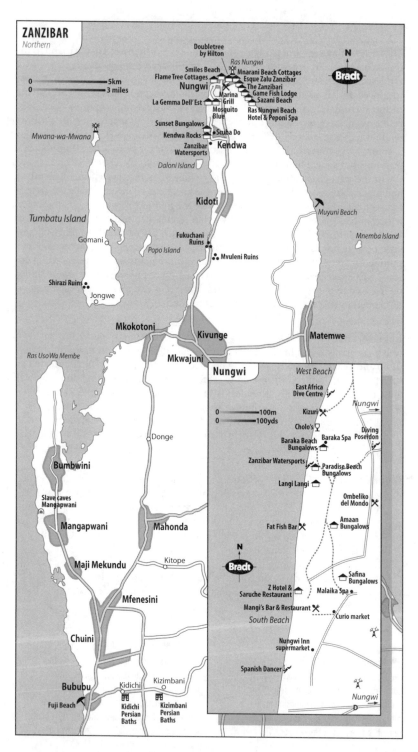

ZANZIBAR
Northern

0 —————5km
0 —————3 miles

N

Doubletree
by Hilton
Ras Nungwi
Smiles Beach   Mnarani Beach Cottages
Flame Tree Cottages   Esque Zalu Zanzibar
Nungwi   The Zanzibari
                        Game Fish Lodge
                    Marina   Sazani Beach
                    Grill
La Gemma Dell' Est   Mosquito   Ras Nungwi Beach
                      Blue   Hotel & Peponi Spa

Sunset Bungalows
Kendwa Rocks   Scuba Do
         Zanzibar
         Watersports   **Kendwa**
Daloni Island

Mwana-wa-Mwana

Kidoti
                        Muyuni Beach

Tumbatu Island

Gomani   *Popo Island*   Fukuchani
                           Ruins   *Mnemba Island*
                           Mvuleni Ruins

Shirazi Ruins
         Jongwe

Mkokotoni
         Kivunge   **Matemwe**

Ras Uso Wa Membe   **Mkwajuni**

Donge

Bumbwini

Slave caves
Mangapwani
Mangapwani   **Mahonda**

Maji Mekundu   Kitope

Mfenesini

Chuini

Bububu   Kidichi   Kizimbani
Fuji Beach   Kidichi   Kizimbani
              Persian   Persian
              Baths   Baths

Nungwi

West Beach

0 —————100m
0 —————100yds

East Africa
Dive Centre
              Kizuri   *Nungwi*
         Cholo's
                            Diving
Baraka Beach   Baraka Spa Poseidon
Bungalows
Zanzibar Watersports
              Paradise Beach
              Bungalows
Langi Langi
                        Ombeliko
                        del Mondo
Fat Fish Bar   Amaan
                Bungalows

N
Bradt
                        Safina
                        Bungalows
         Z Hotel &   Malaika Spa
         Saruche Restaurant
Mangi's Bar & Restaurant
                        Curio market
South Beach

         Nungwi Inn
         supermarket

Spanish Dancer

Nungwi

Bradt

US$55), which doubles as a gallery for showcasing worldwide artists. The on-site Zalu Retreat spa & Petit VIP kids club aim to treat parents and children alike. *US$640 dbl, FB.*

⌂ **Ras Nungwi Beach Hotel** (33 rooms)
☏ 024 223 3767/2512; e info@rasnungwi.com; www.rasnungwi.com. This perennially popular choice for honeymooners lies at the southern end of Nungwi's beach. Rooms of various categories are set in well-tended gardens & include AC, safes & neatly tiled bathrooms, though those situated further back have no sea view. Alongside the central bar & split-level dining room are a games area, a small swimming pool & a spa. Activities include snorkelling, diving, fishing & kayaking. The exceptional food & great wine list are highlights of any stay, with the occasional seafood BBQ featuring Swahili cuisine classics. *US$220–810 dbl, B&B.*

⌂ **The Zanzibari** (8 rooms, 2 suites)
☏ 024 550 0590; m; 0772 222919; e info@thezanzibari.com; www.thezanzibari.com. Formerly the Golden Dragon Lodge, the Zanzibari has undergone significant transformation & is far better for it. The original accommodation blocks have a Mediterranean apt appearance, but have been improved with extensive tropical climbers & flowering shrub borders. Rooms are cool & clean, with a private balcony or terrace. The new family suites are right above the raised beach. Complete with their own plunge pool & comfortably sleeping 5, they are a good option for families who want some private space alongside regular hotel facilities. There's a large pool with loungers dotted around the stone patio, & a pole & bougainvillea shade for sunbathers; & 3 cliff-top Jacuzzi pools for dhow-spotting dips. *US$240–345 dbl, HB.*

⌂ **Z Hotel** (35 rooms) m 0774 266266; e info@theZhotel.com, reservations@theZhotel.com; www.thezhotel.com; ⏰ closed mid Apr–end May. Lording over South Beach & bringing a degree of city-boy bling to Nungwi, rooms here are divided into 6 levels of luxury, but all boast indulgences from iPod docking stations, AC & plasma TVs to White Company toiletries & stocked minibars. Every room has a balcony with a sea view, of varying degrees, from each one. Elsewhere in the compact complex, the busy stone pool above the beach is a fine hangout, whilst the Cinnamon Bar & Saruche Restaurant are evening hotspots. The biggest issue for style-seekers may prove to be the less salubrious surrounding sprawl. *US$220–440 dbl, B&B.*

Moderate

⌂ **Doubletree by Hilton Resort** (103 rooms)
☏ 024 224 0476; m 0779 999056; e znzdt_reservations@hilton.com; www.doubletree.com. Taken over & spruced up by Hilton resorts in 2010, the accommodation is clean & tidy with a touch more character than you might expect from an international hotel chain. The well-kept standard rooms come with en-suite bathrooms with showers or baths, AC, mosquito nets & depending on location, have either a pool or a sea view. Larger ocean-view suites are bright, airy & spotless with the usual mod-cons. The 2-storey restaurant hosts themed evenings where local musicians entertain. An array of water activities is available, along with table tennis, pool & volleyball, plus a gym with state of the art fitness equipment. *US$210–400 dbl, B&B.*

⌂ **Mnarani Beach Cottages** (37 rooms)
☏ 024 224 0494; m 0777 415551/0713 334062; e mnarani@zanlink.com; www.lighthousezanzibar.com. Close to the northernmost tip of the island, Mnarani overlooks a beautiful stretch of beach, & is separated by dense vegetation from the lighthouse; unlike most other plots on this coast, it feels less boxed in by development. Some of its en-suite rooms have sea views; others are set in lush, tropical gardens close to the pool. There are also new self-catering cottages & flats. Kayaks, windsurfers & surfboards can be hired, & the lagoon in front of the hotel is a great place for kitesurfers. The bar has a cool, relaxed vibe, & the staff are some of the friendliest on the north coast. *US$120–250 dbl, B&B.*

⌂ **Flame Tree Cottages** (16 rooms) ☏ 024 224 0100; m 0777 479429/0713 262151; e etgl@zanlink.com; www.flametreecottages.com. On the edge of Nungwi village, these whitewashed bungalows & a new house are spread across extensive gardens, beside the beach. Immaculate en-suite rooms have shady verandas, AC & fans, & a shared or private kitchenette. Flame Tree also offers one of Nungwi's best dining experiences (think delicious fish goujons with tartare sauce US$5.50, or steamed chilli crab claws US$9). There is a real feeling of space & peace, with a lovely pool & staff who are genuinely happy to help. Activities range from yoga to snorkelling trips aboard the owner's dhow. *US$130–150 dbl, B&B.*

⌂ **Langi Langi Beach Bungalows** (31 rooms)
☏ 024 224 0470; e langi_langi@hotmail.com. The hotel is divided by a footpath, with newer rooms

on the seafront & the original rooms by the pool in a lush gardenr. Although all are en suite with AC & fans, the latter are probably still the rooms of choice. On the seafront, aim for rooms higher up for the best views. The reasonably good Langi Langi Café is a popular hangout for visitors & expats, serving good curries; bring your own alcohol. The owners are friendly, employing only local staff, & are genuinely hospitable. *US$100–220 dbl, B&B.*

⌂ **Smiles Beach Hotel** (16 rooms) ☎ 024 224 0472; m 0774 444334; e info@smilesbeachhotel. com; www.smilesbeachhotel.com. One of the best-quality quiet options in Nungwi, Smiles is a firm favourite with overland groups & repeat visitors. Around a flower-filled, semi-circular garden are 4 striking villas, resplendent in pale yellow & white, with pagoda-like roofs & exterior spiral staircases. High-quality en-suite rooms are Indian in flavour, & all are immaculate. Expect sliding mosquito nets, AC, satellite TV & beach towels. For those who can drag themselves the few metres to the beach, there's an onsite restaurant (no alcohol) & regular beach BBQs. *US$120 dbl, B&B.*

Budget

⌂ **Amaan Bungalows** (58 rooms) ☎ 024 5501152; m 0775 044719; e info@ amaanbungalows.com; www.amaanbungalows. com. This sprawling complex is popular with a young, lively crowd. Of its deluxe, garden & sea-view rooms, the last – perched on a cliff above the sea – more than justify the higher cost, though all are clean & well cared for, with en-suite bathrooms, fans &, in deluxe & sea-view rooms, AC. A grocery shop, bureau de change & internet café add to the package. The affiliated Marina Grill & Infusion, immediately opposite on the seafront, are good places to eat pizza & seafood & drink virtually anything all day (HB rates include meals at either place). *US$80–150 dbl.*

⌂ **Safina Bungalows** (30 rooms) m 0777 415726; e newsafina@hotmail.com. Despite the lack of sea view, Safina is a comfortable & spotlessly clean retreat, & benefited enormously when the main road was diverted away from its garden. The staff remain as accommodating as ever, & the flower-filled garden continues to flourish. All rooms have 24hr electricity, AC & hot water in en-suite bathrooms. If post-beach chilling on the veranda isn't enough, there is a massage room. *US$40–60 dbl, B&B.*

⌂ **Baraka Beach Bungalows** (9 rooms) m 0777 422910/415569; e barakabungalow@ hotmail.com; http://barakabungalow.atspace. com. In the shadow of Paradise Beach Bungalows, these surround a small garden. Simple, en-suite rooms are dark but fairly clean with fans, electricity & hot water. Proximity to West Beach is ideal for sun-worshippers, but music from Cholo's is likely to prevent any sleep before midnight. At the beachfront restaurant, the coconut curries (US$6–8) are good; also check out the adjoining Baraka Spa.

Kendwa
Upmarket

⌂ **Kilindi** (15 rooms) ☎ 024 223 1954; e reservations@kilindi.com; www. elewanacollection.com. Kilindi's unique design is a first for Zanzibar, & it's created quite a stir. Exclusive & upmarket without being pretentious, it offers 15 bright white pavilions spread out over 20ha & overlooking a sweep of beach. Reminiscent of Greek Orthodox churches, the domed, 2-tier pavilions are dotted among the dense, indigenous shrubbery & each is accessed through heavy wooden Zanzibari doors, through which is a serene sanctuary shielded from the view of others by yet more luscious plants. With a personal butler to bring you whatever you may desire, including your meals, you may never wish to leave your pavilion. However, if you can be tempted away, there's an attractive, colonial chic restaurant & bar, a bijoux spa and gorgeous infinity pool. For style, space & service, most definitely one of Zanzibar's top spots! *US$1,300–1,600 dbl, FB.*

⌂ **La Gemma Dell'Est** (138 rooms) ☎ 024 224 0087; e info.gemma@planhotel.com; www.planhotel.com. This stylish resort at the northern end of Kendwa Beach is one of Zanzibar's best choices for families. Comfortable but contemporary rooms, with all mod-cons, are designed to give each a sea-view veranda, while remaining fairly unobtrusive. Exotic plants characterise the sloping gardens, & the beach is backed by an enormous pool with a children's area, jacuzzi & swim-up bar. Guests have the choice of several bars & restaurants, serving anything from pizza to Mediterranean buffets – although the seafood restaurant is charged extra. Activities range from diving (run by Scuba Do) & other watersports to quizzes & Swahili BBQs. *US$250–500 dbl, FB.*

Moderate

🏠 **Kendwa Rocks Resort** (35 rooms) m 0777 415473/5; e booking@kendwarocks.com; www. kendwarocks.com. Kendwa Rocks is totally chilled, so don't expect anything to happen fast. Its clifftop bungalows, beach bungalows, motel-style rooms & an 11-bed dormitory get booked up in that order. Bungalows are all en suite, with those on the beach having a particularly good location. There's a beach bar, a Finnish steam bath (*US$6.50/2 persons*), & a huge, refurbished cargo ship (*www.jahazihouseboat. com*) which offers a seductive overnight trip for US$500. Every evening, a US$15 dhow cruise leaves for Tumbatu laden with island punch, & at full moon there's a lively beach party. *US$40–218 dbl, B&B.*

🏠 **Sunset Bungalows** (80 rooms) m 0777 413818/414647; e sunsetbungalows@hotmail. com/sunsetbungalows@gmail.com; www. sunsetkendwa.com. A faded surfboard in the sand marks Sunset Bungalows' location – & its bar, where US$6 lunches feature everything from fresh fish to egg & chips. Pleasant bungalows (some with AC) have been built on the beach behind, with en-suite bathrooms & a shady terrace. Other rooms (no AC) are in thatched cottages in a colourful garden, with the most recent housed in 6 huge buildings at the rear. Whilst these have taken away a lot of the beach retreat vibe, Sunset remains a reliable choice & is remarkably convenient for divers using Scuba Do on the foreshore. *US$50–98 dbl, B&B.*

✖ **WHERE TO EAT AND DRINK** Nearly all the hotels and guesthouses in Nungwi and Kendwa have attached restaurants, many of which are open to guests and non-guests alike. Others are stand-alone places that tend to close and spring up again as if with the tide. A few stand out as worth investigating in their own right, as listed below, but do ask around for the current culinary hotspots.

✖ **Marina Grill** Bright & breezy Marina Grill is relaxed by day but livens up during the 17.00–19.00 happy hour, when a selection of cocktails is offered. The expansive, mangrove-pole terrace is cantilevered over the beach, affording diners uninterrupted views out to sea & a welcome breeze. The speciality here is fish, which features in a range of salads, sandwiches & pasta dishes (*US$7*). Seafood is served freshly grilled or fried, & the piri piri prawns with chips are a popular choice (*US$13*). Although the staff could be friendlier, it's a welcoming enough place & there's also a satellite TV for catching up on international sporting events.

✖ **Langi Langi** On the hotel's large seaside deck, this is a relaxed coffee shop by day, & a Swahili restaurant by night. It's a popular place & worth booking for dinner (*US$8–12*), inside or out. Alcohol is not sold, but bring your own & it'll be chilled & served.

✖ **Ombeliko del Mondo** This pleasant *cucina Italiana* is tucked behind Amaan Bungalows, with precious little view but a menu full of traditional Italian delicacies: seafood antipasti, pastas, risottos & tempting *dolcis*. Mains are US$5–10, & while reviews are consistently good, portions are on the small side.

✖ **Saruche Restaurant** The formal restaurant at Z Hotel, Saruche serves an à la carte menu of African–European fusion food with a heavy emphasis on seafood. Accompanied by an international wine list, ocean views & island antiques, it's one of the smartest options currently in Nungwi. There are traditional music & entertainment nights throughout the week.

🍷 **Cholo's Bar** Tucked at the back of West Beach, this perennial favourite is well known for its music, cool crowd, & free-flowing alcohol. Beach bonfires are a periodic evening attraction along with ad hoc BBQs & dining at upturned dhow tables. Once the place to drink when everywhere else had shut, this long-standing bar has been taken over & given a facelift. Its late-night opening & idiosyncrasies have been retained but it's smartened up a little & added daytime appeal with a raft of 4-poster timber daybeds, each swathed in billowing white cotton, on the beach in front. Good spot if you like a mojito whilst sunbathing, though expect a reasonable amount of attention.

🍷 **Cinnamon** Cinnamon is part of the Z Hotel complex but welcomes non-residents, too. With its 1st-floor location, overlooking the South Beach scene & sparkling sea, the young & beautiful are attracted by its contemporary décor & fabulous tropical cocktails (*US$5*). Sipped at cushion-clad white baraza benches, surrounded by ever-changing mood lights & chilled tunes, this is a great pre-dinner drinks spot. Stay for sushi & tempting tasting platters (*US$5–15*) for lunch or dinner, or just work your way through the extensive cocktail list. There is a cool vibe here & it's the only place by the beach where fashionable ladies won't feel out of place in high heels. Alternatively, head downstairs to Saruche (see page 377).

✗ **Kizuri** This 2012 addition to the Nungwi bar scene is raising the bar in the sand-under-foot, beach bar scene. It's a bijou place, with thatched shade, cushioned concrete *baraza* booths, chilled music & mean mojitos! Offering a range of cocktails & cool drinks, it also has a restaurant serving pan-African/European fusion food. Success has come quickly here & upward expansion is likely if things continue, but hopefully the quality & chilled-out vibe will remain.

♀ **Mangi's Bar & Restaurant** Long-running Mangi's is on a sandy, shaded spot beside Nungwi Inn Hotel. It's a relaxed hangout serving fresh juices, US$4 cocktails (the *Zanzibar Mzungu* concoction of banana, rum, milk & vodka appearing popular), & snacks (samosas US$4.50; chapattis US$5; baked potatoes US$6.50).

HEALTH AND BEAUTY Temporary henna tattoos seem to be *de rigueur* in Nungwi, painted on to your skin by friendly local ladies as you lie under their makeshift palm shades on the beach. Be warned, however, the henna can badly mark bed linen, and many hotel owners will charge for stains. It is also important to avoid black henna (pico): it is a synthetic dye and often results in bad allergic reactions, sometimes delayed by a few weeks, which requires medical treatment. For all-out African beach chic, hair-braiding services are also available from the same ladies, along with basic beach massages. For a less-public massage experience, try one of the following:

Baraka White House Spa & Boutique (*Body treatments US$20/hr; manicures US$10*) In a small, immaculate room, adjoining Baraka's Restaurant on West Beach, Harriet & Tina offer excellent treatments on *kanga*-covered massage tables. From deep muscle rubs to facials, their super little business offers them all. The standard is above that available on the beach; though this is not in any way a 'spa'.

Malaika Spa (*Body treatments US$30/hr; manicures US$10*) Alongside & linked with Safina Bungalows, this small, neat massage room is home to friendly Conchesta. Trained in Dar, she offers scrubs, facials, beauty treatments & spice oil massages, both aromatherapy & Ayurvedic. The room is fan cooled & she tries hard to ensure guests relax & enjoy their treatment.

Peponi Spa e peponi-spa@rasnungwi.com (*Body treatments US$50–120/40–80mins; manicures US$40/1hr; waxing & eyebrow tinting/threading US$10–35*) Set in the tropical gardens of Ras Nungwi Beach Hotel, Peponi offers guests & non-residents 'an array of rejuvenating, pampering & holistic treatments'. It is the area's best spa by far. Run by internationally qualified therapists & using natural oils & ingredients, treatments are wonderfully relaxing.

The Zalu Zanzibar Spa ☏0778 683960; e ezz.retreat@essquehotels.com (*Facials US$120/90mins; body treatments US$80–280/60mins–3.5hrs; manicures US$55/1hr*) Within the Essque Zalu Hotel, this small spa pavilion fans out into sweet-smelling treatment rooms, a Vichy shower room, a sauna/steam & gym area. Using *healingEARTH* products, which blend the organic oils of indigenous African plants, the small team of therapists offer a range of beauty treatments, massages, body polishes & finishing touches from waxing to manicures. There are loungers amid the encircling gardens for pleasant pre- & post-treatment chilling, though the space is limited and it's not a place for all-day relaxing.

Zanzi Yoga m 0776 310227; e info@ yogazanzibar.com; www.yogazanzibar.com. Founded in 2009, Yoga Zanzibar offers yoga classes & longer retreats. Based at Flame Tree Cottages, individual yoga tuition & longer retreats are available year-round by registered teacher, Marisa. Relaxation, pranayama (breathing techniques), sun salutations, asanas (postures), & reiki available.

SHOPPING

Nungwi There are several small shops in Nungwi village, where you'll find an array of cheap souvenirs, including carvings, paintings and jewellery, as well as essential items. In the village itself, the well-equipped Nungwi School computer room has email and internet services (see *Other practicalities*, below), and adjoining **Choices** sells souvenirs and swimwear.

There's an ever-changing array of beauticians, barbers, local cafés, as well as the long-standing **Nungwi Supermarket**. It's a veritable Aladdin's den of imported luxuries, from toothpaste and toiletries to chocolate and Pringles. Further on, the **New Nungwi Salon** offers the brave bikini waxing. **Amaan Bungalows Supermarket** has a selection of knick-knacks and food and drink basics, whilst behind Paradise Beach Bungalows, Mr Alibaba sells everything from kangas to cold drinks, postcards and tours. The **post box** outside their shop offers a twice-daily mail collection for those all-important postcards home. Alternatively, there are now a couple of places open on South Beach: well laid out **Nungwi Inn Supermarket** and **New Worldwide Supermarket**, beside the curio market. For artwork and souvenirs, a fairly contained **curio market** has grown on the alley running perpendicular to South Beach, alongside Z Hotel. Known locally as the Maasai Market, on account of the traders' tribal background, you'll find some entertainingly named shacks – IKEA Zanzibar, Leonardo da Vinci, Gucci – displaying an array of colourful paintings, carvings and beadwork.

Kendwa With the increase in accommodation and visitors, Kendwa now also has two small, local-style 'supermarkets': **Ndiro Supermarket** on the very edge of the coral cliff at the southern end of the beach and **Mwakamini Supermarket** on the village side of Kendwa Rocks. Both sell basic supplies of tinned food, crisps, sweets and water, but little else. For curios, the ever-increasing span of Maasai-manned stalls on the beach bordering La Gemma offers colourful paintings, beaded jewellery and occasionally carvings. Quality varies considerably so shop around and don't be blinded by the sun into making second-rate purchases.

OTHER PRACTICALITIES Several of the larger hotels have internet facilities, many with Wi-Fi, and a reasonable number of the smaller backpacker places will let you use an office PC to check email quickly. **Amaan Bungalows** has three PCs available for general use, however, we would like to recommend the reliable **Nungwi School** IT centre as a first choice (e *bbs@zanlink.com;* ⏰ *08.00–20.00 Mon–Fri, 08.30–19.30 holidays & w/ends; rates are very low at US$0.60/30min or US$1/hr*), as its income is used to reinvest in the school's excellent computer initiative. The centre is clearly signposted beside the football field, on the right as you approach the beach.

SPORTS AND ACTIVITIES If you want peace, quiet and fewer people, you will probably need to head to a different corner of the island; if not, then here are details of the area's main activities:

Watersports The sweeping cape on which Nungwi is sited is surrounded by sparkling, warm, turquoise seas, making it a perfect spot to engage in countless water activities. Prices are all very similar; quality is highly variable. Listen to your instinct and other travellers' advice carefully when deciding who is currently offering the best trip.

Snorkelling
North Coast Snorkelling Shop ⏰ 06.00–18.00. With a prime location on the coral rock above South

Beach, at the entrance to the curio market, the entrepreneurial Hamadi Ali has established a small hire shop for masks, snorkels, fins & fishing rods. He buys kit from tourists in Stone Town who don't want to carry it home, & rents it out here. The quality is variable but you are free to try things on & select the best for you, & there is a range of good brands available as well as adult & child sizes. Rates are US$5 snorkelling kit/day; US$10 fishing rod/day. For fishing, see opposite.

Diving There are currently six dive operations in Nungwi and two in Kendwa. Listed in alphabetical order, the centres below are each very different in feel and ethos, and divers are advised to talk seriously to the individual operators about safety and experience before signing up for courses or sub-aqua excursions.

✓ **Divine Diving** ✆0777 771914/0772 299395; e info@scubazanzibar.com; www.scubazanzibar. com. Based at Amaan Bungalows, Divine Diving is a newcomer on the northern diving scene, offering both yoga & scuba, hence the breathing technique classes to improve underwater air consumption that sit alongside a range of PADI courses. This centre is affiliated with Zanzi Yoga (see *Health and beauty*, page 378). *US$55/95/175/385 (plus US$30 to Mnemba Atoll) for 1/2/4/10 dives; Discover Scuba US$85; Open Water US$450; Advanced US$365; Night dive US$75.*

✓ **Diving Poseidon** ✆0777 720270; www. divingposeidon.com. Owned by Austrian couple, Ilse & Bernhard Kotlar (dive master & PADI Master Scuba Diver Trainer respectively) this relatively new dive PADI centre is located away from the shoreline, between Baraka Beach Bungalows & Nungwi village. Dives are usually led by local dive masters. *US$60/95/180/390 (plus US$30 to Mnemba Atoll) for 1/2/4/10 dives; Discover Scuba US$75; Open Water US$360; Advanced US$270; Night dive US$80.*

✓ **East Africa Diving & Watersport Centre (EADC)** m 0777 416425/420588; e eadc@ zitec.org; www.diving–zanzibar.com. Owned & operated by an experienced, straight–talking German–South African couple, Michael & Delene Kutz, this is the oldest dive centre on the north coast. On the beach in front of Jambo Brothers Guesthouse, this efficient, safety-conscious PADI 5* Gold Palm Resort offers very well-priced courses up to Dive Master & a host of scuba trips. EADC also has bases within Essque Zalu, Royal Zanzibar, Z Hotel & Doubletree by Hilton; for hotel guests confined water assessments take place in the pool at Z or Royal Zanzibar. *US$70/110/190/400 (plus US$30 to Mnemba Atoll) for 1/2/4/10 dives; Discover Scuba US$95; Open Water US$480; Advanced US$380; Nitrox US$300.*

✓ **Rising Sun Diving Centre** m 0777 440883-5/88; e bookings@risingsun-zanzibar.com; www.risingsun-zanzibar.com. Operating out of the all-inclusive Royal Zanzibar Hotel, this is a fully accredited PADI 5* Gold Palm Resort with National Geographic Status & has state-of-the-art technology, quality equipment & experienced staff. *US$85/170/464/695 for 1/2/6/10 dives; Open Water US$672. Digital Photography US$386: daily equipment rental (regulator, BCD, wetsuit, mask & fins) US$39; underwater digital camera rental (inc CD of images) US$46.*

✓ **Scuba Do Diving** ✆(UK) +44 (0)1326 250773; m 0777 417157/0748 415179; e do-scuba@scuba-do-zanzibar.com; www.scubado. demon.co.uk/www.scuba-do-zanzibar.com. Until recently, Scuba Do was Kendwa's only dive operation: & very good it is too! Owned & operated by Christian & Tammy, Scuba Do is a highly professional & well-equipped dive centre, based on the beach next to Sunset Bungalows (& at La Gemma for resort guests). As well as a thoroughly nice guy, Christian is a PADI Master Instructor & the only Emergency First Response Instructor Trainer in Tanzania; Tammy is a PADI Master Scuba Diver Trainer & exceptional at teaching even the youngest children to snorkel & dive. Out of the water, the team here are also involved in extensive community work. *Snorkelling trips US$45–85 Tumbatu/Mnemba; US$120/230/330/420 for 2/4/6/8 dives; scuba equipment hire US$15/day; digital camera hire (inc CD of images) US$50.*

✓ **Spanish Dancer Dive Centre** ✆024 224 0091; m 0777 417717/430005; e contact@spanishdancerdivers.com; www. spanishdancerdivers.com. Based in an open *rondavel* on South Beach, Spanish Dancer is run by David & Shee, with 3 other expat dive instructors & a dive master. The dive centre is PADI accredited & teaches courses in German, French, Spanish, Hebrew & English. There is a live-aboard diving option available on catamaran *Julia*. *Dive packages*

US$132/226/320/475 (plus US$47 for Mnemba); for 2/4/6/10 dives; Discover Scuba US$117; Open Water US$585; Dive Master US$1,169; Course Manual US$62.

Zanzibar Watersports 📞 024 223 3309; m 0773 165862; e info@zanzibarwatersports.com; www.zanzibarwatersports.com. With PADI 5* Gold Palm Instructor Development Centre status, offering all PADI qualifications to instructor level, Zanzibar Watersports has 2 Nungwi outlets: one at Ras Nungwi Beach Hotel for guests only, & one within the central Paradise Beach Bungalows complex, which is open to one & all, & a newer base in Kendwa. This is a highly organised, safe & energetic operation. There are also 1- & 2-man kayaks, waterskiing & wakeboarding equipment available & sunset dhow cruises for the more sedentary visitor. Prices vary by booking location. *US$55/100/295/460 (plus US$65 for Mnemba) for 1/2/6/10 dives excluding equipment; Refresher US$30; Open Water US$550; Advanced US$440; US$15 equipment hire (mask, fins, BCD, regulator, wetsuit); kayaks US$10pp/hr; waterskiing US$70/15mins; windsurfing US$30/hr.*

Sailing
Aside from local sunset dhow trips, there are few opportunities to sail on board more modern vessels on this stretch of coast. For dive live-aboard and 'learn-to-sail' options, *Julia*, listed below, is the only real option.

△ **Dive 'n' Sail Zanzibar** m 0774 441234; e info@dive-n-sail.com/yachtjulia@hotmail.com; www.dive-n-sail.com. If sailing appeals, Dive 'n' Sail operates a lovely 50ft Admiral catamaran, *Julia*, specialising in live-aboard dive trips & fishing excursions to Pemba & Mafia. Available for charter with its own professional skipper, chef, deckhand & optional dive instructor, the boat is fully equipped for diving & deep-sea fishing. With some notice, PADI Advanced Open Water & speciality courses can be taught on board. All rates are subject to periodic change. *US$1,320/day private boat charter (1–5 persons) for min 4 days, excluding dives. Dives US$42/dive for first 10 dives, then US$36. US$108 pp Mnemba Island snorkelling day trip (min 4 persons); US$66 dive supplement; US$480 half-day fishing*

Fishing
Nungwi's proximity to some of Africa's best deep-sea fishing grounds – Leven Bank and the deep Pemba Channel – offers serious anglers outstanding fishing opportunities. **North Coast Snorkelling Shop**'s Hamadi Ali (see page 379) will take you out fishing, it's US$200 for a half-day on his boat, complete with sunshade. In addition to the weather-beaten local dhows that plough the coastal waters, three operators currently offer game fishing in fully equipped, custom-built boats.

Fishing Zanzibar e gerry@fishingzanzibar.com, info@fishingzanzibar.com; www.fishingzanzibar.com. Operated by Gerry Hallam, Fishing Zanzibar have 4 sport-fishing boats based in Nungwi: *Unreel, Surreel, Cobia & Sansuli*, as well as a 50ft sailing yacht, *Walkabout*. The sport-fishing boats are fully kitted out & take small charter groups (max 4 anglers). *US$500–1,000 half-day; US$1,000–2,000 full day, inc lunch; live-aboard US$1,300–2,500/day for 4 persons; rates vary by boat.*

Game Fish Tours m 0753 451919; e gamefish@zanlink.com; www.gamefishlodge.2itb.com. Based out of Game Fish Lodge, this South African operation runs half-day, night fishing & 2-day Pemba tours for reef & bottom fishing. They have 2 boats: *El Shaddai* & *Karambisi*, the latter has a toilet & sleeping facilities so is used for the multi-day Pemba trips. *US$220 pp/6hr charter (max 2 persons) on El Shaddai; US$165 pp/6hrs (max 3–4 persons) on Karambisi; 2-day Pemba US$550 pp on Karambisi*

Zanzibar Big Game Fishing 📞 024 223 3767/2512; e info@rasnungwi.com; www.rasnungwi.com. Arguably the best game-fishing operation on Zanzibar, & certainly the longest established, Zanzibar Big Game Fishing is a division of Zanzibar Watersports (see overleaf). They are extremely well kitted out for both professional fishermen & have-a-go holidaymakers, with 3 new professional sport-fishing boats, professional tackle & international safety equipment. *US$400/550 half-/full day on Suli Suli; US$550/750 half-/full day on Timimi; US$650/950 half/full day on Haraka.*

Kiteboarding In recent years, kiteboarding has grown in popularity and Nungwi is no exception. Steady winds (approximately 15–20 knots) for most of the year, level beaches, warm clear water and protected, shallow lagoons make it a great place for both beginners and more experienced kiters. Check centres are certified by the International Kiteboarding Organisation (IKO) if you are interested in quality assurance and training courses.

Kiteboarding Zanzibar

e kiteboardingzanzibar@gmail.com. Opened in 2009, Kiteboarding Zanzibar is IKO certified, using up-to-date Cabrinha, NPX & Dakine equipment, with qualified & experienced staff on hand for safety & lessons. Their Nungwi base is in a small but neat, thatched chalet alongside Parasailing Zanzibar, whilst a kite-mobile is used to transfer kit & kiters to selected beaches in Nungwi & Matemwe (season dependent – Nungwi Jun–end Sep; Matemwe end Dec–Mar), & perform on the spot maintenance & repairs. You can hire equipment here, and sign up for lessons.

Motorised watersports Nungwi now has several companies offering increasingly thrilling, motorised watersports. From stunt wakeboarding to sedate parasailing, and jet-ski safaris to fast-paced banana boats, the coastal waters are significantly busier and the range of activities vastly increased.

Zanzibar Parasailing ✆0779 073078; e hello@zanzibarparasailing.com; www. zanzibarparasailing.com. This Turkish-run company opened in Jan 2011 alongside Cholo's Bar.

JET–SKIS … THINK BEFORE YOU HIRE

Jet-skiing is one of the fastest growing watersports; but its arrival on the north coast is understandably controversial. For some it is a thrilling addition to the aquatic activity selection, for others a cause for very real concern. If you do choose to take to the waves, make it an informed decision.

Firstly, remember that you would be unable to hire a motorbike or a speedboat without proper training and a licence; a jetski is an equally powerful machine yet neither of these is required. Very careful consideration of your own abilities and experience is necessary before you hire. The waters around Nungwi are full of activity: local dhows and *ngalawas* sailing, women fishing, carefree holidaymakers swimming and snorkelling, and dive operators doing scuba training. The risk of collision is potentially quite high if you find yourself out of control, and the results horrendous to contemplate.

In addition to the safety issues, there are also areas of shallow reef and diverse resident marine life here, so the environmental impact must be considered. Underwater sound pollution is one of the likely reasons for the decline in north shore dolphin sightings, there have already been cases of damage to the reefs at low tide, and the local concerns about the impact on fish breeding habits are understandable.

If you are still keen to hire, the operators listed in this book are reliable: the machinery is good quality and well maintained. However, there is a danger in this part of the world that the visible success of this company will spawn less reputable individuals to begin hiring out secondhand, poorly maintained jet-skis. This would likely result in more sound and fuel pollution, and a rise in accidents, so do avoid any casual approaches, however good a deal they appear to strike.

Parasailing flights are consequently a very recent arrival in Nungwi, & already a popular one. Solo or tandem 'flights' are possible, as are escorted Tumbatu jet-ski safaris, stereo or mono waterskiing with lessons available too, wakeboarding, kneeboarding, & an 8-person banana boat or ringos are also on offer for fun-filled adrenalin action. *Parasailing US$80/120 solo/tandem; jet-ski safari US$200/220 1/2 riders per bike; jet-ski rental US$50/15mins; waterskiing US$45/10mins;* *wakeboarding US$45/10mins; banana boat US$15pp/15mins; ringos US$30pp/10mins.*

Zanzibar Watersports Escorted jet-ski safaris (1hr 15mins) head from the Paradise Beach base in Nungwi to Tumbatu, where riders can have a quick, cooling swim before pushing on to Kendwa & back around the coast to the watersports centre. 2011 Yamaha 110 HP 4-Stroke jet-skis can also be hired for individual use. *Jet-ski safari US$180/200 1/2 riders per bike; jet-ski rental US$50/15mins.*

WHAT TO SEE AND DO Most visitors come to this area to relax on the beach, swim in the sea and perhaps party at night. For local attractions, the small turtle sanctuary and terrific local coral reefs are still a draw. If you want a more cultural experience, head down the coast to the 16th-century Swahili ruins at Fukuchani and Mvuleni, the bustling, ramshackle market at Mkokotoni, or venture across the water to Tumbatu Island. Note that the lighthouse at Ras Nungwi is still in operation and, although it is not open to visitors anyway, no photography is allowed.

Mnarani Natural Aquarium (⏱ *09.00–18.00 daily; US$5, 50% discount for children*) Hawksbill turtles have traditionally been hunted around Zanzibar for their attractive shells, and green turtles for their meat. In 1993, with encouragement and assistance from various conservation bodies and some dedicated marine biologists, the local community opened the Mnarani Natural Aquarium.

In the shadow of the lighthouse (Mnarani meaning 'place of the lighthouse' in Swahili), at the northernmost tip of Zanzibar Island, the aquarium was created around a large, natural, tidal pool in the coral rock behind the beach. Originally set up to rehabilitate and study turtles that had been caught in fishing nets, the aquarium project expanded to ensure that local baby turtles were also protected.

Turtles used to nest frequently on Nungwi Beach, though sadly, in some part due to hotel lighting, this is now a rare occurrence. If a nest is found, village volunteers now mark and monitor new nests, whilst local fishermen rescuing turtles caught in their nets receive a small fee. The resulting hatchlings are carried to small plastic basins and small concrete tanks at the aquarium where they remain for ten months. By this time, they have grown to 25cm and their chances of survival at sea are dramatically increased. All bar one of these turtles are then released into the sea, along with the largest turtle from the aquarium pool. The one remaining baby turtle is then added to the pool, ensuring a static population of 17 turtles.

Currently, this equates to four hawksbills (Swahili: *ng'amba*), identified by the jagged edge on their shell, sharper beak and sardine diet, and 13 seaweed-loving green turtles (Swahili: *kasakasa*). The aquarium manager, Mr Mataka Kasa, keeps a log book detailing all eggs, hatchlings and releases. On 5 June 2005, the sanctuary released its first tagged turtle, as part of a worldwide monitoring programme, and now all large turtles are released with an 'address tag' to track their movements.

In spite of the aquarium being little more than a glorified rock pool, it's fascinating to see the turtles at close quarters. Further, the money raised secures the project's future, and goes towards local community schemes – in a bid to demonstrate the tangible value of turtle conservation to the local population. With luck, this will lessen the trade in souvenir shell products and ensure the species' survival.

On a practical note, when timing your visit, the water is clearest about two hours before high tide (Swahili: *maji kujaa*).

Dhow-building and harbour activity Nungwi is also the centre of Zanzibar's traditional dhow-building industry, where generations of skilled craftsmen have worked on the beach outside the village, turning planks of wood into strong ocean-going vessels, using only the simplest of tools. It is a fascinating place to see dhows in various stages of construction, but do show respect for the builders, who are generally indifferent towards visitors, and keep out of the way. Most do not like having their photos taken (ask before you use your camera), although a few have realised that being photogenic has a value, and will reasonably ask for payment.

Fishing continues to employ many local men, who set out to sea in the late afternoon, returning at around 06.00 the following morning, taking their catch to the beach fish market. The spectacle is worth the early start, but if you don't make it, there's a smaller rerun at around 15.00 each day.

As on the east coast, the other key marine industry here centres on seaweed. Local women tend this recently introduced crop on the flat area between the beach and the low-tide mark. The seaweed is harvested, dried in the sun and sent to Zanzibar Town for export.

Cultural Village Tour (*US$15 pp*) The base for the Nungwi Cultural Village Tours is adjacent to Mnarani Aquarium, and indeed run by the same volunteers. From the clearly marked bungalow, the two hour walks operate as and when visitors wish, and take in the aquarium, fish market (best visited early morning when the day's catches are landed), mosques, dhow builders, basket-weavers and even touches on the uses of surrounding medicinal trees. A pleasant, guided trip, it does offer visitors a different view of the community here, and gives photographers a great opportunity to capture the dhow builders (always ask permission first). The money generated from these tours goes back into the community and is donated to a range of beneficiaries, from the kindergarten to the dhow builders.

THE EAST COAST

The east coast of Zanzibar is where you will find the idyllic tropical beaches you dreamed about during those interminable bus rides on the mainland: clean white sand lined with palms, and lapped by the warm blue water of the Indian Ocean. Some travellers come here for a couple of days, just to relax after seeing the sights of Zanzibar Town, and end up staying for a couple of weeks. Visitors on tighter time restrictions always wish they could stay for longer.

The east coast is divided into two discrete stretches by Chwaka Bay, which lies at the same latitude as Zanzibar Town on the west coast. Traditionally, the most popular stretch of coast is to the south of this bay, between Bwejuu and Makunduchi, but recent years have seen an increasing number of developments further north, between Matemwe and Chwaka. Most hotels have restaurants, and you can usually buy fish and vegetables in the villages, but supplies are limited. If you are self-catering, stock up in Zanzibar Town.

GETTING THERE AND AWAY The east coast can easily be reached by bus or dala-dala from Zanzibar Town. North of Chwaka Bay, No 6 buses go to Chwaka (some continue to Uroa and Pongwe), No 13 to Uroa via Chwaka, No 15 to Kiwengwa and No 16 to Matemwe. South of the bay, No 9 goes to Paje (sometimes continuing to Bwejuu or Jambiani) and No 10 to Makunduchi. Chwaka Bay can sometimes be crossed by boat between Chwaka and Michamvi, with the help of local octopus fishermen. Most travellers prefer to use private transport to the east coast: several tour companies and some independent guides arrange minibuses (US$5–8 pp each way). Unless you specify where you want to stay, minibus drivers are likely to take you to a hotel that gives them commission.

NORTHEASTERN ZANZIBAR Stretching from Nungwi on the northernmost tip of the island to the mangrove swamps of Chwaka Bay, the sand beaches of the northeastern coastline are breathtaking in length and beauty. Less than 1km offshore, waves break along the fringe reef that runs the length of the island, and the warm, turquoise waters of the Indian Ocean attract divers, swimmers and fishermen. Bordering the sand, an almost unbroken strip of picturesque coconut palms provides shade for traditional fishing villages and sunbathing honeymooners, and completes many people's vision of paradise.

The beaches along Zanzibar's east coast slope very little. Consequently, when the tide is out, the water retreats a long way, making swimming from the beach difficult. It does, however, allow for fascinating exploration along the top of the exposed reef.

Where to stay The roughly 40km of coastline north of Chwaka Bay is lined with numerous lovely beaches and punctuated by a number of small traditional fishing villages, the most important of which – running from north to south – are Matemwe, Pwani Mchangani, Kiwengwa, Uroa and Chwaka. Hotels along this stretch of coast mostly fall into the mid-range to upmarket bracket, though good budget accommodation is available at Kiwengwa.

Exclusive

🏠 **Matemwe Retreat** (3 rooms) m 0777 475788/0774 414834; e reservations@ asilialodges.com, matemweretreat@asiliaafrica. com; www.matemwe.com, www.asilialodges. com. Matemwe Bungalows' new sibling is one of Zanzibar's most impressive & exclusive places to stay, its exceptional villas creatively designed with panoramic ocean views, an infinity plunge pool & a private, 2-tier roof terrace that catches the sunrise. A butler takes care of your every need & almost anything seasonally available is prepared on request & served where you like. There are no public areas, but guests can use the facilities at Matemwe Bungalows (see below). *Lodge US$468–571 pp, FB; Beach House US$468–571 pp, FB.*
🏠 **Kasha Boutique Hotel** (11 villas) m 0776 676611/22; e info@kashazanzibar.com; www. kashazanzibar.com. Kasha's substantial villas are in 2 rows on coral cliffs above the beach. Spacious interiors lead onto a patio, with a plunge pool & cushioned *baraza*. Sadly, paths mean the 2nd row of villas are totally lacking in privacy. There's

an infinity pool with views across to Mnemba, a simple spa & a coastal path leading down to the sea. The high-thatched main area contains the Nargili bar and the Sama restaurant, where à la carte b/fasts & pretty basic European-style dinners are served. Although well-finished with plenty of comforts, it's a fairly pricey place which doesn't quite live up to expectation. *US$420–560 dbl, FB.*
🏠 **Green and Blue** (14 rooms, 1 villa) m 0772 390086; e welcome@greenandbluezanzibar. com; www.greenandbluezanzibar.com. Green & Blue is a terrific lodge that opened for business in late 2011. On a pleasantly large & strikingly landscaped plot, the 2-person bungalows are all identical bar their view, whilst the Ocean Front Villa, which is larger, sleeps up to 4. Colourful interiors are meticulously designed & laid out, but the beachfront public areas are the real draw. The lounge, bar & restaurant are cantilevered over the beach, offering fabulous sea views, & food from Michelin-starred chefs. 2 large swimming pools run down to the beach & there's the refreshingly simple Tulia Spa. *Garden US$235–330 pp; Pool US$250–340 pp; Ocean US$330–430 pp, FB.*

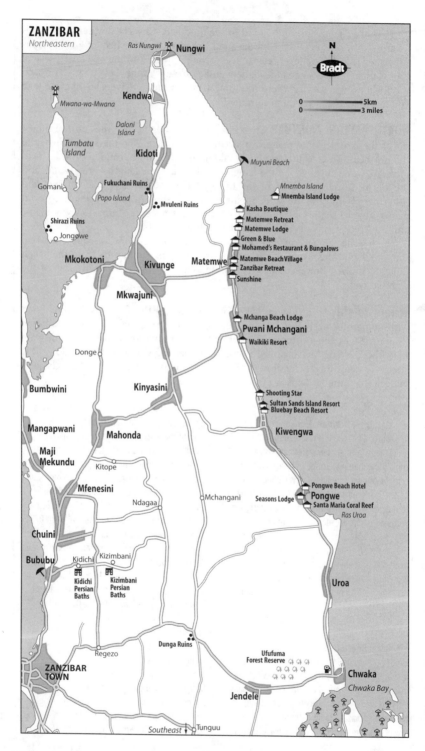

ZANZIBAR
Northeastern

N

Bradt

0 ———— 5km
0 ———— 3 miles

Ras Nungwi   Nungwi

Mwana-wa-Mwana

Kendwa

Daloni
Island

Tumbatu
Island

Kidoti

Muyuni Beach

Gomani

Fukuchani Ruins

Mnemba Island

Popo Island

Mnemba Island Lodge

Mvuleni Ruins

Kasha Boutique

Shirazi Ruins

Matemwe Retreat

Jongowe

Matemwe Lodge

Green & Blue

Mohamed's Restaurant & Bungalows

Mkokotoni

Kivunge

Matemwe

Matemwe Beach Village

Zanzibar Retreat

Sunshine

Mkwajuni

Mchanga Beach Lodge

Pwani Mchangani

Waikiki Resort

Donge

Bumbwini

Kinyasini

Shooting Star

Sultan Sands Island Resort

Bluebay Beach Resort

Mangapwani

Mahonda

Kiwengwa

Maji
Mekundu

Kitope

Mfenesini

Pongwe Beach Hotel

Ndagaa

Mchangani

Seasons Lodge

Pongwe

Santa Maria Coral Reef

Ras Uroa

Chuini

Bububu

Kidichi   Kizimbani

Uroa

Kidichi
Persian
Baths

Kizimbani
Persian
Baths

Regezo

Dunga Ruins

Ufufuma
Forest Reserve

Chwaka

Chwaka Bay

ZANZIBAR
TOWN

Jendele

Southeast   Tunguu

🛏 **Matemwe Lodge** (12 rooms) m 0777 414834; e matemwe@asiliaafrica.com; www. asiliaafrica.com; ⏲ Jun–Mar. Smart yet informal, the quiet Matemwe Lodge is popular with couples. Each of its thatched cottages is perched on the edge of a low coral cliff, with a superb view across to Mnemba Island. All have been upgraded into stylish suites, with electricity, mosquito nets, fan (on request), a day bed & an area to chill out as standard. Lush tropical gardens lead to the swimming pools, dining area & sandy beach. Activities include snorkelling & sailing in dhows, fishing, diving, & escorted reef walks. The lodge supports the local community through the provision of fresh water, a primary school, 2 deep-sea dhows for fishing, & teaching English. *US$288–337pp, FB.*

Upmarket

🛏 **Mchanga Beach Lodge** (8 rooms) m 0773 952399/569821; e tradewithzanzibar@zantel. com; www.mchangabeachlodge.com. Simple, stylish construction, high-quality interiors & a happy, efficient staff characterise Mchanga, & the location near Pwani Mchangani is stunning. Thatched rooms have a 4-poster bed, as well as a *baraza* alcove & small terrace. A thoughtful mix of wooden shutters, ceiling fans, AC & high-beamed ceilings ensure that rooms remain cool. Outside are a pool, open-sided bar & a restaurant serving a range of Swahili specials. Mchanga's understated vibe & vista make one of Zanzibar's best beach havens. *US$306–336 dbl, FB.*

🛏 **Shooting Star** (16 rooms) m 0777 414166; e star@zanzibar.org; www.zanzibar.org/star. Above Kiwengwa Beach, about 8km south of Matemwe, this is a delightfully social place, whose garden rooms, sea-view cottages & suites all feature Zanzibari beds & colourful Tingatinga pictures. An infinity pool & sundeck afford views over the ocean, reef & beach below. Dining is split across 3 shady areas, offering simple & filling meals, but it's the lively bar & relaxed lounge area that are the true heart of Shooting Star – & especially the lobster beach BBQ (*extra US$45 pp*). Diving, snorkelling & fishing trips can be organised. *US$235–610 dbl, FB.*

🛏 **Seasons Lodge Zanzibar** (11 rooms) m 0776 107225; e info@seasonszanzibar. com/seasonslodge@gmail.com; www. seasonszanzibar.com. The 7 bright cottages & 4 top-floor rooms are bathed in sunlight from the numerous windows & all have fans & folding

louvered doors to allow the sea breezes to enter, so no AC is necessary. The owners have made a conscious & commendable effort to lower their carbon footprint by growing their own produce, composting their waste, & employing local staff. After a hard day's sunbathing lie back in an easy chair & sip on a Scottish malt whisky in 'Bar Es Salaam', which has a large wall-mounted TV catering to sports fans. The Temple Bar, a throwback to the owner's Irish roots, offers similar fare down on the sand. The romantic cottages, privacy & sweeping vistas would suggest this is a honeymooner's dream, but children are warmly welcomed, too. *US$160 dbl.*

🛏 **Sultan Sands Island Resort** (76 rooms) m 0777 422137. This Moorish hillside resort shares an activity centre & spa with neighbouring Bluebay. Rooms are in planted terraces above the beach, but few have a sea view. In the reception, alongside the lounge & restaurant, arches, fountains & potted palms set the tone, while outside, water from the pool laps gently beside comfortable loungers. The lack of activities makes this a place to relax, although energetic guests can venture next door to Bluebay where facilities abound. *US$118–278 pp, FB.*

🛏 **Sunshine Hotel** (16 rooms) m 0774 388 662/0773 236 578; e office@sunshinezanzibar. com; www.sunshinezanzibar.com; ⏲ Jun–Apr. On a sweeping curve of white sand, the vibrant Sunshine Hotel occupies a relatively small plot of land. The immaculate gardens of raked stones & tropical trees, stylish architectural touches & calm efficiency lend this place a cool intimacy & prevent it from feeling claustrophobic. 16 light rooms set in 2-storey chalets, some with private plunge pools & beach bandas, On the beach front, the 2-tier main area houses the restaurant, lounge & overlooks a small, sail-cloth shaded infinity pool. Sunshine has a lively buzz, which would appeal to sociable young couples as much as urban escapists. *US$103–136 pp, HB.*

🛏 **Pongwe Beach Hotel** (16 rooms) m 0784 336181/0773 169096; e info@pongwe.com; www. pongwe.com. In its own quiet cove, in the shade of coconut palms, this lodge is well managed & good value. Airy bungalows have simple furniture, en-suite bathrooms (brackish water), & limited electricity. The barrier reef is only 15 mins offshore & the resort has its own dhow for sailing, snorkelling trips (*US$15*), & fishing. A large infinity pool has recently opened to the north of the beach. Pongwe serves tasty lunches from US$5 & varied set menus at dinner, including succulent spiced meats. With a little notice, children are welcome. *US$105–135 pp, HB.*

🏠 **Matemwe Beach Village** (22 rooms) 📞 024 2238374; m 0777 417250; e matemwebeachvillage@zitec.org; www. matemwebeach.net; ⏰ Jun–Mar. Firmly a place to relax, this simple, unassuming beach resort is popular with family groups & honeymooners. Simple but stylish en-suite rooms (2 with AC) are a mere hop, skip & a jump from the beach, while newer thatched suites, though very classy, are set well back with limited views. The resort's raised lounge area, overlooking the beach, encourages lazy afternoons & evenings, while the adjoining restaurant offers an à la carte menu. There's an attractive pool & an excellent on-site dive centre. *US$85–105 dbl/US$250–450 suite, HB.*

Moderate

🏠 **Panga Chumvi** (4 rooms) m 0772 177204/0777 862899; e pangachumvi@gmail.com; www.pangachumvi.com. This small locally owned place offers surprisingly good accommodation, a stone's throw from a pretty quiet stretch of beach. Mchanga Mdogo Villa has 2 dbl & 2 twin rooms; all with a pleasant veranda & some rooms interconnecting. The terraced bungalow rooms have been built with an eye on traditional Swahili design while the beachfront Baharini bungalow & banda offer sea-facing rooms. There is a small on-site restaurant & bar, complete with pizza oven, offering the usual fish & rice fare, but otherwise it's quite a private place to be. *US$70–90.*

🏠 **Waikiki Resort & Restaurant** (15 rooms) m 0773 286881/0777 877329; e waikikibooking@ hotmail.com; www.waikikiafrica.com. This delightful 15-room hotel is refreshingly small & personal, run enthusiastically by husband and wife team, Flavio & Sarah. Life here focuses on the buzzing central restaurant & the funky beached dhow bar 'Cassiopeia'. The multi-lingual staff check everyone's happy & a vibrant atmosphere prevails. Every Fri from 22.00, Flavio DJs on the beach to a large party crowd (up to 400 revellers). All bungalows are individually decorated with striking tropical murals & contain lovely bijou rooms. There is some basic activity equipment, free Wi-Fi, & a small massage zone. Kitesurfing courses & equipment available with on-site operator Kite Zanzibar. *US$70–90 dbl.*

Budget

🏠 **Santa Maria Coral Reef** (10 rooms) m 0777 432655; e info@santamaria-zanzibar. com; www.santamaria-zanzibar.com. This is a delightful hideaway, set in a coconut grove. Both bandas & bungalows are basic with solid wooden beds, coconut-rope & timber shelves & colourful mats. All are en suite with flush toilets & showers, & there is generator for electricity 18.00–midnight. For lunch & dinner expect freshly cooked fish or chicken with rice (around US$6). There's a simple thatched lounge/library area, & dhow snorkelling trips can be arranged. *US$60–80 dbl.*

🏠 **Mohamed's Restaurant & Bungalows** (4 rooms) m 0777 431881. The beachfront location & budget continue to make this a great backpacker option. Follow the sign from the main road & you'll find the cottages behind a high wall in the heart of Matemwe village. Rooms are basic but fairly clean & bed linen can usually be arranged. Simple meals can be organised with a day's notice. *US$50–70 dbl, B&B.*

Mnemba Island The tiny island of Mnemba, officially titled Mnemba Island Marine Conservation Area (MIMCA), lies some 2.5km off the northeastern coast of Zanzibar, and forms part of the much larger submerged Mnemba Atoll. It is now privately leased by &Beyond (formerly Conservation Corporation Africa, or CCAfrica) and has become one of Africa's ultimate beach retreats. It cannot be visited without a reservation.

The island itself boasts wide beaches of white coral sand, fine and cool underfoot, backed by patches of tangled coastal bush and a small forest of casuarina trees. The small reefs immediately offshore offer a great introduction to the fishes of the reef for snorkellers, while diving excursions further afield allow you to explore the 40m-deep coral cliffs, a good place to see larger fish including the whale shark, the world's largest fish. The bird checklist for the island, though short, includes several unusual waders and other marine birds.

Where to stay

🏠 **Mnemba Island Lodge** (10 bandas)
📞 (South Africa) +27 (0)11 809 4300;
e inboundsales@andbeyond.com; www.
andbeyond.com; ⊕ Jun–Mar. The *crème de la
crème* of &Beyond's impressive portfolio, Mnemba
Island Lodge is the height of rustic exclusivity.
Overlooking the beach from the forest's edge,
its secluded, split-level bandas are constructed
entirely of local timber & hand-woven palm fronds.
Large, airy & open-plan, each has a huge bed &
solid wooden furniture, softened with natural-
coloured fabrics. A 'butler' is assigned to each room
to ensure that everyone is content. The cuisine
is excellent, with plenty of fresh seafood, fruit &
vegetables, though guests may choose what, when
& where to eat. A number of superb dive sites are
within 15 mins of the lodge. Up to 2 dives a day
are included for qualified PADI divers, though
courses are charged extra. There's also snorkelling,
dbl kayaks, windsurfing, power-kiting, sailing, &
fly or deep-sea fishing. Hot stone, aromatherapy,
deep-tissue massage & reiki are all available, too.
Mnemba is unquestionably expensive, but its
flexibility & service levels are second to none, & its
idyllic location & proximity to outstanding marine
experiences are very hard to match. *US$1,250 pp/
night, inc FB & activities.*

Ufufuma Forest Habitat The Ufufuma Forest conservation project, set up
by the people of nearby Jendele village, aims to protect the forest habitat and to
educate the villagers in sustainable use. The local volunteers, led by the dedicated
and charismatic Mr Mustafa Makame, hope to make it a place for both locals and
foreigners to visit, and to preserve the traditional worship of *shetani*, or spirits,
that is performed here. Of the many underground caves hidden in the dense forest
undergrowth, three are shetani caves being used by the local traditional healer (or
'witch-doctor'), which tourists may also visit.

The forest area is at present only 1km², but the villagers are leaving the
surrounding 4km² area uncultivated to allow the forest habitat to expand in size. A
visit here is not a great wildlife experience, nor is it meant to be, although you might
be fortunate enough to see skittish red colobus (apparently early morning is best),
island birdlife, snakes and lizards. The villagers who act as guides are not wildlife
specialists but they are trying to learn and, meanwhile, they are very enthusiastic
about Ufufuma's cultural importance – which is the primary reason to visit.

Six villages in the vicinity already benefit from the forest income. All of the money
goes directly to the community leaders, who assess their village's primary needs, and
channel the money as appropriate. If more people visit the forest, accepting that it's
not a slick tourism enterprise, the village coffers will slowly increase, and in turn the
communities will begin to see the benefits of preserving rather than plundering their
surroundings. We wish the Ufufuma Forest conservation project every success.

Arranging your visit To visit Ufufuma Forest, it is best to make contact in
advance (*Mr Mustafa Makame Ali;* m *0777 491069;* e *himauje@yahoo.com*), to
ensure that an English-speaking guide will be available. Costs are variable, but for
a guided forest walk lasting a few hours, a visit to the caves, and usually a gift of
fresh fruit or coconut refreshment, expect to pay US$5 per person per guide, and
then volunteer to make a larger donation to the community fund. A full shetani
ceremony, consisting of about seven hours of singing, dancing and assorted rituals,
costs US$50 (*1–2 pax*), and must be booked in advance for a time convenient to
the local 'doctor'.

Getting there From Zanzibar Town, take the road east towards Chwaka: the
forest is on the left, about 5km before Chwaka. If you have contacted the Ufufuma
volunteers in advance, a welcoming party will likely be waiting for you, but if your

visit isn't scheduled, stop at Jendele village and ask in the market area for an official forest guide. Take sturdy shoes and, in the hot season, plenty of water to drink.

To reach the forest by **public transport**, talk to the dala-dala drivers heading towards Chwaka (No 206 or 214), and ask to be dropped in Jendele village: be aware that this is a sprawling village with little tourism connection so it may not be an easy task.

SOUTHEASTERN ZANZIBAR The coastline south of Chwaka Bay caters better to budget travellers than the coast further north, though a few relatively upmarket hotels are also found in the area. Until a few years ago, the southeast stretch of coast had the most crowded beaches on Zanzibar, but these days the area is quieter than Nungwi on the north coast.

Coming from Zanzibar Town along the main road through Jozani Forest, the first coastal settlement you'll hit is Paje, a small fishing village situated at a junction, from where minor roads run north and south along the coast. The most important settlement north of Paje and south of Chwaka Bay is Bwejuu, a fishing village whose livelihood is linked to the gathering and production of seaweed. Several resorts catering to all budgets lie within a few kilometres' radius of Bwejuu. South of Paje, Jambiani is a substantial village that runs for several kilometres along the beach, while the more southerly town of Makunduchi lacks any real tourist development.

The Michamvi Peninsula, which demarcates Chwaka Bay, is very similar to the northeast of the island, with the same stunning powder-white beaches, barrier reef, palm trees and a significant tidal change.

Where to stay

Exclusive

Baraza (30 rooms) e info@baraza-zanzibar. com; www.baraza-zanzibar.com. The youngest sibling of The Palms & Breezes, Baraza offers an all-inclusive option at a similar high level to The Palms, but more child-friendly. With strong Omani influences in its architecture, ornate gardens & plunge pools in every room, it aims at affluent families who are not interested in the island's activity-focused mega-resorts. Villas, divided into categories based on their proximity to the sea & size, are spacious & well kitted out. Public areas are spacious & guests also have access to the activities and dive centre at Breezes. *Public areas are spacious & guests also have access to the activities and dive centre at Breezes US$730-1035 dbl, all inclusive.*

The Palms (6 villas) m 0774 440882; e info@palms-zanzibar.com; www.palms-zanzibar.com. Adjacent to Breezes & owned by the same family, The Palms is small & stylish, with a colonial feel, attracting affluent honeymooners lured by image & intimacy. That said, the family-friendly Breezes (see overleaf) shares the same beach, so romantic dinners for 2 on the sand may be subject to intrusion. In the colonnaded Plantation House, housing a bar/lounge, dining room & mezzanine library, antique furniture rests on highly polished floors, while old-fashioned fans spin in the high makuti thatch. In the villas, huge rooms are classically elegant but with all mod-cons & a private outdoor plunge pool. They share a small swimming pool, & each has a private banda overlooking the beach. Most activities take place at Breezes. Min age 16. *US$685-1,025 dbl, all inclusive.*

Upmarket

Anna of Zanzibar (5 villas) m 0773 999387; e info@annaofzanzibar.com; www. annaofzanzibar.com. Staying here feels like being welcomed into a friend's home, & the 5 spacious villas are cosy & full of old world charm. Split into 3 rooms – a living room, bedroom & bathroom – all are filled with homely touches, & surround the pool, which sits behind a lovely section of powdery sand. The lounge is a popular place to kick back; there's a large satellite TV & DVD collection, plus a good range of novels. Free, reliable Wi-Fi is available all over the property, & laptops are available to take to rooms. Meals are served at the formal dining table or at tables dotted around the garden. For more indulgent

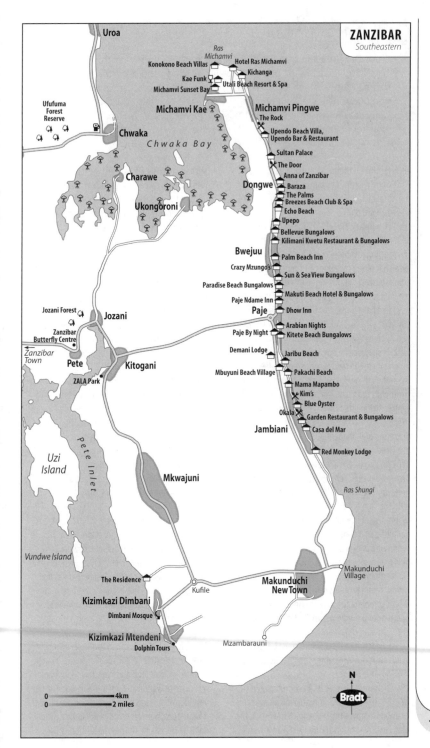

ZANZIBAR
Southeastern

Uroa

Ras
Michamvi

Konokono Beach Villas   Hotel Ras Michamvi
                         Kichanga
Kae Funk
Michamvi Sunset Bay   Utali Beach Resort & Spa

Ufufuma
Forest
Reserve

Chwaka

Michamvi Kae   Michamvi Pingwe
                The Rock
                Upendo Beach Villa,
                Upendo Bar & Restaurant

Chwaka Bay

Sultan Palace
The Door
Anna of Zanzibar

Charawe   Dongwe   Baraza
                                 The Palms
Ukongoroni   Breezes Beach Club & Spa
                                 Echo Beach
                                 Upepo
                                 Bellevue Bungalows
                                 Kilimani Kwetu Restaurant & Bungalows

                       Bwejuu   Palm Beach Inn

              Crazy Mzungo's   Sun & Sea View Bungalows
         Paradise Beach Bungalows   Makuti Beach Hotel & Bungalows
              Paje Ndame Inn
Jozani Forest   Dhow Inn
                       Paje
Jozani
Zanzibar   Arabian Nights
Butterfly Centre   Paje By Night   Kitete Beach Bungalows

*Zanzibar
Town*   Demani Lodge   Jaribu Beach
Pete   Kitogani
                   Mbuyuni Beach Village   Pakachi Beach
ZALA Park   Mama Mapambo
                                            Kim's
                                            Blue Oyster
                                      Okala   Garden Restaurant & Bungalows
                              Jambiani   Casa del Mar

*Uzi
Island*   Red Monkey Lodge

                   Mkwajuni

P e t e   I n l e t   Ras Shungi

Vundwe Island

The Residence   Makunduchi
                   Kufile   Village
Kizimkazi Dimbani   Makunduchi
                               New Town
Dimbani Mosque
Kizimkazi Mtendeni
Dolphin Tours   Mzambarauni

0 ———— 4km
0 ———— 2 miles

N

Bradt

From December to mid-February, some of the beaches on the east coast have large patches of brown seaweed washed ashore by the wind. This can be quite a shock if you expect pristine, picture-postcard tropical beach conditions. The seaweed normally stays on the beaches until the start of the rainy season, when it is carried back out to sea. After March, and up until November, the beaches are mostly clear.

entertainment, there's an outside bathtub & 2 massage treatment rooms (*$40 p/hr*), or the hotel also has a telescope for star-gazing. *US$440–580 dbl, FB.*

🏠 **Echo Beach Hotel** (12 rooms) **m** 0773 593260/593286; **e** echobeachhotel@hotmail.com; www.echobeachhotel.com. This small, friendly lodge has high aspirations and continues to receive admirable reviews. Arranged in a dbl arc behind the inviting swimming pool, the vast majority of its rooms have a sea view from a private terrace, all enjoying a 4-poster dbl bed swathed in a mosquito net, AC, fans & an open, en-suite bathroom with walk-in shower. The open-sided lounge/dining room, where the food is consistently very good, is a stone's throw from a lovely stretch of beach. Hydrophiles can head for the on-site watersports centre, African Blue Divers, to arrange dive trips (*US$80/dive*) & courses. Children stay at the discretion of management.

🏠 **Breezes Beach Club** (74 rooms) **m** 0774 440883/5; **e** info@breezes-zanzibar.com; www. breezes-zanzibar.com. A perennial favourite with honeymooners & families, Breezes is a large, efficient, family-run beach resort. Comfortable rooms are set in whitewashed villas with all the amenities of a good hotel. Facilities include a large swimming pool & a great stretch of sandy beach, plus plenty of watersports, including a dive centre. For landlubbers, there's a modern spa, yoga studio, fitness centre & tennis court. Several restaurants & bars complete the package, including a carved beach hut for dining *à deux* (but note that dinner at the smaller restaurants is not included in HB rates). Beach weddings, which must be arranged in advance, are increasingly popular here. *US$154–480 dbl, HB.*

🏠 **Michamvi Sunset Bay** (20 rooms) **m** 0777 878136/ 0778 662872; **e** matt@michamvi.com, brad@michamvi.com; www.michamvi.com. The only east coast resort facing west across water,

Michamvi Sunset Bay is a relaxed, family-friendly resort with a casual atmosphere & a keen sense of community empowerment. There's a small open-sided restaurant & a breezy bar overlooking the pretty beach. The bedrooms are in 4 large, 2-storey villas set out around the mosaic pool. Sunset mangrove safaris (*US$50 up to 4 pax*) are available & several watersports are possible from the quiet beach – from canoeing to windsurfing & snorkelling – whilst divers are collected by the off-site Peponi Diving PADI centre, & village tours are encouraged. Children are warmly welcomed by the hands-on management, with under 12s staying free of charge. *US$380–500 dbl, HB.*

🏠 **Dhow Inn** (6 rooms) **m** 0777 525828; **e** info@dhowinn.com; www.dhowinn.com. Dhow Inn's Dutch owners are on site & keen to warmly welcome guests & live up to their 'come as a guest, leave as family' motto. Set 40m back from the water's edge, the modern rooms don't have a sea view but the atmospheric 2-storey bar-restaurant does. There is a flexible dining programme with Full moon pool parties & regular poolside BBQs. 28 additional rooms will open in 2013. *US$100–150 dbl, B&B.*

🏠 **Sultan Palace** (22 rooms) **** 024 224 0173; **m** 0777 423792 **e** Sultanpalacezanzibar@ zanlink.com; www.sultanpalacezanzibar.com. The Sultan Palace reopened in Aug 2011, brighter & even lovelier than before. Set high on a coral cliff, overlooking a deserted pristine beach, this elegant place has lost none of its olde-worlde charm. The 22 rooms, identical apart from the view, are gorgeous & extremely spacious, with beautifully ornate Zanzibari furniture, antiques & pictures. The Arab-esque main area is laid out in a circle, with stained glass windows, fading old Africa maps & photos, & an intimate bar. The upper level restaurant has a breezy interior, great view over the sea & serves some of the most delicious food on the island. Outdoors, the infinity pool is a recent addition, & has a stunning clifftop location, or there are snaking pathways to a lovely beach. The gracious & attentive owner Paola is on hand & her enthusiasm for this lovely place is infectious. *US$380–750 dbl, FB.*

Moderate

🏠 **Hotel Ras Michamvi** (15 rooms) 📞 024 223 1081; e info@rasmichamvi.com; www. rasmichamvi.com. This little resort sits high up on the coral cliffs at the very tip of the peninsula. It's in a very quiet corner of the island, so unless you have your own transport or enjoy extremely long walks, it's really quite remote; this is also its charm for the escapist. Rooms are surprisingly pleasant, & tthe restaurant offers fabulous reef panoramas & glimpses into the open kitchen. Steep steps lead down to a small private cove, where the sand is at its deepest & best in Jun/Jul. **$$$**

🏠 **Blue Oyster Hotel** (13 rooms) 📞 024 224 0163; m 0713 33312; e blueoysterhotel@gmx. de; www.zanzibar.de. In lovely gardens, Blue Oyster remains one of the friendliest, most cared for & best-value hotels in its range. Ground-floor rooms are around a palm courtyard & others in a trio of smaller 2-storey buildings, all with en-suite facilities & balconies. The wonderfully breezy 1st-floor restaurant, with a wide veranda overlooking the sea, offers snacks (around US$5), delicious salads (US$4) or pizzas & evening meals like coconut-infused octopus with rice (around US$10). In front of the hotel a raised stretch of sand is perfect for sunbathing, or for a coconut-oil massage (US$20). *US$90–180 dbl, HB.*

🏠 **Bellevue Bungalows** (9 rooms) m 0777 209576; e bellevuezanzibar@gmail.com; www. bellevuezanzibar.com. On the top of a high rise of coral rock, this is a thoroughly relaxed, gentle place offering one of the best budget deals on the island. Bellevue has flourished under its young Dutch owners, with pretty gardens surrounding the simple, spacious accommodation & vibrant restaurant. Here, Chef Chulla makes terrific tapas as well as a variety of fresh European & Swahili cuisine (US$5–7). Scrumptious b/fasts of spice-infused juices, fresh bread, pancakes, locally produced honey & homemade jams are a great start to the day, too. With a 50m walk down to the beach & free transfers to the owner's kitesurfing school in Paje, the focus is on traditional seaside

activities & the chance to chill under the storm lanterns with a cold beer in the evening. *US$55–100 dbl, B&B.*

🏠 **Paje By Night** (21 rooms) m 0777 460710; e info@pajebynight.net; www.pajebynight.net. The row of hammocks at the entrance hints at the pervading mood of this unpretentious joint. Set 50m back from the beach, & without a sea view, the bar is the hub with an adjoining TV lounge showing international news & sport virtually all day. The food is good with an Italian bent; seafood & Swahili BBQs are a weekly occurrence & the cocktail bar is open 24hr. Spacious en-suite rooms & rustic 2-storey 'jungle bungalows' are available. *US$60–90 dbl, B&B.*

Budget

🏠 **Casa Del Mar** (14 rooms) m 0777 455446; e info@casa-delmar-zanzibar.com; www. casa-delmar-zanzibar.com; lodge ⊕ Jun–Mar. Casa del Mar is run with impressive enthusiasm, skill & environmental awareness. Rooms are in thatched 2-storey houses, made almost entirely of organic material. The majority of the staff are Jambiani residents, & the school & clinic receive regular support. These credentials aside, the accommodation & friendly vibe are good reasons to stay, too. En-suite rooms are either 1- or 2-storey, both with balconies & the latter with a galleried bedroom high in the thatch, & a lounge (or children's room). Good food is served in the cool, shady restaurant. There's a range of activities & excursions & the lodge has its own boat for snorkelling trips (US$15 pp/day). *US$90–110 dbl, B&B.*

🏠 **Garden Restaurant & Bungalows** (6 rooms) m 0776 586193; e info@ gardenbungalows-zanzibar.com/ gardenbungalows@gmail.com; http:// gardenbungalows-zanzibar.com This is one place where the Sau Inn's fire has had a positive effect – the damage spurred the British owner on to get renovating & improving, & they're doing a great job. New fixtures & fittings have updated the spacious rooms and manager Jenny has redesigned the garden, which she hopes will grow to a lush & green space to live up to its name. Meanwhile a brand new kitchen & bar should smarten up the restaurant, which is popular for its curries & crêpes. The whole place has a lot of potential, & with Jenny's enthusiasm & dedication, there are hopes that this could be a high quality operation in the near future. *US$20–115 dbl, B&B.*

⌂ **Makuti Beach Hotel & Bungalows**
(11 bungalows) m 0774 372947; www.makuti-beach-hotel.com. Just metres from the beach on a beautiful patch of soft white sand speckled with shrubs, these cool & simple bungalows are shaded by makuti thatch. 9 pristine dbls & trpls are compact but contain all you really need, & outside is a small deck with a sofa & a fabulous sea view. The bar & restaurant is little more than a few kanga-covered chairs & tables dotted around in the sand under thatch, while upstairs the lounge is strewn with animal appliqué cushions, a few books & a world map. Come here to get away from it all. *US$55–175 dbl, B&B.*

⌂ **Mama Mapambo** (5 rooms) m 0772 671073/0774 134767; e mamamapambo@gmail.com; www.mamamapambo.altervista.org. Mama Mapambo adds a splash of much-needed colour & character to the guesthouses along this stretch of Jambiani beach. A wonderfully vibrant sign will direct you to this Italian-owned place, where the sunny yellow exterior matches the owners' warm disposition. 3 rooms have a sea view & all have 4 poster beds, walk-in wardrobes & stylised modern bathrooms; whilst 2 jaunty 'jungle rooms' are up a spiral staircase. Unsurprisingly, the food is most definitely Italian with large bowls of spaghetti & cheesy pizzas being the staples. The owners have put their hearts & souls into this project, & it shows. *US$55–105 dbl, B&B.*

⌂ **Sun & Sea View Bungalows** (11 rooms) m 0718 102633; e info@sunandseaviewbungalows.com; www.sunandseaviewresort.com. On a large, open plot by the beach, this is a relaxed place with cheerful African music playing at the bar. Large rondavels contain 2 independent rooms, each simple & clean with nets, mains electricity & fans. There's plenty of natural light, & a bath as well as a shower in the en-suite bathrooms. The hospitable owner is often around & his views on the island, its people & politics are enlightening; with time he can arrange village tours. There is no gate to the property, so self-drivers may prefer a more physically secure option, but otherwise this is a reasonable budget choice. *US$70–110 dbl, B&B.*

⌂ **Kilimani Kwetu Restaurant & Bungalows**
(4 rooms) ℡ 024 224 0235; m 0777 465243/0777 214133; e info@kilimani.de; www.kilimani.de. A partnership between 5 Germans & the village of Bwejuu, Kilimani Kwetu is rooted in community development & has already financed the construction of an adult education centre & library. Built on a hill overlooking the sea by local people from local materials, this is a relaxed, hassle-free spot. Rooms in 2 thatched bungalows are basic if a little uninspiring, with a fan & en-suite bathrooms (cold-water shower & squat, flush toilet). Fresh fish is served in the restaurant, & vegetarian dishes on request. Just 50m along a zigzag path leads to a private beach area & beach bar. *US$55 dbl, B&B.*

⌂ **Pakachi Beach Hotel** (8 rooms) m 0777 423331; e pakachi@hotmail.com; www.pakachi.net. Appropriately, *pakachi* means border, for this pleasant little hotel is situated roughly halfway between Paje & Jambiani. It's a friendly, rustic haven, its simple thatched bungalows set amid flower-filled gardens. Spotlessly clean en-suite rooms have ceiling fans, & there's also a 2-bedroom family house. The bar/restaurant overlooks the sea, where a range of boats is available, though it's not ideal for swimming. The chef rustles up both local & international dishes, with his pizzas recommended. A much-needed pool & a simple Island Spice spa have been added for guest enjoyment. *US$50–60 dbl, B&B.*

⌂ **Crazy Mzungo's Flashpackers & Beach Lounge** (5 rooms) m 0779 912498; e vanillaarches@gmail.com. Under joint South African–New Zealand ownership, Crazy Mzungos started life as a trendy beach lounge in 2010. Soon a chic beach house was added, & hey presto, some of the most stylish, chilled-out budget beach accommodation in the area appeared. It's easy to spot from the road with its eye-catching orange sign depicting a deranged cartoon monkey, or from the beach by a Jack Daniels' VW Beetle wedged into the sand. The Beach Lounge is still the main attraction, but next door a well-finished villa contains 5 rooms. It's a lovely spot for families & groups, but couples taking the rooms individually may find their style cramped by fellow guests. The rooms share 2 modern kitchens, of which the downstairs one is slightly better equipped, & can be used by either guests or a private chef. *US$76–210 dbl, B&B.*

⌂ **Demani Lodge** (11 rooms) m 0772 263115/0777 460079; e demanilodge@gmail.com; www.demanilodge.com. In 2011, Swedish-managed Demani opened up on a previously barren stretch of road between Paje & Jambiani. Catering for those on a tight budget who still want a decent standard, Demani is truly a backpackers place, filled with chill-out music, good vibes & offbeat characters. The simple but well-constructed thatched bandas are well looked after, & all rooms share neat bathrooms. The dormitories have 6–9 beds, & the largest one's a bargain at $12 per bed. The bar features swings, benches & a fire pit, & the upper chill-out zone is strung with rainbow coloured hammocks & scattered with floor cushions. Tasty meals are served here for rock bottom prices too – check out the blackboard marked 'cheap shit', filling comfort food for those on even the tightest of budgets. Demani helpfully offers both Wi–Fi & internet access for US$0.30/day & rents out bikes for US$4/day. *US$30–40 dbl, B&B.*

🏠 **Paradise Beach Bungalows** (12 rooms) 📞 024 223 1387; m 0777 414129; e paradisebb@ zanlink.com, saori@cats-net.com; www. geocities. jp/paradisebeachbungalows. Opened 20 years ago by a diminutive Japanese lady, Saori Miura, Paradise is a cheap beach retreat offering basic facilities & great sushi. The new chalets, with European toilets & showers, are a better bet than the original, basic rooms, with their squat toilets & cold showers. Despite storm lanterns, frequent power cuts make a torch essential. Good-quality home-cooked food include fresh sushi & tempura, but supplies are limited so order well in advance. Paradise can get very busy, so advance booking is advisable. And be aware that there are a number of not-so-docile dogs around the gardens! *US$65–80 dbl, B&B.*

🏠 **Red Monkey Lodge** (12 rooms) m 0777 713366; e info@redmonkeylodge.com; www. redmonkeylodge.com. About 2km from the centre of Jambiani, on an increasingly bumpy track, Red Monkey is set on the low coral cliffs, & named after the Kirk's red colobus monkeys that live in the adjacent forest & pass through the grounds most days. Standards & quality have risen recently; as has cost. The German–Zanzibari staff are very friendly, rooms are clean & spacious, complete with moulded concrete beds, large ceiling fan, mosquito nets & high-pressure en-suite showers, making this one of the better budget deals in this part of Zanzibar. *US$60–90 dbl, B&B.*

🍴 Where to eat and drink

🍴 **Albi's Well** m 0786231988; 🕐 11.30–17.00. Part of the Jambiani Tourism Training Institute (JTTI), Albi's Well is staffed by local students gaining experience in the tourism industry. Tasty fusion food such as wraps & pizzas are on the light bites menu, as well as rich coffee & tempting cakes for whiling away the afternoon. Colourful cocktails are shaken & stirred at the pretty pink bar & there's also a deck overlooking the sea. Dinner is served on some Fri nights only & must be pre-booked, & the varied menu takes on a different theme each week – Japanese & Italian are some of the more popular choices. This is a spot to support.

🍴 **The Door** m 0777 414962; 🕐 lunch & dinner daily. This is a good place for fresh seafood, though book in advance for dinner. It's a sizeable shady restaurant with friendly staff & a great outlook over the waving palm fronds to the Blue Lagoon (the only place where swimming is possible in this area of coast at low tide). After some fried squid with lemon rice (US$6.50) or a divine 2-person whole grilled lobster (US$40), leave your things behind the bar & take a cooling dip or snorkel.

🍴 **Crazy Mzungo's Beach Lounge** m 0779 912498; e vanillaarches@gmail.com. Relaxed Crazy Mzungo's is popular with partygoers & locals alike – the former attracted by the Crazy Cocktail specials, including Crazy Juice (US$15), the Zanzibaris for the international football broadcast on a tiny TV. All day b/fasts & fresh organic food are a real draw, plus the BBQ night on Wed. After all that gorging, replete diners can head for the beach bed, or wear it all off with a spot of volleyball. Internet access costs $7/hr.

🍴 **Okala Restaurant** m 0777 430519. In a small, unremarkable makuti building, between the Nuru Beach Resort & Oasis Beach hotels, Okala's food far exceeds any expectations arising from its architecture. It's run by a small co-operative of Jambiani families, & the Zanzibari food is excellent by any standards. With some notice, the team can prepare a fabulous *meze* of Swahili curries, grilled seafood & tasty vegetable accompaniments. Filling up on fresh coconut rice, wilted spinach with lime & rich tomato fish curry is a real Zanzibari treat. Individual dishes, such as grilled octopus or fish, are US$5–6, with special items, like the amazing (& enormous!) coconut–crusted jumbo prawns, at US$10. Short courses in Zanzibari cooking are also offered. The team here is closely involved with several community projects, so ask them if you're interested in what's happening, or arrange to end your Eco+Culture village tour (see *What to see and do*, below) with a satisfying lunch.

✗ **The Rock Restaurant** m 0777 840724/490681; www.therockrestaurantzanzibar. com. Probably the most remarkable location of any Zanzibar restaurant, The Rock is perched on top of a marooned, seriously undercut coral-rock outcrop, just off the shore of the Michamvi Peninsula. Accessed by wandering across the sand at low tide, or by boat or breaststroke at high tide, the local team in this dilapidated building, with its cheery yellow window frames (no glass) & sea-life murals, serve up a simple 'catch of the day' menu (US$21–6, with some pasta dishes (*US$16*) & tropical salad). It's very basic, quirky & often empty, but the views are terrific & the experience unique. Calling in advance to arrange food is recommended. $$$

✗ **Upendo Bar & Restaurant** m 0777 244492; e info@upendozanzibar.com; www. upendolounge.com. On the gorgeous sweep of beach directly opposite The Rock, Upendo is the perfect hideaway to while an afternoon by the sea. Opened in May 2009 by a flamboyant British lady, Trish Dhanak, this is a chilled-out, funky beach bar – try the US$6 Upendo signature drink (Sky vodka shaken with guava juice & honey, then topped with sparkling wine). Lounge music is piped into the shady, cushion covered beach barazas, & tasty treats are cooked to order, slowly but beautifully. Delights range from salt & pepper squid (US$5) to loaded beef tacos (US$9) & the 'So Loaded' seafood fiesta sharing platter (US$100), comprising 1kg

rock lobster, slipper lobster, crab, prawns, octopus, calamari and catch of the day! Sun brunches could well become an island institution here, but anytime it's worth a trip. Rooms are also available in the upmarket villa next door & there's a pool.

✗ **Upepo** m 0784 619579; e shareefznz71@ hotmail.com; www.zanzibarhotelbeach.com. You can't fail to hear the Cuban beats emanating from this chilled out restaurant cum bar, which, with only 6 tables, offers a personal touch on local & international cuisine, influenced by the joint Tanzanian–Canadian ownership. Thirsty beachgoers can cool off with a fruity sangria, but there's also a range of seasonal fish dishes, curries, bowls of pasta & pancakes for the hungry. There's a good vibe here, & you may well find that you linger longer than intended. *US$65–70*.

⌂ **Kae Funk** m 0777 439059/ 0777 222346/ 0777 001692/ 0779351382 e kaefunk@hotmail.com. Tucked away along a sandy road at the northern end of Michamvi Kae, the bar itself is impressively constructed from multiple boats, driftwood, rusted bicycles, & all manner of flotsam & jetsam. There's a massive array of liqueurs & spirits lining the multi-tier bar, cushioned swings in the shady garden, & *ngalawa* tables for enjoying US$6 coconut spice curry (lunch & dinner; 1 days' notice required). Music is played all day, & fireside beach parties a regular occurrence. Open 24/7, this Rasta hangout is as chilled & entertaining as you'd expect, & a hangout for social backpackers & open-minded travellers.

What to see and do While most visitors are here for the beach and watersports, two community projects in this area are well worth the support of visitors.

Eco+Culture Jambiani Cultural Tours Probably the island's best insight into genuine rural life is afforded by Eco+Culture's village tours. Meet in the small, signposted hut in the centre of the village (opposite the school), or be collected on foot from your hotel for these well-run, enlightening community-focused walks, organised & guided by resident Kassim Mande and his colleagues. A percentage of your fee goes directly towards community development initiatives, a direct result of the organisation's original NGO status.

Depending on your enthusiasm and heat tolerance, tours last anything from a few hours to the best part of a day and take in many aspects of everyday life. Spend time helping the women make coconut paste, reciting the alphabet in unison at the efficient kindergarten and meeting the *mganga* (traditional healer). Kassim's presence, reputation within the community and ability to translate allow for genuine interaction with the Jambiani residents and a thoroughly engaging time.

The trip be arranged directly through Kassim (m *0777 469118; kassimmande@ hotmail.com*) or in in advance through Eco+Culture's Stone Town office (☏ *024 223*

3731; m 0777 410873; e ecoculturetours@gmail.com, hajihafidh@yahoo.co.uk; www. ecoculture-zanzibar.org; see *Zanzibar Town, Tour operators*, page 350). Do be aware that of late there are a few villagers operating apparently copycat walks. It is well worth taking the time to seek out Kassim or the Eco+Culture office, not only for his knowledge & friendliness, but also to be sure that your money is directed back into vital village projects.

Jambiani Wellness Centre (e *habszanzibar@yahoo.ca; www.handsacrossborders society.org;* ⏲ *09.00–14.00 Mon/Tue & Thu/Fri*) Opened in 2003 by a joint Canadian–Zanzibari NGO, Hands Across Borders, the Jambiani Wellness Centre primarily offers chiropractic treatment, homeopathic remedies and other therapy free of charge to the local community. Tourists are welcome to visit for massage, acupuncture, *breema* or homeopathic treatments. A donation of at least US$15 is asked in lieu of a fee. The charitable work of the group now extends well beyond the clinic boundaries, with current community projects including the Jambiani Tourism Training Institute (JTTI), a vocational school that educates adults about tourism and starting up a business, and also provides on-the-job training at the Albi's Well Restaurant (see *Where to eat*, page 395).

THE WEST COAST

SOUTHWESTERN ZANZIBAR For most overseas visitors, Zanzibar's southwest corner holds little more than day trip opportunities to see dolphins from Kizimkazi or troops of red colobus monkeys in Jozani Forest. As a result, few people stay in this area, with most opting instead for the endless beaches of the east coast or the buzz of Zanzibar's Stone Town. Away from the main tourist attractions, the villagers in these parts rarely encounter visitors, and their welcome is one of genuine friendliness and interest. It's a refreshing contrast to the more crowded and visitor-centric feeling taking over significant parts of the island's north and east coasts.

 Where to stay and eat

Exclusive

🏠 **The Residence** (66 rooms) ✆024 555 5000; e info-zanzibar@theresidence.com; www. theresidence.com. Just 3km north of Kizimkazi Dimbani stands one of the most talked about hotels on the island, a place where movie stars & supermodels wouldn't seem out of place: The Residence. This glossy, big-budget resort opened in 2011. Set on a delightfully calm, mile-long stretch of powdery beach, its 66 plush villas, each with its own generously sized swimming pool & personal butler, are highly contemporary & impeccably kitted out. The main complex is vast, including 2 restaurants, a raised glass-sided pool, tennis courts, a nature trail & serious spa. There's certainly plenty to keep you amused, though some may find it a bit sterile – you could be anywhere in the world, albeit a very nice part of it. *US$500–1,065 dbl, HB.*

Upmarket

🏠 **Chumbe Island Lodge** (7 rooms) ✆024 231 040; m 0777 413232; e chumbe@zitec.org; www.chumbeisland.com; ⏲ mid Jun–mid Apr. Part of the Chumbe Island Coral Park (CHICOP), this superb, trail-blazing lodge is an example of truly eco-friendly accommodation. Bungalows are simple, clean, ingeniously designed & genuinely ecologically sensitive. The central area is a huge, star-shaped *makuti* structure – perfect for catching the sea breeze in the heat of the day. Fresh meals & drinks are served on the terrace (on the sounding of a gong), & there's a lovely upper deck of hammocks & chairs. Activities are all escorted & focus on learning about the surrounding environment & ecology, & include snorkelling (scuba diving is prohibited) on the nearby reefs; forest walks along the nature trail; & walks across the inter-tidal zone, with its plethora of rock pools. *US$520–560 dbl, all inclusive.*

15

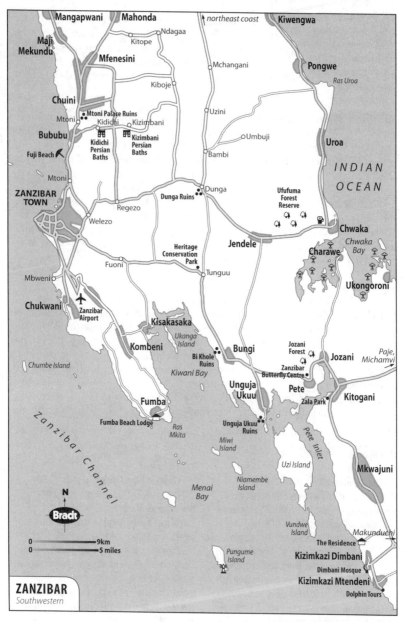

ZANZIBAR
Southwestern

⌂ **Unguja Lodge** (12 rooms) m 0774
477477/857234; e info@ungujalodge.com; www.
ungujaresort.com. Unguja Lodge at Kizimkazi
Mkunguni is up with the best on the island, its style
a mix of modern & traditional. Enormous rooms
under steep makuti roofs are set in densely planted
gardens. Inside each, sinuous walls enclose a lounge,
shower room, mezzanine seating area & bedroom. 3
'baobab villas' each have a small plunge pool, whilst
others have a sea view. For a cool dip, try the pool
or make for the crushed-shell beach. There's a PADI
dive centre, with shore diving & boat dives possible.
Other activities include dhow cruises, dolphin
viewing & a village tour. *US$320–430.*

☗ **Fumba Beach Lodge** (26 rooms) m 0777 860504/878025; e info@fumbabeachlodge.co.tz; www.fumbabeachlodge.com. To the south of Zanzibar Town, & created in line with contemporary, upmarket safari camps, this is one of the islands' more stylish places to stay. Rooms & suites are beach-chic understated & spacious with lovely vistas. A large infinity pool lies next to the lounge & open-sided restaurant, while an African spa & efficient on-site dive centre keep guests entertained. The full-day picnic sailing trip around Menai Bay's islands make for one of Zanzibar's most beautiful & indulgent outings. *US$220–360 dbl, HB.*

Moderate

☗ **Karamba** (20 rooms) m 0773 166406; e karamba@zanlink.com; www.karambaresort. com. This appealing clifftop lodge at Kizimkazi Dimbani has smart, en-suite bungalows, each thoughtfully decorated & with a sea view. In the restaurant, try fresh sushi (US$20 sharing platter) & tapas dishes (US$3–6 each), or just a sunset cocktail overlooking the bustling dhow harbour below. There's a lovely pool, & yoga, reiki & Ayurvedic therapies are also available. *US$42–204 dbl, B&B.*

Jozani–Chwaka Bay National Park (⊕ 07.30–17.00 daily; admission US$8)

This national park incorporates Jozani Forest, protecting the last substantial remnant of the indigenous forest that once covered much of central Zanzibar. It stands on the isthmus of low-lying land that links the northern and southern parts of the island, to the south of Chwaka Bay. The water table is very high and the area is prone to flooding in the rainy season, giving rise to this unique 'swamp-forest' environment. The large moisture-loving trees, the stands of palm and fern, and the humid air give the forest a cool, 'tropical' feel.

Jozani's main attraction is Kirk's red colobus (see box overleaf), a beautiful and cryptically coloured monkey with an outrageous pale tufted crown. Unique to Zanzibar, Kirk's red colobus was reduced to a population of around 1,500 individuals a few years back, but recent estimates now place it at around 2,700.

The forest used to be the main haunt of the Zanzibar leopard, a race that is found nowhere else, but which recent research suggests may well be extinct. The forest is also home to Ader's duiker, a small antelope that effectively may now be a Zanzibar endemic, as it is probably extinct and certainly very rare in Kenya's Sokoke Forest, the only other place where it has ever been recorded. Several other mammal species live in Jozani, and the forest is one of the best birding sites on the island, hosting a good range of coastal forest birds, including an endemic race of the lovely Fischer's turaco.

A network of nature trails has been established. The main one takes about an hour to follow at a leisurely pace, with numbered points of interest that relate to a well-written information sheet you can buy for a nominal cost at the reception desk. There are also several shorter loops. As you walk around the nature trails, it's possible to see lots of birds and probably a few colobus and Sykes monkeys, but these animals are shy, and will leap through the trees as soon as they hear people approaching. On the south side of the main road live two groups of monkeys that are more used to humans and with a guide you can watch these at close quarters. This is ideal animal viewing – the monkeys are aware of your presence but not disturbed. Some visitors have been tempted to try to stroke the monkeys or give them sweets, which is not only bad for the monkeys, but can be bad for tourists too – several people have been given a nasty nip or scratch.

South of the forest, a long thin creek juts in from the sea, and is lined with mangrove trees.

A new development in the area, based in the village of Pete, 1km from the entrance to the forest, is a mangrove boardwalk, allowing visitors a rare view into the unique mangrove habitat.

Kirk's red colobus (*Procolobus kirkii*) is named after Sir John Kirk, the 19th-century British consul-general in Zanzibar, who first identified these attractive island primates. They are endemic to the archipelago and one of Africa's rarest monkeys. Easily identified by their reddish coat, pale underside, small dark faces framed with tufts of long white hairs, and distinctive pink lips and nose, the monkeys are a wildlife highlight for many visitors to Zanzibar.

Kirk's red colobus live in gregarious troops of five to 50 individuals, headed by a dominant male and comprising his harem of loyal females and several young (single births occur year-round). They spend most of the day hanging out in the forest canopy, sunbathing, grooming and occasionally breaking away in small numbers to forage for tasty leaves, flowers and fruit. Their arboreal hideouts can make them hard to spot, but a roadside band at the entrance to Jozani–Chwaka Bay National Park allow for close observation and photography.

Timber felling, population expansion and a rise in agriculture have resulted in the rapid destruction of the tropical evergreen forests in which the Kirk's red colobus live, thus dramatically reducing population numbers. Researchers estimate that around 2,700 of these monkeys currently exist, a fact verified by their classification as 'endangered' on the IUCN Red List (2004) and their inclusion in Appendix II of the Convention on International Trade in Endangered Species of Wild Flora and Fauna (CITES).

Human behaviour has undoubtedly caused the decline in Kirk's red colobus population numbers, yet now tourism may help to save the species. With national park status now protecting their habitat in Jozani Forest, and visitor numbers increasing, the local communities are beginning to benefit from the tangible economic rewards that come from preserving these striking monkeys. If this continues, the future survival of the species should be secured.

When to visit Keen naturalists who want to watch wildlife undisturbed, or those who just like a bit of peace and quiet, should try to visit the reserve either very early or in the middle of the day, as most groups come at about 09.00–10.00 on their way to the coast, or 15.00–16.00 on their way back. The monkeys and birds seem subdued in the midday heat, so about 14.00–15.00 seems to be the best time for watching their behaviour.

Getting there and away The entrance to the National Park is clearly signposted on the main road between Zanzibar Town and the southern part of the east coast, north of the village of Pete. You can visit at most times of the year, but in the rainy season the water table rises considerably and the forest paths can be under more than 1m of water. The entrance fee includes the services of a guide and the mangrove boardwalk.

Many **tour companies** include Jozani on their east-coast tours or dolphin tours, but you can easily get here by frequent **public bus** (routes 9, 10 or 13), **dala-dala** (nos 309, 310, 324 or 326), hired **bike** or **car**. Alternatively, take a **tourist minibus** heading for the east coast, and alight here. This road is well used by tourist minibuses and other traffic throughout the day, so after your visit to the forest you could flag something down and continue to the coast or return to Zanzibar Town.

Around Jozani Also of interest in the Jozani area are the Zanzibar Butterfly Centre and the Bi Khole Ruins.

Zanzibar Butterfly Centre (ZBC; e *mail@zanzibarbutterflies.com; www. zanzibarbutterflies.com;* ⏰ *09.00–17.00 daily; admission US$5 pp*) The Zanzibar Butterfly Centre aims to show visitors the forest's fluttering friends close up, as well as generating an income for local villagers and preserving the forest. Participants (currently 26 farmers) are taught to identify butterfly species, gently capture female butterflies, net small areas for breeding, harvest eggs, plant appropriate caterpillar fodder, and ultimately collect the resulting pupae for breeding the next generation and for sale back to the centre. The pupae are then sold on to overseas zoos and live exhibits, or displayed for visitors to the centre in the large, netted tropical garden. Here, 200–300 colourful butterflies can be seen in the enclosure, making for a fascinating diversion and one of Africa's largest butterfly exhibits. There are good guides and clear informative signs to explain the project and butterfly lifecycle, and experienced photographers can get some wonderful shots. The income generated from visitors to ZBC is channelled back into further funding local conservation and poverty-alleviation projects, whilst the message is made clear to the communities that protecting the natural habitat of these insects provides much-needed income. The centre is a fun, worthwhile 30 minute stop, and its location, just outside Jozani Forest, makes it a convenient addition to a forest trip.

Bi Khole Ruins The Bi Khole ruins are the remains of a large house dating from the 19th century. Khole was a daughter of Sultan Said (Bi is a title meaning 'lady') who came to Zanzibar in the 1840s, after Said moved his court and capital from Oman. With her sister, Salme (see box, page 370), she helped their brother, Barghash, escape after his plans to seize the throne from Majid were discovered. Khole had this house built for her to use as a private residence away from the town; she is recorded as being a keen hunter and a lover of beautiful things. The house had a Persian bathhouse where she could relax after travelling or hunting, and was surrounded by a garden decorated with flowering trees and fountains. The house was used until the 1920s but is now ruined, with only the main walls standing.

The main front door has collapsed into a pile of rubble but this is still the way into the ruin. Directly in front of the door is a wide pillar, designed so that any visitor coming to the door would not be able to see into the inner courtyard, in case Khole or other ladies of the court were unveiled. In this room are alcoves and niches with arabesque arches, although the windows are rectangular. With some imagination, it's possible to see what an impressive house this once was.

The ruins lie a few kilometres to the west of the main road from Zanzibar Town to the southern part of the east coast, about 6km south of the village of Tunguu. The road passes down a splendid boulevard of gnarled old mango trees, supposed to have been planted for Khole (although they may date from before this period): about halfway along is the track to the ruins. If you're travelling on **public transport**, take any of the buses (routes 9, 10 or 13) or dala-dalas (No 309, 310, 324 or 326) heading southeast and ask the driver to tell you when to alight.

Kizimkazi The small town of Kizimkazi lies on the southwestern end of the island, and is best known to tourists as the place to see humpback and bottlenose dolphins, both of which are resident in the area.

Getting there and away Most tourists visit Kizimkazi on an **organised day tour** out of Zanzibar Town, which costs US$25–100 per person, depending on group size, season and trip quality, including transport to/from Kizimkazi, the boat, all snorkelling gear and lunch. Alternatively, the town can be reached independently in a **hired car**, or with a No 326 **dala-dala** from Zanzibar Town.

Dolphin watching The best time of year to see the dolphins is between October and February. From June to September, the southerly winds can make the seas rough, while during the rainy season (March to May) conditions in the boat can be unpleasant. However, out at sea you're likely to get wet anyway. You should also protect yourself against the sun. Sightings used to be almost guaranteed, but it's not unusual now for groups to return without having seen a single dolphin. Sadly, as the disturbances from too many boats and people increasingly outweigh the benefits of food and shelter, this trend is likely to continue, with fewer and fewer dolphins appearing in Kizimkazi's waters in the future.

Never encourage your pilot to chase the dolphins or try to approach them too closely yourself. With up to 100 people visiting Kizimkazi daily in the high season, there is genuine cause to fear that tourism may be detrimental to the animals. If you do get close enough and you want to try your luck swimming with the dolphins, slip (rather than dive) into the water next to the boat, and try to excite their interest by diving frequently and holding your arms along your body to imitate their streamlined shape.

Kizimkazi Mosque Hidden behind its new plain walls and protective corrugated-iron roof, the mosque at Kizimkazi Dimbani is believed to be the oldest Islamic building on the East African coast. The floriate Kufic inscription to the left of the *mihrab* (the interior niche indicating the direction of Mecca) dates the original mosque construction to AD1107 and identifies it as the work of Persian settlers. The silver pillars on either side of the niche are decorated with pounded mullet shells from the island of Mafia, and the two decorative clocks, which show Swahili time (six hours different from European time), were presented by local dignitaries. However, though the fine-quality coral detailing and columns date from this time, most of the building actually dates from an 18th-century reconstruction. The more recent additions of electrical sockets and flex have not been installed with a comparable degree of style or decoration.

Outside the mosque are some old tombs, a few decorated with pillars and one covered by a small makuti roof. The pieces of cloth tied to the edge of the tomb are prayer flags. The raised aqueduct that carried water from the well to the basin where hands and feet were washed is no longer used: running water is piped straight into a more recently built ablution area at the back of the mosque.

Archaeological evidence suggests that when the mosque was built Kizimkazi was a large walled city. Tradition holds that it was founded and ruled by a king, Kizi, and that the architect of the mosque itself was called Kazi. Legend has it that when the city was once attacked by invaders, Kizi prayed for divine intervention and the enemies were driven away by a swarm of bees. Later the enemies returned, but this time Kizi evaded them by disappearing into a cave on the shore. The cave entrance closed behind him and the enemies were thwarted once again.

Today, very little of the old city remains, but non-Muslims, both men and women, are welcome to visit the mosque and its surrounding tombs. It's normally locked, and you'll probably have to find the caretaker with the key (he lives nearby, but is usually under the trees near the beach a few hundred metres further down the road). Show respect by removing your shoes and covering bare arms and legs (this part of the island is very traditional so, out of politeness, your arms and legs should be covered anyway). On leaving you'll be shown the collection box and be able to make a donation.

Menai Bay excursions The Menai Bay Conservation Area has a number of picturesque, uninhabited islands and sandbanks to explore, as well as some fascinating marine life. It's well worth taking a full-day excursion, either through Fumba Beach Lodge (see *Where to stay*, page 399), if you're a guest, or with one of the two operators running trips: Safari Blue or Eco+Culture, see below. Take towels, and waterproof shoes for wading out to the boat across coral rock.

Tour operators

Eco+Culture ☎ 024 223 3731; m 0777 410873; e ecoculture@gmx.net; www.ecoculture-zanzibar. org. This full-day excursion on a traditional dhow departs from Unguja Ukuu, taking small groups (max 8 pax) past mangrove forests to the pristine beaches of Miwi, Nianembe or Kwale islands & accessible sandbanks. Snorkelling kit is provided, & a BBQ lunch is prepared on the beach. An English-speaking guide with knowledge of the surroundings & local traditions is always on board. The company's policy of limiting numbers on their trips, & taking out max 2 boats at any time, makes this a firm favourite. Trips leave Stone Town at 08.00, returning at 17.00. *US$70 pp for 4 pax, or US$55 pp for groups of 8.*

Safari Blue m 0777 423162; e adventure@ zanlink.com; www.safariblue.net. Traditional sailing dhows kitted out with safety & comfort in mind offer time to explore some of the bay's islands & sandbanks, guided snorkelling trips & watching for humpback & bottlenose dolphins, as well as a tasty lunch on Kwale Island. It may also be possible to have a go at sailing a *ngalawa*, to swim in a mangrove lagoon, & to go for an island walk. Bear in mind that there are no changing facilities, & note that these popular excursions can get very busy. Boats leave from close to Fumba Beach at 09.30, returning about 17.00. *US$60/30 adult/child. Stone Town transfer an additional US$60/vehicle.*

PEMBA ISLAND

Lying to the northeast of the larger island of Zanzibar, directly east of the mainland port of Tanga, Pemba is visited by few travellers. While tourist facilities on Zanzibar have mushroomed in recent years, Pemba has changed little over the last decade, making it a particularly attractive destination for those seeking to 'get away from it all'.

Pemba has a more undulating landscape than Zanzibar, and is more densely vegetated with both natural forest and plantation. The main agricultural product is cloves, which Pemba produces in far greater abundance than Zanzibar, with the attendant heady aroma permeating much of the island.

There is nothing on Pemba to compare with Zanzibar's Stone Town, but it does boast a number of attractive beaches, as well as some absorbing ruins dating to the Shirazi era. During holidays, traditional bullfights are sometimes held, presumably introduced during the years of Portuguese occupation. The island is also a centre for traditional medicine and witchcraft, and it is said that people seeking cures for spiritual or physical afflictions come from as far away as Uganda and the Congo to see Pemba's doctors.

Accommodation is limited to just a handful of lodges, hotels and guesthouses. Most are geared to the diver in search of the island's renowned underwater attractions, including some exciting drift dives and the possibility of seeing some of the larger pelagics.

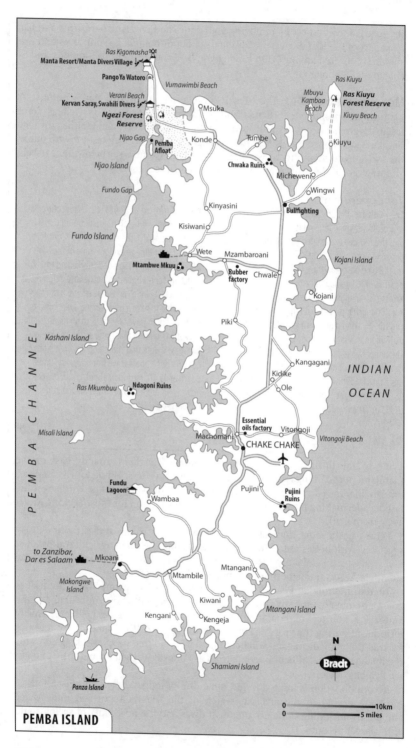

Ras Kigomasha

Manta Resort/Manta Divers Village

Pango Ya Watoro

Verani Beach

Kervan Saray, Swahili Divers

Ngezi Forest Reserve

Njao Gap

Pemba Afloat

Njao Island

Fundo Gap

Fundo Island

Kashani Island

Ras Mkumbuu
Ndagoni Ruins

Misali Island

Vumawimbi Beach

Msuka

Konde

Kinyasini

Kisiwani

Wete
Mzambaroani

Mtambwe Mkuu

Rubber factory

Chwale

Piki

Kidike
Ole

Kangagani

Essential oils factory

Machomani
Vitongoji

CHAKE CHAKE

Tumbe

Chwaka Ruins

Micheweni

Wingwi

Bullfighting

Kojani

Kojani Island

Mbuyu
Kambaa
Beach

Ras Kiuyu
Forest Reserve

Kiuyu Beach

Kiuyu

Ras Kiuyu

INDIAN

OCEAN

Vitongoji Beach

Fundu Lagoon

Wambaa

Pujini

Pujini Ruins

to Zanzibar,
Dar es Salaam   Mkoani

Makongwe
Island

Mtambile

Kiwani

Kengani

Kengeja

Mtangani

Mtangani Island

Shamiani Island

Panza Island

P E M B A   C H A N N E L

N

Bradt

0   10km
0   5 miles

PEMBA ISLAND

The island's largest town is Chake Chake. To the north lies the port of Wete, while to the southwest is the port of Mkoani, used by most passenger ferries. There are banks and post offices in Chake Chake, Wete and Mkoani, but only the Chake Chake bank can change travellers' cheques and none have ATMs, so taking cash is advisable. The main hospital is in Chake Chake, where there is also a ZTC office, opposite the ZTC Hotel.

GETTING THERE AND AWAY

By air ZanAir operates two daily flights between Dar es Salaam and Pemba: 09.00 from Dar via Zanzibar, arriving Pemba at 10.15, and a direct service, departing Dar at 13.45 and arriving in Pemba at 14.30. Fares on this route are US$300 return, including tax.

Coastal Aviation operates two daily flights from Dar to Pemba, which travel via Zanzibar then onwards to Tanga on the Tanzanian mainland. Flights depart Dar at 10.45 and 14.00, arriving in Zanzibar at 11.15 and 14.30 before arriving in Pemba at 11.45 and 15.05, with the later flight waiting for earlier connections from Selous and Ruaha. The one-way fare from Dar is US$130 and from Zanzibar US$95. The onward 20-minute flight to Tanga leaves Pemba at 15.15, and costs US$95. For return journeys, the flights leave Pemba at 12.00 and 16.35, arriving in Zanzibar at 12.30 and 17.05, and landing back in Dar at 13.20 and 17.35. Fares are the same as for the outbound trip.

Tropical Air also flies from Zanzibar to Pemba daily, leaving Zanzibar at 08:00 for the half-hour flight. Return flights depart Pemba at 10:05. Flights cost US$90 one way. These can be used to connect with flights to/from Tanga and Dar.

On leaving Pemba by air, there is a US$6 departure tax and be prepared to hand this over in cash.

By boat The main ferry port on Pemba is at Mkoani on the south end of the island.

🚢 **MV *Kilimanjaro* & *Seabus I, II & III*** Run by Azam Marine, these boats share the Dar–Zanzibar–Pemba route. Departures from Dar are at 07.00 on Mon, Thu & Sat, & after a 30 min stopover in Zanzibar the ferries leave at 09.30 for Pemba. Returning, ferries depart Pemba at 12.30 & Zanzibar at 16.00. These can all be booked online at www.azammarine.com. *One-way fare, non-residents from Dar–Pemba, US$75.*

🚢 ***Noora*** In theory, there is a weekly Sun service on the *Noora* between Tanga & Wete, leaving Wete at 08.00. The return journey on Tue leaves Tanga at 08.00 but timings are erratic & this service is none too reliable; for the current state of play, & for details of any other boats on this route, contact one of the tour operators in Chake Chake (see overleaf).

🚢 ***Sea Express I & II*** These speedboats owned by Fast Ferries Ltd commenced operations between Dar, Zanzibar & Mkoani on Pemba in 2005. At the time of writing, 1 of the 2 Fast Ferries was departing Zanzibar every day at 07.00, 09.45 or 10.00 (depending on the day) for the 3hr crossing to Pemba; for the return Pemba to Zanzibar, boats were departing at 11.00 or 13.30. Journeys from Dar to Zanzibar depart 07.00 & 09.00, arriving 2–3hrs later. *One-way fare, non-residents for Zanzibar–Pemba US$45; Dar–Pemba US$65.*

🚢 ***Serengeti*** The most reliable of the slow boats is the passenger ship *Serengeti*, operated by JAK Enterprises. The 6–8hr crossing between Zanzibar Town & Mkoani runs 3 times a week (currently Tue, Thu & Sun), departing at 22.00, returning the following day. *One–way US$20.*

GETTING AROUND Pemba's road system was given a boost in 2005 with the completion of the tarred road across the island from Mkoani to Konde, paid for by the World Bank. North of Konde, and elsewhere, however, most of the roads are pretty poor, with access to some of the outlying villages requiring **4x4** vehicles, particularly in the rainy season. A network of inexpensive **dala-dalas** connects most main points of interest on Pemba, starting up at 06.00 (or 04.00 during Ramadan), with the regularity of the service depending on the popularity of the route; one of the most frequent is the No 606, with several buses each day. Services to and from Mkoani are tied in closely with ship arrivals. Fares on the longer routes, such as Chake Chake to Mkoani, are around US$1 one way, with shorter trips about half that. The most useful routes are listed below (though note that dala-dalas will stop to collect or drop off passengers at any point along their route):

601	Wete to Konde	316	Chake Chake to Vitongoji (5km east of Chake Chake)
602	Chake Chake to Konde		
603	Chake Chake to Mkoani	319	Chake Chake to Pujini
606	Chake Chake to Wete	330	Chake Chake to Wambaa
305	Chake Chake to Wesha (Chake's port)	10	Wete to Wingwi/Micheweni

Other **buses** connect Chake Chake and, to a lesser extent, Wete with outlying villages; for details, check with the station manager at the bus depot in each town.

Most **tour companies** on the island can arrange car hire with a driver at around US$70 per day. Recommended drivers include Said (m 0777 430201) and Suleiman (m 0777 431793). **Self-drive** would cost around Tsh45,000 per day, but it is rare for tourists to hire cars in Pemba, and it's not the easiest thing to organise. With some effort it can be done through a few tour companies in Chake Chake, but it is not for the faint-hearted.

It's normally possible to arrange **bicycle hire** through your hotel reception for around US$10 per day, and **motorbike hire** for around US$22 per day.

CHAKE CHAKE This is the largest town on Pemba, and several centuries old, but it has never achieved a degree of importance comparable to Zanzibar Town. The busy market area and old port are pleasant to walk around, and seem very relaxed and untouristy after Zanzibar, but sightseeing is pretty much limited to the remains of an Omani fort near the modern hospital, part of which is now a good little museum.

Tour operators
For tours, transport bookings and most other travel services, **Treasure Island Travel & Tours** (\ *024 245 2278*), next to Le Tavern, has a range of tours and will help with ferry tickets.

Where to stay and eat
Chake Chake's renowned Old Mission Lodge, for years the home of Swahili Divers, has closed its doors and the operation has moved north to Kervan Saray Beach (see *Wete and the north, Where to stay and eat,* page 411), leaving something of an accommodation vacuum in the town. Fortunately, there are a couple of decent and central alternatives, of which the Samail is probably your best bet.

Pemba Island Hotel (16 rooms) \024 245 2215; e pembaislandhotel@yahoo.com. Run by strict Muslims, this welcoming & pleasant place is in the centre of town, just down the hill from the People's Bank of Zanzibar. En-suite rooms have dbl beds with AC/fans, nets, TV & fridge. In keeping with the hotel's Muslim ethos, no alcohol is permitted on the premises, & a marriage certificate is required for a couple to share a room. There's a rooftop restaurant. *US$50 dbl, B&B.*

Hotel Le Tavern (8 rooms) \024 245 2660. On the main street, opposite the People's Bank of Zanzibar, Le Tavern is above a small row of shops. If you're asking for directions; it's pronounced 'lay' Tavern. Clean, en-suite rooms with sgl beds have mosquito nets, fans & crackling TVs, but are in

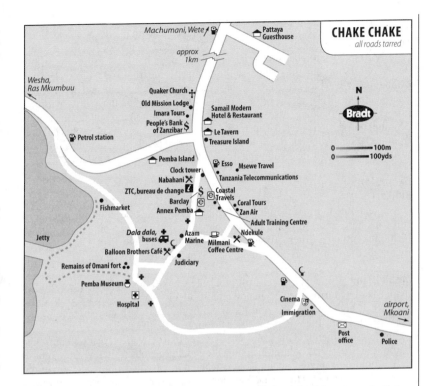

CHAKE CHAKE
all roads tarred

Machumani, Wete

approx
1km

Pattaya
Guesthouse

Wesha,
Ras Mkumbuu

Quaker Church
Old Mission Lodge
Imara Tours
People's Bank
of Zanzibar

Samail Modern
Hotel & Restaurant

Petrol station

Le Tavern
Treasure Island

Pemba Island
Clock tower
Nabahani
ZTC, bureau de change
Barclay
Annex Pemba
Fishmarket

Esso
Msewe Travel
Tanzania Telecommunications
Coastal
Travels
Coral Tours
Zan Air
Adult Training Centre
Ndekule

Jetty

Dala dala,
buses
Azam
Marine
Milmani
Coffee Centre
Balloon Brothers Café
Remains of Omani fort
Pemba Museum
Judiciary

Hospital

Cinema
Immigration

airport,
Mkoani

Post
office
Police

N

Bradt

0 ————— 100m
0 ————— 100yds

desperate need of a fresh coat of paint. *Meals to order around US$5. US$40 dbl, B&B.*

🏠 **Samail Modern Hotel & Restaurant**
(16 rooms) **m** 0776 627619/0718 010960;
e samailmodernhotel@yahoo.com. Samail opened in Apr 2012 in a 3-storey building next door to Le Tavern. Light & bright restaurant, where a selection of spiced chicken & fish dishes are served with rice or biriyani (US$3.50). Cakes, bread & fresh fruit juices make for quick snacks & there's even an ice cream machine. Upstairs, 16 identical & spacious rooms have AC & fans, & TVs; bathrooms are fine & functional. *US$50 dbl, B&B.*

Alternatively, to the north of the town, reached by taking a No 606 dala-dala towards Wete:

🏠 **Pemba Misali Sunset Beach**
(20 villas) 📞 024 223 3882 **m** 0775 044713/7;
e info@pembamisalibeach.com; www. pembamisalibeach.com. North of Chake Chake, near the village of Wesha, Pemba Misali Sunset Beach's row of 20 pea-green villas occupies a pretty waterfront spot, with sea views for all. Despite the bright exterior, a neutral colour scheme runs through the pleasant rooms. There's plenty of privacy & space, & outside a small terrace faces the sunset. Cantilevered over the sea, the restaurant serves up an eclectic mix of Indian, Arabic, Swahili & European meals along with the fisherman's daily catch. Diving is arranged through the onsite Pemba Misali Divers. Camping facilities are available. *US$120–150 dbl, B&B.*

🏠 **Pattaya Guesthouse** (6 rooms) **m** 0773 172445. This simple local guesthouse is fine if you want a feel of Pemba-style suburban living. Simple suppers of chicken & rice cost US$4 & must be ordered in advance. *US$30 dbl, B&B.*

What to see and do Chake Chake has a dusty charm that repays a walk through its small market and around its narrow streets and alleys crowded with shops selling a wide range of goods. Worth a visit is the **Pemba Museum** (⏲ *08.30–16.30 Mon–Fri, 09.00–16.00 Sat & Sun; admission US$3*). Located in part of the town's 18th-century Arab Fort, it retains the original wooden door, but other features were lost during restoration, and the cannons at the entrance came from Wete. Clearly laid out exhibits cover every aspect of Pemba's history, economy and culture and of particular interest are the display on the ruins of Pemba, and the room on the island's maritime history and boatbuilding. Also, several rooms are set out to represent the interior of a Swahili house, while related displays focus on individual aspects of Swahili culture, from initiation and burial rituals to the use of herbal plants and traditional musical instruments. Visitors are accompanied around the exhibitions by a guide.

Excursions
Kidike (⏲ *08.00–18.00 daily; admission US$3.50*) Just 7km north of Chake Chake is Kidike, home to more than half of Pemba's flying foxes. Several **tour operators** run trips here, and individual drivers charge around US$25 from Chake Chake, including entrance. Alternatively you can take a **dala–dala** from Chake Chake, then walk the 45 minutes or so along the 3.5km track to the reserve.

Misali Island This small island west of Chake Chake, an easy boat ride from the main island, is surrounded by a coral reef. Its idyllic beach is good for swimming, whether at high or low tide, and it's worth bringing a mask and snorkel for the excellent reef fish. The waters are also a favourite with divers.

The forested interior of the island, criss-crossed by a network of clear walking trails, harbours a rich variety of birds including the endemic Pemba white-eye and sunbird.

The notorious pirate Captain Kidd is reputed to have had a hideout here in the 17th century, but today the island and the surrounding reef are incorporated within the Misali Island Marine Conservation Area.

Ras Mkumbuu Ruins About 14km west of Chake Chake, these well-preserved ruins lie at the tip of a long peninsula. Thought to have been one of the largest towns on the coast during the 11th century, Ras Mkumbuu may also have been the site of the earlier port of Qanbalu. Today, the remains of a mosque are visible, albeit overgrown, along with several pillar tombs.

The most enjoyable way to reach Ras Mkumbuu is by **boat**, perhaps combined with a visit to Misali Island. While there is a road from Chake Chake, the final 5km is negotiable only on foot or by bike.

Pujini Ruins This site is about 10km southeast of Chake Chake. You can walk there and back in a day, but it is easier to travel by **hired bike** or **car**. The ruins are the remains of a 13th-century Swahili town, known locally as Mkame Ndume ('milker of men'), after a despotic king who forced the inhabitants to carry large stones for the town walls while shuffling on their buttocks. The overgrown remains of the walls and ditches can be seen, as can a walkway which joined the town to the shore, some wide stairways that presumably allowed access to the defensive ramparts, and the site of the town's well.

Chwaka Ruins More ruins can be found on the island's northeast coast, close to the village of Tumbe (whose fish market is worth a visit in itself). Dating from as early as the 9th century, the town of Chwaka, or Harouni, was active as a port in the 15th century. In addition to the ruins of two small mosques, there are also remains of houses and tombs.

Ngezi Forest Reserve (⏰ *07.30–15.30 daily; admission short tour US$5 pp, longer tour or birdwatching US$10; transit fee US$2; night walks by prior arrangement*) This small reserve in the north protects the last of the indigenous forest that used to cover much of the island. The forest supports an interesting range of vegetation, including the most substantial patch of tropical moist forest on Pemba. It is a good place for birders, who can seek out the Pemba white-eye, green pigeon, scops owl and sunbird, all of which are endemic to the island. Mammals include the endemic Pemba flying fox, Kirk's red colobus, vervet monkey, blue duiker, marsh mongoose and a feral population of European boars, introduced by the Portuguese and left untouched by their Muslim successors, who don't eat pork. A short nature trail runs through the forest. Not far from here, the open sandy beach at Vumawimbi is a great place to chill out.

The lighthouse (*Admission US$2 pp*) The west of the Ngezi peninsula is flanked by the long expanse of **Verani Beach**, with a lighthouse at Ras Kigomasha marking its northern tip. At low tide, it's possible to walk along the beach to the lighthouse, but when the water is up you'll need to take the path across the fields. If you want to climb to the top, ask at the house nearby for the lighthouse keeper; the views from the top both out to sea and across Pemba certainly repay the effort.

MKOANI AND THE SOUTH The smallest of the three main towns on Pemba, Mkoani is also the busiest tourist centre, thanks to the boat services connecting it to Zanzibar and Dar es Salaam.

Where to stay and eat

Fundu Lagoon (18 rooms) Reservations ☎024 223 2926; hotel m 0777 438668; e info@fundulagoon.com; www.fundulagoon.com. In the south of the island, this upmarket & romantic hideaway is accessed by boat from Mkoani, & is extremely popular with honeymooners. En-suite tented rooms, with verandas overlooking the sea, nestle among the trees. Meals, predominantly seafood, are served in the restaurant or at the end of the jetty, with regular BBQ & Swahili nights. Snorkelling, kayaking & fishing are on offer, & there's a fully equipped dive centre; less strenuous are sunset dhow cruises, boat trips to Misali Island, & village excursions. There's also a treatment room, & a games room with satellite TV. *US$740–1,500 dbl, FB.*

Pemba Eco Lodge (5 bungalows) m 0732 495077/88; e info@pembalodge.com; www.

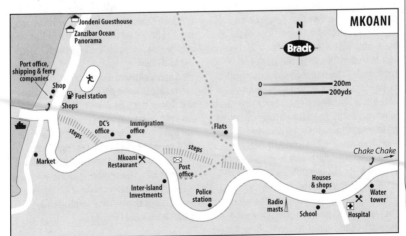

pembalodge.com; ⊕ May–Mar. Pemba Eco Lodge, with an emphasis on the 'eco', is the vision of enthusiastic Nassor Ali. The 4 dbl & 1 family timber frame bungalows are constructed from natural materials, feature solar-powered lighting & composting toilets, but also a building design that harnesses the breeze from the Pemba Channel. Access to the lodge is an adventure by traditional (though motorised) boat through the beautiful mangroves, dinner is 'catch of the day' cooked over a gas flame, & there's an honesty bar. Come for ecological sensibility & peace on a deserted beach, not luxury. *US$440 dbl, FB.*

⌂ **Zanzibar Ocean Panorama**
(4 rooms) \024 245 6166 m 0773 545418; e info@zanzibaroceanpanorama.com; www.zanzibaroceanpanorama.com. Zanzibar Ocean Panorama opened in 2012 – the name inspired by the excellent sea view from its hillside location. Don't let the slightly ramshackle exterior of the bungalows put you off; inside, the rooms are simple but better than expected, with cool stone floors & reasonable facilities. Outside, each has a tidy terrace with a hammock facing the sea. B/fast is served in the shaded terrace restaurant (other meals with advanced notice, dinner $15). *US$50 dbl, B&B.*

⌂ **Jondeni Guesthouse** (8 rooms) \024 245 6042; e pembablue@hotmail.com. To the north of town, a dusty 10–15min walk uphill from the port, this bungalow is set in lush gardens, & the friendly staff make staying here a pleasure. Clean, simple rooms – some en suite – have fans & mosquito nets & there's a 6-bed dorm. Drinks & meals (around US$7) are taken on the shady terrace overlooking the sea. Snorkelling, sailing & fishing trips, & island tours can be arranged. *US$30 dbl, B&B.*

WETE AND THE NORTH The quiet and pleasant town of Wete, the second largest on the island, lies on a large inlet on the northwest coast.

⌂ **Where to stay and eat** Wete itself has several small guesthouses, as well as the run-down Wete Hotel, but most visitors head north to one of the beach lodges. All the hotels and guesthouses serve food with advance notice, and Wete also has a choice of local eating houses, most open until the last buses have left at 16.00. The pick of the eateries are: **Green Garden Refreshments**, a pleasant open-air café selling omelette and chips or beans and rice for around US$1; **Times Restaurant**, is worth going to for the AC alone, but it also serves up good pizza, curries and grilled meats (all US$4) accompanied by English language newspapers; and up towards clocktower, the **Al Falahy Hotel**, for tasty snacks and fried bread.

In town

⌂ **Pemba Crown Hotel** (12 rooms) \024 245 4191; m 0777 4936667; e sales@pembacrown.com; www.pembacrown.com. Pemba Crown is a 3-storey hotel above a row of shops on the main street, right in the centre of Wete. It's Wete's best accommodation. The rooms are clean & comfortable, & the staff smiley & helpful. Spotless bedrooms come with AC, fans & TVs. All rooms have a large balcony looking out over a busy street, which may not be the most attractive of views, but it's interesting to see townsfolk going about their everyday business. B/fast is the only meal served, but it's central enough to walk to any of the local cafés for a bite. *US$30–60 dbl, B&B.*

⌂ **Sharook Guesthouse** (5 rooms) \024 245 4386; e sharookguest@yahoo.com. Sharook is in the lower part of town, on a quiet side street near the market & bus station. It's a small, clean, family-run place with a peaceful & friendly atmosphere. With its own generator, the guesthouse offers constant running water & functioning TV. Dinner, with local dishes, must be ordered well in advance. Bike hire (US$10 per day) can be arranged, as can a range of tours around the island. *Dinner US$10. US$40 dbl, B&B.*

⌂ **Sharook Riviera Grand Lodge** (8 rooms) Located in a sleepy, residential area overlooking the harbour, this is the annex to the above & is not nearly as magnificent as the name suggests. The building is newly constructed, & inside are 8 sgl & dbl rooms plus a dorm. The communal space is made up of the b/fast room & a lounge with a computer & TV. Meals can be ordered in advance & are prepared fresh; juices, water & soft drinks are served but no alcohol. There are plans for a roof-top restaurant. *US$40 dbl, B&B.*

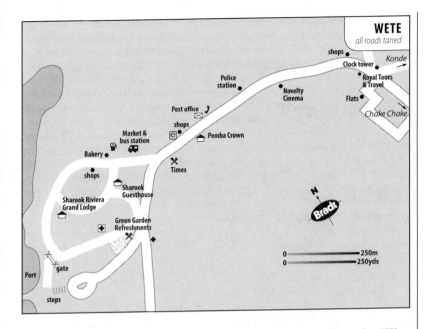

shops
Clock tower
Konde
Royal Tours
& Travel
Police
station
Novelty
Cinema
Flats
Chake Chake
Post office
shops
Pemba Crown
Market &
bus station
Bakery
Times
shops
Sharook
Guesthouse
Sharook Riviera
Grand Lodge
Green Garden
Refreshments
gate
Port
steps

N

Bradt

0 _____ 250m
0 _____ 250yds

North of Wete

The Manta Resort (17 rooms) m 0776 718852; e stacey@themantaresort.com; www. themantaresort.com; ⏳ Jun–Apr. Overlooking the northern end of Verani Beach, in a truly stunning location, The Manta Resort is a smart beach resort catering to divers & landlubbers alike. There are 6 sea-front villas built on stilts affording a panoramic view across the Pemba Channel, plus garden rooms, some family friendly, some basic. A central area serves as dining room, bar, lounge & lobby, with a big terrace looking out to sea & steps leading down to a powder-sand beach, with a 2-tiered beach bar: beware sea urchins. There is a spa, pool & a PADI dive centre. Aside from watersports, guests benefit from a location that boasts a wide range of birdlife & some interesting walks to the lighthouse, Vumawimbi Beach & Ngezi Forest (5km). *US$500 dbl, all inclusive.*

Kervan Saray Beach (22 rooms) m 0773 176737/8; e resort@kayakpemba.com; www. kervansaraybeach.com. Owned & managed by Turkish adventurer Raf Jah & his Dutch anthropologist wife, Cisca, this is a simple & unpretentious affair. Kervan Saray's thatched, cottages are just above a sand & rock beach that is excellent for swimming at high tide. 11 bungalows contain 22 cool & spacious rooms, which are really lovely with oodles of colour. Don't come expecting luxuries; come instead for the informal friendliness of the place & the marine excursions. The lodge boasts a PADI 5* Resort Dive Centre with a team who are experienced in the surrounding reefs & sometimes challenging waters. Kayaking (*$70 pp for a half day*), fishing, local hikes & trips to the Ngezi Forest are also on offer. *US$275 dbl, FB.*

Appendix 1

LANGUAGE

SWAHILI Swahili, the official language of Tanzania, is a Bantu language that developed on the East African coast about 1,000 years ago and has since adopted many words from Arabic, Portuguese, Indian, German and English. It spread into the Tanzanian interior along with the 19th-century slave caravans and is now the lingua franca in Tanzania and Kenya, and is also spoken in parts of Uganda, Malawi, Rwanda, Burundi, Congo, Zambia and Mozambique.

In Dar es Salaam, Zanzibar, Arusha, Moshi and the northern game reserves, you can get by with English well enough. If you travel in other parts of the country, you will need to understand some Swahili. And even if you are sticking to tourist areas, it is polite and can be useful to know a bit of Swahili.

There are numerous Swahili–English dictionaries on the market, as well as phrasebooks and grammar books, and most can be ordered from online sellers such as Amazon. For anybody serious about learning Swahili, Joan Russell's longstanding but recently upgraded *Teach Yourself Swahili* (TY Complete Courses, 2010) is the best choice, and the book comes with two invaluable CDs, though it is quite pricey at around US$40. A useful dictionary for travellers is Nicholas Awde's *Swahili-English/English-Swahili Practical Dictionary* (Hippocrene Books, 2000), which costs around US$30. For casual visitors, the Lonely Planet or Rough Guide *Swahili* phrasebooks are both very handy and cost less than US$10. Also recommended is *Swahili for Beginners*, the 5th edition of which was published in Tanzania by Kiswahili na Utamaduni (KIU) in 2011.

For short-stay visitors, all these books have practical limitations. Wading through a phrasebook to find the expression you want can take ages, while trying to piece together a sentence from a dictionary is virtually impossible. In addition, most books available are in Kenyan Swahili, which often differs greatly from the purer version spoken in Tanzania.

The following introduction is not a substitute for a dictionary or phrasebook. It is not so much an introduction to Swahili as an introduction to communicating with Swahili-speakers. Before researching this guide, my East African travels had mainly been in Kenya, Uganda and parts of Tanzania where English is relatively widely spoken. We learnt the hard way how little English is spoken in most of Tanzania. I hope this section will help anyone in a similar position to get around a great deal more easily than we did at first.

Pronunciation Vowel sounds are pronounced as follows:

a	like the a in *father*
e	like the e in *wet*
i	like the ee in *free*, but less drawn out
o	somewhere between the o in *no* and the word *awe*
u	similar to the oo in *food*

The double vowel in words like *choo* or *saa* is pronounced like the single vowel, but drawn out for longer. Consonants are in general pronounced as they are in English. *L* and *r* are often interchangeable, so that *Kalema* is just as often spelt or pronounced *Karema*. The same is true of *b* and *v*.

You will be better understood if you speak slowly and thus avoid the common English-speaking habit of clipping vowel sounds – listen to how Swahili-speakers pronounce their vowels. In most Swahili words there is a slight emphasis on the second last syllable.

Basic grammar Swahili is a simple language in so far as most words are built from a root word using prefixes. To go into all of the prefixes here would probably confuse people new to Swahili – and it would certainly stretch my knowledge of the language. They are covered in depth in most Swahili grammar books and dictionaries. The following are some of the most important:

Pronouns

ni	me	*tu*	us
u	you	*wa*	they
m-	yu (plural)	*a*	he or she

Tenses

na	present
ta	future
li	past
ku	infinitive

Tenses (negative)

si	present
sita	future
siku	past
haku	negative, infinitive

From a root word such as *taka* (want) you might build the following phrases:

Unataka soda	You want a soda
Tutataka soda	We will want a soda
Alitaka soda	He/she wanted a soda

In practice, *ni* and *tu* are often dropped from simple statements. It would be more normal to say *nataka soda* than *ninataka soda*.

In many situations there is no interrogative mode in Swahili; the difference between a question and a statement lies in the intonation.

Greetings There are several common greetings in Swahili. Although allowances are made for tourists, it is rude to start talking to someone without first using one or another formal greeting. The first greeting you will hear is *Jambo*. This is reserved for tourists, and a perfectly adequate greeting, but it is never used between Tanzanians (the more correct *Hujambo*, to which the reply is *Sijambo*, is used in some areas).

The most widely used greeting is *Habari?*, which more or less means *What news?* The normal reply is *Nzuri* (good). *Habari* is rarely used by Tanzanians on its own; you might well be asked *Habari ya safari?*, *Habari yako?* or *Habari gani?* (very loosely, *How is your journey?*, *How are you?* and *How are things?* respectively). *Nzuri* is the polite reply to any such request.

A more fashionable greeting among younger people is *Mambo*, especially on the coast and in large towns. Few tourists recognise this greeting; reply *Safi* or *Poa* and you've made a friend.

In Tanzanian society it is polite to greet elders with the expression *Shikamu*. To the best of my knowledge this means *I hold your feet*. In many parts of rural Tanzania, children will greet you in this way, often with their heads bowed and so quietly it sounds like *Sh...oo*.

Don't misinterpret this by European standards (or other parts of Africa where *Mzungu give me shilling* is the phrase most likely to be offered up by children); most Tanzanian children are far too polite to swear at you. The polite answer is *Marahaba* (I'm delighted).

Another word often used in greeting is *Salama*, which means peace. When you enter a shop or hotel reception, you will often be greeted by a friendly *Karibu*, which means *Welcome*. *Asante sana* (thank you very much) seems an appropriate response.

If you want to enter someone's house, shout *Hodi!* It basically means *Can I come in?* but would be used in the same situation as *Anyone home?* would in English. The normal response will be *Karibu* or *Hodi*.

It is respectful to address an old man as *Mzee*. *Bwana*, which means *Mister*, might be used as a polite form of address to a male who is equal or senior to you in age or rank, but who is not a *Mzee*. Older women can be addressed as *Mama*.

The following phrases will come in handy for small talk:

Where have you just come from?	*(U)natoka wapi?*
I have come from Moshi	*(Ni)natoka Moshi*
Where are you going?	*(U)nakwenda wapi?*
We are going to Arusha	*(Tu)nakwenda Arusha*
What is your name?	*Jina lako nani?*
My name is Philip	*Jina langu ni Philip*
Do you speak English?	*Unasema KiIngereza?*
I speak a little Swahili	*Ninasema KiSwahili kidogo*
Sleep peacefully	*Lala salama*
Bye for now	*Kwaheri sasa*
Have a safe journey	*Safari njema*
Come again (welcome again)	*Karibu tena*
I don't understand	*Sielewi*
Say that again	*Sema tena*

Numbers

1	*moja*	30	*thelathini*
2	*mbili*	40	*arobaini*
3	*tatu*	50	*hamsini*
4	*nne*	60	*sitini*
5	*tano*	70	*sabini*
6	*sita*	80	*themanini*
7	*saba*	90	*tisini*
8	*nane*	100	*mia (moja)*
9	*tisa*	150	*mia moja na hamsini*
10	*kumi*	155	*mia moja hamsini na tano*
11	*kumi na moja*	200	*mia mbili*
20	*ishirini*	1,000	*elfu (moja)* or *mia kumi*

Swahili time Many travellers to Tanzania fail to come to grips with Swahili time. It is essential, especially if you are catching buses in remote areas. The Swahili clock starts at the equivalent of 06.00, so that *saa moja asubuhi* (hour one in the morning) is 07.00, *saa mbili jioni* (hour two in the evening) is 20.00, etc. To ask the time in Swahili, say *Saa ngapi?*

Always check whether times are standard or Swahili. If you are told a bus leaves at nine, ask whether the person means *saa tatu* or *saa tisa*. Some English-speakers will convert to standard time, others won't. This does not apply so much where people are used to tourists, but it's advisable to get in the habit of checking.

Day-to-day queries The following covers such activities as shopping, finding a room, etc. It's worth remembering that most Swahili words for modern objects, or things for which there would not have been a pre-colonial word, are often similar to the English. Examples are *resiti* (receipt), *gari* (car), *polisi* (police), *posta* (post office) and – my favourite – *stesheni masta* (station master). In desperation, it's always worth trying the English word with an *ee* sound on the end.

Shopping The normal way of asking for something is *Ipo?* or *Zipo?*, which roughly means *Is there?*, so if you want a cold drink you would ask *Soda baridi zipo?* The response will normally be *Ipo* or *Kuna* (there is) or *Hamna* or *Hakuna* (there isn't). Once you've established the shop has what you want, you might say *Nataka koka mbili* (I want two Cokes). To check the price, ask *Shillingi ngapi?* It may be simpler to ask for a brand name: Omo (washing powder) or Blue Band (margarine), for instance.

Accommodation The Swahili for guesthouse is *nyumba ya wageni*. In my experience *gesti* works as well, if not better. If you are looking for something a bit more upmarket, bear in mind *hoteli* means restaurant. We found self-contained (*self-contendi*) to be a good keyword in communicating this need. To find out whether there is a vacant room, ask *Nafasi zipo?*

Getting around The following expressions are useful for getting around:

Where is there a guesthouse?	*Ipo wapi gesti?*
Is there a bus to Moshi?	*Ipo basi kwenda Moshi?*
When does the bus depart?	*Basi itaondoka saa ngapi?*
When will the vehicle arrive?	*Gari litafika saa ngapi?*
How far is it?	*Bale gani?*
I want to pay now	*Ninataka kulipa sasa*

Foodstuffs

avocado	*parachichi*	food	*chakula*
bananas	*ndizi*	fruit(s)	*(ma)tunda*
bananas (cooked)	*matoke/batoke*	goat	*(nyama ya) mbuzi*
beef	*(nyama ya) ngombe*	mango(es)	*(ma)embe*
bread (loaf)	*mkate*	maize porridge	
bread (slice)	*tosti*	(thin, eaten at	
coconuts	*nazi*	breakfast)	*uji*
coffee	*kahawa*	maize porridge	
chicken	*kuku*	(thick, eaten as	
egg(s)	*(ma)yai*	staple with	
fish	*samaki*	relish)	*ugali*
meat	*nyama*	rice	*pilau*
milk	*maziwa*	salt	*chumvi*
onions	*vitungu*	sauce	*mchuzi/supu*
orange(s)	*(ma)chungwa*	sugar	*sukari*
pawpaw	*papai*	tea	*chai*
pineapple	*nanasi*	(black/milky)	*(ya rangi/maziwa)*
potatoes	*viazi*	vegetable	*mboga*
rice (cooked plain)	*wali*	water	*maji*
rice (uncooked)	*mchele*		

Days of the week

Monday	*Jumatatu*	Friday	*Ijumaa*
Tuesday	*Jumanne*	Saturday	*Jumamosi*
Wednesday	*Jumatano*	Sunday	*Jumapili*
Thursday	*Alhamisi*		

Useful words and phrases

afternoon	*alasiri*	night	*usiku*
again	*tena*	no	*hapana*
and	*na*	no problem	*hakuna matata*
ask (I am		now	*sasa*
asking for …)	*omba (ninaomba …)*	only	*tu*
big	*kubwa*	OK or fine	*sawa*
boat	*meli*	passenger	*abiria*
brother	*kaka*	pay	*kulipa*
bus	*basi*	person (people)	*mtu (watu)*
car (or any		please	*tafadhali*
vehicle)	*gari*	road/street	*barabara/mtaa*
child (children)	*mtoto (watoto)*	shop	*duka*
cold	*baridi*	sister	*dada*
come here	*njoo*	sleep	*kulala*
excuse me	*samahani*	slowly	*polepole*
European(s)	*mzungu (wazungu)*	small	*kidogo*
evening	*jioni*	soon	*bado kidogo*
far away	*mbale kubwa*	sorry	*pole*
father	*baba*	station	*stesheni*
friend	*rafiki*	stop	*simama*
good	*mzuri*	straight or direct	*moja kwa moja*
(very good)	*(mzuri sana)*	thank you	*asante*
goodbye	*kwaheri*	(very much)	*(sana)*
here	*hapa*	there is	*iko/kuna*
hot	*moto*	there is not	*hamna/hakuna*
later	*bado*	thief (thieves)	*mwizi (wawizi)*
like	*penda*	time	*saa*
(I would like …)	*(ninapenda …)*	today	*leo*
many	*sana*	toilet	*choo*
me	*mimi*	tomorrow	*kesho*
money	*pesa/shillingi*	want	*taka*
more	*ingine/tena*	(I want …)	*(ninataka …)*
morning	*asubuhi*	where	*(iko) wapi*
mother	*mama*	yes	*ndiyo*
nearby	*karibu/mbale*	yesterday	*jana*
	kidogo	you	*wewe*

Useful conjunctions include *ya* (of) and *kwa* (to or by). Many expressions are created using these; for instance *stesheni ya basi* is a bus station and *barabara kwa Mbale* is the road to Mbale.

Health

flu	*mafua*	recover	*pona*
fever	*homa*	treatment	*tiba*

malaria	*malaria*	cure	*ponyesha*
cough	*kikohozi*	injection	*sindano*
vomit	*kutapika*	bone	*mfupa*
swollen	*uvimbe*	death	*mauti*
injure	*jeraha*	to examine	*vipimo*
weak	*dhaifu*	to fall down	*kuanguka*
pain	*maumizu*	to bleed	*kutokwa na damu*

MAA

Emma Thomson

Maa is the language of the Maasai. It does not exist in written form, so the spellings below are approximate.

Greetings

Father/elderly man, I greet you	*Papa … supai*
Warrior/middle-aged man, I greet you	*Apaayia … supai*
Young woman, I greet you	*Siangiki … supai*
Boy, I greet you	*Ero … supai*
Girl, I greet you	*Nairo … supai*
Mother/middle-aged woman, I greet you	*Yeyio … takwenya*
Grandmother/elder woman, I greet you	*Koko … takwenya*
How are you?	*Koree indae?*
Are you fine/healthy?	*Kira sedan/kira biot?*
My name is …	*Aji …*
What is your name?	*Kekijaa enkarna?*
I come from …	*Aingwaa …*
Where do you come from?	*Kaingwaa?*
Goodbye	*Serae*

Numbers

1	*nabo*	13	*tomon ok ooni*
2	*are*	14	*tomon o ongwan*
3	*ooni*	15	*tomon o imiet*
4	*ongwan*	16	*tomon o ille*
5	*imiet*	17	*tomon o opishana*
6	*ille*	18	*tomon o isiet*
7	*naapishana*	19	*tomon o odo*
8	*isiet*	20	*tikitam*
9	*naudo*	100	*iip nabo*
10	*tomon*	1,000	*enchata nabo*
11	*tomon o obo*	2,000	*inkeek are*
12	*tomon o are*	3,000	*inkeek ooni*

Shopping

How much does it cost?	*Empesai aja?*
I want/need it	*Ayieu*
I don't want/need it today	*Mayieu taata*
I will buy this one	*Ainyang ena*
I will buy these	*Ainyang kuna*
I won't buy anything today	*Mainyang onyo taata*
I haven't got any money	*Maata empesai*

Useful words and phrases

Thank you	*Ashe*
Thank you very much	*Ashe naleng*
Take it (used when giving a gift)	*Ngo*
I receive it (used when accepting a gift)	*Au*
Leave me/it alone (to children)	*Tapala*
Go outside (to children)	*Shomo boo*
May I take a picture?	*Aosh empicha?*
Yes	*Ee*
OK	*Ayia*
No, I don't want you to	*A-a, mayieu*
Stop it	*Tapala*
Expression of sympathy (like '*pole*' in Swahili)	*Kwa adei*

AFRICAN ENGLISH Although many Tanzanians speak a little English, not all speak it fluently. Africans who speak English tend to structure their sentences in a similar way to how they would in their own language: they speak English with Bantu grammar.

For a traveller, knowing how to communicate in African English is as important as speaking a bit of Swahili, if not more so. It is noticeable that travellers who speak English as a second language often communicate with Africans more easily than first-language English-speakers.

The following ground rules should prove useful when you speak English to Africans:

- *Unasema Kilngereza?* (Do you speak English?). This small but important question may seem obvious. It isn't.
- Greet in Swahili then ask in English. It is advisable to go through the Swahili greetings (even *Jambo* will do) before you plough ahead and ask a question. Firstly, it is rude to do otherwise; secondly, most Westerners feel uncomfortable asking a stranger a straight question. If you have already greeted the person, you'll feel less need to preface a question with phrases like 'I'm terribly sorry' and 'Would you mind telling me', which will confuse someone who speaks limited English.
- Speak slowly and clearly. There is no need, as some travellers do, to speak as if you are talking to a three year old; just speak naturally.
- Phrase questions simply and with Swahili inflections. 'This bus goes to Dodoma?' is better than 'Could you tell me whether this bus is going to Dodoma?'; 'You have a room?' is better than 'Is there a vacant room?' If you are not understood, don't keep repeating the same question; find a different way of phrasing it.
- Listen to how people talk to you, and not only for their inflections. Some English words are in wide use, others are not. For instance, lodging is more likely to be understood than accommodation.
- Make sure the person you are talking to understands you. Try to avoid asking questions that can be answered with a yes or no. People may well agree with you simply to be polite.
- Keep calm. No-one is at their best when they arrive at a crowded bus station after an all-day bus ride; it is easy to be short-tempered when someone cannot understand you. Be patient and polite; it's you who doesn't speak the language.

GLOSSARY

Acacia woodland	type of woodland dominated by thorny, thin-leafed trees of the genus *Acacia*

AICC	Arusha International Conference Centre
banda	a hut, often used to refer to hutted accommodation at hotels and lodges
boma	traditional enclosure or homestead; administration building of the colonial era
bui-bui	black cloth worn veil-like by women, mainly in Islamic parts of the coast
bwana	mister (polite term of address to an adult man)
brachystegia woodland	type of woodland dominated by broad-leaved trees of the genus *Brachystegia*
Chama Cha Mapinduzi	ruling party of Tanzania since independence (CCM)
cichlid	family of colourful fish found in the Rift Valley lakes
closed canopy forest	true forest in which the trees have an interlocking canopy
dala-dala	light vehicle, especially minibus, serving as public transport
dhow	traditional wooden seafaring vessel
duka	kiosk
endemic	unique to a specific country or biome
exotic	not indigenous; for instance plantation trees such as pines and eucalyptus
forex bureau	bureau de change
fly-camping	temporary private camp set up remotely from a permanent lodge
guesthouse	cheap local hotel
hoteli	local restaurant
indigenous	naturally occurring
kanga	colourful printed cloth worn by most Tanzanian women
KIA	Kilimanjaro International Airport
kitenge (pl *vitenge*)	similar to *kanga*
koppie (or *kopje*)	Afrikaans word used to refer to a small hill such as those on the Serengeti
mandazi	deep-fried doughball, essentially the local variant on a doughnut
mishkaki	meat (usually beef) kebab
mzungu (pl *wazungu*)	white person
NCA	Ngorongoro Conservation Area
ngoma	Swahili drumming
Omani era	period when the coast was ruled by the Sultan of Oman, especially 19th century
self-contained room	room with en-suite shower and toilet
savanna	grassland studded with trees
Shirazi era	medieval period during which settlers from Shiraz (Iran) dominated coastal trade
taarab	Swahili music and dance form associated particularly with Zanzibar
TANAPA	Tanzania National Parks
ugali	stodgy porridge-like staple made with ground maize meal
woodland	area of trees lacking a closed canopy

Appendix 2

BOOKS

History and biography A limited number of single-volume histories covering East Africa and/or Tanzania are in print, but most are rather textbook-like in tone, and I've yet to come across one that is likely to hold much appeal for the casual reader. About the best bet is Iliffe's *Modern History of Tanganyika* (Cambridge, 1979). For a more general perspective, Oliver and Fage's *Short History of Africa* (Penguin, sixth edition, 1988) is rated as providing the best concise overview of African history, but it's too curt, dry, wide-ranging and dated to make for a satisfying read.

If I were to recommend one historical volume to a visitor to Tanzania, it would have to be Richard Hall's *Empires of the Monsoon: A History of the Indian Ocean and its Invaders* (HarperCollins, 1996). This highly focused and reasonably concise book will convey a strong historical perspective to the general reader, as a result of the author's storytelling touch and his largely successful attempt to place the last 1,000 years of East and southern African history in an international framework.

Considerably more bulky, and working an even broader canvas, John Reader's *Africa: A Biography of the Continent* (Penguin, 1997) has met with universal praise as perhaps the most readable and accurate attempt yet to capture the sweep of African history for the general reader.

Several books document specific periods and/or regions in African history. Good coverage of the coastal Swahili, who facilitated the medieval trade between the gold fields of Zimbabwe and the Arab world, is provided in J de Vere Allen's *Swahili Origins* (James Currey, 1992). Among the better popular works on the early era of European exploration are Hibbert's *Africa Explored: Europeans in the Dark Continent* (Penguin, 1982) and two excellent biographies by Tim Jeal: *Livingstone: Yale Nota Bene* (Yale University Press, 2001) and *Stanley: The Impossible Life of Africa's Greatest Explorer* (Faber & Faber, 2007), the latter voted Sunday Times 'Biography of the Year' in 2007. For an erudite, compelling and panoramic account of the decade that turned Africa on its head, Thomas Pakenham's gripping 600-page tome *The Scramble for Africa* was aptly described by one reviewer as '*Heart of Darkness* with the lights switched on'. For a glimpse into the colonial era itself, just about everybody who sets foot in East Africa ends up reading Karen Blixen's autobiographical *Out of Africa* (Penguin, 1937).

Field guides and natural history

General East African Wildlife by Philip Briggs (Bradt, 2008) is a handy and lavishly illustrated one-stop handbook to the fauna of East Africa, with detailed sections on the region's main habitats, varied mammals, birds, reptiles and insects. It's the ideal companion for first-time visitors whose interest in wildlife extends beyond the Big Five but who don't want to carry a library of reference books.

Mammals Dorst and Dandelot's *Field Guide to the Larger Mammals of Africa* (Collins) and Haltennorth's *Field Guide to the Mammals of Africa (including Madagascar)* (Collins), were the standard mammal field guides for years, but have been rendered obsolete by several newer and better books. The pick of these, especially if your interest extends to bats and other small mammals, is Jonathan Kingdon's *Field Guide to African Mammals* (Princeton University Press, 1997), which also contains a goldmine of information about the evolutionary relationships of modern species. Its more compact counterpart is the same author's *Kingdon Pocket Guide to African Mammals* (Princeton Pocket Guides, 2005). Chris and Tilde Stuart's *Field Guide to the Larger Mammals of Africa* (Struik Publishers, 1997) is well suited to space-conscious travellers who are serious about putting a name to all the large mammals they see. For backpackers, the same authors' *Southern, Eastern and Central African Mammals: A Photographic Guide* (Struik Publishers, 1993) is far lighter and still gives adequate detail for 152 mammal species.

Not a field guide in the conventional sense so much as a guide to mammalian behaviour, Richard Estes's superb *The Safari Companion* (Green Books UK, Chelsea Green USA, Russell Friedman Books South Africa, 1992) is well organised and informative but rather bulky for casual safari-goers.

Birds Zimmerman, Turner, Pearson, Willet and Pratt's *Birds of Kenya and Northern Tanzania* (Russell Friedman Books, 1996) is a contender for the best single-volume field guide available to any African country or region. I would recommend it to any serious birder sticking to northern Tanzania, since it provides complete coverage for the northern safari circuit, the Usambara and Pare mountains and Pemba Island, and although it stops short of Dar es Salaam and Zanzibar, this wouldn't be a major limitation. Unfortunately, it's too bulky, heavy and expensive to be of interest to any but the most bird-obsessed of backpackers, and the gaps in its coverage would limit its usefulness south of Dar es Salaam or in the Lake Victoria and Lake Tanganyika region.

For any birding itinerary extending to parts of Tanzania west of the Serengeti or south of the Usambara, the best option is the *Field Guide to the Birds of East Africa* by Stevenson and Fanshawe. Published in early 2002, this field guide provides comprehensive coverage for the whole of Tanzania, as well as Kenya, Rwanda and Burundi, and based on limited field usage to date it seems excellent, with accurate plates, good distribution maps and adequately detailed text descriptions.

Another quality field guide that provides full coverage of East Africa is *Birds of Africa South of the Sahara: A Comprehensive Illustrated Field Guide* by Ian Sinclair and Peter Ryan (Struik Publishers, 2003), which describes and illustrates the 2,100-plus species recorded in the region. Should you already own it, or be planning more extensive travels in Africa, then this guide will more than suffice for northern Tanzania. But if your African travels will be restricted to East Africa, you are probably better off buying a more focused field guide.

Ber Van Perlo's *Illustrated Checklist to the Birds of Eastern Africa* (Collins, 1995) is a useful, relatively inexpensive and admirably compact identification manual describing and illustrating all 1,488 bird species recorded in Eritrea, Ethiopia, Kenya, Uganda and Tanzania. Unfortunately, however, the distribution maps and colour plates are often misleading, and the compact format means that descriptions are too terse and pictures too cluttered to allow identification of more difficult genera. It is, however, far more useful than John Williams's pioneering but now obsolete *Field Guide to the Birds of East Africa*, also published by Collins and still referred to in many brochures and guides.

Other field guides The past few years have seen the publication of a spate of high-quality field guides to other more specialised aspects of East Africa's fauna and flora.

Among the more interesting of these titles are Najma Dharani's *Field Guide to Common Trees and Shrubs of East Africa* (Struik, 2002) and a simply magnificent *Field Guide to the Reptiles of East Africa* by Stephen Spawls, Kim Howell, Robert Drewes and James Ashe (A & C Black, 2004). Alan Channing and Kim Howell's *Amphibians of East Africa* (Comstock Books in Herpetology, 2006) is also highly worthwhile. Matt Richmond and Irene Kamau's *East African Marine Ecoregion* (World Wide Fund for Nature USA, 2005) examines the whole of the East African coast.

National parks An excellent introductory handbook to all Tanzania's national parks and other major conservation areas is Olli Marttila's misleadingly named *The Great Savanna* (Auris Publishers, Finland, 2011). This includes a very useful overview of conservation in Tanzania, and detailed (20–30 page) description of each park and reserve, including lesser-known ones such as Rubondo Island, Mkomazi and Amani. There is also a useful pocket field guide to mammals and select birds at the back. The only place where it seems to be sold in northern Tanzania is the branch of A Novel Idea in the TFA Centre (see page 117), where it costs US$50.

In the early 1990s, Jeanette Hanby and David Bygott wrote a series of excellent booklets covering Serengeti National Park, Tarangire National Park and Lake Manyara National Park. These were published by Tanapa and can still be bought for US$5–10 from street vendors and bookshops in Arusha, and possibly at some safari lodges. The same authors have written an equally informative and widely available self-published booklet covering the Ngorongoro Conservation Area. These older guides have now been formally superseded by a series of glossier booklets covering each of the four major reserves, published by the African Publishing House in association with Tanapa. However, while these newer booklets are more up to date and colourful than the older ones, they are also pricier and not substantially more informative.

Giovanni Tombazzi's lively, colourful and accurate maps covering (among other places) the Serengeti, Lake Manyara, Tarangire and the Ngorongoro Conservation Area are probably the most user-friendly maps I've seen in East Africa. Each map shows details of the appropriate conservation area in both the dry and wet seasons, and is liberally dotted with illustrations of common trees and other points of interest. Giovanni has also produced a map covering the whole northern safari circuit, useful to those who don't want to splash out on the whole series of more detailed maps. As with the booklets mentioned above, these maps are widely available in Arusha and at the national park lodges, but vary in price depending on where you buy them.

Bernhard Grzimek's renowned book *Serengeti Shall Not Die* (Collins, 1959) remains a classic evocation of the magic of the Serengeti, and its original publication was instrumental in making this reserve better known to the outside world. Iain Douglas-Hamilton's *Amongst the Elephants* (Penguin, 1978) did much the same for publicising Lake Manyara National Park, although the vast herds of elephants it describes have since been greatly reduced by poaching.

Travel guides Bradt also publishes Philip Briggs's *Tanzania Safari Guide* (2013) aimed at those who want to explore this vast and varied country's wildlife destinations outside of the northern safari circuit, while *Zanzibar, Pemba & Mafia: The Bradt Travel Guide* (2013) by Chris McIntyre and Susan McIntyre is the most useful book for those visiting the islands in isolation. Travellers with limited mobility may also be interested in Bradt's *Access Africa: Safaris for People with Limited Mobility* (2009) by Gordon Rattray. For people combining a visit to Tanzania with one or other of its neighbours, there are also detailed Bradt guides available to Kenya, Ethiopia, Uganda, Zambia, Congo, Mozambique, Malawi and Rwanda.

Coffee-table books The best book of this sort to cover Tanzania as a whole is Paul Joynson-Hicks's *Tanzania: Portrait of a Nation*, which contains some great down-to-earth cultural photography and lively anecdotal captions. Also recommended is *Journey through Tanzania*, photographed by the late Mohammed Amin and Duncan Willets and published by Camerapix in Kenya. Both of the above books are stronger on cultural, landmark and scenic photography than on wildlife photography, for which M Iwago's superb *Serengeti* (Thames and Hudson, 1987) has few peers, although Reinhard Kunkel's stunning *Ngorongoro* (Welcome Enterprises, 2006) is certainly one, while Boyd Norton's more

TANZANIA ON CD

From traditional percussion and chants to Congolese-style guitar pop and a home-grown style of contemporary hip hop called bongo flava, Tanzania has a rich and varied musical culture, and – unlike a few years back – it is increasingly well represented on CD and on download sites such as emusic and iTunes. The following short list includes some of the most interesting material on offer:

Bi Kidude: Zanzibar (Retroafric, 2007) The first solo recordings by the gravel-voiced Queen of Taarab, a centurion who first performed in the 1920s and it still an active member of the Zanzibari music scene today.

Lady Jaydee: Ya 5 – The Best of Lady Jaydee (Machozi, 2012) The cream of the four studio CDs recorded by this very popular and multiple award-winning artist, one of the few to have given international exposure to bongo flava.

Mohamed Ilyas: Taarab (Chitu-Taku, 2009) A soulful modern taarab recording by one of Zanzibar's most legendary singers backed by a 16-piece orchestra.

Various Artists: Bongo Flava – Swahili Rap from Tanzania (Out Here, 2006) A rare international release featuring 70 minutes of modern Swahili hip-hop by 14 artists, mostly recorded in Dar Es Salaam.

Various Artists: Rough Guide to the Music of Tanzania (Rough Guides, 2009) Traditional music, 80s guitar pop and bongo flava all get an airing on this genre-spanning and highly recommended introduction to Tanzania's musical heritage.

Various Artists: Taarab 3 – Music of Zanzibar (Globestyle 1989) Excellent and well-annotated introduction to Zanzibar's distinctive taarab music, mostly played by small bands and recorded in the 1980s, also featuring one of the best recordings by the legendary Bi Kidude.

Various Artists: Tanzania Instruments (SWP, 2009) A fascinating countrywide tour of traditional instrumentals performances – ranging from Lake Victoria to Zanzibar – recorded by the legendary Hugh Tracey in 1950.

Various Artists: Tanzania Vocals (SWP, 2009) Another culture-hopping rerelease of material recorded by Hugh Tracey in 1950, this *a capella* selection includes atmospheric Maasai chants and a 600-strong mixed-sex Chagga choir recorded on the footslopes of Kilimanjaro.

Various Artists: Zanzibara Vol. 3 – The 1960s Sound of Tanzania (Buda, 2007) Highlife-influenced and infectiously poppy guitar-driven *muziki wa dansi* (dance music) recorded by the likes of the Jamhuri Jazz Band and Atomic Jazz Band in the late 1960s and early 1970s.

Vijana Jazz Band: The Koka Koka Sex Battalion (Sterns Africa, 2011) Showcasing one of the most exciting and popular purveyors of East African rumba-style *muziki wa dansi*, this includes a great selection of toe-tappers recorded in the 1970s and 1980s.

recent *Serengeti: The Eternal Beginning* (Fulcrim, 2011) is also very handsome and has better text. Javed Jafferji's atmospheric photographs are highlighted in *Images of Zanzibar*, while *Zanzibar – Romance of the Ages* makes extensive use of archive photographs dating to before the turn of the century. Both were originally published by HSP Publications in 1996, and are readily available on the island.

Health

Self-prescribing has its hazards so if you are going anywhere very remote consider taking a health book. For adults there is *Bugs, Bites & Bowels: The Cadogan Guide to Healthy Travel* by Jane Wilson-Howarth (2006); if travelling with the family look at *Your Child Abroad: A Travel Health Guide* by Jane Wilson-Howarth and Matthew Ellis, published by Bradt in 2005.

Fiction

Surprisingly few novels have been written by Tanzanians or about Tanzania. An excellent novel set in World War I Tanzania is William Boyd's *An Ice-cream War*, while the same author's *Brazzaville Beach*, though not overtly set in Tanzania, devotes attention to aspects of chimpanzee behaviour first noted at Gombe Stream.

A Tanzanian of Asian extraction now living in Canada, M G Vassanji, is the author of at least one novel set in Tanzania and the Kenyan border area, the prize-winning *Book of Secrets* (Macmillan, 1994). This is an atmospheric tale, with much interesting period detail, revolving around a diary written by a British administrator in pre-war Kenya and discovered in a flat in Dar es Salaam in the 1980s. Vassanji is also the author of *Uhuru Street*, a collection of short stories set in Dar es Salaam. The most prominent Tanzanian-born novelist is Abdulrazak Gurnah, a Zanzibari now living in the UK whose books are mostly set in East Africa. His best known novels are *Desertion* (Bloomsbury, 2005), *Paradise* (Bloomsbury, 1994) which was shortlisted for the Booker and the Whitbread Prize, and *By the Sea* (Bloomsbury, 2001), which was shortlisted for the Los Angeles Times Book Award. Novels set elsewhere in Africa, but which may be of interest to visitors to Tanzania, include the following:

Brink, A *An Act of Terror* or *A Dry White Season*
Cartwright, J *Maasai Dreaming*
Conrad, J *Heart of Darkness*
Dagarembga, T *Nervous Conditions*
Gordimer, N *July's People*
Kingsolver, B *The Poisonwood Bible*
Lambkin, D *The Hanging Tree*
Lessing, D *The Grass is Singing, Children of Violence* (5 volumes)
Mazrui, A *The Trial of Christopher Okigbo*
Mungoshi, C *Coming of the Dry Season*
Mwangi, M *Going down River Road*
Naipaul, V S *A Bend in the River*
Okri, B *The Famished Road*
Theroux, P *Jungle Lovers*
Thiong'o, N *Petals of Blood* or *A Grain of Wheat*
Slaughter, C *Antonia saw the Oryx First*
Van der Post, L *A Story like the Wind*

MAPS

A number of maps covering East Africa are available. The best is the Austrian-published Freytag-Berndt 1:2,000,000 map. By far the most accurate and up-to-date dedicated map of Tanzania is the 1:400,000 *Tanzania Travel Map* published by Harms Verlag (*www.harms-ic-verlag.de*).

A series of excellent maps by Giovanni Tombazzi covers most of the northern reserves, as well as Kilimanjaro, Mount Meru and Zanzibar. Colourful, lively and accurate, these maps are widely available throughout northern Tanzania. Also recommended are the new Harms Verlag maps to Ngorongoro Conservation Area, Lake Manyara National Park and Zanzibar Island.

TRAVEL MAGAZINES The quarterly magazine *Kakakuona: African Wildlife* (e *kakakuona@africaonline.co.tz*), which is produced by the Tanzania Wildlife Protection Fund, frequently includes several good articles about conservation in Tanzania. For readers with a broad interest in Africa, an excellent magazine dedicated to tourism throughout Africa is *Travel Africa*, which can be visited online at www.travelafricamag.com. Recommended for their broad-ranging editorial content and the coffee-table standard photography, the award-winning magazine *Africa Geographic* can be checked out at the website www.africageographic.com (see also advert on page 245). Also recommended is *Ujumbe* (*www.ujumbemagazine.com*), a quarterly magazine published from Karatu.

WEBSITES The following offer information on northern Tanzania and Zanzibar:

www.allaboutzanzibar.com
www.intotanzania.com
www.mambomagazine.com
www.ntz.info
www.tanzaniatouristboard.com
http://updates.bradtguides.com/tanzania

Index

Entries in **bold** indicate main entries; those in *italics* indicate maps

INDEX OF ADVERTISERS